HA'IL   oasis city of Saudi Arabia

HA'IL

oasis city of Saudi Arabia

PHILIP WARD

The Oleander Press
Cambridge · New York

LC

The Oleander Press
17 Stansgate Avenue
Cambridge CB2 2QZ

The Oleander Press
210 Fifth Avenue
New York
N.Y. 10010, U.S.A.

ISBN 0 900891 75 0

British Library Cataloguing in Publication Data

Ward, Philip
   Ha'il: oasis city of Saudi Arabia. — (Arabia
   past & present; v.11)
   1. Ha'il, Arabia — History
   I. Title   II. Series
   953'.8   DS248.H/

   ISBN 0-900891-75-0

Printed and bound in Great Britain

P-16-87

Contents

List of Illustrations

Preface

In January 1976 the city of Ha'il made such an indelible impression on my mind that I determined to discover as much as possible about the city's past and present, and present a documentary history of the city using as far as possible the authentic voices of earlier visitors.

Following sketches of the geographical and historical setting, I have reproduced, in their own words as far as possible, the writings of the great travellers. In the case of Yrjö Aukusti Wallin, I prepared a complete edition of his *Travels in Arabia 1845 and 1848* (The Oleander Press, 1979), with ample introductory material by M. Trautz and W.R. Mead, and a new bibliography. Since Wallin's work on Ha'il is in print in this same "Arabia Past & Present" series, there is no need to do more than refer readers to his pioneering account of Ha'il; the first by a European.

In the following generation, Palgrave and Guarmani visited Ha'il. I have cited Palgrave in full, and summarised the less brilliant record by Guarmani.

Our view of Ha'il is particularly clear during the period 1877-84. First in chronological order (though not in date of publication), comes the magisterial account of Doughty, whose literary style, once an effort of imagination has been made, remains an enchantment - an evocation of Chaucerian pilgrimage in a sharply-etched antique mode which, for me among many other readers, makes *Travels in Arabia Deserta* a key book in English literature.

After Doughty come Wilfrid and Anne Blunt, also excellent prose stylists in the *Pilgrimage to Nejd*.

Charles Huber's *Journal* is by contrast a sequence of notes, with fascinating insights here and there but lacking any attempt at organisation. I have chosen to translate from Huber's French only selectively.

Julius Euting, Huber's travelling companion, wrote in swashbuckling German with a Swabian tinge. A vivid writer and talented artist, Euting is a strong personality with the typical European faults of impatience and intellectual snobbery. Where Doughty can sense a pattern of nobility among certain of the beduin he meets, Euting is by contrast a colonial type, sure of his own superiority and a compelling narrator for his zest in every detail of life, from his drawing of named kitchen utensils to his games and unlucky ibex hunts. It is time he was rendered into English, and the task of translating him accounts in large measure for the delay between this book's conception and its completion seven years later.

Ten years after Huber and Euting, Eduard Nolde offered his own *Reise,* and this too has been translated in full from the German as regards all references to Ha'il and the Jabal Shammar.

These are the principal sources, then. For the rest, I have summarised visits by the Muslim Williamson, by Gertrude Bell (in the words of D.G. Hogarth), by Eldon Rutter, and by Bawden the painter and Berman the photographer.

'Ha'il Today' brings the story up to date by describing the growth of the city since World War II, and its place in the Kingdom of Saudi Arabia. *Ha'il* concludes with an appendix of E.C. Ross's notes on the Rashid dynasty, a chronology, a gene-

alogy of the Rashids of Jabal Shammar, and a
bibliography.

The book would not have been possible without
many friends and associates. Firstly, thanks for
hospitality in 1976 are gratefully tendered to
Shaikh ^CAbdullah ibn ash-Shaikh, Deputy Governor of
Ha'il and District, for permission to use the
government guest-house and to visit the old and new
areas of Ha'il, as well as zones beyond the city.

His Royal Highness Prince Muqrin ibn ^CAbdulaziz,
Governor of Ha'il since 1980, has answered questions, provided a series of photographs, and supplied the basic document *Ha'il baina al-madi wa 'l-
hadir* (1401=1981).

To Angelo Pesce, with his unrivalled first-hand
knowledge of the Kingdom of Saudi Arabia gained
from travels and discussions over twenty years, I
am indebted for advice, assistance, and photographs.

The Royal Geographical Society has kindly granted permission for the reproduction of Hogarth's
'Gertrude Bell's Journey to Hail' in *The Geographical Journal*, with photographs and subsequent discussion. Edward Bawden and the Imperial War Museum
are duly thanked for permission to use the artist's
words and pictures. Photographs by Sergeant-
Photographer Berman are reproduced by permission of
The Architectural Review. Thanks are extended to
Jonathan Cape (for *Arabia Deserta*) and to all other
publishers whose out-of-copyright works are reprinted in facsimile.

My wife Audrey and my daughters Carolyn and Angela
have, as always, offered the space and time for the
translations from French and German, the correspondence and compilation, and the consultation with
Arab friends and non-Arabs alike, among whom I
should like to mention the late Faisal al-Waili of
Baghdad, Mr & Mrs Gant, Saffron Walden and Douglas
Gregor, Northampton.   Mrs C. Carpenter redrew

some of the early maps for the sake of clarity.
Staff of the Cambridge University Library offered
their usual impeccable services.

If the book succeeds in enhancing understanding
between Europeans and Saudi Arabs I shall have
achieved my primary objective. If I have drawn
particular attention to the story of the Rashid
dynasty, understated in most histories of Northern
Arabia, I shall have also achieved my secondary
aim. A tertiary aim is to provide by example one
documentary history of an Arabian city in the hope
that other writers may be inspired toward similar
enterprises devoted to Ta'if, perhaps, to al-Qasim,
or to al-Jawf.

Cambridge, 1983   Philip Ward

1
Ha'il in its Geographical Setting

Situated in the Jabal Shammar, a mountain mass-
if in the desert region of Najd, Saudi Arabia,
Ha'il stands strategically equidistant between al-
Qasim (Buraidah and 'Anaizah) in the south and al-
Jawf (Sakakah and Daumat al-Jandal) in the north
at the farther edge of the Sand Sea called the
Nafud.

Ha'il is a man-made fortress sheltering under
the northeastern end of the natural fortress of
the Aja' mountains. Against the reddish-grey
granite cliffs of Aja', Ha'il became a camel-brown
citadel which has seen numerous vicissitudes of
supremacy and subjection in the centuries since it
became capital of Jabal Shammar.

The village, then town, now an oasis city, is
situated at an altitude of 979 metres. Jabal Samra
or Mawqida bounds Ha'il on the east, and the ridge
Umm Arqab on the northern side. The shorter granite range of Jabal Salma lies fifty kilometres to
the south-east.

The wadi itself was once known as Ha'il, and
the village simply al-Qurayyah (the little village). But since numerous other villages were
known as al-Qurayyah, the name Qurayyat Ha'il
gradually took over, and then this in turn was
abbreviated to Ha'il. The pre-Islamic poet Imr al-
Qais praises his secure encampment in the Aja'
mountains, with good grazing for his camels in the
wadi near al-Qurayyah, and the hospitality of the
Tu'l tribe near the village.

1

Wherever there is good natural water accumulation there are large date-palm groves. Elsewhere, smaller level areas were traditionally sown with wheat or barley and irrigated. But the produce of the Jabal Shammar oases, from classical Faid to modern Ha'il, has never been sufficient for local demands. Before the foundation of the Kingdom, successive Amirs ordered caravans of food and other supplies from Najaf and Samawah, Damascus and Gulf cities to the north. In 1916, *A Handbook of Arabia* declared: 'Like the nomads in all other parts of Arabia, the Shammar must go beyond thier own borders for much of their supplies, food, clothing, and for the utensils which even the most primitive desert existence demands. Since the Damascus trade has diminished they have become the more dependent on Mesopotamia and the Gulf. Indian brocades are worn by the Amir's harem, and every house in Ha'il is lighted by oil lamps from Baghdad. Any interruption of this traffic would seriously embarrass the inhabitants of the Jabal. In short, here as elsewhere in Arabia, it must be borne in mind that those who hold the settled lands and their markets can control the interior'.

The old capital of the Jabal Aja' was Faid, near Jabal Salma, seat of the Asad and Tai tribes. In 657 A.D., ^CAli, son-in-law of the Prophet Muhammad (salla Allahu ^Calayhi wa sallam), mounted a camel and rode to Faid, where he was greeted with acclamation by the tribespeople, on his way to Basra, as Tabari relates. In 762, the Caliph Abu Ja^Cfar al-Mansur sent a strong force to seize and reinforce Faid which they surrounded with a moat, his purpose being to eliminate traffic between Kufa and the rebel followers of ^CAli in Medina. In his *Buldan,* Ya'qubi indicates that Faid was the capital of a district traversed by pilgrims on their way to Mecca. Ibn Rustah conforms this, adding that the Tai people of Faid irrigated their fields of grain from an aqueduct, and that a Friday Mosque had been built in the town. Muqaddasi writes in

Traditional Ha'il - note the stout doors and wooden
pipes draining the flat roofs. (Photo: Berman,
1944.) Almost all of these nineteenth-century
houses have been demolished in recent urban modernisation.

his *Ahsan* that in 985 A.D. Faid was a small town fortified with iron gates, baths, and a pool. Well watered by springs, cisterns and wells, the town was plentifully supplied with goods for its inhabitants and pilgrims alike.

In the second half of the tenth century, Faid fell under the control of the Carmathians, so no sermons were preached in the Friday Mosque. Ibn Jubair, visiting Faid in the spring of 1185, found a strong fort provided with towers beside a town protected by old ramparts and inhabited by Arabs who traded with the pilgrims. Yaqut adds to the above the observation that the people of Faid grew fodder the whole year round to sell to pilgrims for their animals during the time of the Haj. Ibn Battuta (*Tuhfa*, vol.1, pp. 409 ff.), saw Faid towards the end of 1329, when pilgrims had learnt to don full battle array against marauders. 'The Arab population', he writes, 'trades with the pilgrims. The latter enter Faid in battle array with weapons in their hands to intimidate the Arabs, who gather there in the hope of easy spoils.' He met two Arab princes, sons of Muhanna ibn ^cIsa who, with a train of mounted and foot attendants, looked after the pilgrims and their pack beasts.

When Faid declined, Ha'il assumed capital status of Jabal Aja', and its communications node. The only other settled areas of any note have been ^cAqdah, with scattered villages, and palm-groves which at their peak numbered seventy-five thousand trees; Qafar, a broad oasis inhabited by Bani Tamim under the slopes of Jabal Aja'; and Mustajiddah, on the southwestern spurs of Jabal Salma.

Ptolemy's Arre Kome (named thus in the second century A.D.) was identified with Ha'il by Alois Sprenger in his *Die alte Geographie Arabiens*, but D.G. Hogarth disputes this, in *The Penetration of Arabia*, suggesting that it is Ptolemy's Aine.

Sprenger is probably correct, since both the Ptolemaic Arre and Ha'il lie north-east of Jabal Salma.

Jabal Aja' rises from a vast erosion plain at about latitude 27° 30' N and longitude 41°E. It is over 700 kilometres southwest of Baghdad and more than 800 kilometres southeast of Damascus. Human settlement in the area has been possible from the earliest times because spring water is abundant in the mountains for several months of the year, and wells for domestic and agricultural purposes have been easy to exploit.

Water from the mountains remains on the granite floor of the valley under a surface of protective gravel derived from mountain erosion. As freshets and weathering break up the gravel, the resulting soil becomes productive for agriculture, in particular for date palms and other hardier plants.

The districts of Ha'il city were listed by J.G. Lorimer in his *Gazetteer of the Persian Gulf, Oman, and Central Arabia* (Vol.IIA, 1908, reprinted by Gregg, 1970) as, in roughly west-east order: Samah, Barzan (with the main castle), Subhan, ᶜAbid, Lubdah (with the main *suq* or bazaar), Mughaithah, ᶜAtiq, Jubarah, Jarad, Quraishi, Rakhis, Faraikh, Dubaᶜan, Ziqdi, and Wasitah (fertile in date palms but depopulated when visited in 1787, probably as a result of the cholera epidemic of 1871.

Lorimer describes the main square, or Mishab, as being 250 yards long and 25 wide, with the castle on one side and the guest rooms on the other. The main suq, called Mabiᶜ, is a continuation of the Mishab; it was 200 yards long in Lorimer's time, and had about 140 shops belonging to the Amir, who rented them out. 'The shopkeepers', according to Lorimer, 'are generally natives of Najaf, Qasim or Madinah. Cloth, calico, spices, metals and European goods are imported from

Basrah, Najaf and Madinah; corn from Suq ash-Shuyukh'. As regards the typical Ha'il townsman of the period, he 'is of slender build. All classes and both sexes wear next their skin the Haqu, a plaited leather belt, and in this they resemble the Arabs of the desert'. The houses of Ha'il during the early years of the 20th century often had an upper storey, and were built of small sun-dried bricks and date-palm or *ithl* (tamarisk) wood. 'The coffee rooms and the guests' quarters pertaining to them are usually in an adjoining quadrangle with a separate entrance. Rooms, which are ordinarily few but large commodious, are lighted only by the doorways and by unglazed openings in the walls just below the ceilings'.

As regards the human population of Ha'il, figures must be regarded with extreme suspicion: Doughty estimated it at 3,000 in 1877, while the official estimate for the whole of the administrative district in 1976 was 260,000, comprising 143,000 bedu and 117,000 settled inhabitants. J. Mandaville, author of the article on Ha'il in *The Encyclopedia of Islam,* cites a figure of 20,000 for the town itself in 1965. *A Handbook of Arabia* suggested a figure of 4,000 for the town in 1916.

The position of Ha'il has led to the construction of notable roads from the classical period to the motorways of the present day. A significant road probably ran in ancient times from Gerrha and other ports on the Gulf to Ha'il and thence to Taima and Damascus.

A track led north-west over the Sand Sea via the oasis of Jubbah to al-Jawf. Northeast a road passes by al-Luwaimi to meet the Tapline road just south of Rafha.

A new road southeast links Ha'il with al-Qasim, Riyadh and the Eastern Province's oilfields. An excellent motorway runs southwest to Medina, Yanbu[c], and Jiddah or Mecca.

The last link in the communications chain was
wrought when Saudia began to operate flights between Ha'il and the rest of the Kingdom of Saudi
Arabia.

A spring in the Jabal Aja'

2
Ha'il in its Historical Setting

The district of Ha'il has been inhabited for many
centuries by the southern Shammar, to be distinguished from the Shammar of Jazirah and the Shammar
of Iraq. The southern Shammar are northern Arabs:
a mixture of ^CAbs and Hawazin (deriving from the
Mudhar division) and the Taghlib (deriving from
the Rabi^Cah division) of the ^CAbdah tribe. It is
not clear whether the southern Shammar have dis-
placed the ancient Tayy people, deriving from the
Qahtan, recorded in the district from pre-Islamic
times, or whether they have absorbed the Tayy into
their own stock.

In the mid-seventeenth century the Shammar
stretched their northern boundaries deep into the
Syrian desert. They defeated the Mawali tribe,
then the most awesome military power in the region,
and dispersed the Mawali into the northeastern
corner of Syria.

The Shammaris of Ha'il submitted to Wahhabi rule
in 1201 A.H. (1786-7 A.D.). Early in the nineteenth century, the 'Anaizah forced the Shammaris
northward across the Euphrates, and it was at this
moment that they split into northern and southern
Shammar, even if ethnically they are indissoluble.
Ibrahim Pasha, leading an Ottoman campaign, sub-
jugated Ha'il 1233 A.H. (1818 A.D.), following the
fall of Dira^Ciyah, and the town was again seized
by foreign troops in 1253, two years after the
House of Rashid had taken over as masters of Ha'il,
under the general overlordship of the Al Sa^Cud.

9

At the beginning of the nineteenth century, the master of Jabal Shammar was Muhammad ibn ᶜAbdulmuhsin ibn ᶜAli, of the al-Jaᶜafrah clan of the Rabiᶜah. The main rival to the ibn ᶜAli house was the ibn Rashid house of the al-Jaᶜafrah clan. At first, events and alliances seemed to favour the ibnᶜAli faction, for when Muhammad ibn ᶜAli's son-in-law Muhammad ibn Rashid tried to gain too much power, he was forced to flee with his family to Iraq. He nevertheless sought the influence of Faisal ibn Turki ibn Saᶜud in Riyadh and, in 1827, compelled the lord of the Jabal Shammar, then ᶜIsa ibn ᶜAli, to recognise the sovereignty of ibn Saᶜud. Hamad ibn Shuwair was then installed at Ha'il as ibn Saᶜud's representative.

Within ten years the ibn Rashid house had expanded its sway, offering real or token allegiance to the Al Saᶜud in Riyadh, according to changes in fortune. ᶜAbdullah ibn Rashid was nominated Hakim (Governor) of Ha'il by Faisal after helping the latter to overthrow the rebel Mashari ibn ᶜAbdurrahman ibn Saᶜud and Mashari's ally Salih ibn Muhsin ibn ᶜAli. The latter fled from Ha'il, seeking refuge in Buraidah, but on the journey he was caught and killed.

But in 1837 ᶜAbdullah and his brother ᶜUbaidallah were forced to seek refuge at the oasis Jubbah, in the Nafud, and ᶜIsa ibn ᶜAli, supported by Turkish troops, took over the reins of government in Ha'il. When the Turkish soldiery left for al-Qasim, ᶜAbdullah's next ploy was not to attack Ha'il, but to take the large oasis of Qafar, occupied by supporters of ibn ᶜAli, and to carry out sorties against Ha'il from this neighbouring stronghold. When ᶜAbdullah learned that Turks under Khurshid Pasha were coming from Medina, early in 1838, ᶜAbdullah met them with gifts at Mustajiddah, vowing allegiance to the Sublime Porte if Khurshid would name ᶜAbdullah Hakim of Ha'il and repudiate ᶜIsa. This tactic success-

fully concluded, ^cAbdullah and Khurshid marched
on Ha'il, and the banished ^cIsa was overtaken on
his flight to Medina and murdered by ^cUbaidallah.

In this way ^cAbdullah, with the help of 'the
Wolf' ^cUbaidallah, his brother, cemented his hold
over Jabal Shammar, and became the strongest of the
ibn Rashid until his son Muhammad won wide renown
as a munificent and shrewd ruler over a quarter of
a century from 1872.

It was ^cAbdullah who was responsible for the
enlargement of the official governor's residence
known as the Barzan, begun by Muhammad ibn ^cAli
and continued by the latter's son ^cIsa. Strategically, he won respect for maintaining the balance of
power between the Turko-Egyptian governor Khurshid
Pasha, and his own overlord, Prince ibn Sa^cud, who
opposed the Egyptians. ^cAbdullah's own bodyguard
included two hundred and fifty Turko-Egyptian
troops who had deserted with their arms. He forced
the warring oases of al-Jawf to pay him tribute
from 1838. He supported Khurshid Pasha in raids
against the Harb and Hutaim, rich tribes gradually
weakened by unexpected depredations. Finally, in
1843 he supported Faisal ibn Sa^cud against the
claims of ^cAbdullah ibn Thunayyan. As his wealth
increased, so did the number and valour of his
allies. As he strengthened the defences of Ha'il
against sudden attack, the town's prosperity increased, its population swelled, and its opponents
dwindled in importance.

When ^cAbdullah died a natural death in April
1847, he was succeeded by his eldest son Talal. It
was a sign of the times that Talal was to commit
suicide, and none of his sons was to die a natural
death. Talal married a daughter of his overlord
Faisal ibn Sa^cud, but his token subjection was confined to sending seven mares each year as tribute
to Riyadh.

Talal was by the standards of the age a peaceable ruler, leaving his uncle ^cUbaidallah to root out and destroy opposition to Rashidi sovereignty, including the destruction of robber bands which preyed on luckless villages, travellers, and pilgrim caravans. Devastated palm-groves were restored to use, choked wells were cleared and made useable once more, fortified houses were erected in palm gardens to defend cultivators from sudden raids, and trade connections were renewed with north and south. Nomads of the Shammar once more chose to transact their business in Ha'il, instead of in Iraq or Syria.

When al-Jawf, in 1853, sent word that no more tribute was to be paid to Ha'il, Talal sent his brother Mit^cab with his uncle ^cUbaidallah to restore Rashidi powers. Al-Jawf, rebelling again in 1855, felt the fury of Talal himself, who used Egyptian guns to destroy the hitherto unvanquished fortress of al-Qara, and to breach the historic castle of Marid in Daumat al-Jandal. He became master of al-Jawf by placing his own governor in the restored Qasr al-Marid and lodging a permanent garrison in both Daumat al-Jandal and Sakakah. It was Talal too who completed the building of Qasr Barzan in Ha'il, settled eight hundred families of loyal servants in Qafar to guarantee the rival village's future allegiance, and enclosed the greater city of Ha'il within a new defensive circuit of thick mud-brick walls.

It is generally thought that Talal's death on 11 March 1868 at the age of 45 was by suicide, after years of torture by an abscess which, ineptly treated, poisoned his system.

After Talal's death, there was no obvious claimant to lordship of Ha'il. The tribal chiefs of the Shammar confederation, and the older members within the Rashidi clan, supported the candidacy of Talal's brother Mit^cab. The younger Rashidis supported

Talal's eldest son Bandar. Mit^Cab was chosen, but
Bandar's adherents increased in power and influence,
and Bandar thought he would win general support as
lord of Ha'il by ambushing Mit^Cab outside the Qasr
Barzan in January 1869. Bandar took over, but the
old ^CUbaidallah and Bandar's uncle Muhammad ibn
^CAbdullah sought refuge in Riyadh while they concerted opposition to the young assassin. Bandar's
luck appeared to be holding when ^CUbaidallah died
a natural death, of old age, and when Muhammad his
uncle agreed to return to Ha'il, with Hamud, son
of ^CUbaidallah, Bandar was unduly heartened.

Muhammad did not return directly, however, but
joined a trade caravan to Iraq. On his way back
he induced ibn Suwait and a large body of his Zafir
followers to continue southward beyond their own
borders. Bandar, sensing disaster, rode out from
Ha'il to meet Muhammad before the latter could
join Hamud and his allies within the city, but
was cut down north of Ha'il, and his followers
pursued and massacred within the city streets as
they sought asylum there. Bandar's brothers
Maslat and Badr managed to elude their pursuers,
but were tracked down to their refuge in the Jabal
Aja' and murdered there. Three years later
Muhammad put to death the next two sons of Talal,
^CAbdullah and Nahar, and in 1881 it was the turn
of Talal's youngest son Na'if to die, again with
the knowledge of Muhammad. Thus did he guarantee
the stability of his rule, having wiped out all
six sons of his eldest brother.

Muhammad's sovereignty dates from 25 December
1869, and it is his rule that is best chronicled –
by Doughty, Huber, Euting, the Blunts, Nolde, and
Williamson. It was Muhammad who forced the pilgrim caravans to pass through Ha'il levying a toll
of 30 *majidis* on the way to Mecca and 15 on the
way back. Since as many as ten thousand pilgrims
may have had to pay this toll on water and camel-
fodder each year, it is obvious that Muhammad ibn

Rashid, and incidentally also the merchants of
Ha'il, stood to gain great wealth from the stability of his realm, and from his insistence that
the caravans should take the route through Ha'il.
Furthermore, a fraction of all the goods imported
or transported by the pilgrims was exacted. Since
even the trade caravans from al-Qasim were compelled to traverse Ha'il, their rulers joined
Prince ^CAbdurrahman of Riyadh in the spring of 1891
to destroy Muhammad ibn Rashid and with him the
strength of Ha'il. But even so Muhammad was too
cunning and powerful for their combined might.
Zamil as-Salim of ^CAnaizah was killed in combat,
while Prince ^CAbdurrahman and Hasan al-Muhanna of
Buraidah were taken captive.

But as his dominions grew in extent, they
weakened in loyalty. Pockets of rebellion arose
and his forces splintered on all sides in trying to
put down resistance to demands for tribute. He
decided to release Prince ^CAbdurrahman as a subject
viceroy in Riyadh, but the resentful prince, once
installed in Riyadh, fled late in 1891 to the
protection of the Sabah family in Kuwait, awaiting
deliverance from Rashidi rule. Muhammad ibn Rashid
then replaced ^CAbdurrahman with Prince ^CAbdullah's
brother Muhammad. It was at this point that
Muhammad ibn Rashid's sway reached its zenith.
Strategically, he was vulnerable from both Red Sea
and Gulf ports, for he held no access to the sea
at all. He was also constantly in need of fresh
arms to put down incipient revolts. He therefore
had to seize the Turkish-held port of al-^CUqair or
the port of Kuwait, held by Sabah, the ally of his
enemy ^CAbdurrahman. He could hardly take on the
might of the Ottoman Empire, declining though it
was, so he resolved to attack and seize Kuwait,
hoping at the same time to oust ^CAbdurrahman, and
carried out attacks on the port from 1895 until, on
3 December 1897, he was poisoned according to local
rumour possibly Majid ibn Hamud ibn ^CUbaidallah.

14

Majid did not succeed the sonless Muhammad: the lordship of Ha'il fell to ^cAbdulaziz, son of Muhammad's brother and victim Mit^cab. ^cAbdulaziz feared the treachery that had stalked his father, and never once entered the gates of Ha'il, where ^cUbaidallah's family bore him little goodwill. Though a capable fighter, he preferred to show mercy to the Al Sa^cud captives interned in Ha'il with a view to their future collaboration. But in this, as in so much else, he was to be disappointed. He was confronted with internal dissension, which festered in his continuous absence from Ha'il, and with the external warfare waged from Kuwait by the supporters of Prince ^cAbdurrahman ibn Sa^cud, from Mecca, where the formerly-interned ^cArayif urged military action against him on the Grand Sharif, and from Riyadh, home of so many of his foes.

In spring 1900, Mubarak ibn Sabah of Kuwait carried off several thousand camels in a *ghazu* on Shammari allies of ^cAbdulaziz ibn Rashid. In January 1901, Mubarak advanced westward again, this time with allies of the Al Sa^cud from the south and disgruntled tribesmen anxious to rid themselves of the burden of paying tribute to Ha'il. The combined force was defeated at al-Bukairiyah, where the tribesmen again vowed allegiance to Ha'il, abandoning the force of Mubarak to total slaughter at as-Sarif on 17 March 1901.

^cAbdulaziz now intended to wipe out all resistance by Mubarak in the autumn of 1901, but his advance eastward was halted when messengers brought news of a general rising in the south, led by opponents in Riyadh and vicinity who refused to pay taxes to the Rashidi or to their viceroy in Riyadh, at that time Muhammad ibn Sa^cud.

Intending to march against Riyadh early in 1902, he was told that his deputy in Riyadh, ^cAjlan, had been assassinated, by the Al Sa^cud, and replaced

Above left, the inner
courtyard, showing a low sunbaked-clay wall with
crenellations dividing the shaded coffee-hearth
from the uncovered section of the courtyard, with a
typical wooden door. Below left, the social hub of
the home: the coffee-hearth, with a rifle to hand.
The 'shelves' are simply modelled in wet clay, and
allowed to harden.

Right, one of the remarkable
doors, locks and keys of Ha'il which are fast
disappearing, though some keys are preserved in
museums. Only the side of the door facing the
street is painted. The large wooden key has a set
of unique metal prongs releasing wooden pegs in the
vertical bar corresponding to a set of holes in the
horizontal bolt.

17

by the venerable ^CAbdurrahman ibn Faisal, emerging from his refuge in Kuwait. ^CAbdulaziz, son of ^CAbdurrahman, now sought arms, men, and gold to extend the new Riyadh regime's power northward, with the ultimate objective of taking Ha'il and the Jabal Shammar. To remain in power, the Rashidi dynasty now required wholehearted military assistance from its Turkish allies, and the active support of settlers and nomads in the region, as well as complete co-operation within the dynasty itself. But ^CAbdulaziz could not command any such crucial allegiance, and he was killed in the Battle of Tarafiyyah, north of Buraidah, on 12 April 1906.

A glance at the genealogical table will show that the succession of Mit^Cab, son of ^CAbdulaziz, could satisfy only his father's adherents; it could only sow further discontent into the hearts of ^CUbaidallah's side of the clan, and further divide the settled folk of Ha'il. Finally, early in 1907 Mit^Cab ibn ^CAbdulaziz and his brother Mish^Cal were killed by Sultan ibn Hamud ibn ^CUbaidallah, and Sultan took over the government of Ha'il. Feeling insecure, and fearful of the vengeance of the family of ^CAbdullah ibn Rashid, the ruling faction caused ^CAbdulaziz's third son Muhammad to be killed five months after the death of his brothers. His eight-year-old brother Sa^Cud, fourth son of ^CAbdulaziz, was taken into protective custody at Medina by Sa^Cid, finance minister to ^CAbdulaziz ibn Rashid.

Sultan's rule marked the disintegration of Ha'il from the powerful capital of Muhammad ibn Rashid to a ruined dependency of Riyadh. Sultan lost first al-Qasim, then al-Khaibar. The inhabitants of Ha'il, forced to take sides between the two warring factions, experienced the anxieties of civil war and sudden treachery. Moreover, the lucrative pilgrim trade was diverted through Riyadh and away from Ha'il, reducing income of rulers and ruled alike. Sultan was powerless to prevent looting in

the Jabal Shammar region by forces belonging to
the Al Sa^{c}ud. In January 1908 he was killed by his
brothers Sa^{c}ud and Faisal. Sa^{c}ud took over the
rule of Ha'il and Faisal appointed himself governor
of al-Jawf. Now bitter hatred divided the
^{c}Ubaidallah clan of the Rashid, some supporting
Sa^{c}ud and Faisal; others, who had been loyal to
Sultan, continued raids against his enemies within
the clan.

Taking advantage of the bloodshed and fatal
rivalries within their kinsmen's ranks, the family
of Muhammad ibn ^{c}Abdullah and its supporters devised a plan to take power as regents through the
rule of the minor Sa^{c}ud ibn ^{c}Abdulaziz. These
would-be regents were Hamud and Zamil of the Subhan
clan, both cousins of Sa^{c}ud's mother. Taking
advantage of the hatred felt by Shammari hillfolk
towards the murderous regent Sa^{c}ud, many joined
Hamud and Zamil in attacking the oasis city. It
fell, and Sa^{c}ud ibn Hamud ibn ^{c}Ubaidallah was
assassinated in his turn. The ten-year-old Sa^{c}ud
ibn ^{c}Abdulaziz was installed as governor, while his
supporters relentlessly pursued and cut down the
supporters of the ^{c}Ubaidallah clan. Of the survivors, perhaps the most notable was Faisal ibn Hamud,
who escaped from al-Jawf to sanctuary with
^{c}Abdulaziz ibn Sa^{c}ud in Riyadh.

His maternal uncle Hamud's having been poisoned
in the spring of 1909, Zamil now ruled as the
eminence grise behind the throne of Sa^{c}ud ibn
Rashid, but his period of power was tainted by out-
bursts of vendetta killings. The Jabal Shammar
became depopulated as refugees from vengeance and
tribal law sought refuge in Riyadh with the Al
Sa^{c}ud in the south, and the nomads of Nuri ibn
Sha^{c}lan in the more turbulent north. From January
1909 ibn Sha^{c}lan had received submission from all
parts of al-Jawf except for a garrison in Qasr
Marid loyal to the other faction, which eventually
fell before close-range gunfire. The Rashidi out-

post of Taima fell in 1909, and Zamil as-Subhan recognised the *fait accompli* by accepting the over-lordship of the Al Sa^{c}ud of Riyadh, and restoring order under threat of reprisals from the south.

Zamil heard that the ^{c}Ali and Sulaiman tribes to the West had yielded to the Turks, thus safeguarding the Hijaz Railway. In 1910 he marched on the tribes, retook Taima in June, and raided the Turkish station at Mada'in Salih.

Zamil's next opportunity came in spring 1913, when ibn Sa^{c}ud felt strong enough to incorporate within his realm the coastal district of al-Hasa and sent the Turkish officials packing. Zamil en-trusted his ambassador in Damascus, Rashid Pasha, with the delicate task of obtaining secret support for Zamil against the Al Sa^{c}ud. Thus, early in 1914 a Turkish gift of 6,000 rifles, 60,000 cart-ridges, a car, and a great deal of money arrived at al-Mu^{c}azzam station on the Hijaz Railway bound for Taima and Ha'il. Apparently successful in playing off the Turks against Riyadh, Zamil had however overlooked the most persistent and the most effect-ive of all curbs on Rashidi sovereignty: assassina-tion by treachery. In spring 1914 he was murdered by the young Sa^{c}ud ibn Salih as-Subhan, who was to become regent in his turn.

In 1914 Gertrude Bell visited Ha'il, but Captain Shakespear did not. Alois Musil writes: 'While Sa^{c}ud ibn Rashid's representative in Damascus was negotiating with the French consul there about taking over the protectorate of Ha'il, his minister Sa^{c}ud said to have concluded an agreement with the British political officer, Captain W.H.I. Shakespear, who visited him in Ha'il in the late Spring of 1914' (*Northern Negd*, p. 248). However, as Victor Winstone has shown in *Captain Shakespear* (London, 1976), Shakespear never entered Ha'il, but during his 1914 trans-Arabian crossing skirted the city at the northeast, touching Hayaniah and the Sarut Plain. And he met his death from Shammar tribesmen, who

attacked the forces of ibn Sa^{c}ud while Shakespear
was negotiating with them. Armed only with his
revolver, he was cut down by Shammari, then shot in
the arm as he fell, and finally shot through the
head, at the age of 36, on 24 January 1915, not far
from the battlegrounds of Tarafiyyah and Sarif,
where the Shammari had defeated the forces of
Mubarak and ibn Sa^{c}ud's father in 1901, and where
^{c}Abdulaziz had annihilated the forces of ^{c}Abdulaziz
ibn Rashid in 1906.

However, the minister Sa^{c}ud, leading the Shammar
attack, had been unable to secure total victory,
and chose to retreat at night; on the way back he
was alarmed to learn that his camp at Umm Juraif
was being raided by the Mutair from the east, and
by pursuing troops from the west, to such devastating effect that no food or arms were left. The
minister Sa^{c}ud slaughtered twenty-nine relatives of
the exiled ruling family in 1915, leaving alive
only the prince and two youths surviving from the
direct dynastic descendants. Late in 1916 he felt
so secure that he tried to set himself up as prince,
despite the likely resistance of the many who feared him. He had bought with gold the allegiance of
numerous retainers, some of the Aslam tribespeople,
and some of the Ja^{c}afarah families of the ^{c}Abdah
confederation, but the majority of the Shammari
hill people and the settled population of Ha'il
abhorred the mass murderer, and drove him to the
Budur tribes between al-Khamisiyyah and Zubair,
east of the Euphrates. He was killed in 1919.

Who was now to rule Ha'il? The northern tribes
looked for security to Nawwaf ibn Nuri ibn Sha^{c}lan
of al-Jawf, while the southern tribes were begin-
ing to lean towards the burgeoning power of the Al
Sa^{c}ud in Riyadh. The young Sa^{c}ud ibn Rashid found
his dominions shrunk to the immediate vicinity of
Ha'il and the Jabal Aja', though even there he felt
unsure of the loyalty of his 'subjects', incapable
of offering substantial rewards for loyalty, or

effective intimidation against non-payment of taxes. Ever less secure in his rule, therefore, he left for the Ottoman-held railway settlement of Mada'in Salih, relinquishing his rule to ʿAqab bin ʿAjal, his father-in-law, who played off against each other the Turks on the one hand and on the other the rebelling Grand Sharif of Mecca, claiming to be allied to each in turn, for rewards and arms.

The position at the end of World War I was menacing for Saʿud ibn Rashid at Mada'in Salih and his father-in-law ʿAqab at Ha'il. With little support in the Jabal Shammar, ever-diminishing resources, and the disappearance from northern Hijaz and Iraq of his former allies the Turks, the Rashidi dynasty was threatened from the north by tribes of the ʿAnaizah confederation, and from the south by the growing might of the Al Saʿud. They could expect no support from the British in Iraq, who traditionally favoured the Al Saʿud. The Rashidi therefore determined to obtain support from King Husain of Hejaz, enemy of the Al Saʿud, and subject of the detailed biography by Randall Baker, *King Husain and the Kingdom of Hejaz* (Cambridge, The Oleander Press, 1979). Husain was delighted with this new subject, and readily granted arms, ammunition, and money in payment for Rashidi loyalty. Ha'il was to harass Nawwaf in Jawf and the Al Saʿud in Riyadh, a policy successful to the point that Nawwaf again submitted to the overlordship of ʿAqab, so that early in 1920 Ha'il once again controlled al-Jawf. But within two months the people of al-Jawf were persuaded to join ʿAbdullah ibn Talal ibn Rashid against the young Prince Saʿud and his father-in-law ʿAqab. In March 1920 Saʿud was captured and killed, but his servants retaliated at once, murdering ʿAbdullah ibn Talal. To restore order, ʿAqab ibn ʿAjal and his camp reached agreement with the followers of ʿAbdullah ibn Mitʿab that the latter should govern Jabal Shammar. But these endless internecine murders, feuds and vendettas had so sundered the Rashidi dynasty, so weakened it in numbers and in the very will to rule, that each succeeding day seemed likelier to encompass its final downfall. Ibn Saʿud, having concerted an attack with the northern foes of Ha'il, advanced from the south in summer 1921, raiding the ʿAbdah encampments in the Shammar plains. From the north, the northern ʿAnaizah again took arms against Ha'il, together with the Awlad ʿAli, the Awlad Sulaiman, the Huwaitat, and the Ruwala. Ibn Saʿud's forces, led by his brother Muhammad, were unexpectedly defeated at al-Ajfar, but ʿAbdullah ibn Rashid recognised the inevitability of eventual defeat and sued for peace. Ibn Saʿud refused to deal with the ruling dynasty, but only with the Shammar tribes. The ultimatum required that the Rashidi themselves would live in Riyadh, renouncing all claims on Ha'il and the Jabal Shammar. ʿAbdullah at once rejected these terms and continued the unequal struggle, maintaining a lifeline by sending Shammar tribesmen to King Faisal of Iraq, who supplied them with arms, food and money, and encouraged them to continue their inveterate harassment of ibn Saʿud's tribes.

Ibn Saʿud now ordered Faisal ibn Dawish, imposing shaikh of the Mutair, to make a direct attack on Ha'il. In September 1921, ʿAbdullah ibn Rashid was seized at al-Jitamiyyah and surrendered. The Shammar tribesmen now named Muhammad ibn Talal as successor, whereupon ʿAbdullah ibn Saʿud himself arrived to conduct the final siege of Ha'il.

Early in December 1921, the Al Saʿud captured the oasis city of Ha'il, bringing to an end the long-established Rashidi dynasty. Ha'il was declared a district in the province of al-Qasim, and Ibrahim as-Subhan named governor of Ha'il. Sultan ibn Nawwaf of the Shaʿlan was appointed governor of al-Jawf, his father Nawwaf having died only a few months earlier.

Though each succeeding Governor of Ha'il has since brought progress, the best-known Governor in

Sa^{C}udi times has been ^{C}Abdulaziz ibn Mus^{C}ad ibn
Jiluwi, ruler of Ha'il under the leadership of King
^{C}Abdulaziz from 1923. Ha'il has subsequently been
governed, with ever-increasing prosperity and progress, by Prince Fahd ibn Sa^{C}d ibn ^{C}Abdurrahman
(1971-2), Prince Sa^{C}d ibn Fahd ibn Sa^{C}d (1972-4),
and most recently by Prince Muqrin ibn ^{C}Abdulaziz
(b. 1943), son of the late King ^{C}Abdulaziz and
brother of King Fahd.

3
Yrjö Aukusti Wallin, 1845 and 1848

A Swedish-speaking Finn is our first authoritative
informant on Ha'il. The contributions resulting
from visits in the 1840s by Wallin (1811-1852) can
hardly be overestimated, and Arabia exploration
suffered an immeasurable loss by his premature
death, on the eve of his 41st birthday.

His two important articles, written in English,
were originally published in the journal of the
Royal Geographical Society. They have been reprinted with additional material by W.R. Mead and
M. Trautz, a portrait, a map, and a select Wallin
bibliography by Philip Ward, in *Travels in Arabia
(1845 and 1848)* (The Oleander Press, 1979). Since
Wallin's Travels are now in print for the first
time in book form, there is no need to reproduce
those pages (60-93) which deal with Ha'il in 1845,
or the scant notes on his shorter visit in 1848.

Called 'the last of the original pioneers' in
Arabia, and the first 'scientific explorer of the
best modern type', Wallin - or 'Abdu-el-Wali' as he
called himself - took it upon himself to live in
Cairo for fifteen months so totally as an Arab that
he would thereafter be taken for an Arab in speech,
gesture, and appearance.

Eventually reaching Ha'il across the Nafud on
20 September 1845 after tremendous hardships, Wallin
spent two happy months there as the guest of Amir
ᶜAbdullah ibn Rashid. He spent six days eating with
the Amir and sleeping in a mosque, then managed to

rent a small house with a garden and to hire a poor
Persian dervish as servant. 'The Shammar are at
present the mightiest Badawin tribe', Wallin was to
write, and his host was virtually the founder of
the Shammar dynasty. He was victorious in raids,
but so open-handed that his enemies began to sue
for his favour. He steered a prudent course between such potential overlords as the Sharif of
Mecca, Faisal ibn Al-Saud, the Pasha of Egypt, and
the Sublime Porte. Though ^cAbdullah acknowledged
Faisal's power in southern Najd, it was then Ha'il
in northern Najd which men regarded as the focal
power of Central Arabia.

Wallin also reached Ha'il from the direction of
Tabuk and Taima on 3 May 1848, and records meeting
Mit^cab, the younger brother of the new ruler, Talal.
He writes very little about these latter experien-
ces for, hearing of disturbances in eastern Najd, he
determined to take the direct road back to Baghdad.

Wallin's love of the desert can stand for that
of all the travellers whose experiences can be read
at much greater length, and of those who have left
no record at all: 'I do not know where my love of
the desert comes from - all too well I know that
nothing awaits me there but hunger and thirst; the
hot sun without shade; every hour the fear of being
snapped up by my friends the Badawins, and being
left, cruelly stripped, to die of hunger; or else
the prospect of having to pit my strength against a
nature that is as cruel as the sons of the desert;
yet I know that in all Persia's luxuriance, and the
superfluities of the English colony at Baghdad, as
among the fleshpots of Egypt, I longed continually
for the desert.'

4
William Gifford Palgrave, 1862

The Englishman William Gifford Palgrave (1826-88) spent only a relatively unimportant part of his life in Arabia, but nevertheless produced a classic of travel and literature in his *Personal narrative of a year's journey through Central and Eastern Arabia (1862-63)* which was published in London in 1865.

Like Wallin, Palgrave claimed to be a doctor, acquiring goodwill through simple remedies to real or imagined ailments. T.E. Lawrence rated Palgrave's achievements far above his own, and there is no doubt that Palgrave possessed unusual assurance, amounting to arrogance. After an interlude with the army in Bombay (1847-9), he became a passionate convert to Roman Catholicism and spent the period up to 1864 as a student and Jesuit missionary, in Negapatam, Rome, Syria, Paris, and Arabia, before returning to Europe in 1863. The years from 1865 to his death in 1888 were passed in the diplomatic service in places as diverse as Manila and Sofia, Bangkok and Montevideo.

Palgrave chose to travel in Arabia with a young Greek schoolmaster from Zahleh called Geraigeri, who spoke Arabic even more fluently than did Palgrave himself. Palgrave travelled as Salim Abu Mahmu al-ᶜAis ('The Quiet One'), while his Greek companion assumed the name of Barakat ash-Shami.

In Ha'il, Palgrave was recognised three times. First, by a middle-aged merchant who had met him

six months earlier in Damascus. Second, by a man
of al-Qasim who had also met him in Damascus.
Third, by a Ha'ili who claimed to have known him in
Cairo, and to have seen his 'daughter' riding a
beautiful horse. Palgrave was fortunate to be delivered from each of these mischances. The merchant,
told he had made a mistake, apologised for confusing Palgrave with someone else. The Qasimi left
Ha'il the next day. The Ha'ili, once assured that
Palgrave was unmarried and had no daughter, freely
confessed his error.

When Salim and Barakat left Ha'il for Riyadh,
they bore letters from Talal for Faisal and from
^CUbaid for ^CAbdullah, Faisal's eldest son. Mis-
trusting ^CUbaid, Palgrave opened the second letter
and discovered that he was 'recommended' as having
a good knowledge of magic, at that time a capital
crime in Wahnabi Riyadh. Palgrave delivered the
goodwill message from Talal and withheld the
missive from ^CUbaid.

On two occasions, H. St John Philby categoric-
ally claimed that much of Palgrave's narrative was
a fabrication. 'If [Palgrave] ever reached Hayel,
that was his farthest limit in Arabia, and I do not
think that he ven did that. His clever and
romantic story has taken the fancy of the world,'
stated Philby in *Arabian days*, 'but it is little
more, in my opinion, than a "traveller's tale".'

Philby repeated this accusation again in 1947,
basing his case on Palgrave's alleged visit to the
small oasis of al-^CUyun in al-Qasim. Here are
'several huge stones like enormous boulders, placed
endways perpendicularly on the soil, while some of
them yet upheld similar masses laid transversely
over their summit. They were arranged in a curve
once forming a part, it would appear, of a large
circle.' Though he sought this locality, Philby
never identified it and consequently assumed it to
be imaginary. Mea Allan, in her biography of
Palgrave of Arabia (1972), was more pertinacious,

asking the opinion of Dr ^{c}Abdullah Wuhaibi of the University of Riyadh. Dr Wuhaibi quickly confirmed the existence of a stone circle well-known to the people of al-^{c}Uyun as Mawa'in ^{c}Antar ('The Utensils of ^{c}Antar, the Arabian folk hero'). Stone circles of this kind are also found near Henakiyah and at Ras. Palgrave, vindicated in this particular, is not necessarily vindicated in every particular, but we can certainly enjoy today as much as ever his narrative for its lively evocation of the Jabal Shammar under Prince Talal.

Typical street-scene in old Ha'il. (Photo: Berman, 1944). The wall on the left protects a huge date-palm grove, while that on the right is a domestic wall behind which family privacy was (and still is) jealously protected. The horizontal protuberances from the house wall are wooden drainpipes.

CHAPTER III

The Nefood and Djebel Shomer

Per correr miglior acqua alza le vele
Omai la navicella del mio ingegno,
Che lascia dietro a se mar si crudele.—*Dante*

DAUGHTERS of the Great Desert, to use an Arab phrase, the
"Nefood," or sand passes, bear but too strong a family resemblance to their unamiable mother. What has been said
elsewhere about their origin, their extent, their bearings, and
their connection with the D'hanā, or main sand waste of
the south, may exempt me from here entering on a minute
enarration of all their geographical details; let it suffice for
the present that they are offshoots—inlets, one might not un-
suitably call them—of the great ocean of sand that covers about
one-third of the Peninsula, into whose central and comparatively
fertile plateau they make deep inroads, nay, in some places

Palgrave's Plan of Hail (1863)

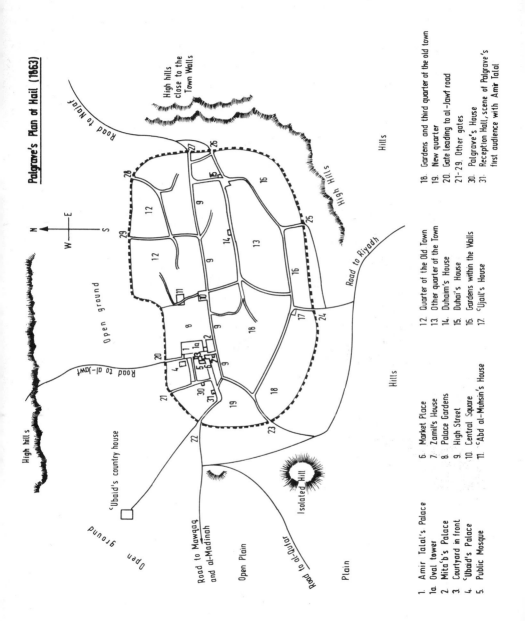

High hills

High hills close to the Town Walls

Road to Najaf

High hills

High Hills

Hills

Road to Riyadh

N
E
S
W

Open ground

Road to al-Jawf

High hills

'Ubaid's country house

Open ground

Road to Mawqaq and al-Madinah

Open Plain

Road to al-Quiar

Plain

Isolated Hill

Hills

1. Amir Talal's Palace
1a. Oval tower
2. Mita'b's Palace
3. Courtyard in front
4. 'Ubaid's Palace
5. Public Mosque

6. Market Place
7. Zamil's House
8. Palace Gardens
9. High Street
10. Central Square
11. 'Abd al-Muhsin's House

12. Quarter of the Old Town
13. Other quarter of the Town
14. Duhaim's House
15. Duhai's House
16. Gardens within the Walls
17. 'Ujail's House

18. Gardens and third quarter of the old town
19. New quarter
20. Gate leading to al-Jawf road
21-29. Other gates
30. Palgrave's House
31. Reception Hall, scene of Palgrave's first audience with Amir Talal

32

almost intersect it. Their general character, of which the
following pages will, I trust, give a tolerably correct idea, is
also that of the Dahnä, or "red desert," itself. The Arabs,
always prone to localize rather than generalize, count these
sand-streams by scores, but they may all be referred to four
principal courses, and he who would traverse the centre must
necessarily cross two of them, perhaps even three, as we did.

The general type of Arabia is that of a central table-land,
surrounded by a desert ring, sandy to the south, west, and east,
and stony to the north. This outlying circle is in its turn girt by
a line of mountains, low and sterile for the most, but attaining
in Yemen and 'Omän considerable height, breadth, and fertility,
while beyond these a narrow rim of coast is bordered by the
sea. The surface of the midmost table-land equals somewhat
less than one-half of the entire Peninsula, and its special
demarcations are much affected, nay, often absolutely fixed,
by the windings and in-runnings of the Nefood. If to these
central high-lands, or Nejed, taking that word in its wider
sense, we add the Djowf, the Ṭä'yif, Djebel 'Aaseer, Yemen,
'Omän, and Ḥasa, in short, whatever spots of fertility belong
to the outer circles, we shall find that Arabia contains about
two-thirds of cultivated, or at least of cultivable land, with a
remaining third of irreclaimable desert, chiefly to the south.
In most other directions the great blank spaces often left in
maps of this country are quite as frequently indications of
non-information as of real non-inhabitation. However, we
have just now a strip, though fortunately only a strip, of pure
unmitigated desert before us, after which better lands await
us; and in this hope let us take courage with the old poet,
who has kindly furnished me with a very appropriate heading
to this chapter, and boldly enter the Nefood.

Much had we heard of them from Bedouins and countrymen,
so that we had made up our minds to something very terrible
and very impracticable. But the reality, especially in these
dog-days, proved worse than aught heard or imagined.

We were now traversing an immense ocean of loose reddish
sand, unlimited to the eye, and heaped up in enormous ridges
running parallel to each other from north to south, undulation
after undulation, each swell two or three hundred feet in average

33

height, with slant sides and rounded crests furrowed in every
direction by the capricious gales of the desert. In the depths
between the traveller finds himself as it were imprisoned in a
suffocating sand-pit, hemmed in by burning walls on every side ;
while at other times, while labouring up the slope, he overlooks
what seems a vast sea of fire, swelling under a heavy monsoon
wind, and ruffled by a cross-blast into little red-hot waves.
Neither shelter nor rest for eye or limb amid torrents of light
and heat poured from above on an answering glare reflected
below.

> Tale scendeva l' eternale ardore ;
> Onde la rena s' accendea com' esca
> Sotto focile, a doppiar lo dolore.

Add to this the weariness of long summer days of toiling—I
might better say wading—through the loose and scorching soil,
on drooping half-stupefied beasts, with few and interrupted hours
of sleep at night, and no rest by day because no shelter, little
to eat and less to drink, while the tepid and discoloured water in
the skins rapidly diminishes even more by evaporation than by
use, and a vertical sun, such a sun, strikes blazing down till
clothes, baggage, and housings all take the smell of burning,
and scarce permit the touch. "Were this eternal it were hell,"
said I to my comrade, who, drooping on his camel, gave no
answer. The boisterous gaiety of the Bedouins was soon ex-
pended, and scattered, one to front, another behind, each
pursued his way in a silence only broken by the angry snarl of
the camels when struck, as they often were, to improve their
pace.

It was on the 20th of July, a little after noon, that we had
left Be'er Shekeek. The rest of that day and almost all night
we journeyed on, for here three or four hours of repose at a
time, supper included, was all that could be taken, since, if we
did not reach the other side of the Nefood before our store of
water was exhausted, we were lost for certain. Indeed, during
the last twenty-four hours of these passes, to call them by
their Arab name, we had only one hour of halt. Monday, the
21st of July, wore slowly away, most slowly it seemed, in the
same labour, and amid the same unvarying scene. The loose
sand hardly admits of any vegetation ; even the Ghada, which,

like many other Euphorbias, seems hardly to require either earth or moisture for its sustenance, is here scant and miserably stunted; none can afford either shelter or pasture. Sometimes a sort of track appears, more often none; the moving surface has long since lost the traces of those who last crossed it.

About this time we noticed in the manner of our Sherarat companions, especially the younger ones, a certain insolent familiarity which put us much on our guard; for it is the custom of the Bedouin, when meditating plunder or treachery, to try the ground first in this fashion, and if he sees any signs of timidity or yielding in his intended victim, he takes it as a signal for proceeding further. The best plan in such cases is to put on a sour face and keep silence, with now and then a sharp reprimand by way of intimidation, and this often cows the savage just as a barking dog will shrink back under a steady look. Such was accordingly our conduct on the present occasion. We kept apart for hours at a time, and when alongside of the brigands, said little, and that little anything but friendly. Before long the more impudent appeared abashed or embarrassed and fell back, while an old 'Azzām chief, with a dry face like a withered crab-apple, pushed his dromedary up alongside of mine, under pretext of seeking medical advice, but in reality to make thus a proffer of friendliness and respect. Of course I met his advances with cold and sullen reserve; and hereon he began to apologize for the " Ghushm," "ill-bred clowns" of his party, assuring us that they had, however, no bad intention; that it was merely want of good education; that all were our brothers, our servants, &c. &c. We received his apology with an air of dignified importance, talked big of what we could or would do—very little, I fear, had matters been brought to the test—and then condescended to friendly chat and professional information, according to what his ailments might require or his intelligence admit.

But I afterwards learnt from the Shomer Bedouins and from the men of Djowf, that the worthy Sherarats, supposing us to have amassed great wealth under Hamood's patronage, had seriously proposed to take the opportunity of this desert solitude to pillage us, and then leave us without water or camels to find our way out of the Nefood as best we might, that is, never.

This little scheme they had communicated to the Shomer, hoping for their compliance and aid. But these last, more accustomed to the restraints of neighbouring rule, were afraid of the consequences; knowing, too, that Telāl, if anyhow informed of such proceedings, might very possibly constitute himself our sole legatee, executor, and something more. Accordingly they refused to join, and the conspirators, who perceived from our manner that we already had some suspicion about their intentions, hastened to plaster matters over before we should be in a way to compromise their position at Ḥā'yel, by complaints of their meditated treachery.

If accompanied on a journey by Bedouins of a number less than or equal to your own, do as you think best—talk, joke, or keep silence, it is all one. But should they be many and you few, your only security is in a serious, steady, and rather sulky manner. Above all, never let them grow familiar; the proverb of giving an inch and taking an ell, must have been first made for these people.

Near sunset of the second day we came in sight of two lonely pyramidal peaks of dark granite, rising amid the sand-waves full in our way. " 'Aalām-es-Sa'ād," the people call them, that is, " the signs of good luck," because they indicate that about one-third of the distance from Be'er-Shekeek to Djebel Shomer has been here passed. They stand out like islands, or—rather like the rocks that start from the sea near the mouth of the Tagus, or like the Maldive group in the midst of the deep Indian Ocean. Their roots must be in the rocky base over which this upper layer of sand is strewn like the sea-water over its bed; we shall afterwards meet with similar phenomena in other desert spots. Here the under stratum is evidently of granite, often it is of basalt, sometimes it is calcareous. As to the average depth of the sand, I should estimate it at about four hundred feet, but it may not unfrequently be much more; at least I have met with hollows of full six hundred feet in perpendicular descent.

On we journeyed with the 'Aalām-es-Sa'ād looming dark before us, till when near midnight, so far as I could calculate by the stars, our only timepiece (and not a bad one in these clear skies), we passed close under the huge black masses of

rock. Vainly had I flattered myself with a halt, were it but
of half an hour, on the occasion. "On we swept," and not till
the morning star rose close beneath the Pleiades was the word
given to dismount. We tumbled rather than lay down on the
ground; and before sunrise were once more on our way.

Soon we reached the summit of a gigantic sand ridge. "Look
there," said Djedey' to us, and pointed forwards. Far off on
the extreme horizon a blue cloud-like peak appeared, and
another somewhat lower at its side. "Those are the mountains
of Djobbah, and the nearest limits of Djebel Shomer," said
our guide. Considering how loose the water-skins now flapped
at the camel's side, my first thought was, "how are we to reach
them?": all the band seemed much of the same mind, for they
pushed on harder than before.

Near this we fell in with a small party of roving Bedouins,
from the south; and by their conversation received our first
news of the war then raging in the province of Kaseem, between
the Wahhabee monarch and the partisans of 'Oneyzah,—war of
which we shall afterwards see and hear our fill, and of which we
shall learn also, though not till the following year and when
on the very point of quitting Arabia, the disastrous conclusion.

Meanwhile with no slight difficulty we slid down the sand,
descending from our elevated position, and at once lost sight,
much to my regret, of the peaks of Djobbah; nor did we
view them again till when close under their base, at the verge
of the Nefood.

But the further we advanced the worse did the desert grow,
more desolate, more hopeless in its barren waves; and at noon
our band broke up into a thorough " sauve qui peut;" some had
already exhausted their provisions, solid or liquid, and others
were scarcely better furnished; every one goaded on his beast
to reach the land of rest and safety.' Djedey', my comrade, and
myself, kept naturally together. On a sudden my attention
was called to two or three sparrows, twittering under a shrub by
the wayside. They were the first birds we had met with in this
desert, and indicated our approach to cultivation and life. I
bethought me of tales heard in childhood, at a comfortable fireside, how some far-wandering sailors, Columbus and his crew, if
my memory serves me right, after days and months of dreary

ocean, welcomed a bird that, borne from some yet undiscovered coast, first settled on their mast. My comrade fell a crying for very joy.

However we had yet a long course before us, and we ploughed on all that evening with scarce an hour's halt for a most scanty supper, and then all night up and down the undulating labyrinth, like men in an enchanter's circle, fated always to journey and never to advance. During the dark hours that immediately precede the dawn, we fell in with a band of some sixty horsemen, armed with matchlocks and lances; they formed part of a military expedition directed by order of Telāl against the insolence of some Tey'yāhha Bedouins in the neighbourhood of Teymah.

The morning broke on us still toiling amid the sands. By daylight we saw our straggling companions like black specks here and there, one far ahead on a yet vigorous dromedary, another in the rear, dismounted, and urging his fallen beast to rise by plunging a knife a good inch deep into its haunches, a third lagging in the extreme distance. Every one for himself and God for us all; so we quickened our pace, looking anxiously before us for the hills of Djobbah, which could not now be distant. At noon we came in sight of them all at once, close on our right, wild and fantastic cliffs, rising sheer on the margin of the sand sea. We coasted them awhile, till at a turn the whole plain of Djobbah and its landscape opened on our view.

Here we had before us a cluster of black granite rocks, streaked with red, and about seven hundred feet, at a rough guess, in height; beyond them a large barren plain, partly white and encrusted with salt, partly green with tillage, and studded with palm groves, amongst which we could discern, not far off, the village of Djobbah, much resembling that of Djowf in arrangement and general appearance, only smaller, and without castle or tower. Beyond the valley glistered a second line of sand-hills, but less wild and desolate looking than those behind us, and far in the distance the main range of Djebel Shomer, a long purple sierra of most picturesque outline. Had we there and then mounted, as we afterwards did, the heights on our right, we should have also seen in the extreme south-west a green patch near the horizon, where cluster the palm plantations of Teymah, a place famed in Arab history, and by some supposed identical with the Teman of Holy Writ.

But for the moment a drop of fresh water and a shelter from the July sun was much more in our thoughts than all the Teymahs or Temans that ever existed. My camel, too, was not at his wits' end, for he never had any, but quite at the end of his legs, and hardly capable of advance, while I was myself too tired to urge him vigorously, and we took a fair hour to cross a narrow white strip of mingled salt and sand that yet intervened between us and the village.

Without its garden walls was pitched the very identical tent of our noble guide, and here his wife and family were anxiously awaiting their lord. Djedey' invited us—indeed he could not conformably with Shomer customs do less—to partake of his board and lodging, and we had no better course than to accept of both. So we let our camels fling themselves out like dead or dying alongside of the tabernacle, and entered to drink water mixed with sour milk, and to repose in the equivocal shade afforded by a single tattered covering of black goat's hair.

As evening drew on, Djedey', after giving his camels a well-earned draught from the garden well close by, invited us to pay a visit of ceremony to the local governor 'Aaḳil, a native of the village itself, but invested by Ṭelál with vicarious authority. Now our friend's real object in calling in at this hour was to ensure a good supper, a thing which his own domicile could hardly have mustered. No dowager lady in Young's time or our own ever better deserved the satirical description of one who

> For her own breakfast will devise a scheme,
> Nor take her tea without a stratagem,

than does a Bedouin on parallel occasions. But you must substitute " supper " for " breakfast," and " dates " for " tea."

To the great delight of my comrade, whom the wretchedness of Djedey's hovel had led to anticipate a correspondingly miserable kitchen, our guide's manœuvres, the most intellectual of which a Bedouin is capable, met with deserved success. 'Aaḳil honoured us with the desired invitation ; and the day closed in a good supper and a lively evening, during which

Djedey' amused the whole party, by an uncouth dance with the coffee-making negro of the governor.

Next day we remained quiet; all glad of an interval of repose before the three days' journey which was to lead us to Ḥā'yel. Sometimes we climbed the heights to get a wider range of view, sometimes we strolled about the irregular village and talked with its inhabitants; and here first we met with unmistakable proofs of that deep half-idolizing attachment which the very name of Ṭelāl claims throughout the whole of Djebel Shomer. The quiet and settled state of all things here much contrasted with the half anarchical condition lately witnessed in the Djowf, and its war-seamed features. But the soil of Djobbah is poor, and its produce, though of the same kind with that we had left behind us, was in every way inferior to it. A curiosity of this valley is the capricious intermixture of salt and fresh water springs; they are often separated from each other by only a few yards of distance, and jotted seemingly at random all over the level.

The village itself so far resembles the Djowf, that I may be excused from entering on particular details regarding houses, gardens, and the like. I may here add, as an apology for brevity of description, while we pass by the different localities of Djebel Shomer, that they have almost all of them, whether large or small, much the same straggling appearance, the same mixture of dwellings and cultivation, of plantations and byeways, the same neglect of fortification and defence, which distinguishes them from the compact and well-guarded villages of Nejed Proper, and denotes habitual security; but also, alas! a total disregard for ,whatever is known in Europe by the name of symmetry, of which no true Arab of the north, whether sleeping or waking, had ever an idea. I say of the north, for in Ḥasa and 'Omān the laws of architectural proportion are known and observed, nor are they wholly absent from middle and southern Nejed.

About sunrise on the 25th of July we left Djobbah, crossed the valley to the south-east, and entered once more on a sandy desert; but a desert, as I have before hinted, of a milder and less inhospitable character than the dreary Nefood of two days back. Here the and is thickly sprinkled with shrubs, and not

40

altogether devoid of herbs and grass ; while the undulations of the surface, running invariably from north to south, according to the general rule of that phenomenon, are much less deeply traced, though never wholly absent. We paced on all day ; at nightfall we found ourselves on the edge of a vast funnel-like depression, where the sand recedes on all sides to leave bare the chalky bottom-strata below ; here lights glimmering amid Bedouin tents in the depths of the valley invited us to try our chance of a preliminary supper before the repose of the night. We had, however, much ado to descend the cavity, so steep was the sandy slope ; while its circular form and spiral marking would have reminded me of Edgar Poe's " Maelstroom," had I then been acquainted with that most authentic narrative. The Arabs to whom the watch-fires belonged were shepherds of the numerous Shomer tribe, whence the district, plain and mountain, takes its name. They welcomed us to a share of their supper ; and a good dish of rice, instead of insipid samḥ or pasty Djereeshah, augured a certain approach to civilization. The limestone rock, at whose edge the tents were pitched, furnishes through its clefts a copious supply of water, and hence this hollow is a common resort for Bedouins and their beasts, like the wells of Magoowa' mentioned in a former chapter.

Such cavities are not uncommon amidst the sands, and occur in a very arbitrary manner, independent it would seem of the general laws of the desert ; nor could I hit on any passable hypothesis to explain their formation. Their great size secures them against filling up ; the pit in which we passed that night could not have measured much less than a quarter of a mile at its upper diameter, from rim to rim, and its depth was certainly about eight hundred feet. The huge undulations of sand, rolling apparently from west to east, and never failing in the Nefood of Arabia, may, if a hypothesis be permitted, find their cause in the diurnal rotation of the globe, and the imperfect communication of its rapid surface movement to the loose material here strewn over it. But this affords no clue to the capricious pits dug out by nature from time to time in these very wastes, and hollowed with an exactness of circular form truly surprising. I met them alike in the Nefood and Dahna, in the northern and southern desert ; the phenomenon belongs to the vast aggregation of sand, not to any particular wind, or meteorological phase of a local nature. The parallel waves of the desert are also the same everywhere, on condition of a sufficient depth in the sand itself.

At break of day we resumed our march, and met with camels and camel-drivers in abundance, besides a few sheep and goats. Before noon we had got clear of the sandy patch, and entered in its stead on a firm gravelly soil. Here we enjoyed an hour of midday halt and shade in a natural cavern, hollowed out in a high granite rock; itself an advanced guard of the main body of Djebel Shomer. This mountain range now rose before us, wholly unlike any other that I had ever seen; a huge mass of crag and stone, piled up in fantastic disorder, with green valleys and habitations intervening. The sun had not yet set when we reached the pretty village of Kenah, amid groves and waters, no more, however, running streams like those of Djowf, but an artificial irrigation by means of wells and buckets. At some distance from the houses stood a cluster of three or four large over-shadowing trees, objects of peasant veneration here, as once in Palestine. The welcome of the inhabitants, when we dismounted at their doors, was hearty and hospitable, nay, even polite and considerate; and a good meal, with a dish of fresh grapes for dessert, was soon set before us in the verandah of a pleasant little house, much reminding me of an English farm-cottage, whither the good man of the dwelling had invited us for the evening. All expressed great desire to profit by our medical skill; and on our reply that we could not conveniently open shop except at the capital Hā'yel, several announced their resolution to visit us there; and subsequently kept their word, though at the cost of about twenty-four miles of journey.

We rose very early. Our path, well tracked and trodden, now lay between ridges of precipitous rock, rising abruptly from a level and grassy plain; sometimes the road was sunk in deep gorges, sometimes it opened out on wider spaces, where trees and villagers appeared, while the number of wayfarers, on foot or mounted, single or in bands, still increased as we drew nearer to the capital. About noon we came opposite to a large village called Lakeetah, where we turned aside to rest a little during the heat in the house of a wealthy inhabitant. There was an air of

newness and security about the dwellings and plantations hardly
to be found now-a-days in any other part of Arabia, 'Omān
alone excepted. I may add also the great frequency of young
trees and ground newly enclosed, a cheerful sight, yet further
enhanced by the total absence of ruins, so common in the East,
and above all in the Ottoman dominions ; hence the general effect
produced by Djebel Shomer, when contrasted with most other
provinces or kingdoms around, near and far, is that of a newly
coined piece, in all its sharpness and shine, amid a dingy heap
of defaced currency. It is a fresh creation, and shows what Arabia
might be under better rule than it enjoys for the most part : an
inference rendered the more conclusive by the fact that in natural
and unaided fertility Djebel Shomer is perhaps the least favoured
district in the entire central peninsula.

Lakeetah contains about four hundred houses, and in consequence two thousand four hundred inhabitants, more or less,
according to the broad computation common in these countries,
which allows six or seven individuals for each domicile. After
remounting and riding a little further on, we saw, not far from
the main road, the larger village of Woseyṭah, whither Djedey'
would fain have turned aside for the evening. But we were
now thoroughly impatient to be at our journey's end, and stoutly
declared that we would not, on any consideration, halt short of
Ḥā'yel itself.

We were here close under the backbone of Djebel Shomer,
whose reddish crags rose in the strangest forms on our right and
left, while a narrow cleft down to the plain-level below gave
opening to the capital. Very hard to bring an army through
this against the will of the inhabitants, thought I ; fifty
resolute men could, in fact, hold the pass against thousands ;
nor is there any other approach to Ḥā'yel from the northern
direction. The town is situated near the very centre of the
mountains ; it was as yet entirely concealed from our view by the
windings of the road amid huge piles of rock. Meanwhile from
Djobbah to Ḥā'yel, the whole plain gradually rises, running up
between the sierras, whose course from north-east to south-
west crosses two-thirds of the upper peninsula, and forms the
outwork of the central high country. Hence the name of
Nejed, literally " highland," in contradistinction to the coast

and the outlying provinces of lesser elevation.   Hence, too, in
popular phrase, the word " talaa', " or " went up," is applied to
those who journey from the circumference inland ; while
" anhader," that is, " went down," is said of travellers whose
way lies from the centre to Mecca, Ḥaṣa, the Djowf, and so
forth.

I must insert a line or two of explanation regarding the deno-
mination "Nejed" itself.   It is commonly enough applied to
the whole space included between Djebel Shomer on the north
and the great desert to the south, from the extreme range of
Djebel Toweyḳ on the east to the neighbourhood of the Turkish pilgrim-road, or Derb-el-Ḥajj, on the west.   However, this
central district, forming a huge parallelogram, placed almost
diagonally across the midmost of Arabia, from north-east-by-east
to south-west-by-west, as a glance at the map may show, is
again subdivided by the natives of the country into the Nejed-el-
'aalā, or Upper Nejed, and the Nejed-el-owṭā, or Lower Nejed,
a distinction of which more hereafter, while Djebel Shomer is
generally considered as a sort of appendage to Nejed, rather
than as belonging to that district itself.   But the Djowf is
always excluded by the Arabs from the catalogue of upland
provinces, though strangers sometimes admit it also to the title
of Nejed by an error on their part, since it is a solitary oasis,
and a door to highland or inner Arabia—not, in any strict
sense, a portion of it.

I trust that these topographical details, and more are yet to
come, may perhaps lend an aid to rectify in some degree the
current but too often erroneous nomenclature which has crept
into maps of the region; not that a name is in itself of any
great importance, but that mistakes on these points give rise at
times to incorrect ideas, and thus the whole picture of Arabia
in all its bearings comes to be distorted.

The sun was yet two hours' distance above the western
horizon, when we threaded the narrow and winding defile, till we
arrived at its further end.   Here we found ourselves on the verge
of a large plain, many miles in length and breadth, and girt on
every side by a high mountain rampart, while right in front of
us, at scarce a quarter of an hour's march, lay the town of
Ḥā'yel surrounded by fortifications of about twenty feet in

height, with bastion-towers, some round, some square, and large folding gates at intervals; it offered the same show of freshness and even of something like irregular elegance that had before struck us in the villages on our way. But this was a full-grown town, and its area might readily hold three hundred thousand inhabitants or more, were its streets and houses close packed like those of Brussels or Paris. But the number of citizens does not, in fact, exceed twenty or twenty-two thousand, thanks to the many large gardens, open spaces, and even plantations, included within the outer walls, while the immense palace of the monarch alone, with its pleasure grounds annexed, occupies about one-tenth of the entire city. Our attention was attracted by a lofty tower, some seventy feet in height, of recent construction and oval form, belonging to the royal residence. The plain all around the town is studded with isolated houses and gardens, the property of wealthy citizens, or of members of the kingly family, and on the far-off skirts of the plain appear the groves belonging to Kafar, 'Adwah, and other villages, placed at the openings of the mountain gorges that conduct to the capital. The town walls and buildings shone yellow in the evening sun, and the whole prospect was one of thriving security, delightful to view, though wanting in the peculiar luxuriance of vegetation offered by the valley of Djowf. A few Bedouin tents lay clustered close by the ramparts, and the great number of horsemen, footmen, camels, asses, peasants, townsmen, boys, women, and other like, all passing to and fro on their various avocations, gave cheerfulness and animation to the scene.

We crossed the plain, and made for the town gate opposite the castle; next, with no little difficulty, prevailed on our camels to pace the high-walled street, and at last arrived at the open space in front of the palace. It was yet an hour before sunset, or rather more; the business of the day was over in Ḥā'yel, and the outer courtyard where we now stood was crowded with loiterers of all shapes and sizes. We made our camels kneel down close by the palace gate, alongside of some forty or fifty others, and then stepped back to repose our very weary limbs on a stone bench opposite the portal, and waited what might next occur.

But before we verify the Arab proverb which attributes ill-

luck to occurrences of the evening, let us cast around a look on this
strange scene, strange, that is, to a foreigner, but completely in
harmony with the genius of the country and people. Before us
are the long earth walls of the palace, enormously thick, and about
thirty feet in height, pierced near the summit with loopholes
rather than windows, and occupying an extent of four hundred
and fifty to five hundred feet in length. The principal gate is
placed, according to approved custom, in a receding angle of the
wall, and flanked by high square towers; semicircular bastions
advance too from space to space all the length of the front.
Immediately under the shadow of the wall runs a long bench of
beaten earth and stone; we observe too, about half way in its
line, a sort of throne or raised seat, to be occupied by the
monarch's most sacred person when giving public audience.
The palace of Meta'ab, the king's second brother, is included in
the same mass of building, but has its own entrance apart.

On the other side of the open area, that is, where we are now
seated, stands a long range of warehouses and small apartments,
each under lock and key. Here is stowed away the merchan-
dize which belongs exclusively to the government; here, too,
Telāl, as a general rule, lodges his guests; for no stranger, be he
who he may, is ever allowed to sleep within the palace walls.
In the same direction, but farther up the area, and opposite to
the residence of Meta'ab, is the large public mosque, or Djāmia'.
At its angle the court opens out into the new market-place,
which we will visit to-morrow. On the other side of this
opening, but on the same line as the Djāmia', rises the sump-
tuous house of Zāmil, the chief treasurer and prime minister too.
I do not say that the union of such offices in one person is exactly
constitutional, but it seems to work here very well, besides
simplifying government salaries, a positive advantage in poor
Arab states. Lastly, a tall gate ends the area, and gives admittance into the more plebeian High Street, which here crosses
at right angles, and leads up and down through the whole
breadth of the town.

At the opposite extremity of this great courtyard, and communicating with a second gate through which we had just passed,
enters another large street, leading out at some distance on the
plain. Towards this end of the enclosure, and still opposite the

46

palace itself, are the dwellings of two or three principal officers
of the household ; and lastly, a low door, in all " the pride that
apes humility," gives entrance to the abode and spacious gardens
of 'Obeyd, the present king's uncle, a very important character
he, and already mentioned on occasion of his first expedition
against the Djowf.   Enough of him for the present ; he will end
by becoming a personal and even too intimate an acquaintance.

About the portal, some standing, some seated on the stone
platform near its entrance, are several of the subordinate officers
in waiting.   These men are neatly and, all things considered,
cleanly clothed, in white robes and black cloaks, much like
Hamood, whose dress we have not long since described ; long
silver-tipped wands, strongly resembling those wielded by that
venerable class of men whom mortals call Beadles, distinguish
those among them who are charged with household employment ; but the greater number are of a military character, and
wear silver-hilted swords.   The neighbouring benches on one
side of the court and on the other are thronged by a crowd of
the better sort of citizens, come from their shops or houses to
hear and chat over news, and to take the evening air.   Few of
them, save those of noble birth, wear arms ; but their general
appearance is every way decorous.   Some, in plainer clothes,
have a peculiar and puritanical look, they will be from Nejed ;
a slightly rakish air, on the contrary, points out the man of
Ḳaseem.   In the middle of the courtyard itself, or seated
among the well-dressed citizens with true Arab fraternity and
equality, are not a few whose dingy garments and coarse features
bespeak them of mechanical profession, or at least poor.   Some
Bedouins are mixed with the rest, and may at once be known
by their scanty ragged dress and cringing attitude.   The lowest
in the nomade scale here present are the uncouth Sherarat,
and the still more uncouth Ṣolibah ; while the Shomer, near
akin to many of the townsmen, and somewhat polished by
more frequent intercourse with the civilized world, may stand
highest in this category.

At our first appearance a slight stir takes place.   The
customary salutations are given and returned by those nearest at
hand ; and a small knot of inquisitive idlers, come up to see
what and whence we are, soon thickens into a dense circle.   Many

questions are asked, first of our conductor, Djedey', and next of ourselves ; our answers are tolerably laconic. Meanwhile a thin middle-sized individual, whose countenance bears the type of smiling urbanity and precise etiquette, befitting his office at court, approaches us. His neat and simple dress, the long silver-circled staff in his hand, his respectful salutation, his politely important manner, all denote him one of the palace retinue. It is Seyf, the court chamberlain, whose special duty is the reception and presentation of strangers. We rise to receive him, and are greeted with a decorous, " Peace be with you, brothers," in the fullness of every inflection and accent that the most scrupulous grammarian could desire. We return an equally Priscianic salutation. " Whence have you come? may good attend you !" is the first question. Of course we declare ourselves physicians from Syria, for our bulkier wares had been disposed of in the Djowf, and we were now resolved to depend on medical practice alone. " And what do you desire here in our town ? may God grant you success !" says Seyf. " We desire the favour of God most high, and, secondly, that of Telāl," is our answer, conforming our style to the correctest formulas of the country, which we had already begun to pick up. Whereupon Seyf, looking very sweet the while, begins, as in duty bound, a little encomium on his master's generosity and other excellent qualities, and assures us that we have exactly reached right quarters.

But alas ! while my comrade and myself were exchanging side-glances of mutual felicitation at such fair beginnings, Nemesis suddenly awoke to claim her due, and the serenity of our horizon was at once overcast by an unexpected and most unwelcome cloud. My readers are doubtless already aware that nothing was of higher importance for us than the most absolute incognito, above all in whatever regarded European origin and character. In fact, were we once known for Europeans, all intimate access and sincerity of intercourse with the people of the land would have been irretrievably lost, and our onward progress to Nejed rendered totally impossible. These were the very least inconveniences that could follow such a detection ; others much more disagreeable might also be well apprehended. Now thus far nothing had occurred capable of exciting serious suspicion, no one had recognized us, or pretended to recognize. We, too, on our part, had thought that Gaza, Ma'ān, and perhaps the Djowf, were the only localities where this kind of recognition had to be feared. But we had reckoned without our host; the first real danger was reserved for Ḥā'yel, within the very limits of Nejed, and with all the desert-belt between us and our old acquaintances.

For while Seyf was running through the preliminaries of his politeness, I saw to my horror amid the circle of bystanders a figure, a face well known to me scarce six months before in Damascus, and well known to many others also, now merchant, now trader, now post-contractor, shrewd, enterprising and active, though nigh fifty years of age, a zealous Mahometan, yet intimate with many Europeans of considerable standing in Syria and Bagdad—one, in short, accustomed to all kinds of men, and not to be easily imposed on by any.

While I involuntarily stared dismay on my friend, and yet doubted if it could possibly be he, all incertitude was dispelled by his cheerful salutation, in the confidential tone of an old acquaintance, followed by wondering enquiries as to what wind had blown me hither, and what I meant to do here in Ḥā'yel.

Wishing him most heartily—somewhere else, I had nothing for it but to " fix a vacant stare," to give a formal return of greeting, and then silence.

But misfortunes never come single. While I was thus on my defensive against so dangerous an antagonist in the person of my free and easy friend, lo! a tall, sinister-featured individual comes up, clad in the dress of an inhabitant of Ḳaseem, and abruptly breaks in with, " And I too have seen him at Damascus," naming at the same time the place and date of the meeting, and specifying exactly the circumstances most calculated to set me down for a European bone and marrow, body and soul.

Had he really met me as he said? I cannot precisely say; the place he mentioned was one whither men, half spies, half travellers, and whole intriguers from the interior districts, nay, even from Nejed itself, not unfrequently resort; and as I myself was conscious of having paid more than one visit there, my officious interlocutor might very possibly have been one of those present on some such occasion. So that although I did not now

recognize him in particular, there was a strong intrinsic probability in favour of his ill-timed veracity; and his thus coming
in to support the first witness in his assertions, rendered my
predicament, already unsafe, yet worse.

But ere I could frame an answer or resolve what course to
hold, up came a third, who, by overshooting the mark, put the
game into our hands. He too salaams me as an old friend, and
then, turning to those around, now worked up to a most extraordinary pitch of amazed curiosity, says, " And I also know him
perfectly well, I have often met him at Cairo, where he lives
in great wealth in a large house near the Ḳaṣr-el-'Eynee ; his
name is 'Abd-es-Ṣaleeb, he is married, and has a very beautiful
daughter, who rides an expensive horse," &c. &c. &c.

Here at last was a pure invention or mistake (for I know not
which it was) that admitted of a flat denial. " Aṣlaḥek' Allah,"
" May God set you right," said I ; " never did I live at Cairo,
nor have I the blessing of any horse-riding young ladies for
daughters." Then, looking very hard at my second detector,
towards whom I had all the right of doubt, " I do not remember
having ever seen you ; think well as to what you say; many a
man besides myself has a reddish beard and straw-coloured
mustachios," taking pains however not to seem particularly
" careful to answer him in this matter," but as if merely questioning the precise identity. But for the first of the trio I knew
not what to do or to reply, so I continued to look at him
with a killing air of inquisitive stupidity, as though not fully
understanding his meaning.

But Seyf, who had appeared at first somewhat staggered by
this sudden downpour of recognition, was now reassured by
the discomfiture of the third witness, and came to the convenient conclusion that the two others were no better worthy
of credit. " Never mind them," exclaimed he, addressing
himself to us, " they are talkative liars, mere gossipers ; let
them alone, they do not deserve attention ; come along with
me to the Ḳ'hāwah in the palace, and rest yourselves." Then
turning to my poor Damascene friend, whose only wrong was to
have been over much in the right, he sharply chid him, and
next the rest, and led us off, most glad to follow the leader,
through the narrow and dark portal into the royal residence.

After passing between files of wandsmen and swordsmen, Arabs and negroes, we entered on a small court, where, under a shed, was arranged the dreaded artillery of Ṭelāl, nine pieces in all, of different calibre, four only mounted on gun carriages, and out of the four just three serviceable. Of this last number were the two large iron mortars that had played so important a part in the siege of the Djowf. The third, a long brass field-piece, bore the date of 1810, with a very English " G. R." (illegible, I need hardly say, for its actual possessors) embossed above. The other guns were all more or less injured, and quite unfit for duty, but this was a circumstance unknown to the Arabs around, and perhaps to Ṭelāl himself, and "all the nine " military muses seemed to impress equal awe on the minds of the beholders. This tremendous battery had been in part furnished by the Wahhabee monarch to 'Abd-Allah, father and predecessor of Ṭelāl, and in part procured by the agents of the present reign at the seaport of Koweyt on the Persian Gulf, an active and thriving little town, of whose doings with the Wahhabees on the south, and with Ṭelāl on the west, we shall see more hereafter.

We traversed this court, and entered a second, one side of which was formed by the ladies' apartments, duly separated by a high blind wall from profane intercourse, and the other by the Ḳ'hāwah or guest-room. This apartment was about eighty feet in length by thirty or more in breadth, and of height proportionate; the beams of the flat roof (for vaulting is here unknown) rested on six large round columns in a central row. It was of evidently recent construction, well lighted, and perfectly neat. The coffee furnace was of dimensions proportionate to those of the hall, and by its side was seated a sturdy negro, who rose at our approach. A few guests from the neighbouring provinces, and some of the court attendants, were present. Two men, whose feet were loosely chained with heavy iron links, shuffled about the hall. They were state prisoners, and condemned to incarceration at his Majesty's royal will and pleasure, but were permitted the entrance of the Ḳ'hāwah by way of recreation; a curious instance of the humanity of the Arab character, even in the infliction of punishment. Imagine how the appearance of a convicted rebel in the saloons of the

Tuileries or of Buckingham Palace would surprise the court!
One of these men was a chieflet of Djowf, brought hither by
Telāl on his conquest of that district, and not yet liberated, nor
likely to be so in a hurry. But neither he nor his companion
looked particularly miserable.

Here we remained whilst coffee was, as wont, prepared and
served. Seyf, who had left us awhile, now came back to say
that Telāl would soon return from his afternoon walk in a
garden where he had been taking the air, and that if we would
pass into the outer court we should then and there have the
opportunity of paying him our introductory respects. He
added that we should afterwards find our supper ready, and be
provided also with good lodgings for the night; finally, that
the K'hāwah and what it contained were always at our disposition
so long as we should honour Hā'yel by our presence.

We rose accordingly and returned with Seyf to the outside
area. It was fuller than ever, on account of the expected
appearance of the monarch. A few minutes later we saw a
crowd approach from the upper extremity of the place, namely,
that towards the market. When the new-comers drew near,
we saw them to be almost exclusively armed men, with some
of the more important-looking citizens, but all on foot. In
the midst of this circle, though detached from those around
them, slowly advanced three personages, whose dress and
deportment, together with the respectful distance observed
by the rest, announced superior rank. "Here comes Telāl,"
said Seyf, in an undertone.

The midmost figure was in fact that of the prince himself.
Short of stature, broad-shouldered, and strongly built, of a very
dusky complexion, with long black hair, dark and piercing eyes,
and a countenance rather severe than open, Telāl might readily
be supposed above forty years in age, though he is in fact
thirty-seven or thirty-eight at most. His step was measured,
his demeanour grave and somewhat haughty. His dress, a
long robe of Cachemire shawl, covered the white Arab shirt,
and over all he wore a delicately worked cloak of camel's hair
from 'Omān, a great rarity and highly valued in this part of
Arabia. His head was adorned by a broidered handkerchief, in
which silk and gold thread had not been spared, and girt by a

broad band of camel's hair entwined with red silk, the manufacture of Meshid 'Alee. A gold-mounted sword hung by his side, and his dress was perfumed with musk in a degree better adapted to Arab than to European nostrils. His glance never rested for a moment; sometimes it turned on his nearer companions, sometimes on the crowd; I have seldom seen so truly an " eagle eye " in rapidity and in brilliancy.

By his side walked a tall thin individual clad in garments of somewhat less costly material, but of gayer colours and embroidery than those of the king himself. His face announced unusual intelligence and courtly politeness; his sword was not, however, adorned with gold, the exclusive privilege of the royal family, but with silver only.

This was Zāmil, the treasurer and prime minister—sole minister, indeed, of the autocrat. Raised from beggary by 'Abd-Allah the late king, who had seen in the ragged orphan signs of rare capacity, he continued to merit the uninterrupted favour of his patron, and after his death had become equally, or yet more dear to Ṭelāl, who raised him from post to post till he at last occupied the highest position in the kingdom after the monarch himself. Faithful to his master, and placed by his plebeian extraction beyond reach of rival family jealousy, his even and amiable temper had made him eminently popular without the palace, and as cherished by his master within, while his extraordinary application to business, joined with a ready but calm mind, and the great services he rendered the state in his double duty, merited, in the opinion of all, those personal riches of which he made a very free and munificent display.

Of the demurely smiling 'Abd-el-Maḥsin, the second companion of the king's evening walk, I will say nothing for the moment; we shall have him before long for a very intimate acquaintance and a steady friend.

Every one stood up as Ṭelāl drew nigh. Seyf gave us a sign to follow him, made way through the crowd, and saluted his sovereign with the authorized formula of " Peace be with you, O the Protected of God!"—no worse a title than " Protector " anyhow, and more modest. Ṭelāl at once cast on us a penetrating glance, and addressed a question in a low voice to Seyf, whose answer was in the same tone. The prince then looked again towards us, but with a friendlier expression of face. We approached and touched his open hand, repeating the same salutation as that used by Seyf. No bow, hand-kissing, or other ceremony is customary on these occasions. Telāl returned our greeting, and then, without a word more to us, whispered a moment to Seyf, and passed on through the palace gate.

" He will give you a private audience to-morrow," said Seyf, " and I will take care that you have notice of it in due time ; meanwhile come to supper." The sun had already set when we re-entered the palace. This time, after passing the arsenal, we turned aside into a large square court, distinct from the former, and surrounded by an open verandah spread with mats. Two large ostriches, presents offered to Telāl by some chiefs of the Solibah tribe, strutted about the enclosure, and afforded much amusement to the negro-boys and scullions of the establishment. Seyf conducted us to the further side of the court, where we seated ourselves under the portico.

Hither some black slaves immediately brought the supper ; the " pièce de résistance " was, as usual, a huge dish of rice and boiled meat, with some thin cakes of unleavened bread and dates, and small onions with chopped gourds intermixed. The cookery was better than what we had heretofore tasted, though it would, perhaps, have hardly passed muster with a Vatel. We made a hearty meal, took coffee in the Ḳ'hāwah, and then returned to sit awhile and smoke our pipes in the open air. Needs not say how lovely are the summer evenings, how cool the breeze, how pure the sky, in these mountainous districts.

Seyf, on his side, got our night quarters ready, and, by his orders, one of the king's magazines (I have already mentioned them) had been emptied, swept, and matted for our reception. My readers are, I should think, sufficiently acquainted with eastern customs to know that neither chairs nor tables, tubs nor washhand basins, can reasonably be expected. We entered our lodgings, closed and locked the outer door, and then fell into deep consultation and weighty debate.

What were we to say to Telāl on our morrow's meeting ? what line of conduct to hold ? how obviate suspicion ? Such and similar topics were now long and carefully discussed. A reception evidently favourable, and good promises for the future,

were so far encouraging signs. But the untimely encounter
of our Damascene acquaintances, though patched up for the
moment, could not but have produced a certain sinister effect
on the public mind. Besides, Ṭelál was, if fame said true, the
most discerning of men, and certainly he looked it. Might it
not, all things considered, be the better plan to let him at once,
though privately, into our full confidence, and thus prevent the
dangers of an afterhand detection? But again, we did not, we
could not, as yet precisely know what might be his feelings
towards foreigners, Europeans especially. All we had for
certain was, that his kingdom had been originally founded by
Wahhabee influence and support; but whether he himself was
an independent sovereign or merely a vassal of Nejed, was a point
far from clear to us amid the contradictory statements given on
the matter thus far. With the extreme aversion of the Wahhabees for Europeans we were already acquainted : now Ṭelál
might perhaps be of their way of thinking. On the other hand,
I could not but suspect the existence of something like that
rival jealousy and ill-feeling between him and his Nejdean
neighbours, which, as we ere long found out, was really the
case. But the ground was at best uncertain, and might prove
a quicksand.

Our final conclusion was to be extremely cautious, to stick
close by our original disguise, and to give Ṭelál those answers,
and those only, which might serve to fix his ideas on Syria and
on our medical profession. Perhaps had we then known all that
we discovered some days later, our determination might have
taken a different turn. But for our then circumstances and
degree of information, I do not think that we resolved or
acted unwisely, much less, I am sure, will my readers censure
the corollary of our conference, which was to betake ourselves
to a sound and early sleep.

While we are thus, to borrow Madge Wildfire's phrase, " in
the land of Nod," it may perhaps be well, instead of recounting
our dreams, to gratify the curiosity of those who would desire
to learn whether we had any further encounter with our unwelcome friends from the north, and what was the sequel of
their history. Be it known, then, that the first and worthiest
of the two, the trader-post-contractor, had been so utterly

puzzled by our chilling " cut," and subsequently by the rebukes
he received from Seyf and others, that he ended in doubting
his own eyes, and concluded that he must have made some
strange mistake about our identity, or perhaps even his own ;
for, on the third day, when we once more came across each
other in the street, he began a confused discourse much like
that of the old woman in the ballad, " Oh dear me, it is not
I," and made such very humble apologies for his past conduct,
that I felt half disposed out of sheer pity to set his mind at
ease with a " no mistake at all, old fellow, you were perfectly
in the right." But prudence would not permit of this extra
kindness ; and besides, his public abjuration produced the best
imaginable effect on those present, so I left him to his regrets,
in which he may be plunged up to the present day, for aught I
know. The following morning he left Ḥā'yel, nor have I since
seen him anywhere.

For the man of Ḳaseem, his stay in this capital was yet
shorter, and the next day saw him on his way home, nor did
we again meet him ; thus his tale, true or not, fell to the ground
for want of repetition and confirmation.

As to the third, who had so obligingly set me up with house
and family, he was a citizen of the town itself, and we had in
consequence frequent interviews during the following weeks.
But he readily gave up his unfounded pretensions to previous
intimacy, and declared before all that he had mistaken his man.
And thus the triple cloud, fraught with distrust and danger,
passed away without further ill consequences, at least of a direct
nature. But the morrow's sun is up, and we must up with him.

Our door was yet unopened, when a low rap announces a
visitor. My companion undoes the bolt with a " samm',"
equivalent on these occasions to " come in."

It is 'Abd-el-Maḥsin, the same whom we had seen the evening
before as companion of Ṭelāl. He enters with a " hope I don't
intrude " air, and begins by excusing himself for breaking in on
us so early, asks after our health, trusts that we are somewhat
refreshed from the fatigues of our journey ; in short, makes no
less display of politeness, though without any overdoing or
affectation soever, than a French marquis of the old school
could to guests newly arrived at his château. He then proceeds

56

to enquiries about our road hither, how we had fared on the
way, laments over the coarse manners and ill breeding of
Bedouins, and the heat of the desert. Next he shows a great
desire to be instructed in medicine, adding that he is not
altogether ignorant of the healing art, and in a word directs
his whole conversation so as to make us feel perfectly at home,
and thus proceeds to sound us on the purport of our visit to
Ḥā'yel, and who we really were.

His appearance was certainly much in his favour, and one
that inspired confidence, or even familiarity. He could not have
been under fifty, but bore his years well; his complexion equal
in fairness to that of most Italians, his eye large and intelligent,
his features regular; in youth he must have been positively
handsome; his person was slender and a little bent by advancing
age; his dress extremely neat, though unadorned; a plain wand
in his hand bespoke his pacific and unmilitary turn; in short,
he had the look of a scientific or literary courtier, perhaps
an author, certainly a gentleman. A curious half-smile, but
partially disguised by the ceremonious gravity of a first visit,
showed him to be no enemy to a joke, while it tempered the
thoughtful expression of his large forehead and meaning eye.

Such was 'Abd-el-Maḥsin, the intimate friend and inseparable
companion of the prince. He belonged to the ancient and
noble family of 'Aleyyān, chiefs of the town and district of
Bereydah in Ḳaseem. There he had once enjoyed the confidence
of his own fellow-citizens, and the boon fellowship of Khursheed
Basha the Egyptian governor, during the period that this latter
held Ḳaseem before the final re-establishment of the Wahhabee
dynasty. Avoiding any open part in political affairs, and
devoting himself in appearance to literature and society, he
was, in fact, the deepest intriguer of the province, and guided
all the machinations of his relatives to deliver his country from
foreign occupation. How this was at last brought about, and
the part borne by the Wahhabee prince, Feyṣul, in the execution
of the scheme, belongs to the history of the Nejdean dynasty,
and we must reserve it accordingly for a future chapter. But
when a few years later 'Abd-el-Maḥsin found that Feyṣul had
only concurred in freeing them from the tyranny of Egypt in
order the better to subject them to his own, he became once

more the active though secret agent of his powerful family in opposing the progress of Wahhabee preponderance and rule. At last came the ruin of the 'Aleyyān family, consummated by one of the blackest acts of perfidy that stain the annals of central Arabia. 'Abd-el-Mahsin escaped the first fury of the massacre that destroyed most of his relatives, but was involved in the proscription which followed immediately after, and had to flee for his life. After some months of concealment on the outskirts of the province, finding that no hope was left in his native country, he took refuge with Ṭelāl, and had now lived for about ten years in the palace of the Shomer prince, first a guest, then a friend and favourite, welcomed in moments of relaxation on account of his gaiety, his natural elegance, and his extensive knowledge of Arab history and anecdote ; but prized in more serious hours for his shrewd advice and wise counsel. When on our way home a year later my companion and myself beguiled the long hours of horseback in the plains of Mosool or the hills of Orfah by passing in review the events of our Arabian journey, we readily agreed that from Gaza to Rās-el-Hadd we had not met with any one superior, or perhaps equal, in natural endowments and cultivated intellect to 'Abd-el-Mahsin 'Aleyyān.

Hardly had he entered on conversation than we guessed, and rightly guessed, that he had been sent by Ṭelāl in a preparatory way to the audience fixed by the king for a few hours later. We were accordingly on our guard, and stuck perseveringly to Damascus, Syria, and doctoring. On any other topics started by our friend while beating the bush, we gave very off-hand answers, implying that these things did not regard us, and to a few hesitating questions about Egypt, and even about Europe, we put on an appearance of great ignorance and unconcern.

Meanwhile it was our turn to find out everything possible about Ṭelāl and his real position, especially in what regarded the Wahhabee dynasty, and his own fashion of government. 'Abd-el-Mahsin's answers were naturally cautious and guarded enough ; yet we were able this very morning to discover much that we had been previously ignorant of. My readers may think this a suitable place, before we go any further in our narrative, to put together these first glimpses obtained from

'Abd-el-Maḥsin with the fuller information of a few days later,
and to give here a brief account, derived from the past history
of Djebel Shomer, and the foundation and progress of its present
prosperity.

And here, as an apology necessary perhaps in regard to some
who may think unworthy of even this slight record the history of
a small country, little known beyond the homogeneous limits of
its peninsula, and almost isolated century after century by the
encircling desert, I shall venture to make my own the elegant
paragraph with which the author of " Waverley " concludes the
fifth chapter of that incomparable tale, and copy his very words,
with a few slight substitutions alone required by the difference
of subject. So, " I beg pardon, once and for all, of those readers
who take up travels merely for amusement, for plaguing them
so long with Arab politics and history, with Bedouin and
Wahhabee, Shomer and Nejed. The truth is, I cannot promise them that this narrative shall be intelligible, not to say
probable, without it. My plan requires that I should explain
the motives on which events proceeded, and these motives
necessarily arose from the feelings, prejudices, and parties of
the times. I do not invite my fair readers, whose sex and
impatience give them the greatest right to complain of these
circumstances, into a flying chariot drawn by hippogriffs or
moved by enchantment. Mine is a humble English post-
chaise, drawn upon four wheels, and keeping his Majesty's
highway. Such as dislike the vehicle may leave it at the
next halt, and wait for the conveyance of Prince Hussein's
tapestry, or Malek the weaver's flying sentry-box. Those who
are contented to remain with me will be occasionally exposed
to the dulness inseparable from heavy roads, steep hills,
sloughs, and other terrestrial retardations ; but with tolerable
horses and a civil driver, as the advertisements have it, I
engage to get as soon as possible into a more picturesque and
romantic country, if my passengers incline to have some
patience with me during my first stages." And having thus
invoked the Muse, or better, the Genius of Abbotsford to my
aid, I continue.

At an early, indeed the earliest known period in the history of
central Arabia, the numerous and powerful tribe of Ṭā'i, first

arrived from Yemen, occupied the district included by the parallel
mountain chains of which the northernmost was then entitled
Djebel 'Aja, now Djebel Shomer, and its southerly sister Djebel
Salma, a name it has preserved to the present day. Some of
the clan dwelt in the towns and villages scattered through the
valleys, while others followed the roving life which forms and
maintains the Bedouin.

About the year 500 of our era occurred the celebrated conflict
between the tribes of Nejed, headed by Koleyb Wā'il, chief of
Taghleb, and the armies of Yemen led by the Lakhmite chiefs,
which ended in the overthrow of the latter, and the entire
deliverance of Nejed from the Kahtanite yoke. In this war
Tā'i, though of Yemenite origin, sided with the Nejdean clans
of Rebeea'. Soon after followed the civil war between those
very clans, on occasion of the death of Koleyb, treacherously
murdered by his kinsman Djessās. This caused many important changes in the relative position of the central tribes, and a
large settlement of Beni Taghleb, Beni 'Abs, and Howāzin took
place within the limits of Djebel Shomer, where the new settlers
united with the elder inhabitants, or Beni Tā'i, and from this
union sprang the tribe of Shomer, whose appellation has remained unchanged to our time. Such is at least the account
given by the inhabitants themselves; and though imaginative
fiction has been busy at adorning it with many marvellous
episodes, yet its historical veracity in the main cannot, I think,
reasonably be called in doubt.

Coming down to the earlier years of Mahometan rule, we
find this district still powerful and independent, resisting
successfully all the efforts of the Ommiade Caliphs, whose armies
suffered a signal defeat at the entrance of these very mountains
during the reign of Merwan, towards the beginning of the
eighth century. This event is followed by a long period of time
during which little or nothing authentic has been recorded
in Shomer history. One principal reason of this silence was
that these mountains lay at a considerable distance from
the ordinary pilgrim roads to Mecca, and were too far removed from Bagdad or Cairo to be much influenced by the
Abbaside or Fatimite caliphates, and by the various dynas-
ties or anarchies that succeeded them, down to the final

conquest of Syria and Egypt by the Ottoman Sultans in the
sixteenth century. Hence they were left with the rest of Nejed
to their own resources, nor perhaps fared the worse for that,
while at the same time want of external communication cut
them out of the general volume of Oriental annals. A large
portion of the tribes that had coalesced to form the great
clan of Shomer had once been Christians, and they appear to
have remained so still, at the epoch when they repelled the
invasion of the Ommiade troops. The clan of Bedr, to whom
belonged the easterly range of 'Aja, was entirely Christian.
Probably a time came when all more or less professed Islamism.
But at last we find them relapsed into a state of semi-barbarism,
having resumed the old Pagan forms of worship, and subdivided
themselves into as many rival or hostile chieftainships as there
were villages in the land ; nay often a single town was rent into
two or more contending factions, resembling what we have
seen exemplified in the Djowf, to the utter ruin of all civilization and prosperity. Here again we are reminded of the
European middle ages. Arabia repeats, so to speak, in a faint
reflection the course of the Western world. " There is a kind
of circle in events," says Tacitus ; history comes round like the
seasons.

There has been a tendency, I hardly know why, to praise the
clannish system, and decorate it with the title of " patriarchal."
But the patriarchs were not a nation, nor even a people, and
when the Jewish race did at last become such, one has only to
look over their national history from Judges to Chronicles, to
find painful evidence that the ruin of Israel was, humanly
speaking, owing for the most part to that very clannish spirit,
which set " Manasses against Ephraim and Ephraim against
Manasses, and these together against Judah." But whatever
may have been the case with the Jews, it is certain that this
persistence in hereditary classification, stronger habitually
among the Arabs than all ties of government and of patriotism, or even of religion, has been and always will be a bar
to the permanence of institutions for the common good, and
to any general advancement of the entire race. The rods,
so long as some strong hand binds them together, may seem to
unite and form themselves into a single stem ; but no sooner

is the blending hand withdrawn, than they start asunder, and resume their former severance. Or, to take another and a not inappropriate metaphor, if the elements mix together awhile, it is only mechanically, never chemically. This remark applies more especially to the inhabitants of the north and centre ; those of Southern Arabia present, as we shall afterwards see, a remarkable and advantageous difference in this respect. So much for " clans " in general ; let us now return to Djebel Shomer, and its more recent phases.

This province, in common with the rest of the peninsula, underwent the short-lived tyranny of the first Wahhabee empire at the beginning of the present century, and, like many other districts, was but transiently affected by it. The storm soon blew over, and left matters religious and political pretty much where they were before. At this period the town of Ḥā'yel was already looked on as in a manner the capital of Djebel Shomer, a distinction which it owed partly to its superior size and resources and partly to its central position ; yet its chiefs could not enforce their authority over any great distance beyond the walls of the town, at least in a regular way. The supreme rule was held by the family of Beyt 'Alee, ancient denizens of the city, and who seem to have fully appreciated both in theory and practice " the right divine of kings to govern wrong."

But there lived then in the same town of Ḥā'yel a young and enterprising chief, of the family Rasheed, belonging to the clan of Dja'afer, the noblest branch of the Shomer tribe. Many of his near relations were Bedouins, though his own direct ancestors had long occupied the social position of townsmen. His name was 'Abd-Allah-ebn-Rasheed ; wealthy, as wealth here goes, high-born, and conscious of ability and vigour, he aspired to wrest their hitherto undisputed pre-eminence from the chiefs of Beyt 'Alee ; his own powerful and numerous relatives lent their aid to his endeavour. The inhabitants of Ḥā'yel favoured some the one and some the other party, and on the whole 'Abd-Allah's faction was the stronger within the walls of the capital. But the neighbouring village of Kefar held to a man for Beyt 'Alee, and Kefar was at that time almost equal in strength and population to Ḥā'yel ; indeed, to judge by popular song and local tradition, our only guide here, Kefar was considered the more aristocratic town of the two.

After many preliminary bickerings, the struggle between 'Abd-Allah and Beyt 'Alee began; but the result proved unfavourable to the young competitor for sovereignty, and he was driven into exile. This happened about the year 1818 or 1820.

With a few of his relatives, fugitives like himself, he took the road of the Djowf, in hopes of refuge and alliance; but not finding either, he passed on to Wadi Sirhan, whose depths have ever been a common asylum for men in a similar predicament up to the present time. While he and his followers were wandering amid the labyrinths of the valley, they were suddenly attacked by a strong party of 'Anezeh Bedouins, hereditary enemies of the Shomer clan. 'Abd-Allah and his companions fought well, but numbers gained the day. The Benoo-Dja'afer fell without exception on the field of battle; the victorious 'Anezeh " stripped and gashed the slain;" none of 'Abd-Allah's companions remained alive, and he himself was left for dead amid the corpses on the sand.

What follows, I give as I heard it in Djebel Shomer, without anywise vouching for its accuracy or even veracity; Arab imagination, that most inventive faculty, has here done its utmost; yet the tale is worth recording for the illustration it at least affords of the mind of those who tell or who believe it.

The 'Anezeh had, as is often their wont, " made assurance doubly sure " by cutting the throats of the wounded where they lay on the ground; and in this respect 'Abd-Allah had fared no better than his comrades. But the destined possessor of a throne was not thus to perish before his time. While he lay senseless, his blood fast ebbing from the gaping gash, the locusts of the desert surrounded the chief, and with their wings and feet cast the hot sand into his wounds, till this rude styptic stayed the life-stream in its flow. Meanwhile a flock of Ḳaṭa, a partridge-like bird common in these regions, hovered over him to protect him from the burning sun—a service for which unwounded travellers in the Arabian wilds would be hardly less grateful.

A merchant of Damascus, accompanied by a small caravan, was on his way home to Syria from the Djowf, and chanced to pass close by the scene of carnage and miracle. He saw the wounded youth, and the wondrous intervention of Heaven in his behalf. Amazed at the spectacle, and conjecturing no ordinary future for one whose life was so dear to Providence, he alighted by his side, bound up his wounds, applied what means for reviving suspended animation the place and circumstances could allow of, placed him on one of his camels, and took him to Damascus.

There 'Abd-Allah, now the charitable merchant's guest, and treated by him like a son, speedily recovered strength and vigour. His generous preserver then supplied him with arms and provision for the way, and sent him back with a well-stored girdle to Arabia once more.

But to Djebel Shomer he could not return as a prince, and would not return as a subject. So, following a circuitous track, he passed on to the inner Nejed, and there offered his services in quality of " condottiere " to Turkee, son of 'Abd-Allah-ebn-Sa'ood, a prince whose despotic reign and tragical end we shall relate further on, with the fortunes of his dynasty. Turkee was then actively engaged in reconstructing his father's kingdom, ruined by the Egyptian invasion, and in recovering one after another the provinces formerly subject to Wahhabee domination. From such a prince 'Abd-Allah naturally found a ready welcome, and work in abundance. He was the foremost in every fray, and soon became the head of a considerable division in the Wahhabee army.

In 1830 or thereabouts, for I have been unable to procure from Arab negligence the exact date of this and of many other important incidents, Turkee resolved on the conquest of Hasa, one of the richest appanages of the old Nejdean crown. But since public affairs did not permit the withdrawing of his own personal presence from Ri'ad, his capital, he placed his eldest son Feysul at the head of the royal armies, and sent them to the invasion of the eastern coast. 'Abd-Allah as a matter of course joined the expedition, and, though a stranger by birth, was much looked up to by Feysul and his officers, and was almost their leader in all military operations.

Hardly had the Wahhabee army reached the frontiers of Hasa, and, having passed the narrow defiles of Ghoweyr, where we too, gentle reader, will pass in due time, were just proceeding to lay siege to the town of Hofhoof, when news reached them that Turkee had been treacherously assassinated during the evening prayers in the great mosque of the city by his own cousin Meshāree, and that the murderer had already occupied the vacant throne.

A council of war was at once called. The " Hushais " there present, and they were the greater number, advised Feyṣul to continue the war in Ḥaṣa, and after the conquest of that opulent province, return rich with its spoils to wrest the crown from his usurping relative. But 'Abd-Allah, a very Ahithophel in counsel, observed that such delay would only serve to give Meshāree better leisure for collecting troops, fortifying the capital, and thus becoming a yet more dangerous, if not an insurmountable enemy. Accordingly, he insisted on Feyṣul's immediate return with all his troops to Ri'aḍ, as the surest way to take Meshāree unprepared, avenge the yet warm blood of Turkee, and secure the capital and the central provinces for the rightful heir. For what concerned Ḥaṣa, its conquest could be only all the more certain for being a moment deferred.

Feyṣul, wiser than Absalom, subscribed to 'Abd-Allah's opinion, and the event fully justified him. Without loss of time the camp was broken up, and the whole army in movement on its backward way for Ri'aḍ, under whose walls forced marches speedily brought them, while Meshāree yet imagined his competitor far off on the other side of the passes in the distant plains of Ḥaṣa.

On the first appearance of the lawful prince, all Nejed rose round his banner. The capital followed the example, the gates were thrown open, and Feyṣul entered Ri'aḍ amid enthusiastic acclamations, and without striking a blow.

But Meshāree still occupied the palace, whose high walls and massive outworks could stand a long siege, as sieges go in Arabia; while within the fortress he had at his disposition all the state treasury, artillery, and ammunition, beside good store of provisions in case of blockade; lastly, he was protected by a powerful garrison of his own retainers, well paid and well armed. Thus provided, he determined to hold out, and wait a turn of fortune. It came, but against him.

Feysul, on his side, ordered an immediate assault on the fortress. It was delivered, but the thick walls and iron-bound gates, joined to the desperate valour of the defenders, baffled all efforts; and the assailants were reduced to wait the slow results of a regular siege.

This lasted twenty days without bringing material advantage to either party. But on the twenty-first night, 'Abd-Allah, desirous to bring matters to a conclusion by any means, however hazardous, took with him two sturdy companions of his Shomer kinsmen, refugees like himself, and, under cover of darkness, went roaming round the castle walls in hopes of detecting some unguarded spot. At a narrow window high up under the battlements (it was afterwards pointed out to me when I was at the very place) a light was glimmering. 'Abd-Allah drew close underneath, took a pebble, and threw it up against the window. A head appeared and called out in a muffled tone, " Who are you ?" 'Abd-Allah recognized the voice of an old palace retainer, long in the service of the deceased monarch, and his own intimate friend. He answered by his name. "What is your purpose ?" said the old man. " Let us down a cord, and we will arrange the rest."

Presently the rustling of a rope came down the wall. 'Abd-Allah and his two companions clambered up one after the other, and soon stood together within the palace chamber. "Where does Meshāree sleep?" was the ominous question. The servant of Turkee indicated the way. Threading the dark corridors, barefoot and in silence, the three adventurers reached the door of the usurper's bedchamber. They tried it; it was bolted from within. " In the name of God !" exclaimed 'Abd-Allah, and with one vigorous thrust burst the lock, and the room lay open.

There lay Meshāree, with a pair of loaded pistols under his pillow. At the noise he started up, and saw three dark outlines before him. Seizing his weapons, he fired them off in quick succession, and the two companions of 'Abd-Allah fell, one dead, the other death-wounded, yet alive. But 'Abd-Allah remained unscathed, and rushed on his victim, sword in hand. Meshāree, a man of herculean size, seized the arms of his enemy and grappled with him. Both fell on the floor, but Meshāree kept firm hold on the sword-arm of 'Abd-Allah, and bent him-self to wrest the weapon from his hand. While thus they rolled together in doubtful struggle, the dying comrade of 'Abd-Allah, collecting his last strength, dragged himself to their side, and seized the wrist of Meshāree with such convulsive force, that it made him for an instant relax his hold. That instant 'Abd-Allah freed his sword, and plunged it again and again into the body of his antagonist, who expired without a struggle.

Not a cry had been raised, not an alarm given. 'Abd-Allah cut off the head of Meshāree where he lay, and with it in his hand returned to the chamber where the servant of Turkee awaited trembling the result of the attempt. By the lamplight both made themselves sure that the disfigured features were indeed those of the usurper. Then without a moment's loss 'Abd-Allah went to the window and, leaning out, raised his voice to its utmost pitch to alarm the camp of Feyṣul, whose advanced guard was not far from the palace. Several soldiers started up, and when they approached the wall, "Take the dog's head," exclaimed 'Abd-Allah, and flung his bloody trophy in the midst. A shout of triumph echoed throughout the city. Meanwhile the servant of Turkee rushed down to the outer palace gates, and threw them open, proclaiming Amān, or quarter, to all of Meshāree's retinue who would acknowledge Feyṣul for their master. A few minutes more, and Feyṣul himself stood within his father's walls, now his own.

No resistance was offered. "God has willed it," was the only comment of Meshāree's followers as they presented unhesitating allegiance to their new sovereign. Feyṣul was now undisputed master throughout Nejed, and the circumstances of his accession only secured him the more the attachment of his subjects.

The son of Turkee was not ungrateful to him whose intre-pidity had placed him on his father's throne. He openly ac-knowledged—an honourable proceeding in a king—the eminent services of 'Abd-Allah, and determined to requite his daring mercenary with a crown, bestowed in return for the crown thus acquired. To this end he named him absolute governor of his native province, Shomer, with right of succession, and supplied him with troops and all other means for the establishment of his rule.

'Abd-Allah returned to Ḥā'yel, now no longer a proscribed exile, but a powerful and dreaded chieftain, with an army at his bidding. He soon drove out the rival family of Beyt 'Alee from the town, where his own authority was henceforth supreme. Here he fixed his residence, while he intrusted the fullness of his vengeance on the ill-fated chieftains of Beyt 'Alee to his younger brother 'Obeyd, "the Wolf," to give him the name by which he is commonly known, a name well earned by his unrelenting cruelty and deep deceit. 'Obeyd with his horsemen dislodged Beyt 'Alee from Kefar, though not till after an obstinate struggle, and then pursued them from town to town till he drove them into Ḳaseem. The inhabitants of Ḳaseem rose to defend the fugitives. 'Obeyd called for fresh troops from Nejed, and engaged to put his conquests at the disposal of Feyṣul. On this condition· supplies were furnished, and " the Wolf" at their head laid waste the fertile lands of Ḳaseem with such savage fury, that to this day his name is a curse throughout the province, like that of Cromwell or Claverhouse in Ireland and Scotland. The Beyt 'Alee were cut off root and branch ; one child alone, hidden in a small village on the outskirts of Ḳaseem, escaped the slayers. When Ṭelāl years after ascended the throne, he sent for the lad, the only representative now surviving of his hereditary enemies, gave him estates and riches, and installed him in a handsome dwelling within the capital itself, thus with rare but politic generosity obviating the last chances of a rival faction.

While 'Obeyd was wolfing it in Ḳaseem, 'Abd-Allah's main care was to consolidate his power in Djebel Shomer itself. Kefar had been already won, next the large and neighbouring villages of Woseyṭah, Laḳeeṭah, Moḳah, and others, fell one by one under his rule in spite of much opposition and bloodshed, and before long he saw himself sole master of the whole mountain district. But beyond 'Āja' and Solma his sway did not extend, and the conquests made by his brother in the south were according to the previous stipulation given over to the Wahhabee monarch. 'Abd-Allah too all his lifetime paid a stated tribute to Feyṣul, of whom he was in fact a mere viceroy, while, the more to ensure the support of his powerful neighbour and jealous benefactor, he caused the Wahhabee religion to be re-

cognized officially for that of the new state, and encouraged the
Nejdean Meṭow'wā'as (a term already explained) in their zeal
for the extirpation of the many local superstitious practices
still observed in Djebel Shomer. This was a very unpopular
measure, nor did 'Abd-Allah adopt it from any motive, it
would seem, of real religious conviction, but merely to avoid
being deposed sooner or later by the same hand that had
raised him to the throne. He did not, however, neglect the
while to strengthen his own national influence, and to this
end he had at an early period contracted a marriage alliance
with a powerful chieftain's family of Dja'afer, his near kinsman
by blood. Strong in the support of this restless clan, who
cared little about Wahhabee dogmas and enactments which
they well knew could never reach them, he subdued with their
help the rivalry of town and country nobles, and gratified at
once his own ambition and the rapacity of his Bedouin allies
by the measures that crushed his domestic enemies and
ensured his pre-eminence. Plots were formed against him,
broken, and formed again; hired assassins dogged him in the
streets, open rebellion broke out in the province, but 'Abd-Allah
escaped every danger and prostrated every opponent, till his
" star," less fickle if less famous than that of the Corsican,
became a proverb for good fortune in Shomer; it was no other
than his own calculating courage and inflexible resolve. Yet
his memory is scarcely a favourite with the citizens of Ḥā'yel,
little disposed to sympathize with Wahhabees and Bedouins ;
and the weight of the new government pressed heaviest, as
needs was, on the best and most thriving portion of the general
population.

Towards the latter part of his reign 'Abd-Allah took a measure eminently calculated, at least under the actual circumstances, to secure the permanence of his dynasty. Hitherto he
had dwelt in a quarter of the capital which the old chieftains
and the nobility had mainly chosen for their domicile, and
where the new monarch was surrounded by men his equals in
birth and of even more ancient title to command. But now he
added a new quarter to the town, and there laid the foundations
of a vast palace destined for the future abode of the king and
the display of all his grandeur, amid streets and nobles of his

own creation. The walls of the projected edifice were fast
rising when he died, almost suddenly, in 1844 or 1845, leaving
three sons, Ṭelāl, Meta'ab, and Moḥammed, the eldest scarce
twenty years of age, besides his only surviving brother 'Obeyd,
who could not then have been much under fifty.

Ṭelāl was already highly popular, much more so than his
father, and had given early tokens of those superior qualities
which accompanied him to the throne. All parties united to
proclaim him sole heir to the kingdom and lawful successor to
the regal power, and thus the rival pretensions of 'Obeyd, hated
by many and feared by all, were smothered at the outset and
put aside without a contest.

The young sovereign possessed, in fact, all that Arab ideas
require to ensure good government and lasting popularity.
Affable towards the common people, reserved and haughty with
the aristocracy, courageous and skilful in war, a lover of commerce and building in time of peace, liberal even to profusion,
yet always careful to maintain and augment the state revenue,
neither over strict nor yet scandalously lax in religion, secret
in his designs, but never known to break a promise once given,
or violate a plighted faith ; severe in administration, yet averse
to bloodshed, he offered the very type of what an Arab prince
should be. I might add, that among all rulers or governors,
European or Asiatic, with whose acquaintance I have ever
chanced to be honoured, I know few equal in the true art of
government to Ṭelāl, son of 'Abd-Allah-ebn-Rasheed.

His first cares were directed to adorn and civilize the capital.
Under his orders, enforced by personal superintendence, the
palace commenced by his father was soon brought to completion.
But he added, what probably his father would hardly have
thought of, a long row of warehouses, the dependencies and
property of the same palace ; next he built a market-place
consisting of about eighty shops or magazines, destined for
public commerce and trade, and lastly constructed a large
mosque for the official prayers of Friday. Round the palace,
and in many other parts of the town, he opened streets, dug
wells, and laid out extensive gardens, besides strengthening
the old fortifications all round and adding new ones. At the
same time he managed to secure at once the fidelity and the

absence of his dangerous uncle by giving him charge of those military expeditions which best satisfied the restless energy of 'Obeyd. The first of these wars was directed, I know not on what pretext, against Kheybar. But as Ṭelāl intended rather to enforce submission than to inflict ruin, he associated with 'Obeyd in the military command his own brother Meta'ab, to put a check on the ferocity of the former. Kheybar was conquered, and Ṭelāl sent thither, as governor in his name, a young man of Ḥāʾyel, prudent and gentle, whom I subsequently met when he was on a visit at the capital.

Not long after, the inhabitants of Ḳaseem, weary of Wahhabee tyranny, turned their eyes towards Ṭelāl, who had already given a generous and inviolable asylum to the numerous political exiles of that district. Secret negotiations took place, and at a favourable moment the entire uplands of that province—after a fashion not indeed peculiar to Arabia—annexed themselves to the kingdom of Shomer by universal and unanimous suffrage. Ṭelāl made suitable apologies to the Nejdean monarch, the original sovereign of the annexed district; he could not resist the popular wish; it had been forced on him, &c. &c. &c.;—but Western Europe is familiar with the style. Feyṣul felt the inopportuneness of a quarrel with the rapidly growing power to which he himself had given origin only a few years before, and, after a wry face or two, swallowed the pill. Meanwhile Ṭelāl, knowing the necessity of a high military reputation both at home and abroad, undertook in person a series of operations against Teyma' and its neighbourhood. Everywhere his arms were successful, and his moderation in victory secured the attachment of the vanquished themselves.

Of the war of Djowf and the conquest of that province I have already spoken. Other expeditions of minor consequence, but always fortunate in their result, were headed by Ṭelāl; while 'Obeyd is said to have taken the field above forty times. These military doings, in which there was often more display than slaughter, were principally directed against the Bedouins, who occupied, as a glance at the map will show, a very large portion of Ṭelāl's domains, and whom that prince made it his capital business to put down everywhere. With the nomades of the outer districts he had no great difficulty;

but he found much more with his own kinsmen and near neighbours, the Arabs of Shomer.

In order to carry out his views for enriching the country by the benefits of free and regular commerce, security on the high roads and the cessation of plundering forays were indispensable. Now the tribe of Dja'afar, his own blood relations, had grown especially insolent through the favour of 'Abd-Allah, whose instruments they had been in subduing the towns and villages of the mountain. Telâl, who had not the same need of them, now played his father's game backwards, subduing these same Bedouins by the means of the very populations whom they had formerly oppressed, and who were naturally eager for their turn of revenge; while the quarrels of the clansmen among themselves afforded him frequent occasion for setting them one against another, till, weakened and divided, they all in common submitted to his yoke. "Divide et impera," is a maxim known to Arab, no less than to European statesmanship. Henceforth no Bedouin in Djebel Shomer, or throughout the whole kingdom, could dare to molest traveller or peasant.

This obstacle removed, Telâl applied himself with characteristic vigour and good sense to the execution of more pacific projects. Merchants from Basrah, from Meshid 'Alee and Wâsit, shopkeepers from Medinah and even from Yemen, were invited by liberal offers to come and establish themselves in the new market of Hâ'yel. With some Telâl made government contracts equally lucrative to himself and to them; to others he granted privileges and immunities; to all, protection and countenance. Many of these traders belonged to the Shiya'a sect, hated by all good Sonnites, doubly hated by the Wahhabees. But Telâl affected not to perceive their religious discrepancies, and silenced all murmurs by marks of special favour towards these very dissenters, and also by the advantages which their presence was not long in procuring for the town. He even exerted his ability to persuade Jews and Christians from the north to take up their abode in his capital, where he promised them entire security and free exercise of religion. But the great distance of Hâ'yel from all Christian or Jewish centres has hitherto hindered this liberal-minded design from taking effect. Meanwhile the desired impulse had been given; the town became a centre of trade and industry, and many of its inhabitants followed the example of the foreigners thus settled among them, and rivalled them in diligence and in wealth.

All this, however, could not but irritate the Wahhabee faction of the country, at whose head stood the sanguinary fanatic 'Obeyd. Feyṣul, too, already annoyed by the Ḳaseem annexation, now sent forth from his Nejdean fastnesses loud protestations against the laxity of his "brother," Ṭelāl. Besides, horrible to Wahhabee thought and hearing, Ṭelāl was rumoured to indulge in the heretical pleasures of tobacco, to wear silk, and to be very seldom seen in the mosque; though indeed it might be charitably hoped that he said his prayers at home. Lastly, and this was no good sign in Wahhabee eyes, he showed much more disposition to pardon prisoners or criminals than to behead them; and the encouragement he gave to commerce did not seem at all consistent with the character of a true Muslim, who should only know three legitimate sources of profit or pleasure—war, prayer, and women.

In spite of all Ṭelāl steadily pursued his way, while his dexterous prudence threw over these enormities a veil sufficient for decency, if not for absolute concealment. If he smoked, it was only in private, and by way of remedy, prescribed by the best physicians, for some occult disease, which admitted of no other means of cure; no sooner shall the malady be removed, than he will give it up. If he harboured Shiya'as, it was that they had to his own personal knowledge declared themselves sincere converts to the Sonnee creed. The commerce of Ḥā'yel was not his, but the work of private individuals, with whom, much to his regret, he could not interfere. What excuse he made for his unorthodox leniency in war and judgment I did not hear, but I doubt not that it was a plausible one. And finally, if he was obliged by business to absent himself sometimes from the mosque, he always took care that his uncle or some one of the family should be there to represent him :—

> Ne'er went to church, 't was such a busy life;
> But duly sent his family and wife.

But above and besides apologies, judicious presents despatched

from time to time to the Nejed, and an alliance brought about
with one of Feysul's numerous daughters, went far to appease
the Wahhabee.   In his own kingdom also Telāl made suitable
concessions to orthodox zeal.   The public sale of tobacco was
prohibited; and if any went on in a contraband way in back-
shops or under private roofs, government could not be held
responsible.   Although silk was tolerated for wear, orders were
given that the ungodly material should be mixed with so much
cotton as to render it no longer an object of strict and legal
animadversion.   In the capital, where Nejdean spies often
came, the inhabitants were requested to pay fitting attendance
on public prayers, and the mosque became tolerably full.
Besides 'Obeyd was so regular and devout, so far from the
abominations of silk and tobacco, so frequent in long recita-
tions of the Coran and invectives against infidels, that his good
example might almost atone for and cover the scandals given
by his nephew, and yet more by Meta'ab, a very "wild young
man," whose eternal Nargheelah and silken dress, unsanctified
by a single thread of cotton, shocked pious noses and eyes,
and constituted a crime of which said one day a Nejdean
Metow'waa', pointing to the gay head-dress of the prince, "all
other wickedness may be forgiven by God, but *that* never."
But of Wahhabee action in these countries, and of the Arab reaction against it, I shall have afterwards occasion to say more;
let us now return to Telāl.

His conduct towards the Ottoman government is not less
skilful, nor is the position a whit less delicate.   For if his
southern and eastern frontiers border the Wahhabee, his
northern boundaries are marked out by the pashalics of Bagdad
and Damascus; while the great Mecca road, itself regarded as
Ottoman territory, forms his western limit beyond Teyma and
Kheybar.   Constant commerce with Meshid 'Alee, with Sook-
esh-Sheyook, and other localities near the Euphrates, bring him
into frequent contact with Turkish subjects, and even with Turks
themselves; while an equally active trading intercourse with
Medinah and the pilgrim caravans produces the same result on
the opposite side of the kingdom.   Hence he is continually
obliged to conciliate favour and to elude quarrels; while every
forward step in these directions, however desirable, is fraught

with danger.   In truth, whatever passes at Ḥā'yel is sure to be reported sooner or later at Bagdad and Medinah, nay even at Damascus; this my readers may well understand from the very events of our own first arrival here.   I should add that the knowledge so acquired of what passes in Arabia seldom goes beyond Mahometan limits, nor is shared in by others than men of office and government; the Bashas learn something, the ordinary crowd less, and Europeans least of all.   From these last, indeed, even though long resident in the East, I have heard few statements relative to inner Arabia which were corroborated, or even which were not contradicted, by facts on the spot.

In accordance with the policy just described, the name of the Sultan, with its pompous appendix of now unmeaning titles, is proclaimed every Friday with a loud voice in the public prayer of Ḥā'yel, and profession is made that Ṭelāl is only his vicegerent, and from him derives all authority.   Not that a single " para " is ever sent from Djebel Shomer to the treasuries of Constantinople, nor a soldier furnished to the Turkish battalions from the entire extent of Ṭelāl's dominion.   But no one is allowed to speak otherwise than with respect of 'Abd-el-'Azeez, who is always to be styled " Sultan " and Ruler; and though Wahhabees call him an " infidel," and the men of Shomer " a Turkish mule," such courteous sayings can only be uttered in private.   Should a Turkish officer, and this will sometimes happen, take his returning course from the pilgrimage by the passes of Ḥā'yel, or direct his route that way to Medinah, he meets with nothing but courtesy, hears nothing but loyalty. And, to come to more ticklish matters, if Ṭelāl himself conquers Kheybar and Teyma, both within the imaginary limits of the Porte, and attacks and subdues the western tribes from Medā' in Sāleḥ to Kerak, on the very ground of the Sultan, it is all in the service of his Ottoman Majesty, and to ensure the tranquillity and subordination of the Turkish frontier.   Nay, if he place governors in the Djowf, without a single with your leave or by your leave from Constantinople, and send expeditions to the limits of the Belḳā, and under the walls of Meshid 'Alee, it is in the name of 'Abd-el-'Azeez, and all for his Majesty's profit.

Thus, closely watched on all sides by rivals and enemies, and guiding his newly-constructed bark between the Wahhabee Scylla and the Ottoman Charybdis, Ṭelāl has to look out for allies and friends against the hour of danger, which, with all his prudence, he can hardly hope to avert for many years. With Europeans, indeed, of whatever nation, he wisely declines any intercourse, except that of mere courtesy, should occasion offer, well persuaded by the events of other and even of neighbouring countries, that the interference of such is but too often either unavailing or pernicious. But with Egypt to the west and with Persia to the east, he keeps up a very frequent and a more congenial intercourse; from the latter he procures considerable commercial advantages, besides moral support at Bagdad, while from the former he may reckon on military aid and a strong arm, should need require.

Towards his own subjects his conduct is uniformly of a nature to merit their obedience and attachment, and few sovereigns have here met with better success. Once a day, often twice, he gives public audience, hears patiently, and decides in person, the minutest causes with great good sense. To the Bedouins, no insignificant portion of his rule, he makes up for the restraint he imposes, and the tribute he levies from them, by a profusion of hospitality not to be found elsewhere in the whole of Arabia from 'Akabah to 'Aden. His guests at the midday and evening meal are never less than fifty or sixty, and I have often counted up to two hundred at a banquet, while presents of dress and arms are of frequent if not of daily occurrence. It is hard for Europeans to estimate how much popularity such conduct brings an Asiatic prince. Meanwhile the townsfolk and villagers love him for the more solid advantages of undisturbed peace at home, of flourishing commerce, of extended dominion, and military glory.

Very seldom does this remarkable sovereign inflict capital punishment, and the severest penalty with which he has hitherto chastised political offences is banishment or prison. Indeed, even in cases of homicide or murder, he has been known not unfrequently to avail himself of the option allowed by Arab custom between a fine and retaliation, and to buy off the offender, by bestowing on the family of the deceased the allotted price of blood from his own private treasury, and that from a pure motive of humanity. When execution does take place, it is always by beheading; nor is any other mode of putting to death customary in Arabia; indeed Ottoman and Persian barbarity, with their impalings, burnings, and the like, are strongly reprobated here. In Nejed we shall afterwards meet with one and one only exception to this general rule. Stripes, however, are not uncommon, though administered on the broad back, not on the sole of the foot. They are the common chastisement for minor offences, like stealing, cursing, or quarrelling; in this last case both parties usually come in for their share.

With his numerous retainers he is almost over-indulgent, and readily pardons a mistake or a negligence; falsehood alone he never forgives; and it is notorious that whoever has once lied to Ṭelāl must give up all hopes of future favour.

In private life he relaxes much of his official gravity; laughs, jokes, chats, enjoys poetry and tales, and smokes, but only in presence of his more intimate friends. He has three wives, taken each and all, it would seem, from some political motive. One is the daughter of Feyṣul, the Wahhabee monarch, a second belongs to a noble family of Ḥāʾyel, a third is from among his kinswomen of the tribe of Djaʾafar; thus in a way conciliating three different interests, but uniting them in one household. He has three sons: the eldest named Bedr, a clever and handsome lad of twelve, or thereabouts; the second, Bander; the third is ʾAbd-Allah, a very pretty and intelligent child of five or six. He has some daughters, too, but I do not know their number, for here, as elsewhere in the East, they are looked on as something rather to be ashamed of than otherwise, and accordingly are never mentioned. It will be long before this ungallant indication of ancient barbarism, fostered by Mahometan influences, disappears from Oriental manners.

Such is Ṭelāl. His reign has now lasted nearly twenty years, and hitherto with unvaried and well-deserved prosperity. He has gone far to civilize the most barbarous third of the Arabian continent, and has established law and security where they had been unknown for ages past. We shall now see him in a more intimate and personal point of view.

ʾAbd-el-Maḥsin stayed with us awhile, and then left us, saying that the public audience of the day was drawing nigh, and that

his attendance there would be expected; for ourselves we were
to be admitted immediately afterwards to a private interview.
Meanwhile we may reasonably conjecture that he went to tell
Telāl of his own espionage, and conjectures regarding the Syrian
adventurers.

The sun was now tolerably high in heaven; but as the long
palace wall faced the west, the seats beneath it and even a good
part of the courtyard were yet in shade.   When morning
advanced this space gradually filled up with groups of citizens,
countrymen, and Bedouins, some to despatch business, others
merely as lookers on.   About nine, if I judged correctly of the
time from the solar altitude, Telāl, "dressed in all his best,"
and surrounded by a score of armed attendants, with his third
brother Mohammed at his side (for the second, Meta'ab, was
absent from Hā'yel, nor did he return till some days later),
issued in due state and gravity from the palace portal, and took
his seat on the raised dais in the centre against the wall.   'Abd-
el-Mahsin and Zāmil placed themselves close by, while officers
and attendants, to the number of sixty or thereabouts, filled up
the line.   Immediately in front of Telāl, but squatted on the
bare ground, were our Sherarat companions, the 'Azzām chiefs,
every one with his never-failing camel-switch in his hand;
around and behind sat or stood a crowd of spectators, for the
occasion was one of some solemnity.

" How many of those I know would give half their having to
be present at such a scene and in such a locality," thought
I, while almost wondering at our own quiet and secure position
amid the multitude; for, to say truth, how little of Arab rule
or life has yet been witnessed by Europeans, how little faithfully
described?   Half romantic and always over-coloured scenes of
wild Bedouins, painted up into a sort of chivalresque knight-
errants and representatives of unthralled freedom; or, perhaps,
the heavy and hollow formalities of some coast or frontier
courtlet, more than half Ottomanized : apocryphal legends, like
those of Lamartine, and the sentimental superficialities of his
school,—such is almost all that we possess on these subjects, and
from which we are invited to form our criterion and appreciation
of Arabia and its people.   But not in the Syrian desert, nor on
the limits of the Hejāz, not in the streets of Mokha, nor in the

markets of Meshid 'Alee, still less at Bagdad or Damascus, is the true idea of genuine Arab ways and manners to be sought or found.

The researches of Pococke, the incomparable exactitude of Niebuhr, the varied information of Burckhardt, the minute accuracy of Wallen, the sailor-like daring of Welsted, deserve indeed the highest praise as well as the fullest confidence. Nor is it in a spirit of idle rivalry, far less of depreciation, that while mentioning names of such justly earned celebrity, I beg permission to point out the limits within which circumstances, those impassable boundary-walls of human life and enterprise, confined their experience of Arabia. This was for the most part derived from the frontier provinces and the outer surface; of the interior, whether physical or moral, they have less to tell. Yet a description of the foot or of the hand, however trustworthy, does not always furnish a complete idea of the body or the head, still less of the anatomical structure within. " Ex pede Herculem," is an excellent adage, but not always applicable to living nations and to human nature.

While I was occupied in these reflections, and my companion in his, of which I cannot pretend to give an account, but I suppose them to have been what a youth of Zaḥlah might be expected to make in similar circumstances, the audience went on ; and the 'Azzám chieftains or ragamuffins presented their coarse Bedouin submission, much like runaway hounds crouching before their whipper-in, when brought back to the kennel and the lash. Ṭelál accepted it, though without giving them to understand his own personal intentions respecting them and their clansmen, and detained them for several days without any decisive answer, thus affording them suitable leisure to experience the profusion of his hospitality, and to become yet more deeply impressed with the display of his power.

" The Arab's understanding is in his eyes," is here a common proverb, and current among all, whether Bedouins or townsmen. It implies, "the Arab judges of things as he sees them present before him, not in their causes or consequences :" keen and superficial. This is eminently true of the Bedouin, though more or less of every Arab whatsoever; it is also true in a measure of all children, even European, who in this resemble

79

not a little the "gray barbarian." A huge palace, a few large pieces of artillery, armed men in gay dresses, a copious supper, a great crowd, there are no better arguments for persuading nomades into submission and awe; and one may feel perfectly safe that they will never enquire too deeply whether the cannon are serviceable, the armed men faithful, the income of the treasury sure, or the supper of wholesome digestion. This Telāl knows right well, and in this he seems to have the advantage over many who have attempted to establish their influence, partial or total, over the Arab race.

Other minor affairs are now concluded; the audience is at last over, Telāl rises, and, accompanied by Zāmil, Mohammed, Sa'eed (his head cavalry officer), a Meshid merchant named Hasan, and two or three others, slowly moves off towards the farther end of the court where it joins the market-place. Seyf comes up to us, and bids us follow.

CHAPTER IV

Life in Ḥā'yel

Ueberall regt sich Bildung und Streben,
Alles will sich mit Farben beleben,
Doch an Blumen fehlt's in Revier,
Sie nimmt geputzte Menschen dafür.
Kehre dich um von diesen Höhen
Nach der Stadt zurück zu sehen.—*Goethe*

PRIVATE AUDIENCE OF ṬELĀL—HIS SUSPICIONS—OUR HOUSE—REMARKS ON
NATIONALITY — WE BEGIN DOCTORING — PLAN OF LIFE AND ACTION —
STATE OF MEDICAL KNOWLEDGE PAST AND PRESENT IN ARABIA—INFLU-
ENCE OF MAHOMETANISM — NATIVE REMEDIES AND PRACTITIONERS —
THE ṢOLIBAH—OUR DAILY LIFE—A WALK OUT OF TOWN; VIEW ROUND
ḤAY'EL—MARKET-PLACE EARLY—VISITORS AND PATIENTS—'OJEYL AND
HIS BROTHER—'ABD-EL-MAḤSIN AND ṬELĀL'S THREE CHILDREN—MOḤAM-
MED-EL-ḲADEE — PEASANT OF MOGAH — DOHEYM—ḲASEEM IMMIGRATION
—MARKET NEAR NOON — INTERIOR OF ḤA'YEL — DOHEYM'S HOUSE AND
FAMILY — A FEVER CASE — ḲASEEM POLITICS; STATE OF THE PROVINCE
UNDER ṬELĀL—THE 'ALEY'YĀNS OF BEREYDAH—THEIR DESTRUCTION—
FIRST WAR OF 'ONEYZAH—INTERVENTION OF THE SHEREEF OF MECCA—
SECOND WAR—ZĀMIL AND HIS PARTISANS—CHARACTER AND PROGRESS
OF THE WAR—REFLECTIONS ON ARAB CAPABILITY OF PROGRESS—WALK
THROUGH THE TOWN—MIRAGE—PRAYERS OF THE 'AGR AND SERMON—
PURITY OF ELOCUTION IN ḤA'YEL—ṬELĀL AT THE MOSQUE—HIS AFTER-
NOON AUDIENCES—THE EMEER ROSHEYD—DOḤEY'S HOUSE AND FAMILY
— LITERARY MEETINGS IN A GARDEN — EVENINGS AT ḤA'YEL — NEW
COURSE OF EVENTS.

ṬELĀL once free from the mixed crowd, pauses a moment till
we rejoin him. The simple and customary salutations are given
and returned. I then present him with our only available
testimonial, the scrap written by Ḥamood from the Djowf. He
opens it, and hands it over to Zāmil, better skilled in reading
than his master. Then laying aside all his wonted gravity, and
assuming a good-humoured smile, he takes my hand in his right
and my companion's in his left, and thus walks on with us
through the court, past the mosque, and down the market-
place, while his attendants form a moving wall behind and on
either side.

81

He was in his own mind thoroughly persuaded that we were, as we appeared, Syrians; but imagined, nor was he entirely in the wrong thus far, that we had other objects in view than mere medical practice. But if he was right in so much, he was less fortunate in the interpretation he chose to put on our riddle, having imagined that our real scope must be to buy horses for some government, of which we must be the agents; a conjecture which had certainly the merit of plausibility. However, Ṭelāl had, I believe, no doubt on the matter, and had already determined to treat us well in the horse business, and to let us have a good bargain, as it shortly appeared.

Accordingly he began a series of questions and cross-questions, all in a jocose way, but so that the very drift of his enquiries soon allowed us to perceive what he really esteemed us. We, following our previous resolution, stuck to medicine, a family in want, hopes of good success under the royal patronage, and much of the same tenor. But Ṭelāl was not so easily to be blinkered, and kept to his first judgment. Meanwhile we passed down the street, lined with starers at the king and us, and at last arrived at the outer door of a large house near the further end of the Sook or market-place; it belonged to Ḥasan, the merchant from Meshid 'Alee.

Three of the retinue stationed themselves by way of guard at the street door, sword in hand. The rest entered with the king and ourselves; we traversed the courtyard, where the remainder of the armed men took position, while we went on to the Ḳ'hāwah. It was small, but well furnished and carpeted. Here Ṭelāl placed us amicably by his side in the highest place; his brother Mohammed and five or six others were admitted, and seated themselves each according to his rank, while Ḥasan, being master of the house, did the honours.

Coffee was brought and pipes lighted. Meantime Ebn-Rasheed renewed his interrogatory, skilfully throwing out side remarks, now on the government of Syria, now on that of Egypt, then on the Bedouins to the north of Djowf, or on the tribes of Ḥejāz or the banks of Euphrates, thus to gain light whence and to what end we had in fact come. Next he questioned us on medicine, perhaps to discover whether we had the right professional tone; then on horses, about which same noble animals we affected an ignorance unnatural and very unpardonable in an Englishman ; but for which I hope afterwards to make amends to my readers. All was in vain ; and after a full hour our noble friend had only managed by his cleverness to get himself farther off the right track than he had been at the outset. He felt it, and determined to let matters have their own course, and to await the result of time. So he ended by assuring us of his entire confidence and protection, offering us to boot a lodging on the palace grounds. But this we declined, being desirous of studying the country as it was in itself, not through the medium of a court atmosphere ; so we begged that an abode might be assigned us as near the market-place as possible : and this he promised, though evidently rather put out by our independent ways.

Excellent water-melons, ready peeled and cut up, with peaches hardly ripe, for it was the beginning of the season, were now brought in, and we all partook in common. This was the signal for breaking up ; Ṭelāl renewed his proffers of favour and patronage ; and we were at last reconducted to our lodgings by one of the royal guard.

Seyf now went in search of a permanent dwelling-place wherein to instal us ; and before evening succeeded in finding one situated in a street leading at right angles to the market, and at no unreasonable distance from the palace. The house itself consisted of two apartments, separated by an unroofed court, with an outer door opening on the road ; over the rooms was a flat roof surrounded by a very high parapet, thus making an excellent sleeping-place for summer. The locality had been occupied by one of the palace retinue, Ḥoseyn-el-Miṣree, who at Seyf's bidding evacuated the premises in our favour, and moved off to take up his quarters in the neighbourhood. We examined the dwelling-place, and found it tolerably convenient ; the rooms were each about sixteen feet in length by eight or nine in breadth, and of corresponding height ; one of them might officiate as a store-room and kitchen, while the other should be fitted up for a dwelling apartment. It was the zenith of the dog-days, and a bedchamber would have been a mere superfluity ; the roof and open air were every way preferable, nor had we to fear intrusion, the court-walls being sixteen feet high or more. Every door was provided with its own distinct lock; the keys here are made of iron, and in this respect Ḥá'yel has the better of any other Arab town it was my chance to visit, where the keys were invariably wooden, and thus very liable to break and get out of order.

Before nightfall we had transferred all our goods and chattels to our new abode, and taken leave of Seyf, who, sweetly smiling, informed us that whenever we chose to take our meals at the palace we should always find them ready, and that our present lodgings were entirely at the king's cost, whose guests we were accordingly to consider ourselves, however long our stay might prove. We begged him to express our gratitude to Ṭelál, and once arrived " at home," shut the street door, made sundry arrangements the result of which shall be visible on the morrow, and thanked God for dangers averted, and for a prosperous outset to the more important part of our journey. Hitherto we had been merely on the threshold, now we were fairly in the " promised land," and we felt all the importance of every step and every word.

Besides, in our quality of civilized men, more or less, the general appearance of power, of order, of populousness and prosperity, of vigour and rule, the extent of the palace, the fortifications, in a word, the whole " ensemble " of the capital, added to the person and character of its ruler, had not failed to produce a certain impression on our minds and senses, habituated for some months past to the loneliness of the desert, the semi-barbarism of Ma'án and Djowf, nay, and before that, to the anarchy of Turkish misrule or no-rule in Syria. " This is a government in good earnest " said, at his first arrival, my companion, who had all his life before seen nothing better than the squabbles of Lebanon and the anarchy of its districts. Indeed Ṭelál's administration is in no respect less unquestionably superior to the Ottoman than the English or Prussian may be to Ṭelál's.

After all, nationality is a good thing, and foreign rule but a poor compensation for it. Here was an Arab governing Arabs after their own native Arab fashion, and thus succeeding infinitely better in securing the peace of his lands, the happiness of his subjects, the regular administration of law and justice, and

the maintenance of quiet and good order, than any Constanti-
nople-sent Khoorshid Basha, or Foo'ad Basha, or 'Omar Basha
ever did in their respective provinces, or ever can. Needs hardly
say the why and wherefore ; a thinking mind (and Eastern politics require one) may fill up the rest. But it would be well
for Syria, well for Bagdad, well for the valley of Mosool and the
Mesopotamian uplands, were the same principles that preside
at Ḥā'yel applied there. It is beyond the writer's province to
speak of Europe, where Poles, Servians, Sicilians, and other
races may have to work out the same problem. But of Asia,
at least so much of it as lies between Kara-Dagh and 'Aden,
I would unhesitatingly say that its specific remedy (and very
sick it is wherever it forms part of the great " sick man") is to
be found first and foremost in the redintegration of its nationality. *Forsan—hæc olim meminisse juvabit.*

Next morning, the 29th of July, about an hour after sunrise,
the loiterers of the town—and they are numerous here as those
who ever hung on the bridge at Coventry—had in us and our
dwelling a new centre of curiosity and attraction. This was
just what we wanted ; so our outer door had been purposely left
open, and the interior spectacle displayed to the delighted
beholders.

Round the walls of the courtyard and following the shade
they afforded, we had arranged ends of carpet, empty saddle-bags,
and the like, for the convenience of whoever might come to
visit or to consult the great doctor. Once for all, I beg pardon
of the medical faculty for my assumed title. I had taken no
degree, not even at Aberdeen. In short, it was a horrid, a most
scandalous imposture, an unpardonable cheat, whatever you
choose ; but I could not help it. I trust that extenuating
circumstances and previous good character may save me from a
" prosecution according to law." True, I had seriously availed
myself, during past years, of opportunities for the European
study and the Asiatic practice of an amateur in the " leech's "
art, and might securely trust to acquired experience for
ordinary cases. The inner room on the left of the court
had been decently carpeted, and there I sat in cross-legged
state, with a pair of scales before me, a brass mortar, a glass
ditto, and fifty or sixty boxes of drugs, with a small flanking

line of bottles.   Two Arab books of medical science by my side
answered all the purposes of a diploma; of English or French
" vade-mecums " I had but two, and they were concealed behind
the cushion at the back, to be consulted in secret, if necessary.
My companion, who did his best to look like a doctor's serving-
man, sat outside near the door; his duty was to enquire of
comers-in what they wanted, and to admit them one by one
to the professional sanctuary.   In the opposite room, to the
right, a cauldron, a pile of wood, two or three melons, bread,
dates, and so forth, promised something better than the purga-
tives and emetics on the left.   We had, of course, put on our
Sunday's best, that is, clean shirts, a more decent head-gear, and
an upper garment or Combaz—Zaboon they here style it—in
England it would pass for a flowered dressing-gown.   Such was
our appearance on setting up business in Ḥá'yel, while we
awaited the first onset of its custom.

Nor had we long to wait.   The courtyard was soon thronged
with visitors, some from the palace, others from the town.   One
had a sick relation, whom he begged us to come and see,
another some personal ailment, a third had called out of mere
politeness or curiosity; in short, men of all conditions and of
all ages, but for the most part open and friendly in manner, so
that we could already anticipate a very speedy acquaintance
with the town and whatever it contained.   In order not to lose
time, and to preserve at once the dignity and the popularity of
our position, we concerted a methodical system, to which I
adhered in every town we stopped in throughout the rest of our
journey: it succeeded admirably well both for our real and
apparent ends; and I shall here explain it accordingly, for the
benefit of quacks, impostors, and travellers.

In the first place, it was resolved to refuse steadily all
medical practice among women and small children.   A measure
absolutely necessary, considering the very limited bounds of our
science, if we wished to avoid failure, and to husband leisure
for more interesting game.

Secondly, though not till after some observation of Arab
town-life, we arranged our daily occupations on a settled plan,
of which I will subsequently give some description.

Thirdly, it was resolved that among the men of a reasonable

age who should visit or apply to us, we would reject no one
at first sight, but give a courteous welcome to one and all,
nor let any individual go away till after drawing him out in
conversation to the best of our ability; but that, at the same
time, we would undertake a regular treatment of no one with
whose social position, general tenor of life, and other circumstances, we should not have first rendered ourselves sufficiently
familiar.

Obvious motives of prudence in a strange land might suffice
to make these precautions advisable, but there was here a
special reason for taking them.   Arabs never, or hardly ever,
pay the physician except in case of a recovery.   Their way is to
make from the very first a stipulation or agreement " 'Ala-el-
bar'," as they call it, that is, " under contingency of cure : "
and offer payment in such event, of a larger or smaller sum,
according to the gravity, tediousness, or other circumstances of
the case.   Should recovery not follow, the doctor has nothing to
expect.

I do not know how far this system would be relished by our
own M.D.'s; though mayhap the patients might occasionally be
the gainers by it.   But this way of proceeding exacts, it is
evident, many precautions on the part of the doctor, if he
would not see his labour and fair fame speedily thrown away.
Good assurance touching the character and solvency of the con-
tracting party is, above all, necessary.   Then witnesses must be
called in, and the definition of what is precisely meant by " recovery " be exactly fixed, to ensure against evasion and chicane.
And, lastly, the doctor, (if, at any rate, no better a one than
myself, though I should be sorry to think that,) would do
well to assure himself, so far as possible, of the prognosis of the
disease, and if he sees the case to be an unfavourable one, let
him decline it.

But since this, if done in too straightforward a way, might
give the public a limited idea of his skill, he must resort to
sundry little expedients, according to the circumstances before
him.   Thus if he sees that death is certainly imminent, let him
at once declare that the Divine decrees must have their course,
and that from Heaven alone can any suspension or alleviation
be expected.   More than once, where the signs of approaching

dissolution, though unmistakeable enough to practised eyes and
fingers, were yet of a character to escape the notice of the very
unscientific bystanders, the sudden verification within a few days
or hours of some similar announcement on my part, procured me a wonderful name for extraordinary science. So easy
a task has *monoculus inter cæcos.*

In less ominous but still unfavourable cases, I found it an
excellent plan to exact for price of cure, something very exorbi-
tant, say, the value of ten pounds or thereabouts, and which I
was confident that no Arab would dream of agreeing to ; and
thus get off with fair words and a steady refusal.

However, now and then I did come across some exceptionally
reasonable individuals, who when informed that all the resources
of art could only act as palliatives, or if they chanced to be followed by amelioration, it must be after much time and attendance, consented even thus to accept of my aid, offered a fixed
sum to be paid whatever the result might be, and conscien-
tiously kept their word. But these were very rare exceptions
to a far more general rule.

My readers must already understand that to distribute medicine or to afford assistance " gratis " in the usual way, in Arabia,
would be sheer madness ; such a line of conduct would inevitably
betray the stranger, and perhaps imply the spy. One should,
on the contrary, appear more eager than any attorney after one's
fees, and make it seem that they are the main or indeed the
only object of one's travels.

However, whatever dexterity the real or pretended man of
prescriptions may possess, he will find the Arabs of the interior
queer patients, and " kittle cattle " to shoe behind or before.
For although they are fairly civilized in many other respects,
and do not want either clearness of perception or local knowledge, they are mere children in medical matters, and do not
muster the very first data or ideas of that science. Hence their
Æsculapius has need of much patience and good-humour, and
even of a little innocent quackery from time to time. For his
clients will look on the medicines asked for or administered as
hardly less than charms expected to produce a visible and tangible amendment on the very spot, and that quite independently
of any regulations respecting diet, clothing, and the like, from

which in real fact two-thirds of success must often depend in
Asia quite as much as in Europe. If after a day or two the
sick man does not appear cured, or at least on the high road to
being so, they will say, " We do not see any good come of it," and
forthwith abandon physic and physician. In consequence it is
best to adopt, when one can in conscience do it, an energetic
treatment from the very outset; homœopathy and " *la médecine
expectante*" would here have little success. I may add that
the tough Arab fibre generally requires doses which might be
almost fatal in Europe ; and experience soon taught me to
multiply by two most of the prescription-formulas at the end of
my manual.

Perhaps my readers may wish to hear what is the exact
degree of medical lore or ignorance in Modern Arabia : the
more so because Arabs are not uncommonly supposed in Europe
to have been if not the authors at least the restorers of the
healing art.

But this is a popular error. Whatever the Eastern physicians
of Bagdad, or their westerly brethren of Cordova, might know,
was derived from translations of Hippocrates or Galen, from the
Physics of Aristotle and the treatises of Celsus, embodied in
Byzantine compilations, and the works of modern Greeks. These,
rendered with more or less accuracy into the vernacular tongue,
and in the hands of men who had, without exception, so far as
I have been able to investigate, nothing of the Arab except that
they wrote in Arabic, (much in the way that a Prussian of Dussel-
dorf may occasionally publish in French,) and that they professed
the Mahometan belief, became at once the base and the super-
structure, the alpha and the omega, of the whole science ; to this
their successors added nothing, unless it be some scanty and
inaccurate lists of Persian, African, or Egyptian herbs ; and their
confused and unscientific treatises have remained to the present
day the *ne plus ultra* of Arab medical learning.

But even their first glimmerings of science and of method
were soon effectually closed and cross-barred by Islamitic im-
mobility, and its misplaced supernaturalism. The traditional
sayings of Mahomet, whether really his or not, but which at
any rate are little calculated to give the Prophet place among
the ranks of those who can heal the body, were intermixed with

or substituted for the formulas of Galen and the precepts of
Hippocrates; and to deny or evade the hygienic theories of the
Meccan camel-driver might render one suspected of heresy at
the least, and bring down the most awkward consequences.
The fated and all-pervading interference, for such Islam makes
it, of the Divine Omnipotence came in to preclude research, by
reducing every phenomenon at once to the one immediate
universal and arbitrary cause, and thus cut every knot instead
of untying it. Moreover, autopsy and anatomical studies were
held, and still are so, in horror, because a violation of the rights
of Munkar and Nekeer, the grave-angels; while to insist on the
healing or noxious qualities of this or that, appears a downright
transfer made to the creature of an honour exclusively due to
the Creator. This is no exaggeration; not one of these ideas
but I have heard fifty and a hundred times from orthodox and
otherwise intelligent Muslims. Thus, without knowledge alike
of the human frame and of the chemical pharmacopœia, pre-
cluded from experimental science, and rejecting theoretical,
they came at the very outset to a dead stand, and there to the
present day they have remained crystallized, one might almost
say, in complacent and conscientious ignorance.

Thus much for the schools of Syria, Bagdad, Spain, and even
of Egypt down to the reign of Mahommed 'Alee. The Arabs
of Arabia itself, though much freer in general from the stifling
influences of Islám, which their practical good-sense rejected
even where they admitted it in speculation and name, could
however only learn of the medical sciences so much as its
masters chose to teach them in the few torn and dingy manuscripts that might eke their way into the interior of the
Peninsula. Iron sharpens iron, and man's wits sharpen man's,
and intercourse is the first and most essential condition of
advancement. But of this, the Arabs were almost totally
deprived by their isolated position girdled round by the sand
sea of their country, and thus they have been left without most
of those intellectual advantages which a freer communication
with other nations might and would have bestowed on them.
The wonder is not that they failed to acquire new civilization
and learning, but that they managed to maintain their own;
not that they did not advance, but that they lost so little

ground. Less unfavourable circumstances have sufficed to sink many races into utter barbarism. Here the soil was good, but, for the sciences we are now speaking of, there was neither seed nor sower. And at last the noxious Wahhabee atmosphere, the purest azote of Mahometanism, overspread the better half of the land, to stifle what latent vitality it yet retained.

The result is what might naturally be expected. To come to particulars : senna and colocynth, both indigenous products, and whose effect on the animal economy is equally evident and energetic, are almost the only vegetable drugs used or understood. Sulphur, the sulphuret of mercury, and that of arsenic, constitute the entire ordinary list of external applications. On a certain draught derived from the cameline kingdom, and much in use among constipated Bedouins, no need to dilate. Bleeding, especially from the arm, is known, but seldom practised, few having either the skill or the instruments necessary for the operation. A friend of mine, by name Hannoosh, once performed it with a hatchet ! and, stranger still, without cutting off the arm or causing phlebitis. One only remedy is lavishly employed, and borne with amazing patience,—the actual cautery. Whatever be the ailment, wherever the pain fixes itself, the hot iron is forthwith applied ; and should an individual be so unlucky or so unadvised as to complain of pain " all over," he is pretty sure to be seamed all over also.

But ignorance would be a trifle, were it not united with a pretence to knowledge. Everyone, even the very negro slaves, have learned by rote the famous quadruple division of the human constitution; and " am I bilious? or sanguine? or lymphatic? or melancholic?" is asked by each and all, and they attach the greatest importance to the answer on this abstruse point. Any theory that they have, and no man however uninstructed can do without one altogether, is founded on the four temperaments. And accordingly the real or soi-disant doctor, whatever value he may in his own mind assign to this superannuated classification, will do well to bear it in mind, and to bring it perforce into his decisions, if he wishes not to pass for an absolute ignoramus in Nejed and Hâ'yel.

However, the prevailing good humour and urbanity of this people, joined with their large stock of natural sound sense and keen though not deep observation, does much to alleviate the difficulties of the physician. So let no one despair; should London or Brussels prove unkind, a few years of Nejdean practice may perhaps mend matters.

Before leaving this subject, I must add a concluding word on the ordinary practitioners now in vogue throughout Arabia Proper. From the frontiers of Syria to the innermost valleys of Nejed is scattered a tribe of a very peculiar character and name, everywhere the same, and everywhere distinct from the surrounding clans, easily distinguishable, and well known to all conversant with the desert and its wanderers. Should any one of my readers be of this number, he will readily understand that I speak of the Ṣolibah tribe, whose very title, immediately derived as it is from Ṣaleeb, or the Cross, together with external and internal tradition, may seem to confirm their Christian origin. But this betrays itself too in other ways. Among these is their mode of life, never taking part in the wars and disputes of the remaining clans, never allying with them in marriage or otherwise; their main, indeed almost their only occupation, is the chase of ostriches and gazelles, and in this they are unrivalled. Though retaining, so far as I could discover, but very faint traces of the more positive features of Christianity, they have yet one of its negative marks in a strong unchanging hatred to Mahometanism, which they not only neglect in common with the great mass of Bedouins, but openly and positively disavow. They are evidently strangers to the Arab stem, and by their own account belong to a more northerly extraction. And in support of this, their fair complexion and open, sometimes handsome, features and light eyes show the Syrian rather than the Arabian type; while their careless gaiety of manner strongly contrasts with the cloudy and suspicious physiognomy of the wanderers among whom they live. I often fell in with these men, and mention will be made of them again in the course of this work.

Now to these same Ṣolibah Bedouins the ordinary inhabitants of the peninsula attribute a knowledge of the healing art far exceeding their own; nor, it would seem, altogether without reason. It is a common saying among Mahometans that medical science is the offspring and heritage of the Christians; and they readily avow their own inferiority in this respect. Hence they think it natural enough to look for it among the Ṣolibah. Of these, and of their skill, I have heard many stories, some wild enough, though not totally incredible. But having never had the good luck to see any fact of the sort with my own eyes, I do not think it advisable to prolong my tale with episodes of but a doubtful value; suffices to say that paracentesis, lithotomy, and still more difficult operations worthy of an Astley Cooper or a Brodie, have been often in my hearing ascribed to the Ṣolibah surgeons, and that with such circumstantial detail in the narrative as to give it at least an air of truth, besides medical treatments of all kinds and qualities for sundry and complicated diseases. So that I really suppose the reputation of this errant faculty to be somehow founded in fact.

Besides these rather mysterious practitioners, Mughrabee and Belooch quacks occasionally wander over the peninsula, and profess to heal, but with little success either for the bodies of their patients or for their own pockets. I never heard them well spoken of, nor should I indeed have expected it.

What has been now said may be enough to give an idea of the line we had to hold in our simulated profession. Throughout the remainder of our travels, we kept up our medical character, making it our exclusive title of introduction among whatever people we had to deal with, and never permitted anyone of low or high degree to know anything else of us, unless some very peculiar circumstances rendered an opposite conduct necessary or expedient in individual instances, one of which happened in fact only a few weeks later.

The nature of our occupations now led to a certain daily routine, though it was often agreeably diversified by incidental occurrences. Perhaps a leaf taken at random from my journal, now regularly kept, may serve to set before my readers a tolerable sample of our ordinary course of life and society at Ḥā'yel, while it will at the same time give a more distinct idea of the town and people than we have yet supplied. It is, besides, a pleasure to retrace the memories of a pleasant time, and such on the whole was ours here; and I trust that the reader will not be wholly devoid of some share in my feelings.

Be it, then, the 10th of August, whose jotted notes I will put together and fill up the blanks. I might equally have taken

the 9th or the 11th, they are all much the same; but the day
I have chosen looks a little the closer written of the two, and
for that sole reason I prefer giving it; nor does it seem to me
devoid of calm and real though not stirring interest. However,
for the consolation of those who delight in recitals of desperate
battles, grisly murder, and all that, I forewarn that an episode
thick-set with these agreeable and soul-stirring events must of
necessity be introduced into its course like a crimson patch on
a ground of quiet green.

On that day, then, in 1862, about a fortnight after our
establishment at Ḥá'yel, and when we were, in consequence,
fully inured to our town existence, Seleem Abou Maḥmood-
el-'Eys and Barakát-esh-Shámee, that is, my companion and
myself, rose, not from our beds, for we had none, but from
our roof-spread carpets, and took advantage of the silent
hour of the first faint dawn, while the stars yet kept watch
in the sky over the slumbering inhabitants of Shomer, to
leave the house for a cool and undisturbed walk ere the
sun should arise and man go forth unto his work and to his
labour. We locked the outer door, and then passed into the
still twilight gloom down the cross-street leading to the market-
place, which we next followed up to its farther or south-
western end, where large folding-gates separate it from the rest
of the town. The wolfish city-dogs, whose bark and bite too
render walking the streets at night a rather precarious business,
now tamely stalked away in the gloaming, while here and there
a crouching camel, the packages yet on his back, and his
sleeping driver close by, awaited the opening of the warehouse
at whose door they had passed the night. Early though it was,
the market-gates were already unclosed, and the guardian sat
wakeful in his niche. On leaving the market we had yet to go
down a broad street of houses and gardens cheerfully intermixed, till at last we reached the western wall of the town, or,
rather, of the new quarter added by 'Abd-Allah, where the high
portal between round flanking towers gave us issue on the open
plain, blown over at this hour by a light gale of life and coolness. To the west, but some four or five miles distant, rose the
serrated mass of Djebel Shomer, throwing up its black fantastic
peaks, now reddened by the reflected dawn, against the lead-

blue sky.   Northward the same chain bends round till it meets
the town, and then stretches away for a length of ten or twelve
days' journey, gradually losing in height on its approach to
Meshid 'Alee and the valley of the Euphrates. On our south we
have a little isolated knot of rocks, and far off the extreme
ranges of Djebel Shomer or 'Aja', to give it its historical name,
intersected by the broad passes that lead on in the same direction to Djebel Solma.   Behind us lies the capital.   Telāl's
palace, with its high oval keep, houses, gardens, walls, and
towers, all coming out black against the ruddy bars of eastern
light, and behind, a huge pyramidical peak almost overhanging
the town, and connected by lower rocks with the main mountain range to north and south, those stony ribs that protect the
central heart of the kingdom.   In the plain itself we can just
distinguish by the doubtful twilight several blackish patches irregularly scattered over its face, or seen as though leaning upward
against its craggy verge; these are the gardens and country-
houses of 'Obeyd and other chiefs, besides hamlets and villages,
such as Kefar and 'Adwah, with their groves of palm and "Ithel"
(a tree which I will describe farther on), now blended in the
dusk.   One solitary traveller on his camel, a troop of jackals
sneaking off to their rocky caverns, a few dingy tents of Shomer
Bedouins, such are the last details of the landscape.   Far away
over the southern hills beams the glory of Canopus, and announces a new Arab year ; the pole-star to the north lies low
over the mountain tops.

   We pace the pebble-strewn flat to the south, till we leave behind
us the length of the town wall, and reach the little cluster of
rocks already mentioned.   We scramble up to a sort of niche
near its summit, whence, at a height of a hundred feet or more,
we can overlook the whole extent of the plain and wait the sunrise.   Yet before the highest crags of Shomer are gilt with its
first rays, or the long giant shadows of the easterly chain have
crossed the level, we see groups of peasants, who drawing their
fruit and vegetable-laden asses before them, issue like little
bands of ants from the mountain gorges around, and slowly
approach on the tracks converging to the capital.   Horsemen
from the town ride out to the gardens, and a long line of camels
on the westerly Medinah road winds up towards Ḥā'yel.   We

wait esconced in our rocky look-out and enjoy the view till the
sun has risen, and the coolness of the night air warms rapidly
into the sultry day; it is time to return. So we quit our
solitary perch, and descend to the plain, where keeping in
the shadow of the western fortifications we regain the town
gate and thence the market. There all is now life and movement; some of the warehouses, filled with rice, flour, spices, or
coffee, and often concealing in their inner recesses stores of the
prohibited American weed, are already open; we salute the
owners while we pass, and they return a polite and friendly
greeting. Camels are unloading in the streets, and Bedouins
standing by, looking anything but at home in the town. The
shoemaker and the blacksmith, those two main props of Arab
handicraft, are already at their work, and some gossiping bystanders are collected around them. At the corner where our
cross street falls into the market place, three or four country
women are seated, with piles of melons, gourds, egg-plant
fruits, and the other garden produce before them for sale. My
companion falls a haggling with one of these village nymphs, and
ends by obtaining a dozen " badinjans " and a couple of water
melons, each bigger than a man's head, for the equivalent of an
English twopence. With this purchase we return home, where
we shut and bolt the outer door, then take out of a flat basket
what has remained from over night of our wafer-like Ḥā'yel
bread, and with this and a melon make a hasty breakfast. I
say a hasty one, for although it is only half an hour after sunrise, repeated knocks at our portal show the arrival of patients
and visitors: early rising being here the fashion, and reason
must wherever artificial lighting is scanty. However, we do not
at once open to our friends, nor will they take offence at the
delay, but remain where they are chatting together before our
door till we admit them; of so little value is time here. Our
drink is water, for which we address ourselves to a goat-skin
filled from the neighbouring well by Fatimah, daughter of our
landlord Ḥasan-el-Miṣree, and suspended against the wall in
the shady corner of the court. We untie its mouth where it
hangs, and let out the contents into a very rude but strong
brass cup of town manufacture, and with this teetotaller draught
content ourselves. I hardly know why we had not yet begun

at Ḥā'yel to make our own coffee; we became better house-keepers in the after course of the journey. We then arrange the carpets, and I retire to my doctoral seat within, taking care to have the scales and an Arab book in ostentatious evidence before me, while Barakāt-esh-Shāmee opens the entrance.

In comes a young man of good appearance, clad in the black cloak common to all of the middle or upper classes in central Arabia; in his hand he bears a wand of the Sidr or lotos-wood. A silver-hilted sword and a glistering Ḳafee'yah announce him to be a person of some importance, while his long black ringlets, handsome features and slightly olive complexion, with a tall stature and easy gait, declare him native of Djebel Shomer, and townsman of Ḥā'yel; it is 'Ojeyl, the eldest born of a large family, and successor to the comfortable house and garden of his father not long since deceased, in a quarter of the town some twenty minutes' walk distant. He leads by the hand his younger brother, a modest-looking lad of fair complexion and slim make, but almost blind, and evidently out of health also. After passing through the preliminary ceremonies of intro-duction to Barakāt, he approaches my recess, and standing without, salutes me with the greatest deference. Thinking him a desirable acquaintance, I receive him very graciously, and he begs me to see what is the matter with his brother, describing to me all the boy's various ailments with much exactness, though with scrupulous decorum in the choice of words, a point in which the Arabs of the towns are remark-ably skilful, unless perhaps when they choose to be rude on purpose. I examine the case, and find it to be within the limits of my skill, nor likely to require more than a very simple course of treatment. Accordingly I make my bargain for the chances of recovery, and find 'Ojeyl docile to the terms pro-posed, and with little disposition, all things considered, to backwardness in payment. Arabs, indeed, are in general close in driving a bargain and open in downright giving; they will chaffer half a day about a penny, while they will throw away the worth of pounds on the first asker. But 'Ojeyl was one of the best specimens of the Ḥā'yel character, and of the clan Ṭā'i, renowned in all times for their liberal ways and high sense of honour. I next proceed to administer to my patient

such drugs as his state requires, and he receives them with
that air of absolute and half religious confidence which well-
educated Arabs show to their physician, whom they regard as
possessed of an almost sacred and supernatural power—a feeling,
by the way, hardly less advantageous to the patient than to the
practitioner, and which may often contribute much to the
success of the treatment.

During the rest of my stay at Ḥá'yel, 'Ojeyl continued to be
one of my best friends, I had almost said disciples; our mutual
visits were frequent, and always pleasing and hearty. His
brother's cure, which followed in less than a fortnight, confirmed
his attachment, nor had I reason to complain of scantiness in
his retribution. From him also I obtained what I valued much
more, namely, considerable information about the political and
religious state of the " past and present " of Shomer; I will
give it interwoven into the course of the narrative when occasion
offers.

Meanwhile the courtyard has become full of visitors. Close
by my door I see the intelligent and demurely-smiling face of
'Abd-el-Maḥsin, where he sits between two pretty and well-
dressed boys; they are the two elder children of Telál, Bedr and
Bander; their guardsman, a negro slave with a handsome cloak
and sword, is seated a little lower down. Farther on are two
townsmen, one armed, the other with a wand at his side. A
rough good-natured youth of a bronzed complexion, and whose
dingy clothes bespeak his mechanical profession, is talking with
another of a dress somewhat different in form and coarser in
material than that usually worn in Ḥá'yel; this latter must be a
peasant from some one of the mountain villages. Two Bedouins,
ragged and uncouth like all their compeers, have straggled in
with the rest; while a tall dark-featured youth, with a gilded
hilt to his sword, and more silk about him than a Wahhabee
would approve, has taken his place opposite to 'Abd-el-Maḥsin,
and is trying to draw him into conversation. But this last has
asked Barakát to lend him one of my Arabic books to read, and
is deeply engaged in its perusal.

'Ojeyl has taken leave, and I give the next turn of course to
'Abd-el-Maḥsin. He informs me that Telál has sent me his
two sons Bedr and Bander that I may examine their state of

health, and see if they require doctoring. This is in truth a little stroke of policy on Telāl's part, who knows equally with myself that the boys are perfectly well and want nothing at all. But he wishes to give us a mark of his confidence, and at the same time to help us in establishing our medical reputation in the town ; for though by no means himself persuaded of the reality of our doctoral title, he understands the expediency of saving appearances before the public.

Well, the children are passed in review with all the seriousness due to a case of heart-complaint or brain-fever, while at a wink from me, Barakāt prepares in the kitchen a draught of cinnamon water, which with sugar, named medicine for the occasion, pleases the young heirs of royalty and keeps up the farce ; 'Abd-el-Maḥsin, like the Chorus in Euripides, expatiating all the time to the bystanders on the wonderful skill with which I have at once discovered the ailments and their cure, and the small boys thinking that if this be medicine, they will do their best to be ill for it every day.

'Abd-el-Maḥsin now commits them to the negro, who, however, before taking them back to the palace, has his own story to tell of some personal ache, for which I prescribe without stipulating for payment, since he belongs to the palace, where it is important to have the greatest number of friends possible, even on the back-stairs. But 'Abd-el-Maḥsin remains, reading, chatting, quoting poetry, and talking history, recent events, natural philosophy, religion, or medicine, as the case may be.

But let us see some of the other patients. The gold-hilted swordsman has naturally a special claim on our attention. It is the son of Rosheyd, Telāl's maternal uncle. His palace stands on the other side of the way, exactly opposite to our house ; and I will say nothing more of him for the present, intending to pay him afterwards a special visit, and thus become more thoroughly acquainted with the whole family.

Next let us take notice of those two townsmen who are conversing, or rather " chaffing," together. Though both in plain apparel, and much alike in stature and features, there is yet much about them to distinguish the two ; one has a civilian look, the other a military. He of the wand is no less a personage than Moḥammed-el-Ḳādee, chief justice of Ḥā'yel, and of course a very important individual in the town. However his exterior is that of an elderly unpretentious little man, and one, in spite of the proverb which attributes gravity to judges, very fond of a joke, besides being a tolerable representative of what may here be called the moderate party, neither participating in the fanaticism of the Wahhabee, nor yet, like the most of the indigenous chiefs, hostile to Mahometanism; he takes his cue from the court direction, and is popular with all factions because belonging properly to none.

He requires some medical treatment for himself, and some for his son, a big heavy lad with a swollen arm, who has accompanied him hither. Here too is a useful acquaintance, well up to all the scandal and small-talk of the town, and willing to communicate it. Our visits were frequent, and I found his house well stored with books, partly manuscript, partly printed in Egypt, and mainly on legal or religious subjects. Among those of the latter description were, by way of example, a collection of Khoṭbahs or sermons for all the Fridays in the year, and the Lives of the Prophets from Seth downwards, written with an historical accuracy and critical discernment worthy of the stories of Baron Munchausen or Jack and the Beanstalk. Moḥammed was a great talker, and exercised on all matters a freedom of remark common though not peculiar to men of the legal profession; he became in short our " daily news " for court intrigue and city gossip, what had been said in public, and what done in private, who ran away with whom, and so forth. Yet on the whole the portrait he thus laid before us of Ḥā'yel and its inhabitants, noble or commoners, was a favourable one, more so perhaps than could be in justice given of most capitals. This might be the result of the character of those tribes who, as Arab annals have it, coalesced into the present population, namely, Ṭā'i and Wā'il, with their kindred clans, and who were, so fame assures us, the flower of Arab enterprise and generosity, the most affable in peace, the most daring in war, and the most honourable at all times amid the inhabitants of Nejed and Upper Arabia. In later ages the civilization of town-life has cast an agreeable varnish over their rougher qualities, while that civilization itself is of too simple a character to render them artificial or corrupt.

Of the country folks in the villages around, like Mogah, Delhemee'ch, and the rest, Mohammed-el-Kadee used to speak with a sort of half-contemptuous pity, much like a Parisian talking of Low Bretons; in fact, the difference between these rough and sturdy boors, and the more refined inhabitants of the capital, is, all due proportion allowed, no less remarkable here than in Europe itself. We will now let one of them come forward in his own behalf, and my readers shall be judges.

It is accordingly a stout clown from Mogah, scantily dressed in working wear, and who has been occupied for the last half-hour in tracing sundry diagrams on the ground before him with a thick peach-tree switch, thus to pass his time till his betters shall have been served. He now edges forward, and taking his seat in front of the door, calls my attention with an "I say, doctor." Whereon I suggest to him that his bulky corporation not being formed of glass or any other transparent material, he has by his position entirely intercepted whatever little light my recess might enjoy. He apologizes, and shuffles an inch or two sideways. Next I enquire what ails him, not without some curiosity to hear the answer, so little does the herculean frame before me announce disease. Whereto Do'eymis, or whatever may be his name, replies, "I say, I am all made up of pain." This statement, like many others, appears to me rather too general to be literally true. So I proceed in my interrogatory : "Does your head pain you?" "No." (I might have guessed that; these fellows never feel what our cross-Channel friends entitle "*le mal des beaux esprits.*") "Does your back ache?" "No." "Your arms?" "No." "Your legs?" "No." "Your body?" "No." "But," I conclude, "if neither your head nor your body, back, arms, or legs pain you, how can you possibly be such a composition of suffering?" "I am all made up of pain, doctor," replies he, manfully intrenching himself within his first position. The fact is, that there is really something wrong with him, but he does not know how to localize his sensations. So I push forward my enquiries, till it appears that our man of Mogah has a chronic rheumatism ; and on ulterior investigation, conducted with all the skill that Barakāt and I can jointly muster, it comes out that three or four months before he had an attack

of the disease in its acute form, accompanied by high fever,
since which he has never been himself again.

This might suffice for the diagnosis, but I wish to see how he
will find his way out of more intricate questions; besides, the
townsmen sitting by, and equally alive to the joke with myself,
whisper "Try him again." In consequence, I proceed with
"What was the cause of your first illness?" "I say, doctor,
its cause was God," replies the patient. "No doubt of that,"
say I; "all things are caused by God: but what was the
particular and immediate occasion?" "Doctor, its cause was
God, and, secondly, that I ate camel's flesh when I was cold,"
rejoins my scientific friend. "But was there nothing else?"
I suggest, not quite satisfied with the lucid explanation just
given. "Then, too, I drank camel's milk; but it was all, I
say, from God, doctor," answers he.

Well, I consider the case, and make up my mind regarding
the treatment. Next comes the grand question of payment,
which must be agreed on beforehand, and rendered conditional
on success, as my readers know. I enquire what he will give
me on recovery. "Doctor," answers the peasant, "I will give
you, do you hear? I say, I will give you a camel." But I
reply that I do not want one. "I say, remember God," which
being interpreted here means, "do not be unreasonable; I will
give you a fat camel, every one knows my camel; if you
choose, I will bring witnesses, I say." And while I persist in
refusing the proffered camel, he talks of butter, meal, dates,
and suchlike equivalents.

There is a patient and a paymaster for you. However, all
ends by his behaving reasonably enough; he follows my prescriptions with the ordinary docility, gets well, and gives me
for my pains an eighteenpenny fee.

So pass two or three hours, during which the remaining
visitors already mentioned take each their turn, others come
and go, and the sun nears the zenith. For brevity's sake, I
pass on at once to the mechanic, who, after long waiting in the
shade with genuine Arab patience, now advances, and with a
good-natured grin on his broad features begs me to accompany
him to his house, where his brother is lying ill of a fever.
After a short conversation, I direct Barakāt to stay at home till

my return, and gratify my petitioner by consenting to his invitation.

Small of stature, dusky in complexion, strongly built, and with a sly expression about his face which resembles almost strikingly that of Murillo's Spanish beggar-boy, Doheym (literally "blacky,") may stand for a not unfair specimen of a large class among the central Nejdean population. Partly from a desire of increasing gain, partly from dislike to Wahhabee puritanism, his family has not long since emigrated northward from Kaseem to Ḥā'yel, where they have fixed their residence, but still retain many of the distinctive ways and habits of their native district. Such immigrations have of late become very common, and have greatly contributed to the numerical and military strength of Djebel Shomer, while they add much to its industrial and commercial prosperity. My readers will perhaps call to mind Louis XIV and the repeal of the Nantes edict, and add one parallel more between Arabia and Europe. For the civilization of Kaseem is of ancient date, and its inhabitants possess traditional skill in all kinds of handicraft and trade, far superior to anything found among the recently organized tribes of the north, while the memories of former independence, protracted wars and victories, have given to their character a steadiness and resolution in all their undertakings very unlike the unsustained though dashing bravery of the north, formed in brief forays and in Bedouin feuds. The good-natured and social disposition common to Arabs in general has been also fostered among them by centuries of city and town life till it occasionally attains the level of sprightliness, while it bestows on them a more decided turn of ease and urbanity in their conversation than is general in Shomer and its dependencies. It is natural enough that such men should for the most succeed well in obtaining easy admittance and speedy success in a strange land, though they readily after a short sojourn avail themselves of any good opportunity for returning to their native country, a land favoured both by nature and art much more than the stony precincts of Ḥā'yel and the rough sierras of Sulma and 'Aja'.

Doheym takes up his thin black cloak, and wraps it round him in folds that a sculptor might admire, and out we set together. As we go on to the Sook, he nods and smiles to some

fifty acquaintances, or stops a moment to interchange a few
words with those of his own land. The market-place is now
crowded from end to end; townsmen, villagers, Bedouins, some
seated at the doors of the warehouses and driving a bargain
with the owners inside, some gathered in idle groups, gossiping
over the news of the hour. For the tongue is here what printed
paper is in Europe, and I doubt whether an Arab loses more
time in hearing and retailing the occurrences of the day than
an Englishman every morning over his " Times," although the
latter has at least the advantage of looking the more studious.
I might here enter on a most interesting investigation touching
the comparative amount of individual and of united action in
the East and West, whereby it should appear by way of conclusion that the Occidental has much more the advantage over
the Oriental hemisphere in the combination of work than in
the quantity of the work itself gone through. Thus it might
be shown that an Arab and an Englishman, take them man
for man, perform each about the same portion of day's-work
in the twenty-four hours, with this difference, that the Arab
works for himself and by himself, while the Englishman works
for society, and with all the assistance and durability of result
that society affords, like one who builds with cement and mortar, compared with him who merely piles up loose stones on
stones. This and more; but I should tire my reader's patience,
while he stands by me in the dust and sun of a Ḥāʾyel fore-
noon, with a Gladstone or a Bright oration on the use of combined labour, even had I their mastery of words and command
of the subject.

Groups of lading and unlading camels block up the path; I
look right and left; there within the shops I see one merchant
laboriously summing up his accounts (I know not whether the
Arabs were ever good mathematicians, certainly at present a
simple reckoning of addition poses nine out of the ten); another,
for want of customers, is reading in some old dog-eared manuscript of prayers, or of natural history, or of geography—such
geography, where almost all the world except Arabia is filled up
with " Anthropophagi and men whose heads do grow beneath
their shoulders." The Coran is little dealt in here, " thank
God for that;" but the Shiya'ees of Meshid 'Alee may per-

chance have in their hands some small illuminated treatise on the imaginary excellencies of 'Alee or one of his family, or very likely a most unscriptural, or more truly antiscriptural narrative of the amours of Joseph with Zuleykha, Potiphar's traditionary wife; the history of David's frailties, wherein the monarch's fault is made to consist not, as some innocently suppose, in taking his neighbour's wife, but in the extravagance of adding a hundredth to the ninety-nine he is supposed to have already, but lawfully, possessed, and suchlike edifying tales. For to idolize 'Alee and his race, and to wallow in the swine-trough of sensuality, is the *dernier mot* and turning-point of Shiya'ee doctrine and practice.

Mixed with the city crowd, swordsmen and gaily-dressed negroes, for the negro is always a dandy when he can afford it, belonging mostly to the palace, are now going about their affairs, and claim a certain amount of deference from the vulgar cits, though we see nothing here of the Agha and Basha style of the overbearing and despotic Turk. Nor do these government men ever dream of taking aught without purchase, or of compelling those they can lay hold of to gratuitous labour, Ottoman fashion; such proceedings, also, being repugnant to that independent high-mindedness which stamps the genuine Arab caste. The well-dressed chieftain and noble jostles on amid the plebeian crowd on terms of astounding familiarity, and elbows or is elbowed by the artisan and the porter; while the court officers themselves meet with that degree of respect alone which indicates deference rather than inferiority in those who pay it. A gay and busy scene; the morning air in the streets yet retains just sufficient coolness to render tolerable the bright rays of the sun, and everywhere is that atmosphere of peace, security, and thriving known to the visitors of inner Arabia, and almost or wholly unknown to the Syrian or Anatolian traveller. Should you listen to the hum of discourse around, you will never hear a curse, an imprecation, or a quarrel, but much business, repartee, and laughter. Doheym and I slowly pick out our way through the crowd amid many greetings on either hand, till we reach the open space of the palace court where the Sook falls into it; and thence we pass through the high gateway, and enter the main artery of the town.

It is a broad and level road, having on its left the walls of the palace gardens, overtopped here and there by young date trees, for this plantation is quite recent, and the work of the present reign only; on its right a succession of houses, scattered among gardens of older growth and denser vegetation; the trees overhang the walls, and we are glad to avail ourselves of their deep dark shade. Doheym entertains me with descriptions of Nejed and Kaseem, and extols in no measured terms the land of his birth; he has seen too the Wahhabee monarch in person, though not in Riad his capital. Thus we beguile a quarter of an hour's leisurely walk (it were superfluous to say that no one hurries his pace in these semi-tropical regions, especially in the month of August), till we reach an open space behind the palace garden, where a large and deep excavation announces the Maslakhah, or slaughter-house (literally " skinning place ") of the town butchers. In any other climate such an establishment would be an intolerable nuisance to all neighbours if thus placed within the city limits, and right in the centre of gardens and habitations. But here the dryness of the atmosphere is such that no ill consequence follows; putrefaction being effectually anticipated by the parching influence of the air, which renders a carcass of three or four days' standing as inoffensive to the nose as a leather drum; and one may pass leisurely by a recently deceased camel on the road-side, and almost take it for a specimen prepared with arsenic and spirits for an anatomical museum.

At this point the street leads off to the interior of the capital. The part hitherto traversed on our walk is the new quarter, and dates almost entirely from the accession of the actual dynasty; but now we are to enter on the original town of Ḥá'yel, where everything announces considerable though not remote antiquity. The two main quarters which form the old city are divided by a long road, narrower and less regular than that we have yet followed. Nor was this line of demarcation more to indicate a division of the buildings than of the inhabitants, split up as they formerly were by civil and internecine hostility. But to this the strong hand of Ebn-Rasheed has at last put an end. Right and left crossways, branching out of the main path, lead to side streets and lesser subdivisions. We take a very narrow and winding lane on the right, by which Doheym leads me awhile through a labyrinth of gardens, wells, and old irregular houses, till we reach a cluster of buildings, and a covered gallery, conducting us through its darkness to the sun-glare of a broad road, bordered by houses on either side, though a low court wall and outer door, generally intervenes between them and the street itself. The arch is here unknown, and the portals are all of timber-work enclosed in brick, and equally rough and solid in construction. My guide stops before one such and knocks. "Samm'" ("come in") is heard from within-side, and immediately afterwards some one comes up and draws back the inner bolt. We now stand in a courtyard, where two or three small furnaces, old metal pots and pans of various sizes, some enormously big—for the Arabs pique themselves now, like their ancestors of two thousand years since, in having cauldrons large enough to boil an entire sheep—sheets of copper, bars of iron, and similar objects, proclaim an Arab smithy. Some brawny half-naked youths covered with soot and grime come up to present a shake of their unwashed hands, while they exchange Nejdean jokes with Doheym. His elder brother So'eyd, whose gravity as head of the family has been a little ruffled by the sportiveness of his younger relatives, rebukes the juveniles, hastens to purify his own face and hands, and then introduces me to the interior of the house, where in a darkened room lies another brother, the sick man on whose behalf I have been summoned; he is in a high fever and hardly able to speak, though there is fortunately no immediate danger. I take my seat by the patient and address a few preliminary questions to the bystanders, intermixed with hopeful prognostics, while the sick man tries to look cheerful, and shows that he expected my coming to see him, and is pleased at it. To put out the tongue even unasked, and to hold forth the hand that the doctor may feel the pulse, are customary proceedings here; but, if you do not wish to pass for an ignoramus, you must successively try both wrists, either radial being supposed entirely independent of its fellow, and each with a separate story to tell; whence my readers may deduce that the real theory of the circulation of the blood is equally unknown with the name of Harvey. When I have

played my part, the elder brother takes me aside and enquires
about the diagnosis and prognosis, or, in plain English, what is
the matter, and what may be the consequences. On my guarded
reply, he promises compliance with whatever I may prescribe,
and then invites me to sit down and take coffee before any
further doctorings. I show a desire of at once getting things
in order for the patient, but the patient himself in a low voice,
eked out with signs, indicates his wish that I should first and
foremost partake of their hospitality. Were he actually dying
I doubt whether matters could hold another course in these
countries. So dates are brought, pipes are lighted, Doheym
prepares coffee, and the room in which (mind you) the sick man
is lying, fills with visitors. Seclusion makes no part of Arab
treatment; on the contrary it is considered almost a sacred
duty to visit and enliven the sufferer by the most numerous
and the most varied society that can be got together. The
Arab invalid himself has no idea of being left alone; to be
kept in company is all his desire; nay, the same system is
observed even when death occurs in a family, and the survivor's nearest of kin, son, wife, or husband, keep open house
for many days after in order to receive the greatest amount
of consolatory calls possible, so that the solitude of woe has few
advocates here.

My readers, conversant, I doubt not, with the scenes and the
injunctions of the Old and of the New Testament also, may here
recall to mind many an example and many an apophthegm to
this same purport, in the book of Job and elsewhere.

In Doheym's house the visitors are mainly natives of Ḳaseem,
or Upper Nejed. It was easy to perceive from their bearing
and from the tone of their conversation that the inhabitants of
the above-named provinces were no less superior to those of
Djebel Shomer in whatever is understood by civilization and
general culture, than the Shomerites to those of Djowf, or the
people of Djowf to the Bedouins. Indeed, if my readers will
draw a diagonal line across the map of Arabia from north-west
to south-east, following the direction of my actual journey
through that country, and then distinguish the several regions
of the peninsula by belts of colour brightening while they
represent the respective degrees of advancement in arts, com-

merce, and their kindred acquirements, on the Dupin system, they will have for the darkest line that nearest to the north, or Wadi Serḥān, while the Djowf, Djebel Shomer, Nejed, Ḥaṣa, and their dependencies, grow lighter in succession more and more, till the belt corresponding to 'Omān should show the cheerfullest tint of all. In fact, it is principally owing to the circumstance that the northern and western parts of Arabia have been hitherto those almost exclusively visited by travellers, that the idea of Arab barbarism or Bedouinism has found such general acceptance in Europe ; the centre and the east of what lies between the Red Sea and the Gulf of 'Omān would have supplied a much more favourable criterion. But I anticipate : let us return to our hosts and their friends.

Here we are now in Ḥā'yel, yet in the midst of Nejdean politics and debate, where the bigotry and tyranny of the Wahhabee meet with oft-recurring and cordial detestation. The siege of 'Oneyzah, its latest news, conjectures, hopes and fears relative to its duration and result, are the chief topic of conversation. Already, indeed, when hardly beyond the boundaries of the Djowf, had we heard of that great event of the Arabian day. But here it was the all-engrossing subject of anxious enquiry and speculation, and the real though disguised cause of the frequent visits paid by the chiefs of Ḳaseem to Ṭelāl, and of their endless rendezvous in the apartments of 'Abd-el-Maḥsin. To render this matter intelligible, and to serve also for a key to much which must needs be alluded to hereafter, I will now briefly sketch what was at the very time passing in Ḳaseem, with the necessary supplement of the previous circumstances that brought on the memorable events of 1862 and 1863 in central Arabia, events to be long remembered and deeply deplored.

When Feyṣul, the reigning monarch of the Wahhabee or Ebn-Sa'ood dynasty, returned for the third time in 1843 or 1844 (for I am not sure of the precise date) to his native Nejed and hereditary throne, he found in the rich and populous province of Ḳaseem his foremost auxiliaries for re-establishing his sway and expelling the last remnants of Egyptian occupation. The indwellers of this district took the opportunity of incorporating themselves into the great

Wahhabee empire; more, however, from hatred to the stranger
Bashas of Egypt than from any particular sympathy with the
natives of Nejed, against whom, indeed, they had often waged
war in former times. They now consented to furnish Feysul
with an annual contingent of tribute, and of troops also, should
such be required, but on condition of non-interference with
their own indigenous chiefs, municipal administration, and local
customs. Matters continued on this footing for seven or eight
years, till Feysul, after having not only thoroughly secured his
supremacy over the central provinces, namely, Sedeyr, Woshem,
'Aared, Yemāmah, Ḥareek, Aflaj, and Dowāsir, but also conquered Ḥasa and Kateef, besides considerable successes obtained
in the direction of Baḥreyn and 'Omān, felt at last the sceptre
strong enough in his hand to crush the surviving liberties of
Kaseem, and to reduce its chiefs and people to that degree of
servitude which in Wahhabee eyes is the only fitting condition
of all except the true " Muslemeen " or Mahometans, that is, of
course, of all men but themselves.

The first and principal step in this direction was to annihilate
the great families that had from time immemorial ruled in
Kaseem, or at least to deprive them of all authority and power.
Now the two most important towns in that province were
Bereydah and 'Oneyzah, whose respective chieftains exercised an
undisputed influence over the third emporium of commerce,
namely, the town of Rass, and over the fifty or sixty other
towns and villages scattered throughout the land. The nobles
of Bereydah, amongst whom was our friend 'Abd-el-Maḥsin,
belonged to the family of 'Aleyy'ān, those of 'Oneyzah to that of
'Ātee'yah. But Bereydah was somewhat lesser in importance, and
inferior in numerical strength and in wealth to her sister town;
in antiquity I believe them equal. The inhabitants of 'Oneyzah
are reckoned at about thirty thousand souls, those of Bereydah
between twenty and twenty-five thousand. Against the latter
town Feysul directed his first efforts, trusting here to find an
easier prey.

He picked a quarrel with the 'Aleyy'ān chieftains, and harassed
them for a while by continual forays under the command of
his eldest son, the talented but ferocious and unprincipled
'Abd-Allah. A considerable period thus passed in desultory

attack and delusive truce, till the nobles of Bereydah, finding their commerce almost cut off, and their strength unequal to the contest, began to desire peace at whatever price. In reply to their embassies Feysul sent them word, not by 'Abd-Allah, whose position as heir-apparent gives an official character to whatever passes in his name, but by his third son Mohammed, that he pardoned their rebellion, and invited them to Riad, where suitable terms of pacification should be arranged between both parties. But the message was verbal only, and without a sufficient guarantee in the person of him who delivered it, and the 'Aleyy'ans hung back awhile, suspecting, and with good cause, some hidden snare: However, their hesitation was at last overcome by repeated assurances of safe-conduct and honourable treatment, backed by a written summons bearing the signature of the heir-apparent, 'Abd-Allah himself, and in which the name of God was solemnly invoked to attest that neither guile nor treachery lurked under his own and his father's invitation. Then in an evil hour 'Oley', the chief of Bereydah, accompanied by two of his sons and several other near kinsmen, set out for Riad, escorted by Mohammed.

Ten days at an easy travelling pace separate Bereydah from the capital of Nejed. The 'Aleyy'an nobles were received with the distinction due to their rank all the way, till they reached Riad; where, to their great surprise, they found no one ready to meet them according to Arab custom without the walls. Mohammed apologized, and said that his brother 'Abd-Allah was doubtless taken up in preparing a fit place for their reception, and that they would find him within waiting for them at his palace-door. Whatever suspicions might arise in the minds of the victims were now unavailing; it was too late either to attempt flight or to parley on conditions. Surrounded by a crowd of the fanatical denizens of Riad, the 'Aleyy'ans reached the outer gate of 'Abd-Allah's best residence. Before it in the street was 'Abd-Allah himself on horseback, surrounded by armed retainers. Hardly had he seen 'Oley's approach, than he hastily turned his horse and re-entered the portal, without waiting to receive the salutation of his guests. They followed; but 'Abd-Allah had already concealed himself from view in an inner apartment, and in his place they found the courtyard filled with armed men and drawn swords. The doors were immediately barred behind them, and the massacre began.

'Oley', his eldest son, and all his relatives and companions, were cut to pieces on the spot, and their blood overflowed the threshold of their perfidious host. The younger son of the ill-starred chieftain was alone reserved alive, as hostage for those of the family who yet remained in Ḳaseem.

Without a moment's delay 'Abd-Allah and his murderous band set out for that province, where the arrival of the traitor almost outstripped the news of his treachery. He fell at once on the town of Bereydah, now in the confusion of recent terror, and involved all whom he could seize of the 'Aleyy'ān family in the fate of their relatives at Riaḍ. A few, amongst whom was 'Abd-el-Maḥsin, escaped the sword: their heads were set at a price. The townsmen, thus deprived of their chieftains, submitted after a brief struggle, and a native of Riaḍ, Mohanna by name, was appointed governor of Bereydah in quality of vice-gerent of Feysul, but with almost absolute power. When all opposition seemed thus at an end, 'Abd-Allah gave orders for putting to death the only surviving son of 'Oley', whom he had hitherto retained in prison; and then, profiting by the consternation spread throughout Ḳaseem, attempted to strike a final and decisive blow at 'Oneyzah itself.

That large town had been for centuries the capital of the province, or rather of a full third of Arabia, namely, of what we may call its north-western centre. Its commerce with Medinah and Mecca on the one hand, and with Nejed, nay, even with Damascus and Bagdad, on the other, had gathered in its warehouses stores of traffic unknown to any other locality of inner Arabia, and its hardy merchants were met with alike on the shores of the Red Sea and of the Persian Gulf, and occasionally on the more distant banks of the Euphrates, or by the waters of Damascus. Meanwhile the martial and energetic character of its population prevented a too exclusive predominance of the commercial over the military spirit, and the warriors of 'Oneyzah had twice at a recent period been seen beneath the walls of Bahholah in the very heart of 'Omān, though separated from them by three months' distance of Arab march. 'Oneyzah itself boasted a double enclosure of fortifications, unbaked brickwork it is true, but in their height and thickness no less formidable to Arab besiegers in their present state of obsidionary science, than the defences of Antwerp or of Badajoz to a European army. The outer circle of walls, with its trench and towers, protected the gardens, while the inner range surrounded the compact mass of the town itself. Here a young and courageous chief Zâmil, or, to give him the name by which he is often familiarly styled, Zoweymil-el-'Āṭeeyah, was adored by his fellow citizens and subjects for his gentleness and liberality in peace, and his daring in war. His head officer or lieutenant, a mulatto called El-Khey'yāṭ, was hardly less renowned for his skill and valour. And the fighting men of 'Oneyzah and its dependent villages, reckoned at five thousand matchlocks, with an equal or greater number of mercenary troops, collected chiefly from among the Bedouins of the surrounding districts, and especially from the powerful tribes of Ḥarb and 'Oṭeybah, were all in readiness at the bidding of Zāmil and his council.

'Abd-Allah tried a sudden and violent assault, but was repulsed. He sent word to his father Feyṣul, who in all speed collected the whole force of Upper Nejed, and marched with them in person to 'Oneyzah, hoping by this juncture of his own and of his son's armies, to carry the place by storm before the sympathy of Ḳaseem, already enlisted in the cause of the capital, should bring about a general levy to its defence. But Zāmil had already sent word of these events to 'Abd-el-Moṭṭalib the Shereef of Mecca, and laid before him the danger impending over the sacred city itself from Wahhabee encroachments, should 'Oneyzah, the sole existing barrier between it and Nejed, be thus swept away. The Shereef perceived the reality of the peril announced, and with what few troops he could muster came to the scene of action. There he met with Feyṣul and 'Abd-Allah, and proposed to act as mediator between them and Zāmil. Feyṣul saw that to continue the war after the intervention of the Shereef, and in his despite, might well draw down on himself and on his empire consequences no less fatal than what had once followed on the rupture between his grandfather and the Ottoman power, which the Shereef represented. Reluctantly he abandoned his prey, accepted the offered terms of pacification " on the hand " (an Arabian expression) of the

governor of Mecca, and retired with his army to the mountains
of Nejed, leaving Zámil and his supporters to themselves;
while 'Abd-el-Moṭṭalib, after exacting and obtaining from
the Wahhabee the strongest assurance that no new attempt
should be made upon the liberty of 'Oneyzah, returned to the
Ḥejáz.

Six or seven years passed before the Wahhabee ventured on
an open violation of the treaty ratified by so high an authority.
But he never lost sight of his first design, and with true
Nejdean perseverance carried steadily on all this while a series
of measures calculated to render easier its after execution, so
soon as time and opportunity should come round to his turn.
One after another he attacked and crushed the tribes of 'Oṭeybah,
Ḥarb, and whatever others were likely to furnish contingents to
the army of 'Oneyzah. Meanwhile the power of Mohanna in
the neighbouring town of Bereydah received further and further
accessions, till it extended over almost the whole of Ḳaseem,
while 'Oneyzah became in a manner isolated and cut off from its
main sources of strength alike in commerce and in war. At last
nothing remained between Feyṣul and his hopes but the risk of
provoking the hostility of the Shereef of Mecca, and thereby of
Egypt or Constantinople. Events which occurred without the
Arabian limits in 1861, left him at liberty to raise the mask
and commence direct hostilities. Certain news was brought
that the change of politics occasioned at Constantinople by the
death of the Sultan 'Abd-el-Mejeed, and the accession of his
brother 'Abd-el-'Azeez, had been highly unfavourable to the
Shereef 'Abd-el-Moṭṭalib, and that he would in all probability
be soon displaced to make room for another known as a friend
to the principles and progress of the Wahhabee. Besides the
growing illness of Sa'eed Basha, and his unprofitable voyage to
Europe, nullified all chance of Egyptian interference in behalf
of 'Oneyzah. Feyṣul's moment was now come, yet he hesitated.
Old and infirm, he may have felt himself unequal to the activity
and cares inseparable from such an undertaking, while twinges
of a conscience not wholly seared even by thirty years of reign
are said to have deterred him awhile from the breach of his
own most solemn engagements plighted to Zámil and his
townsmen. But the less scrupulous council of the Muddey'-

yeeyah, or "Zelators" (of whom more hereafter), urged him to action, and at last he consented.

A quarrel was sought, and soon found on occasion of the annual tribute due from 'Oneyzah to the central government at Riad. Feyṣul pretended that the money raised fell short of the sum stipulated on in the treaty, and sent an armed force to exact a larger supply. This too was furnished, but the Wahhabee was not so to be satisfied. He brought in a claim of arrears, said by him to have been fraudulently kept back, and inculpated Zāmil, whom he summoned to answer for himself at the capital of Nejed. To this summons Zāmil very naturally refused consent, and Feyṣul proclaimed war. The people of 'Oneyzah sent envoy on envoy to beg for peace, and offered to submit to any conditions imposed, except the surrender of their chief. But Feyṣul was inexorable, and the conflict went on.

At the period when I arrived at Ḥā'yel, the 'Oneyzah war had lasted for four or five months without any decisive result, or even any very considerable advantage on either side. Feyṣul sought to weaken the partisans of Zāmil by dragging on the campaign till its duration should have thoroughly harassed and wearied out his enemies, intending then only to gather all his force and strike the final blow when morally sure of speedy and complete success. This plan seemed excellently calculated to obviate the dangers consequent on any reverse at the first outset, and to ensure final triumph. And so, in fact, it proved.

To this end he sent his younger son Moḥammed with small bands of Nejdean troops renewed from time to time, and enjoined him to second the operations of Mohanna, who from his central position at Bereydah was carrying on a sort of loose blockade against 'Oneyzah, much resembling the siege of Troy in character, and destined in all appearance to scarce a less duration. Zāmil and his men retaliated by frequent sallies against the aggressors, and by inroads on the lands and gardens belonging to Bereydah or other towns subject to Mohanna, and the result of these partial operations had hitherto been on the whole in their favour.

The whole of Kaseem with the exception of a very small party sympathized with the warriors of 'Oneyzah and desired their success; but the fear of Mohanna and the constant arrival of

fresh Nejdeans, those Romans of Arabia, kept most of the
natives of the land from open action. Zámil and El-Khey'yát,
sent repeated messages to the governor of Mecca and to Telál
at Ḥá'yel, earnestly requesting their assistance or at least their
mediation. But neither of the parties thus appealed to could
afford any useful succour. Telál for his part was unwilling to
provoke a downright war between himself and the Wahhabee,
whose armies surpassed his own in the proportion of three to
one, and whatever proposals of truce or treaty he could make
were rejected or evaded at Riaḍ. Equally fruitless were the
pacific endeavours of Abd-el-Mottalib, now feeble, because un-
supported. Egypt, the last hope of Zámil, proved, not for the
first time in history, a broken reed. Nor could any clear-sighted
eye fail to perceive that, whatever temporary success might
yet attend the extraordinary efforts of the 'Átee'yah and their
retainers, it must ultimately become impossible for one isolated
town, though well defended and garrisoned, to resist alone the
whole weight of Nejed, and the multiplied resources of the
Wahhabee. However the partisans of 'Oneyzah still continued
to hope against hope, and the wish being in this as in too many
other instances parent to the thought, flattered themselves with
the promise of a result no less unlikely in the natural course of
events than the emancipation of Poland, or the triumph of
Sertorius over the legions of Pompey.

Such was the position of affairs in August 1862; the rest of
my stay in Arabia exactly coincided with the continuation and
catastrophe of this bloody drama, of which I was in part
rendered by circumstances a very unwilling eyewitness. And
accordingly I do not think this cursory sketch of the origin and
progress of these events superfluous or uninteresting, though at
the expense of a somewhat long digression.

We left Doheym and his friends or relatives in earnest discussion of these same topics. However, their conversational
powers were nowise confined to war and politics; medicine and
surgery (for the Arabs hardly distinguish the one from the
other, whether in theory or practice; indeed, their favourite
remedy or panacea, the actual cautery, belongs rather to the
latter than the former) were often brought on the carpet, and I
was pleased to find my Ḳaseem acquaintances speak on these

matters with much good sense, all due allowances made, and
even with some slight tinge of experience. Many plants that
grow hereabouts possess some medicinal virtue, tonic, sedative,
or narcotic, and are occasionally employed by the more knowing
inhabitants. The use, too, of fomentations and other external
remedies or palliatives is not entirely beyond their skill, and
natural quickness may and does fill up to a certain measure the
deficiencies of theoretical ignorance.

Some authors, travelled or otherwise, have represented the
Arabs of the interior as a race absolutely incapable of any real
attainment or progress in practical and material science, and
have supposed that branch of knowledge to be the exclusive
portion of Japhet, to borrow for an instant the typical but convenient classification used by many, while Shem and his descendants, amongst whom the Arabs hold a distinguished place, are to
be allowed neither part nor lot in this matter. My own experience, if indeed it may bear the name of experience, would
lead me to a very different conclusion ; and I am rather inclined
to regard the Arabs, taken in themselves and individually, as
endowed with a remarkable aptitude for these very pursuits, and
hardly less adapted " to the railroad, to the steam-ship," or any
other nineteenth-century invention or natural research than the
natives of Sheffield or Birmingham themselves. But lack of communication with other countries, and especially with those which
were in former times, and yet are, the fountain-heads of that
special activity ; and, in addition, the Mahometan drug which
paralyzes whatever it does not kill outright, have kept them
back in the intellectual race, to be outrun by others more
favoured by circumstance, though not perhaps by nature. When
the Coran and Mecca shall have disappeared from Arabia, then,
and then only, can we seriously expect to see the Arab assume
that place in the ranks of civilization from which Mahomet
and his book have, more than any other individual cause, long
held him back.

I do not exactly know how far these remarks may have their
analogical application among Turks or Persians. The former,
whether in their Pagan or in their Mahometan phase, have
hardly ever appeared on the world's scene except to destroy,
rarely to construct ; neither literature nor arts owing aught

to the Turk but progressive debasement and decay. As to
the Persians, they appear to me, at least in their national character, essentially and irretrievably rotten, whatever be their
religion, dynasty, or organization. Their influence on the
Eastern mind has been undeniably great; but only productive
of extravagance in speculation, bad taste in literature, and
perversity in art. Again and again they have fermented the
masses around them, but with a fermentation which a Liebig
himself could hardly distinguish from putrefaction. Very
different is the aspect afforded by the better days of Arab preponderance; and the decline and extinction of its early promise
can only be explained, partly by the foreign influences, national
or intellectual, of Ispahan and Tartary, and still more by the
Mahometan principle of decay, first developed in the Ḥejāz.

Here at Ḥạ'yel, and in other parts of central Arabia where
Wahhabeeism is in the minority or, happily, unknown, one is
much less wearied with the eternal " There is no God but God,"
the " If it please God," " There is no strength nor power save
in God," and the whole catalogue of phrases with which the
Mahometan encourages his growing apathy or bars the onward
road to enquiry and exertion. On the other hand, " There
is no denying the efficiency of secondary causes," " Everything
has its own cause," are current expressions here, and are often
made use of in reply to the fatalistic interjections of some
fervent Musselman. This is more especially the case among
those who, like the party now assembled in Doheym's house, are
in an actual state of irritation against the Wahhabee and his
ways. " Belaa'na Allah," literally " God has devoured us up,"
have I repeatedly heard from these men, when alluding to the
" Allah, Allah," in season and out of season of the Wahhabee
fanatic or politician. And since Mahometanism in general is
only known to them through the Nejdean medium, the reaction
against the doctrines of Moḥammed, the son of 'Abd-el-Wah-
hāb, is not far from involving the system of the yet more famous
Moḥammed, son of 'Abd-Allah, of Mecca. For further illustration of this and of the preceding remarks, I must refer my
reader to the onward progress of our journey.

In a narrative like this, where personal adventures and
the process of days and months are intermingled with general

reflections and national or religious speculation, many statements must needs occur here and there which may at first sight
appear overcharged, or at least not enough propped up by
immediate argument and proof. Should my reader find it so,
I would beg him to suspend awhile his critical judgment, and
to wait till facts and scenes unavoidably reserved by the date of
their occurrence to a later period of my story may have filled
up the outlines thus broadly traced beforehand. My book is —
at least I mean it to be—a whole, and cannot be taken otherwise, under penalty of misunderstanding; nor do I believe
that I have advanced anything in one page which is not fairly
borne out by the contents of another, though perhaps after an
interval of a few chapters. Where, however, I touch on lands
or races external to the Arabian Peninsula, brevity compels me
to dispense in some measure with minute corroboration, or complete explanation and research. Were I now and here to enter
full sail on so vast a sea, the result would be an encyclopædia
rather than a journey, and of this the limits of a volume destined
simply to the recital of travels in Central and Eastern Arabia
will hardly permit. And with this apology given, and I hope
admitted, let us return to our patchwork tale.

An hour wears away in agreeable and lively talk. Some
other patients are offered to my care, and visits are arranged,
till, after suitable prescriptions for the invalid, I rise to take
my leave. Doheym's eldest brother offers to accompany me to
some of the neighbouring houses, where he expects that mutual
advantage may be derived for the sick and for the doctor.

This part of the town is composed of large groups or islands
of houses, arranged with some approach to regularity amid
gardens and wells : but it possesses neither market nor mosque,
an additional evidence of the prevailing want of organization
before the Ebn-Rasheed dynasty. The streets or lanes are
cleaner than I had expected to find them, much more so,
certainly, than those of any Turkish or Curdish village ; but
this is due in part to the remarkable dryness of the climate.
We stroll about here and there, sometimes drawing near to the
high craggy rock that overhangs the eastern town wall, sometimes winding through the groves that border the inner line
of the southern fortifications, till noon is past, and the heat

renders further walking unadvisable. So'eyd reconducts me to
the main road, and there quits me with a promise to send
Doheym in the evening to inform me of the state of my patient.

I now return homewards alone ; the streets and the market are
nearly solitary ; the small black shadows lie close gathered up
at the stems of the palm-trees or under the walls, everything
sleeps under the heavy glare of noon. Perhaps, instead of going
on directly to our domicile, curiosity and the pleasure of being
alone leads me on some minutes farther up to the western gate,
thence to look out on the great plain between Ḥā'yel and the
mountain. That plain now appears transformed into one wide
lake, whose waters seem to bathe the rocky verge of Shomer,
while nearer to the town they fade into deceptive pools and
shallows ; it is the every-day illusion of the mirage. If we
return when the meridian heat is passing away, we may see the
fairy lake shrunk up to a distant pond, and before evening it
will quite disappear, to return next day an hour or two before
noon. Meanwhile this semblance of water, " the eye of the
landscape," as the Arabs not inappropriately call that element,
renders the view, which would else be too arid and rough, very
lovely. Were it but real !

After feasting my gaze on this beautiful though now familiar
phenomenon, I regain our dwelling. Barakāt and myself make
our dinner, and talk over the visits and affairs of the morning.
We have then two hours or so of quiet before us, for it is
seldom that any one calls at this period of the day, hardly less
a siesta here than in Italy or Spain. At last the 'Asr approaches, a division of time well known in the East, but for
which European languages have no corresponding name; it
begins from the moment when the sun has reached half-way in
his declining course, and continues till about an hour and a half
or rather less before his setting. We now leave the house together, and direct our steps towards the palace by a cross-way
leading between the dwellings of some court retainers and an
angle of the great mosque. In this latter there will generally
be a decent number of worshippers for the Salāt-el-'Asr, or
afternoon prayers, especially since this is the hour chosen by
Ṭelāl and Zāmil out of the five legal periods for performing
their devotions in public, though even then they are not un-

frequently absent. These prayers are invariably followed by the reading aloud of a chapter or section selected from some traditionary work, and to this often succeeds a short extemporary sermon or commentary on what has been read. We were known to all for Christians, but nobody made any difficulty about admitting our presence on these occasions, and we often took advantage of this tolerance or indifference, be it which it may,—and indeed the words are at times synonymous.

Concerning the ceremonies of the prayer itself—though slightly different among the Hambelees and Mālekees of Central Arabia, from those in fashion with the Wahhabees, on the one hand, and from what is generally observed among the Shāfi'ees and Haneefees more frequently met with in Syria or in Turkey, on the other —I will not here detain my reader, nor puzzle him with the complicated minutiæ of sunneh and fard, rek'aas, and tekbeers. These scarcely perceptible discrepancies have no real moment or meaning at Hā'yel; and for a correct idea of Mahometan worship in its ordinary form, I would beg leave to refer such as desire it to the third chapter of Lane's Egypt, where they will find whatever instruction they may need on this and on analogous subjects given in clear and interesting detail, and with incomparable accuracy upon all points.

When indeed we reach the Upper Nejed, it must be my task to indicate several variations in the form and manner of worship, which help to draw the line between the Wahhabees and all other orthodox or heterodox Muslims. For in that land religion has a real import, being interwoven into every fibre of the national, nay, almost of the individual frame, and hence such details have there a peculiar value, not, perhaps, exactly on their own account, but in the way of illustration and of completing the principal view. On the contrary, in Hā'yel and Djebel Shomer, the Mahometan prayers and usages are rather polite ceremonies adopted out of courtesy to their neighbours than an intimate expression of national belief and thought. Hence their practice is almost exclusively confined to the great official mosque of the capital, and a few similar localities. It is more an expedient than a faith, and an act of prudence rather than of conviction, and because such offers little worthy of remark except its hollowness. The real state of mind touching religious matters is throughout this region uncertainty and fluctuation; there is much of Paganism, something of Islamism, a lingering shade of Christianity, and great impatience of any definite code or dogma.

When the formulas of prayer are over, about half the congregation rise and depart. Those who remain in the mosque draw together near the centre of the large and simple edifice, and seat themselves on its pebble-strewn floor, circle within circle; some lean their backs against the rough square pillars, I might better call them piers, that support the roof, some play with the staff or riding-switch in their hands. In the midmost of the assembly a person selected as reader, but neither Imām nor Khaṭeeb, who is supposed to be better acquainted with letters than are the average of his countrymen, besides being gifted with a good and sonorous voice, holds on his knees a large manuscript, which might be an object of much curiosity at Berlin or Paris; it contains the traditions of the prophet, or the lives of his companions, or perhaps El-Bokhāree's commentaries, or something else of the kind. Out of this he reads in a clear but somewhat monotonous tone, accompanying each word by an inflexion and accentuation worthy of Sibawee'yah or Kosey', and hardly to be attained by the best professional grammarian of Syria or Cairo. And reason clear; here it is nature, there art. This kind of lecture lasts ordinarily from ten minutes to a quarter of an hour, and is listened to in decorous silence, while all who have any pretensions to religious feeling, and these form of course a large proportion of those present on such occasions, look down on the ground, or fix their eyes on the reader and his volume. Others, of a less serious turn of mind, and the younger auditors, put themselves at their ease; and others, again, whisper sceptical criticism to their neighbours, or interchange glances of sarcasm at the recital of some portentous exploit, or totally incredible vision. For although Arabs are a credulous race, much that is readily gulped down at Mecca and Bagdad, will not pass here. I regret to say that Telāl himself, when he honoured these meetings with his presence, set invariably a very bad example of attention, giving the time to studying the faces of the congregation, and showing by the expression of his quick-glancing eye, that his thoughts were much more occupied by questions of actual life and politics, than by the wise sayings of the Prophet, or the glorious achievements of his companions. The man is in fact just enough of a Mahometan for state business, and not a tittle more.

If the prince were in the mosque his custom was after about ten minutes' patience to give the reader a sign that he had had enough of it, on which the latter would close his book, and the assembly break up without further ceremony. But if the prince were absent, the reader's place would be taken by one of the elder and more respectable individuals belonging to the semi-literary semi-religious class, or by the Imām or the Khaṭeeb himself, who would then give a short verbal explanation of the chapter just read, or at times an extemporary sermon, but sitting, and in a familiar way. I have often heard much good sense and practical morality enounced on these occasions both here and in Kaseem. In the Wahhabee provinces matters often took a different turn; but of this hereafter.

When the reading, or the reading and sermon together, are concluded, every one would remain seated in silence for a minute or so, partly as though to reflect on what they had heard, and partly to give the more important personages present free time to retire before the press of the throng. Telāl would naturally be the first to rise and leave the building, accompanied by Zāmil and his brothers or 'Abd-el-Maḥsin, and take his place on a stone bench in the courtyard without, there to hold a short afternoon audience. On this occasion minor causes, and whatever had not been deemed of sufficient importance to occupy the morning hours, would often be discussed; and Telāl himself would occasionally relax into a condescending smile when some Bedouin presented his uncouth complaint, or two townsmen, guilty of having called each other hard names, were brought into his presence. I was more than once an amused spectator of these scenes; Telāl's manner was concise and sarcastic; the decision very frequently to administer a few stripes, nowise severe ones, to both parties; the royal judge wisely observing that insult was almost always the offspring of provocation, and that where the fault was equally divided, the punishment should be so too. But it was a very mild

one; a Charterhouse boy in my time (1838–44) might have
thought himself lucky had three marks in the Black Book
brought him no more from the dreaded head-master of that
day.

We now mix with the crowd; sometimes 'Abd-el-Maḥsin
would single us out, and enter into deep discussion of Arab
literature and history; or a friend from among the townsmen,
often one of the younger chiefs who had become in a certain
way our clients and companions, would invite us to peaches and
dates, with a cup of that coffee which Arabia alone can
afford, in his father's or uncle's house.   Or we would return
straight home to meet the many visits and consultations
already awaiting us there, and while I prescribe or operate,
according to circumstances, Barakát prepares our supper of rice
and pumpkins, with occasionally a piece of meat by way of
luxury.   For we made little use of our standing invitation to
the palace, and did not often accept a supper in a private house,
wishing to keep a little time to ourselves, and to avoid over-
publicity, where not necessary or evidently advantageous.

I may add that this degree of reservedness on our part helped
to raise us much in the esteem of the town, and to avert from
us the dangerous appearance of busybodies, or of inquisitive and
meddlesome men.   I say dangerous, because we were already
close watched by Wahhabee spies, ready to lay us any snare and
proceed to any extremity, as the next chapter will bring to
light.   Dangerous, too, though in another way, from its consequences with Ṭelál himself, who, far too prudent to compromise himself, or to allow others to compromise him, would not
have hesitated an instant, if dissatisfied with us, to send us
" back on our heels," in Arab phrase, and thus prostrate all our
intentions for the remainder of our journey.   But an open and
familiar manner wherever business was concerned, mixed with
reserve on other occasions, won us a good place in popular
feeling, did away with the suspicions of some, and prevented
those of the rest from passing on to probability, much less
certainty.

However, when any more distinguished individual, some
member of the royal family, or wealthy and respectable citizen,
invited us—for example, the judge Moḥammed or the courtly

'Abd-el-Mahsin, or the opulent Dohey', an elderly merchant in
whose house my medical assistance had been of service, we
would relax from our ordinary austerity, and accept the honourable invitation. Of these dinners or suppers, for either name
may suit the evening meal, I have already spoken at sufficient
length, and need not here go through the scene again. *Ex
uno disce omnes,* at least in what regards the comestibles
through the whole of inner Arabia from the Djowf to the neighbourhood of Riad. Never had a nation less idea of cookery
than the Arabs; in this science, anyhow, Turks, Persians, and
Indians leave them immeasurably behind; they know no more
of it in truth than just enough to bring them within the
" cooking animal " definition of man. Rice and boiled mutton,
all piled in one large dish, a little indifferent bread, dates, perhaps a hard-boiled egg or two, hashed gourds or something of
the kind for garnish ; the monarch of all Shomer cum Djowf and
Kheybar has no more at his table. Wash your hands, say
Bismillah (unless you desire to pass for an atheist), fall to, eat as
fast as though you were afraid that the supper would run away,
then say, " El hamdu l'Illāh," or " thanks to God," with an
added compliment to your host if you wish to be polite, wash
your hands again, with soap or with potash, for sometimes the
one will be brought you and sometimes the other, and all is
over so far as the meal is concerned. You have smoked a
pipe or two and drunk three or four cups of coffee before supper ;
you may now smoke and drink one only, for that is the etiquette
after eating, and then wish your friends good evening and go
away.

Rosheyd, Telāl's maternal uncle, and our next-door neighbour, as I have before mentioned, invited us not unfrequently
to his house. He was a rather shrewd, amusing, but very superficial character, proud of his knowledge of foreign lands, having
travelled farther than almost any other man in Hā'yel. He
had even reached Kerkook, seven days' journey north of Bagdad,
and was besides no stranger to Egypt, both Upper and Lower.
Like too many travellers of more cultivated races, he had
managed to see the outside of everything and the inside of
nothing, and would spin long yarns of grotesque adventures and
exotic singularities, much reminding one of the way in which

men are apt to talk of other countries than their own when they
have visited them without previous knowledge of language,
history, and manners. He believed himself, too, possessed of
unusual discernment, and imagined that he was drawing us out,
while in reality he was only unveiling himself and his family.
But his heart was better than his head, and if not a wise he was
at least a kind and steady friend.

Doḥey's invitations were particularly welcome, both from the
pleasantness of his dwelling-place, and from the varied and
interesting conversation that I was sure to meet with there.
This merchant, a tall and stately man of between fifty and sixty
years of age, and whose thin features were lighted up by a lustre
of more than ordinary intelligence, was a thorough Ḥā'yelite of
the old caste, hating Wahhabees from the bottom of his heart,
and with small sympathy for Mahometanism in general, eager for
information on cause and effect, on lands and governments, and
holding commerce and social life for the main props if not the
ends of civil and national organization. His uncle, now near
eighty years old, to judge by conjecture in a land where regis-
ters are not much in use, had journeyed to India, and traded at
Bombay; in token whereof he still wore an Indian skull-cap
and a Cachemire shawl. The rest of the family were in keeping with the elder members, and seldom have I seen more
dutiful children or a better educated household. My readers
will naturally understand that by education I here imply its
moral not its intellectual phase. The eldest son, himself a
middle-aged man, would never venture into his father's presence without unbuckling his sword and leaving it in the
vestibule, nor on any account presume to sit on a level with
him or by his side in the divan.

The divan itself was one of the prettiest I met with in these
parts. It was a large square room, looking out on the large
house-garden, and cheerfully lighted up by trellised windows
on two sides, while the wall of the third had purposely been
discontinued at about half its height, and the open space thus
left between it and the roof propped by pillars, between which
" a fruitful vine by the sides of the house " was intertwined so
as to fill up the interval with a gay network of green leaves and
tendrils, transparent like stained glass in the eastern sunbeams.

Facing this cheerful light the floor of the apartment was raised about two feet above the rest, and covered with gay Persian carpets, silk cushions, and the best of Arab furniture. In the lower half of the K'hāwah, and at its farthest angle, was the small stone coffee-stove, placed at a distance where its heat might not annoy the master and his guests. Many of the city nobility would here resort, and the talk generally turned on serious subjects, and above all on the parties and politics of Arabia ; while Dohey' would show himself a thorough Arab patriot, and at the same time a courteous and indulgent judge of foreigners, qualities seldom to be met with together in any notable degree, and therefore more welcome.

Many a pleasant hour have I passed in this half greenhouse, half K'hāwah, mid cheerful faces and varied talk, while inly commenting on the natural resources of this manly and vigorous people, and straining the eye of forethought to discern through the misty curtain of the future by what outlet their now unfruitful because solitary good may be brought into fertilizing contact with that of other more advanced nations, to the mutual benefit of each and all. " It is not good that the man should be alone " was said from the beginning by a very high Authority, no, nor the nation either. Time, not perhaps distant, may help to solve the problem.

Or else some garden was the scene of our afternoon leisure, among fruit-trees and palms, by the side of a watercourse, whose constant supply from the well hid from view among thick foliage, seemed the work not of laborious art but of unassisted nature. Here, stretched in the cool and welcome shade, would we for hours canvass with 'Abd-el-Mahsin, and others of similar pursuits, the respective merits of Arab poets and authors, of Omar-ebn-el-Fārid or Aboo'l 'Ola, in meetings that had something of the Attic, yet with just enough of the Arab to render them more acceptable by their Semitic character of grave cheerfulness and mirthful composure.

Or when the stars came out, Barakāt and myself would stroll out of the heated air of the streets and market to the cool open plain, and there pass an hour or two alone, or in conversation with what chance passer-by might steal on us half unperceived and unperceiving in the dusk, and amuse ourselves with his simplicity if he were a Bedouin, or with his shrewdness if a townsman.

Thus passed our ordinary life at Ḥāyel. Many minor incidents occurred to diversify it, many of the little ups and downs that human intercourse never fails to furnish; sometimes the number of patients and the urgency of their attendance allowed of little leisure for aught except our professional duties; sometimes a day or two would pass with hardly any serious occupation. But of such incidents, though invested at the period of their occurrence with actual and local interest, and even at this distance of time and place to me at least the source of much pleasant remembrance, I will say nothing more here; my readers have a sufficient sample in what has been already set down. From the 27th of July to the 8th of September we remained doctoring in the capital or in its immediate neighbourhood. But during this time was also carried on what might almost have seemed an episode, but which was in reality the main plot of the drama, and it became more and more inwoven with our other circumstances and occupations, till the exoteric veil of medicine could barely suffice to cover much of more genuine interest and importance. My readers may easily guess that I alluded to our position relatively to Ṭelāl, to his family and government, for with these and with him we were now unavoidably in frequent and significant contact. Here began a long series of events to be continued on through the rest of our journey, sometimes in accordance with our desires and sometimes against them—a very parti-coloured skein, reaching from Ḥāyel to the Persian Gulf, and even farther. But this will be fittingly explained in a separate chapter.

CHAPTER V

Court Incidents at Ḥā'yel

Yet though thou stand'st more sure—
Thou art not sure enough, since griefs are green,
And all thy friends, which thou must make thy friends,
Have but their stings and teeth newly ta'en out. —
Be it thy course to busy giddy minds
With foreign quarrels.—*Shakespeare*

ṬELĀL'S CONDUCT TOWARDS US — HIS BROTHER META'AB — PALACE OF
META'AB, HIS Ḳ'HĀWAH AND CONVERSATION — 'ABBAS BASHA AND HIS
INTRIGUES WITH THE BEDOUINS AND WAHHABEES: WHY BOTH FRUIT-
LESS—LASCARIS AND FATḤ 'ALLAH—WHERE LIES ARAB NATIONALITY—
CORRESPONDENCE BETWEEN ḤĀY'EL AND EGYPT—ṬELĀL'S POLICY TO
OBTAIN THE PATRONAGE OF THE PERSIAN CARAVAN—DEPUTATIONS FROM
ḲASEEM — OUR OWN POSITION GROWS CRITICAL — ZĀMIL, HIS CHA-
RACTER—OUR CONFIDENCE IN HIM—HIS CONDUCT—SECOND INTERVIEW
WITH ṬELĀL — ITS RESULT—NEJDEAN SPIES — 'OBEYD — HIS HISTORY
AND CHARACTER — WAHHABEE PARTY IN SHOMER — 'OBEYD'S CONDUCT
TOWARDS US — WARNINGS OF 'ABD-EL-MAḤSIN — 'OBEYD'S OUTBREAK —
HE TAKES COMMAND OF AN EXPEDITION AGAINST THE ḤARB TRIBE—
GATHERING OF THE TROOPS—'OBEYD'S LETTER ON OUR ACCOUNT TO
'ABD-ALLAH AT RIAḌ — THIRD INTERVIEW WITH ṬELĀL; ITS CONSE-
QUENCES—A SHOMER PASSPORT—REASONS FOR LEAVING ḤĀ'YEL—OUR
GUIDES FOR ḲASEEM — FAREWELL VISITS OF 'ABD-EL-MAḤSIN, ZĀMIL,
AND OTHERS—MUTUAL REGRETS—WE QUIT ḤĀ'YEL.

WE have seen that Ṭelāl, although somewhat, so to speak,
put off the scent by our conduct at our first entrance in his
capital, and in some measure acquiescing in our medical disguise, had yet by no means laid aside his general idea that
something more was meant by our visit to his dominions than
met the eye or ear of ordinary observation. Accordingly he
continued for a time to watch us closely by means of 'Abd-el-
Maḥsin and others of the palace, and the frequent visits with
which we were honoured from that quarter were no less
prompted by the curiosity of the king to know all about us
than by an excess of courtesy or thirst after science on the
part of our friends themselves. Of this we could not but be
aware, and kept constant to our first plan, nor allowed word or

129

jest to escape us otherwise than in strict conformity with what we had announced at the very outset.

Before many days had passed a second invitation of Ṭelâl's reached us, purporting that we should do well to exchange our present abode for more spacious and convenient lodgings close by the royal palace. Its master hoped to have us thus immediately under his eye and hand. But a polite refusal on our side, tempered with suitable excuses on plausible grounds, baffled his desire. He felt the check, and henceforth returned our salutations at the public audience or in chance meetings with something less of cordiality than before.

Meanwhile his gay dashing brother Meta'ab, the second of the family, returned from the pasture-lands, where he had been looking after the well-doing of the royal stud in the meadows of Ḥafr Ma'ad, at some distance from Ḥâ'yel. His long jetty ringlets, his gorgeous dress and easy demeanour contrasted with the more sober-coloured apparel and serious ways of his elder brother and sovereign. He was a travelled man, had often visited Meshid 'Alee and its confines, and had even more than once entered Bagdad, and discoursed with Bashas and Consuls. But, while the levity both of his outer and inner man rendered him unsuited for the weightier business of the State, his agreeable manners and quickness of perception made him remarkably successful in those petty intrigues, which in the East and the West alike may often prepare the way for affairs of greater moment; and in such preliminary manœuvres Meta'ab was a known and willing instrument.

A man of this character could not fail to be soon informed of our arrival and of all concerning us; and he had no need of further instigation to desire our better acquaintance. The very second day after his return from the country, that is, about the tenth since our establishment in Ḥâ'yel, he honoured us with a morning visit; wished to see the medicines, the books, everything; talked in a random way about Egypt and Syria, and took a hasty leave. But the same evening a handsome negro of his retinue came up to me while I was walking in the neighbourhood of the palace, and informed me that the Emeer Meta'ab requested me to take coffee with him at his dwelling.

His palace, about the size of three large Belgrave Square houses,

is close by that of Ṭelāl, and joins on to it by a long covered
gallery, with windows at regular intervals, and resembling a
cloister were it vaulted instead of flat-roofed. Into this passage
I now entered, escorted by the black, till after traversing its
whole length we reached a vestibule, where a confusion of swords
and shoes left outside announced the presence of several visitors
within. There in a lofty Ḳ'hāwah sat Meta'ab, and before him
a Persian pipe or Nargheelah, from which he was busily in-
haling exotic vapours. Several of the courtsmen and townsmen
were seated near, and a thick cloud, but not of incense, went up
on every side.

A cordial welcome greeted my entrance, and Meta'ab rose to
present me his open hand in half-Arab, half-English fashion.
While coffee and the ceremonies which accompany it went round,
our host began a very free and easy chat about Bagdad, its
Basha, the English and French consuls, their horses and their
politics, what he had seen and what heard, to discover whether
all this would take with me. But having at that time not
yet visited Bagdad, it was easy for me to look blank, and to
show little interest in these matters; Meta'ab then changed his
key-note, and tried Egypt.

Here the case was changed. I was really very desirous to
know what intercourse might exist between Djebel Shomer and
the valley of the Nile, and accordingly let him understand that
I was no stranger to Cairo and its neighbourhood. The Emeer,
delighted to find a better opening in this quarter, launched out
into much and curious, though desultory, discourse about Sa'eed
Basha and his journey to Europe, about 'Abbas Basha and his
intrigues with the Arab chiefs, and explained the actual position
of his brother towards the reigning viceroy.

In this and in the following interviews with Met'aab, who
became more intimate day by day, I obtained a tolerably
distinct idea of what I had heard about before, but only con-
fusedly—I mean the strange Arab intrigues of 'Abbas Basha.
That prince had devised a scheme for not only rendering himself independent of the Ottoman Porte, but even of becoming
in person sole sovereign of the Arabian Peninsula, by means of
a double alliance, linked with the Bedouins to the north, and
the Wahhabee to the south. In the view of ensuring the

sympathy of the former, he consigned his eldest son, then a
mere child, to the well-known Feyṣul-ebn-Shaaʾlān, chief of the
great Ruʾala tribe, intending thus to have his heir brought up
like one of the clan, and in all the perfection of wild ways
and customs.   Besides this singular measure, he sent abundant
largesses to the other contiguous tribes ; while any Bedouin
who approached his palace was sure of a favourable reception,
and was readily admitted to experience the effects of his lavish
liberality, if one may term liberality what was in fact mere
waste.   Nay, the infatuated viceroy went to the extent of
affecting the Bedouin in his own person and manners, would
imitate the nomade style of dress, relish, or seem to relish,
their fare, and live with them on a footing of sham familiarity,
fancying the while that he was gaining their affection to his
service.

It may be said in the way of apology for the extravagancies
of ʾAbbas Basha, that others of more pretensions than ever were
his to intellectual discernment, have now and then committed
a somewhat similar miscalculation regarding the supposed
importance of the Bedouin tribes, and the advantages to be
derived from their alliance.   But what rendered the Egyptian
governor particularly inexcusable in his error, was the contrary
example of his own uncle Ibraheem Basha, and the success
which had attended him in an exactly opposite course of policy.
The neglect of family lessons and hereditary experience is of all
others the hardest to pardon in a ruler.

" The man who relies on Bedouin assistance is like one who
should build his house on the face of the water," said Metaʾab
to me, while describing the conduct of ʾAbbas, and he said true.
This assertion he proved by reasons not unworthy of record, since
assigned by one whom long experience had rendered every way
capable of forming a correct estimate of the subject.   " The
Bedouins," thus continued the Emeer, the sense of whose
words I give, though not the words themselves, " besides their
little weight in serious warfare, owing to their deficiency in
arms, accoutrements, and military discipline, besides their utter
incapacity of combined action, because split up into infinitesimal
factions by continual and childish feuds that never permit them
to unite for any real purpose a month together, are besides

the mere creatures of the moment, to whom the present hour
alone is something, yesterday and to-morrow alike nothing.
Without either national or religious aim or principle, without
social bonds or patriotic feeling, every one isolated in his own
petty and personal interests, all against all, and all equally
without purpose or meaning, they neither care for those out
of their clan, nor even for their own tribesmen, except just so
far as they may chance to receive from them some immediate
gain, or suffer some actual detriment—friends to-day, enemies
to-morrow, friends again the day after. Now if such is their
condition with those of their own 'skin' (race), much more
so must it be with respect to strangers. Sultan, Viceroy, Turk,
Egyptian, English, French, all is one with them—they have
no sympathy with any one of all these, and are no more disposed to attach themselves to the one rather than to the other.
Their only real partiality is for the highest bidder; and while,
to use their own expression, 'his food is yet in their bellies,'
they may possibly do his work, but even that so far only as it
is evidently profitable to themselves, and not over-dangerous
either. In such a case one may reckon that they will furnish
camels and bring water, or even take courage to attack and
plunder a neighbouring village or a weaker tribe; but these
services are simply in the view of hire or booty, not in the
least from any liking to or esteem for their employer, much less
from aught approaching to patriotism and national feeling.
And in proof of this they will be perfectly ready to turn on
and plunder their former ally and friend, the very first hour
that they see him unable to afford them advantage or to offer
resistance."

Thus far Meta'ab. But I have often been amused by
thinking how ill bestowed were the labours of Lascaris and his
companion Fatḥ-Allah during the seven years they passed
lavishing the money of their imperial master in getting up a
Bedouin alliance on national and philanthropic principles. And
I trust that I may be pardoned for smiling at what I have more
than once heard the very objects of their misplaced largesses,
the Ru'ala, Sebaa', and Ḥasinah Bedouins ridicule themselves,
and that heartily. Not only within the limits of the Syrian
desert, but even farther inland up to Ḥā'yel, I met with some

133

remembrance of this wild scheme, and Meta'ab had learnt from the Ru'ala, in their occasional visits to Djebel Shomer, all the main facts and features of its progress.   Not that the wonderful events of wars and combats with which Lamartine in his version of Fath-Allah's journal has swollen the bulk of his second volume about Syria, have any historical reality, at least to the best of what I could discover, nor did any one pretend to the faintest remembrance of seven days' battles on the banks of the Orontes, or expeditions conducted into the heart of Persia and Beloochistan. The same must be said of the pretended embassy to the Wahhabee monarch at Derey'eeyah, and whatever other episodes the author's vivid imagination has tacked on to his story.   But of presents offered and received, of largesses made and tribes enriched with European gold, there was remembrance enough.   To conclude, the whole business was a capital "catch" for the Bedouins, and so was 'Abbas Basha and his intrigues.

His bounty—for to him we now return—was of course gladly pocketed or eaten, promises were signed and sealed, and a faith which had never existed was solemnly pledged.   Then all disappeared like a ripple on the water.   No sooner had the news of the Basha's death reached Syria, than Feysul-ebn-Shaa'lān got rid of his benefactor's son by a dose of poison, if report say true, and thus ended the Egypto-Bedouin alliance, with no more utility for those who made it than that of Lascaris before.   In one thing only 'Abbas Basha succeeded, namely, in convincing all Arabia that he was a fool; a compendious result, and likely to be attained by any one who may choose to tread in the steps of the Egyptian viceroy.

Nor was 'Abbas Basha more lucky in his Wahhabee alliance, though here his mistake was much worthier of excuse; indeed, it would have required a very thorough acquaintance with the political condition of inner Arabia not to have anticipated a more advantageous termination to this measure. The Wahhabees certainly presented an organized government and a central power, acting on and guided by well-defined principles of religion and nationality, all so many points whereon to fix the Egyptian lever ; and besides, it would be a great injustice to the sturdy and dogged denizens of Nejed to compare them with the fickle and undependable Bedouins either in moral or in military value. Yet here again 'Abbas had mistaken his men. The Wahhabees were too consistent in their peculiar dogmas not to regard the Egyptian as a polytheist and an infidel, one of those whose friendship was enmity with God, and his professions of orthodoxy met with as little credence among the Nejdeans as the Islamism of Kleber or of Bonaparte (I mention not to stigmatise but to illustrate), found among the Egyptians themselves. No one believed him, no one trusted; and the true believers of Riad showed a steadfastness in holding back from the flattering offers of Eygpt, greater than that which Jeremiah vainly sought to obtain in his day from the inhabitants of Jerusalem, and on somewhat analogous grounds. In addition, the Wahhabees were yet smarting from the blows inflicted on them by Mohammed 'Alee and Ibraheem Basha, and ill-disposed to unite with the grandson of the one and the nephew of the other. However, the desire of expected profit led them not wholly to reject the tendered alliance, nor rudely interrupt the stream of envoys, every one of whom filled their hands with the good things of Egypt; and they continued to hold out hopes of compliance and co-operation, like angling lines to catch the silly fish of the Nile, till the presents of 'Abbas Basha had well replenished the coffers of Feysul-ebn-Sa'ood, while the Nejdean monarch's daughters, (as I myself witnessed, when his guest some months later at Riad), glistened in pearls and gold-net of Cairo workmanship. Thus the Wahhabee, like the Bedouins, though from different motives, pocketed the gifts and laughed at the giver.

In all this there was yet a deeper and more pernicious error. 'Abbas Basha did not, indeed he could not know the immense reaction existing throughout the Arabian Peninsula against the overbearing tyranny of the Wahhabee dynasty, and greatly overrated the real strength and influence of the latter, while he neglected the proper source of Arab vigour, and missed the chord which, if skilfully touched, might have vibrated in his favour, from the shores of the Red Sea to the Indian Ocean. A few words will explain this. Take the Wahhabees, that is, those who are really such, and the Bedouins together, they will not exceed one-fourth of the denizens of Arabia. The remaining three-fourths consist of townsmen and peasants spread through-

out the land, enthusiastic partisans of their local chiefs and
rulers, and true lovers of Arab freedom—patriots, in short, but
alike hostile to Bedouin marauders and to Wahhabee coercion.
They cling to a national glory and patriotic memories of a
date much older than the recent honours of Ebn-Sa'ood, and
rivalling or surpassing in antiquity those of Koreysh itself.
Love of order and commerce renders them also the enemies of
nomadic anarchy. Lastly, they far outweigh their antagonists
collectively in numbers no less than in national importance,
and to them alone, if to any, are reserved the destinies of
Arabia.

Mahomet, a master mind, saw this in his time, and it was exactly by enlisting this part of the Arab commonwealth and these
feelings in his cause, that he secured his ascendency over the
whole peninsula. The Coran and cotemporary tradition give no
other clue to his able line of conduct, and to the prodigious success
that justified it. Had he stopped here he would have been the
first and greatest benefactor of his native country. But the
prophet marred what the statesman had begun, and the deadening
fatalism of his religious system, that narcotic of the human mind,
stopped for ever the very progress to which he had himself half
opened the way by his momentary fusion of Arabia into a
common nation with a common aim. Again, the Judaical
narrowness and ceremonial interferences of his law soon fretted
the impatient and expansive mind of his countrymen into that
almost universal revolt which accompanied rather than followed
the news of his death. The revolt was indeed repressed for a
moment, but soon reappeared, nor ceased till the final and
lasting disintegration of the Arab empire in Arabia.

Now, if ordinary Islam proved too strait-laced for Arabia,
Wahhabeeism is of necessity even more so, and the men who had
broken asunder the yoke of Mahomet himself were very unlikely
long to bow their necks under that of Ebn-Sa'ood and 'Abd-el-
Wahhāb. Thus it was that 'Abbas Basha had chosen his starting point ill, and his partiality for Riad and its rulers tended
to estrange yet more from him the nation at large.

In Ḥā'yel 'Abd-Allah-ebn-Rasheed and his family kept
wisely aloof from the manœuvres of the Egyptian viceroy, and
awaited better times. These seemed at hand when the murder

of 'Abbas placed Sa'eed Basha on the throne. The known
inclination of this prince for European alliances was not an
unfavourable circumstance in the views of Telāl, who knew
that from this latter quarter he might have much to gain where
industry and commerce were concerned, while he could have
but little to fear in the way of aggression and war. Surrounded on every side by a broad and almost trackless desert,
with no ports or coast line to defend against the " dogs of the
sea," as Europeans, and particularly the English, are often,
though most impolitely, denominated in the East, and nestled
amid a labyrinth of mountains and crags, the provinces of Ḥā'yel
were the last place in the world to dread a French invasion or
an English occupation, while on the other hand they might
derive considerable profit from an interchange at arm's-length,
so to speak, of material or mental goods. In this idea the
negotiations between Ḥā'yel and Cairo, interrupted awhile by the
ill-starred reign of 'Abbas Basha, were renewed after his death.
But the frivolity of Sa'eed was not long in displaying itself,
and Telāl, while he continued to keep up a series of friendly
messages and greetings to and fro, soon ceased to flatter himself
with the hope of any effective support from that quarter against
Wahhabite encroachments or Turkish hostility. Still, in the
actual position of affairs, Egypt may be considered his best
friend and ally in case of extreme need—a fact noticed on a
former occasion.

I mentioned then, too, but in a general way, that Telāl was
careful to maintain his correspondence with Persia. It is now
time to explain his special reasons for so doing, and what the
Arab prince could look for from the decrepit despotism of
Teheran. The solution of this problem lies in the geographical
conditions of the land. I must here beg my readers to give a
look to the map. There they will see that Djebel Shomer
exactly crosses the line drawn from the central and upper provinces of Persia to the Ḥejāz, and thus is right in the track
which Persian pilgrims would naturally follow in their annual
visits to the Meccan Ca'abah, or the tombs of Medinah, whether
those of Mahomet and his companions, or the more equivocal
monuments of Shiya'ee devotion. Similar bodies of travellers
benefit the towns and countries through which they pass by

their wayfaring expenditure, no less than by the example of
their piety, perhaps even more.   To draw this yearly current of
pilgrim wealth within the limits of his dominions, and to make
it flow through the very gates of Ḥá'yel, was Ṭelál's great
desire; the more so because such a measure would not only
ensure him the transient though oft-recurring advantages
already alluded to, but would also serve to encourage the
sectaries of Meshid 'Alee, Bagdad, and that whole region, in
their trade with Djebel Shomer, a trade created by Ṭelál, and
highly beneficial to his entire kingdom, but especially to the
capital.   Many circumstances combined to favour this project.
The road from Teheran and Bagdad by Djebel Shomer, traversing the narrower neck of the Arabian continent, and leading
right to the sacred cities whither the pilgrims were bound, was in-
disputably more commodious and more secure, besides involving
far less expense, than the circuitous routes followed so often by
the Persian caravans through Syria, or southward down the
Persian Gulf and along the coasts of 'Omán, Ḥaḍramaut and
Yemen to Djiddah.   There remained, indeed, the road across
the centre of Arabia through Nejed, a comparatively short and
easy track, but this was rendered almost impracticable for the
votaries of 'Alee by the bigoted intolerance of the Wahhabees,
who deemed their land polluted if trodden by such mis-
believing wretches.   How far " a consideration " in old Trapbois'
phrase, might prevail in mitigating this abhorrence, we shall
afterwards see.   But with Ṭelál, Sonnite and Shiya'ee were all
one, and it was not his way to impose extra dues or exact any
special perquisites from a pilgrim because his religious opinions
chanced to be of this or of that colour.

Accordingly he employed all his diligence and skill to
negotiate the annual transit of the Perso-Meccan caravan by
Ḥá'yel in preference to the other routes just mentioned, and
kept up a continual correspondence on the subject at Bagdad
and Meshid 'Alee.   There he found the Persian authorities
well disposed to come into his ideas, and the Shah himself,
when informed of the project, notified his entire approbation.
Yet its full and entire execution has not yet taken place, owing
to circumstances whose explanation can only be given when
we reach Nejed itself.   However, in spite of all opposition

a numerous band of conical caps and furred robes appear
every pilgrim-season in Ḥā'yel; I was myself witness of one
caravan, and all the Persians in it expressed their gratitude
in very bad Arabic for the gracious treatment they had met
with from Ṭelāl and Meta'ab, and their entire satisfaction with
the Shomer government.

Such and similar were the subjects of conversation in the
Ḳ'hāwah of Meta'ab and his friends. I have recorded them at
some length hoping thereby to afford some kind of insight into
that real and living Arabia so often left a blank in many narra-
tives, no less than its geographical surface in many maps. To
determine the positions of mountains, the course of rivers, the
gradations of climate, the geological character of rocks, and
whatever else relates to physical and inanimate nature, is certainly of high and serious importance, and here too I have tried
to do my best, although with what imperfect results, from want of
preparation and of opportunity for scientific observation, I am
regretfully conscious. But to sum up much in that most hackneyed of all hackneyed quotations, " The proper study of mankind is man ;" and it is perhaps an even higher service rendered
to science and to Europe if we attempt to draw aside at least a
little the veil so thickly cast over human-Arabia, its parties and
politics, its mind and movement. I return to my story.

About twenty days had passed at Ḥā'yel, when we began
seriously to consider whether and how far we should acquaint
Ṭelāl with the real main object of our journey. We had by
this time sufficiently ascertained his position, his views, his
system, his projects. We had learnt his exact bearings with the
Wahhabee and the Turk, how far he might be considered their
ally, how far their enemy. We were no longer ignorant of the
general feeling and tendency of his government and people,
while the daily arrival of envoys from Kaseem and 'Oneyzah
revealed more and more the intimate nature of politics and
religion in Djebel Shomer. These very envoys had often sat
hours together in our courtyard, and discussed with us and
before us the means and ends of Ṭelāl, and the degrees of
alliance which linked him with the chiefs of Kaseem in one
way, and with their enemy the monarch of Nejed in another.
Information thus obtained seemed to me in a certain measure

more dependable than what I received from the born subjects and vassals of Ṭelál.

Nor did we hold it fair to keep longer in the dark one who had so cordially welcomed us and treated us so well. Hitherto we had in fact requited his openness by reserve, and met his advances with something like chilliness. To put him in possession of a secret which he evidently desired to unravel, and which there seemed hardly any danger that he would abuse, might be reckoned no more than natural equity and justice towards our royal host.

Besides, though Ṭelál seemed to think well of us on the whole, yet he could not but look on us with some suspicion, however slight; and such vague suspicion is apt to take a sinister turn. Now it was utterly impossible for us to pursue our journey into the Wahhabee territory except with Ṭelál's cognizance, and by his good will. A passport bearing the royal signature is indispensable for whoever desires to journey on in that direction, much more to cross the frontier; without such a document in hand no one would venture to conduct us; and to attempt the road furtively and alone would have been to run a madman's risk. But that Ṭelál would furnish us with the requisite passport while he yet felt uneasy about us and our intentions was highly improbable; whereas to tell him frankly the real object of our wanderings, and the course we meant to hold, was the likeliest way to procure from him a consent which doubt and mistrust otherwise might, nay, certainly would, deny.

Such was our position, and whatever step we might decide on was attended by its unavoidable difficulties; but after much discussion it was at last resolved in the cabinet council of myself and my companion that we should ask for a private interview with Ṭelál, and then and there let him know all. However, to proceed in the most approved court-fashion, we determined first to secure an intermediary agent in our favour, and that we soon found in the person of the treasurer Zámil.

This individual, so highly placed in the good graces of Ṭelál, had all along approved himself equally intelligent and well-disposed. Medical duties and friendly invitations had already given me free access to himself and to his family; while he on his part, in spite of the great press of business which hardly left him a moment's leisure, had paid us frequent though cursory visits at our domicile. Participating fully in Ṭelāl's views, and having a considerable share in most of his administrative measures, he was decidedly of a brighter and more open character than his master, much easier of access, and giving in himself the rare example of a man raised from the lowest ranks of society to the highest degree of wealth and influence (at Ḥā'yel, I mean), without having thereby contracted anything of the arrogant and ungainly manners common to the *parvenu*. Lastly, he possessed a clear and capacious mind, Arab prudence, great moderation and tact, and much good nature. The only faults ascribed to him by that nice censor, popular rumour, and in a degree confirmed by the costly elegance of his dress and all about his handsome person, was a certain ostentation, and a love of pleasure carried even beyond the bounds of what one may call standard Arab morality; a fault, it may be added, from which his master Ṭelāl was not held exempt. But this weak point of Zāmil's character did not come in the way of the business we required him for; we trusted to his better qualities and influential position, nor had we after-reason to repent our trust.

Accordingly we took a suitable opportunity for informing him that we desired a secret interview with Ṭelāl on matters of considerable import, and begged him to procure it for us. Subsequently we went yet further, and explained to our ambassador the entire case, and what it was that we desired to lay before the monarch.

Zāmil very properly took time to deliberate, and after demanding and receiving our consent, acquainted Ṭelāl with the reasons of our request. For two days he came regularly to our apartments, with the precaution, however, of selecting the hours which were least liable to observation, and conned over with us every point of the projected colloquy in the minutest detail. At last he informed us that on such and such a morning (it was the 21st of August) Ṭelāl would receive our communications.

I ought to say that in Arab no less than in European courts, personal and private audiences of the sovereign are looked upon as a high favour, not to be lightly demanded nor

easily conferred. Etiquette has something to do with this,
policy more : something also is due to the fear of treachery,
and more than one instance is recorded in the chronicles of
the land of a supplicant admitted to privacy and there proving
an assassin. Of public and official audiences, where " sun-like
majesty " in its attendant pomp is alike secure from the felon's
dagger, and from the cheapness of vulgar company, Telāl is
liberal enough, more so indeed by far than the monarchs of
Nejed and 'Omān.

On the appointed day, a little before sunrise, my companion
and myself sought out by circuitous side-lanes and by-ways
Zāmil's house, and there seated ourselves in the empty K'hāwah,
for the family were not yet stirring, and it was too early for
guests. Zāmil himself had already gone to Telāl, doubtless to
concert with him how we were to be received. We had not
waited long when a negro belonging to the palace entered the
K'hāwah, and made us a signal to follow him. We entered the
royal residence by a private door, generally kept shut, and
after traversing several small apartments ascended a flight of
stairs constructed in the central oval tower. At about mid-
height the greater part of its width was occupied by a large and
well-furnished room ; and here sat Telāl with Zāmil only by
his side. Slaves and armed attendants were in waiting in an adjoining apartment, but too distant to overhear our conversation.
After the first salutations in their wonted simplicity, the king
said, " What do you wish to speak of ?" and, seeing me hesitate
a moment in my answer, added with a glance towards Zāmil,
" Never mind his presence, you may consider him as myself."

Thus encouraged, I began, and gave a brief but clear account
of the circumstances and object of our journey, whence and
whither, what we desired, and what expected. A conversation of at least an hour ensued ; it consisted principally of
interrogations on Telāl's part, and of explanations and answers
on ours. His queries were always to the point ; his remarks
concise but uncommonly shrewd, and going to the bottom of
things. Much that I said was met half-way by assent, on other
points he suggested difficulties or proposed modifications. He
took particular care not to commit himself by assurances of
adhering to any definite line of conduct, and we of course

avoided with equal scrupulosity all appearance of a desire to
lead him farther or faster than he chose to follow. But
he insisted much on the necessity of entire secrecy, saying,
" Were what now passes between us to be known at large, it
might be as much as your lives are worth, and perhaps mine
also."

In the course of this interview I took the opportunity to
mention certain ambiguous and sinister reports which I had
been told circulated regarding us among some classes of the
people. " Does the town say so ?" exclaimed Telāl in an half-
scornful voice ; and then placing his hand on his breast, added,
with a gesture and a tone that Louis XIV in council might
have envied, " I am the town!" subjoining, " Never fear; from
none of my subjects shall you ever again hear the like. But,"
continued he, " there are others for whom I cannot answer
equally well."

At last, when all had been sufficiently canvassed, Telāl expressed his wish that we should continue to sift these matters
with Zāmil, promised a second audience, in which he was to
give us a more definite answer ; " though," said he, " that cannot
be in a hurry," and then called out to a slave who stood waiting
behind the door, sword in hand. The negro thus summoned
put his head into the room, and then vanished a moment,
to return with ready-made coffee. After all had drunk, two
other servants brought in a large round dish, laden with excellent peaches, of which Telāl partook along with us, in sign of
entire confidence and good will. When all was concluded,
Zāmil, with a highly satisfied air (for he was by this time an
enthusiastic participator in our views), rose, and conducted us
downstairs and so from the palace to his own house. Several
days passed, during which we met frequently ; but Telāl continued to defer his ultimatum, nor were we inclined to urge
him out of season.

Meanwhile, the " others," at whom our royal friend had
hinted, were not idle : indeed, we had been long before made
aware of their existence. More than once a Nejdean, in the
plain cotton dress of a Metow'waa' or disciplinarian of the
Wahhabee sect, had presented his pharisaical demeanour and
sour face in our courtyard. These men were spies in the service

of the Riaḍ government, sent express to see what was going on
in Ḥá'yel; they were often to be met with in the streets and
market-place, observing all, shunned by all, yet treated by all
with cautious respect.   Strangers and Christians like ourselves
could not expect to escape their notice, indeed we had a very
considerable share of it, and the antipathy which their words
did not express was yet no secret.   " Hearts see each other," is
a common and very expressive Arab saying; and an enemy is
soon distinguished, however disguised in language, and even in
features.   Nor are the Arabs remarkably skilful in concealing
their feelings, I should rather say the contrary ; their emotions
are for the most part too impetuous not to betray themselves in
gest and expression ; certainly, taking them altogether, they
are far outdone by Turks and Indians in the science of dissimulation ; nay, even by some branches of the great European
family.   However, the Nejdeans, who are the calmest, have
also the reputation of being the deepest among their countrymen.

But a more important lesson was yet to learn.   'Obeyd-ed-
De'eb, or " 'Obeyd the wolf," to give him his popular surname,
the same of whom I have before spoken as brother of the deceased prince 'Abd-Allah, and uncle of Ṭelál, had been absent
from Ḥá'yel during the first three weeks of our stay, or nearly
so.   He now returned, and at once occupied himself with the
two foreigners who had found their way into his nephew's
capital.

That a Wahhabee party should exist in a government first
founded by Wahhabee influence, close watched by Wahhabee
jealousy, and nominally itself tributary to Nejed ; that this
party should reckon in its ranks men even of the highest birth
and influence, of the royal family and near the throne, cannot
be wondered at ; indeed, the wonder would be were it otherwise.
This party is, indeed, at the present epoch small in number, but
is formidable through its unity of purpose, and the powerful support given it from the southern or Wahhabee frontier.
The most and chiefest of its partisans are gathered together
in Ḥá'yel, but no small number of its members are scattered
throughout the province.   Its head and pivot is 'Obeyd.

We have already seen his elder brother 'Abd-Allah a volunteer of high trust and consideration in the armies of Turkee, and bearing a conspicuous part in the eventful fortunes of the Nejdean dynasty during its most critical period. But 'Abd-Allah, though intimately connected, whether soldier or prince, with the Wahhabee government, seems to have had personally very little or perhaps no sympathy with the dogmas of the sect; he was a political ally, nowise a disciple. Not so his haughty and hot-headed brother 'Obeyd. His mind found in the fanaticism of Nejed its congenial element, and he plunged into it heart and brain, till it may be doubted whether Riad itself contains a more thorough-going Wahhabee than 'Obeyd-ebn-Rasheed of Hā'yel.

An excellent warrior, of undisputed skill and valour, versed alike in all the resources of deceit and violence, of bloodshed and perjury, he was eminently qualified to become the apostle of his sect in Shomer and its provinces. With his own hand, if report say true, he had slain no less than eight hundred "infidels" (that is, enemies), not to count the thousands slaughtered by his followers, and many were the trees once consecrated by popular veneration that he had cut down, many the sepulchres, honoured for centuries by devout visits and sacrifices, he had levelled with the surrounding dust, in compliance with the expressive laconism of the Wahhabee formula, "Kheyr el keboor ed-dowāris," "The best sepulchres are those which have ceased to exist." My readers will probably remember how the same sectaries treated the tomb of their own avowed prophet Mahomet at Medinah, and may hence imagine what little grace monuments of more equivocal orthodoxy would find in the eyes of 'Obeyd and his fellows.

During the reign of 'Abd-Allah the greater part of the external administration, summed up pretty nearly in the successive subjugation of villages, towns, and provinces, was left to the " Wolf," who assuredly did his best to deserve his name; thirty years of peace have not sufficed to re-people several of the tracts which he then ravaged. His princely brother profited by the acquisitions of territory thus obtained, and contented himself with the quieter but humaner work of organisation at Hā'yel. But when 'Abd-Allah died, the ambition of 'Obeyd, no longer satisfied with the blood-stained laurels of his campaign, aspired to a regal crown, and the boyish age of Telāl, then barely in his twenty-first year, seemed to leave him an open field. But Telāl though young in days was old in counsel, and had so effectually attached to his interests the town nobility and the other local chiefs who had small relish for the revival of the Coran, that 'Obeyd was speedily compelled to desist from his pretensions.

Henceforth Telāl employed his uncle much in the way that a surly mastiff is kept in the farmyard of some wealthy proprietor, where his duty is to growl at or to bite, and at times to range about the grounds and worry strangers. The young monarch entrusted 'Obeyd with distant forays, where there was more need of killing than of permanent conquest, and above all those directed against Bedouin tribes or the rougher mountain districts—not perhaps without a secret hope that his dear uncle might on some such occasion eternize his earthly honours by the unfading glories of martyrdom. But the proverb, equally current in Arabia and in England, "'tis long ere the devil dies," has met with another exemplification in the person of this bloody and deceitful but long-lived man.

Similarity of character and of religious opinions had led to an intimacy of long standing between 'Obeyd and 'Abd-Allah, son of Feyṣul, at Riad. A close and loving correspondence was kept up between these well-matched friends, altogether in the interests of the Wahhabee party, and not over favourable to Telāl, whom 'Obeyd denounced as a mere latitudinarian, little better than a disguised infidel, and one who basely preferred the visible and material prosperity of his kingdom and subjects to the unity of the true faith and the triumph of Wahhabee monotheism. 'Obeyd, on the contrary, was now the mainspring of the faction in Shomer, and his palace the daily resort of Nejdean zealots and disciplinarians. Here all whom the desire of plunder and the love of despotism drew into the cause would meet together and inveigh against the prevailing laxities and abominations; against commerce, tobacco, and polytheism. Never absent from public prayers in the mosque, 'Obeyd would there take the precedence, which his nephew readily abandoned him, and often go through the duties of Imām and preacher too, with a zeal more worthy of imitation than successful in obtaining it.

Lastly, to prove himself deficient in no point of the most correct orthodoxy, he built for himself a spacious harem in a rural palace without the town, and there the number of his wives and concubines befitted a genuine disciple of him " whose delight " (to quote Mahomet's own words about himself) " God had ordained to be in women." Indeed, at the age of seventy, or more, and while we were ourselves at Ḥā'yel, he added a new partner to the long list of ladies already in hand.

Such was 'Obeyd, who now returned to the capital from a foray in which he had shown all the vigour and ferocity of youth, and found the Christian doctors established within its precincts. Had he been absolute lord and master here, our stay would not have been much prolonged. But aware of the favour we enjoyed at court and among the townsmen, he restrained himself; and where the wolf's skin was not long enough, eked it out with the fox's, after the prudent counsel of the Macedonian Philip.

On the second day of his arrival, towards noon, he came to our door on horseback, accompanied by a dozen retainers. His greeting was that of the greatest apparent cordiality ; he offered his hand for a downright shake, and expressed his satisfaction at finding us the guests of his nephew, and, consequently, his own.

We had not even yet been fully informed of his real character. Arabs, even when most communicative in their talk, never forget the laws of prudence when a third party has to be mentioned, and do not like to discuss an absent individual, especially if his presence may be shortly expected. So that general phrases and anecdotes of no particular bearing were all that, up to this date, we had heard of 'Obeyd. His tall stature, absolutely unbowed by years, his strongly-marked features, and his easy, soldier-like manner, told much in his favour at a first appearance. But I cannot easily forget the effect produced on me by the cold look of his large grey eye ; it seemed to belong to a different face, so strangely did it contrast with the expression of the rest of his countenance.

Nothing could be more open and cheerful than the tone of his conversation, and he showed a strong desire to be fully acquainted with all about us, merely in order to help us according to his means. His visits to our lodgings were almost

daily, and he begged us in return to be his guests as frequently
as we could. His town palace was, my readers may remember,
nearly opposite to that of Ṭelál; and here 'Obeyd possessed a
large garden, newly planted and uncommonly well arranged, for
he brought his energetic activity to bear on whatever he undertook, and showed no less vigour in digging a well or conducting
a water channel than in burning a village and cutting infidels to
pieces. Within this garden it was his wont to have carpets spread
at evening under the trees near the palace wall, and here he
would pass the first hours of the night with friends selected
to suit his purposes or agree with his tastes. To these " soirées "
he often called us, and would then, in the freedom of the dusk,
hold discourse on religion or politics in the manner best adapted
to discover from our answers what were our personal opinions
and intentions. At last, between direct enquiry and close observation, he ended by forming an approximately correct idea
of who we were and what had brought us to Ḥá'yel. All this
took place near the date of our familiar interviews with Zámil
and Ṭelál.

A display of friendship above what circumstances seemed
exactly to warrant had put us somewhat on our guard at the
outset, and a hint thrown out now and then by those who
noticed 'Obeyd's growing familiarity tended still more to awake
our mistrust. But it was not long before we obtained a fuller
knowledge of our dangerous friend.

'Abd-el-Maḥsin had not been put into the secret, at least we
had determined to make him no special communications on
that point. But perhaps he had heard from Ṭelál something of
what was going on, or perhaps native sagacity and old experience led him to conjectures not far removed from the truth.
Whatever it were, he was much too polite to make us aware in
a direct manner that he saw through an incognito which we
had not thought fit to unveil for him. But when he became
aware of the attentions paid us by 'Obeyd, and our frequent
meetings, friendship or prudence prompted him to put us on
our guard. He therefore acquainted us with all the previous
history and actual position of this chief, and concluded by describing him as the very representative of the anti-government
or opposition party in Shomer. What 'Abd-el-Maḥsin stated,

'Obeyd himself confirmed shortly after in a curious manner, when, like most men who act a part, he for an instant forgot his mask and allowed us a glimpse of his true face—momentary, but more than sufficient.

One morning he had sent for me to see an individual of his household who stood in need of medical treatment. I came, accompanied by my acting servant, Barakāt. While we were yet within 'Obeyd's palace, we fell into conversation with him touching the events then going on in the neighbouring pashalics of Syria and Bagdad, on Christian influence and Mahometan reaction. 'Obeyd kept up awhile the impartial style which he usually affected before us, and seemed to take pleasure in the prospects of advancement and amelioration opening in the East. Suddenly an electric shock of his genuine feelings got the better of his assumed demeanour; his conciliatory tone and smooth phrases changed into the language of hate and open defiance, and he burst out into violent invectives against innovators, Christians, temporizers, and all who did not hold fast by the old purity and exclusiveness of Islam; till, with a hideous expression of concentrated rage, he said, " But you, whoever you may be, know this, that should my nephew and his people and all Arabia with them think fit to apostatize, and there be left in the entire world only one Muslim, I will be that one." Then all at once, feeling that he had gone too far, he broke off, and returned without transition or gradation like the shifting of a scene to his open smile and friendly chat, as though he had never known suspicion or anger. But we had seen enough, and from that hour visits and intercourse were at an end.

Soon after Zāmil brought us the news that 'Obeyd had sought out Telāl, who in general kept out of his way the utmost possible, and had held a long and secret conversation with him, about what was easy to guess. This explained why the monarch hesitated to give us an answer, and put off our second audience from day to day. He had in his path one almost his equal in birth and power, a near relative and a yet nearer enemy, who could and did report his every word and step to the Wahhabee despot, and who might bring him into serious difficulties. In truth the position was not a pleasant one, but Telāl was not to be so baffled ; he took his time and his measures.

The pilgrim road in the neighbourhood of Medinah was infested by marauding bands of the Ḥarb and Benoo-'Āteeyah Bedouins whom Ṭelāl had promised to punish. He now persuaded 'Obeyd, always ready for military work, to take the lead of an expedition against these robbers, meaning thus to procure his absence for a few days from Ḥā'yel. Orders were given to collect a suitable number of troops. Ḥā'yel itself furnished about a hundred, an equal contingent was supplied by Kefār, and the villages of the vicinity were laid under contribution, till four hundred armed men were ready to take the field. The common rendezvous was at the capital, without the northern gate, for it is the custom to set out a few miles in the opposite direction to that really intended, which was here the south-west. In this way rumour is often baffled, and the enemy led to suppose the attack destined for some other than himself. For the same reason the ultimate object in view is commonly kept a secret from the soldiers themselves, who only know in a general way that they have to march somewhere and fight somebody. When the day came for starting (it was the 4th of September), 'Obeyd caused his tent to be pitched in the plain without the northern walls; and there reviewed his forces. About one-third were on horseback, the rest were mounted on light and speedy camels; all had spears and matchlocks, to which the gentry added swords; and while they rode hither and thither in sham manœuvres over the parade-ground, the whole appearance was very picturesque and tolerably martial. 'Obeyd now unfurled his own peculiar standard, in which the green colour distinctive of Islam had been added border-wise to the white ground of the ancestral Nejdean banner, mentioned fourteen centuries back by 'Omar-ebn-Kelthoom, the poet of Ṭaghleb, and many others. Barakāt and myself mixed with the crowd of spectators. 'Obeyd saw us, and it was now several days since we had last met. Without hesitating, he cantered up to us, and while he tendered his hand for a farewell shake, he said : " I have heard that you intend going to Riaḍ ; there you will meet with 'Abd-Allah the eldest son of Feyṣul ; he is my particular friend ; I should much desire to see you high in his good graces, and to that end I have written him a letter in your behalf, of which you yourselves are to be the bearers ;

you will find it in my house, where I have left it for you with
one of my servants." He then assured us that if he found us
still at Ḥà'yel on his return, he would continue to befriend us
in every way; but that if we journeyed forward to Nejed, we
should meet with a sincere friend in 'Abd-Allah, especially if
we gave him the letter in question.

He then took his leave with a semblance of affectionate cordiality that made the bystanders stare; thus supporting to the
last the profound dissimulation which he had only once belied
for a moment. The letter was duly handed over to us the same
afternoon by his head-steward, whom he had left to look after the
house and garden in his absence. Doubtless my readers will be
curious to know what sort of recommendation 'Obeyd had provided
us with. It was written on a small scrap of thick paper, about
four inches each way, carefully folded up and secured by three
seals. However, "our fears forgetting manners," we thought
best with Hamlet to make perusal of this grand commission
before delivering it to its destination. So we undid the seals
with precautions admitting of reclosing them in proper form,
and read the royal knavery. I give it word for word; it ran
thus: "In the Name of God, the Merciful, the Compassion-
ate, We 'Obeyd-ebn-Rasheed salute you, O 'Abd-Allah son of
Feysulebn-Sa'ood, and peace be on you, and the mercy of
God and His blessings." (This is the invariable commencement
of all Wahhabee epistles, to the entire omission of the com-
plimentary formulas used by other Orientals.)   " After which,"
so proceeded the document, " we inform you that the bearers
of this are one Seleem-el-'Eys, and his comrade Barakāt-esh-
Shāmee, who give themselves out for having some knowledge
in "—here followed a word of equivocal import, capable of
interpretation alike by " medicine " or " magic," but generally
used in Nejed for the latter, which is at Riaḍ a capital crime.
" Now may God forbid that we should hear of any evil having
befallen you. We salute also your father Feysul, and your
brothers, and all your family; and anxiously await your news
in answer. Peace be with you." Here followed the signet
impression.

A pretty recommendation, especially under the actual circumstances. However, not content with this, 'Obeyd found means

to transmit further information regarding us, and all in the same tenour, to Riad, as we afterwards discovered. For his letter, I need hardly say that it never passed from our possession, where it yet remains as an interesting autograph, to that of 'Abd-Allah; with whom it would inevitably have proved the one only thing wanting, as we shall subsequently see, to make us leave the forfeit of our lives in the Nejdean man-trap. Meanwhile it helped us thus far, by giving us a clue to the conduct we had to observe in the Wahhabee court.

Without showing the epistle itself to Zámil, we let him know in a casual manner that 'Obeyd had written for us an introduction to the son of Feysul. Zámil, fearing that we might be less aware of 'Obeyd's intentions than we really were, begged us most earnestly not to be the bearers of the letter, of whose contents he had a shrewd guess. We promised him to be discreet, but did not tell him more, satisfied with this additional proof of his sincerity.

'Obeyd was now at a distance, and Telál felt himself at liberty to proceed with us ; and accordingly on the 6th of the month we received his orders to meet him privately in Zámil's K'hāwah an hour or so after noon. To the K'hāwah we went, and a slave was stationed at the outer door to prevent interruption from unseasonable visitors. We had not been ten minutes at the rendezvous when Telál came, accompanied by two swordsmen, whom he left outside. He was plainly dressed, his look was serious even more than wont, and after seating himself he remained some time in a silence which we did not interrupt. At last he raised his eyes, and looking me hard in the face, said : " You would not be imprudent enough to require, nor I to give, a formal and official answer to communications like yours, and in such a state of things. But this much I, Telál, will say : be assured now and ever of my good will and countenance ; you must now continue your journey ; but return in whatever fashion you may, and I hope it will be before long, your word shall pass here as law, and whatever you may wish to see done, shall be exactly complied with throughout the limits of my government. Does this satisfy you ? " added he. I replied that my utmost desires went no further ; and we shook hands in mutual pledge.

He then declared that he had no objections to our visiting the
Wahhabee capital, but that he much recommended us to be
prudent and wary, and that, in a word, least said there would be
soonest mended ; nor were we likely to find in Riad any one high
or low fitted for our confidence.   He added that 'Obeyd might
return shortly, and that in consequence we had better lose no
time in setting out, that he had already given orders to a party
of Kaseem travellers who were bound for Bereydah to take us
with them, and that they were awaiting our leisure.

He was evidently in some anxiety about the result of our
expedition, both on his own account and ours, and seemed to
consider the remainder of our journey likely to turn out more
hazardous than we yet thought it.   His fears were nohow
exaggerated, as we found when once within the Nejdean
territory.

I asked him, more out of trial than anything else, if he would
not give us an introductory letter in his name to the Wahhabee
monarch.   " There would be little use in that," said he, " and
a recommendation of mine would hardly make him think the
better of you."   In its place he then dictated to Zámil, for
Telál himself is no scribe, a passport or general letter of safe
conduct, enough to ensure us good treatment within the limits
of his rule, and even beyond.   I subjoin the translation for the
benefit of the Foreign Office and all therein employed.

" In the name of God the Merciful, we, Telál-ebn-Rasheed,
to all dependent on Shomer who may see this, peace be with
you and the mercy of God.   Next, we inform you that the
bearers of this paper are Seleem-el-'Eys-Abou-Mahmood and
his associate Barakát, physicians, seeking their livelihood by
doctoring, with the help of God, and journeying under our
protection, so let no one interfere with or annoy them, and
peace be with you."   Here followed the date.

When this was written, Telál affixed his seal, and rose to
leave us alone with Zámil, after a parting shake of the hand,
and wishing us a prosperous journey and speedy return.   We,
too, had at that time some idea of repassing by Há'yel on our
homeward way, but after circumstances conducted us by
a different and a more instructive, though a longer route.
Nothing now remained but to make our preparations for

departure; we had obtained sufficient knowledge of the Shomer capital and its denizens, while far the greater part of our journey lay yet before us, and the autumn was already drawing on. Besides, any notable prolongation of our stay at Ḥā'yel might be dangerous both for ourselves and for Ṭelāl; we were watched by the spies of 'Obeyd and Feyṣul, and so was the monarch also. The Bagdad merchants, too, who formed a numerous and not uninfluential body in the town, looked on us with positive dislike, supposing us in reality Damascenes, for whom the Shiy'aees bear an especial and hereditary hatred, that twelve centuries have rather increased than diminished. Accordingly, though in most respects so dissident from the Wahhabee sectarians, they now sided with them in one thing, and that was in giving us askance looks of no friendly import, and in saying of us all the harm imaginable, whenever they could safely do so, I mean among themselves and behind our backs. Moreover, my stock of remedies was limited, and I had cause to fear lest too much expenditure of them in one place might barely leave us enough to suffice for the practice awaiting us in the rest of our long journey. Lastly, it need hardly be said that Ṭelāl's recommendation to set out was, in our position, fully equivalent to a command. Yet with all these motives for going, I could not but feel reluctant to quit a pleasing town, where we certainly possessed many sincere friends and well-wishers, for countries in which we could by no means anticipate equal favour or even equal safety. Indeed, so ominous was all that we heard about Wahhabee Nejed, so black did the landscape before us look, on nearer approach, that I almost repented of my resolution, and was considerably inclined to say, "Thus far enough, and no farther."

But "over shoes over boots," and the "tra Beatrice e te è questo muro" of the Florentine, though in a somewhat altered sense, ran in my memory, and gave me courage. And then we had already got so far that to turn back from what was yet to traverse, be it what it might, would have been an unpardonable want of heart. Hardly had Ṭelāl left the Ḳ'hāwah, when we requested Zāmil to let us know where we were to find out our destined companions for the road. He answered that they had received orders to come in quest of us, and that they would unfailingly present themselves at our house the very same day.

Before evening three men knocked at our door; they were our future guides. The eldest bore the name of Mubārek, and was a native of the suburbs of Bereydah; all three were of the genuine Ḳaseem breed, darker and lower in stature than the inhabitants of Ḥā'yel, but not ill-looking, and extremely affable in their demeanour. Mubārek told us that their departure from Ḥā'yel had been at first fixed for the morrow, or the 7th of the month, but that owing to some delay on the part of their companions, for the band was a large one, it had been subsequently put off to the 8th or the day after. Such procrastinations are of continual occurrence in the East, where the mode of travelling renders them unavoidable, and one must be prepared for them and take them as they come, under penalty of making oneself ridiculous by unavailing impatience. We now struck a bargain with Mubārek for the hire of two of his camels to bear ourselves and our chattels; the price was almost ridiculously small, even after making allowance for the comparatively high value of money in these inland regions; and we were glad to see that the polite and chatty manners of our new guides promised us an agreeable journey.

We had soon made all necessary arrangements for our departure, got in a few scattered debts, packed up our pharmacopœia, and nothing now remained but the pleasurable pain of farewells. They were many and mutually sincere. Meta'ab had indeed made his a few days before, when he, a second time, left Ḥā'yel for the pastures; Ṭelāl we had already taken leave of, but there remained his younger brother Moḥammed to give us a hearty adieu of good augury. Most of my old acquaintance or patients, Ḍoḥey' the merchant, Moḥammed the judge, Doheym and his family, not forgetting our earliest friend Seyf the chamberlain, Sa'eed the cavalry officer, and others of the court, freemen and slaves, white or black (for negroes readily follow the direction indicated by their masters, and are not ungrateful if kindly treated while kept in their due position), and many others of whose names Homer would have made a catalogue and I will not, heard of our near departure, and came to express their regrets, with hopes of future meeting and return. For my own part, I then felt as if I should be well pleased were such hopes one day to be realized; yet how improbable!

'Abd-el-Maḥsin, too, accompanied by Bedr, the eldest of Ṭelāl's sons, came a little before evening to see us a last time and bid us God-speed. All along he had been our daily and welcome companion, and his cultivated and well-stored mind, set off by ready eloquence, had done much to charm our stay and to take off the loneliness that even in the midst of a crowd is apt to weigh on strangers in a foreign land. The boy, too, Bedr, was much what his father must have been at that age; we had helped to cure him of some slight feverish attacks not uncommon at that time of life, and our young patient showed in return steady gratitude and simple attachment, more, perhaps, than is customary among children, at least of high birth, while his modest and polite manners would have done credit to a European court education. 'Abd-el-Maḥsin assured us, in Ṭelāl's name and his own, that we carried with us the good-will of all the court, and we sat thus together till sunset, staving off the necessity of separating by word and answer that had no meaning, except that we could not make up our minds to part.

But at fall of night, our last night at Ḥāʼyel, we had a more important visit to receive. In the dusk Zāmil came, and having stationed his negro Soueylim at the street door, to preclude chance intruders, remained with us in long and affectionate talk, pledging his active support and entire cooperation for whatever measures after times might bring, renewing his recommendations of the greatest caution to be observed among the Wahhabees, pointing out the dangers possibly before us, and the means to avoid, or at least diminish them, and finally entreating us to send him a few lines from Riad, whereby to inform his master and himself, under covert phrases worded in seemingly medical import, of our own personal safety, and the result of our proceedings at the capital. We, too, begged him to assure Ṭelāl of our entire confidence in his good faith and honour, and to put his mind at rest about our discretion and wariness in word and deed. He embraced us, and departed under the star-light.

Early next morning, before day, Mubārek and another of his countrymen, named Dahesh, were at our door with the camels.

Some of our town friends had also come, even at this hour, to accompany us as far as the city gates.   We mounted our beasts, and while the first sunbeams streamed level over the plain, passed through the south-western portal beyond the market-place, the 8th of September 1862, and left the city of Ḥā'yel.

5
Carlo Guarmani, 1864

Carlo Claudio Guarmani was born at Leghorn on 11
December 1828, emigrating to Beirut with his family
in 1850. Disliking office work, he obtained the post
of agent for the Imperial French Postal Service at
Jerusalem and was soon travelling and trading among
the bedouin who roam the desert lands of Syria and
northern Najd. His first book was *El Kamsa: il cav-
allo arabo puro sangue: studio di sedici anni in
Siria, Palestina, Egitto e nei deserti dell' Arabia*
(Bologna, 1864; reprinted first in 1866, and recently
by The Falcon Press of Italy, 1977, with an introduction by Angelo Pesce), written in French and translated into Italian by Ansaldo Feletti. This dealt
with the breeds of Arabian horse and the system suggested by Guarmani to improve the breed. The book
reveals little overtly about the author's travels,
though we may infer that he frequented encampments
of the Bishr, Bani Sakhr, and Ruwala bedouin. His
translator, who had made Guarmani's acquaintance in
Jerusalem, tells us that the author of *El Kamsa* (The
'Five' in question being the original (mythical)
strains of noble pedigree: Kuhailan, Ubayyan, Saqlawi,
Hamdani and Habdan) "is gifted with an adventurous
spirit, great courage, and a thorough knowledge of
Arabic. He frequently lives among the nomads. Inured
to fatigue and other hardships, thoroughly conversant
with local usage, dressed as a bedu and mounted on
horseback he penetrates far into the desert. There he
spends many days under canvas, studying all aspects of
the Arabian horse, and becoming so deeply acquainted
with all the various tribes that I believe him to be
the only European who can wander throughout the desert

without risk. He knows the cunning and the ingenuity of the bedouin, expertly selecting and buying the most splendid stallions."

Such a shrewd judge and bargainer might well expect to be commissioned by the wealthy and powerful, so it is hardly surprising that in 1863 Guarmani had been summoned both to Paris and to Turin, where he had been charged with buying stallions for the Government of France and for Vittorio Emanuele II, King of Italy. Hence the journey made from January to April 1864 recorded in *Il Neged settentrionale* (Jerusalem, 1866), a book translated by Lady Capel-Cure in 1916 and published first 'for official use only' by the Arab Bureau, Cairo in 1917 and subsequently in an edition limited to 475 copies by The Argonaut Press of London in 1938, the latter, with a useful introduction by Douglas Carruthers, having been reprinted in 1971 by N. Israel of Amsterdam with Da Capo of New York. A virtually complete French translation appeared in the *Bulletin de la Société de Géographie,* (5th ser., Vol. IX, 1865) and a German précis by H.G. Rosen (with a map by H. Kiepert) in the *Zeitschrift für Allgemeine Erdkunde* (N.s., Vol. XVIII, 1865).

We shall never know to what extent - if at all - the French commission to Guarmani carried with it political overtones (even if we are familiar with French intentions at that period to occupy Syria), but Guarmani's journey brought geographical knowledge enhancing the experiences already recorded by Wallin and Palgrave, the former sober in scholarship for a restricted circle, the latter ornate and 'literary', for the widest public possible. Like the Jesuit Palgrave, Guarmani travelled under an assumed name, an assumed nationality, an assumed religion: Khalil Agha, a Turkish Muslim.

Talal ibn Rashid had ruled the Jabal Shammar strongly and prosperously from 1847 until Guarmani's arrival in 1864, and was to survive for another four years. Talal paid lip service to the Wahhabi empire to the

south ruled by Faisal ibn Al Sa^{C}ud through his sons
Muhammad, Sa^{C}ud, and ^{C}Abdullah, but to all intents and
purposes the Rashidi dynasty then represented by Talal
was not only strong and resilient but, under Muhammad
ibn Rashid, it was to hold all of Najd, the pilgrim
routes north as far as Iraq and Palmyra, and even
obstinate Qasim, from which the Saudi family still
surviving managed to reach exile, a tale retold in
every history of the Kingdom of Saudi Arabia.

Indeed, Guarmani's only moments of anxiety occurred
during an unexpected clash between the ^{C}Utaiba tribesmen and the forces of the Amir ^{C}Abdullah ibn Faisal
ibn Al Sa^{C}ud and during a *ghazu* in Wadi Sirhan on the
way back: the rest of his four-month journey, largely
in Rashidi-held territory, was as tranquil as if he had
been making the Grand Tour in Europe.

Just as Philby cast doubt on the veracity of
Palgrave's narrative, Doughty and Zehme questioned
certain aspects of Guarmani's route, even denying
that the Italian had ever visited Khaibar. Doughty,
who claimed to have been the first European in Khaibar,
was also "obliged to doubt if he has seen Aneyza".
Later writers have absolved Guarmani from deceit,
however. Carruthers avers: "There is no doubt in my
mind that Guarmani went to Khaibar. I can see no
reason for Zehme's opinion to the contrary." We should
thus view Guarmani's comments on Ha'il as authentic,
though his estimate of the oasis-city population at
7,500 should probably be scaled down to something like
4,000, and the Jabal Shammar district had probably no
more than 40,000 inhabitants (both sedentary and
nomadic), and not the 75,000 suggested by Guarmani.

Guarmani left Jerusalem on 26 January 1864, arriving
in Taima on 11 February, Khaibar on 29 February,
^{C}Anaiza on 22 March, Faid on 26 March, and Ha'il late
on 1 April. Departing from Ha'il on 4-5 April, he
reached Bedan on 11 April, visited Taima, returning to
Bedan on 24 April, and was back in Ha'il on 28 April.
Leaving Ha'il on 4 May, he reached Hayaniah on the
edge of the Nafud next day, and thence made his way to

al-Jauf and al-Kaf via the wells of Jubba, in the Sand Sea.

While still south of Jabal Salma, before approaching Ha'il from the south, Guarmani encountered the encampment of Bandar, the Amir Talal's eldest son, who would then have been about fourteen. Some three hundred retainers were guarding five hundred thoroughbred mares at grass. Some were put to stallions each morning, and then were immediately separated and sent away to other pasture.

Accompanied by the Ethiopian ^cAnaibar (who claimed to be a subject of Faisal ibn Al Sa^cud but obeyed only Talal ibn Rashid), Guarmani paid a visit to the young prince in his encampment. Let Carlo Guarmani himself take up the story as Khalil Agha, head of the stables of the Ottoman Sultan H.E. Fuad Pasha.

'No sooner did the slaves perceive us than they fired a few shots to warn us off, no one being permitted, as Aneibar informed me, to go near the mares for fear of the evil eye. The slaves, seeing we paid no attention to their eloquent rebuke, came yelling and shaking their *nabbuts* at us. Aneibar laughed in return, and they soon recognised him and treated him with much deference, kissing his hand and congratulating him on his return. The young prince, when informed of his arrival, sent for him to his tent, and after five minutes' talk with his father's faithful servant, he invited me to enter, saying, with much courtesy, that an official of H.E. Fuad Pasha should expect civility from the princes who wield the sword for the Sultan and consider themselves his slaves; further, that his father, far from seeking freedom, thought himself honoured in serving the Government. He was surprised at my refusal to smoke and enquired laughingly if it was "because the Uakabite exists no longer in the Neged", the princes of that sect having invaded Constantinople! He would not help himself to coffee before me, and, as I refused, he took the *findgian* from the slave's hand and personally offered it to me. When the coffee was finished, he had my beard scented and

persuaded me to stay three days in his tent, telling
me he was sent for by his father to Kail and would like
to present me to him himself. He chaffed Aneibar about
having accepted the office of policeman over me, and
that if I had been a spy, the faithful subjects of the
Sultan might well be proud of me.

Aneibar left after dinner. Ali had stayed on at
Tabe. On the 31st we left for Seban, passing Tabe in
order to pick up Ali. After sunset on April 1st we
entered Kail.

At the gate the corpse of a Persian Jew lay rotting,
he having been massacred by the populace for pretending to be a Mussulman and then refusing to repeat the
formula: "God and the Prophet". The unfortunate man
had penetrated into Neged from the Kammad to buy
horses for H.M. the Shah of Persia.   If his fate was
a sad one, it must be owned he had deserved it. When
a man decides to risk himself in a great adventure, he
must use every means in his power and be prepared to
suffer all consequences of the enterprise. His death
was believed to be my own both in Palestine and Egypt;
the news reached Teime and spread to Tebuk and the
other caravan stations of the Mecca pilgrims! The
news was known at Cairo, where Monsignor Samuel Gobat
(the Anglican Bishop in Jerusalem) was; and our Latin
Patriarch in Jerusalem, S.E. Monsignor Giuseppe
Valerga (brother of the celebrated Father Leonardo, one
of the most distinguished prelates who have worked in
the Holy Land during this century), was advised of it
when in Alexandria. My poor family were informed
through the tactlessness of a friend, and mourned me
in earnest, whilst all the time I was in excellent
health, eating *pilaff* or *temmen*, and making my *rikat* to
God in my heart, but to Mahomet with my lips, in all
due reverence; and, remembering Christ's Sermon on the
Mount, not to mention the stench of that Jew's rotting
corpse, I was determined not to be amongst the poor in
spirit and enter Paradise with the fools.

Dismounting from my dromedary at the door of the
mosque, in the square which separates it from the

prince's palace, I went in with Bedar to say seven *rikat*, not having prayed during the day. The *mihrab* was turned to the south (and not in the direction of the "Kaaba"), like all those I had seen hitherto; this was not from ignorance but from custom. In the neighbouring provinces it was believed that the central niche, originally meant in the Syrian villages to indicate the south (*keblek*, pronounced ordinarily *kiblak*), could not be turned in any other direction.

Bendar, having finished his prayers before I had, went outside to give some orders; he came in again whilst I, turning my face to the right and left (the mosque was empty), stroked my beard and murmured the *salem aleikam*. On leaving be bade me good night and begged me to follow his slave, Mahbub. I crossed the square with my inseparable Ali and entered the prince's castle by a little gateway cut in the great door of the central gate which was shut during the night. Mahbub conducted me to the coffee hall, which was about fourteen metres long by five wide and six high; the ceiling was supported by a row of five columns, and the grey walls were smudged over with rude arabesques in white. The fireplace was on the right as one entered, where a youth of about twenty was boiling the black drug. I drank two half *findgians* or small cups, which it is an insult to fill to the brim. I was then led under the arches of a very long narrow courtyard; a slave offered me a *senie* of dates and fresh butter. The dates are eaten dipped in butter, which brings out the taste. I had no wish to return to the coffee hall, so enquired after our dromedaries and belongings. Mahbub replied that, according to Bendar's orders, our dromedaries were in the enclosure reserved for the Emirs' and every morning they were to be taken out to graze. Our baggage was already in the house prepared for us.

The Emir Talal had constructed several guest-houses all on the same plan, namely a courtyard for dromedaries and horses, one room with a gateway without a door, for receiving visitors and drinking coffee, and a smaller room for sleeping. The latter has a door made of slabs of palm wood with a lock and key in wood, as used in Lebanon. The outside doors opened and shut in the same way. Each ceiling is supported by a pillar; on the top of mine I carved in an idle hour: "Zulima, 1864" - my daughter's name and the year of my journey.

Should anyone ever follow in my track and wish to find my house, let him cross the square from the great door leading into the prince's castle, to the archway in front of it; he must follow the road starting from this arch until coming to another street leading to the market; my house was the one at the corner, detached on three sides. I found it clean; a good fire of palms was burning in the hole dug by the door on the left; the room was well provided with mattings, rugs and cushions; a jar of water with a copper cup forming a stopper stood in a corner, and our belongings were hung on the walls.

I woke up early on the 2nd; the Emir's doorkeeper brought me some camel's milk, with fried honey and grapes, advising me to go out and see the country, as I could not see the Emir Talal until after the *asser* prayers. After breakfast I repaired to the market-place and found it very poor after Aneizeh. Many of the merchants were natives of Mesced-Ali, others of Bagdad, Bassora, the Gezire villages, and of the Izak or Arak-Arabi. I went into the shops and spent two hundred true piastres on Ali, for I gave him a new *abah*, a *keffieh* and a white shirt, not wishing to have disparaging remarks made on the colour of his blue shirt such as his tribe wear, and which is usually only worn by women. I say "true" piastres, because in that market the piastre has a conventional value corresponding to seven and a half piastres. Wholesale goods are always paid for in "thaler megidi". In the Cassim it is the same as at Colannati di Spagna. Most of the shops close from ten till three.

Mahbub, who had been looking for me for an hour, conducted me to the same courtyard, as on the previous evening, where I was again offered *pilaff* and *temmen*. Ali

shared my repast. I went for a moment into the coffee
hall before returning to my house, where I wrote and
slept.

The muezzin from the minaret of the mosque (in Neged
"meschit") was calling the faithful to the *asser* prayer when Bendar came to fetch me to present me to his
father. My preparations were not completed before the
prayers were over.

The Emir Talal-eben Rascid was a man of forty: short,
fat and dark, with sharp black eyes and an aquiline
nose. He wore a very fine brown Hassa *abah*, a *keffieh-
allas* from Bagdad, an *aarkal* tied with silk and gold
cords; a dark-green cloth coat and a long white shirt.
He had already left the mosque and was holding a tribunal at the door, seated on the western side of the
mosque with his chief officials sitting on his left,
according to their rank, in rows one behind another.
Twenty slaves and servants sat in a semicircle on the
ground in front of him, all well dressed in fine black
abahs, with red or blue cloth coats heavily embroidered with gold; in their hands they held, as did the
prince and all his followers, a scimitar in a silver
scabbard, which they only buckle on when on horseback.
From the other side of the semicircle a poor woman was
asking for justice against the governor of the village
of Usseta who had taken her ass and, when she asked
him the reason, had ill-treated her. The prince gave
orders that two horsemen should accompany her to the
village to choose the best ass belonging to the govern-
or and give it to the poor woman as recompense for the
loss of her own; also as compensation for her ill-
treatment at the hands of the governor, he was condemned to buy a *kessue*, or entire new garment. The woman
departed calling down blessings on the ruler.

The prince did not rise to receive me. He put out
his hand; I touched it with mine, which I then lifted
to my mouth, kissing the fingers, and then to my forehead, while he did the same with his, and at a sign
from him, and without uttering a word, I seated myself

on the ground at his right hand on the step of the mosque.

He got rid of eight lawsuits in two hours, put on his sandals and broke up the court. He then saluted me, smiling, with his hand on his heart, and I did the same, trying not to laugh, for I was not used to a dumb reception. Bendar went away with his father.

Mahbub announced dinner. This time he took me up to the roof over the gateway and spread out a large carpet; a black boy brought a round table a few inches high and two others laid a *senie* on it, with *temmen,* meat and bread. When I had dined I washed my hands, having helped myself, like the Beduin, with Adam's forks.

Whilst I was dining, the Emir's women looked at me through the wooden grating of a window. I thought I could distinguish among the whispers of the women the male voices of the Emir Talal and of Bendar. There is always an occasion in his life when the wisest man forgets himself and unknowingly makes a fool of himself! I descended the steps without glancing towards the harem, pretending to be deaf, and was going to the usual place to drink my coffee, when Bendar ran after me to invite me into his father's private apartments.

The prince welcomed me with embraces and kept me talking about five hours. From time to time he had my beard perfumed and offered me both black and white coffee.

He had heard that my horses were still at Mestegeddeh, where my Ehteim were sheltering for fear of the Meteir, who were harrying the southern frontiers. Bendar requested to be allowed to accompany me and was given permission, it being understood that I first accepted three days of their hospitality. Aneibar was to command the escort of twenty horsemen which the Emir provided, and we were permitted to travel by day. I made no mention of the recommendation from the Emir Abdalla-eben-Feisal.

Until the 5th I could eat, drink, rest and write. I
spent several hours every day in the shops, and always
attended the morning tribunal at the castle gate, and
the evening one at the door of the mosque. The Emir
Talal availed himself of the Gospel precept, "All who
use the sword shall perish by the sword." He ordered
death for assassins, cut off the hand of those who
wounded another in a quarrel; for liars and false witnesses he ordered their beards to be burnt over a fire,
which often ended in their eyes being burnt as well;
imprisonment was the punishment for thieves; rebels had
their goods confiscated. He constantly told me that he
held widows and orphans dearer than his own family.
His sentences were just and his generosity excessive.
When he did not receive me in his own apartments in the
evening, he would come to the coffee hall for an hour,
where poets of Cassim improvised verses in his honour.
He gave a poet of Eben-Sehud, one blind as Homer, a
complete suit of clothes, a hundred megidi, a dromedary
and a horse, all for a poem ending with this line:

"And Eben-Rascid has all Neged with him."'

On 28 April 1864, Guarmani 'returned with a certain
amount of satisfaction' to his little house at Ha'il
(or 'Kail', in his spelling). The young prince Bandar
had gone to the village of Biqa$^{C'}$ ('Bahcaa'); Guarmani
did not follow. 'Instead, I climbed a neighbouring hill
whence I could see the surrounding mountains, so as to
be able to discover in which direction this village lay.
Some days later', continues Guarmani, 'having occasion
to accompany the princes ^{C}Abdurrahman and Rashid ibn
Rashid (relatives of Amir Talal) to see their mares on
the road to Bahcaa, and over which we journeyed for
eight hours, we reached a mountain after seven hours
which was said to be halfway to this same village'.

Biqa$^{C'}$ is in fact not a village at all, but as its
Arabic name suggests, a depression. It is roughly fifteen miles in circumference, with a high water table
which turns Biqa$^{C'}$ into a lake after heavy rains. Small

farms and houses are dotted around the edge of the depression. Amir Talal was planning a raid, or *ghazu*, against the Shararat tribesmen, rallying his allies at Hayaniah, northeast of Ha'il, and on 30 April Guarmani went to the fortified zone below Jabal Aqda to bring the arms which were left there in peacetime. The weapons were sufficiently numerous to load forty camels. The narrow entrance to the enclosed valleys of Aqda was boarded up with wood and strengthened with sheets of iron. Before, during, and after Guarmani's time the Amirs of Ha'il used Aqda not only as an armoury but also as a refuge, since the many palm gardens were inhabited (if occasionally and if sparsely) and almost always well watered by seasonal rains.

The promised *ghazu* began early on 4 May. The banner of Amir Talal was flying on a flagpole before the gateway of his castle in Ha'il, and Guarmani rose early because he had been warned that he was to accompany the *ghazu* as far as the rallying-place - Hayaniah. The prince was already at work. 'I found him assisting in the distribution of arms and dromedaries to the volunteers who required them; he gave away about six hundred dromedaries. At ten o'clock a slave seized the banner, vaulted onto his horse and began the march; all the troops, nearly a thousand men, followed him; then came the Amir, with ^CAli (son of ^CUbaid), his cousin, and lastly ^CAnaibar with myself. ^CAnaibar distributed coins of twenty *paras* to the wives and children of the slaves, who accompanied us for half an hour beyond the town yelling (or as they believed, singing) in honour of their great and liberal master.'

At al-Waqid, the party was further reinforced by three hundred or so horsemen from the Sulaimi and ^CAbda tribes; 'the Dagheret and Singhiara contingents joined us at Lechite (Laqita), where we passed most of the night. Three hours before daylight we started again, reaching Haianie (Hayaniah) after sunset, and were received with acclamation by the five hundred volunteers who had preceded us. The following morning I was sent for by the prince, who exchanged my dromedary, which was beginning to lose his hump, for his own; he also sought to make me accept other presents, endeavouring in every way to overcome the diffidence on my part; he placed me under the care of a Shammari, and a Ruwaili on the Mashhur side, who were to conduct me to Jubba and al-Jauf. Just as I was leaving I bought (from a bedu Hutaiba spy) a young grey stallion of the celebrated Kubaishan breed. El-Haianie, being only recently built, can boast so far only a fort and three houses: it is surrounded by the Nafud sands. I believe it to be another place of safety prepared by the Amir Talal in the event of fortune's forsaking him.'

The castle of Hayaniah, to be visited by Captain Shakespear and Gertrude Bell in 1914, was indeed built by Talal and not, as Miss Bell asserted, by Abdullah ibn Rashid. However, Guarmani is only partly correct in assuming that Qasr Hayaniah was built as a place of refuge, for its foremost significance was a redoubt to guard the wells against unauthorised use by others than Shammari tribespeople. It is also misleading to suggest that the Qasr is 'surrounded' by the sand-sea: it is on the edge of the Nafud, and four rock-hewn wells there were noted by Charles Huber.

On 9 May 1864, having rested for two nights at Jubba, Guarmani left the Jabal Shammar for good. 'In silence I meditated on my experiences! ... The Jabal Shammar had at last opened its secrets to Europe, and I was leaving it without having encountered the least trouble: in fact I had received great kindnesses and might also have received as many presents.'

6
Charles Montagu Doughty, 1877 and 1878

In 1906-7, six volumes of an epic poem *The Dawn in Britain* appeared in London, crowning a lifetime's dedication to the grand style. The author was Charles Doughty, who had arabicised his Christian name to Khalil and achieved world fame in 1888 with the publication of one of the major classics of English literature, *Travels in Arabia Deserta*. Though the book is read nowadays (most commonly in Edward Garnett's skilful abridgment) for the details of bedu̇in life in northern Arabia during the 1870s, 'wherein is set forth faithfully some parcel of soil of Arabia, smelling of *samn* and camels', Doughty's main intention was not so much specifically 'the setting forth of personal wanderings among a people of Biblical interest, as the ideal endeavour to continue the older tradition of Chaucer and Spenser, resisting to my power the decadence of the English language: so that whilst my work should be the mere verity for Orientalists, it should be also my life's contribution, so far to literature.'

Doughty's *Travels in Arabia Deserta* is all the more remarkable for the author's ancestry - conservative, Anglican, and patriotic as only a Victorian landed family could be. Quickly baptized because he was expected not to live long, he failed the Navy because of a slight speech impediment, and turned instead to the study of geology at Cambridge, beginning his scientific career with the study of glaciers in Norway. He fell deeply in love with the resonance of Chaucerian English, and of Spenserian, ceaselessly practising what he preached: that the degeneration of English speech could be halted only by a return to mediaeval and Elizabethan vocabulary in all their wealth of allusion and breadth of reference, with meandering periods, Biblical overtones, dignified archaicisms just managing to avoid pomposity or tedium.

Doughty's *Wanderjahre* began in 1870 with the Low Countries, northern Italy, Florence, Rome, Vesuvius, Sicily, and Algeria. He explored Palestine, Syria, and Egypt, with visits to Sinai and Petra. In Petra he learned of the Nabataean city of Mada'in Salih, and determined to set out from Damascus on the pilgrim caravan which passed through Mada'in Salih, leaving the *hajjis* there and joining them again on their way back from Mecca. But he never returned with the *Hajj*, preferring to live with the nomads of northern Arabia despite his refusal to disavow his religion.

He stayed with the Fajr, and travelled with them as far as Taima, then wandered for four long months over the barren black wilderness of the Harra, making his way eventually to the Ha'il of Muhammad ibn Rashid.

Let Khalil take up the story as he enters with fear and trembling on 22 October 1877 the seat of that bloodthirsty ruler of the Jabal Shammar, he whose own Beduins confessed 'had committed crimes which before were not known in the world.'

Charles M. Doughty.

1921

Beyond Gofar orchard walls is that extreme barrenness of desert plain (máhal) which lies before Hâyil; the soil, a sharp granite-grit, is spread out between the desolate mountains Ajja and *Selma*, barren as a sea-strand and lifeless as the dust of our streets; and yet therein are hamlets and villages, upon veins of ground-water. It is a mountain ground where almost nothing may spring of itself. but irrigated it will yield barley and wheat, and the other Nejd grains. Though their palms grow high they bear only small and hot, and therefore less wholesome kinds of date-berries. We found hardly a blade or a bush besides the senna plant, flowering with yellow pea-like blossoms. The few goats of the town must be driven far back under the coast of Ajja to find pasture. After two hours Nasr said, " Hâyil is little further, we are here at the mid-way ; women and children go between Hâyil and Gofar before their (noon) break-fast." Thus the road may be eleven miles nearly. Hâyil was yet hidden by the brow of the desert,—everywhere the horizon seemed to me very near in Nomad Arabia. Between these towns is a trodden path; and now we met those coming out from Hâyil. They were hareem and children on foot, and some men riding upon asses : " Ha ! (said a fellow, and then another, and another, to Nasr) why dost thou bring him ? " —So I knew that the Nasrâny's coming had been published in Hâyil ! and Nasr hearing their words began to be aghast. ' What, he said, if his head should be taken off ! '—" And Khalîl, where is the tobacco-bag ? and reach me that galliûn, for billah, my head turns." We had ridden a mile further, when I espied two horsemen galloping towards us in a great dust. I began to muse, were these hot riders some cruel messengers of the Emir, chevying out from Hâyil upon my account ?—The name of Nasrâny was yet an execration in this country, and even among nomads a man will say to another, " Dost thou take me for a Nasrâny! that I should do such [iniquitous] thing."— Already the cavaliers were upon us, and as only may riders of the mild Arabian mares, they reined up suddenly abreast of us, their garments flying before them in the still air ; and one of them shouted in a harsh voice to Nasr (who answered nothing, for he was afraid), " All that baggage is whose, ha ? "—so they rode on from us as before ; I sat drooping upon my camel with fatigue, and had not much regarded what men they were.

We saw afterward some high building with battled towers. These well-built and stately Nejd turrets of clay-brick are shaped like our light-houses ; and, said Nasr, who since Telâl's time had not been to Hâyil, " That is the Emir's summer residence." As we approached Hâyil I saw that the walls extended backward, making of the town a vast enclosure of palms. Upon our right hand I saw a long grove of palms in the desert, closed by high walls; upon the left lies another outlying in the wilderness and larger, which Abeyd planted for the inheritance of his children. Now appeared as it were suspended above the town, the whitened donjon of the *Kasr*,—such clay buildings they whiten with jiss. We rode by that summer residence which stands at the way-side; in the tower, they say, is mounted a small piece of artillery. Under the summer house wall is a new conduit, by which there flows out irrigation water to a public tank, and townswomen come hither to fetch water. This, which they call *mâ es-Sáma*, is reckoned the best water in the town; from all their other wells the water comes up with some savour of salty and bitter minerals, "which (though never so slight) is an occasion of fever." We alighted, and at my bidding a woman took down the great (metal) water-pan upon her head to give us to drink. Nasr spoke to me not to mount anew; he said we had certain low gateways to pass. That was but guile of the wild Beduwy, who with his long matted locks seemed less man than satyr or werwolf. They are in dread to be cried down for a word, and even mishandled in the towns; his wit was therefore not to bring in the Nasrâny riding at the (proud) height of his camel.

I went on walking by the short outer street, and came to the rude two-leaved gateway (which is closed by night) of the inner sûk of Hâyil. There I saw the face of an old acquaintance who awaited me,—Abd el-Azîz, he who was conductor of Ibn Rashîd's gift-mare, now twelve months past, to the kella at el-Héjr. I greeted him, and he greeted me, asking kindly of my health, and bade me enter. He went before me, by another way, to bring the tiding to the Emir, and I passed on, walking through the public sûk, full of tradesmen and Beduw at this hour, and I saw many in the small dark Arab shops, busy about their buying and selling. Where we came by the throng of men and camels, the people hardly noted the stranger; some only turned to look after us. A little further there stepped out a well-clad merchant, with a saffron-dye beard, who in the Arabian guise took me by the hand, and led me some steps forward, only to enquire cautelously of the stranger ' From whence I came? ' A few saffron beards are seen at Hâyil: in his last years Abéyd ibn Rashîd had turned his grey hairs to a saffron beard. It is the Persian manner, and I may put that to my good fortune, being a traveller of the English colour, in Arabia. The welfaring men stain their eyes with kahl; and of these bird-like Arabians it is the male sex which is bright-feathered and adorned. Near the sûk's end is their corn market, and where are sold camel-loads of fire-wood, and wild hay from the wilderness. Lower I saw veiled women-sellers under a porch with baskets where they sit daily from the sunrise to sell dates and pumpkins; and some of them sell poor ornaments from the north. for the hareem.

We came into the long-square public place, *el-Méshab*, which is before the castle, *el-Kasr.* Under the next porch, which is a refuge of poor Beduin passengers, Nasr couched my camel, hastily, and setting down the bags, he withdrew from me ; the poor nomad was afraid. Abd el-Azîz, coming again from the Kasr, asked me why was I sitting in that place ? he sat down by me to enquire again of my health. He seemed to wish the stranger well, but in that to have a fear of blame,—had he not also encouraged my coming hither ? He left me and entered the Kasr gate, to speak anew with the Emir. Abd el-Azîz, in the rest a worthy man, was timid and ungenerous, the end of life to them all is the least displeasure of Ibn Rashîd, and he was a servant of the Emir. A certain public seat is appointed him, under the Prince's private kahwa upon the Méshab, where he sat in attendance with his company at every mejlis. The people in the square had not yet observed the Nasrâny, and I sat on three-quarters of an hour, in the midst of Hâyil ;—in the meanwhile they debated perhaps of my life within yonder earthen walls of the castle. I thought the Arabian curiosity and avarice would procure me a respite : at least I hoped that someone would call me in from this pain of famine to breakfast.

In the further end of the Méshab were troops of couched thelûls ; they were of Beduin fellowships which arrived daily, to treat of their affairs with the Emir. Certain of the Beduw now gathered about me, who wondered to see the stranger sitting under this porch. I saw also some personage that issued from the castle gate under a clay tower, in goodly fresh apparel, walking upon his stick of office, and he approached me. This was *Mufarrij, rájul el-Mothíf,* or marshal of the Prince's guest-hall, a foreigner, as are so many at Hâyil of those that serve the Emir. His town was Aneyza in Kasîm (which he had forsaken upon a horrible misadventure, afterwards to be related). The comely steward came to bid the stranger in to breakfast ; but first he led me and my nâga through the Méshab, and allotted me a lodging, the last in the row of guest-chambers, *mákhzans,* which are in the long side of this public place in front of the Kasr : then he brought me in by the castle-gate, to the great coffee-hall, which is of the guests, and the castle service of the Emir. At this hour—long after all had breakfasted and gone forth—it was empty, but they sent for the coffee-server. I admired the noble proportions of this clay hall, as before of the huge Kasr ; the lofty walls, painted in device with ochre and jiss, and the rank of tall pillars, which in the midst upheld the simple flat roof, of ethel timbers and palm-stalk mat-work, goodly stained and varnished with the smoke of the daily hospitality. Under the walls are benches of clay overspread with Bagdad carpets. By the entry stands

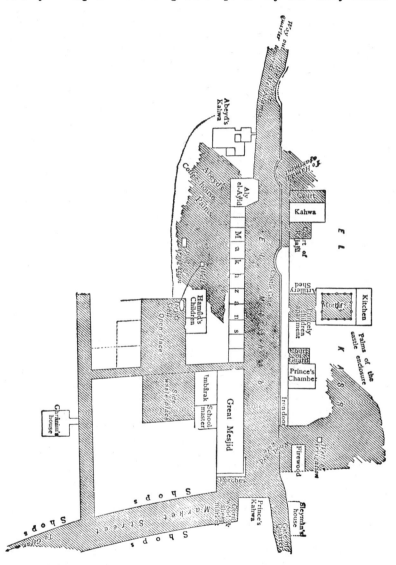

a mighty copper-tinned basin or " sea " of water, with a chained cup (daily replenished by the hareem of the public kitchen from the mâ es-Sáma); from thence the coffee-server draws, and he may drink who thirsts. In the upper end of this princely kahwa are two fire-pits, like shallow graves, where desert bushes are burned in colder weather; they lack good fuel, and fire is blown commonly under the giant coffee-pots in a clay hearth like a smith's furnace. I was soon called out by Mufarrij to the guest-hall, *mothíf;* this guest-house is made within the castle buildings, a square court cloistered, and upon the cloisters is a gallery. Guests pass in by the Prince's artillery, which are five or six small pieces of cannon; the iron is old, the wood is ruinous.

The Beduins eat below, but principal sheykhs and their fellowships in the galleries; Mufarrij led me upstairs, to a place where a carpet was belittered with old date-stones. Here I sat down and dates were brought me,—the worst dates of their desert world—in a metal standish, thick with greasy dust; they left me to eat, but I chose still to fast. Such is the Arabian Ruler's morning cheer to his guests—they are Beduw—and unlike the desert cleanness of the most Arabian villages, where there is water enough. Till they should call me away I walked in the galleries, where small white house-doves of Irâk were flittering, and so tame that I took them in my hands. I found these clay-floor galleries eighty feet long; they are borne upon five round pillars with rude shark's-tooth chapiters. Mufarrij appearing again we returned to the kahwa where coffee was now ready. A young man soon entered shining in silken clothing, and he began to question me. This Arabian cockney was the Prince's secretary, his few words sounded disdainfully : " I say, eigh ! what art thou ?—whence comest thou, and where-fore hast thou come ? " I answered after the nomad sort, " Weled, I can but answer one question at once ; let me hear what is thy first request : " he showed himself a little out of countenance at a poor man's liberal speech, and some friendly voice whispered to me, " Treat him with more regard, for this is *Nasr.*" So said this Nasr, " Up ! the Emir calls thee : " and we went out towards the Prince's quarters.

There is made a long gallery under the body of the clay castle-building, next the outer wall upon the Méshab ; by this we passed, and at the midst is an iron-plated door, kept by a young Galla slave within ; and there we knocked. The door opens into a small inner court, where a few of the Emir's men-at-arms sit in attendance upon him ; at the south side is his chamber. We went through and entered from the doorway of his open chamber into a dim light, for their windows are but casements to the air, and no glass panes are seen in all Nejd. The ruler Mohammed—a younger son of Abdullah ibn Rashîd, the first prince of Shammar, and the fourth Emir since his father—was lying half along upon his elbow, with leaning-cushions under him, by his fire-pit side, where a fire of the desert bushes was burning before him. I saluted him "*Salaam aleyk*, Peace be with thee;" he lifted the right hand to his head, the manner he had seen in the border countries, but made me no answer;—their hostile opinion that none out of the saving religion may give the word of God's peace! He wore the long braided hair-locks for whose beauty he is commended in the desert as 'a fresh young man.' His skin is more than commonly tawny, and even yellowish; lean of flesh and hollow as the Nejders, he is of middle height: his is a shallow Nejd visage, and Mohammed's bird-like looks are like the looks of one survived out of much disease of the world,—and what likelihood was there formerly that he should ever be the Emir?

"Sit down!" he said. Mohammed, who under the former Princes was conductor of the "Persian" Haj, had visited the cities of Mesopotamia, and seen the manners of the Dowla.— The chief of the guard led me to the stranger's seat. In the midst of a long carpet spread under the clay wall, between my place and the Emir, sat some personage leaning upon cushions; he was, I heard, a kinsman of Ibn Rashîd, a venerable man of age and mild countenance. The Emir questioned me, "From whence comest thou, and what is the purpose of thy voyage?"—"I am arrived from Teyma, and el-Héjr, and I came down from Syria to visit Medáin Sâlih."—"*Rájul sadúk*, wellah! a man to trust (exclaimed that old sheykh). This is not like him who came hither, thou canst remember Mohammed in what year, but one that tells us all things plainly." *Emir*: "And now from Teyma, well! and what sawest thou at Teyma—anything?"—"Teyma is a pleasant place of palms in a good air."—"Your name?"—"Khalîl."—"Ha! and you have been with the Beduw, eigh Khalîl, what dost thou think of the Beduw? *Of the Beduw there are none good:*—thou wast with which Beduins?" "The Fukara, the Moahîb, the Sehamma beyond the Harra."—"And what dost thou think of the Fejîr, and of their sheykhs? Motlog, he is not good?"—"The Fukara are not unlike their name, their neighbours call them Yahûd Kheybar." The Emir, half wondering and smiling, took up my words (as will the Arabians) and repeated them to those present: "He says they are the Yahûd Kheybar! and well, Khalîl, how did the Aarab deal with thee? they milked for thee, they showed thee hospitality?"—"Their milk is too little for themselves." The Emir mused and looked down, for he had heard that I wandered with the Beduins to drink camel milk. "Ha! and the Moahîb, he asked, are they good? and Tollog, is he good?"—The Emir waited that I should say nay, for Tollog was an old enemy or 'rebel' of theirs.—"The man was very good to me, I think he is a worthy Beduin person." To this he said, "*Hmm hmm!*—and the Sehamma, who is their sheykh?"—"Mahanna and Fóthil."—"And how many byût are they?"

He said now, "Have you anything with you (to sell)? and what is thy calling?"—"I have medicines with me, I am an hakîm."—"What medicines? *kanakîna* (quinine)?"—"This I have of the best."—"And what besides?"—"I have this and that, but the names are many; also I have some very good *chai*, which I will present to thee, Emir!"—"We have chai here, from Bagdad; no, no, we have enough." [Afterward it was said to me, in another place,—"He would not accept thy chai, though it were never so good: Ibn Rashîd will eat or drink of nothing which is not prepared for him by a certain slave of his; he lives continually in dread to be poisoned."] *Emir:* "Well! thou curest what diseases? canst thou cure the mejnûn?" (the troubled, by the jan, in their understanding):— the Emir has some afflicted cousins in the family of Abeyd, and in his heart might be his brother Telâl's sorrowful re-membrance. I answered, "*El-mejnûn hu mejnûn*, who is a fool by nature, he is a fool indeed." The Emir repeated this wisdom after me, and solemnly assenting with his head, he said to those present, "*Hu sâdik*, he saith truth!" Some courtiers answered him "*Fi tarîk*, but there is a way in this also." The Aarab sup-pose there is a *tarîk*, if a man might find it, a God-given way, to come to what end he will.—"And tell me, which beasts thou sawest in the wilderness?"—"Hares and gazelles, I am not a hunter."—"Is the hare unlawful meat!—you eat it? (he would know thus if I were truly a Christian). And the swine you eat?" I said, "There is a strange beast in the Sherarát wilder-ness, which they call wild ox or wothŷhi, and I have some horns of it from Teyma."—"Wouldst thou see the wothŷhi? we have one of them here, and will show it thee." Finally he said, "Dost thou 'drink' smoke?" The use of tobacco, not yet seen in the Nejd streets but tolerated within doors, is they think un-becoming in persons of more than the common people's dignity and religion. Mohammed himself and Hamûd his cousin were formerly honest brothers of the galliûn; but come up to estimation, they had forsaken their solace of the aromatic Hameydy. The Emir said further, "So you are Mesîhy?"

—that was a generous word! he would not call me by the reproachful name of Nasrâny; also the Emir, they say, "has a Christian woman among his wives."—Christians of the Arabic tongue in the great border lands name themselves *Mesíhiyûn.*

He bade Nasr read in a great historical book which lay upon a shelf, bound in red (*Akhbâru-'d-Dúal wa athâru-'l-Uwwal*), what was written therein of the prophet *Isa ibn Miriam;*—and the secretary read it aloud. The Mohammedan author tells us of the person, the colour, the human lineaments of Jesus, "son of the virgin;" and the manner of his prophetic life, how he walked with his disciples in the land of Israel, and that his wont was to rest in that place where the sun went down upon him. The Emir listened sternly to this tale, and impatiently.—"And well, well! but what could move thee (he said) to take such a journey?" I responded suddenly, "*El-elûm!* the liberal sciences;" but the sense of this plural is, in Nejd and in the Beduin talk, *tidings.* The Ruler answered hastily, "And is it for this thou art come hither!" It was difficult to show him what I intended by the sciences, for they have no experience of ways so sequestered from the common mouth-labours of mankind. He said then, "And this language, didst thou learn it among the Beduw, readest thou *Araby?*"— He bade Nasr bring the book, and put it in Khalîl's hands. Mohammed rose himself from his place, [he is said to be very well read in the Arabic letters, and a gentle poet though, in the dispatch of present affairs of state, he is too busy-headed to be longer a prentice in unprofitable learning]— and with the impatient half-childish curiosity of the Arabians, the Emir Ibn Rashîd himself came over and sat down beside me.—"Where shall I read?"—"Begin anywhere at a chapter,— there!" and he pointed with his finger. So I read the place, '*The king* (such an one) *slew all his brethren and kindred.*' It was *Sheytán* that I had lighted upon such a bloody text; the Emir was visibly moved! and, with the quick feeling of the Arabs, he knew that I regarded him as a murderous man. "Not there! he said hastily, but read here!—out of this chapter above" (beating the place with his finger); so I read again some passage. *Emir:* "Ha, well! I see thou canst read a little," so rising he went again to his place. Afterward he said, "And whither wouldst thou go now?"—"To Bagdad."—"Very well, we will send thee to Bagdad," and with this word the Emir rose and those about him to go forth into his palm grounds, where he would show me the 'wild kine.' Nasr then came with a letter-envelope in his hand, and

asked me to read the superscription. " Well, I said, this is not
Arabic ! "—" Ay, and therefore we wish thee to read it."—" From
whom had ye this letter ? "—" From a Nasrâny, who came from
the Haurân hither, and *this we took from him.*" Upon the seal I
found in Greek letters *Patriarchate of Damascus,* and the legend
about it was in Latin, *Go ye into all the world and preach
this gospel to every creature.* They were stooping to put on
their sandals, and awaited a moment to hear my response ;
and when I recited aloud the sense *Ukhruju fî kulli el-
âlam......* the venerable sheykh said piously to the Emir :
" Mohammed, hearest thou this ?—and they be the words of
the Messîah ! "

All they that were in his chamber now followed abroad with
the Emir ; these being his courtier friends and attendance.
Besides the old sheykh, the captain of the guard, and Nasr,
there was not any man of a good countenance amongst them.
They of the palace and the Prince's men wear the city gown,
but go ungirded. Mohammed the Emir appeared to me, when
we came into the light, like a somewhat undergrown and hard-
favoured Beduwy of the poorer sort ; but he walked loftily and
with somewhat unquiet glancing looks. At the irrigation well,
nigh his castle walls, he paused, and showing me with his
hand the shrill running wheel-work, he asked suddenly, " Had I
seen such gear ? "—" How many fathoms have ye here ? "—
" Fifteen." He said truly his princely word, though I thought
it was not so,—for what could it profit them to draw upon the
land from so great depths ? I walked on with Mohammed
and the old sheykh, till we came to his plantation, enclosed
in the castle wall ; it seemed to me not well maintained. The
Emir stayed at a castor-oil plant (there was not another in
Hâyil) to ask " What is that ? " He questioned me, between
impatient authority and the untaught curiosity of Arabians,
of his plants and trees,—palms and lemons, and the thick-
rinded citron ; then he showed me a seedling of the excellent pot-herb *bâmiya* and thyme, and single roots of other
herbs and salads. All such green things they eat not ! so unlike is the diet of Nejd Arabia to the common use in the Arabic
border countries.

Gazelles were running in the further walled grounds ; the
Emir stood and pointed with his finger, " There (he said) is
the wothŷhi ! " [*v.* p. 327—8.] This was a male of a year and
a half, no bigger than a great white goat ; he lay sick under
a fig-tree. *Emir :*—" But look yonder, where is a better, and
that is the cow."—" Stand back for fear of her horns ! the
courtiers said about me, do not approach her." One went

out with a bunch of date twigs to the perilous beast, and stroked her ; her horns were like sharp rods, set upright, the length I suppose of twenty-seven inches. I saw her, about five yards off, less than a small ass ; the hide was ash-coloured going over to a clear yellow, there was a slight rising near the root of her neck, and no hump, her smooth long tail ended in a bunch. She might indeed be said " to resemble a little cow " ; but very finely moulded was this creature of the waterless wilderness, to that fiery alacrity of their wild limbs. " *Uktub-ha !* write, that is portray, her ! " exclaimed the Emir. As we returned, he chatted with me pleasantly ; at last he said " Where are thy sandals ? "— " Little wonder if you see me unshod and my clothing rent, it is a year since I am with the Beduw in the khála."—" And though he go without soles (answered the kind old sheykh), it is not amiss, for thus went even the prophets of Ullah."—This venerable man was, I heard, the Emir's mother's brother : he showed me that mild and benevolent countenance, which the Arabs bear for those to whom they wish a good adventure.

The Emir in his spirituous humour, and haughty familiar manners, was much like a great sheykh of the Aarab. In him is the mark of a former contrary fortune, with some sign perhaps of a natural baseness of mind ; Mohammed was now " fully forty years old," but he looked less. We came again into the Kasr yard, where the wood is stored, and there are two-leaved drooping gates upon the Méshab ; here is the further end of that gallery under the castle, by which we had entered. The passage is closed by an iron-plated door ; the plates (in their indigence of the arts) are the shield-like iron pans (*tannúr*) upon which the town housewives bake their girdle-bread.—But see the just retribution of tyrants ! they fear most that make all men afraid. Where is—the sweetest of human things— their repose ? for that which they have gotten from many by their power, they know by the many to be required of them again ! There the Emir dismissed the Nasrány, with a friendly gesture, and bade one accompany me to my beyt or lodging.

CHAPTER XXII.

WHEN this day's sun was setting, Mufarrij called me to the
Mothîf gallery, where a supper-dish was set before me of
mutton and temmn. When I came again into the coffee-hall,
as the cup went round there began to be questioning among
the Beduin guests and those of the castle service, of my
religion. I returned early to my beyt, and then I was called
away by his servants to see one, whom they named " The Great
Sheykh."—' Who was, I asked, that great sheykh?' they answered
" *El-Emir!* " So they brought me to a dàr, which was nearly
next by, and this is named Kahwat Abeyd. They knocked and
a Galla slave opened the door. We passed in by a short entry,
which smelled cheerfully of rose-water, to that which seemed
to my eyes full of the desert a goodly hall-chamber. The
Oriental rooms are enclosures of the air, without moveables,
and their only ornaments are the carpets for sitting-places,

here laid upon the three sides of the upper end, with pillowed places for "the Emir" and his next kinsman. All was clay, the floor is beaten clay, the clay walls I saw were coloured in ochre; the sitters were principal persons of the town, a Beduin sheykh or two, and men of the princely service; and bright seemed the civil clothing of these fortunate Arabs.—They had said 'The Emir'! and in the chief place I saw a great noble figure half lying along upon his elbow!—but had I not seen the Prince Ibn Rashîd himself this morning? If the common sort of Arabs may see a stranger bewildered among them, it is much to their knavish pleasure.

This personage was *Hamûd*, heir, although not the eldest son, of his father Abeyd; for *Fâhd*, the elder, was *khíbel*, of a troubled understanding, but otherwise of a good and upright behaviour; the poor gentleman was always much my friend.—The princely Hamûd has bound his soul by oath to his cousin the Emir, to live and to die with him; their fathers were brethren and, as none remain of age of the Prince's house, Hamûd ibn Rashîd is next after Mohammed in authority, is his deputy at home, fights by his side in the field, and he bears the style of Emir. Hamûd is the Ruler's companion in all daily service and counsel.—The son of Abeyd made me a pleasant countenance, and bade me be seated at his right hand, and when he saw I was very weary, he bade me stretch' the legs out easily, and sit without any ceremony.

Hamûd spoke friendly to the Nasrâny stranger; I saw he was of goodly great stature, with painted eyes, hair shed [as we use to see in the images of Christ] and hanging down from the midst in tresses, and with little beard. His is a pleasant man-like countenance, he dissembles cheerfully a slight crick in the neck, and turns it to a grace, he seems to lean forward. In our talk he enquired of those marvellous things of the Nasâra, the telegraph, 'and glass, was made of what? also they had heard to be in our Christian countries a palace of crystal; and Baris (Paris) a city builded all of crystal; also what thing was rock oil,' of which there stood a lamp burning on a stool before them: it is now used in the principal houses of Hâyil, and they have a saying that the oil is made from human urine. He wondered when I told them it is drawn from wells in the New World; he had heard of that *Dínya el-jedîda*, and enquired to which quarter it lay, and beyond what seas. He asked me of my medicines, and then he said, "Lean towards me, I would enquire a thing of thee." Hamûd whispered, under the wing of his perfumed kerchief, "Hast thou no medicine, that may enable a man?" I answered immediately, "No, by thy life."—

" No, by my life ! " he repeated, turning again, and smiled
over to the audience, and laughed cheerfully, " ha ! ha ! "—for
some crabbed soul might misdeem that he had whispered of
poison. Also that common oath of the desert, " By thy life,"
is blamed among these half-Wahábies. Hamûd said, with the
same smiling demeanour, " Seest thou here those two horsemen
which met with thee upon the road ? "—" I cannot tell, for I was
most weary."—" Ay, he said with the Arabian humanity, thou
wast very weary ; ask him ! " Hamûd showed me with his finger
a personage, one of the saffron-beards of Hâyil, who sat leaning upon cushions, in the place next by him, as next in dignity
to himself. This was a dull-witted man, *Sleymàn*, and his
cousin. I asked him, " Was it thou ? " but he, only smiling,
answered nothing. *Hamûd:* " Look well ! were they like us ?
be we not the two horsemen ?—It was a match, Khalîl, to try
which were the better breathed of our two mares ; how seest
thou ? the horses of the Engleys are better, or our Nejd horses ? "
—Hamûd now rising to go to rest (his house is in another
part), we all rose with him. In that house—it stands by the
public birket which is fed from the irrigation of this kahwa
palm-yard—are his children, a wife and her mother, and
his younger brothers ; but, as a prince of the blood, he has a
lodging for himself (where he sleeps) within the castle building.
The Hâyil Princes are clad as the nomads, but fresh and cleanly
and in the best stuffs ; their long wide tunic is, here in the town,
washed white as a surplice, and upon their shoulders is the
Aarab mantle of finer Bagdad woollen, or of the black cloth of
Europe. They wear the haggu upon their bodies, as in all
nomad Arabia.

I was but ill-housed in my narrow, dark, and unswept cell :—
they told me, a Yahûdy also, at his first coming, had lodged
there before me ! This was a Bagdad Jew, now a prosperous
Moslem dwelling at Hâyil and married, and continually increasing with the benediction of the son-in-law of Laban ; the
man had a good house in the town, and a shop in the sûk,
where he sold clothing and dates and coffee to the nomads : his
Hâyil wife had borne him two children. The gaping people
cried upon me, " Confess thou likewise, Khalîl, ' There is one
God, and His apostle is Mohammed,' and thine shall be an
equal fortune, which the Emir himself will provide." From the
morrow's light there was a gathering of sick and idle townsmen to the Nasrâny's door, where they sat out long hours
bibble-babbling, and left me no moment of repose. They asked
for medicines, promising, ' If they found them good remedies
they would pay me, but not now.' When I answered they

might pay me the first cost for the drugs, this discouraged them; and nothing can be devised to content their knavish meaning. I said at length, "None of you come here to chaffer with me, for I will not hear you," and putting my door to upon them, I went out. As I sat at my threshold in the cool of the afternoon, Hamûd went by with his friends; he stayed to greet me, and bade me come to supper, and showed me his sword, which he carries loosely in his hand with the baldric, like the nomads, saying, "What thinkest thou of it?"—they suppose that every son of the Nasâra should be schooled in metal-craft. As I drew his large and heavy blade out of the scabbard—the steel was not Damascened—Hamûd added, "It is Engleys" (of the best Christian countries' work): he had this sabre from Ibn Saûd, and "paid for it one thousand reals." "It seems to be excellent," I said to him, and he repeated the words smiling in their manner, "It is excellent." The sword is valued by the Arabians as the surest weapon; they all covet to have swords of the finest temper.

At sunset came a slave from Abeyd's coffee-hall to lead me to supper. Hamûd sups there when he is not called to eat with the Emir; his elder son *Májid*, and the boy's tutor, eat with him; and after them, the same dish is set before the men of his household. His simple diet is of great nourishment, boiled mutton upon a mess of temmn, with butter, seasoned with onions, and a kind of curry. When the slave has poured water upon our hands, from a metal ewer, over a laver, we sit down square-legged about the great brazen tinned dish upon the carpet floor. "*Mudd yédak*, Reach forth thine hand" is the Arabs' bidding, and with "*Bismillah*, In the name of God," they begin to eat with their fingers. They sit at meat not above eight or ten minutes, when they are fully satisfied; the slave now proffers the bowl, and they drink a little water; so rising they say "*El-hamd illah*, The Lord be praised," and go apart to rinse the mouth, and wash their hands:—the slave lad brought us grated soap. So they return to their places refreshed, and the cheerful cup is served round: but the coffee-server—for the fear of princes—tasted before Hamûd. There is no banqueting among them. Arabians would not be able to believe, that the food-creatures of the three inhabited elements (in some happier lands) may hardly sustain an human entrail; and men's sitting to drink away their understanding must seem to them a very horrible heathenish living. Here are no inordinate expenses of the palace, no homicide largesses to smooth favourites of the spoil of the lean people. Soon after the sunrising, the Shammar princes breakfasted of girdle-bread and butter with a draught of milk; at noon a dish of dates is set before them; at sunset they sup as we have now seen: Prince and people, they are all alike soberly dieted. The devil is not in their dish; all the riot and wantonness of their human nature lies in the Mohammedan luxury of hareem.— I remember to have heard, from some who knew him, of the diet of the late Sultan of Islam, Abd el-Azîz, otherwise reproached for his insatiable luxury. Only one dish—which his mother had tasted and sealed—was set before him, and that was the Turks' every-day *pilaw* (which they say came in with Tamerlane) of boiled rice and mutton; he abstained (for a cause which may be divined) from coffee and tobacco. I heard Hamûd say he had killed the sheep in my honour; but commonly his supper mutton is bought in the sûk.

An hour or two after, when the voice of the muétthin is heard in the night calling to the last prayer, Hamûd never fails to rise with the company. A slave precedes him with a flaming palm leaf-branch; and they go out to pray in the mosque, which is upon the further part of the Méshab, [*v.* the fig. p. 587,] ranging with the guest-chambers, but separated by a small thoroughfare from them.—Princes of men, they are bond-servants to a doting religion!

When Hamûd returns, a little *sajjeydy* or kneeling-carpet reserved only to this use is unrolled by the slave in waiting before him; and the princely man falling upon his knees towards Mecca says on to great length more his formal devotion. One evening I asked him, ' But had he not already said his prayers in the mesjid ? '—" Those, Hamûd answered, which we say in the mesjid are a man's legal prayers, and these are of the tradition, sunna." The sitters in the coffee-hall did not stint their chatting, whilst Hamûd prayed,—there prayed no man with him. The rest were not princes, why should they take upon them this superfluous religion! and the higher is a Moslem's estate, by so much the more he must show himself devoted and as it were deserving of God's benefits. Hamûd never fails at the mosque in the hours; and in all the rest with the cheerful air of a strong man he carries his own great fortune, and puts by the tediousness of the world. He might be a little less of age than the Emir; in his manly large stature he nearly resembles, they say, the warlike poet his father: Hamûd and the Emir Mohammed are not novices in the gentle skill inherited from their fathers in this princely family; —their new making is extolled by the common voice above the old.

The Prince Mohammed goes but once at el-assr to prayers

in the great mesjid ; he prays in an oratory within the castle, or standing formally in his own chamber. And else so many times to issue from the palace to their public devotion, were a tediousness to himself and to his servitors, and to the towns-people, for all fear when they see him, since he bears the tyrant's sword. And Mohammed fears !—the sword which has entered this princely house ' shall never depart from them —so the Aarab muse—until they be destroyed.' He cut down all the high heads of his kindred about him, leaving only Hamûd ; the younger sort are growing to age ; and Mohammed must see many dreams of dread, and for all his strong security, is ever looking for the retribution of mankind. Should he trust himself to pass the Méshab oftentimes daily at certain hours ?—but many have miscarried thus. Both Hamûd and the Emir Mohammed affect popular manners : Hamûd with an easy frankness, and that smiling countenance which seems not too far distant from the speech of the common people ; Mohammed with some softening, where he may securely, of his princely asperity, and sowing his pleasant word between ; he is a man very subtle witted, and of an acrid understanding. Mohammed as he comes abroad casts his unquiet eyes like a falcon ; he walks, with somewhat the strut of a stage-player, in advance of his chamber-followers, and men-at-arms. When Hamûd is with him, the Princes walk before the rout. The townspeople (however this be deemed impossible) say ' they *love him and fear him :* '—they praise the prince under whose sufficient hand they fare the better, and live securely, and see all prosper about them ; but they dread the sharpness, so much fleshed already, of the Ruler's sword.

The evening after, Mohammed sent for me to his apart-ment : the clay walls are stained with ochre. When I said to the Emir, I was an Englishman, this he had not understood before ! he was now pleasant and easy. There sat with him a great swarthy man, Sâlih, (I heard he was of the nomads,) who watched me with fanatical and cruel eyes, saying at length in a fierce sinister voice, " Lookest thou to see thy land again ? " —" All things, I answered, are in the power of Ullah."—" Nay, nay, Sâlih ! exclaimed the Emir, and Khalîl has said very well, that all things are in the hand of Ullah." Mohammed then asked me nearly Hamûd's questions. " The telegraph is what ? and we have seen it (at Bagdad in time of his old conductorship of the ' Persian ' pilgrims) : but canst thou not make known to us the working, which is wonderful ? "— "It is a trepidation—therewith we may make certain signs—engendered

189

in the corrosion of metals, by strong medicines like vinegar."
Emir : " Then it is an operation of medicine, canst thou not
declare it ? "—" If we may suppose a man laid head and heels
between Hâyil and Stambûl, of such stature that he touched
them both ; if one burned his feet at Hâyil, should he not feel it
at the instant in his head, which is at Stambûl ? "—" And glass
is what ? " He asked also of petroleum ; and of the New Continent, where it lay, and whether within ' the Ocean.' He listened
coldly to my tale of the finding of the New Land over the great
seas, and enquired, " Were no people dwelling in the country
when it was discovered ? " At length he asked me, ' How did
I see Hâyil ? and the market street, was it well ? but ah (he
answered himself) it is a *sûk Aarab !* ' little in comparison
with the chief cities of the world. He asked ' Had I heard of
J. Shammar in my own country ? ' The ruler was pleased to
understand that the Nasâra were not gaping after his desert
provinces ; but it displeased the vain-glory of the man that
of all this troublous tide of human things under his govern-
ance, nearly no rumour was come to our ears in a distant
land. Hamûd asked of me another while the like question,
and added, " What ! have ye never heard of Ibn Saûd the
Waháby ! " When I had sat two hours, and it might be
ten o'clock, the Emir said to the captain of the guard, who
is groom of his chamber, " It is time to shut the doors ; " and
I departed.

In the early days of my being in Hâyil, if I walked
through their sûk, children and the ignorant and poor Beduw
flocked to me, and I passed as the cuckoo with his cloud of
wondering small birds, until some citizen of more authority
delivered me, saying to them, ' Wellah, thus to molest the
stranger would be displeasing to the Emir ! ' Daily some
worthy persons called me to coffee and to breakfast ; the
most of them sought counsel of the hakîm for their diseases,
few were moved by mere hospitality, for their conscience
bids them show no goodness to an adversary of the saving
religion ; but a Moslem coming to Hâyil, or even a Frankish
stranger easily bending and assenting to them, might find
the Shammar townspeople hospitable, and they are accounted
such.

And first I was called to one *Ghrânim,* the Prince's
jeweller, and his brother *Ghruneym.* They were rich men,
of the smiths' caste, formerly of Jauf, where are some of
the best sânies, for their work in metal, wood, and stone,
in nomad Arabia. Abeyd at the taking of the place found
these men the best of their craft, and he brought them

perforce to Hâyil. They are continually busied to labour
for the princes, in the making and embellishing of sword-
hilts with silver and gold wire, and the inlaying of gun-
stocks with glittering scales of the same. All the best
sword-blades and matchlocks, taken (from the Beduw) in
Ibn Rashîd's forays, are sent to them to be remounted, and
are then laid up in the castle armoury. Of these, some
very good Persian and Indian blades are put in the hands
of the Emir's men-at-arms. In his youth, Ghrânim had
wandered in his metal trade about the Haurân, and now he
asked me of the sheykhs of the Druses, such and such whom
he had known, were they yet alive. The man was fanatical,
his understanding was in his hands, and his meditations
were not always of the wise in the world : so daily meeting me, Ghrânim said before other words, " Khalîl, I am
thine enemy ! " and in the end he would proffer his friendly
counsels.—He had made this new clay house and adorned it
with all his smith's art. Upon the earthen walls, stained with
ochre, were devices of birds and flowers, and koran versets in
white daubing of jiss,—which is found everywhere in the desert
sand : the most houses at Hâyil are very well built, though
the matter be rude. He had built a double wall with a casement in each, to let the light pass, and not the weather. I saw
no sooty smith's forge within, but Ghrânim was sitting freshly
clad at his labour, in his best chamber ; his floor was spread with
fine matting, and the sitting places were Bagdad carpets. His
brother Ghruneym called away the hakîm to his own house
to breakfast : he was hindered in his craft by sickness and the
Emir ofttimes threatened to forsake him. His son showed
me an army rifle [from India] whereupon I found the Tower
mark ; the sights—they not understanding their use !—had
been taken away.

The Jew-Moslem—he had received the name *Abdullah,* " the
Lord's servitor," and the neophyte surname *el-Moslemanny*—
came to bid me to coffee. His companion asked me, ' Did
my nation love the Yahûd ? ' " We enquire not, I answered,
of men's religions, so they be good subjects." We came to
the Jew's gate, and entered his house ; the walls within were
pleasantly stained with ochre, and over-written with white
flowerets and religious versets, in daubing of gypsum. I read :
" THERE IS NO POWER BUT OF GOD ; " and in the apostate's
entry, instead of Moses' words, was scored up in great letters
the Mohammedan testimony, " There is none other god than
(very) God, and Mohammed is the apostle of (very) God."
Abdullah was a well-grown man of Bagdad with the pleasant

elated countenance of the Moslemîn, save for that mark (with peace be it spoken) which God has set upon the Hebrew lineaments. Whilst his companion was absent a moment, he asked me under his breath "Had I with me any—" (I could not hear what).—"What sayest thou?" "*Brandi*, you do not know this (English Persian Gulf word)—brandi?" His fellow entering, it might be his wife's brother, Abdullah said now in a loud voice, 'Would I become a Moslem, his house should be mine along with him.' He had whispered besides a word in my ear—"I have a thing to say to thee, but not at this time." It was seven years since this Bagdad Jew arrived at Hâyil. After the days of hospitality he went to Abeyd saying, he would make profession of the religion of Islam ' upon his hand ' ; —and Abeyd accepted the Jew's words upon his formal hand full of old bloodshed and violence. The princely family had endowed the Moslemanny at his conversion with " a thousand reals," and the Emir licensed him to live at Hâyil, where buying and selling,—and Abdullah knew the old art,—he was now a thriving tradesman. I had heard of him at Teyma, and that ' he read in such books as those they saw me have ': yet I found him a man without instruction,—doubtless he read Hebrew, yet now he denied it.

A merchant in the town, *Jâr Ullah*, brought me a great foreign folio. It was a tome printed at Amsterdam in the last century, in Hebrew letters ! so I said to him, " Carry it to Abdullah, this is the Jews' language."—" Abdullah tells me he knows it not."—This book was brought hither years before from the salvage of a Bagdad caravan, that had perished of thirst in the way to Syria. Their dalîl, " because Ullah had troubled his mind," led them astray in the wilderness ; the caravaners could not find the wells, and only few that had more strength saved themselves, riding at adventure and happily lighting upon Beduins. The nomads fetched away what they would of the fallen-down camel-loads, ' for a month and more.' There were certain books found amongst them, a few only of such unprofitable wares had been brought in to Hâyil.

It was boasted to me that the Jew-born Abdullah was most happy here ; ' many letters had been sent to him by his parents, with the largest proffers if he would return, but he always refused to receive them.' He had forsaken the Law and the Promises ;—but a man who is moved by the affections of human nature, may not so lightly pass from all that in which he has been cherished and bred up in the world !

Jâr Ullah invited me to his spacious house, which stands

in the upper street near the Gofar gate : he was a principal corn-merchant. One *Nasr*, a fanatical Harb Beduwy of the *rajajîl*, meeting with us in the way, and *Aneybar* coming by then, we were all bidden in together : our worthy host, otherwise a little fanatical, made us an excellent breakfast. Aneybar was a *Hábashy*, a home-born Galla in Abdullah ibn Rashîd's household, and therefore to be accounted slave-brother of Telâl, Metaab and Mohammed : also his name is of the lord's house, Ibn Rashîd. This libertine was a principal personage in Hâyil, in affairs of state-trust under the Emirs since Telâl's time. The man was of a lively clear understanding, and courtly manners, yet in his breast was the timid soul-not-his-own of a slave : bred in this land, he had that suddenness of speech and the suspicious-mindedness of the Arabians.— When I came again to Hâyil Aneybar had the disposing of my life ;—it was a fair chance, to-day, that I broke bread with him !

Hamûd bade me again to supper, and as I was washing, " How white (said one) is his skin ! " Hamûd answered in a whisper, " It is the leprosy."—" Praised be God, I exclaimed, there are no lepers in my land."—" Eigh ! said Hamûd (a little out of countenance, because I overheard his words), is it so ? eigh ! eigh ! (for he found nothing better to say, and he added after me) the Lord be praised." Another said, " Wellah in Bagdad I have seen a maiden thus white, with yellow hair, that you might say she were Khalîl's daughter."— " But tell me (said the son of Abeyd), do the better sort in your country never buy the Circass women ?—or how is it among you to be the son of a bought-woman, and even of a bond-woman, I say is it not-convenient in your eyes ? "—When it seemed the barbaric man would have me to be, for that un-common whiteness, the son of a Circass bond-woman, I re-sponded with some warmth, " To buy human flesh is not so much as named in my country : as for all who deal in slaves we are appointed by God to their undoing. We hunt the cursed slave-sail upon all seas, as you hunt the hyena." Hamûd was a little troubled, because I showed him some flaws in their manners, some heathenish shadows in his religion where there was no spot in ours, and had vaunted our naval hostility, (whereby they all have damage in their purses, to the ends of the Mohammedan world).—" And Khalîl, the Nasâra eat swine's flesh ? "—" Ay billah, and that is not much unlike the meat of the wabar which ye eat, or of the porcupine. Do not the Beduw eat wolves and the hyena, the fox, the thób, and the spring-rat?—owls, kites, the carrion eagle? but I would taste of none such." Hamûd answered, with his easy humanity, "My meaning was not to say, Khalîl, that for any filth or sickliness of the meat we abstain from swine's flesh, but because the Néby has bidden us;" and turning to Sleymàn, he said, " I remember *Abdullah*, he that came to Hâyil in Telâl's time, and cured *Bunder*, told my father that the swine's flesh is very good meat."—" And what (asked that heavy head, now finding the tongue to utter his scurvy soul) is the wedlock of the Nasâra? as the horse covers the mare it is said [in all Nejd] the Nasâra be engendered,—wellah like the hounds! "

And though they eat no profane flesh, yet some at Hâyil drink the blood of the grape, *mâ el-enab*, the juice fer· mented of the fruit of the few vines of their orchards, here ripened in the midsummer season. Mâjid told me. that it is prepared in his father's household; the boy asked me if I had none such, and that was by likelihood his father's request. The Moslemîn, in their religious luxury, extremely covet the forbidden drink, imagining it should enable them with their wives.

When coffee was served at Hamûd's, I always sat wonder· ing that to me only the cup was not poured; this evening, as the servitor passed by with the pot and the cups, I made him a sign, and he immediately poured for me. An· other day Mâjid, who sat next me, exclaimed, " Drinkest thou no kahwa, Khalîl? " As I answered, " Be sure I drink it," the cup was poured out to me,—Hamûd looked up to· wards us, as if he would have said something. I could suppose it had been a friendly charge of his, to make me the more easy. In the Mohammedan countries a man's secret death is often in the fenjeyn kahwa. The Emir where he enters a house is not served with coffee, nor is coffee served to any in the Prince's apartment, but the Prince called for a cup when he desired it; such horrible apprehensions are in their daily. lives !

Among the evening sitters visiting Hamûd in the Kahwat Abeyd was a personage whom they named as a nobleman, and yet he was but a rich foreign merchant, *Seyyid Mahmûd*, the chief of the *Meshâhada* or tradesmen of Méshed, some thirty-five families, who are established in Hâyil; the bazaar merchan-dise (wares of Mesopotamia) is mostly in their hands; Méshed (place of the martyrdom of) Aly is at the ruins of *Kúfa*, they are Moslems of the Persian sect in religion.

These ungracious schismatics are tolerated and misliked in Ibn Rashîd's town, howbeit they are formal worshippers with the people in the common mesjid. They are much hated by the fanatical Beduins, so I have heard them say, " Nothing, billah, is more néjis than the accursed Meshâhada." Men of the civil North, they have itching ears for political tidings, and when they saw the Engleysy pass, some of them have called me into their shops to enquire news of the war,—as if dwelling this great while in the deserts I had any new thing to relate !—for of the Turkish Sûltàn's " victories " they believed nothing ! The (Beduin-like) princes in Hâyil have learned some things of them of the States of the world, and Hamûd said to me very soberly : " What is your opinion, may the Dowlat of the Sûltàn continue much longer ? "—" *Ullah Âlem* (God knoweth)."—" Ay ! ay ! but tell us, what is that your countrymen think ? "—" The Sûltàn is become very weak."—Hamûd was not sorry (they love not the Turk), and he asked me if I had been in el-Hind ;—the Prince every year sends his sale-horses thither, and the Indian govern-ment they hear to be of the Engleys. Hamûd had a lettered man in his household, Mâjid's tutor, one formed by nature to liberal studies. The tutor asked me tidings of the several Nasâra nations whose names he had heard, and more especially of Fransa and Brûssia, and *el-Nemsa*, that is the Austrian empire. " All this, I said, you might read excellently set out in a book I have of geography, written in Arabic by one of us long resident in es-Sham, it is in my chamber." —" Go Khalîl, and bring it to me," said Hamûd, and he sent one of his service to light before me, with a flaming palm-branch.

" How ! (said Hamûd, when we came again,) your people learn Arabic ! " I opened my volume at the chapter, *Peninsula of the Aarab.* Hamûd himself turned the leaves, and found the sweet verses, " Oh ! hail to thee, beloved Nejd, the whole world to me is not as the air of Nejd, the Lord prosper Nejd ; " and with a smile of happiness and half a sigh, the patriot, a kassâd himself, gave up the book to his man of letters, and added, wondering, " How is this ?—are the Nasâra then *ahl athâb*, polite nations ! and is there any such beautiful speaking used amongst them ? heigh !—Khalîl, are there many who speak thus ? " For all this the work was unwelcome among them, being written by one without the saving religion ! I showed the lettered man the place where Hâyil is mentioned, which he read aloud, and as he closed the book I said I would lend it him, which was (coldly) accepted. I put also in their hands the Psalter in Arabic of " Daûd Father of Sleymàn," names which they hear with a certain reverence, but whose *kitâb* they had never seen. Even this might not please them! as coming from the Nasâra, those 'corruptors of the scriptures'; and doubtless the title savoured to them of 'idolatry,'—*el-Mizamîr* (as it were songs to the pipe); and they would not read.

"Khalîl, said Hamûd, this is the Seyyid Mahmûd, and he is pleased to hear about medicines; visit him in his house, and he will set before thee a water-pipe,"—it is a keyif of foreigners and not used in Nejd. Hamûd told me another time he had never known any one of the tradesmen in Hâyil whose principal was above a thousand reals; only the Seyyid Mahmûd and other two or three wholesale merchants in the town, he said might have a little more. Of the foreign traders, besides those of Méshed, was one of Bagdad, and of Medina one other;—from Egypt and Syria no man. Hamûd bade me view the Emir's cannon when I passed by to the Mothîf:—I found them, then, to be five or six small ruinous field-pieces, and upon two were old German inscriptions. Such artillery could be of little service in the best hands; yet their shot might break the clay walling of Nejd towns. The Shammar princes had them formerly from the Gulf, yet few persons remembered when they had been used in the Prince's warfare, save that one cannon was drawn out in the late expedition with Boreyda against Aneyza; but the Emir's servants could not handle it. Two shots and no more were fired against the town; the first flew sky-high, and the second shot drove with an hideous dint before their feet into the desert soil.

—To speak now of the public day at Hâyil: it is near two hours after sunrise, when the Emir comes forth publicly to the Méshab to hold his morning mejlis, which is like the mejlis of the nomads. The great sheykh sits openly with the sheukh before the people; the Prince's mejlis is likewise the public tribunal, he sitting as president and judge amongst them. A bench of clay is made all along under the Kasr wall of the Méshab, in face of the mesjid, to the tower-gate; in the midst, raised as much as a degree and in the same clay-work (whereupon in their austere simplicity no carpet is spread), is the high settle of the Emir, with a single step beneath, upon which sits his clerk or secretary Nasr, at the Prince's feet. Hamûd's seat (such another clay settle and step, but a little lower) is that made nigh the castle door. A like ranging bank and high settle are seen under the opposite mesjid walls, where the sheukh sit in the afternoon shadow, holding the second mejlis, at el-assr. Upon the side, in face of the Emir, sits always the kâdy, or man of the religious law; of which sort there is more than one at Hâyil, who in any difficult process may record to the Emir the words, and expound the sense, of the koran scripture. At either side of the Prince sit shoykhly men, and court companions; the Prince's slaves stand before them; at the sides of the sheukh, upon the long clay bank, sit the chiefs of the public service and their companies; and mingled with them all, beginning from the next highest place after the Prince, there sit any visiting Beduins after their dignities. —You see men sitting as the bent of a bow before all this mejlis, in the dust of the Méshab, the *rajajil*, leaning upon their swords and scabbards, commonly to the number of one hundred and fifty; they are the men-at-arms, executors of the terrible Emir, and riders in his ghrazzus; they sit here (before the tyrant) in the place of the people in the nomads' mejlis. The mejlis at Hâyil is thus a daily muster of this mixed body of swords-men, many of whom in other hours of the day are civilly occupied in the town. Into that armed circuit suitors enter with the accused and suppliants, and in a word all who have any question (not of state), or appear to answer in public audience before the Emir; and he hears their causes, to every one shortly defining justice: and what judgments issue from the Prince's mouth are instantly executed. In the month of my being at Hâyil might be daily numbered sitting at the mejlis with the Emir about four hundred persons.

The Emir is thus brought nigh to the people, and he is acquainted with the most of their affairs. Mohammed's judg-ment and popular wisdom is the better, that he has some-time himself tasted of adversity. He is a judge with an indulgent equity, like a sheykh in the Beduin commonwealths, and just with a crude severity: I have never heard anyone speak against the Emir's true administration of justice. When I asked if there were no handling of bribes at Hâyil, by those who are nigh the Prince's ear, it was answered, " Nay." The Byzantine corruption cannot enter into the eternal and noble simplicity of this people's (airy) life, in the poor nomad country; but (we have seen) the art is not unknown to the subtle-headed Shammar princes, who thereby help themselves with the neighbour Turkish governments. Some also of Ibn Rashîd's Aarab, tribesmen of the Medina dîras, have seen the evil custom. a tale was told me of one of them who brought a bribe to advance his cause at Hâyil, and when his matter was about to be examined he privily put ten reals into the kâdy's hand. But the kâdy rising, with his stick laid load upon the guilty Beduin's shoulders until he was weary, and then he led him over to the Prince, sitting in his stall, who gave him many more blows himself, and commanded his slaves to beat him. The mejlis is seldom sitting above twenty minutes, and commonly there is little to hear, so that the Prince being unwell for some days (his ordinary suffering of headache and bile), I have seen it intermitted ;—and after that the causes of seven days were dispatched in a morning's sitting! The mejlis rising and dispersing, as the Prince is up, they say *Thâr el-Emir!*—and then, what for the fluttering of hundreds of gay cotton kerchiefs in the Méshab, we seem to see a fall of butterflies. The town Arabians go clean and honourably clad ; but the Beduins are ragged and even naked in their wandering villages.

The Emir walks commonly from the mejlis, with his companions of the chamber, to a house of his at the upper end of the Méshab, where they drink coffee, and sit awhile : and from thence he goes with a small attendance of his rajajîl to visit the stud ; there are thirty of the Prince's mares in the town, tethered in a ground next the clay castle, and nearly in face of the Kahwat Abeyd. After this the Emir dismisses his men, saying to them, "Ye may go, *eyyâl*," and re-enters the Kasr ; or sometimes with Hamûd and his chamber friends he walks abroad to breathe the air, it may be to his summer residence by the mâ es-Sáma, or to Abeyd's plantation : or he makes but a passage through the sûk to visit someone in the town, as Ghrânim the smith, to see how his orders are executed ;—and so he returned to the castle, when if he have any business with Beduins, or men from his villages, and messengers awaiting him, they will be admitted to his presence. It is a busy pensive life to be the ruler at Hâyil, and his witty head was always full of the perplexity of this world's affairs. Theirs is a very subtle Asiatic policy. In it is not the clement fallacy of the (Christian) Occident, to build so much as a rush upon the natural goodness (fondly imagined to be) in any man's breast ; for it is certain they do account most basely of all men, and esteem without remorse every human spirit to be a dunghill solitude by itself. Their (feline) prudence is for the time rather than seeing very far off, and always savours of the impotent suddenness of the Arab impatience. He rules as the hawk among buzzards, with eyes and claws in a land of ravin, yet in general not cruelly, for that would weaken him. An Arab stays not in long questioning, tedious knots are in peril to be resolved by the sword. Sometimes the Prince Ibn Rashîd rides to take the air on horseback, upon a white mare, and undergrown, as are the Nejd horses in their own country, nor very fairly shaped.

I was sitting one after-sunset upon the clay benching at the castle-gate when the Prince himself arrived, riding alone : I stood up to salute the Emir and his horse startled, seeing in the dusk my large white kerchief. Mohammed rode with stirrups, he urged his mare once, but she not obeying, the witty Arab ceded to his unreasonable beast ; and lightly dismounting the Emir led in and delivered her to the first-coming hand of his castle service.

Beduin companies arrived every day for their affairs with the Prince, and to every such company or *rubba* is allotted a makhzan, and they are public guests (commonly till the third day) in the town. Besides the tribesmen his tributaries, I have seen at Hâyil many foreign Beduins as *Thuffir* and *Meteyr*, that were friendly Aarab without his confederacy and dominion, yet from whom Ibn Rashîd is wont to receive some yearly presents. Moreover there arrived tribesmen of the free Northern Annezy, and of Northern Shammar, and certain migrated Kahtân now wandering in el-Kasîm.

An hour before the morning's mejlis the common business of the day is begun in the oasis. The inhabitants are husbandmen, tradesmen (mostly strangers) in the sûk, the *rajajîl es-sheukh,* and the not many household slaves. When the sun is risen, the husbandmen go out to labour. In an hour the sûk is opened : the *dellâls,* running brokers of all that is put to sale, new or old, whether clothing or arms, cry up and down the street, and spread their wares to all whom they meet, and entering the shops as they go with this illiberal noise, they sell to the highest bidders ; and thus upon an early day I sold my nâga the Khuèyra. I measured their sûk, which is between the Méshab and the inner gate towards Gofar, two hundred paces ; upon both sides are the shops, mall ware-rooms built backward, into which the light enters by the doorway,—they are in number about one hundred and thirty, all held and hired of the Emir. The butchers' market was in a court next without the upper gate of the sûk : there excellent mutton was hastily sold for an hour after sunrise, at less than two-pence a pound, and a small leg cost sixpence, in a time when nine shillings was paid for a live sheep at Hâyil, and for a goat hardly six shillings. So I have seen Beduins turn back with their small cattle, rather than sell them here at so low prices : —they would drive them down then, nearly three hundred miles more, to market at Medina ! where the present value of sheep they heard to be as much again as in the Jebel. The butchers' trade, though all the nomads are slaughterers, is not of persons of liberal condition in the townships of Nejd.

Mufarrij towards evening walks again in the Méshab : he comes forth at the castle gate, or sends a servant of the kitchen, as often as the courses of guests rise, to call in other Beduin rubbas to the public supper, which is but a lean dish of boiled temmn seconds and barley, anointed with a very little samn. Mufarrij bids them in his comely-wise, with due discretion and observance of their sheykhly or common condition, of their being here more or less welcome to the Emir, and the alliance or enmities of tribesmen. Also I, the Nasrâny, was daily called to supper in the gallery ; and this for two reasons I accepted,— I was infirm, so that the labour had been grievous to me if I must cook anything for myself, and I had not fuel, and where there was no chimney, I should have been suffocated in my makhzan by the smoke, also whilst I ate bread and salt in the Mothîf I was, I thought, in less danger of any sudden tyranny of the Emir ; but the Mothîf breakfast I forsook, since I might have the best dates in the market for a little money. If I had been able to dispend freely, I had sojourned more agreeably at Hâyil ; it was now a year since my coming to Arabia, and there remained but little in my purse to be husbanded for the greatest necessities.

In the Jebel villages the guest is bidden with : *summ !* or the like is said when the meat is put before him. This may be rather *'smm* for *ism,* in *b' ismi 'llah* or bismillah, " in God's name." But when first I heard this summ ! a a boy of the Mothîf set down the dish of temmn before me, I thought he had said (in malice) *simm,* which is ' poison,' and the child was not less amazed, when with the suddenness of the Arabs I prayed Ullah to curse his parentage :—in this uncertainty whether he had said poison I supped of their mess, for if they would so deal with me I thought I might not escape them. From supping, the Beduins resort in their rubbas to the public kahwa : after the guests' supper the rajajîl are served in like manner by messes, in the court of the Mothîf ; there they eat also at noon their lean collation of the date-tribute, in like manner as the public guests. The sorry dates and corn of the public kitchen have been received on account of the government-tax of the Emir, from his several hamlets and villages ; the best of all is reserved for the households of the sheykhly families. As the public supper is ended, you may see many poor women, and some children, waiting to enter, with their bowls, at the gate of the Kasr. These are they to whom the Emir has granted an evening ration, of that which is left, for themselves. and for other wretched persons. There were daily served in the Mothîf to the guests, and the rajajîl, 180 messes of bariey-bread and temmn of second quality, each might be three and a quarter pints; there was a certain allowance of samn. This samn for the public hospitality is taken from the Emir's Beduins, so much from every beyt, to be paid at an old rate, that is only sometimes seen in the spring, two shillings for three pints, which cost now in Hâyil a real. A camel or smaller beast is killed, and a little flesh meat is served to the first-called guests, once in eight or ten days. When the Prince is absent, there come no Beduins to Hâyil, and then (I have seen) there are no guests. So I have computed may be disbursed for the yearly expenses of the Prince's guest-house, about £1500 sterling.

—Now in the public kahwa the evening coffee is made and served round. As often as I sat with them the mixed rubbas of Beduins observed towards me the tolerant behaviour which is used in their tents ;—and here were we not all guests together of the Emir? The princely coffee-hall is open, soon after the dawn prayers, to these bibbers of the morning cup; the door is shut again, when all are gone forth about the time of the first mejlis. It is opened afresh, and coffee is served again after vespers. To every guest the cup is filled twice and a third is offered, when. if he would not drink, a Beduwy of the Nejd tribes will say shortly, with the desert courtesy, *Káramak Ullah*, ' the Lord requite thee.' The door of the kahwa is shut for the night as the coffee-drivelling Beduw are gone forth to the last prayers in the mesjid. After that time, the rude two-leaved gates of this (the Prince's) quarter and the market street are shut,—not to be opened again ' for prayer nor for hire ' till the morrow's light; and Beduins arriving late must lodge without :—but the rest of Hâyil lies open, which is all that built towards Gofar, and the mountain Ajja.

The Emir Mohammed rode out one half-afternoon with the companions of his chamber and attendance to visit *ed-dubbush*, his live wealth in the desert. The Nejd prince is a very rich cattle-master, so that if you will believe them he possesses " forty thousand " camels. His stud is of good Nejd blood, and as *Aly el-Aŷid* told me, (an honest man, and my neighbour, who was beforetime in the stud service,—he had conducted horses for the former Emirs to the Pashas of Egypt,) some three hundred mares, and an hundred horses, with many foals and fillies. After others' telling Ibn Rashîd has four hundred free and bond soldiery, two hundred mares of the blood, one hundred horses : they are herded apart in the deserts ; and he has " an hundred bond-servants " (living with their families in booths of hair-cloth, as the nomads), to keep them. Another told me the Emir's stud is divided in troops of fifty or sixty, all mares or all horses together ; the foals and fillies after the weaning are herded likewise by themselves. The troops are dispersed in the wilderness, now here, now there, near or far off,—according to the yearly springing of the wild herbage. The Emir's horses are grazed in nomad wise ; the fore-feet hop-shackled, they are dismissed to range from the morning. Barley or other grain they taste not : they are led home to the booths, and tethered at evening, and drink the night's milk of the she-camels, their foster mothers.—So that it may seem the West Nejd Prince possesses horses and camels to the value of about a quarter of a million of pounds sterling ; and that has 'been gotten in two generations of the spoil of the poor Beduw. He has besides great private riches laid up in metal, but his public taxes are carried into the government treasury, *beyt el-mâl*, and bestowed in sacks and in pits. He possesses much in land, and not only in Hâyil, but he has great plantations also at Jauf, and in some other conquered oases.—I saw Mohammed mount at the castle gate upon a tall dromedary, bravely caparisoned. In the few days of this his peaceable sojourn in the khála, the Prince is lodged with his company in booths like the Beduins. He left Hamûd in Hâyil, to hold the now small daily mejlis ;—the son of Abeyd sits not then in the Prince's settle, but in his own lower seat by the tower.

Hamûd sent for me in his afternoon leisure : " Mohammed is gone, he said, and we remain to become friends." He showed me now his cheap Gulf watches, of which he wore two upon his breast, and so does his son Mâjid who has a curious mind in such newels.—it was said he could clean watches ! and that Hamûd possessed not so few as an hundred, and the Emir many more than he. Hamûd asked me if these were not " Engleys," he would say ' of the best Nasâra work.' He was greedy to understand of me if I brought not many gay things in my deep saddle-bags of the fine workmanship of the Nasâra : he would give for them, he promised me with a barbarous emphasis, FELÛS ! ' silver scales ' or money, which the miserable Arab people believe that all men do cherish as the blood of their own lives. I found Hamûd lying along as the nomads, idle and yawning, in the plantation of Abeyd's kahwa, which, as said, extends behind the makhzans to his family house in the town (that is not indeed one of the best). In this palm-ground he has many gazelles, which feed of vetches daily littered down to them, but they were shy of man's approach : there I saw also a bédan-buck. This robust wild goat of the mountain would follow a man and even pursue him, and come without fear into the kahwa. The beast is of greater bulk and strength than any he-goat, with thick short hair ; his colour purple ruddle or nearly as that blushing before the sunset of dark mountains.

This is a palm-ground of Abeyd, planted in the best manner. The stems, in the harsh and lean soil of Hâyil, are set in rows, very wide asunder. I spoke with Aly, that half-good fanatical neighbour of mine, one who at my first coming had felt in my girdle for gold, he was of Môgug, but now overseer at Hâyil of the Prince's husbandry. This palm foster answered, that ' in such earth (granite grit) where the palms have more room they bear the better ; the manner which I showed him of setting trees could not avail them.' Hamûd's large well in this ground was of fifteen fathoms, sunk in that hard gritty earth ; the upright sides, baked in the sun, stand fast without inner building or framework. The pit had been dug by the labour of fifteen journeymen, each receiving three or four piastres, in twenty days, this is a cost of some £10. Three of the best she-camels drew upon the wheels, every one was worth thirty-five reals. The price of camels in Arabia had been nearly doubled of late years after the great draughts for Egypt, the Abyssinian wars, and for Syria. It surprised me to hear a Beduwy talk in this manner,—" And billah a cause is the lessened value of money ! " If rainless years follow rainless years there comes in the end a murrain. It was not many years since such a season, when a camel was sold for a crown by the nomads, and languishing thelûls, before worth sixty in their health, for two or three reals, (that was to the villagers in Kasîm,) sooner than the beasts remaining upon their hands should perish in the khála.

Mâjid, the elder of Hamûd's children, was a boy of fifteen years, small for his age, of a feminine beauty, the son (the Emirs also match with the nomads) of a Beduin woman. There accompanied him always a dissolute young man, one Aly, who had four wives and was attached to Hamûd's service. This lovely pair continually invaded me in my beyt, with the infantile curiosity of Arabs, intent to lay their knavish fingers upon any foreign thing of the Nasâra,—and such they hoped to find in my much baggage · and lighting upon aught Mâjid and his villanous fellow Aly had it away perforce.—When I considered that they might thus come upon my pistol and instruments, I wrested the things from their iniquitous fingers, and reminded them of the honest example of the nomads, whom they despise. Mâjid answered me with a childish wantonness : " But thou, Khalîl, art in our power, and the Emir can cut off thy head at his pleasure ! " One day as I heard them at the door, I cast the coverlet over my loose things, and sat upon it, but nothing could be hidden from their impudence, with *bethr-ak ! bethr-ak !* " by thy leave ; "—it happened that they found me sitting upon the koran. " Ha ! said they now with fanatical bitterness, he is sitting upon the koran ! "—this tale was presently carried in Mâjid's mouth to the castle ; and the elf Mâjid returned to tell me that the Emir had been much displeased.

Mâjid showed himself to be of an affectionate temper, with the easy fortunate disposition of his father, and often childishly exulting, but in his nature too self-loving and tyrannical. He would strike at the poorer children with his stick as he passed by them in the street and cry, " Ullah curse thy father ! " they not daring to resent the injury or resist him,—the best of the *eyyâl es-sheukh ;* for thus are called the children of the princely house. For his age he was corrupt of heart and covetous ; but they are all brought up by slaves ! If he ever come to be the Prince, I muse it will be an evil day for Hâyil, except, with good mind enough to amend, he grow up to a more humane understanding. Mâjid, full of facility and the felicity of the Arabs, with a persuading smile, affected to treat me always according to his father's benevolence, naming me ' his dear friend '; and yet he felt that I had a cold insight into his ambitious meaning. So much of the peddling Semite was in him, that he played huckster and bargained for my nâga at the lowest price, imagining to have the double for her (when she would be a milch cow with the calf) in the coming spring : this I readily yielded, but ' nay, said then the young princeling, except I would give him her harness too,' (which was worth a third more).— I have many times mused what could be their estimation of honour ! They think they do that well enough in the world which succeeds to them ; human deeds imitating our dream of the divine ways are beautiful words of their poets, and otherwise unknown to these Orientals.

As I walked through their clean and well-built clay town I thought it were pleasant to live here,—save for the awe of the Ruler and their lives disquieted to ride in the yearly forays of the Emir : yet what discomfort to our eyes is that squalor of the desert soil which lies about them ! Hâyil for the unlikelihood of the site is town rather than oasis, or it is, as it were, an oasis made *ghrôsb,* perforce. The circuit, for their plantations are not very wide, may be nearly an hour ; the town lies as far distant from the Ajja cliffs (there named *el-M'nîf*). Their town, fenced from the wholesome northern air by the bergs *Sumrâ Hâyil*, is very breathless in the long summer months. The Sumrâ, of plutonic basalt, poured forth (it may be seen in face of the Méshed gate) upon the half-buried grey-red granite of Ajja, is two members which stand a little beyond the town, in a half moon, and the seyl bed of Hâyil, which comes they say from Gofar, passes out between them. That upon the west is lower ; the eastern part rises to a height of five hundred feet, upon the crest are cairns ; and there was formerly the look-out station, when Hâyil was weaker.

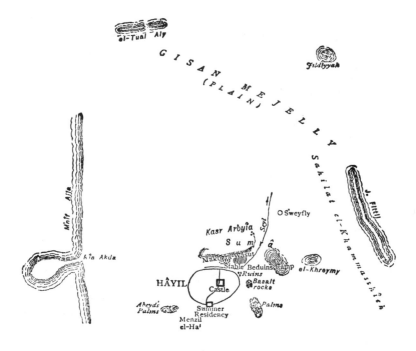

The higher Samrâ, *Umm Arkab*, is steep, and I hired one morning an ass, *jáhash*, for eightpence to ride thither. The thick strewed stones upon this berg, are of the same rusty black basalt which they call *hurrî* or *hurra*, heavy and hard as iron, and ringing like bell-metal. Samrâ in the nomadic speech of Nejd is any rusty black berg of hard stone in the desert ; and in the great plutonic country from hence to Mecca the samrâs are always basalt. The same, when any bushes grow upon it, is called *házm*, and házm is such a vulcanic hill upon the Harras. I saw from the cairns that Hâyil is placed at the midst in a long plain, which is named *Sâhilat el-Khammashieh*, and lies between the M'nîf of Ajja (which may rise in the highest above the plain to 1500 feet), and that low broken hilly train, by which the Sâhilat is bounded along, two leagues eastward, toward Selma, *J. Fittij ;* and under us north-eastward from Hâyil is seen *el-Khreyma*, a great possession of young palms,—the Emir's ; and there are springs, they say, which water them !

Some young men labouring in the fields had seen the Nasrâny ascending, and they mounted after us. In the desert below, they said, is hidden much treasure, if a man had wit to find it, and they filled my ears with their " *Jebel Tommieh !* " renowned, " for the riches which lie there buried," in all Nejd ; —Tommîeh in the Wady er-Rummah, south of the *Abanát* twin mountains. After this, one among them who was lettered, sat down and wrote for me the landmarks, that we saw in that empty wilderness about us. Upon a height to the northward they showed me *Kabr es-Sâny,* ' the smith's grave,' laid out to a length of three fathoms : " Of such stature was the man ; he lived in time of the Beny Helál : pursued by the enemies' horsemen, he ran before them with his little son upon his shoulder, and fell there." All this plain upon the north is *G(k)isan M'jelly*, to the mountain peaks, *Tuâl Aly,* at the borders of the Nefûd, and to the solitary small mountain *Jildíyyah,* which being less than a journey from Hâyil, is often named for an assembling place of the Emir's ghrazzus. There is a village northward of Hâyil two miles beyond the Sumrâ, *S'weyfly ;* and before S'weyfly is seen a ruined village and rude palm planting and corn grounds, *Kasr Arbÿiyyah.* Arbŷiyyah and S'weyfly are old Hâyil ; this is to say the ancient town was built, in much better soil and site, upon the north side of the Sumrâ. Then he showed me with his hand under the M'nîf of Ajja the place of the *Rîa Ag(k)da,* which is a gap or strait of the mountain giving upon a deep plain-bosom in the midst of Ajja, and large so that it might, after their speaking, contain *rúba ed-dínya,* " a fourth part of their (thinly) inhabited world." There are palms in a compass of mighty rocks ; it is a mountain-bay which looks eastward, very hot in summer. The narrow inlet is shut by gates, and Abeyd had fortified the passage with a piece of cannon. The Riâ Agda is accounted a sure refuge for the people of Hâyil, with all their goods, as Abeyd

had destined, in the case of any military expedition of the
Dowla, against "the JEBEL," of which they have sometimes
been in dread. Northward beyond el-M'nîf the Ajja coast is
named *el-Aucyrith*.

I came down in the young men's company, and they invited
me to their noonday breakfast of dates which was brougnt out
to them in the fields. Near by I found a street of tottering
walls and ruinous clay houses, and the ground-wall of an ancient
massy building in clay-brick, which is no more used at Hâyil.
The foundation of this settlement by Shammar is from an
high antiquity ; some of them say "the place was named at
first, *Hâyer*, for the plentiful (veins of ground-) water," yet
Hâyil is found written in the ancient poem of Antar. [Ptolemy
has here Ἀρρη κώμη.—*v*. Sprenger in *Die alte Geogr. Arabiens.*]
The town is removed from beyond the Sumrâ, the cause was,
they say, the failing little and little of their ground-water.
Hâyil, in the last generation, before the beginning of the
government of Ibn Rashîd, was an oasis half as great as Gofar,
which is a better site by nature ; yet Hâyil, Abdullah Ibn
Rashîd's town, when he became *Muhafúth*, or constable under
the Waháby for West Nejd, was always the capital. To-day
the neighbour towns are almost equal, and in Hâyil I have
estimated to be 3000 souls ; the people of Gofar, who are Beny
Temîm, and nearly all husbandmen, do yet, they say, a little
exceed them. In returning home towards the northern gate, I
visited a ruined suburb *Wâsit* "middle" (building), which by
the seyl and her fields only is divided from Hâyil town. There
were few years ago in the street, now ruins, "forty kahwas," that
is forty welfaring households receiving their friends daily to
coffee.

Wâsit to-day is ruins without inhabitant ; her people (as
those in the ruined quarter of Gofar and in ruined Môgug) died
seven years before in the plague, *wába*. I saw their earthen
house-walls unroofed and now ready to fall, for the timbers had
been taken away : the fields and the wells lay abandoned.
The owners and heirs of the soil had so long left the waterer's
labour that the palm-trees were dead and sere : few palms
yet showed in their rusty crowns any languishing greenness.
Before I left Hâyil I saw those lifeless stems cut down, and
the earth laid out anew in seed-plots. There died in Wâsit
three hundred persons ; in Hâyil, 'one or two perished in
every household (that were seven hundred or eight hundred) ;
but now, the Lord be praised, the children were sprung up
and nearly filled their rooms.' Of the well-dieted princely
and sheykhly families there died no man ! Beduins that

visited Hâyil in time of the pestilence perished sooner than
townsfolk ; yet the contagion was lighter in the desert and
never prevailed in their menzils as a mortal sickness. The
disease seized upon the head and bowels ; some died the
same day, some lingered awhile longer. Signs in the plague-
struck were a black spot which appeared upon the nose, and
a discolouring of the nails ; the sufferings were nearly those of
cholera. After the pest a malignant fever afflicted the country
two years, when the feeble survivors loading the dead upon
asses (for they had no more strength to carry out piously
themselves) were weary to bury. A townsman who brought
down, at that time, some quinine from the north, had dispensed
' ten or twelve grains to the sick at five reals ; and taken
after a purging dose of magnesia, he told me, it commonly
relieved them.' This great death fell in the short time of
Bunder's playing the Prince in Hâyil, and little before the
beginning of Mohammed's government, which is a reign they
think of prosperity, " such as was not seen before, and in which
there has happened no public calamity." Now first the lordship of Shammar is fully ripe : after such soon-ripeness we
may look for rottenness, as men succeed of less endowments
to administer that which was acquired of late by warlike
violence, or when this tide of the world shall be returning from
them.

After Wâsit, in a waste, which lies between the town walls
and the low crags of the Sumrâ, is the wide grave-yard of
Hâyil. Poor and rich whose world is ended, lie there alike
indigently together in the desert earth which once fostered
them, and unless it be for the sites here or there, we see
small or no difference of burial. Telâl and Abeyd were laid
among them. The first grave is a little heap whose rude head-
stone is a wild block from the basalt hill, and the last is like
it, and such is every grave ; you shall hardly see a scratched
epitaph, where so much is written as the name which was a
name. In the border Semitic countries is a long superstition
of the grave ; here is but the simple nomad guise, without
other last loving care or adornment. At a side in the mákbara
is the grave-heap of Abeyd, a man of so much might and
glory in his days : now these are but a long remembrance ;
he lies a yard under the squalid gravel in his shirt, and upon
his stone is rudely scored, with a nail, this only word, *Abeyd
bin-Rashîd.* When I questioned Mâjid, ' And did his grandsire, the old man Abeyd, lie now so simply in the earth ? ' my
words sounded coldly and strange in his ears ; since in this
land of dearth, where no piece of money is laid out upon

thing not to their lives' need, they are nearly of the Wife of Bath's opinion, " it were but waste to bury him preciously," —whom otherwise they follow in her luxury. When one is dead, they say, *khálas!* " he is ended," and they wisely dismiss this last sorrowful case of all men's days without extreme mourning.

Between the mákbara and the town gate is seen a small menzil of resident nomads. They are pensioners of the palace ; and notwithstanding their appearance of misery some of them are of kin to the princely house. Their Beduin booths are fenced from the backward with earthen walling, and certain of them have a chamber (kasr) roofed with a tent-cloth, or low tower of the same clay building. They are Shammar, whose few cattle are with their tribesfolk in the wilderness ; in the spring months they also remove thither, and refresh themselves in the short season of milk. As I went by, a woman called me from a ragged booth, the widest among them ; ' had I a medicine for her sore eyes ? ' She told me in her talk that her sister had been a wife of Metaab, and she was " aunt " of Mohammed now Emir. Her sons fled in the troubled times and lived yet in the northern dîras. When she named the Emir she spoke in a whisper, looking always towards the Kasr, as if she dreaded the wings of the air might carry her word into the Prince's hearing. Her grown daughter stood by us, braying temmn in a great wooden mortar, and I wondered to see her unveiled ; perhaps she was not married, and Moslems have no jealous opinion of a Nasrâny. The comely maiden's cheeks glowed at her labour ; such little flesh colour I had not seen before in a nomad woman, so lean and bloodless they all are, but she was a stalwart one bred in the plenteous northern dîras. I counted their tents, thirty ; nearer the Gofar gate were other fifteen booths of half-resident Shammar, pitched without clay building.

TRAVELS IN ARABIA DESERTA

VOLUME TWO

CHAPTER I.

IBN RASHÎD'S TOWN.

Curious questioning of the townspeople. A Moor hakîm had visited Hâyil. He cast out demons. The jins. Superstitious fears of the Arabs. Exorcists. A counterfeit Christian vaccinator cut off in the desert. Advantage of the profession of medicine. Hamûd sends his sick infant son to the Nasrâny hakîm, who cures also Hamûd's wife. Diseases at Hâyil. The great Kasr. The guest-chambers. Hâyil house-building. Wards of the town. Artificers. Visit to S'weyfly. The mákbara has swallowed up the inhabitants. Deaf and dumb man-at-arms of the Emir. Mâjid shooting with ball. English gunpowder. Gulf words heard at Hâyil. Palms and a gum-mastic tree in Ajja. 'The coming of Mohammed foretold in the Enjîl.' Hamûd's tolerant urbanity. Another audience. The princely family of Ibn Rashîd. Telâl a slayer of himself. Metaab succeeded him. His nephews, Telâl's sons, conspire to kill him. Metaab dies by their shot. Bunder prince. Mohammed who fled to er-Riâth returns upon assurance of peace. He is again conductor of the Bagdad pilgrims. He comes again to Hâyil with the yearly convoy of temmn for the public kitchen. Bunder rides forth with his brother Bedr and Hamûd to meet him. Mohammed slays (his nephew) Bunder. Hamûd's speech to the people. Tragedies in the Castle. Mohammed's speech in the Méshab. He sits down as Muhafúth. Bedr taken and slain. Mohammed slays the slayer. Hamûd's nature. Mohammed the Emir is childless. His moderation and severity. The princely bounty. The Shammar state. Villages and hamlets. The public dues and taxes and expense of government. The Prince's horses sold in India. His forces. Ibn Rashîd's forays. He "weakens" the Aarab. The Shammar principality.

WHEN I returned in the afternoon from the ascent of the Sumrâ I found it was already a matter of talk in the town. The first persons met with approached to ask me, "What have you found there—anything? tell us! certainly you went to see something yonder,—and else wherefore had the Nasrâny climbed upon those high rocks, and paid pence for an ass?" As I passed by the sûk tradesmen beckoned to me from the shops, they too would speak with me of the adventure.

My former friends durst no more be seen openly in the

211

Naṣrâny's company ; it might be laid to their charge, that they also favoured the kafir. As I walked on the morrow in the town, one of the young patricians of those daily about the Emir came to question me :—the most of these complacent young gallants, as I might perceive them, through their silken shining petticoats, are some of the vilest spirits in Hâyil. With many shallow impatient gestures, and plucking my mantle, " Khalîl, said he, what dost thou here, so far from the sûk ? Why wander round about ? what brings thee into this place ? what seekest, what seest thou ? Is Hâyil a good town ? the air, is it well ?—and when wilt thou depart ? " As I came again a Beduwy who sat in the upper end of the Méshab saluted me friendly, he was of the Wélad Aly sheykhs, and had seen the Naṣrâny at el-Héjr. We sat down together, and another came to me of those effeminate young silken Arabs, masking in the insolent confidence of the Emir. The cockerel disdainfully breaking our talk, I cut him off with—" Pass on, young man, my ears ache of thy ignorance and malevolent speech." The young man left us in anger, and as he was gone, " Khalîl, said the friendly Beduwy, I speak it of fellowship, deal not so plainly with this townspeople ; believe me they will take up thy words, he also that you now sent away will not cease to hate thee extremely ; and billah the young man is of their principal houses, and one nigh to the Emir.—Ay ! here is another manner of life, than that to which thou hast been wont in the desert, and we are not here in the desert, neither be these the Beduw : "—and himself, a messenger from the rebellious tribe, he seemed somewhat to be daunted in the tyrannical shadow of the place.

Some friendly persons coming to visit me, after I had flitted from my old beyt to the next makhzan, said, " Khalîl is the second hakîm we have seen in this lodging."—" Who was the hakîm in this chamber before me ? "—" A Moghreby, a doctor indeed, [better than Khalîl,] there was none like him to write hijâbs, and upon every one he received three reals :—why, Khalîl, write you no hijâbs ? Write, man, and the whole town will be at thy door, and every one with two dollars, or three, in his hand. Thou mightest be enriched soon, that now never canst thrive in this selling of medicines, the Arabs desire no medicines.—But the Moghreby, wellah, holding his hijâbs a moment in the smoke, delivered them to those who paid him reals, and the people found them very availing. If such were the Moghreby's hijâbs, is not Khalîl a Naṣrâny, and therefore one who might write even better than he ?—Ah ! how that man was powerful in his 'reading' (spells)! He cast out the demons of possessed persons, and he bound the jân, wellah, in yonder corner."—"What bound he in that corner?"—"*Ahl el-aard*, (the demon-folk, which inhabit under the earth,) they make men sick, and the possessed beat themselves, or they fall down, raging and foaming."

Aly el-Aŷid, my neighbour in the next houses, who was beholden to me for some faithful (medical) service, brought me a lamp of tallow, saying, 'He would not have a friend sleep here in the darkness, the demons might affray me;' and, looking round, "This makhzan, he said, is full of jân (since the Moghreby's casting out so many), I myself durst not sleep in this place."—"But tell me, who has seen these jân, and what is their likeness?"—"I have seen them, Khalîl, some tall, and some be of little stature, their looks are very horrible; certain of them have but one eye in the midst of their faces; other jins' visages be drawn awry in fearful manner, or their face is short and round, and the lips of many jins hang down to their middles." Aly el-Aŷid came early on the morrow to my beyt to know how I fared, and seeing not an hour of his tallow burned, he called me foolhardy to sleep without light. But pointing upward, he showed me a worse case, the great beam was half broken in the midst! the load of the earthen heaped ceiling threatened ruin and destruction, and therefore they had lodged none here of late :—but even that abandoned makhzan Hamûd had conceded to the Nasrâny unwillingly. The wavering branches of a palm which grew in Hamûd's orchard-grounds, sliding ghostly in the open casement by night, might, I thought, be the jân of their unquiet consciences. By day little chirping sparrows of the Méshab were my guests, and more than other, amiable company.

I found professors of exorcism (as before said) at Hâyil : they were two vile and counterfeit persons. One of them was a man growing into years; I had seen him at Abeyd's kahwa, and by certain of his answers he surprised me, and by his know-ledge of letters : this person was a foreigner from East Nejd, but now he dwelt at Gofar. He seemed afraid in that presence to answer me; perhaps he durst not speak frankly, or much above his breath. That other was a young man of Hâyil, and he came secretly to my makhzan, to learn some mastery in the art, from the Nasrâny. He asked me, 'what were my manner to lay strong constraint upon the demons, and the words of my powerful spells, *kerreya*.' 'He had a book too written full of very strong *readings* at home, and he sped very well by it, for he could cast out the jins more than any person besides.

This was a smooth fellow, Nature had favoured him in all, and for his sweet voice the shrew was sometimes called in (he boasted) to sing before the Emir.

That Moghreby, with his blind arts, lived at Hâyil in the popular favour, and he had won much silver; also to the lone man they lent a pretty widow to wife,—" wherefore should he live without housewifery ? " Abdullah, a slave of the Emir, came to the Nasrâny upon a day with a like proffer, and Mâjid showed me a pleasant Galla maiden of his father's household, saying, that did I consent, she should be mine. The poor girl was gentle and modest, and without unwillingness ; but because I would not lead my life thus, they ascribed it to the integrity of the Christian faith, and had the more tolerance of me in the rest. Word that ' the Princes suffered at Hâyil, and even favoured the Nasrâny ' was spread by Beduins returning from the capital, into all the next parts of Arabia ; and afterward I came nowhither in Nejd, until I arrived at the Kasîm villages, where they had not heard of the wandering Nasrâny, and by the signs they all knew me. They told me also of a Nasrâny (some Syrian by likelihood or Mesopotamian), who years before, coming to Hâyil, had taken the people's money for pretended vaccination. " But Ullah, they said, cut him off, for he was met with and slain in the desert by the Aarab."

Little was my practice of medicine, yet this name procured me entrance amongst them, and the surest friends. A man of medicine is not found in Nejd ; but commonly they see some Ajamy hakîm, once a year, at Hâyil amongst the Persian pilgrims. I was called to visit suffering persons ; yet because they would not leave with me the smallest pledge of their good faith, I remained with hardly any daily patients. Hamûd now sent to me an infant son, *Feysal,* that seemed to be of a very good disposition, and was sick of fever and dysentery. The child whom they brought to me, languishing and likely to die, I left, when I departed from Hâyil, nearly restored to health. I was called also to Hamûd's wife in his family house. I found her clad as other Arabian women in a simple calico smock dyed in indigo, her face was blotted out with the heathenish veil-clout ; I gave her a medicine and she in a few days recovered. Of all their ailings most common (we have seen already) are eye-diseases,—it is the poorer, that is the misdieted people, who are the sooner affected— then diseases of the intestines, agues, old rheumatism ; and men, the ignominy of the Meccawy's religion, too often complain of inability. The morbus gallicus is common at Hâyil, and in the neighbourhood ; I saw many hypochondriacs [they are a third of all the Arabians]. There were brought to me cases of a sudden kind of leprosy ; the skin was discoloured in whitish spots, rising in the space of two or three days in the breast and neck. Cancer was not uncommon, and partial paralysis with atrophy of the lower limbs.

I enquired when was the Kasr founded ?—which though clay-built is of a certain noble aspect. The wall is near eight feet in thickness at the ground, and more than forty in height, and seems to be carried about a great space. Upon the public place, I measured this castle building, one hundred and ten paces, with two towers. The doorway of the Kasr, under the tower in the midst, is shut at evening by a rude door of heavy timber, in which is a little wicket, only to be entered stooping—and that before dark, is put-to. The wall and foundation of the huge clay building is from old times and was laid by some of the former sheykhs (surely men of ambitious mind) at Hâyil, before Abdullah. The Méshab in front is twenty-five paces over, and the makhzans built in face of the castle are nine in number. [*v.* the fig., Vol. I. p. 587.] To every makhzan is a door with a wooden lock opening into a little court, and beyond is the guest-chamber without door, square and dark, some fifteen feet by twelve feet. If any rubba would have fuel in the cold winter days, they must ask it of the Emir sitting in the public mejlis. Telâl built the makhzans, and the great mesjid ; his father Abdullah had ended the building of the Kasr, only one year before his decease. The clay of the house-building at Hâyil is disposed in thick layers, in which are bedded, as we saw at Môgug, flat brick-blocks, long dried in the sunny air, set leaning wise, and very heavy, of great strength and endurance. The copes of the house-walling at Hâyil, and the sills of their casements, are often finished above with a singular stepped pinnacle (fig., Vol. I. p. 106), which resembles the strange sculptured cornice of the Petra and Héjr frontispices.

Their streets—I came in then from living long in the wilderness—I thought well set out ; the rows are here of one-storied houses. There is no seeming of decay, but rather of newness, and thriving and spending : their capital village is seen, as her inhabitants, well arrayed. Hâyil is divided into eleven wards, a twelfth is S'weyfly. All the settlements in nomad Arabia, even the smallest hamlets, with the incorrupt desert about them, have a certain freshness and decent aspect above that which the traveller arriving from the West may have seen in Syria. The village Arabians—come of the nomad blood—are happy (where God's peace is not marred by striving factions) under the mild and just government of their home-born sheykhs ; and in their green palm islands, they have much of the free-born and civil mind of the desert. At Hâyil, and Teyma, the stranger's eye may mark certain little close frames set high upon the front walling of many dàrs, and having the form of right-angled triangles ; he will see them to be timbered above the doorways. These are shooting-down sconces (like the machicolations of our mediæval fortresses), for defence of the door of the household.

As for the administration of the town, there are no dues at Hâyil for maintenance of ways or public lighting,—which is unknown even at Damascus—nor so much as for watchmen : yet the streets are clean, and draffe is cast out into certain pits and side places. Irrigation water drawn by camel labour from their deep wells, though not of the best, is at hand in sebîls and conduits ; to these common pools the town housewives resort to fill their pans and their girbies, and for the household washing. Dogs are not seen by day in any Nejd villages, but some lost hounds which remain without the most oases, will prowl by their streets in the night-time. Of household animals, there are in nearly all the settlements small kine for their sweet milk and as light plough-beasts, asses for riding and carriage, cats to quit them of vermin, besides poultry.

The artificers in Hâyil are few and of the smiths' caste, workers in metal and wood, in which there are some who turn small and brittle ethelware bowls. Their thelûl saddle here is other than that of Teyma and westwards, in which the pillars are set upright. There is a petty industry among women of sewing and embroidering, with silk and metal thread, the mantles which are brought down (in the piece) from Jauf and Bagdad,—none are made here. I saw in the sûk fine skein-silks, folded in printed papers, and such the shopkeepers oft-times put in my hands to read for them ;—but the language was English ! and when I found the title it was THE BOMBAY GAZETTE. Their hareem plait the common house-matting of the tender springing palm-leaf, as in all the oases. There are besides a few men of builders' and carpenters' craft, rude workers, nearly without tools, and pargeters in jiss or *jips*, a gypsum-stone which is brought from the mountain, and found clotted together, like mortar, in the desert sand. The jips, broken and ground to a flour-like powder, they mix with water, and spread it for the border and lining-walls of hearth-pits :

this dries quickly to a hard white crust, shining like marble, that will bear the fire. The wood and hay gatherers who go far out into the wilderness, are *Kusmán*, laborious foreigners from el-Kasîm; the nomad-spirited townspeople of Jebel Shammar are not good for such drudging labour.

I went out of Hâyil another day towards S'weyfly. Beyond Wâsit I walked by fields where men were labouring, and one threw clods at the Nasrâny, but the rest withheld him; I went on between the two Samras, and beside the wide seyl bed, being there half a stone-cast over. The soil is now good loam, no more that sharp granite grit of Hâyil; the dates are good, they are the best of the country.—The first houses I found to be but waste walls and roofless, and the plantations about them forsaken; the languishing palm-stems showed but a dying crown of rusty leaves. I had not perceived a living person in these fields, that were once husbanded upon both sides of the large-bedded torrent. The pest, which destroyed the Jebel villages, came upon them after a year of dearth, when the date harvest had failed, and the price of corn (three sahs to the real) was risen more than twofold. Strange it seems to us, used to public remedies, that in none of the merchants, more than in cattle, nor in the Prince himself, was there any readiness of mind to bring in grain from a distance :—the Moslem religion ever makes numbness and death in some part of the human understanding. The wába being come upon them there died in two months in this small village two hundred persons. The few which remained at S'weyfly were feeble even now, and had lost their health, so that it was said of them "They might hardly bear the weight of their mantles." The cruel disease seized upon men sooner than women and children.

At length I came where a few persons were loitering abroad; I saluted them in passing, and asked "Who has here a coffee-house, and where are the inhabitants?" They saw he was a stranger who enquired this of them and responded with a desolate irony, "They lie in yonder mákbara!" I went forward where I heard the shrilling of a suâny. A woman (since the men were dead) was driving that camel-team at the well. It is eight fathoms here to water; all their wells are brackish, and sweet water to drink must be fetched from Hâyil 'for money.' Brackish water in a sweet soil is best for the palm irrigation; but if the palms be rooted in any saltish or bitter earth, as at Kheybar, they have need of a fresh irrigation water : and always for some little saltiness in the soil or water, palm-plants thrive the better. Such water to drink is very unwholesome in these climates, and was a cause they think of so many dying here in the pestilence. In old time, they say, when S'weyfly was ancient Hâyil, the wells in this part were sweet, that is until the new planting above them had spent the vein of good water. One led the stranger in hospitable manner to the best house which remained, to drink coffee. We entered a poor clay room, long unswept, and in the sun a swarming place of flies ; this was their kahwa. The three or four ghastly looking and weakly speaking men who followed us in to drink were those that survived in the neighbourhood ; and it seemed as if the nightmare lay yet upon them. Kindly they received the guest, and a tray was presently set before me of their excellent dates. The S'weyfly villagers, for this hospitable and gentle humour, are said to resemble rather the Beduw than Hâyil towns-people. Enough it seemed to them that the stranger was the hakîm, they would not cavil with a guest or question of his religion.

Whilst I sat with them at the coffee, there entered, with his sword, a deaf and dumb young man, whom I knew in Hâyil, one of the Prince's armed rajajîl : and with vehement signs and maffling cries he showed us he was come out from Hâyil to seek me. The poor fellow had always a regard of me in the town, and would suffer none to trouble me. I have seen him threaten even Mâjid in my chamber with angry looks, and shake his stick at the princeling boy, who too much, he thought, molested me. He now made them signs—drawing the first finger across his throat—that he feared for me so far abroad. All the way homeward the poor man blamed me, as if he would say " Why adventure so far alone, and thou art in danger to be waylaid ? " I made him signs I went to visit sick people, that were in need of medicines. Lower where we passed he showed me smiling a few palm trees and a field which were his own. I heard he was a stranger (as are so many of the Emir's men) from el-Aruth. At my first arriving at Hâyil, when they beckoned to him that I was not of their religion, he quickly signified his friendly counsel that ' I should pray as the rest.' The poor Speechless uttered his soul in a single syllable, *Ppahppah ;* that is nearly the first voice in children and dumb creatures, beginning in M-, B-, W-, which is all one. This P is not found in all the large Arabic alphabet, but any foreign taken-up words having in them that initial letter they must pronounce with F- or else with B-. All his meaning was now very well understood by the people of Hâyil ; they made him kindly answers with movement of the lips, as in speaking, and of his wistful life-

long comparison, he could guess again their minds : but if
any mocked, with great bursting forth of *Ppahs* and chatter-
ing, and furious eyes, and laying hand upon his sword, he
threatened their lives, or suddenly he drew it forth rattling,
to the half, in the scabbard. Of his long sufferance of the
malice of the world might be this singular resolution in him,
to safeguard another manner of deaf and dumb person. He
rode in the band upon his thelûl, and served very well, they
said, in the Prince's ghrazzus.

As I returned to town I met with Mâjid and his company
carrying guns in the fields, his uncle Fáhd was with them.
Thus they went out daily, shooting with ball at a white paper
set up in an orchard wall at a hundred and twenty paces.
I sat down with Fáhd to see the practice ; their shots from
the long Arabic matchlocks struck at few fingers' distance
all round the sheet, but rarely fell within it. The best was
Ghrânim, when he was one amongst them, for looking through
spectacles, he would send his ball justly at the first shot into
the midst of the white ;—this firing with the match does not
unsettle the aim. They shot with ' powder Engleysy,' of a tin
flask, whereupon I read in a kind of stupor, HALL, DART-
FORD ! There are many sea-borne wares of the Gulf-trade seen
at Hâyil, and the people take as little thought from whence
they come to them, as our country people of China tea-chests ;
European are many things of their most necessary use, as
the husbandmen's spades and crowbars, pigs of lead with the
English stamp, iron and tinning metal ; their clothing is calico
of Manchester and Bombay. All their dealings are in foreign
money ; reals of Spain, Maria Theresa dollars, and Turkish
mejîdy crowns ; gold money is known more than seen among
them. They call *doubloon* the piece of 5 Turkish pounds,
English sovereigns *ginniyát* or *bintu*, and the 20 fr. piece *lira
fransâwy*. For small silver in the Hâyil sûk they have Austrian
sixpences, and certain little gross Persian coins, struck awry,
and that for the goodly simplicity of the workmanship resemble
the stamps of the old Greek world. With the love of novelty
which is natural even to Semitic souls, they are also importers
with their foreign merchandise of some Gulf words, especially
from the Persian, as they will say for a dromedary *shittr*, rather
than of their own wealth in the current Arabic, (*hajín*,) *thelûl*,
rikâb, (*hadùj*), *mátiyah*, *rohòl*, *hâshy*, *hurra*.

Mâjid invited me, if I stayed till winter, to take part in
their hunting expeditions in Ajja. Then the young franklins
and men of Hâyil, and even the Princes, go out to the mountain
to shoot at the bedûn, driving asses with them to carry their

water : they commonly stay out a week thus and trust to
shooting the game for their supper. In many small wadies
of Ajja are wild palms watered by springs, or growing with
their roots in the seyl ground. The owners are Beduin families
which come thither only in the time of the date gathering :
the date is smaller than the fruit of trees which are husbanded.
There grows a tree in Ajja, named *el-aràr*, from which flows
a sort of gum-mastica, " it resembles the tamarisk." Ajja is
greater, and a score of miles longer, than the sister mountain
Selma.

Hamûd I saw daily ; I went to dine with him again, and
as we sat in the evening, he said to me, " Is there not something written in the Enjîl, of Mohammed ? "—" Nay, nothing,
and I know of it every word."—" But is there not mentioned
that a prophet, by name *Hamed*, should come after ;—and
that is Mohammed ? "   I answered shortly again : " No, there
is not." Hamûd startled, he believed me, his humanity persuaded him that I could not intend any offence—and that
were without remission—towards the religion. I said further :
" If such were found in the Enjîl, I would be a Mosleman ;
do you read this word in the koran ! " Hamûd did not answer, he sat on gravely musing. It was an enigma to me
what they might mean by a prediction of Hamed or Mohammed (which is one) in the Christian scriptures.—We read
in the sixth verset of the koran chapter 61, " *And said Îsa-bin-*
Miriam, O Beny Israel, I am the apostle of Ullah, to confirm
the Towrât (Mosaic Scriptures) *and to show unto you the coming*
of an apostle,—his name shall be Ahmed " (The Glorious). To
such Ahmed or Glorious One responds in the tongue of the
New or Hellenic Scriptures the word Περικλυτός, ' very illus-
trious.' Therefore their barbaric doctors bray that the malicious
Nasâra have miswritten Παράκλητος, ' COMFORTER ' [which word
is but four times found, and namely, in the last testament of
Christ, from the xiv. to the xvi. chapters of St. John].

Hamûd took pleasure to question, and commune with me
of our religion ; he smiled with pious admiration to hear
the Nasrâny stranger repeat after him some part of their
canonical prayers, and say ' he held them thus far for godly,'
as the fâtiha, commonly said in the beginning of their devotion, which sounds in their full and ripe Nejd utterance of a
certain surprising beauty and solemnity : the sense of the text
is this : " In the name of the God of the Bowels of Mercies.
The praise be unto God, the Lord of all worlds [creatures], the
God of the Bowels and Mercies, Sovereign of the day of doom ;
we adore Thee, we for help do cry unto Thee. Lead us in

the right way; the way of those unto whom Thou hast been
gracious, with whom Thou art not wroth, and which be not
gone astray." Hamûd, even in his formal religion, was of a
tolerant urbanity : religion was in him the (politic) religion
of rulers. In the palm ground without his kahwa, he has
(in their town manner) a raised place for prayers ; this was
a square platform in clay, with a low cornice, bestrewn with
clean gravel, and so large that a coffee company might kneel
in it and bow themselves to the ground. Hamûd prayed
in this oratory in the day-time, as imâm, before the men
of his household. Some day whilst they prayed, Aly, that
ribald foot-follower of Mâjid, laid hands suddenly on my
mantle to have drawn me among them. But Hamûd stayed
in his prayers to smile towards one and the other, and with
a sign forbade that the stranger should suffer any displeasure.
In all the house-courts at Hâyil, and in their orchard grounds,
there is made some such praying-stand ; it may be a manner
of the reformed religion in Nejd, and like to this we have
seen prayer-steads in the open deserts defended from the
common by a border of stones. Every such raised clay *masálly*,
littered with pure gravel, is turned towards the sanctuary of
Arabia.

A week passed and then the Emir Mohammed came again
from the wilderness : the next afternoon he called for me after
the mejlis. His usher found me slumbering in my makhzan ;
worn and broken in this long year of famine and fatigues, I was
fallen into a great languor. The Prince's man roused me with
haste and violence in their vernile manner : " Stand up thou
and come off ; the Emir calls thee ; " and because I stayed to
take the kerchief and mantle, even this, when we entered the
audience, was laid against me, the slave saying to the Emir
that ' Khalîl had not been willing to follow him ! '
Mohammed had gone over from the mejlis with the rajajîl
to Abeyd's kahwa. The Emir sat now in Hamûd's place,
and Hamûd where Sleymàn daily sat. The light scimitar, with
golden hilt, that Mohammed carries loose in his hand, was
leaned up to the wall beside him ; the blade is said to be of
some extremely fine temper. He sat as an Arabian, in his loose
cotton tunic, mantle and kerchief, with naked shanks and feet,
his sandals, which he had put off at the carpet, were set out
before him. I saluted the Emir, *Salaam aleyk.* No answer :
then I greeted Hamûd and Sleymàn, now of friendly acquaintance, in the same words, and with *aleykom es-salaam* they
hailed me smiling comfortably again. One showed me to a

place where I should sit down before the Emir, who said shortly
" From whence ? "—" From my makhzan."—' And what found I
there to do all the day, ha! and what had I seen in the time
of my being at Hâyil, was it well?'   When the Prince said,
" Khalîl ! " I should have responded in their manner *Aunak*
or *Labbeyk* or *Tawîl el-Ummr*, " O Long-of-age! and what is
thy sweet will ? " but feeling as an European among these light-
tongued Asiatics, and full of mortal weariness, I kept silence.
So the Emir, who had not responded to my salutation, turned
abruptly to ask Hamûd and Sleymàn : *Mâ yarúdd!* ' how!
he returns not one's word who speaks with him ? '   Hamûd
responded kindly for me, ' He could not tell, it might be
Khalîl is tired.'   I answered after the pause, " I am lately
arrived in this place, but *aghrûty*, I suppose it is very well."
The Emir opened his great feminine Arab eyes upon me as if
he wondered at the not flattering plainness of my speech ; and
he said suddenly, with an emphasis, before the company, " Ay,
I think so indeed, it is very well !—and what think you Khalîl,
it is a good air ? "—" I think so, but the flies are very thick."—
" Hmm, the flies are very thick ! and went you in the pilgrimage to the Holy City (Jerusalem) ? "—" Twice or thrice, and to
J. Tôr, where is the mountain of our Lord Mûsa."—Some among
them said to the Emir, " We have heard that monks of the
Nasâra dwell there, their habitation is built like a castle in
the midst of the khála, and the entry is by a window upon
the wall ; and who would come in there must be drawn up by
a wheelwork and ropes."   The Emir asked, " And have they
riches ? "—" They have a revenue of alms."   The Emir rose,
and taking his sandals, all the people stood up with him,—he
beckoned them to be seated still, and went out to the plantation.   In the time of his absence there was silence in all the
company ; when he returned he sat down again without ceremony.   The Prince, who would discern my mind in my answers,
asked me, " Were dates good or else bad ? "   and I answered
" *battâl, battâl,* very bad."—" Bread is better ? and what in your
tongue is bread ? " he repeated to himself the name which he
had heard in Turkish, and he knew it in the Persian ; Mohammed, formerly conductor of the pilgrimage, can also speak
in that language.

    The Emir spoke to me with the light impatient gestures
of Arabs not too well pleased, and who play the first parts,—
a sudden shooting of the brows, and that shallow extending of
the head from the neck, which are of the bird-like inhabitants
of nomadic Nejd, and whilst at their every inept word's end
they expect thy answer.   The Emir was favourably minded to-

ward me, but the company of malignant young fanatics always about him, continually traduced the Nasrâny. Mohammed now Prince was as much better than they, as he was of an higher understanding. When to some new question of the Emir I confirmed my answer in the Beduin wise, By his life, *hayâtak,* he said to Hamûd, "Seest thou? Khalîl has learned to speak (Arabic) among the Annezy, he says *aghrúty.*" —"And what might I say, O el-Muhafûth? I speak as I heard it of the Beduw." The Prince would not that I should question him of grammar, but hearing me name him so justly by his title, Warden (which is nearly that in our history of Protector), he said mildly, "Well, swear By the life of Ullah!" (The other, since they are become so clear-sighted with the Waháby, is an oath savouring of idolatry.) I answered somewhat out of the Prince's season, "—and thus even the nomads use, in a greater occasion, but they say, *By the life of thee,* in a little matter." As the Prince could not draw from me any smooth words of courtiers, Hamûd and Sleymàn hastened, with their fair speech, to help forth the matter and excuse me. "Certainly, they said, Khalîl is not very well to-day, eigh, the poor man! he looks sick indeed!"—And I passed the most daylight hours, stretched weakly upon the unswept floor of my makhzan, when the malignants told the Emir I was writing up his béled; so there ofttimes came in spies from the Castle, who opened upon me suddenly, to see in what manner the Nasrâny were busied.—*Emir:* "And thy medicines are what? hast thou *tiryâk?*" [thus our fathers said treacle, θηριακ-, the antidote of therine poisons]. In an extreme faintness, I was now almost falling into a slumber, and my attention beginning to waver I could but say,—"What is tiryâk?—I remember, but I have it not, by God there is no such thing." *Sleymàn:* "Khalîl has plenty of salts Engleys (magnesia)— hast thou not, Khalîl?" At this dull sally, and the Arabian Emir being so much in thought of poison, I could not forbear to smile,—an offence before rulers. Sleymàn then beginning to call me to give account in that presence of the New Continent, he would I should say, if we had not dates there, but the "Long-of-Days" rose abruptly and haughtily,—so rose all the rest with him, and they departed.

A word now of the princely family and of the state of J. Shammar: and first of the tragedies in the house of Ibn Rashîd. Telâl returning from er-Riâth (whither he was accustomed, as holding of the Waháby, to go every year with a present of horses) fell sick, *musky,* poisoned, it was said, in his cup, in East Nejd. His health decayed, and the Prince fell into a sort of melancholy frenzy. Telâl sent to Bagdad for a certain Persian hakîm. The hakîm journeyed down to Hâyil, and when he had visited the Prince, he gave his judgment unadvisedly : " This sickness is not unto death, it is rather a long disease which must waste thy understanding."—Telâl answered, " Aha, shall I be a fool ?—wellah *mejnûn ! wa ana el*-HÂKIM, and I being the Ruler ? " And because his high heart might not longer endure to live in the common pity, one day when he had shut himself in his chamber, he set his pistols against his manly breast, and fired them and ended. So Metaab, his brother, became Emir at Hâyil, as the elder of the princely house inheriting Abdullah their father's dignity : Telâl's children were (legally) passed by, of whom the eldest, Bunder, afterwards by his murderous deed Emir, was then a young man of seventeen years. Metaab I have often heard praised as a man of mild demeanour, and not common understanding ; he was princely and popular at once, as the most of his house, politic, such as the great sheukh el-Aarab, and a fortunate governor. Metaab sat not fully two years,—always in the ambitious misliking of his nephew Bunder, a raw and strong-headed young man. Bunder, conspiring with his next brother, Bedr, against their uncle, the ungracious young men determined to kill him.

They knew that their uncle wore upon his arm " an amulet which assured his life from lead," therefore the young parricides found means to cast a silver bullet.—Metaab sat in his fatal hour with his friends and the men-at-arms before him in the afternoon mejlis, which is held, as said, upon the further side of the Méshab, twenty-five paces over in face of the Kasr.—Bunder and Bedr were secretly gone up from the apartments within to the head of the castle wall, where is a terrace and parapet. Bunder pointing down his matchlock through a small trap in the wall, fired first ; and very likely his hand wavered when all hanged upon that shot, for his ball went a little awry and razed the thick head-band of a great Beduin sheykh *Ibn Shalàn*, chief of the strong and not unfriendly Annezy tribe er-Ruwàlla in the north, who that day arrived from his dîra, to visit Prince Ibn Rashîd. Ibn Shalàn, hearing the shot sing about his ears, started up, and (cried he) putting a hand to his head, " Akhs, Mohafùth, wouldst thou murder me ! " The Prince, who sat on, and would not save himself by an unseemly flight, answered the sheykh with a constant mild face, " Fear not ; thou wilt see that the shot was levelled at myself." A second shot struck the Emir in the breast, which was Bedr's.

Bunder being now Prince, sat not a full year out, and could not prosper : in his time, was that plague which so greatly wasted the country. Mohammed who is now Emir, when his brother Metaab was fallen, fled to er-Riâth, where he lived awhile. The Waháby prince, Abdullah Ibn Saûd, was a mean to reconcile them, and Bunder, by letters, promising peace, invited his uncle to return home. So Mohammed came, and receiving his old office, was governor again of the Bagdad haj caravan. Mohammed went by with the convoy returning from Mecca to Mesopotamia, and there he was to take up the year's provision of temmn for the Mothîf (if you would believe them, a thousand camel-loads,—150 tons !). Mohammed finding only Thuffîr Aarab at el-Méshed, hired camels of them with promise of safe-conduct going and returning, in the estates of Ibn Rashîd ; for they were Beduw from without, and not friendly with the Jebel. The journey is two weeks' marches of the nomads for loaded camels.—Mohammed approaching Hâyil, sent before him to salute the Emir saying, " Mohammed greets thee, and has brought down thy purveyance of temmn for the Mothîf."—" Ha ! is Mohammed come ? answered Bunder,— he shall not enter Hâyil." Then Bundei, Bedr, and Hamûd rode forth, these three together, to meet Mohammed ; and at Bunder's commandment the town gates behind them were shut.

Mohammed sat upon his thelûl, when they met with him, as he had ridden down from the north, and said Bunder, " Mohammed, what Beduw hast thou brought to Hâyil ?—the Thuffîr ! and yet thou knowest them to be gôm with us ! " *Mohammed :* " Wellah, yâ el-Mohafûth, I have brought them *bi wéjhy,* under my countenance ! (and in the Arabian guise he stroked down his visage to the beard)—because I found none other for the carriage of your temmn." Whilst Bunder lowered upon him, Hamûd, who was in covenant with his cousin Mohammed, made him a sign that his life was in doubt,—by drawing (it is told) the forefinger upon his gullet. Mohammed spoke to one of the town who came by on horseback, " Ho there ! lend me thy mare awhile," making as though he would go and see to the entry and unloading of his caravan. Mohammed, when he was settled on horseback, drew over to the young Prince and caught Bunder's " horns," and with his other hand he took the crooked broad dagger, which upon a journey they wear at the belt.—" *La ameymy, la ameymy,* do it not, do it not, little 'nuncle mine ! " exclaimed Bunder in the horror and anguish of death. Mohammed answered with a deadly stern voice, " Wherefore didst thou kill thine uncle? *wa hu fi batn-ak*, and he is in thy belly (thou hast devoured him, dignity, life, and all)," and with a murderous hand-cast he struck the blade into his nephew's bowels! —There remained no choice to Mohammed, when he had received the sign, he must slay his elder brother's son, or himself be lost; for if he should fly, how might he have outgone the godless young parricides? his thelûl was weary, he was weary himself; and he must forsake the Thuffîr, to whom his princely word had been plighted.—Devouring is the impotent ambition to rule, of all Arabians who are born near the sheykhly state. Mohammed had been a loyal private man under Metaab; his brother fallen, what remained but to avenge him? and the garland should be his own.

Bunder slain, he must cut off kindred, which else would endanger him. The iniquity of fortune executed these crimes by Mohammed's hand, rather than his own execrable ambition.—These are the tragedies of the house of Ibn Rashîd! their beginning was from Telâl, the murderer of himself: the fault of one extends far round, such is the cursed nature of evil, as the rundles of a stone dashed into water, trouble all the pool. There are some who say, that Hamûd made Bunder's dying sure with a pistol-shot,—he might do this, because his lot was bound up in Mohammed's life: but trustworthy persons in Hâyil have assured me that Hamûd had no violent hand in it.—Hamûd turning his horse's head, galloped to town and commanded to 'keep the gates close, and let no man pass out or enter for any cause'; and riding in to the Méshab he cried: "Hearken, all of you! a Rashîdy has slain a Rashîdy,— there is no word for any of you to say! let no man raise his voice or make stir, upon pain of my hewing off his head wellah with this sword."

In Hâyil there was a long silence, the subject people shrunk in from the streets to their houses! Beduins in the town were aghast, inhabitants of the khála, to which no man "may set doors and bars," seeing the gates of Hâyil to be shut round about them.

An horrible slaughter was begun in the Kasr, for Mohammed commanded that all the children of Telâl should be put to death, and the four children of his own sister, widow of one *el-Jabbár* of the house *Ibn Aly*, (that, till Abdullah won all, were formerly at strife with the Rashîdy family for the sheykhship of Hâyil, --and of them was Mohammed's own mother). Their uncle's bloody command was fulfilled, and the bleeding warm corses, deceived of their young lives, were carried out the same hour to the burial; there died with them also the slaves, their equals in age, brought up in their fathers' households,—their servile brethren, that else would be, at any time, willing instruments to avenge them.

All Hâyil trembled that day till evening and the long night till morning, when Mohammed, standing in the Méshab with a drawn sword, called to those who sat timidly on the clay banks,—the most were Beduins—"Yâ Moslemin! I had not so dealt with them, but because I was afraid for this! (he clapped the left palm to the side of his neck), and as they went about to kill me, *ana sabáktahum,* I have prevented them." Afterward he said :—" And they which killed my brother Metaab, think ye they had spared me ? " " And hearing his voice, we sat (an eyewitness, of the Meteyr, told me) astonished, every one seeing the black death before him."—Then Mohammed sat down in the Emir's place as Muhâfuth. By and by some of the principal persons at Hâyil came into the Méshab bending to this new lord of their lives, and giving him joy of his seized authority. Thus ' out dock in nettle,' Bunder away, Mohammed began to rule; and never was the government, they say, in more sufficient handling.

—Bedr had started away upon his mare for bitter-sweet life to the waste wilderness : he fled at assr. On the morrow, fainting with hunger and thirst, and the suffered desolation of mind and weariness, he shot away his spent horse, and climbed upon a mountain.—From thence he might look far out over the horror of the world, become to him a vast dying place ! Mohammed had sent horsemen to scour the khála, and take him ; and when they found Bedr in the rocks they would not listen to his lamentable petitions : they killed him there without remedy, and hastily loading his body they came again the same day to Hâyil. The chief of them as he entered, all heated, to Mohammed, exclaimed joyfully, "Wellah, O Muhafûth, I bring thee glad tidings ! it may please thee come with me where-as I will show thee Bedr lies dead ; this hand did it, and so perish all the enemies of the Emir ! " But Mohammed looked grimly upon the man, and cried, "Who commanded thee to kill him ? I commanded thee, son of an hound ? when, thou cursed one ? Ullah curse thy father, akhs ! hast thou slain Bedr ? " and, drawing his sword, he fetched him a clean back-stroke upon the neck-bone, and swapt off at once (they pretend) the miserable man's head. Mohammed used an old bitter policy of tyrants, by which they hope to make their perplexed causes seem the more honest in the thick eye-sight of the common people. " How happened it, I asked, that Bedr, who must know the wilderness far about, since the princely children accompany the ghrazzus, had not ridden hardily in some way of escape ? Could not his mare have borne him an hundred miles ?—a man of sober courage, in an extremity, might have endured, until he had passed the dominion of Ibn Rashîd, and entered into the first free town of el-Kasîm." It was answered, " The young man was confused in so great a calamity, and jâhil, of an inept humour, and there was none to deliver him."

Hamûd and Mohammed allied together, there was danger between them and Telâl's sons ; and if they had not fore stalled Bunder and Bedr, they had paid it with their lives. The massacres were surely contrary to the clement nature of the strong man Hamûd. Hamûd, who for his pleasant equal countenance, in the people's eyes, has deserved to be named by his fellow citizens *Azîz*, " a beloved," is for all that, when contraried out of friendship, a lordly man of outrageous incontinent tongue and jabbâr, as his father was ; and doubtless he would be a high-handed Nimrod in any instant peril. Besides, it is thus that Arabs deal with Arabs ; there are none more pestilent, and ungenerous enemies. Hamûd out of hospitality, is as all the Arabs of a somewhat miserable humour, and I have heard it uttered at Hâyil, " Hamûd *khára !* " that is draffe or worse. These are vile terms of the Hejâz, spread from the dens of savage life, under criminal governors, in the Holy Cities ; and not of those schools of speaking well and of comely manners, which are the kahwa in the Arabian oases and the mejlis in the open khála.—A fearful necessity was laid upon Mohammed : for save by these murders of his own nigh blood, he could not have sat in any daily assurance. Mohammed is childless, and ajjr, a man barren in himself ; the loyal Hamûd el-Abeyd has many children.

His instant dangers being thus dispersed, Mohammed set himself to the work of government, to win the opinion of his proper merit; and affecting popular manners, he is easier of his dispense than was formerly Telâl. Never Prince used his authority, where not resisted, with more stern moderation at home, but he is pitiless in the excision of any unsound parts of the commonwealth. When Jauf fell to him again by the mutiny of the few Moghrâreba left in garrison, it is said, he commanded to cut off the right hands of many that were gone over to the faith of the Dowla. Yet Jauf had not been a full generation under the Jebel ; for Mohammed himself, then a young man, was with his uncle Abeyd at the taking of it, and he was wounded then by a ball in the foot which lodged in the bone ;—the shot had lately been taken from him in

Hâyil by a Persian hakîm, come down, for the purpose, from Mesopotamia.

As for any bounty in such Arabian Princes, it is rather good laid out by them to usury. They are easy to loose a pound to-day, which within a while may return with ten in his mouth. The Arabs say, " Ibn Rashîd uses to deal with every man *aly aklu*, according to his understanding." Fortune was to Mohammed's youth contrary, a bloody chance has made him Ruler. In his government he bears with that which may not be soon amended ; he cannot by force only bridle the slippery wills of the nomads ; and though his heart swell secretly, he receives all with his fair-weather countenance, and to friendly discourse ; and of few words, in wisely questioning them, he discerns their minds. Motlog, sheykh of the Fejîr, whom he misliked, he sends home smiling ; and the Prince will levy his next year's *miry* from the Fukara, without those tribesmen's unwillingness. The principal men of Teyma, his good outlying town, whose well was fallen, depart from him with rewards. Mohammed smooths the minds of the common people ; if any rude Beduin lad call to him in the street, or from the mejlis (they are all arrant beggers), " Aha ! el-Muhafûth, God give thee long life ! as truly as I came hither, in such a rubba, and wellah am naked," he will graciously dismiss him with " *bismillah,* in God's name ! go with such an one, and he will give thee garments,"—that is a tunic worth two shillings at Hâyil, a coarse worsted cloak of nine shillings, a kerchief of sixpence ; and since they are purchased in the gross at Bagdad, and brought down upon the Emir's own camels, they may cost him not ten shillings.

What is the state and authority for which these bitter Arabians contended ? Ibn Rashîd is master, as I can understand, of some thirty oases, of which there are five good desert towns : Sh'kâky, Jauf, Hâyil, Gofar, Teyma, with a population together of 12,000 to 13,000 souls : others are good villages, as *el-Kasr, Mógug, Aly, Mustajidda, Feyd, er-Rautha, Semîra, el-Háyat,* and more, with hardly 5000 persons. There are, besides the oases, many outlying hamlets in the desert of Jebel Shammar inhabited by a family or two or three households, that are colonists from the next villages ; in the best may be a score of houses, in the least are not ten inhabitants ; such are *Jefeyfa, el-Agella, el-Gussa, Biddía, Haleyfa, Thùrghrod, Makhaúl, Otheym.* Some among them are but granges, which lie forsaken, after the April harvest is carried, until the autumn sowing and the new months of irrigation : but the palm hamlets have stable

inhabitants, as Biddîa, Thùrghrod. So the settled population
of Jebel Shammar may be hardly 20,000 souls : add to these
the tributary nomads, Beny Wáhab,—the Fejîr, 800, and half
tribe of Wélad Aly in the south, 1600—say together 2500 ;
then Bishr in the south, say 3000, or they are less ; northern
Harb in the obedience of Ibn Rashîd, say 2000 ; southern
Shammar, hardly 2000 ; midland Heteym, say 1500 ; Sherarát,
say 2500; and besides them no more. In all, say 14,000 persons or less : and the sum of stable and nomad dwellers may be
not much better than 30,000 souls.

The burden of the Emir's public contribution is levied in the
settlements, upon the fruits of corn and dates,—we have seen
that it was in Teyma nearly £1 sterling for every head ; and
among nomads, (who have little regard of any government set up
for the public advantage,) it was in the Fukara, a poor tribe,
about £1 sterling for eight or ten persons. Other than these
exactions there are certain dues, of which I am not well informed, such as that payment to be made of sixty reals upon
every camel-load of Hameydy tobacco, which is brought in,
at the sûk gates of Hâyil. In this not improbable course of
conjecture I can compute the state revenues of Ibn Rashîd,
partly in kind, and partly paid in silver, to be nearly £40,000,
of which hardly the twentieth part is gathered among his
nomads. The private rents of the Prince are also very large.
The price and fruits of all confiscated possessions are brought
yearly into the beyt el-mâl, or public treasure-house.

The ordinary government expenses, for the castle service,
for the maintenance of the armed band, the slave grooms of his
stud and the herdsmen of his live wealth in the wilderness,
stewards, mutasállims, his residents in outlying towns as
Teyma and Jauf, the public hospitality at Hâyil, and for
the changes of clothing, may be nearly £12,000. His extraordinary expenses are nearly £1000 yearly in gunpowder and
provision for the general ghrazzus, and yearly gifts. His bribes
are according to the shifting weather of the world, to great
Ottoman government men ; and now on account of Kheybar,
he was gilding some of their crooked fingers in Medina. These
disbursements are covered by his selling, most years, Nejd
horses (all stallions) in India ; which, according to the request,
are shipped at Kuweyt, commonly about two score together :—his
stud servants, who convey them, are absent from Hâyil, upon
the India expedition, about two months.

In a necessity of warfare Ibn Rashîd might summon to the
field, I suppose, without much difficulty, 2000 fighting men from
his villages, riders upon camels (the most thelûls), but not all

provided with fire-arms; and to ride in an expedition not easily
to a fourth of the number. Among the subject Beduw he
might raise at a need, of the tribes more bound to him, or
most fearing him as nigh neighbours, Shammar, Bishr, Harb,
Heteym, as I can estimate of my knowledge of the land, eight
hundred or nine hundred : of the B. Wáhab, as borderers,
always of doubtful trust, and not seldom rebels, two hundred
and fifty ; of the oppressed Sherarát, who would gladly turn
from him to the Dowla, if the Syrian government would stand
by them, nearly another two hundred ; that is altogether to the
number of 1300 nomad Arabians, namely dromedary riders
(only a few principal sheykhs are horsemen)—and two-third
parts of them armed with matchlocks, the remnant riding as
they may, with swords, clubs, spears and lances. The Prince
is said to have " four hundred horses," lent out to men of his
trust and interest among the submitted tribes ; they are riders
in his yearly expeditions. In the Prince's general ghrazzus
there ride, his rajajîl and Hâyil townsmen and men of the
next villages, about four hundred men, and nearly as many of
the tributary Beduw that are ready at the word of the Emir
to mount with him in the hope of winning : and to all a day
is given and the assembling place. The Arabians, dwelling
in a dead country, think that a marvellous muster of human
lives which they see assemble to Ibn Rashîd's forays. They
will tell you " All the way was full of riders betwixt Hâyil
and Gofar ! "—since it is hardly twelve miles, that were but
a rider, in their loose array, for every twenty paces; and
eight hundred or nine hundred armed Arabs mounted upon
dromedaries, even in the eyes of Europeans, were a noble
spectacle.

The Prince Mohammed is pitiless in battle, he shoots with
an European rifle ; Hamûd, of ponderous strength, is seen
raging in arms by the Emir's side, and, if need were, since
they are sworn together to the death, he would cover him
with his body. The princes, descended from their thelûls,
and sitting upon horseback in their " David shirts of mail,"
are among the forefighters, and the wings of the men-at-
arms, shooting against the enemy, close them upon either
hand. The Emir's battle bears down the poor Beduw, by
weight and numbers ; for the rajajîl, and his riders of the
villages, used to the civil life, hear the words of command,
and can maintain themselves in a body together. But the
bird-witted Beduins who, in their herding life, have no
thought of martial exercises, may hardly gather, in the day
of battle, under their sheukh, but like screaming hawks they

fight dispersedly, tilting hither and thither, every man with less regard of the common than of his private interest, and that is to catch a beggarly booty : the poor nomads acknowledge themselves to be betrayed by tóma, the greediness of gain. Thus their resistance is weak, and woe to the broken and turned to flight ! None of the Emir's enemies are taken to quarter until they be destroyed : and cruel are the mercies of the rajajîl and the dire-hearted slaves of Ibn Rashîd. I have known when some miserable tribesmen made prisoners were cast by the Emir's band into their own well-pits :—the Arabians take no captives. The battles with nomads are commonly fought in the summer, about their principal water-stations, where they are long lodged in great standing camps.

Thus the Beduins say " It is Ibn Rashîd that weakens the Beduw ! " Their resistance broken, he receives them among his confederate tributaries, and delivers them from all their enemies from his side. A part of the public spoil is divided to the rajajîl, and every man's is that commonly upon which he first laid his hand. Ibrahîm the Algerian, one of them who often came to speak with me of his West Country, said that to every man of the Emir's rajajîl are delivered three or four reals at the setting out, that he may buy himself wheat, dates and ammunition ; and there is carried with them sometimes as much as four camel loads of powder and lead from Hâyil, which is partly for the Beduw that will join him by the way.

But to circumscribe the principality or dominion in the deserts of Ibn Rashîd :—his borders in the North are the Ruwàlla, northern Shammar and Thuffîr marches, nomad tribes friendly to the Jebel, but not his tributaries. Upon the East his limits are at the dominion of Boreyda, which we shall see is a principality of many good villages in the Nefûd of Kasîm, as el-Ayûn, Khubbera, er-Russ, but with no subject Beduw. The princely house of Hâyil is by marriage allied to that usurping peasant *Weled Mahanna* tyrant of Boreyda, and they are accorded together against the East, that is Aneyza, and the now decayed power of the Waháby beyond the mountain. In the South, having lost Kheybar, his limits are at about an hundred miles from el-Medina ; the deserts of his dominion are bounded westwards by the great haj-way from Syria,—if we leave out the B. Atîeh—and all the next territory of the Sherarát is subject to him, which ascends to J. Sherra and so turns about by the *W. Sirhân* to his good northern towns of Jauf and Sh'kâky and their suburbs. In a word, all that is Ibn Rashîd's desert country lying between Jauf, el-Kasîm and the Derb el-Haj ; north and

south some ninety leagues over, and between east and west it
may be one hundred and seventy leagues over. And the whole
he keeps continually subdued to him with a force (by their
own saying) of about five hundred thelûl riders, his rajajîl and
villagers; for who may assemble in equal numbers out of the
dead wilderness, or what were twice so many wild Beduins,
the half being almost without arms, to resist him ?

CHAPTER II.

THE great tribes partly or wholly west of the Derb el-Haj are too far from him ; they fear not Ibn Rashîd in their dangerous encumbered dîras. Beginning from the north, they are the B. Sókhr in the Belka, now submitted to the government of Syria, then B. Atîeh, and backward of them the stout nomad nation of the Howeytát, so far extended betwixt the two seas, Bíllî behind the Harra, and their neighbours the noble and ancient stock of Jeheyna : besides the southern Harb, nomads and villagers, in Hejâz, and all whose soil seyls into the Wady el-Humth. Between Mecca country and el-Kasîm is the great nomad territory, more than one hundred leagues over, (the best I have seen in the wilderness of Arabia,) of the Ateyba nation ; they are stout in arms, and civil-spirited Beduins, and Ibn Rashîd's capital enemies. There hardly passed a year in which Ibn Rashîd did not invade them, and they again were the bane of the next Aarab of his federation, especially of the midland Heteym, upon the W. er-Rummah, and their Harb

234

neighbours.—Such are his estates, and this is the government of Ibn Rashîd, a name now so great in the (after the master-strokes of the Waháby) timid Upper or Nomadic Arabia.

Between affection and fear, the desert people call him, and he will name himself (it is the pleasant oath of his house) *Akhu Noora.* Thus Abdullah, the first Muhafûth, in Hâyil, swore after the Nejd urbanity and magnanimity by his little sister, " As I am akhu (the brother of) Noora." Telâl after him, and Metaab, swore likewise thus, and so does Mohammed ; for a second Noora, Abdullah's daughter, was their sister, now deceased.—That is a formidable utterance of the Ruler, above the jest, were it spoken against a man's life ! I have heard a man, who had no sister, swear pleasantly by his infant daughter, " I am Abu (the father of) *Atheba !* " So it is in friendship a pretty adulation, and may be a knavish irony, to say to one, " O thou akhu of Such (naming her) ; "—as much as " O magnanimous, that even in thy weak things art worthy to be named among the valiant." I have heard nomad lads (Bishr) exclaim, *Ana akhu Chokty* (*ákhty*) ! I am the brother of Sissy, my little sister ; and akin to this, in the Beduin urbanity, is that (old man's) word of sober astonishment, *Ana weled abúy !* I (am) the son of my father.

To speak shortly of the princely families : Mohammed (as said) is ajjr, made sterile by some pernicious medicine, given him in a sickness, " when by this only he might be saved from death." In such he is unhappy, it is impossible he should strengthen himself by his own offspring. Mohammed has the four wives of their religious licence, two are *hathariyát,* ' women of the settlements,' and other two are *beduwiyát.* By strange adventure, one of those townswomen, we have seen, is named " a Christian." This I often heard ; but what truth there might be in their words, I cannot tell. What countrywoman she was, I could not learn of them. ' She came to Hâyil few years before with her brother, a young man who showing them masteries, and fencing with the lance upon horseback,' had delighted these loose riding and unfeaty Arabians. " The Christian became a Mosleman in Hâyil," and departing, he left his sister wife of the lord of the land. Might this, I mused, have been some horse-player from Egypt or the northern border countries ?— but where my words would be quickly misreported by tale-bearers in the Castle, to ask at large of the Prince's matter were not prudent. The other town wife is a sister of *Hásan,* Weled Mahanna, tyrant of Boreyda ; and Hamûd has a daughter of this Emir Hásan, among his wives.

Mohammed puts away and takes new wives, at his list,

" month by month : " howbeit the princely wretch cannot purchase the common blessing ! his children are as dead within
him, and the dreaded inhabitant of yonder castle remains a
desolate man, or less than a man, in the midst of his marriages.
But the childless Emir cherishes as his own son the little orphan
child, *Abd el-Azîz*, the flesh which is left in the world of his
brother Metaab, and has a father's tenderness of his daily thriving
and learning, that he himself oversees. The child brought him
every day his task, versets of the koran, written, as the Arabian
oasis children use, in their ink made of the soot of pome-
granate rinds, upon a wooden tablet, which is whitened with
jiss or pipe-clay : for another school-day the ink is washed out,
and the plate new whitened. Abd el-Azîz came often to my
makhzan, and he asked me to give him some better ink and
sheets of paper, and percussion caps for a little pistol which
had been given him by his uncle Mohammed. If Mâjid came
in then, Abd el-Azîz would rise and go out,—and I saw there
was no word or sign of fellowship between them. Abd el-Azîz
came alone, or with another princely child, (whom Mohammed
had spared,)—it was the orphan of Bunder ! A Galla slave-boy
of a very good nature accompanied them.

Those princely children by an horrible confusion of wedlock
were half-brothers, born of one mother, of an uncle and nephew,
of whom one had murdered the other ! and the young parricide,
whom no man mourned, was now gone by the murderous
avenging hand of Mohammed his next uncle (to-day Emir) to
his bloody grave.—Bunder having murdered the Prince his
uncle, took to wife the widow of the slain and mother of Abd
el-Azîz,—his aunt ; and the parricide begat upon her a son. The
murderous young man spared his uncle's infant, for the present,
and might look, by such an healing of the breach of blood, to
lay up some assurance for himself against a day when this
little orphan of murdered Metaab should be grown.—Would
Abd el-Azîz seek in that day the life of the father of his
half-brother, with whom he had been bred, the same being his
step-father, his " uncle " and his cousin-german, and yet the
same by whom his own father was done to death long ago ?
Now Mohammed succeeding, the danger from the side of the
children is changed : will Bunder's son, if he may come to years,
for Abd el-Azîz's sake, and because he himself was preserved,
pardon in Mohammed his father's cutting off ?—but that horrid
deed was not in men's sight unjust.

The little Abd el-Azîz shows the gait and countenance of
his uncle the Emir, and carries a little sword which his mother
has given him ; yet there is somewhat in the child of sad

orphan looks, of the branch planted alone by waters not of his natural parentage. Already his mind seemed to muse much of these things; I have heard him say to himself, when he came to visit me, "Ha! it was he, *ellathi thábah* —who killed such an one or other," and the horrible word seemed to be of presage, it was so light upon the child's lips.—O God! who can forecast their tragedies to come! what shall be the next vengeance and succession and forestalling of deaths between them? The eyes painted, their long hair shed in the midst and plaited in love-locks all round their orphan heads, and with the white tunics to their feet, these two princely children had the tender fresh looks of little maidens. Upon that other part may stand Mâjid, for who is after the Prince to-day but his cousin Hamûd? Of this perhaps the children's early shunning each other;—it was Abd el-Azîz who shunned Mâjid. But is it for aught that was practised against his parentage by Hamûd? perhaps they already had determined in their young hearts the destruction of each other. Mâjid also is a pleasant grandson of his father's brother, and like a nephew to the Emir. Mâjid, grandson of Abeyd, is as his father, of a cheerful popular spirit, but less loyal; and there is some perilous presentiment in him, an ambitious confidence that he shall himself one day be the Ruler. Abd el-Aziz, grandson of Abdullah, is an eagle's young; and in his day, if he may so long live, he will pierce through an hand that holds him with a stroke of his talons; but he seems to be of a gentle heart, and if God please that this child be afterwards Emir in Hâyil, he is like to be a good princely man, like his father Metaab.—Such for all their high looks, which is but sordid prince-craft, are the secret miseries of the Emirs' lives at Hâyil; and an horror must hang over Mohammed, or he is not a man, in his bloody solitude. In Kasîm I heard men say of Mohammed ibn Rashîd, "He has committed crimes which before were not known in the world!"

To speak then of the family of Abeyd, of which Hamûd is now head. Abeyd was conductor of the military power of J. Shammar, in Abdullah his brother and in his nephew Telâl's days. He was a martial man, and a Waháby more than is now Hamûd, born in easier times. He was a master of the Arabian warfare, a champion in the eyes of the discomfited Aarab. Abeyd, as said, was an excellent kassâd, he indited of all his desert warfare; his boastful rimes, known wide in the wilderness, were ofttimes sung for me, in the nomad booths. The language of the kasasîd is as a language apart from the popular speech; but here I may remember some plain and notable verse of Abeyd, as that which says, " By this hand are fallen of the enemies ninety men. Smitten to death the Kusmân perished before me, until the evening, when my fingers could not be loosed from the handle of the sword ; the sleeve of my garment was stiffened with the blood of war." This he made of the repulse of an ill-commanded and worse starred expedition, sent out by the great Kasîm town Aneyza, against Ibn Rashîd.—" And how happened it, I asked, that Abeyd, one man, could make so monstrous a slaughter of the men contending against him in battle ? " *Answer :* " When the Kusmân were broken and turned to flight, Abeyd pursuing, whilst the day lasted, struck down so many of the fugitives (from the backward) that they were numbered as ninety men ; " and a worthy and principal person who told me the tale put it to Abeyd's glory that he had killed many thus !

Abeyd could be generous, where the Arabs are so least, with an adversary : and clad in his hauberk of mail which they call Davidian,—for David, say they, first found the ringed armour, and Ullah made the crude iron easy to be drawn in his prophetic fingers—the jeopardy of the strong leader was not very great in the field of battle. One day in his bitter warfare with the Annezy *Ibn Mujállad,* Beduins of el-Kasîm and nomad inheritors of the palm valleys *el-Háyat* (in the Harrat Kheybar), the sheykh of the tribe espying this prince their destroyer in the battle, with a great cry defied him, and tilted desperately against him ; but Abeyd (though nettled with his injuries, yet pitying a man whom he had sorely afflicted) let the Beduwy pass under his romhh, calling to him ' that he would not kill a man [having upon him only a cotton tunic] who ran thus wilfully to his own destruction.'

Abeyd was in his latter days the old man of the saffron beard at home, a mild father of the Arabian household ; he was dead, according to their saying, seven years before my coming to Hâyil, and two years after the decease of Telâl. Of Abeyd's children we have seen Fáhd, the elder, had been set aside for the weakness of his understanding, a man now at the middle age, of a very good countenance, well-grown, and of such stature nearly as his next brother Hamûd, who had supplanted him. He was of a gentle virtuous disposition, and with a sort of cheerful humility consenting to the will of others, only some obscure drawing of the brows, a perplexed secret sadness of face and troubled unsteadfastness of the eyes, were tokens in him of the distracted mind. He was an onlooker with the placid day-long musing of the Moslemîn, and little he said ; he was thus in some sort at Hâyil the happiest of mankind,—the only man's life that feared nothing. Fáhd passed his daily hours in Abeyd's kahwa, and Hamûd now sat in their father's hall in Abeyd's room, and next by him in a seat of honour sat Sleymàn: and Fáhd had no stately place, but he sat upon the common sitting-carpet with the younkers of the princely households, and with the officers of the Emir and any visiting sheykhs of the tribes and villages. Fáhd was become as it were a follower of Hamûd and the companion and play-fellow of Hamûd's son Mâjid. Mâjid his nephew said to me, " I love him, he is so quiet and peaceable a man ; " but yet he did not name him *ammy*, mine uncle. At the supper-time Fáhd departed, who was the father of a family. From his home Fáhd returned again to the paternal coffee-house to sit out the evening, and modestly he would attend awhile in the closet where kahwa was made, if he came in then, until " the Emir " (Hamûd) had ended all the saying of his superstitious devotion.

When the princes forayed, Fáhd was left in Hâyil. Upon a time he would needs ride out to them and came to his father in the field ; so said Abeyd, " How now, my son ! why comest thou hither ? "—" Father, I would ride in the ghrazzu and take part in the spoil; " and Abeyd, " Well, go home to thy house in Hâyil and abide our coming again, which shall be soon, it may please Ullah ; this is my will, and thou shalt lose nothing." The Semitic greediness of the poor man brought forth his infirm heart : and another time the poor man brought forth his fair growing daughter to Abeyd, saying, ' It was time now to sell her away ' (to be a bond-woman) ; and Abeyd falling fatherly in with his son's distracted humour gave him *fulús*, silver, for the price of his granddaughter, and bade Fáhd keep her still for him. The third brother, to read anything in his pale vicious looks, was an umbratile young man, and very fanatical; he lived apart near the Méshed gate, and came never to sit amongst his brethren in their father's hall. I met with him one or two times in a month, passing in the public street, and he cast upon me only sour glances ; he passed his time perhaps with the hareem, and seemed not to be held in any estimation at Hâyil. The fourth younger brother was Feyd, a good plain-hearted almost plebeian young man of seventeen years. Yet in him was some misshaping of nature, for I found in his jaws a double row of teeth. Sometimes in the absence of the Princes in the spring holidays or upon warfare, Feyd was left deputy-Emir, to hold the daily mejlis—at such times nearly forsaken—in Hâyil. After him was one Sleymàn, as I remember, a boy of little worth, and another, Abdullah, of his nephew Mâjid's age, sordid spirits and fitter to be bound

prentices to some ratcatcher than to come into any prince's
hall and audience. The last had fallen in his childhood from
a height and put an arm out of joint ; and as a bone-setter is
not found in these countries, and " it were not worth " to send
to Mesopotamia, they had let ' Ullah provide for him,' and
his arm now hanged down withered. He came very often
to my makhzan, to beg some trifle of the stranger : sore
eyes added to his unlovely looks, he asked for medicine, but
" I will not pay thee, said he, and I have not half a dollar."
Fanatical he was, and the dastardly lad would even threaten
me. The Hâyil princes (*bred up in the company of bond-
servants*) are perhaps mostly like vile-spirited in their youth.
When, rarely, Abdullah entered their father's khawa, Hamûd
called the boy cheerfully and made him sit down beside him ;
and casting his brother's arm about the child's neck, as the
Arabians will (caressing equally their own young sons and their
youngest brethren) he asked gently of his mirth and what he
did that day ; but the ungracious boy hardly responded and
soon shrunk sourly away.—Such were the old eagle Abeyd's
children, *affûn*, crow's eggs, all of them born with some
deficiency of nature, except Hamûd only. So it seems the
stock was faulty, it were strange if there lingered no alloy in
the noble substance of Hamûd ; and the temper of his mind,
though good, is not very fine ; but this may be found in the
Emir Mohammed.

Abeyd's family are wealthy, were it only of their landed
possessions in Hâyil ; they have palms also at Jauf,—and an
Arabian man's spending for his household, except it come by
the Mohammedan liberty of wiving, is small in our comparison.
Besides they are rich with the half fruits of el-Hâyat, which
of old appertained to the inheriting Annezy ; but when those
were driven out by Abeyd, their rents were given by Telâl
to his uncle and his heirs. Abeyd's family are also happy
in this, that no vengeance clouds the years before them for
kinsmen's blood. The wild nomads look on and speak with
an awe of the last damnable deeds in the house of Abdullah :
in their own little commonwealths of uncles' sons in the desert,
are not such impious ambitions. Feyd and Abdullah lived yet
minors in their brother Hamûd's house in Hâyil, where almost
daily I came to treat Feysal, and when I knocked at the ring
it was opened to me sometimes by a slave woman, the child's
nurse, sometimes by Feyd himself. I have found him stand
quarrelling with a carpenter, and they scolded together with
the Arabian franchise as equals. Or it was Abdullah that
opened, and sometimes Hamûd's daughter came to the door.

a pleasant girl, with her father's smiling ingenuous looks, clad only in her poor calico smock, dipped in indigo, without any ornament, and not to discern from the other village maidens of like age ; and such perhaps was Tamar David's daughter, who kneaded and baked bread. Simple was their place, a clay court and dwelling-chambers beyond, a house of hareem and eyyâl, where no strangers were admitted. I saw a line and a cross together, rudely chalked upon the wall of the doorway, |X—it is the wasm of Ibn Rashid. The children of the sheukh mingled with the people in the town ; they went only more freshly clad than other men's sons. Girls are like cage birds bred up in their houses ; young maidens are not seen abroad in the public streets. At fifteen years the sheykhly boys ride already in the ghrazzus ; having then almost two years been free of their schoolmaster, of whom there is little to learn but their letters.

To consider the government of Ibn Rashîd, which is for the public security in a great circuit of the nomad country :—the factious strifes had been appeased in the settlements, even the disorders of the desert were repressed by the sword of the Waháby religion, and the land of Ishmael became *béled amân*, a peaceable country. In the second generation a sheykhly man, Abdullah Ibn Rashîd, of one of the chief Hâyil houses, who had become a principal servitor of the Waháby Prince at er-Riâth, was sent home by Ibn Saûd to his own town in Jebel Shammar :—to be his constable of the west marches of Nejd, " TO GOVERN ANNEZY," and namely the southern tribes of that Beduin nation, landlords in the palm valleys of the Harrat Kheybar. Abdullah soon seated himself by the sword at Hâyil, and prevailing all round, he became muhâfuth of a new state, tithing villages and tribes ; yet of the zikâ, brought into his government treasury, yielding no tribute to er-Riâth, other than a present of horses which he led with him in his yearly visit to Ibn Saûd. This homage is now disused,—in the decay of the Waháby state ; and Ibn Rashîd is to-day the greatest prince in Nejd. His is a ruling of factious Arabs by right of the sword ; none of them not persuaded by fear would be his tributaries. The Beduw and oasis dwellers are not liegemen (as they see it) to any but their natural sheykhs. Townsmen have said to me ofttimes of Ibn Rashîd, even in Hâyil, *Henna mamlukin,* ' we dwell here as bondsmen under him.' A northern nomad patient, pointing backward, whilst he sat within my makhzan door, as if he feared to be descried through wood and walls, murmured to me between his teeth, " The Inhabitant of yonder Kasr is ZÂLIM, a strong-handed tyrant." At Hâyil, where are no stocks, tortures, nor prison, punishment is sudden, at the word of the Ruler; and the guilty, after his suffering, is dismissed.

The Emirs in Hâyil have austerely maintained the police of the desert.—This was told me of Metaab's time : One of the few salesmen to the tribes from the Syrian countries, who from time to time have arrived at Hâyil, was stripped and wounded, as he journeyed in the Sherarât dîra. The stranger came to Hâyil and complained of this outrage to the Emir. Metaab sent riders to summon the sheykhs of the Sherarât to find, and immediately deliver the guilty persons, which was done accordingly, they not daring to disobey Ibn Rashîd, an'd the riders returned with a prisoner. Metaab commanded the nomad to stand forth in the mejlis, and enquired of the stranger if this were he ? When he answered, " It is he," said the Emir, " Sherâry hound ! how durst thou do this violence ? " Metaab bade the stranger take the Sherâry's lance which had been brought with him, and as he had done unto him so to do to the fellow again. " What must I do, O el-Muhafûth ! " —" Pierce him, and kill him too, if it please thee ! " But the tradesman's heart was now cold, and he could not strike the man, but entreated the Emir, since he had his things again, to let him go. I have known certain Damascene salesmen to the Beduw, that had visited Hâyil, and one of them was a Christian, who traded every year to the W. Sirhân and Jauf. The man understanding that mantles were dear in the Jebel, had crossed the Nefûd with a camel-load to Hâyil. Telâl, the prince, spoke to him kindly, and was content that he should remain there awhile and sell his wares ; only exhorting him " not to shave the chin,"—the guise of Damascus Christians and the young coxcombs among the town Moslems.

Tribes agreeing ill together in Ibn Rashîd's confederacy (we have seen) are not in general suffered to molest each other : yet there are some nomads (whether because Hâyil would weaken them, or they are too outlying from him, and not so much bound to keeping of good neighbourhood) who complaining to the Emir of inroads made by Aarab of his subjection, have received his hard answer : " This lies between you and I will be no party in your Beduin dissensions." All the great sheykhs of Arabs are very subtle politic heads : and I think *it would be hard to find a fault in Ibn Rashîd's government,*—yet my later Kasîm friends (his enemies at Aneyza) dispraised it.

—A word of the armed band, *rajajîl es-sheukh.* Ibn Rashîd is much served (as said) by foreigners (adventurers, and fugitives) from East Nejd : and such will be faithful servants of the Emir, with whom they stand or fall. Besides these, there are nearly two hundred men in his salary, of the town. Captain of the guard, the Prince's chamberlain at home, and his standard-bearer in battle, was *Imbârak,* a pleasant but fanatic strong man. He was a stranger from el-Aruth, and had been promoted from the low degree by succeeding Emirs, for his manly sufficiency, until he was become now, in his best years, the executive arm of Ibn Rashîd.

Among the strangers, in my time, in Hâyil, that lived of Ibn Rashîd's wages, were certain Moghrebies. These Moors were at the taking of Jauf, in the expedition from Syria. Unto them, at the departure of the Pasha, was committed one of the two towers, *Mârid;* and the other to a few Syrian soldiery. —These were left in garrison with a kaimakàm, or Resident for the Dowla. But when a time passed, and they had not received their stipends, the bitter and hot-headed men of the West said in their disdain, ' They would call in Ibn Rashîd ' ! They went also to assail the soldiery of Syria, who though in the same case, yet as men that would return to their homes, held " for the Sooltàn," against them. The Moors had the upper hand, and when this tiding was brought in haste to Hâyil, the Emir returned with his armed men, and reoccupied the place which he had lately lost with so much displeasure. The Moors, —fifteen persons—were transported to Hâyil ; where they became of the Prince's armed service. One of them (grown unwieldly to ride) has been made the porter of his castle gate, and no man may pass in thereat but by that Moor's allowance. Sometimes when the sheukh are absent, the Moorish men-at-arms are left in Hâyil, and lodged in the Kasr by night, *for fear of any irruption of the wild Beduw,* who have heard marvels reported of Ibn Rashîd's treasury : for *there is no peace among the Ishmaelites, nor assurance even in the Prince's capital !*

Jauf was thus recovered, by the defection of the Moors, four years before my coming to Hâyil. The men were now wedded and established in the town ; only two had departed. Another of them, Haj Ibrahîm an Algerian, who had been a soldier in his youth (he remembered the words of command) in the French service, was little glad of the Arabian Emir's small salary, and the lean diet of the Mothîf ; and he said, as ever his little son, born in Hâyil, should be of age for the journey, he would take his leave. He and the Moors despised the Arabians as ' a benighted wild kind of people.'

The tale of Jauf may help our estimation of the value in the field of Arabian numbers, against troops under Turkish command, armed with rifles. In or about the year 1872, an expedition was sent by the government of Syria (the Turk, at that time, would extend his dominion in Arabia) to reduce the desert town of Jauf, fifty leagues eastward from the haj road, to the obedience of the Sultan. The small force was assembled at Maan camp. Mahmûd, who went with them, has told me they were seventy irregular soldiery, and the rest a motley crew of serving men in arms ; among them those Moghrebies had been hired in Damascus to go upon the expedition. Mohammed Aly, who rode also with the Pasha, gave me their numbers more than the truth,—troopers two hundred, police soldiery (*zabtiyah*) one hundred, besides fifty ageyl of the haj service. The Kurdy Pasha, Mohammed Saîd, commanded them.

Ten marches to Jauf in the desert are counted trom Maan, with laden camels. Great care was had to provide girbies, for there is little water to find by the way. " But, said Mahmûd, by the mercy of Ullah, it rained plentifully, as we were setting out, so that we might drink of the standing pools where we would, in our daily marches." The ninth evening the Pasha halted his soldiery at three or four leagues from Jauf, and bade them kindle many watch-fires in the plain :—and they of the town looking from their towers, saw this light in the sky, as if all the wilderness had burned. In the first watch some Sherarát came by them,—nomads well disposed towards the Dowla, in as much as they think themselves grieved by (the tyranny of) Ibn Rashîd ; they related marvels that night in Jauf of the great army of the askars of the Sooltàn ! " We passed, said they, where they lie encamped ; and they cannot be less than forty thousand men. We saw them, wellah a score or two about every fire ; at some they were beating the tambour, at some they danced ; and their companies are without number : you might walk four hours among their camp-fires !—and what help is there in Ibn Rashîd, O ye inhabitants of Jauf ! "—The sheukh went out and delivered the keys the same night, and surrendered themselves to the Pasha, who in the morning peaceably occupied the place.

When word came to the Prince in Hâyil, that his good town in the North had been taken by the Dowla, Ibn Rashîd sent a letter thus written to the Ottoman Pasha : " As thou hast entered Jauf without fight, now in like manner depart from it again ; and if not, I come to put you out."

Ibn Rashîd rode over the Nefùd from Hâyil, with his

rajajîl and villagers upon thelûls ; and a great cloud of his Beduw followed him (Mohammed Aly said ten thousand in all, that is perhaps one thousand at most). There were some old cannon in the towers : but the Pasha levelled against the Arabians an " English " piece of steel mountain artillery, which had been borne upon a mule's back in the expedition. The first ball struck a Beduin rider in the middle, from a wonderful distance ; and naught remained of him but his bloody legs, hanging in the shidàd. The hearts of the Arabians waxed cold at that sight,—the black death, when they thought themselves secure, was there in the midst of them ! also the bullets of the Dowla fell to them from very far off ; nevertheless they passed on to the assault. Mahmûd and the seventy stood without the gates with their small arms to resist them, and the rest repulsed them with musketry from the towers. Ibn Rashîd perceiving that his rajajîl and the multitude of Beduw could not avail him, that his enemies were within walls, and this beginning against him had been made by the Dowla, invited the Pasha to a parley ; and trusted to find him a Turk reasonable, greedy to be persuaded by his fee. They met and, as the Arabs speak, " understood each other." Mohammed Ibn Rashîd said : " I give you then Jauf."—*Mohammed Said ;* " We are in Jauf ; and if the Lord will we may go on to take Hâyil." In the end it was accorded between them that Jauf should be still the Prince's town but tributary to the Dowla ; Ibn Rashîd covenanted to pay every year for the place, at Damascus, 1500 mejîdy crowns : and a kaimakàm with his Syrian garrison was to be resident in the place. Each of these principal men looked upon the other with a pleasant admiration ; and in that they became friends for their lives.

In the mixed body of the rajajîl, I found some Beduins. Poverty had persuaded them to abandon the wandering life in the desert. Small was the Prince's fee, but that was never in arrear, and a clay house in Hâyil and rations. Certain among the strangers at Hâyil had been formerly servants of the Waháby !—I knew a company of Riâth men, a sort of perpetual guests of the Emir. They rode in all Ibn Rashîd's ghrazzus, and the Prince who lent them their thelûls, bestowed upon them, from time to time, a change of clothing and four or five reals ; and with that won in the forays, there came in, they reckoned, to each of them twenty reals by the year ; and they had their daily rations in the Mothîf. This life they now led six years, they were unwedded, and one among them was a blind man, who when his fellows forayed must abide at home.—Their house was one of the many free lodgings of the Emir,—a walled court, for their beasts, and two clay chambers, beyond the sûk, in the upper street leading to Gofar. There I went to visit them often, for another was a scholar who knew many ancient lays of the nomad tribes and the muallakát, which he read to me from a roll of parchment. They have often told me that if I went to er-Riâth I should be well treated. I asked, " What has brought you to leave your homes and come to encamp without your families at Hâyil ? "— " Ibn Saûd (answered the scholar, with an Arabian gesture, balancing his outstretched hand down to the ground) is every day sinking lower and lower, but Ibn Rashîd is *ha-ha-ha-ha-ha* coming up thus up-up-up ! and is always growing." It was said now at Hâyil " *Ibn Saûd khurbân* " (is ruined).

Abdullah the Waháby prince, son of old blind Feysal, was come himself two years before into these parts, a fugitive, driven from his government by the rebellion of his younger brother Saûd. Abdullah wandered then awhile, bare of all things, pitching his tent among the western Beduw within the jurisdiction of Ibn Rashîd. The Emir Mohammed sent to Abdullah el-Waháby offering him sheep and camels and horses and all things necessary, only forbidding him to enter Hâyil : but Saûd soon dying, Abdullah returned in peace, to that little which remained to him of his former dominion. Abdullah took at that time a sister of Mohammed Ibn Rashîd for one of his wives ;—but she dying he had afterward a sister of Hamûd : yet, since the past year, some enmity was said to be sprung up between them ; and that is in part because Mohammed ever bitterly harries the great tribe of Ateyba, which are the old faithful allies (though no more tributaries) of Abdullah the Waháby.—There came a messenger from er-Riâth whilst I was at Hâyil. As I sat one day with him at coffee, the man seeing me use a lead pencil, enquired of the company, " Tell me, ye who know him, is the Nasrâny a magician ! " other than this he showed no dislike towards me, but looked with the civil gentleness of an Arabian upon the guest and the stranger. And someone saying to him, " Eigh now ! if this (man) go to er-Riâth what thinkest thou, will they kill him ? " he answered mildly, " Nay, I think they would treat him with gentleness, and send him forward on his journey ; have not other Nasrânies visited er-Riâth (peaceably) ! "

Hâyil is now a centre of nomadic Arabia on this side J. *Tueyk*, and within the Syrian haj road. Embassies often arrive from tribes, not his tributaries, but having somewhat to treat with the Emir Ibn Rashîd. Most remarkable of these strange

Aarab were some Kahtân Beduins, of that ancient blood of el-Yémen and called the southern stock of the Arabs,—as is the Abrahamid family of Ishmael of the north Arabians. The men wondered to hear that any named them *Beny Kahtán.* " This (they said) is in the loghrat of Annezy." Jid or grandsire of their nation they told me to be the 'prophet *Húd*,' and their beginning to be from the mountain country *et-Tôr* in *Asîr.* *Ismayin* (Ishmael) they said, was brother of Húd their patriarch. These men had not heard of Húd's sepulchre in the southern country, nor have they any tradition (it sounded like old wives' tales to them) of the dam-breach at *Máreb,* [from which is fabled the dispersion of the ancient Arabs in the little world of Arabia]. One of them sang me some rimes of a ditty known to all the Kahtân, in which is the stave, " The lance of Néby Húd, raught to the spreading firmament." Some of them asked me, " Wellah ! do the Nasâra worship *asnám*," graven images ?—I think this book-word is not in the tradition of the northern Arabs. The Kahtân now in Hâyil were two rubbas : they had ridden with the young man their great sheykh, *Hayzàn,* from el-Kasîm ; in which country their division of the tribe were intruders these two years, and that was partly into the forsaken Annezy dîra of the Ibn Mujállad expelled by Abeyd. They were two hundred tents, and had been driven from their Yémen dîra,—where the rest remain of their nomad kindred.

These southern tribesmen wandering in Ibn Rashîd's borders, sent, now the second time, to treat with the Prince of Shammar, offering themselves to become his Aarab, and pay tithing to Hâyil ; but Ibn Rashîd, not willing that this dire and treacherous tribe should be established in Nejd, dismissed them with such words ;—' They might pasture in his neighbourhood as guests, giving no occasion against themselves, but that he looked upon them as aliens, and should neither tax them, nor give any charge to the tribes concerning them.' The messengers of Kahtân responded, " Wellah ! O Muhafûth, be we not thy brethren ? is not Ibn Rashîd *Jaafary,* of the fendy *Abda Shammar,* which is from the *Abída* of Kahtân ? " But the prince Mohammed responded hardly, " We know you not, your speech is strange in our hearing, and your manners are none of ours : go now, we are not of you, we will neither help you nor hurt you." Abhorred at er-Riâth,—since by their treachery the old power of the Waháby was broken,—the Nejd Aarab pressing upon them, and the Ateyba from the southward, these intruded Kahtân were now compassed in by strong enemies.

The men seemed to me to speak very well in the Nomad Arabic, with little difference from the utterance of Nejd Beduins,

save perhaps that they spoke with a more eloquent fulness.
When they yet dwelt in the south country they drew their provision of dates from the W. Dauâsir; one of them told me the
palms there lasted—with no long intermissions—for three thelûl
journeys : it is a sandy bottom and all their waters are wells.
Those of the valley, he said, be not bad people, but " good to
the guest." It is their factions which so much trouble the
country, the next villages being often in feud one with another.
El-Aflâj (plur. of *Fálaj*—Peleg, as some learned think—which
may signify ' the splitting of the mountain') is in Jebel
Tuey(k)ch, and the villagers are Dauâsiries. From er-Riâth
he counted to el-Aflâj three, and to *W. Bisha* twelve thelûl
journeys, and he named to me these places by the way, *el-Ferra,
el-Suleyl, Leyla, el-Bediya, Sélla, El-Hadda, Hámmr, es-Sihh :*
some of them asked me if I had heard tell of the *Kasr Ibn
Shaddád.* The ' wild oxen ' are in their country, which they also
name wothyhî. Certainly these men of Kahtân differed not in
the least gestures from any other Beduw whom I have known ;
they were light-coloured and not so swarthy, as are many of
the northern Aarab.

The Kahtân who talked with me in the Méshab were
pleased when I confirmed the noble antiquity of their blood,
in the ears of the tribesmen of Nejd, who until that hour
had never heard anything in the matter. The men invited me
to visit them at evening in their makhzan, when they would
be drinking kahwa with the sheykh. These Kahtân came not
into the great public coffee-hall of the Kasr, whether because
of the (profane) bibbing there of tobacco smoke, or that they
were at enmity with most of the tribesmen : they drank the
morning and mid-afternoon and evening cup apart, in their
own makhzan ; but they received the coffee-berries from the
Emir's kitchen. After supper I sought them out : their young
sheykh Hayzàn immediately bid me sit down on the saddle-
skin beside him, and with a good grace he handed to me the
first cup of kahwa. This was a beautiful young man, of manly
face and stature ; there was nothing in him that you would
have changed, he was a flower of all whom I have seen among
the Arabians : his life had never suffered want in the khála.
In his countenance, with a little ferocity of young years, appeared a pleasant fortitude : the milk-beard was not yet sprung
upon Hayzàn's hardy fresh face. His comeliness was endowed
with the longest and greatest braided side-locks, which are seen
among them ; and big he was, of valiant limbs :—but all this
had no lasting !

They were in some discourse of religion ; and their fanatic

young sheykh pronounced the duty of a Moslem to lie in three
things chiefly,—"the five times daily prayers, the fast in Rama-
thán, and the tithe or yielding of zíka."—How the Semites are
Davids! they are too religious and too very scelerat at once!
Their talk is continually (without hypocrisy) of religion, which is
of genial devout remembrance to them, as it is to us a sad, uncomfortable, untimely and foreign matter. Soon after, their discourse began to turn upon my being a Nasrâny. Then Hayzàn
said to one of his rubba, "Give me there my kiddamîyyah,"
which is their crooked girdle-knife. Then holding the large
blade aloft, and turning himself upon me, he said, *Sully aly en-
Néby,* ' Give glory to the apostle,' so I answered, " We all worship
the Godhead. I cannot forsake my name of Nasrâny, neither
wouldst thou thine if thou be'st a worthy man."—But as he yet
held the knife above my breast, I said to him, "What dagger is
that? and tell these who are present whether thy meaning be
to do me a mischief?" Then he put it down as if he were
ashamed to be seen by the company savagely threatening his
coffee guest; and so returning to his former behaviour, he
answered all my questions. " Come, he said, in the morning, and
we will make thee coffee; then ask me of all that you please,
and I will tell thee as it is." When I said, "You have many
Yahùd in your Yémen country," the fanatic young man was
much troubled to hear it. " And that knife, is from whence?"
—" From Nejrân."—" And in Nejrân be not your sânies
Yahùdies? was not the smith who made this dagger-blade a
Yahùdy?" The ignorant young Beduin, who thought I must
know the truth, hissed between his teeth: *Ullah yusullat
aleyhim,* " The Lord have the mastery of them (to bring evil
upon them)."—When I returned on the morrow, I found Hayzàn alone; the young sheykh, with an uncommon courtesy, had
awaited me, for they think it nothing not to keep their
promises. So he said, " Let us go to the rubba in the next
makhzan, they have invited us, and we will drink our coffee
there."

When I came another evening to the Kahtân, to hear their
lays, Hayzàn did not return my greeting of peace. Soon after
I had taken the cup, the young sheykh as before bade one bring
him his kiddamîyyah; and handling the weapon with cruel looks,
he turned himself anew upon me, and insisted, saying, " *Sully
aly en-Néby.*" I answered, "Oh! ignorant Beduwy, how is it
that even with your own religion I am better acquainted than
thyself!"—" Thou art better acquainted with my religion than
myself! *sully aly en-Néby.*"—(Some of the Kahtân company
now said, "Hayzàn, nay! he is a guest.")—" If thou mayest come

even to the years of this beard, thou wilt have learned, young man, not to offer any violence to the guest." I thought if I said 'the guest of the lord of yonder castle,' he might have responded, that the Prince permitted him ! In the same moment a singular presentiment, almost a persuasion, possessed my soul, that the goodly young man's death was near at hand ; and notwithstanding my life daily threatened in a hazardous voyage and this infirm health, that I should survive him. " Your coffee, I added, was in my throat when you lifted the knife against me ; but tell me, O ye of the Kahtân, do ye not observe the rites of the other Aarab ? " Some of them answered me, " Ay, Ullah ! that do we ; " but Hayzàn was silent, for the rest of the company were not with him, and the Arabs are never of one assent, save in blind dogma of religion : this is for one's safety who adventures among them.—Hayzàn, a few months afterward, by the retaliation of fortune, was slain (in battle) by my friends. This case made the next day some idle talk in the town, and doubtless was related in the palace, for Imbârak asked me of it in the great kahwa :—" Khalîl, what of the Kahtân ? and what of Hayzàn, when he took the knife to stab thee, fearedst thou not to die ? "—" If I feared for every word, judge thyself, had I entered your Arabian country ? but tell me, did the young ignorant well, thinkest thou ? "— Imbârak, who was in such times a spokesman for the Emir, kept silence.

Very ugly tales are current of the Kahtân in the mouths of Nejd Arabians. It is commonly reported that they are eaters of the flesh of their enemies ; and there is a vile proverb said to be of these human butchers, ' eth-thail, the rump, is the best roast.' They are esteemed faithless, " wood at a word, and for every small cause ready to pluck out their weapons." A strange tale was told me in Kasîm, by certain who pretended they had it of eye-witnesses : ' Some Kahtân riders returning weary and empty from a ghrazzu passed by er-Russ ; and finding an abd or bondsman of the village without in the khála, they laid hands on him and bound him, and carried the negro away with them. Before evening the Kahtânies, alighted in the Nefûd, the men were faint with the many days suffered hunger ;—and they said among themselves, ' We will kill the captive and eat him : ' they plucked also bushes and gathered fuel for a great fire.— The black man would be cast in, when they had cut his throat, and roasted whole ; as the manner is of passengers and hunters in the wilderness to dress their game. But in that appeared another band riding over the sand-dunes ! The Kahtân hastily

re-mounted on their thelûls ; and seeing them that approached
to be more than their number, they stayed not, but, as Beduw,
they turned their beasts to flight. Those that now arrived
were some friendly Kasîm villagers, who loosing the poor bondsman heard from him his (unlikely) tale.'—But most fanatic are
these scelerats, and very religious even in their crimes. So it
is said of them proverbially in Nejd, " El-Kahtân murder a
man only for his drinking smoke, and they themselves drink
human blood." But sheykhly persons at Aneyza have told me
that " el-Kahtân in el-Yémen do confirm their solemn swearing
together by drinking human gore ; also a man of them may not
wive, nor loose his leathern band, until he have slain an enemy."
Another sheykh of Kahtân visited Hâyil two years before,—and
after discourse of their affairs the Prince Ibn Rashîd said to
him : " In all my riding southwards through the Beduin country
we never saw a Kahtân burying place ! " The sheykh, it is
reported, answered him (in a boast), " Ay wellah Muhafùth, thou
hast seen the graves of Kahtân, *in the air !*—the crows and the
rákham and the ágab : " he would say their carcases are cast
out unburied,—that which happens in the wild battle-fields of
Arabia ; the fallen of the losers' side remain without burial. It
was so with Kahtân when this Hayzàn was slain in the summer : a week after I passed by, and the caravaners avoided
that sinister neighbourhood !

Somewhat has been said of Ibn Rashîd's lineage. Shammar
is not, as the most great nomad tribes, reputed to spring from one
Jid, but according to the opinion in Nejd, is of mixed ancestry.
Others say the name of their patriarch is *Shimmer.* The divisions by fendies or lineages of Shammar were given me by a
lettered nomad of Annezy Sbáa living at Hâyil. The fendy *Abda*
is from the fendy *Abîda* of Kahtân whereof the *Jaafar* kindred,
of which is Ibn Rashîd's house ; the other ˏfendies are many
and not of one descent,—*Sinjâra, Tumân, Éslam, Deghreyrat,
Ghreyth, Amûd, Faddághra, Thâbit, Afarît, ez-Zumeyl, Ham-
mazàn, Saiyeh, Khûrussy, Zúba, Shammar-Toga* (in Irâk).
No man of the inhabitants of the wilderness knows letters ;
and it was a new pleasure to me to meet here with a lettered
Beduwy, as it were an eye among their dull multitude, for he
was well taught and diligent, and his mind naturally given to
good studies. This was one *Rashîd* who had been bred a
scholar at er-Riâth ; but had since forsaken the decaying
Waháby state and betaken himself to Hâyil, where he was
become a man of Hamûd's private trust and service. He made
every year some scholarly journey, into distant provinces. He

was last year, he told me, in the land of Israel, where he had
visited Bethlehem, " the place (he said devoutly) where the
Messiah was born," and the Holy (City). There is in these
Arabians such a facility of mind, that it seems they only lack
the occasion, to speed in any way of learning ;—that were by an
easy imitation. Rashîd was a good man of liberal understanding
[I could have wished for such a rafîk in my Arabian travels],
but too timid as a Beduwy under masters : almost he dared not
be seen in the town to discourse with the Nasrâny, lest it
should displease any great personage. There is reported to be
a far outlying settlement in el-Aruth, of Shammar lineage, the
name of the village is *Aleyî* and the kindred *Kuruníyah*.

One day I found Rashîd carrying my book of Geography in the
Méshab. As he said that Mâjid sent him with it to some learned
man in Hâyil, a kâdy, I accompanied him ; but come to his dàr
we found not the learned person at home. I heard the kâdy had
compiled *shájr*, a tree, of genealogies, in which he exhibited the
branching from the stock of all their Arabian lines. I went another
day to visit him, and could not soon find his distant house, because
a swordsman of the Emir, whom I met stalking in his gay
clothes, sent me upon a false way about ; and when I arrived
I found the shallow fellow sitting there before me ! so knavish
they are in a trifle, and full of Asiatic suspicions. When I reproached him the fellow could not answer a word, only feeling
down the edge of his sword, he let me divine that he had the
best will in the world to have tried his force and the temper
of the metal upon my neck. The same man was afterwards
not less ready to defend me from the insolence of others.

I greeted the kâdy, who hardly saluted me again : *Mâtha
turîd*, quoth the pedant ;—and this is all their learning, to seem
well taught in the Arabic tongue. He was sitting under his
house wall in the dust of the street. All their gravity is akin to
levity, and first showing me his watch, he asked, " What is this
written upon the face of it ? " Then he sent for a book, and showed
me in the fly-leaf his copies of some short antique inscriptions
which he had found scored upon the rocks in this neighbourhood (they were written in a kind of Himyaric character), and
he asked of me, " Are these *Yunâny* (of Javan), in the Greek
tongue, or Muscovy ?—*the Muscovs of old inhabited this country.*"
I answered, " Art thou so ignorant then even of your own
language ! This is the Himyaric, or ancient Yemenish writing
of Arabia. I heard thou wast a learned man, and upon that
common ground we might be friends. Though thy name be
Moslem and mine is Messîhy we all say ' There is an only
Godhead.' "—" The impiety is not unknown to me of the

Messihiyûn ; they say ' Ullah childed, and that the only God is
become more Gods' ! Nay ! but if thou wilt turn from the
way of idolatry to be a Moslem, we may be accorded together.''
—" I become a Moslem ! I think thou wouldst not become a
Nasrâny ; neither will I take on me the name of your religion, *ebeden !* (ever): yet may we be friendly in this world,
and seekers after the true knowledge."—" Knowledge of the
Messihiyûn ! that is a little thing, and next to unlearning."—
" How art thou called learned ! being without knowledge even
of your own letters. The shape is unknown to you of the dry
land, the names of the hundred countries and the great nations ;
but we by navigation are neighbours to all nations, we encompass the earth with our speech in a moment. Says not Sleymàn
bin Daûd, ' It is the glory of man's solicitous spirit to search
out the sovereign works of the Lord ' ? ye know not those
scriptures, but our young children read these things with understanding."—The pedant could not find his tongue ; he might
feel then, like a friar out of his cell, that he was a narrow soul,
and in fault to have tempted the stranger in argument. He
was mollified, and those that sat with him.

Afterwards, meeting with Rashîd, he said, " How found you
him, he knows very much ? "—" The koran, the muallakát, the
kamûs and his jots, and his titles (the vowel points in their
skeleton writing), and he knows nothing else."—" It is the truth,
and I can think thou didst not like him ; " for it seems, the
learned and religious kâdy was looked upon as a crabbed fellow
in his own town. As we were talking of the ancient scored
inscriptions, in Abeyd's kahwa, Mâjid's tutor said to Hamûd,
" Have we not seen the rocks full of them at *Gubba ?* " Gubba
is the outlying small Nefûd village next to J. Shammar, upon
the way to Jauf.

In Nejd I have found the study of letters in most honour
amongst the prosperous merchants at Aneyza. At Hâyil it
was yet in the beginning : though Hamûd and the Prince are
said to be possessors (but who may ever believe them !) of two or
three thousand volumes. I found in Abeyd's kahwa not above
a dozen in their cotton cases, and bound in red leather :—
but the fewer they were, the more happy I esteemed them,
as princes, not to be all their lives going still to school.
Hamûd sometime asked me of the art of printing, ' Could I
not show him the manner ? ' but when I answered he might buy
himself a printer's press from Bagdad, for not much money, he
was discouraged, for they will spend nothing. It is wonderful
in what nomad-like ignorance of the natural world they all pass
their lives ! Some evening Hamûd asked me, " Do the Nasâra,

Khalîl, see the moon?"—his meaning might be—' The new moon is the ensign of the Sultan of Islam, the moon then is of the Moslemîn ;—therefore the moon is not of the other religions !'

There were in Hâyil four common schools. The master of one of them, a depraved looking fanatical young man, daily uttered the presumptuous saws of his self-liking heart of gall to the ignorant assembly in the kahwa: sordid was his voice, and the baseness of his snake-looking eyes a moral pestilence. Upon a day he called upon me loudly, and smiling in his manner, before them all, " Khalîl, why so steadfast in a false way ? Wouldst thou come to my house, to-morrow, I will lay before thee the proofs, and they shall be out of your own scriptures. Thou shalt read the prophecy of *Hazkiyal* and the other testimonies ; and then, if the Lord will, thou mayest say, ' I that was long time blind, do now see and bear witness that God is One, and Mohammed is the apostle of God.' "—" Will you make my head ache in the Prince's coffee-hall about your questions of religion ! where I come but to drink a cup with my friends." The Beduins answered for me, " He has well said ; peace, thou young man, and let this stranger be."—" But it is of the great hope I have, hissed the holy ribald, of this man's conversion ; for was it not so with the Yahûdy before him ? "

Desiring to see a book at Hâyil and in Arabic " of Ezekiel the prophet " ! I went the next afternoon to his dàr, which I found by the Méshab, near the common draught-yard, as unsavoury as himself. " Ah ! he said, welcome, also I hope thou art come disposed to receive the truth." He set dates before the stranger, and fetched me his wise book ; which I found to be a solemn tome of some doctor of Islam, who at a certain place quoted a voice of the prophet, but in other than barbarous ears of little meaning. The Arabs have a curious wit for the use of this world, but they are all half-rational children in religion. " Well ! (I asked) is there no more than this ? and I was almost in hope to have reformed myself ! " But now the young man, who looked perhaps that I should have taken his vanity upon trust, was displeased with himself, and so I left him. This schoolmaster was maintained by the State; he dined miserably in the Mothîf, and received, besides, a few reals in the year, and a change of clothing.

The Arabs are to be won by gentleness and good faith, they yield to just arguments, and before I left Hâyil the most of my old foes wished me well in their hearts. To use an unflattering plainness of speech was also agreeable to the part of sûwahh, or wandering anchorite in the fable of human life. The best that I met with here, were some who had been in Egypt and Syria, or conductors of the Emir's sale-horses to Bombay, where they told me, with a pleasant wonder, they had seen the horse-race ; men who viewed a stranger, such as themselves had been in another soil, with eyes of good-will and understanding. " This people (they would say) have learned no good manners, they have not corrected themselves by seeing foreign countries : else why do they molest thee, Khalîl, about your religion ; in which no man ought to be enforced.—But we have instructed ourselves in travel ; also we have seen the Nasâra, their wealth, their ingenuity, and justice and liberality."

The weather, sultry awhile after my coming to Hâyil, was now grown cold. Snow, which may be seen the most winters upon a few heads of Arabian mountains, is almost not known to fall in the Nejd wilderness, although the mean altitude be nearly 4000 feet. They say such happens about "once in forty years." It had been seen two winters before, when snow lay on the soil three days : the camels were couched in the menzils, and many of them perished in that unwonted cold and hunger.

A fire was kindled morning and evening in the great kahwa, and I went there to warm myself with the Beduins. One evening before almost anyone came in, I approached to warm myself at the fire-pit.—" Away ! (cried the coffee-server, who was of a very splenetic fanatical humour) and leave the fire to the guests that will presently arrive." Some Beduins entered and sat down by me. " I say, go back ! " cries the coffee-keeper. " A moment, man, and I am warm ; be we not all the Prince's guests ? " Some of the Beduw said in my ear : " It were better to remove, not to give them an occasion." That kâhwajy daily showed his rancour, breaking into my talk with the Beduw, as when someone asked me " Whither wilt thou next, Khalîl ? "—" May it please Ullah (cries the coffee-server) to jehennem ! " I have heard he was one of servile condition from Aneyza in Kasîm ; but being daily worshipfully saluted by guesting Beduin sheykhs, he was come to some solemn opinion of himself. To cede to the tyranny of a servant might, I thought, hearten other fanatics' audacity in Hâyil. The coffee-server, with a frenetic voice, cried to a Beduwy sitting by, " Reach me that camel-stick," (which the nomads have always in their hands,) and having snatched it from him, the slave struck me with all his decrepit force. The Beduins had risen round me with troubled looks,— they might feel that they were not themselves safe ; none of these were sheykhs, that durst say any word, only they beckoned me to withdraw with them, and sit down with them at a little distance. It had been perilous to defend myself among dastards ; for if it were told in the town that the Nasrâny laid heavy hands on a Moslem, then the wild fire had kindled in many hearts to avenge him. The Emir must therefore hear of the matter and do justice, or so long as I remained in Hâyil every shrew would think he had as good leave to insult me. I passed by the gallery to the Emir's apartment, and knocking on the iron door, I heard the slave-boy who kept it within say to the guard that it was Khalîl the Nasrâny. The Emir sent out Nasr to enquire my business, and I went to sit in the Méshab. Later someone coming from the Kasr who had been with the Emir, said that the Emir sent for the coffee-server immediately, and said to him, " Why ! Ullah curse thy father, hast thou struck the Nasrâny ? "—" Wellah, O el-Muhafûth (the trembling wretch answered) I touched him not ! "—so he feared the Emir, who said then to some of the guard " Beat him ! "—but Hamûd rose and going over to Mohammed, he kissed his cousin's hand, asking him, for his sake, to spare the coffee-server, ' who was a *mesquin* (meskîn).' " Go káhwajy, said the Emir, and if I hear any more there shall nothing save thee, but thou shalt lose thy office." Because I forsook the coffee-hall, the second coffee-server came many times to my makhzan, and wooed me to return among them ; but I responded, " Where the guests of the Emir are not safe from outrage—!"

Note.—IBN RASHÍD'S HORSES, for the Indian market, are shipped at Kuweyt. The itinerary is, from Hâyil to el-Khâsira, 9 stounds ;— Bak'a, 8 ;—Khathrâ, 18 ;—el-Feṣaṣ, Umm Arthama (the well there 32 fathoms), 28 ;—el-Wakbâ, 24 ;—el-Hafr (in the Wady er-Rummah, the well 35 fathoms), 24 ;—Arrak'i (where there is little water), 16 ;—el-Jahrâ (on the sea coast), 30 ;—el-Kuweyt, 9. [*Abu Daúd, sheykh el-Ageyl, Damascus.*]

CHAPTER III.

DEPART FROM HÂYIL: JOURNEY TO KHEYBAR.

The 'Persian pilgrimage.' Imbârak's words. Town thieves. Jauf pilgrims in Hâyil. Beduins on pilgrimage. The Caravan to Mecca arrives from the North. An Italian hajjy in Hâyil. The Persians passed formerly by el-Kasîm. Murderous dangers in Mecca. Concourse at Hâyil.—The Kheybar journey. Violent dealing of Imbârak. Ibn Rashîd's passport. Departure from Hâyil. Gofar. Seyadîn, Beduin pedlars. El-Kasr village. Biddîa hamlet. Adventure in the desert. Eyâda ibn Ajjuèyn. Kâsim ibn Barâk. Sâlih the rafîk. "It is the angels." The Wady er-Rummah. Kâsim's sister. Set forward again with Sâlih. The Nasrâny abandoned at strange tents. The hospitable goodness of those nomads. Thaifullah. Set forth with a rafîk from the menzil of Eyâda-Ghroceyb. The Harra in sight. Heteym menzil in the Harra. Lineage of the Heteym. The lava-field. The division of waters of Northern Arabia. The dangerous passage. The great Harrat (Kheybar). El-Hâyat, village. Cattle paths in the Harra. An alarm near Kheybar. Locusts. Ghroceyb in trouble of mind. Wady Jellâs. Kheybar village. The Hûsn. An antique Mesjid.

THE Haj were approaching;—this is Ibn Rashîd's convoy from Mesopotamia of the so-called 'Persian pilgrimage' to Mecca:—and seeing the child Feysal had nearly recovered, I thought after that to depart, for I found little rest at all or refreshment at Hâyil. Because the Emir had spoken to me of mines and minerals, I conjectured that he would have sent some with me on horseback, seeking up and down for metals: —but when he added "There is a glancing sand in some parts of the khála like scaly gold," I had answered with a plainness which must discourage an Arab. Also Hamûd had spoken to me of seeking for metals.

Imbârak invited me one morning to go home with him "to kahwa," he had a good house beside the mesjid, backward from the Méshab. We found his little son playing in the court: the martial father took him in his arms with the tenderness of the Arabians for their children. An European would bestow the first home love upon the child's mother; but the Arabian

257

housewives come not forth with meeting smiles and the eyes of love, to welcome-in their husbands, for they are his espoused servants, he purchased them of their parents, and at best, his liking is divided. The child cried out, " Ho ! Nasrâny, thou canst not look to the heaven ! "—" See, my son, I may look upon it as well, I said, as another and better ;—*taal húbbiny!* come thou and kiss me ; " for the Arab strangers kiss their hosts' young children.—When some of the young courtiers had asked me, *Fen rubbuk,* ' Where is thy Lord God ? ' I answered them very gravely, *Fî kull makán,* ' The Lord is in every place : ' which word of the Nasrâny pleased them strangely, and was soon upon all their tongues in the Kasr.

" Khalîl, said Imbârak, as we sat at the hearth, we would have thee to dwell with us in Hâyil ; only become a Moslem, it is a little word and soon said. Also wouldst thou know more of this country, thou shalt have then many occasions in being sent for the Emir's business here and there. The Emir will promote thee to an high place and give thee a house where thou mayest pass thy life in much repose, free from all cares, wellah in only stretching the limbs at thy own hearth-side. Although that which we can offer be not more than a man as thou art might find at home in his country, yet consider it is very far to come again thither, and that thou must return through as many new dangers."—Imbârak was doubtless a spokesman of the Emir, he promised fair, and this office I thought might be the col- lecting of taxes ; for in handling of money they would all sooner trust a Nasrâny.

Those six or seven reals which came in by the sale of my nâga,—I had cast them with a few small pieces of silver into a paper box with my medicines, I found one day had been stolen, saving two reals and the small money ; that either the Arab piety of the thief had left me, or his superstition, lest he should draw upon himself the Christian's curse and a chastisement of heaven. My friends' suspicion fell upon two persons. The dumb man, who very often entered my lodging, for little cause, and a certain Be- duwy, of the rajajîl at Hâyil, of a melancholy malignant humour ; he had bought my camel, and afterward he came many times to my makhzan, to be treated for ophthalmia. I now heard him named a cut-purse of the Persian Haj, and the neighbours even affirmed that he had cut some of their wezands. When I spoke of this mischief to Hamûd, he affected with the barbaric sleight of the Arabs not to believe me. I looked then in my purse, and there were not thirty reals ! I gave my tent to the running broker and gained four or five more. The dellâl sold it to some young patrician, who would ride in this winter pilgrimage of 160 leagues and more in the khála, to Mecca. Imbárak set his sword to the dumb man's throat, but the dumb protested with all the vehement signs in the world that this guilt was not in him. As for the Beduwy he was not found in Hâyil!

Already the fore-riders of the Haj arrived : we heard that the pilgrims this year were few in number. I saw now the yearly gathering in Hâyil of men from the villages and the tribes that would follow with the caravan on pilgrimage, and of petty tradesmen that come to traffic with the passing haj :— some of them brought dates from Kasîm above a hundred miles distant. A company from the Jauf villages lodged in the next makhzans ; they were more than fifty persons, that had journeyed ten days tardily over the Nefûd in winter rain and rough weather : but that is hardly a third of their long march (of seven hundred miles) to Mecca. I asked some weary man of them, who came to me trembling in the chill morning, how he looked to accomplish his religious voyage and return upwards in the cold months without shelter. " Those, he answered, that die, they die ; and who live, God has preserved them." These men told me they reckon from Jauf eight, to el-Méshed and to Damascus nine camel journeys ; to Maan are five thelûl days, or nine nights out with loaded camels. Many poor Jaufies come every year into the Haurân seeking labour, and are hired by the Druses to cleanse and repair their pools of rain-water :— it is the jealous manner of the Druses, who would live by themselves, *to inhabit where there is scarcity of water.* Much salt also of the Jauf deserts is continually carried thither. The Jauf villagers say that they are descended from Mesopotamians, Syrians and from the Nejd Arabians. The sûk in Hâyil was in these days thronged with Beduins that had business in the yearly concourse, especially to sell camels. The Méshab was now full of their couching thelûls. The multitude of visiting people were bidden, at the hours, in courses, by Mufarrij and those of the public kitchen, and led in to break their fasts and to sup in the Mothîf.

Three days later the Haj arrived, they were mostly *Ajam,* strangers ' of outlandish speech ' ; but this word is commonly understood of Persia. They came early in an afternoon, by my reckoning, the 14th of November. Before them rode a great company of Beduins on pilgrimage ; there might be in all a thousand persons. Many of the Aarab that arrived in Hâyil were of the Syrian Annezy, Sbáa, whose dîra is far in the north-west near Aleppo. With this great yearly convoy came down trains of laden camels with wares for the tradesmen of Hâyil; and I saw a dozen camels driven in through the castle gate, which carried bales of clothing, for the Emir's daily gifts of changes of garments to his visiting Beduins. The Haj passed westwards about the town, and went to encamp before the Gofar gate, and the summer residency, and the Mâ es-Sáma. The caravan was twelve nights out from Bagdad. I numbered about fifty great tents : they were not more, I heard, than half the hajjies of the former season ; but this was a year of that great jehâd which troubled el-Islam, and the most Persians were gone (for fear) the long sea way about to the port of Mecca. I saw none of them wear the Persian bonnets or clad as Persians : the returning pilgrimage is increased by those who visit el-Medina, and would go home by el-Méshed.

I wondered to mark the perfect resemblance of the weary, travel-stained, and ruffianly clad Bagdad akkâms to those of Damascus ; the same moon-like white faces are of both the great mixed cities. In their menzil was already a butchers' market, and I saw saleswomen of the town sitting there with baskets of excellent girdle-bread and dates ; some of those wives—so wimpled that none might know them—sold also buttermilk ! a traffic which passes for less than honest, even in the towns of nomad Arabia. Two days the pilgrims take rest in Hâyil, and the third morrow they depart. The last evening, one stayed me in the street, to enquire, whether I would go with the Haj to Mecca ! When I knew his voice in the dusk I answered only, " *Ambar*, no ! " and he was satisfied. Ambar, a home-born Galla of Ibn Rashîd's house, was now *Emir el-Haj*, conductor of the pilgrim convoy—this was, we have seen, the Emir Mohammed's former office ; Aneybar was his elder brother, and they were freemen, but their father was a slave of Abdullah Ibn Rashîd. Aneybar and Ambar, being thus libertine brethren of the succeeding Emirs, were holders of trusts under them ; they were also welfaring men in Hâyil.

On the morrow of the setting out of the Haj, I stood in the menzil to watch their departure. One who walked by in the company of some Bagdad merchants, clad like them and girded in a kumbâz, stayed to speak with me. I asked, ' What did he seek ? '—I thought the hajjy would say *medicines :* but he answered, " *If I speak in the French language, will you understand me ?* "—" I shall understand it ! but what countryman art thou ? " I beheld a pale alien's face with a chestnut beard :— who has not met with the like in the mixed cities of the Levant ? He responded, " I am an Italian, a Piedmontese of Turin."—" And what brings you hither upon this hazardous voyage ? good Lord ! you might have your throat cut among

them ; are you a Moslem ? "—" Ay."—" You confess then their
' none îlah but Ullah, and Mahound, apostle of Ullah '—which
they shall never hear me utter, may Ullah confound them ! "—
" Ay, I say it, and I am a Moslem ; as such I make this
pilgrimage."

—He told me he was come to the Mohammedan countries,
eight years before ; he was then but sixteen years of age, and
from Damascus he had passed to Mesopotamia : the last three
years he had studied in a Mohammedan college, near Bagdad,
and received the circumcision. He was erudite in the not short
task of the Arabic tongue, to read, and to write scholarly, and
could speak it with the best, as he said, " without difference."
For a moment, he treated in school Arabic, of the variance
of the later Arabian from the antique tongue, as it is found
in the koran, which he named with a Mohammedan aspira-
tion *es-sherif,* ' the venerable or exalted scripture.' With his
pedant teachers, he dispraised the easy babble-talk of the
Aarab. When I said I could never find better than a headache in the farrago of the koran ; and it amazed me that
one born in the Roman country, and under the name of
Christ, should waive these prerogatives, to become the brother of Asiatic barbarians in a fond religion ! he answered
with the Italic *mollitia* and half urbanity,—" Aha ! well, a
man may not always choose, but he must sometime go with
the world." He hoped to fulfil this voyage, and ascend with
the returning Syrian Haj : he had a mind to visit the lands
beyond Jordan, and those tribes [B. Hameydy, B. Sokhr], possessors of the best blood horses, in Moab ; but when he understood that I had wandered there, he seemed to pass over so
much of his purpose. It was in his mind to publish his Travels
when he returned to Europe. Poor (he added) he was in the
world, and made his pilgrimage at the charges, and in the company, of some bountiful Persian personage of much devotion and
learning :—but once returned to Italy, he would wipe off all
this rust of the Mohammedan life. He said he heard of me,
" the Nasrâny," at his coming to Hâyil, and of the Jew-born
Abdullah : he had visited the Moslemanny, but " found him to
be a man altogether without instruction."

There was a hubbub in the camp of the taking up tents and
loading of baggage and litters ; some were already mounted :—
and as we took hands, I asked, " What is your name ? and remember mine, for these are hazardous times and places." The Italian
responded with a little hesitation—it might be true, or it might
be he would put me off—*Francesco Ferrari.* Now the caravan
was moving, and he hastened to climb upon his camel.

From Hâyil to Mecca are five hundred miles at least, over vast deserts, which they pass in fifteen long marches, not all years journeying by the same landmarks, but according to that which is reported of the waterings (which are wells of the Aarab), and of the peace or dangers of the wilderness before them. Ibn Rashîd's Haj have been known to go near by Kheybar, but they commonly hold a course from Mustajidda or the great watering of *Semîra,* to pass east of the *Harrat el-Kesshub,* and from thence in other two days descend to the underlying Mecca country by *W. Laymûn.* It is a wonder that the Ateyba, (the Prince's strong and capital enemies) do not waylay them : but a squadron of his rajajîl ride to defend the Haj.

Formerly this convoy from Mesopotamia to Mecca passed by the way of el-Kasîm, with the kâfilas of Aneyza, or of Boreyda ; in which long passages of the deserts, those of the Persian belief were wont to suffer harshness and even violence, especially by the tyranny of Mahanna, the usurping *jemmâl* or " cameleer " sheykh of Boreyda, of whom there is many a tale told. And I have heard this of a poor Ajamy : When the caravan arrived in the town, he was bound at the command of Mahanna and beaten before him ; the Emir still threatening the needy stranger,— " Son of an hound, lay me down thy four *giniyât,* and else thou diest in this place." The town Arabs when crossed are very uncivil spirits, and their hostility turning to a beastly wildness, they set no bounds to their insane cruelty ; it is a great prudence therefore not to move them.—It was now twelve years since all the " Persian " overland pilgrims use to come down from el-Méshed under the strong conduct of the Prince of Shammar :— to him they pay toll, (if you can believe the talk) ' an hundred reals ' for each person.—I saw a mare led through the town, of perfect beauty : the Emir Mohammed sent her (his yearly present) with the Haj to the sherîf of Mecca. It was eight o'clock when the Haj departed ; but thelûl riders of Hâyil were still leaving the town to overtake the slow camel-train till mid-day.

When in the favourable revolution of the stars I was come again to peaceable countries, I left notice of the Italian wanderer " Ferrari " at his consulate in Syria, and have vainly enquired for him in Italy :—I thought it my duty, for how dire is the incertitude which hangs over the heads of any aliens that will adventure themselves in Mecca,—where, I have heard it from credible Moslems, that *nearly no Haj passes in which some unhappy persons are not put to death as intruded Christians.* A trooper and his comrade, who rode with the yearly Haj caravans, speaking (unaffectedly) with certain Christian Damascenes (my familiar acquaintance), the year before my setting out, said

'They saw two strangers taken at Mona in the last pilgrimage, that had been detected writing in pocket-books. The strangers being examined were found to be "Christians"; they saw them executed, and the like happened most years!' Our Christian governments too long suffer this religious brigandage! Why have they no Residents, for the police of nations in Mecca? Why have they not occupied the direful city in the name of the health of nations, in the name of the common religion of humanity, *and because the head of the slave trade is there?* It were good for the Christian governments, which hold any of the Mohammedan provinces, to consider that till then they may never quietly possess them. Each year at Mecca every other name is trodden down, and the "Country of the Apostle" is they pretend inviolable, where no worldly power may reach them. It is "The city of God's house,"—and the only God is God only of the Moslemîn.

Few or none of the pilgrim strangers while lying at Hâyil had entered the town,—it might be their fear of the Arabians. Only certain Bagdad derwishes came in, to eat of the public hospitality; and I saw besides but a company of merry adventurers, who would be bidden to a supper in Arabia, for the novelty. In that day's press even the galleries of the Mothîf were thronged; there I supped in the dusk, and when I rose, my sandals, the gift of Hamûd, were taken. From four till half-past six o'clock rations had been served for "two to three thousand" persons; the Emir's cheer was but boiled temmn and a little samn.

It is a passion to be a pointing-stock for every finger and to maintain even a just opinion against the half-reason of the world. I have felt this in the passage of Arabia more than the daily hazards and long bodily sufferance: yet some leaven is in the lump of pleasant remembrance; it is oftentimes by the hearty ineptitude of the nomads. In the throng of Aarab in these days in the Méshab, many came to me to speak of their infirmities; strangers where I passed called to me, not knowing my name, "Ho! thou that goest by, el-hakîm there!" others, when they had received of me (freely) some faithful counsel, blessed me with the Semitic grace, "God give peace to that head, the Lord suffer not thy face to see the evil." And such are phrases which, like their brand-marks, declare the tribes of nomads: these were, I believe, northern men. One, as I came, showed me to his rafîk, with this word: *Urraie urraie, hu hu!* 'Look there! he (is) he, this is the Nasrâny.'—*Cheyf Nasrâny?* (I heard the other answer, with the hollow drought of the desert in his manly throat). *agûl!*

weysh yúnsurhu? He would say, " How is this man victorious, what giveth him the victory ? " In this strange word to him the poor Beduwy thought he heard *nasr,* which is *victory.* A poor nomad of Ruwàlla cried out simply, when he received his medicines : ' Money he had none to give the hakîm, wellah ! he prayed me be content to receive his shirt.' And, had I suffered it, he would have stripped himself, and gone away naked in his sorry open cloak, as there are seen many men in the indigence of the wilderness and, like the people of India, with no more than a clout to cover the human shame ; and when I let him go, he murmured, *Jízak Ullah kheyr,* ' God recompense thee with good,' and went on wondering, whether the things ' which the Nasrâny had given him for nothing, could be good medicines ? '

I thought no more of Bagdad, but of Kheybar ; already I stayed too long in Hâyil. At evening I went to Abeyd's kahwa to speak with Hamûd ; he was bowing then in the beginning of his private devotion, and I sat down silently, awaiting his leisure. The son of Abeyd at the end of the first bout looked up, and nodding cheerfully, enquired, " Khalîl, is there need, wouldst thou anything immediately ? "—" There is nothing, the Lord be praised."—" Then I shall soon have ended." As Hamûd sat again in his place, I said, ' I saw the child Feysal's health returning, I desired to depart, and would he send me to Kheybar ? ' Hamûd answered, 'If I wished it.'—" But why, Khalîl, to Kheybar, what is there at Kheybar ? go not to Kheybar, thou mayest die of fever at Kheybar ; and they are not our friends, Khalîl, I am afraid of that journey for thee." I answered, " I must needs adventure thither, I would see the antiquities of the Yahûd, as I have seen el-Héjr."—" Well, I will find some means to send thee ; but the fever is deadly, go not thither, eigh Khalîl ! lest thou die there."—Since I had passed the great Aueyrid I desired to discover also the Harrat Kheybar, such another vulcanic Arabian country, and wherein I heard to be the heads of the W. er-Rummah, which westward of the Tueyk mountains is the dry waterway of all northern Arabia. This great valley which descends from the heads above el-Hâyat and Howeyat to the Euphrates valley at ez-Zbeyer, a suburb of Bosra, has a winding course of " fifty camel marches."

Hamûd, then stretching out his manly great arm, bade me try his pulse ; the strokes of his heart-blood were greater than I had felt any man's among the Arabians, the man was strong as a champion. When they hold out their forearms to the hakîm, they think he may well perceive all their health : I was cried down when I said it was imposture. " Yesterday a Persian medicaster in the Haj was called to the Kasr to feel the Emir's pulse. The Persian said, ' Have you not a pain, Sir, in the left knee ? ' the Prince responded, ' Ay I feel a pain there by God ! ' —and no man knew it ! "

The Haj had left some sick ones behind them in Hâyil : there was a welfaring Bagdad tradesman, whose old infirmities had returned upon him in the way, a foot-sore camel driver, and some poor derwishes. The morrow after, all these went to present themselves before the Emir in the mejlis, and the derawîsh cried with a lamentable voice in their bastard town Arabic, *Janâbak !* ' may it please your grace.' Their clownish carriage and torpid manners, the barbarous border speech of the north, and their illiberal voices, strangely discorded with the bird-like ease and alacrity and the frank propriety in the tongue of the poorest Arabians. The Emir made them a gracious gesture, and appointed them their daily rations in the Mothîf. Also to the tradesman was assigned a makhzan ; and at Hâyil he would pass those two or three months well enough, sitting in the sun and gossiping up and down the sûk, till he might ride homeward. Afterward I saw led-in a wretched young man of the Aarab, who was blind ; and spreading his pitiful hands towards the Emir's seat, he cried out, *Yâ Tawîl el-Ummr ! yâ Weled Abdullah !* ' Help, O Long-of-days, thou Child of Abdullah ! ' The Emir spoke immediately to one over the wardrobe, and the poor weled was led away to receive the change of clothing.

Afterwards, I met with Imbârak. " Wouldst thou (he said) to Kheybar ? there are some Annezy here, who will convey thee." When I heard their menzils were in the Kharram, and that they could only carry me again to Misshel, and were to depart immediately : I said that I could not so soon be ready to take a long journey, and must call in the debts for medicines. " We will gather them for thee ; but longer we cannot suffer thee to remain in our country : if thou wouldst go to Kheybar, we will send thee to Kheybar or to el-Kasîm, we will send thee to el-Kasîm."—" To Kheybar, yet warn me a day or two beforehand, that I may be ready."

The morning next but one after, I was drinking kahwa with those of er-Riâth, when a young man entered out of breath, he came, he said, to call me from Imbârak. Imbârak when I met him, said, " We have found some Heteym who will convey thee to Kheybar."—' And when would they depart ? '—" To-morrow or the morning after." But he sent for me in an hour to say

he had given them handsel, and I must set out immediately.
"Why didst thou deceive me with *to-morrow?*"—"Put up
thy things and mount."—"But will you send me with
Heteym!"—"Ay, ay, give me the key of the makhzan and
make up, for thou art to mount immediately."—"And I
cannot speak with the Emir?"—"*Ukhlus!* have done, delay
not, or wellah! the Emir will send, to take off thy head."—"Is
this driving me into the desert to make me away, covertly?"—
"Nay, nothing will happen to thee."—"Now well let me first
see Hamûd." There came then a slave of Hamûd, bringing in
his hand four reals, which he said his "uncle" sent to me.
So there came Zeyd, the Moghreby porter of the Kasr; I
had shown him a good turn by the gift of medicines, but now
quoth the burly villain, "Thou hast no heart (understanding)
if thou wouldst resist Imbârak; for this is the captain and there
ride behind him five hundred men."

I delayed to give the wooden key of my door, fearing lest if
they had flung the things forth my aneroid had been broken, or
if they searched them my pistol had been taken; also I doubted
whether the captain of the guard (who at every moment laid
hand to the hilt of his sword) had not some secret commission to slay the Nasrâny there within. His slaves already
came about me, some plucked my clothes, some thrust me forward; they would drive me perforce to the makhzan.—"Is the
makhzan thine or ours, Khalîl?"—"But Imbârak, I no longer
trust thee: bear my word to the Emir, 'I came from the
Dowla, send me back to the Dowla.'" The Arab swordsman
with *fugh!* spat in my face. "Heaven send thee confusion
that art not ashamed to spit in a man's face."—"Khalîl, I
did it because thou saidst 'I will not trust thee.'" I saw
the Moghreby porter go and break open my makhzan door,
bursting the clay mortice of the wooden lock. The slaves
plucking me savagely again, I let go the loose Arab upper
garments in their hands, and stood before the wondering
wretches in my shirt. "A shame! I said to them, and thou
Imbârak *dakhîl-ak*, defend me from their insolence." As Imbârak
heard 'dakhîl-ak,' he snatched a camel-stick from one who stood
by, and beat them back and drove them from me.

They left me in the makhzan and I quickly put my things
in order, and took my arms secretly. Fáhd now came by, going
to Abeyd's kahwa: I said to him, "Fáhd, I will enter with thee,
for here I am in doubt, and where is Hamûd?" The poor
man answered friendly, "Hamûd is not yet abroad, but it will
not be long, Khalîl, before he come."—*Imbârak:* "Wellah, I say
the Emir will send immediately to cut off thy head!" *Májid*

(who passed us at the same time, going towards Abeyd's kahwa) :
" Eigh ! Imbârak, will the Emir do so indeed ? " and the boy
smiled with a child's dishonest curiosity of an atrocious spectacle.
As I walked on with Fáhd, Imbârak retired from us, and passed
through the Kasr gate, perhaps then he went to the Emir.
—Fáhd sighed, as we were beyond the door, and " Khalîl, please
Ullah, said the poor man, it may yet fall out well, and Hamûd
will very soon be here." I had not sat long, when they came to
tell me, ' the Emir desired to see me.' I said, " Do not deceive
me, it is but Imbârak who knocks." *Fáhd :* " Nay, go Khalîl,
it is the Emir."

When I went out, I found it was Imbârak, who with the old
menaces, called upon me to mount immediately. " I will first,
I answered, see Hamûd : " so he left me. The door had been
shut behind me, I returned to the makhzan, and saw my baggage was safe ; and Fáhd coming by again, " Hamûd, he said,
is now in the house," and at my request he sent back a servant
to let me in. After a little, Hamûd entering, greeted me, and
took me by the hand. I asked, ' Was this done at the commandment of the Emir ? ' *Hamûd :* " By God, Khalîl, I can
do nothing with the Emir ; *hu yáhkam aleyna* he rules
over us all."—" Some books of mine, and other things, were
brought here."—" Ha ! the eyyâl have taken them from
thy makhzan, they shall be restored." When I spoke of a
knavish theft of his man Aly—he was gone now on pilgrimage
—Hamûd exclaimed : " The Lord take away his breath ! "—He
were not an Arab if he had proffered to make good his man's
larceny. " What intended you by that money you lately sent
me ? "—" My liberality, Khalîl, why didst thou refuse it ? "—" Is
it for medicine and a month's daily care of thy child, who is
now restored to health ? "—" It was for this I offered it, and we
have plenty of quinine ; wilt thou buy an handful of me for two
reals ? " He was washing to go to the mid-day public prayer,
and whilst the strong man stayed to speak with me it was late.
" There is a thing, Hamûd."—" What is that, Khalîl ? " and he
looked up cheerfully. " Help me in this trouble, for that bread
and salt which is between us."—" And what can I do ? Mohammed rules us all."—" Well, speak to Imbârak to do nothing
till the hour of the afternoon mejlis, when I may speak with
the Emir."—" I will say this to him," and Hamûd went to the
mesjid.

After the prayer I met the Prince himself in the Méshab ;
he walks, as said, in an insolent cluster of young fanatics, and
a half score of his swordsmen close behind them.—Whenever
I had encountered the Emir and his company of late, in the

streets, I thought he had answered my greeting with a strutting
look. Now, as he came on with his stare, I said, without a
salutation, *Arûhh,* ' I depart.' " *Rûhh,* So go," answered Mohammed. " Shall I come in to speak with thee ? "—" *Meshghrûl !*
we are too busy."

When at length the afternoon mejlis was sitting, I crossed
through them and approached the Emir, who sat enforcing
himself to look gallantly before the people ; and he talked then
with some great sheykh of the Beduw, who was seated next him.
Mohammed Ibn Rashîd looked towards me, I thought with displeasure and somewhat a base countenance, which is of evil
augury among the Arabs. " What (he said) is thy matter ? "—
" I am about to depart, but I would it were with assurance.
To-day I was mishandled in this place, in a manner which has
made me afraid. Thy slaves drew me hither and thither, and
have rent my clothing ; it was by the setting on of Imbârak,
who stands here : he also threatened me, and even spat in my
face." The Emir enquired, under his voice, of Imbârak, ' what
had he done,' who answered, excusing himself. I added, " And
now he would compel me to go with Heteym ; and I foresee only
mischance." " Nay (said the Emir, striking his breast), fear not ;
but ours be the care for thy safety, and we will give thee a
passport,"—and he said to Nasr, his secretary, who sat at his feet
—" Write him a schedule of safe-conduct."

I said, " I brought thee from my country an excellent tele-
scope." The cost had been three or four pounds ; and I thought,
' if Ibn Rashîd receive my gift, I might ask of him a camel ' :
but when he said, " We have many, and have no need," I answered
the Emir with a frank word of the desert, *weysh aad,* as one
might say, ' What odds ! ' Mohammed Ibn Rashîd shrunk back
in his seat, as if I had disparaged his dignity before the people ;
but recovering himself, he said, with better looks and a friendly
voice, " Sit down." Mohammed is not ungenerous, he might
remember in the stranger his own evil times. Nasr having
ended his writing, upon a small square of paper, handed it up
to the Emir, who perused it, and daubing his Arabic copper
seal in the ink, he sealed it with the print of his name. I asked
Nasr, " Read me what is written herein," and he read, " That
all unto whose hands this bill may come, who owe obedience to
Ibn Rashîd, know it is the will of the Emir that no one *yaarud
aley,* should do any offence to, this Nasrâny." Ibn Rashîd
rising at the moment, the mejlis rose with him and dispersed.
I asked, as the Emir was going, " When shall I depart ? "—" At
thy pleasure."—" To-morrow ? "—" Nay, to-day." He had turned
the back, and was crossing the Méshab.

" Mount ! " cries Imbârak : but, when he heard I had not broken my fast he led me through the Kasr, to the Mothîf and to a room behind, which is the public kitchen, to ask the cooks what was ready. Here they all kindly welcomed me, and Mufarrij would give me dates, flour and samn for the way, the accustomed provision from the Emir, but I would not receive them. The kitchen is a poor hall, with a clay floor, in which is a pool and conduit. The temmn and barley is boiled in four or five coppers : other three stand there for flesh days (which are not many), and they are so great that in one of them may be seethed the brittled meat of a camel. So simple is this palace kitchen of nomadic Arabia, a country in which he is feasting who is not hungry ! The kitchen servants were one poor man, perhaps of servile condition, a patient of mine, and five or six women under him ; besides there were boys, bearers of the metal trays of victual for the guests' suppers.—When I returned to the Méshab, a nomad was come with his camel to load my baggage : yet first he entreated Imbârak to take back his real of earnest-money and let him go. The Emir had ordered four reals to be given for this voyage, whether I would or no, and I accepted it in lieu of that which was robbed from my makhzan ; also I accepted the four reals from Hamûd for medicines.

" Imbârak, swear, I said as we walked together to the sûk, where the nomads would mount, that you are not sending me to the death."—" No, by Ullah, and Khalîl nothing I trust will happen to thee."—" And after two journeys in the desert will the Aarab any more observe the word of Ibn Rashîd ? "—" We rule over them !—and he said to the nomads, Ye are to carry him to *Kâsim ibn Barák* (a great sheykh of the midland Heteym, his byût were pitched seventy miles to the southward), and he will send him to Kheybar."—The seller of drugs from Medina, a good liberal Hejâz man, as are many of that partly Arabian city, came out, as we passed his shop, to bid me God speed, " Thou mayest be sure, he said, that there is no treachery, but understand that the people (of Hâyil and Nejd) are Beduw."— " O thou (said the nomad to me) make haste along with us out of Hâyil, stand not, nor return upon thy footsteps, for then they will kill thee."

Because I would not that his camel should kneel, but had climbed upon the overloaded beast's neck standing, the poor pleased nomad cried out, " Lend me a grip of thy five ! " that is the five fingers. A young man, Ibrahîm, one of the Emir's men— his shop was in the end of the town, and I had dealt with him— seeing us go by, came out to bid me farewell, and brought me forward. He spoke sternly to the nomads that they should have a care for me, and threatened them, that ' If anything befell me, the Emir would have their heads.' Come to the Mâ es-Sáma, I reached down my water-skin to one of the men, bidding him go fill it. " Fill the kafir's girby ! nay, said he, alight, Nasrâwy, and fill it thyself." Ibrahîm then went to fill it, and hanged the water at my saddle-bow. We passed forth and the sun was now set. My companions were three,—the poor owner of my camel, a timid smiling man, and his fanatic neighbour, who called me always the Nasrâwy (and not Nasrány), and another and older Heteymy, a somewhat strong-headed holder of his own counsel, and speaking the truth uprightly. So short is the twilight that the night closed suddenly upon our march, with a welcome silence and solitude, after the tumult of the town. When I responded to all the questions of my nomad company with the courtesy of the desert, " Oh! wherefore, cried they, did those of Hâyil persecute him ? Wellah the people of Hâyil are the true Nasâra ! " We held on our dark way three and a half hours till we came before Gofar ; there we alighted and lay down in the wilderness.

Thus it was that our latter-day Chaucerian pilgrim left Ha'il on the thirtieth day of his stay there, on 21 November 1877, in the company of two ruffianly guides of the Hutaim, and one of the Bishr called Salih who also claimed, for safe conduct, to be a Hutaimi. Doughty possessed no more than thirty dollars in cash by this time, and was without a camel of his own, using that of Salih until they arrived at the tents of Hutaim beyond the settlement of Kasim ibn Barak. A short time after Doughty came across by great good fortune a poor camel-owning man called Qurusaib, who escorted Khalil from 25 November until, on 28 November, they came into view of one of the four walled villages together comprising Khaibar. Only one half-page entry covers Doughty's two and a half months in Khaibar after 30 December, presumably because of the capture of his camel-bags. Unlike Ha'il, Khaibar was considered as within sacred Hejazi territory, and no Christian could be tolerated there, so his confession that he was an Englishman and a Christian on the first day argues well for his integrity, and for the humanity of the negro Commandant, ^CAbdullah as-Sirwan of Khaibar and the compassion of the latter's superior, Sabri, Wali of Medina. During Khalil's stay in Khaibar he met his truest friend and an extraordinarily sympathetic character, Muhammad an-Najumi, commonly called ^CAmm Muhammad, 'Uncle'. Muhammad and Doughty spent nearly every day for four months tending palms or digging wells at Khaibar, and Doughty was compelled to report to the Commandant morn and night.

Sabri Pasha at last ordered Doughty to return from Hejazi lands to Ha'il, with his confiscated belongings returned to him and the six Turkish pounds that ^CAbdullah as-Sirwan had taken from him on the day of his arrival.

Doughty could not afford the two Turkish pounds demanded by Dakhil the letter-bearer to transport him back to Ha'il, and settled instead on a five-dollar fee with a Bishr camel-owner called ^CAyyad via Hayat on the east of the *harra* and Mustajiddah. They left with a youth called Marjan and a villager called Hamid on 18 March and rode into Ha'il on 1 April 1878.

At sunrise we saw the twin heads of the Sumrâ Hâyil. Eyâd responded to all men's questions : " We go with this Khalîl to Hâyil, at the commandment of the Bashat el-Medina ; and are bearers of his sealed letter to Ibn Rashîd ; but we know not what is in the writing,—which may be to cut off all our heads ! "—also I said in my heart, ' The Turks are treacherous ! '—But should I break the Pasha's seal ? No ! I would sooner hope for a fair event of that hazard. This sealed letter of the governor of Medina, was opened after my returning from Arabia, at a British Consulate ; and it contained no more than his commending me to ' The Sheykh ' Ibn Rashîd, and the request that he would send me forward on my journey.

I walked in the mornings two hours, and as much at afternoon, that my companions might ride ; and to spare their sickly thelûl I climbed to the saddle, as she stood, like a Beduwy : but the humanity which I showed them, to my possibility, hardened their ungenerous hearts. Seeing them weary, and

271

Eyâd complaining that his soles were worn to the quick, I
went on walking barefoot to Gofar, and bade them ride still.—
There I beheld once more (oh ! blissful sight), the plum trees and
almond trees blossoming in an Arabian oasis. We met with no
one in the long main street ; the men were now in the fields, or
sleeping out the heat of the day in their houses. We went by the
Manôkh, and I knew it well ; but my companions, who had not
been this way of late years, were gone on, and so we lost our breakfast. When I called they would not hear ; they went to knock
at a door far beyond. They sat down at last in the street's end,
but we saw no man. " Let us to Hâyil, and mount thou, Khalîl ! "
said the rafîks. We went on through the ruins of the northern
quarter, where I showed them the road ; and come near the
desert side, I took the next way, but they trod in another. I
called them, they called to me, and I went on riding. Upon
this Eyâd's light head turning, whether it were he had not
tasted tobacco this day, or because he was weary and fasting, he
began to curse me ; and came running like a madman, ' to
take the thelûl.' When I told him I would not suffer it, he
stood aloof and cursed on, and seemed to have lost his understanding. A mile beyond he returned to a better mind, and
acknowledged to me, that ' until he had drunk tobacco of a
morning his heart burned within him, the brain rose in his pan,
and he felt like a fiend.'—It were as easy to contain such a
spirit as to bind water !

I rode not a little pensively, this third time, in the beaten
way to Hâyil ; and noted again (with abhorrence, of race) at
every few hours' end their " kneeling places " ;—those little bays
of stones set out in the desert soil, where wayfarers overtaken by
the canonical hours may patter the formal prayer of their religion.
—About midway we met the morning passengers out from Hâyil :
and looking upon me with the implacable eyes of their
fanaticism, every one who went by uttered the same hard
words to my companions, ' Why bring ye him again ? ' Ambar,
Aneybar's brother, came next, riding upon an ass in a company ;
he went to Gofar, where he had land and palms. But the
worthy Galla libertine greeted us with a pleasant good humour,
—I was less it might be in disgrace of the princely household
than of the fanatical populace. We saw soon above the brow
of the desert the white tower-head of the great donjon of the
castle, and said Merjàn, " Some think that the younger children
of Telâl be yet alive therein. They see the world from their
tower, and they are unseen." Upon our right hand lay the
palms in the desert, es-Sherafa, founded by Metaab :—so we
rode on into the town.

We enterea Hâyil near the time of the afternoon prayers. Because the Emir was absent, there was no business! the most shops were shut. The long market street was silent; and their town seemed a dead and empty place. I saw the renegade Abdullah sitting at a shop door; then Ibrahîm and a few more of my acquaintance, and lastly the schoolmaster. The unsavoury pedant stood and cried with many deceitful gestures, " Now, welcome! and blessed be the Lord !—Khalîl is a Moslem ! " (for else he guessed I had not been so foolhardy as to re-enter Ibn Rashîd's town.) At the street's end I met with Aneybar, lieutenant now in (empty) Hâyil for the Emir; he came from the Kasr carrying in his hand a gold-hilted back-sword: the great man saluted me cheerfully and passed by. I went to alight before the castle, in the empty Méshab, which was wont to be full of the couching thelûls of visiting Beduins: but in these days since Ibn Rashîd was *ghrazzai*, there came no more Beduins to the town. About half the men of Hâyil were now in the field with Ibn Rashîd; for, besides his salaried rajajîl, even the salesmen of the sûk are the Prince's servants, to ride with him. This custom of military service has discouraged many traders of the East Nejd provinces, who had otherwise been willing to try their fortunes in Hâyil.

Some malignants of the castle ran together at the news, that the Nasrâny was come again. I saw them stand in the tower gate, with the old coffee-server; " Heigh! (they cried) it is he indeed! now it may please Ullah he will be put to death."— Whilst I was in this astonishment, Aneybar returned; he had but walked some steps to find his wit. " *Salaam aleyk !* " " *Aleykôm es-salaam,*" he answered me again, betwixt good will and wondering, and cast back the head; for they have all learned to strut like the Emirs. Aneybar gave me his right hand with a lordly grace: there was the old peace of bread and salt betwixt us.—" From whence, Khalîl? and ye twain with him what be ye?—well go to the coffee hall! and there we will hear more." Aly el-Aŷid went by us, coming from his house, and saluted me heartily.

When we were seated with Aneybar in the great kahwa, he asked again, " And you Beduw with him, what be ye? " Eyâd responded with a craven humility : " We are Heteym."— " Nay ye are not Heteym."—" Tell them, I said, both what ye be, and who sent you hither." *Eyâd:* " We are Ageyl from Medina, and the Pasha sent us to Kheybar to convey this Khalîl, with a letter to Ibn Rashîd."—" Well, Ageyl, and what tribesmen? "—" We must acknowledge we are Beduins, we are Anâjy." *Aneybar:* " And, Khalîl, where are your letters? "—

I gave him a letter from Abdullah es-Siruàn, and the Pasha's sealed letter. Aneybar, who had not learned to read gave them to a secretary, a sober and friendly man, who perusing the unflattering titles " *To the sheykh Ibn Rashîd,*" returned them to me unopened.—Mufarrij, the steward, now came in ; he took me friendly by the hand, and cried, " Sum ! " (i.e. short for *Bismillah,* in God's name) and led us to the mothif. There a dish was set before us of Ibn Rashîd's rusty tribute dates, and—their spring hospitality—a bowl of small camel léban. One of the kitchen servers showed me a piece of ancient copper money, which bore the image of an eagle ; it had been found at Hâyil, and was Roman.

The makhzan was assigned us in which I had formerly lodged ; and my rafîks left me to visit their friends in the town. Children soon gathered to the threshold and took courage to revile me. Also there came to me the princely child Abd el-Azîz, the orphan of Metaab : I saw him fairly grown in these three months ; he swaggered now like his uncle with a lofty but not disdainful look, and he resembles the Emir Mohammed. The princely child stood and silently regarded me, he clapt a hand to his little sword, but would not insult the stranger ; so he said : " Why returned, Khalîl Nasrâny ? "—" Because I hoped it would be pleasant to thine uncle, my darling."—" Nay, Khalîl ! nay, Khalîl ! the Emir says thou art not to remain here." I saw Zeyd the gate-keeper leading Merjàn by the hand ; and he enquired of the lad, who was of a vindictive nature, of all that had happened to me since the day I arrived at Kheybar. Such questions and answers could only be to my hurt : it was a danger I had foreseen, amongst ungenerous Arabs.

We found Aneybar in the coffee-hall at evening : " Khalîl, he said, we cannot send thee forward, and thou must depart to-morrow."—" Well, send me to the Emir in the North with the Medina letter, if I may not abide his coming in Hâyil."— " Here rest to-night, and in the morning (he shot his one palm from the other) depart !—Thou stay here, Khalîl ! the people threatened thee to-day, thou sawest how they pressed on thee at your entering."—" None pressed upon me, many saluted me."— " Life of Ullah ! but I durst not suffer thee to remain in Hâyil, where so many are ready to kill thee, and I must answer to the Emir : sleep here this night, and please Ullah without mishap, and mount when we see the morning light."—Whilst we were speaking there came in a messenger, who arrived from the Emir in the northern wilderness : " And how does the Emir, exclaimed Aneybar with an affected heartiness of voice ; and where left you him encamped ? " The messenger, a worthy

man of the middle age, saluted me, without any religious
misliking, he was of the strangers at Hâyil from the East
provinces. *Aneybar:* "Thou hast heard, Khalîl? and he
showed me these three pauses of his malicious wit, on his fingers,
To-morrow! — The light! — Depart! " — " Whither ? " — " From
whence thou camest ;—to Kheybar : art thou of the *dîn* (their
religion) ? "—" No, I am not."—" And therefore the Arabs are
impatient of thy life : wouldst thou be of the dîn, thou mightest
live always amongst them."—" Then send me to-morrow, at my
proper charge, towards el-Kasîm."

They were displeased when I mentioned the *Dowla :* Aneybar answered hardly, " What Dowla ! here is the land of
the Aarab, and the dominion of Ibn Rashîd.—He says Kasîm :
but there are no Beduw in the town (to convey him). Khalîl !
we durst not ourselves be seen in Kasîm," and he made me a
shrewd sign, sawing with the forefinger upon his black throat.—
" Think not to deceive me, Aneybar ; is not a sister of the
Emir of Boreyda, a wife of Mohammed ibn Rashîd ? and are
not they your allies ? "—" Ullah ! (exclaimed some of them), he
knows everything."—*Aneybar :* " Well ! well ! but it cannot be,
Khalîl : how sayest thou, sherîf ? "

—This was an old gentleman-beggar, with grey eyes, some
fortieth in descent from the Néby, clad like a Turkish citizen,
and who had arrived to-day from Medina, where he dwelt. His
was an adventurous and gainful trade of hypocrisy : three months
or four in a year he dwelt at home ; in the rest he rode, or
passed the seas into every far land of the Mohammedan world.
In each country he took up a new concubine ; and whereso he
passed he glosed so fructuously, and showed them his large
letters patent from kings and princes, and was of that honourable
presence, that he was bidden to the best houses, as becometh
a religious sheykh of the Holy City, and a nephew of the
apostle of Ullah : so he received their pious alms and returned
to the illuminated Medina. Bokhâra was a *villegiatura* for this
holy man in his circuit, and so were all the cities beyond as far
as Càbul. In Mohammedan India, he went a begging long
enough to learn the vulgar language. Last year he visited
Stambûl, and followed the [not] glorious Mohammedan arms
in Europe ; and the Sultan of Islam had bestowed upon him
his imperial firmàn.—He showed me the *dedale* engrossed
document, with the sign manual of the Calif upon a half fathom
of court paper. And with this broad charter he was soon to go
again upon an Indian voyage.

—When Aneybar had asked his counsel, " *Wellah yá el-
Mohafûth* (answered this hollow spirit), and I say the same,

it cannot be; for what has this man to do in el-Kasîm? and what does he wandering up and down in all the land; (he added under his breath), *wa yiktub el-bilâd,* and he writes up the country." *Aneybar:* "Well, to-morrow, Khalîl, depart; and thou Eyâd carry him back to Kheybar."—*Eyâd:* "But it would be said there, 'Why hast thou brought him again?' wellah I durst not do it, Aneybar." Aneybar mused a little. I answered them, "You hear his words; and if this rafîk were willing, yet so feeble is their thelûl, you have seen it yourselves, that she could not carry me."—*Eyâd:* "Wellah! she is not able."—"Besides, I said, if you cast me back into hazards, the Dowla may require my blood, and you must every year enter some of their towns as Bagdad and Medina: and when you send to India with your horses, will you not be in the power of my fellow citizens?"—*The Sherîf:* "He says truth, I have been there, and I know the Engleys and their Dowla: now let me speak to this man in a tongue which he will understand,—he spoke somewhat in Hindostani—what! an Engleysy understand not the language of el-Hind?"—*Aneybar:* "Thou Eyâd (one of our subject Beduins)! it is not permitted thee to say nay; I command you upon your heads to convey Khalîl to Kheybar; and you are to depart to-morrow.—Heigh-ho! it should be the hour of prayer!" Some said, They had heard the *ithin* already: Aneybar rose, the Sherîf rose solemnly and all the rest; and they went out to say their last prayers in the great mesjid.

In the next makhzan lodged a stranger, newly come from the wars: and I heard from him the first sure tidings,—'that the Moslemîn had the worse; but the jehâd being now at an end, they returned home. The Muskovs were big, he said, and manly bodies with great beards.' But, of all that he saw in the land of Europe, most strange seemed to him the sheep of the Nasâra, 'that they had tails like camels' [and not the huge tallow laps of the Arabian stock]. He had come lately to Hâyil in company with the great sheykh of el-Ajmân. That sheykh of Aarab had been taken captive by the Turks, in their occupation of el-Hása, and banished to the confines of Russia. There he was seven years in durance; and his Beduin kindred in Arabia had (in the last two years) slain the year's-mind for him,—supposing him to be deceased! But when the valorous (unlettered) man in a strange land heard the cry to warfare for the religion, he made his humble petition to the Sultan; and liberty was granted him to bear a lance to the jehâd in the worship of Ullah and the Apostle.—This Beduin duke was wounded, in the arm. At the armistice the Sultan bade him ask a reward; and he an-

wered, " That I might return to my province, *Hájjar!* "—In
Ramathàn he landed with this companion at Jidda : they visited
Mecca and Medina, and from Medina they rode to Hâyil. Here
Mohammed ibn Rashîd received him kindly, and dismissed him
with his princely gift of three thelûls and a saddle-bag full of
silver reals. The noble Arabian was now gone home to his country ; and we heard that he had submitted himself to the Wahâby.

That stranger, his rafîk, who had but one mocking eye,
which seemed to look askance, said to me he had seen me
three years before in Alexandria, and spoken with me! [I
think it was true,—that one day meeting with him, in the
street I had enquired the way of him.] To my ear the
Arabian speech sounded mincing and affected-like upon his
tongue. He said he was from el-Yémen, but what he was
indeed (in this time of trouble) I might not further enquire.
When I asked him of the sherîf from Medina, he answered
with an incredulous scorn (which might have become an European), " He is no sherîf, I know him well, but a beggar come
all the way hither, from Medina, with a box of candles (which
they have not in these parts) for Ibn Rashîd, only to beg
of him four or five reals, and receive a change of clothing.
He does this every few years, though he has a good house at
Medina ; he runs through all the world a-begging."—" But
wherefore, if he have to live ? "—" It is only his avarice."

The Sherîf came, after prayers, to visit me, and his wayfaring companion, clad in their long city coats, wide girdles,
superfluous slops, and red caps wound about with great calico
turbans. They asked, ' Was there any water ? ' We were all
thirsty from the journey, which is like a fever in Arabia ;
and I went out to ask a little water, for my guests, at the
Kasr gate. It was shut : " What wouldst thou, Khalîl ? " I
heard a voice say in the dark, and I knew it was Aneybar ;
he was sitting there on Hamûd's clay settle. I asked, " Why
made he this ado about my coming again to Hâyil ? and seeing
that I came with a letter from the Pasha of Medina ? "—" Tell
us not of pashas, here is Ibn Rashîd's government : to-morrow
depart, there is no more to say ; " and he turned to a companion, who answered him, " Ay to-morrow early ! away with
the cursed Nasrâny." I asked Aneybar who was his coun-
sellor, since I could not see him : but he answered not.—
The unsavoury schoolmaster went by, and when he knew our
voices, " Akhs ! quoth he, I saluted thee to-day, seeing thee
arrive, as I supposed, a Moslem, but now thou wilt be slain."
Aneybar was not a bad man, or fanatical, but he had a bonds-

man's heart, and the good was easily corrupted in him, by the despiteful reasons of others.

I went on to knock at the door of Aly el-Aȳid and ask a little water. His wife opened with " Welcome Khalîl."—" And where is Aly ? "—" My husband is gone out to sleep in the (ripening) cornfields, he must watch all night ;" she bade me enter, but I excused myself. She was young and pleasant, of modest demeanour, and had many tall children. When I was formerly at Hâyil, I often visited them, and she sat unveiled, before the hakîm, with her husband ; and he would have it so, because I was a Nasrâny. She brought me water and I returned to my makhzan.

The sherîf's companion had been in the Bagdad caravan ; afterwards he lay sick in a hospital at Medina : he met lately with the sherîf, all ready to go upon his northern journey, and they joined company. Some nomads riding to Hâyil, had carried them upon their camels for two reals each, but far ways about, so that they arrived full of weariness and impatience. When they returned to their makhzan I said I would go over presently to visit them.—*Eyâd*, " Is not the sherîf going to el-Méshed ? we will give him money to take thee with him, and let us see what the morning will bring forth ; look, Khalîl ! I will not forsake thee."—When we entered, the sherîf drew me out the Sultan's diploma ; he found his goggle spectacles, and when he had set them solemnly astride on his nose, the old fox took up his candle end and began to read forth. He showed us his other documents and letters mandatory, from princes and pashas, ' Only, quoth he, there lacked him one from the Engleys ! '—He would have me write him a thing, that he might have entrance to the Consulate of our nation at Bagdad ; and he hoped there to obtain a certificate to further him in his Indian voyage. " Reach me the inkhorn, look in the bags, companion," quoth the iniquitous shrew ; who oppressed me here, and would that I should lift him up abroad ! —" Lend me that reed, and I will not fail thee,—what good deeds of thine shall I record ? wilt thou persuade Aneybar ? "— " Ugh ! " (he would as lief that I perished in this wilderness, as to thrive himself in India).

Eyâd : " Sherîf, since thou art going to Méshed, take with thee Khalîl, and we will give thee four reals ; also Khalîl shall deliver thee a writing for the Engleys."—" Ugh ! said the old shrew, four reals, four only, ugh ! we may consider of it to-morrow. He added this miserable proverb—*the Lord may work much mercy before the morning :* and—this is the only word I know of their speech, besides *bret* (*bread*),—el-Engleys *weri-*

gud." I asked, " Did they take thee too for a spy in the Indian country ? "—" Ay, and there only can I blame their government : *I went no whither in all India, but I was watched!* and for such it is that I would obtain a certificate, another time, from a Konsulato."—" And did any threaten thee because of thy religion ? "—" Nay, that I will say for them."—" Be they not just to all without difference ? "—" They are just, out of doubt ; and (he said to Eyâd) I will tell thee a tale. One day as I journeyed in el-Hind, I hastened, I and a concubine of mine, to come to a town not far beyond to lodge : but the night falling on us short of the place, I turned aside, where I saw a military station ; because I feared for the woman, and if we should lie abroad, we were in danger of robbers.

" The [sepoy] sentinel would not suffer me to pass the gate, " The sun, he said is set :" then in my anger I struck him. [This is very unlike the Arabian comity ;. but the holy parasite was town-bred and not wont to suffer contradiction so far from home.] The soldier reported to the guard, and their officer sent for me ; he was an Engleysy,—they are all yellow haired, and such as this Khalîl. When I told him my quality and spread my firmans before him, which ye have seen, the officer commanded to make ready for us a lodging and supper, and to give me twenty-five rupees ; and he said to me, " You may lodge here one month, and receive daily rations."—" I would thou might persuade this people in Hâyil to show some humanity to strangers ! "—" Ha ! (answered the sherîf, as a citizen despising them), they are Beduw ! " and the false old man began to be merry.

" Bokhâra, he told me, is a city greater than Damascus ; the Emir, who—he added mocking—would be called *Sûltàn,* had a wide and good country ; but now (he murmured) the Muskôv are there ! "—" Well, tell us of the jehâd."—" I myself was at the wars, and am only lately come home to Medina ;" where he said, he had heard of me (detained) at Kheybar, when my matter was before the council.—" But, eigh ! the Nasâra had the upper hand ; and they have taken a province."—" Akhs ! cries Eyâd, tell us, sherîf, have the Nasâra conquered any béled of the Sooltàn ? to whom Ullah send the victory !—Can the Nasâra prevail against the Moslemîn ? " The sherîf answered with the Mohammedan solemnity, and cast a sigh, " *Amr Ullah, amr Ullah !* it was God's ordinance."—*Eyâd :* " Ha ! sherîf, what thinkest thou, will the Nasâra come on hither ? "—" That is unlikely ! " Eyâd's busy broken head was full of a malicious subtlety : I said therefore, " Sherîf, thinkest thou that this land would be worth to them a cup of coffee ? "—" Well, it is all chôl, steppes. an open desolation ; aye, what profit might they have in it ! " " And the Engleys ? "—" They were of our part."— " Eyâd you hear this from the sherîf's mouth ! "—*Eyâd :* " But the Nasâra take the Sultan's provinces, says the sherîf : and the Engleys are Nasâra ! "

When the morning sun rose I had as lief that my night had continued for ever. There was no going forward for me, nor going backward, and I was spent with fatigues.—We went over to the great coffee-hall. Aneybar sat there, and beside him was the old dry-hearted sherîf, who drank his morrow's cup with an holy serenity. " Eyâd affirms, I said, that he cannot, he dare not, and that he will not convey me again to Kheybar."— " To Kheybar thou goest, and that presently."

Eyâd was leading away his sick thelûl to pasture under Ajja, but the Moghréby gatekeeper withheld him by force. That Moor's heart, as at my former departure from Hâyil, was full of brutality. " Come, Zeyd, I said to him, be we not both Western men and like countrymen among these Beduw ? "— " Only become a Moslem, and we would all love thee ; but we know thee to be a most hardened Nasrâny.—Khalîl comes (he said to the bystanders) to dare us ! a Nasrâny, here in the land of the Moslemîn ! Was it not enough that we once sent thee away in safety, and comest thou hither again ! " Round was this burly man's head, with a brutish visage ; he had a thick neck, unlike the shot-up growth of the slender Nejd Arabians ; the rest of him an unwieldy carcase, and half a cart-load of tripes.

In the absence of the princely family, my soul was in the hand of this cyclops of the Méshab. I sat to talk peaceably with him, and the brute-man many times lifted his stick to smite the kafir ; but it was hard for Zeyd, to whom I had sometime shown a good turn, to chafe himself against me. The opinions of the Arabs are ever divided, and among three is commonly one mediator :—it were blameworthy to defend the cause of an adversary of Ullah ; and yet some of the people of Hâyil that now gathered about us with mild words were a mean for me. The one-eyed stranger stood by, he durst not affront the storm ; but when Zeyd left me for a moment, he whispered in my ear, that I should put them off, whom he called in contempt ' beasts without understanding, Beduw ! '—" Only seem thou to consent with them, lest they kill thee ; say ' Mohammed is the apostle of Ullah,' and afterward, when thou art come into sure countries, hold it or leave it at thine own liking. This is not to sin before God, when force oppresses us, and there is no deliverance ! "

Loitering persons and knavish boys pressed upon me with insolent tongues : but Ibrahîm of Hâyil, he who before so friendly accompanied me out of the town, was ready again to befriend me, and cried to them, " Back with you ! for shame, so to thrust upon the man ! O fools, have ye not seen him before ? " Amongst them came that Abdullah of the broken arm, the boy-brother of Hamûd.   I saw him grown taller, and now he wore a little back-sword ; which he pulled out against me, and cried, " O thou cursed Nasrâny, that wilt not leave thy miscreance ! "—The one-eyed stranger whispered, " Content them ! it is but waste of breath to reason with them.   Do ye—he said to the people—stand back ! I would speak with this man ; and we may yet see some happy event, it may please Ullah."   He whispered in my ear, " Eigh ! there will be some mischief ; only say thou wilt be a Moslem, and quit thyself of them.   Show thyself now a prudent man, and let me not see thee die for a word ; afterward, when thou hast escaped their hands, *settîn séna,* sixty years to them, and *yulaan Ullah abu-hum,* the Lord confound the father of them all ! Now, hast thou consented ?— ho ! ye people, to the mesjid ! go and prepare the *muzayyîn :* Khalîl is a Moslem ! "—The lookers-on turned and were going, then stood still ; they believed not his smooth words of that obstinate misbeliever.   But when I said to them, " No need to go ! "—" Aha ! they cried, the accursed Nasrâny, Ullah curse his parentage ! "—*Zeyd* (the porter) : " But I am thinking we shall make this (man) a Moslem and circumcise him ; go in one of you and fetch me a knife from the Kasr : " but none moved, for the people dreaded the Emir and Hamûd (reputed my friend).   " Come, Khalîl, for one thing, said Zeyd, we will be friends with thee ; say, there is none God but the Lord and His apostle is Mohammed : and art thou poor we will also enrich thee."—" I count your silver as the dust of this méshab :—but which of you miserable Arabs would give a man anything ? Though ye gave me this castle, and the *beyt el-mâl,* the pits and the sacks of hoarded silver which ye say to be therein, I could not change my faith."—"*Akhs—akhs—akhs—akhs !* " was uttered from a multitude of throats : I had contemned, in one breath, the right way in religion and the heaped riches of this world ! and with horrid outcries they detested the antichrist.

—" Eigh Nasrâny ! said a voice, and what found you at Kheybar, ha ? "—" Plenty of dates O man, and fever."—" The more is the pity, cried they all, that he died not there ; but akhs ! these cursed Nasrânies, they never die, nor sicken as other men : and surely if this (man) were not a Nasrâny, he had been dead long

ago."—" Ullah curse the father of him!" murmured many a
ferocious voice. Zeyd the porter lifted his huge fist; but Aneybar appeared coming from the sûk, and Ibrahîm cries, "Hold
there! and strike not Khalîl."—*Aneybar:* "What ado is here,
and (to Zeyd) why is not the Nasrâny mounted?—did I not
tell thee?"—" His Beduw were not ready; one of them is gone
to bid his kinsfolk farewell, and I gave the other leave to go
and buy somewhat in the sûk."—*Aneybar:* "And you people
will ye not go your ways?—*Sheytàn!* what has any of you to
do with the Nasrâny; Ullah send a punishment upon you all,
and upon him also."

I said to Aneybar, "Let Eyâd take new wages of me
and threaten him, lest he forsake me."—" And what received he
before?"—" Five reals."—" Then give him other five reals. [Two
or three had sufficed for the return journey; but this was his
malice, to make me bare in a hostile land.] When the thelûl
is come, mount,—and Zeyd see thou that the payment is
made;" and loftily the Galla strode from me.—Cruel was the
slave's levity; and when I had nothing left for their cupidity
how might I save myself out of this dreadful country?—*Zeyd:*
"Give those five reals, ha! make haste, or by God—!"—and
with an ugh! of his bestial anger he thrust anew his huge
fist upon my breast. I left all to the counsel of the moment,
for a last need I was well armed; but with a blow, putting to
his great strength, he might have slain me.—Ibrahîm drew me
from them. "Hold! he said, I have the five reals, where is
that Eyâd, and I will count them in his hand. Khalîl, rid
thyself with this and come away, and I am with you." I
gave him the silver. Ibrahîm led on, with the bridle of the
thelûl in his hand, through the market street, and left me at a
shop door whilst he went to seek Aneybar. Loitering persons
gathered at the threshold where I sat; the worst was that
wretched young Abdullah el-Abeyd; when he had lost his
breath with cursing, he drew his little sword again; but the
bystanders blamed him, and I entered the makhzan.

The tradesman, who was a Meshedy, asked for my galliûn
and bade me be seated; he filled it with hameydy, that honey-
like tobacco and peaceable remedy of human life. "What
tidings, quoth he, in the world?—We have news that the
Queen of the Engleys is deceased; and now her son is king
in her room." Whilst I sat pensive, to hear his words! a strong
young swordsman, who remained in Hàyil, came suddenly in
and sat down. I remembered his comely wooden face, the
fellow was called a Moghréby, and was not very happy in
his wits. He drew and felt down the edge of his blade: so

said Hands-without head—as are so many among them, and
sware by Ullah : " Yesterday, when Khalîl entered, I was running with this sword to kill him, but some withheld me ! " The
tradesman responded, " What has he done to be slain by thee ? "
Swordsman : " And I am glad that I did it not : "—he seemed
now little less rash to favour me, than before to have murdered
me.

Aneybar, who this while strode unquietly up and down, in
the side streets, (he would not be seen to attend upon the
Nasrâny), appeared now with Ibrahîm at the door. The Galla
deputy of Ibn Rashîd entered and sat down, with a mighty
rattling of his sword of office in the scabbard, and laid the
blade over his knees. Ibrahîm requested him to insist no
more upon the iniquitous payment out of Khalîl's empty purse,
or at least to make it less. " No, five reals ! " (exclaimed the
slave in authority,) he looked very fiercely upon it, and clattered
the sword. " God will require it of thee ; and give me a schedule
of safe conduct, Aneybar." He granted, the tradesman reached
him an hand-breadth of paper, and Ibrahîm wrote, ' No man
to molest this Nasrâny.' Aneybar inked his signet of brass,
and sealed it solemnly, ANEYBAR IBN RASHID.

" The sherîf (I said) is going to Bagdad, he will pass by the
camp of the Emir : and there are some Beduw at the gate—I
have now heard it, that are willing to convey me to the North,
for three reals. If thou compel me to go with Eyâd, thou
knowest that I cannot but be cast away : treachery O Aneybar
is punished even in this world ! May not a stranger pass by your
Prince's country ? be reasonable, that I may depart from you
to-day peaceably, and say, the Lord remember thee for good."
The Galla sat arrogantly rattling the gay back-sword in his
lap, with a countenance composed to the princely awe ; and at
every word of mine he clapped his black hand to the hilt.
When I ceased he found no answer, but to cry with tyranny,
" Have done, or else by God—" ! and he showed me a hand-
breadth or two of his steel out of the scabbard. " What ! he
exclaimed, wilt thou not yet be afraid ? " Now Eyâd entered,
and Ibrahîm counted the money in his hand : Aneybar delivered
the paper to Eyâd.—" The Emir gave his passport to me."—
" But I will not let thee have it, mount ! and Ibrahîm thou canst
see him out of the town."

At the end of the sûk the old parasite seyyid or sherîf was
sitting square-legged before a threshold, in the dust of the
street. " Out, I said in passing, with thy reeds and paper ; and
I will give thee a writing ? " The old fox in a turban winced,
and he murmured some koran wisdom between his broken

teeth.—There trotted by us a Beduwy upon a robust thelûl. " I was then coming to you, cried the man ; and I will convey the Nasrâny to el-Irâk for five reals." *Eyâd :* " Well, and if it be with Aneybar's allowance, I will give up the five reals, which I have ; and so shall we all have done well, and Khalîl may depart in peace. Khalîl sit here by the thelûl, whilst I and this Beduwy go back to Aneybar, and make the accord, if it be possible ; wellah ! I am sorry for thy sake."—A former acquaint- ance, a foreigner from el-Hása, came by and stayed to speak with me ; the man was one of the many industrious strangers in Hâyil, where he sewed cotton quilts for the richer households. " This people, quoth he, are untaught ! all things are in the power of Ullah : and now farewell, Khalîl, and God give thee a good ending of this adventure."

Eyâd returned saying, Aneybar would not be entreated, and that he had reviled the poor Beduwy. " Up, let us hasten from them ; and as for Merjàn, I know not what is become of him. I will carry thee to Gofar, and leave thee there.—No, wellah Khalîl, I am not treacherous, but I durst not, I cannot, return with thee to Kheybar : at Gofar I will leave thee, or else with the Aarab." —" If thou betray me, betray me at the houses of hair, and not in the settlements ; but you shall render the silver."—" Nay, I have eaten it ; yet I will do the best that I may for thee."

We journeyed in the beaten path towards Goïar ; and after going a mile, " Let us wait, quoth Eyâd, and see if this Merjàn be not coming." At length we saw it was he who approached us with a bundle on his head,—he brought temmn and dates, which his sister (wedded in the town) had given him. Eyâd drew out a leathern budget, in which was some victual for the way that he had received from the Mothîf, (without my know- ledge) : it was but a little barley meal and dates of ill kind, in all to the value of about one shilling. We sat down, Merjàn spread his good dates, and we breakfasted ; thus eating together I hoped they might yet be friendly, though only misfortunes could be before me with such unlucky rafîks. I might have journeyed with either of them but not with both together. Eyâd had caught some fanatical suspicion in Hâyil, from the mouth of the old Medina sherîf !—that the Nasára encroached continually upon the dominion of the Sultàn, and that Khalîl's nation, although not enemies, were not well-wishers, in their hearts, to the religion of Islam. When I would mount ; " Nay, said Eyâd, beginning to swagger, the returning shall not be as our coming ; I will ride myself." I said no more ; and cast thus again into the wilderness I must give them line.—My companions boasted, as we went, of promises made to them both in Hâyil.—Aneybar had said, that would they return hither sometime, from serving the Dowla, they might be of Ibn Rashîd's (armed) service ;—Eyâd an horseman of the Emir's riders, and Merjàn one of the rajajîl.

Two women coming out from Hâyil overtook us, as they went to Gofar. "The Lord be praised (said the poor creatures, with a womanly kindness) that it was not worse. Ah! thou,—is not thy name Khalîl?—they in yonder town are *jabâbara*, men of tyrannous violence, that will cut off a man's head for a light displeasure. Eigh me! did not he so that is now Emir, unto all his brother's children? Thou art well come from them, they are hard and cruel, *kasyîn*. And what is this that the people cry, ' *Out upon the Nasrâny !* ' The Nasâra be better than the Moslemîn." *Eyâd :* "It is they themselves that are the Nasâra, wellah, *khubithîn*, full of malignity." "It is the Meshâhada that I hate, said Merjàn, may Ullah confound them." It happened that a serving boy in the public kitchen, one of the patients whom I treated (freely) at my former sojourning in Hâyil, was Merjàn's brother. The Meshâhadies he said had been of Aneybar's counsel against me.—Who has travelled in Phoenician and Samaritan Syria may call to mind the inhumanity [the last wretchedness and worldly wickedness of irrational religions,— that man should not eat and drink with his brother!] of those Persian or Assyrian colonists, the *Metówali*.

Forsaking the road we went now towards the east-building of Gofar :—the east and west settlements lie upon two veins of ground-water, a mile or more asunder. The western oasis, where passes the common way, is the greater ; but Eyâd went to find some former acquaintance in the other with whom we might lodge. Here also we passed by forsaken palm-grounds and ruinous orchard houses, till we came to the inhabited ; and they halted before the friend's dàr. Eyâd and Merjàn sat down to see if the good man (of an inhospitable race, the B. Temîm), would come forth to welcome us. Children gathered to look on, and when some of them knew me, they began to fleer at the Nasrâny. Merjàn cursed them, as only Semites can find it in their hearts, and ran upon the little mouthing knaves with his camel-stick ; but now our host coming down his alley saluted Eyâd, and called us to the house. His son bore in my bags to the kahwa : and they strewed down green garden stalks before the thelûl and wild herbage.

A bare dish of dates was set before us ; and the good-man made us thin coffee : bye and bye his neighbours entered. All these were B. Temîm, peasant-like bodies in whom is no natural urbanity ; but they are lumpish drudgers, living honestly of their own—and that is with a sparing hand. When I said to one of them, " I see you all big of bone and stature, unlike the (slender) inhabitants of Hâyil!"—He answered, dispraising them, " The Shammar are *Beduw!* " Whilst we sat, there came in three swarthy strangers, who riding by to Hâyil alighted here also to drink coffee.—They carried up their zika to the Prince's treasury; for being few and distant Aarab, his exactors were not come to them these two years: they were of Harb, and their wandering ground was nigh Medina. They mounted again immediately; and from Hâyil they would ride continually to Ibn Rashîd in the northern wilderness.

My rafîks left me alone without a word! I brought in therefore the thelûl furnitures, lest they should lead away their beast and forsake me. Eyâd and Merjàn feared no more that they must give account for me; and their wildness rising at every word, I foresaw how next to desperate, must be my further passage with them: happily for my weary life the milk-season was now in the land.—The water veins upon which their double oasis is founded flow, they say, from Ajja. The water height in their eight-fathom wells falls about a fathom in the long summer season. These B. Temîmy hosts showed a dull countenance towards ' the adversary of Ullah.' Yet the story of my former being in Hâyil was well known to them: they even told me of my old nâga, the *Khueyra*, that she had lately calved:—I would she were yet mine! for her much milk which might sustain a man's life in full health in the desert. The nâga of any good hump has rich milk; if her hump be low she has less and lean milk. The B. Temîm are very ancient in these districts: yet an elder nation, the *B. Taâmir*, they say, inhabited the land before them. They name their jid or patriarch *Temîm;* he was brother of Wâil jid of the Annezy and Maazy [Vol. I. p. 229].—My rafîks came again at evening with treacherous looks.

T.E. Lawrence wrote of Khalil that he went among the Arabs 'dispassionately, looked at their life, and wrote it down word for word. By being always Arab in manner and European in mind he maintained a perfect judgment, while bearing towards them a full sympathy which persuaded them to show him their inmost ideas. When his trial of two years was over he carried away in his note-book (so far as the art of writing can express the art of living) the soul of the desert, the complete existence of a remarkable and self-contained community, shut away from the currents of the world in the unchanging desert, working out their days in an environment utterly foreign to us.'

And yet one cannot evade the conclusion, having studied all aspects of Doughty's life and work until he died on 20 January 1926, that his two years in Arabia were the pretext for a prose epic in the grand style, to display the virtuosity of that technique which he had absorbed from Chaucer and Spenser between 1865 and 1870. He may have survived into the second quarter of the twentieth century, but he felt more alien to contemporary life and letters than to the age of the *Canterbury Tales* or that of *The Faerie Queene*.

7
The Blunts, 1879

After the extraordinary example of Doughty, who
had preceded them by a matter of months, Wilfrid
Scawen Blunt and Lady Anne Blunt were the first
European travellers to Ha'il who made no effort to
conceal their origins or intentions. They came to
look at horses, and possibly acquire some from the
stables of Muhammad ibn Rashid. Having escaped a
ghazu by the Ruwala and reached al-Jawf, they had
to gain permission from the Governor of al-Jawf to
cross the Nafud to visit Ha'il. On their first day
at al-Jawf Blunt identified a Painted Lady butterfly
on a rock; he realised that the nearest food for
caterpillars of the species was at Hebron, four
hundred miles distant. If a Painted Lady could
travel that distance, he calculated, despite an
injured knee, that his own unpainted lady Anne
could cover half that distance across the Nafud.
They were anxious to cross the Nafud, the object of
their wildest dreams in England, rather than take
three days more and travel round the perimeter.
They were astonished by its colour, which Wilfrid
described as 'deep red gravel with a slight layer
of white saltpetre.' Anne was reminded of the
favourite Victorian aperient, rhubarb and magnesia.
'Yet the Nefud it was,' wrote Anne in excitement,
'the great red desert of Central Arabia. In a few
minutes we cantered up to it, and our mares were
standing with their feet in its first waves'.

They were naturally apprehensive of their reception by Amir Muhammad, having heard how he had
murdered all his brothers and nephews. 'Never

mind,' Wilfrid consoled himself as they wrote their
diaries to pass the time while awaiting news from
Ha'il, they would die happy after seeing Jebel
Shammar, 'even if we have our heads cut off in
Ha'il'.

A *Pilgrimage to Nejd* is predominantly Anne's
book, while Wilfrid added scholarly notes on the
life of the nomads and observations on the horses.
She is a direct stylist, diametrically opposite in
tone to the majestic Doughty. Here is the account
of the Blunts' visit to Ha'il.

The Blunts were shown around the private zoo-
logical garden of Amir Muhammad, and then taken to
the stables.

IBN RASHID'S STABLE AT HAÏL.

There were also a couple of ibexes with immense
heads, tame like the gazelles, and allowing themselves to be stroked.   The gazelles seemed especially at home, and we were told that they breed here
in captivity.   The most interesting, however, of all
the animals in this garden were three of the wild
cows (bakar wahhash), from the Nefûd, which we
had so much wished to see.   They proved to be, as
we had supposed, a kind of antelope,* though their
likeness to cows was quite close enough to account
for their name.   They stood about as high as an
Alderney calf six months old, and had humps on
their shoulders like the Indian cattle.   In colour
they were a yellowish white, with reddish legs
turning to black towards the feet.   The face was
parti-coloured, and the horns, which were black,
were quite straight and slanted backwards, and fully
three feet long, with spiral markings.   These wild
cows were less tame than the rest of the animals, and
the slaves were rather afraid of them, for they seemed
ready to use their horns, which were as sharp
as needles.   The animals, though fat, evidently
suffered from confinement, for all were lame, one
with an enlarged knee, and the rest with overgrown
hoofs.   When we had seen and admired the mena-
gerie, and fed the antelopes with dates, we went on
through a low door, which we had almost to creep
through, into another garden, where there were

* Oryx beatrix.

lemon trees (treng), bitter oranges (hámud), and pomegranates (roman). The Emir, who was very polite and attentive to me, had some of the fruit picked and gave me a bunch of a kind of thyme, the only flower growing there. We saw some camels at work drawing water from a large well, a hundred to a hundred and fifty feet deep, to judge by the rope. The Emir then crept through another low door and we after him, and then to our great satisfaction we found ourselves in a stable-yard full of mares, tethered in rows each to a manger. I was almost too excited to look, for it was principally to see these that we had come so far.

This yard contained about twenty mares, and beyond it was another with a nearly equal number. Then there was a third with eight horses, tethered in like manner ; and beyond it again a fourth with thirty or forty foals. I will not now describe all we saw, for the Emir's stud will require a chapter to itself. Suffice it to say, that Wilfrid's first impression and mine were alike. The animals we saw before us were not comparable for beauty of form or for quality with the best we had seen among the Gomussa. The Emir, however, gave us little time for reflection, for with a magnificent wave of his hand, and explaining with mock humility, " The horses of my slaves," he dragged us on from one yard to another, allowing us barely time to ask a few questions as to breed, for the answers to which he referred us to Hamúd We had seen enough, how-

ever, to make us very happy, and Hamúd had promised that we should see them again.   There was
no doubt whatever that, in spite of the Emir's dis-
claimer, these were Ibn Rashid's celebrated mares,
the representatives of that stud of Feysul ibn Saoud,
about which such a romance had been made.

An equally interesting spectacle, the Emir thought
for us, was his kitchen, to which he now showed the
way.   Here, with unconcealed pride, he displayed
his pots and pans, especially seven monstrous
cauldrons, capable each, he declared, of boiling
three whole camels.   Several of them were actually
at work, for Ibn Rashid entertains nearly two
hundred guests daily, besides his own household.
Forty sheep or seven camels are his daily bill of
fare.   As we came out, we found the hungry
multitude already assembling.   Every stranger
in Haïl has his place at Ibn Rashid's table,
and towards sunset the courtyard begins to fill.
The Emir does not himself preside at these feasts.
He always dines alone, or in his harim ; but the
slaves and attendants are extraordinarily well-drilled,
and behave with perfect civility to all comers, rich
and poor alike.   Our own dinner was brought to us at
our house.   Thus ended our first day at Haïl, a day of
wonderful interest, but not a little fatiguing.   " Ya
akhi," (oh my brother), said Mohammed ibn Arûk
to Wilfrid that evening, as they sat smoking and
drinking their coffee, " did I not promise you that
you should see Nejd, and Ibn Rashid, and the mares

of Haïl, and have you not seen them?" We both
thanked him, and, indeed, we both felt very grateful. Not that the favours were all on one side ;
for brotherly offices had been very evenly balanced,
and Mohammed had been quite as eager to make
this journey as we had. But, alas! our pleasant
intercourse with Mohammed was very near its end.

The next few days of our life at Haïl may be
briefly described. Wilfrid and Mohammed went
every morning to the mejlis, and then paid visits,
sometimes to Hamúd, sometimes to Mubarek, sometimes to the Emir. A slave brought us our breakfast daily from the kasr, and a soldier came to
escort us through the streets. Mohammed had now
made acquaintances of his own, and was generally
out all day long. I stayed very much in doors, and
avoided passing through the streets, except when
invited to come to the castle, for we had agreed
that discretion was the better part of valour with
us. That there was some reason for this prudence
I think probable, for though we never experienced
anything but politeness from the Haïl people, we
heard afterwards that some among them were not
best pleased at the reception given us by the Emir.
Europeans had never before been seen in Nejd ; and
it is possible that a fanatical feeling might have
arisen if we had done anything to excite it.
Wahhabism is on the decline, but not yet extinct at
Haïl ; and the Wahhabis would of course have been
our enemies. In the Emir's house, or even under

charge of one of his officers, we were perfectly safe, but wandering about alone would have been rash. The object, too, would have been insufficient, for away from the Court there is little to see at Haïl.

With Hamúd and his family we made great friends. He was a man who at once inspired confidence, and we had no cause to regret having acted on our first impression of his character. He has always, they say, refused to take presents from the Emir; and has never approved of his conduct, though he has sided with him politically, and serves him faithfully as a brother. His manners are certainly as distinguished as can be found anywhere in the world, and he is besides intelligent and well informed. The Emir is different; with him there was always a certain *gêne.* It was impossible to forget the horrible story of his usurpation; and there was something, too, about him which made it impossible to feel quite at ease in his presence. Though he knows how to behave with dignity, he does not always do so. It is difficult to reconcile his almost childish manner, at times, with the ability he has given proofs of. He has something of the spoiled child in his way of wandering on from one subject to another; and, like Jóhar, of asking questions which he does not always wait to hear answered, a piece of ill-manners not altogether unroyal, and so, perhaps, the effect of his condition as a sovereign prince. He is also very naïvely

vain, as most people become who are fed constantly
on flattery; and he is continually on the look-out
for compliments about his power, and his wisdom,
and his possessions. His jealousy of other great
Sheykhs whom we have seen is often childishly
displayed. Hamúd has none of this. I fancy he
stands to his cousin Mohammed somewhat in the
position in which Morny is supposed to have stood
to Louis Napoleon, only that Morny was neither so
good a man nor even so fine a gentleman as Hamúd.
He gives the Emir advice, and in private speaks his
mind, only appearing to the outer world as the
obsequious follower of his prince. Hamúd has
several sons, the eldest of whom, Majid, has all his
father's charm of manner, and has, besides, the
attraction of perfectly candid youth, and a quite
ideal beauty. He is about sixteen, and he and his
brother and a young uncle came to see us the morning after our arrival, sent by their father to pay
their compliments. He talked very much and
openly about everything, and gave us a quantity of
information about the various mares at the Emir's
stable, and about his father's mares and his own.
He then went on to tell us of an expedition he had
made with the Emir to the neighbourhood of Queyt,
and of how he had seen the sea. They had made a
ghazú on the felláhín of the sea-coast, and had then
returned. He asked me how I rode on horseback,
and I showed him my side-saddle, which, however,
did not surprise him. " It is a shedad," he said;

" you ride as one rides a delúl." This young Majid,
though he looks quite a boy, is married ; and we
were informed that here no one of good family puts
off marriage after the age of sixteen. I made
acquaintance with his wife Urgheyeh, who is very
pretty, very small in stature, and very young ; she
is one of Metaab's daughters, and her sister is
married to Hamúd, so that father and son are
brothers-in-law.

Mubarek, the Emir's chief slave, was one of our
particular acquaintances. He inhabits a very handsome house, as houses go in Haïl ; and there
Wilfrid paid him more than one visit. His house
is curiously decorated with designs in plaster of
birds and beasts—ostriches, antelopes, and camels.
Though a slave, Mubarek has not in appearance the
least trace of negro blood ; and it is still a mystery
to us how he happens to be one. He is a well-bred
person, and has done everything in his power to
make things pleasant for us.

On the second day after our arrival, after the
usual compliments and some conversation, I asked
the Emir's permission to pay a visit to the harim.
Mohammed ibn Rashid appeared gratified by my
request, which he immediately granted, saying that
he would send to the khawatin (ladies) to inform
them, and desire them to prepare for my reception.
He accordingly despatched a messenger, but we sat
on talking for a long time before anything came of
the message ; I had grown quite tired of waiting,

and was already wondering how soon we should be at liberty to return home, where I might write my journal in secret, when the servant re-appeared, and brought us word that Amusheh, the Emir's chief wife, was ready to receive me. I fancy that ladies here seldom dress with any care unless they want to display their silks and jewels to some visitor; and on such special occasions their toilet is a most elaborate one, with kohl and fresh paint, and takes a long time. The Emir at once put me in charge of a black slave woman, who led the way to the harim. Hamúd's wives as well as Mohammed's live in the palace, but in separate dwellings. The kasr is almost a town in itself, and I and my black guide walked swiftly through so many alleys and courts, and turned so many corners to the right and to the left, that if I had been asked to find my way back unassisted, I certainly could not have done it. At last, however, after crossing a very large courtyard, we stopped at a small low door. This was open, and through it I could see a number of people sitting round a fire within, for it was the entrance to Amusheh's kahwah. This room had two columns supporting the ceiling, like all other rooms I had seen in the palace, except the great kahwah, which has five. The fire-place, as usual, an oblong hole in the ground, was on the left as one entered, in the corner near the door; in it stood a brazier containing the fire, and between it and the wall handsome carpets had been spread. All the persons present

rose to their feet as I arrived. Amusheh could easily
be singled out from among the crowd, even before she
advanced to do the honours. She possesses a certain
distinction of appearance and manner which would
be recognised anywhere, and completely eclipsed
the rest of the company. But she, the daughter of
Obeyd and sister of Hamúd, has every right to out-
shine friends, relatives, and fellow wives. Her face,
though altogether less regularly shaped than her
brother's, is sufficiently good-looking, with a well-
cut nose and mouth, and something singularly
sparkling and brilliant. Hedusheh and Lulya, the
two next wives, who were present, had gold brocade
as rich as hers, and lips and cheeks smeared as red
as hers with carmine, and eyes with borders kohled
as black as hers, but lacked her charm. Amusheh
is besides clever and amusing, and managed to keep
up a continual flow of conversation, in which the
other two hardly ventured to join. They sat looking pretty and agreeable, but were evidently
kept in a subordinate position. Lulya shares with
Amusheh, as the latter informed me, what they consider the great privilege of never leaving town, thus
taking precedence of Hedusheh, on whom devolves
the duty of following the Emir's fortunes in the
desert, where he always spends a part of the year in
tents. The obligation of such foreign service is
accounted derogatory, and accordingly objected to
by these Haïl ladies. They have no idea of amusement, if I may judge from what they said to me,

but a firm conviction that perfect happiness and dignity consist in sitting still.

This happiness Amusheh and I enjoyed for some time. We sat together on one carpet spread over a mattress, cushions being ranged along the wall behind us for us to lean against, and the fire in front scorching our faces while we talked. On my right sat Hedusheh ; beyond her Lulya and the rest of the company, making a circle round the fireplace. Before long, Atwa, a pretty little girl, who was introduced to me as the fourth wife, came in and took her place beyond Lulya. She looked more like a future wife than one actually married, being very young ; and indeed it presently appeared that she had merely been brought to be looked at and considered about, and that the Emir had decided to reject her as too childish and insignificant.* He was, in fact, casting about in his mind for some suitable alliance which should bring him political support, as well as an increase of domestic comfort. That these were the objects of his new matrimonial projects I soon learned from his own mouth, from the questions he asked me about the marriageable daughters of Bedouin Sheyks. What could, indeed, be more suitable for his purpose than some daughter of a great desert sheykh, whose family should be valuable allies in war, while she herself, the ideal fourth wife, unlike these ladies of the town, should be

* I heard nothing of the fate of Obeyd's widow, and could not inquire.

always ready to accompany her husband to the
desert, and should indeed prefer the desert to the
town ?

Among other persons present were several oldish
women, relatives, whose names and exact relationship have slipped my memory ; also a few friends
and a vast number of attendants and slaves, these
last mostly black.   They all squatted round the fire,
each trying to get into the front rank, and to
seize every opportunity of wedging in a remark, by
way of joining in the conversation of their betters.
None of these outsiders were otherwise than plainly
dressed in the dark blue or black cotton or woollen
stuffs, used by ordinary Bedouin women in this part
of Arabia, often bordered with a very narrow red
edge, like a cord or binding, which looks well.   The
rich clothes worn by Amusheh and her companion
wives are somewhat difficult to describe, presenting
as they did an appearance of splendid shapelessness.
Each lady had a garment cut like an abba, but
closed up the front, so that it must have been put
on over the head ; and as it was worn without any
belt or fastening at the waist, it had the effect of a
sack.   These sacks or bags were of magnificent
material, gold interwoven with silk, but neither
convenient nor becoming, effectually hiding any
grace of figure.   Amusheh wore crimson and gold,
and round her neck a mass of gold chains studded
with turquoises and pearls.   Her hair hung down
in four long plaits, plastered smooth with some

reddish stuff, and on the top of her head stuck a
gold and turquoise ornament, like a small plate,
about four inches in diameter. This was placed
forward at the edge of the forehead, and fastened
back with gold and pearl chains to another ornament resembling a lappet, also of gold and turquoise,
hooked on behind the head, and having flaps which
fell on each side of the head and neck, ending in
long strings of pearls with bell-shaped gold and
pearl tassels. The pearls were all irregularly shaped
and unsorted as to size, the turquoises very unequal
in shape, size, and quality, the coral generally in
beads. The gold work was mostly good, some of it
said to be from Persia, but the greater part of Haïl
workmanship. I had nearly forgotten to mention
the nose-ring, here much larger than I have
seen it at Bagdad and elsewhere, measuring an
inch and a half to two inches across. It consists
of a thin circle of gold, with a knot of gold and
turquoises attached by a chain to the cap or lappet
before described. It is worn in the left nostril, but
taken out and left dangling while the wearer eats
and drinks. A most inconvenient ornament, I
thought and said, and when removed it leaves an
unsightly hole, badly pierced, in the nostril, and
more uncomfortable-looking than the holes in
European ears. But fashion rules the ladies at
Haïl as in other places, and my new acquaintances
only laughed at such criticisms. They find these
trinkets useful toys, and amuse themselves while

talking by continually pulling them out and putting
them in again. The larger size of ring seemed
besides to be a mark of high position, so that the
diameter of the circle might be considered the
measure of the owner's rank, for the rings of all in-
feriors were kept within the inch.

Amusheh was very communicative, but told me
so many new names, that I could not remember all
the information she volunteered about the Ibn
Rashid family and relationships. She remarked
that neither she nor any of Mohammed's wives had
any children, a fact which I already knew, and not
from Radi alone ; for it is the talk of the town and
tribe that this is a judgment for the Emir's crimes.
She spoke with great affection of her nephew Majid
and of her brother Hamúd, and with veneration of
her father Obeyd, but I cannot recollect that she
told me anything new about any of them. She
spoke too of Tellál, but of course made no mention
of Bender. Indeed, anxious as I was for any information she might give, I knew too much of the
family history and secrets to venture on asking
many questions ; besides, any show of curiosity
might have made her suspect me of some unavowed
motive. I therefore felt more at ease when the
conversation wandered from dangerous topics to safe
and trivial ones, such as the manners and customs
of different countries. " Why do you not wear your
hair like mine ? " said she, holding out one of her
long auburn plaits for me to admire ; and I had

to explain that such short locks as mine were not
sufficient for the purpose. "Then why did I not
dress in gold brocade?" "How unsuitable," I replied,
"would such beautiful stuffs be for the rough work
of travelling, hunting, and riding in the desert."
When we talked of riding, Amusheh seemed for a
moment doubtful whether to be completely satisfied
about her own lot in life—she would like, she said,
to see me on my mare; and I promised she should,
if possible, be gratified; but the opportunity never
occurred, and perhaps the supreme authority did not
care that it should. Even she might become discontented. Thus conversing, time slipped away,
and the midday call to prayer sounded. My hostess
then begged me to excuse her, and added, "I wish
to pray." She and the rest then got up and went
to say their prayers in the middle of the room.
After this she returned and continued the conversation where we had left it off.

Some slaves now brought a tray, which they
placed before me. On it was a regular solid breakfast : a large dish of rice in the middle, set round
with small bowls of various sorts of rich and greasy
sauces to be eaten with the rice. I excused myself
as well as I could for my want of appetite, and said
that I had this very morning eaten one of the hares
sent to us by the Emir. Of course I was only
exhorted all the more to eat, and obliged to go
through the form of trying; but fortunately there
were other hungry mouths at hand, and eager eyes

watching till the dishes should be passed on to them, so I got off pretty easily.

Amusheh afterwards invited me to go upstairs, that she might show me her own private apartment, on the floor above the kahwah. I followed her up a steep staircase, of which each step was at least eighteen inches in height. It led nowhere, except to a single room, the same size as the one below, and built in the same way, with two columns supporting the roof, and with a window in a recess corresponding to the door beneath. This apartment was well carpeted, and contained for other furniture a large bed, or couch, composed of a pile of mattresses, with a velvet and gold counterpane spread over it; also a kind of press or cupboard, a box (sanduk) rather clumsily made of dark wood, ornamented by coarse, thin plaques of silver stuck on it here and there. The press stood against the wall, and might be five feet long and two to three feet high, opening with two doors, and raised about two feet from the floor on four thin legs. Underneath and in front of it were three or four rows of china and crockery of a common sort, and a few Indian bowls, all arranged on the carpet like articles for sale in the streets. Amusheh asked what I thought of her house, was it nice? And after satisfying herself of my approbation, she conducted me down again, and we sat as before on the mattress between the brazier and the wall.

During my stay, the Emir paid two visits to the

kahwah, and each time that he appeared at the
door the crowd and the wives, except Amusheh,
rose and remained standing until he left. Amusheh
only made a slight bow or movement, as if about to
rise, and kept her place by me while her husband
stood opposite to us talking. He addressed himself
almost entirely to me, and spoke chiefly in the
frivolous, almost puerile, manner he sometimes
affects. He inquired my opinion of his wives,
whether they were more beautiful and charming
than Ibn Shaalan's wife, Ghiowseh, the sister of El
Homeydi ibn Meshur, or than his former wife,
Turkya, Jedaan's daughter, who had left him and
returned to her father's tent. In the forty-eight
hours since my arrival at Haïl, the Emir had already
asked me many questions about these two ladies,
and I now answered for the hundredth time that
Turkya was pretty and nice, and that Ghiowseh was
still prettier, but very domineering. He was, however, determined on a comparison of the two
families, and it was fortunate that now, having
seen Amusheh, Hedusheh, and Lulya and Atwa, I
could say with truth they were handsomer, even
the poor little despised Atwa, than their rivals. He
was rather impatient of Atwa being classed with
the others, and said, " Oh, Atwa, I don't want
her ; she is worth nothing." His character is, as
I have already said, a strange mixture of remarkable ability and political insight on the one hand,
and on the other a tendency to waste time and

thought on the most foolish trifles, if they touch
his personal vanity.　Of his ability I judge by his
extremely interesting remarks on serious subjects,
as well as by the position he has been able to seize
and to keep.　Of his energy no one can doubt, for he
has shown it, alas, by his crimes ; but he is so eaten
up with petty personal jealousies, that I sometimes
wonder whether these would influence his conduct
at an important political crisis.　I think, however,
that at such a moment all little vanities would be
forgotten, for he is above all things ambitious, and
his vanity is, as it were, a part and parcel of his
ambition.　He is personally jealous of all other
renowned chiefs, because here in Arabia personal
heroism is, perhaps more than anywhere else in the
world since the age of chivalry, an engine of
political power.　He would, I doubt not, make
alliance with Sotamm, if necessary to gain his ends ;
nevertheless, he could not resist talking to me about
Ibn Shaalan at this most inappropriate moment,
evidently hoping to hear something disparaging of
his rival.　I confess I found it embarrassing to
undergo an examination as to the merits of
Ghiowseh and Turkya in the presence of Mohammed's own wives, who all listened with wide
open eyes, breathless with attention.　My embarrassment only increased when, after the Emir was
gone, Amusheh, on her part, immediately attacked
me with a volley of questions.　While he remained
he had persisted in his inquiries, especially about

Turkya, till I, being driven into a corner, at last lost patience, and exclaimed, "But why do you ask me these questions? Why do you want to hear about Turkya? What is it to you whether she is fair or kind? You never have seen her, nor is it likely you ever will see her!" "No," he replied, "I have never seen her. Yet I want to know something about her, and to hear your opinion of her. Perhaps some day I may like to marry her. I might take her instead of this little girl," pointing to Atwa, "who will never do for me, and whom I will not have. She is worthless," he repeated, "worthless." Poor little Atwa stood listening, but I think with stolid indifference, for I watched her countenance, and could not detect even a passing shade of regret or disappointment. Indeed, of all the wives, Amusheh alone seemed to me to have any personal feeling of affection for the Emir. She, the moment he had left, fell upon me with questions. "Who is Turkya?" she asked, almost gasping for breath. It surprised me that she did not know, for she knew who El-Homeydi ibn Meshur was. I had to explain that his sister Ghiowseh had married Sotamm ibn Shaalan, and to tell her the story of Sotamm's second marriage; and of how Ghiowseh had determined to get rid of her rival, and succeeded in making the latter so uncomfortable, that she had left, and had since refused to return. Amusheh certainly cares about Ibn Rashid, and I thought she feared lest a new element of discord should be brought into the family. As to her own position, it could hardly be affected by the arrival of a new wife; she, as Hamúd's sister, must be secure of her rank and influence, and the Emir, with his guilty conscience, would never dare, if he ever wished, to slight her or Hamúd, to whose support he owes so much.

From Amusheh's house I went with a black slave girl to another house also within the kasr, that of Hamúd's wife, Beneyeh, a daughter of Metaab. There I saw Urgheyeh, her sister, married to Majid, son of Hamúd; also another wife of Hamúd's. This last person I found was not considered as an equal, and on asking about her birth and parentage, was told, " She is the daughter of a Shammar." " Who ?" I inquired. " Ahad " (one). "But *who* is he ? " " Ahad,—fulan min Haïl min el belad " (some one, a person of the town). She was hardly considered as belonging to *the* family. The third and fourth wives, whom I afterwards saw, are, like the first, relations, one a daughter of Tellál, and the other of Suleyman, Hamúd's uncle on the mother's side (khal). These four are young; Majid's mother, whose name I never heard, died, I believe, several years ago. Hamúd, like the Emir, keeps up the number of his wives to the exact figure permitted by the law of the Koran, any one who dies or fails to please being replaced as we replace a servant.

Beneyeh met me at her door, and we went

through a little ante-room or vestibule into her
kahwah. Here we remained only a few moments
till, to my surprise, three arm-chairs were brought
and placed in the ante-room. On these I and
Beneyeh and the second class wife sat, drinking tea
out of tea-cups, with saucers and tea-spoons. The
cups were filled to the brim, and the tea in them
then filled to overflowing with lumps of sugar.
It was, however, good. A pile of sweet limes
was then brought; slaves peeled the fruits, and
divided them into quarters, which they handed
round. After these refreshments Beneyeh wished
to show me her room upstairs. It was reached, like
Amusheh's private apartment, by a rugged staircase
from the kahwah, and was built in the same style,
with two columns supporting the rafters, only it
had no outlook, being lighted only by two small
openings high up in the wall. It was, however,
more interesting than Amusheh's room, for its walls
were decorated with arms. There were eighteen or
twenty swords, and several guns and daggers,
arranged with some care and taste as ornaments.
The guns were all very old-fashioned things, with
long barrels, but most of them beautifully inlaid
with silver. Two of the daggers we had already
seen in the evening, when the Emir sent for them to
show us as specimens of the excellence of Haïl goldsmiths' work. The swords, or sword-hilts, were of
various degrees of richness, the blades I did not see.
Unfortunately at the moment I did not think of

Obeyd and his three wishes, and so forgot to ask Beneyeh whether Obeyd's sword was among these ; it would not have done to inquire about the widow, but there would have been no impropriety in asking about the sword, and I afterwards the more regretted having omitted to do so, because this proved to be my only opportunity. It would have been curious to ascertain whether Obeyd wore a plain unjewelled weapon in keeping with Wahhabi austerity. He would surely have disapproved, could he have foreseen it, of the gold and jewels, not to mention silks and brocaded stuffs now worn by his descendants ; for his own children have none of the severe asceticism attributed to him, although they inherit his love of prayer.

Hamúd came upstairs while I was there with Beneyeh, but he only stayed a few minutes. They seemed to be on very good terms, and after he left she talked a great deal about him, and seemed very proud of him. " This is Hamúd's, and this, and this," said she, " and here is his bed," pointing to a pile of mattresses with a fine coverlid. There were several European articles of furniture in the room, an iron bedstead with mattresses, several common looking-glasses, with badly gilt frames, and a clock with weights. Urgheyeh now joined us, and Beneyeh particularly showed me a handsome necklace her sister wore of gold and coral, elaborately worked. " This was my father's," she told me, adding that the ornament came from Persia.

Beneyeh is immensely proud of her son, Abdallah,
a fine boy of four months old. She and her sister
were so amiable and anxious to please, that I could
willingly have spent the rest of the afternoon with
them. But it was now time to pay my next visit.
After many good-byes and good wishes from both
sisters, my black guide seized hold of my hand, and
we proceeded to the apartments of another wife of
Hamúd, Zehowa, daughter of Tellál. She is sympathetic and intelligent, extremely small and slight,
with the tiniest of hands. Like the other ladies,
she wore rings on her fingers, with big, irregular
turquoises. We sat by the fire and ate sweet limes
and trengs and drank tea. Zehowa sent for her
daughter, a baby only nine months old, to show me,
and I told her I had a daughter of my own, and
that girls were better than boys, which pleased her,
and she answered, "Yes, the daughter is the mother's,
but the son belongs to the father."

Presently one of the guards, a tall black fellow,
all in scarlet, came with a message for me, a request
from the Beg that I would join him in the Emir's
kahwah, where he was waiting for me. Zehowa,
like her cousins, begged hard that I would stay, or
at least promise to visit her again as soon as possible,
and I, bidding her farewell, followed the scarlet and
black swordsman through courts, alleys, and passages to the kahwah, where I found Wilfrid. He
was being entertained by an elderly man with coffee
and conversation. This personage was Mubarck,

already mentioned as the chief of the slaves, and he had been giving Wilfrid a vast deal of interesting information about horses, especially the dispersion of Feysul ibn Saoud's stud, and the chief sources from which that celebrated collection was obtained. It had been originally got together, he said, entirely from the Bedouins, both of Nejd and of the north, by purchase and in war.

I never saw Zehowa, Beneyeh, or Amusheh again, for the next few days were fully occupied, and afterwards, owing to our finding ourselves involved in a network of mystery, and subject to an adverse influence, the pressure of which made itself felt without our being able at first to lay hold of anything tangible, or even to conjecture the cause, it became more than ever an object to us to remain quiet and unobserved. But I am anticipating circumstances to be detailed further on.

About three days later I paid a visit to the harim of Hamúd's uncle. This gentleman, Suleyman, we were already acquainted with, from seeing him at Court on several occasions. He had sent me an invitation to visit his family, and two black slaves came to escort me to their house, one of the dependencies of the palace. In a kahwah opening out of a small yard, I found the old man waiting to receive me. He dyes his beard red, and loves books, amidst a pile of which he was sitting. I was in hopes that his conversation would be instructive, and we had just begun to talk when, alas, his wife came in with a rush, followed by a crowd of other women, upon which he hastily gathered up all his books and some manuscripts which were lying about, and putting some of them away in a cupboard, carried off the rest and made his escape.

Ghut, his wife, was the stupidest person I had seen at Haïl, but very talkative, and hospitable with dates, fresh butter floating in its own butter-milk, and sugar-plums. The many-coloured crowd of white, brown, and black attendants, slaves, and children, were not in much awe of her, and chattered away without a check to their hearts' content. All were, however, respectful and attentive to me. Ghut's daughter, another Zehowa, presently arrived with a slave carrying her son, Abderrahman, a child about a year old. This Zehowa was good-looking, but nearly as stupid and tiresome as her mother. She was very much taken up with showing me her box of trinkets, which she sent for on purpose to display before me its contents. These were of the usual sort, gold ornaments for head and arms and ankles, set with turquoises and strings of pearls. The furniture of the room, which she and her mother specially pointed out for my admiration, was also like what I had already seen—presses or boxes on legs, and ornamented with rude silver plaques.

The conversation was dull. Here is a sample : *I.* "What do you do all day long ? *Zeh.* "We live in the kasr." *I.* "Don't you go out at all ?" *Zeh.*

"No; we always stay in the kasr." *I.* "Then you
never ride" (I always ask if they ride, to see the
effect) "as we do?" *Zeh.* "No, we have no mares
to ride." *I.* "What a pity! and don't you ever go
into the country outside Haïl, the desert?" *Zeh.*
"Oh, no, of course not." *I.* "But, to pass the time,
what do you do?" *Zeh.* "We do nothing." Here
a sharp black boy interrupted us, "O, khatûn,
these are daughters of sheykhs, they have no work
—no work *at all* to do, don't you understand?"
I. "Of course, I understand perfectly; but they
might amuse themselves without doing work," and
turning to Zehowa I added, "Don't you even look
at the horses?" *Zeh.* "No, we do nothing." *I.* "I
should die if I did nothing. When I am at home
I always walk round the first thing in the morning
to look at my horses. How do you manage to
spend your lives?" *Zeh.* "We sit." Thus supreme
contentment in the harim here is to sit in absolute
idleness. It seems odd, where the men are so active
and adventurous, that the women should be satisfied
to be bored; but such, I suppose, is the tyranny of
fashion.

Every evening after dinner we used to receive a
message from the Emir, inviting us to spend the
evening with him. This was always the pleasantest
part of the day, for we generally found one or two
interesting visitors sitting with him. As a sample
of these I give an extract from my journal:

"We found the Emir this evening in high good

humour.   News had just come from El-Homeydi
ibn Meshur, a Roala sheykh of the faction opposed
to Sotamm, that a battle was fought about a month
ago between the Roala and the Welled Ali, and that
Sotamm has been worsted.   Sotamm, at the head
of a ghazú numbering six hundred horsemen, had
marched against Ibn Smeyr at Jerud, but the latter
refused to come out and fight him, and so Sotamm
retired.   On his way back home, however, he fell in
with an outlying camp of Welled Ali, somewhere to
the east of the Hauran, and summoned it to surrender.
These, numbering only a hundred and fifty horsemen, at first entered into negotiation, and, it is said,
offered to give up their camp and camels if they
were permitted to retire with their mares (the
women and children would of course not have been
molested in any case), and to this Sotamm wished
to agree.   But the younger men of his party, and
especially the Ibn Jendal family, who had a death
to avenge, would not hear of compromise, and a
battle ensued.   It ended, strangely enough, in
favour of the weaker side, who succeeded in killing
four of the Roala, and among them Tellal ibn
Shaalan, Sotamm's cousin and heir presumptive.
Sotamm himself is said to have been saved only by
the speed of his mare.   Though the forces engaged
were so disproportionate, nobody here seems surprised at the result, for victory and defeat are " min
Allah," " in the hand of God ; " but everybody is
highly delighted, and the Emir can hardly contain

himself for joy. "What do you think now of Sotamm?" he said; "has he head, or has he no head?" "Not much, I am afraid," I answered, "but I am sorry for him. He is weak, and does not know how to manage his people, but he has a good heart." "And Ibn Smeyr, what do you say to Ibn Smeyr?" "He has more head than heart," I said. This delighted the Emir. "Ah," he replied, "it is you, khatûn, that have the head. Now what do you say to me? have I head, or not head?" "You have head," I answered. "And Hamúd?" "You all of you have plenty of head here, more of course than the Bedouins, who are most of them like children." "But we are Bedouins too," he said, hoping to be contradicted. "I like the Bedouins best," I replied; "it is better to have heart than head." Then he went on to cross-question me about all the other sheykhs whose names he knew. "Which," he asked, "is the best of all you have met with?" "Mohammed Dukhi," I said, "is the cleverest, Ferhan ibn Hedeb the best-mannered, but the one I like best is your relation in the Jezireh, Faris Jerba." I don't think he was quite pleased at this. He had never heard, he said, good or bad of Ibn Hedeb, who belonged to the Bisshr. He was not on terms with any of the Bisshr except Meshur ibn Mershid, who had paid him a visit two years ago. We told him that both Meshur and Faris were Wilfrid's "brothers." Meshur he liked, but Faris Jerba was evidently no favourite of his. I fancy the Emir has taken Ferhan's part in the family quarrel. It is certain that when Amsheh, Sfuk's widow and Abdul Kerim's mother, came with her son Faris to Nejd, he would see neither of them. They stayed in the desert all the time they were here, and never came to Haïl. Rashid ibn Ali, too, is Faris's friend, and of course in no favour at this court.* He then asked about Jedaan, touched rather unfeelingly on the idiotcy of Turki, Jedaan's only son, and then cut some jokes at the expense of our old acquaintance, Smeyr ibn Zeydan. "An old fool," the Emir exclaimed, "why did they send him here? They might as well have sent a camel!" This is the Smeyr who came to Nejd a year and a half ago to try and get Ibn Rashid's assistance for Sotamm, and arrange a coalition against Jedaan and the Sebaa. We knew his mission had failed, but the fact is Ibn Rashid is eaten up with jealousy of anyone who has the least reputation in the desert. We are surprised, however, to find him so well informed about everything and everybody in the far north, and we are much interested, as he has solved for us one of the problems about Nejd which used to puzzle us, namely, the relations maintained by the tribes of Jebel Shammar with those of the north. The Emir has told us that the Shammar of the Jezireh and his own Shammar still count each other as near relations. "Our

---

* The Ibn Alis were formerly Sheykhs of the Shammar, but were displaced by the Ibn Rashids fifty years ago.

horses," he said, "are of the same blood." With
the Roala he has made peace, and with Ibn Haddal;
but the Sebaa and the rest of the Bisshr clan are
out of his way. They never come anywhere near
Nejd, except on ghazús, and that very rarely.
Once, however, a ghazú, of Fedaan, had got as far
as Kasím, and he had gone out against them, and
captured a Seglawi Jedran mare of the Ibn Sbeni
strain. He promised to show it to us. We then
talked a good deal about horses, and our knowledge
on this head caused general astonishment. Indeed,
I think we could pass a better examination in the
breeds than most of the Ibn Rashids. By long
residence in town they have lost many of the
Bedouin traditions. Hamúd, however, who takes
more interest in horses than the Emir, has told us
a number of interesting facts relating to the stud
here, and that of the late Emir of Riad, Feysul ibn
Saoud, solving another problem, that of the fabulous
Nejd breed; but we are taking separate notes about
these things.

We had not been talking long with the Emir
and Hamúd, when a fat vulgar-looking fellow was
introduced and made to sit down by us. It was
evident that he was no Haïl man, for his features
were coarse, and his manners rude. He talked
with a strong Bagdadi accent, and was addressed
by everyone as "ya Hajji." It was clear that he
belonged to the Haj, but why was he here? The
mystery was soon cleared up, for after a whispered

conversation with Hamúd, the new visitor turned
to Wilfrid, and began addressing him in what we at
first took to be gibberish, until seeing that we made
no answer, he exclaimed in Arabic, " There, I told
you he was no Englishman ! " Wilfrid then cross-
questioned him, and elicited the fact that he had been
a stoker on board one of the British India Company's
steamers on the Persian Gulf, and that the language
he had been talking was English. Only two
phrases, however, we succeeded in distinguishing,
" werry good," and " chief engineer "—and having
recognised them and given their Arabic equivalents,
our identity was admitted. The fellow was then
sent about his business, and a very small, very
polite old man took his place. He was conspicuous
among these well-dressed Shammar by the plainest
possible dress, a dark brown abba without hem or
ornament, and a cotton kefiyeh on his head, un-
bound by any aghal whatsoever. He was treated
with great respect, however, by all, and it was easy
to see that he was a man of condition. He entered
freely into conversation with us, and talked to
Mohammed about his relations in Aared, and it
presently appeared that he was from Southern
Nejd. This fact explained the severity of his
costume, for among the Wahhabis, no silk or gold
ornaments are tolerated. He was, in fact, the
Sheykh of Harík, the last town of Nejd towards
the south, and close to the Dahna, or great southern
desert. This he described to us as exactly like the

Nefûd we have just crossed, only with more vegetation. The ghada is the principal wood, but there are palms in places.

It is not the custom of Haïl to smoke, either from Wahhabi prejudice, or, as I am more inclined to think, because tobacco has never penetrated so far inland in quantities sufficient to make the habit general. No objection, however, has been made to Wilfrid's pipe, which he smokes when and where he chooses, and this evening when the call to prayer sounded, and the Emir and Hamúd had gone out to perform their devotions, the old man I have just mentioned, Nassr ibn Hezani, hinted without more ceremony that he should like a whiff. He has quarrelled with Ibn Saoud, and probably hates all the Wahhabi practices, and was very glad to take the opportunity of committing this act of wickedness. He was careful, however, to return the pipe before the rest came back. He, at any rate, if a Wahhabi, is not one of the disagreeable sort described by Mr. Palgrave, for he invited us very cordially to go back home with him to Harík. The Emir, however, made rather a face at this suggestion, and gave such an alarming account of what would happen to us if we went to Riad, that I don't think it would be wise to attempt to go there now. We could not go in fact without the Emir's permission. I do not much care, for town life is wearisome ; we have had enough of it, and I have not much curiosity to see more of Nejd, unless we can go

among the Bedouins there. If Ibn Saoud still had
his collection of mares the sight of them would be
worth some risk, but his stud has long since been
scattered, and Nassr ibn Hezani assures us that
there is nothing now in Arabia to compare with Ibn
Rashid's stud. Ibn Hezani, like everybody else, laughs
at the story of a Nejd breed, and says, as everybody
else does, that the mares at Riad were a collection
made by Feysul ibn Saoud in quite recent times.

Later in the evening, a native goldsmith was
introduced, with a number of articles worked by
him at Haïl. They were pretty, but not specially
interesting, or very unlike what may be seen
elsewhere, dagger hilts and sheaths, and a few
ornaments. It was this man, however, who had
made the gold hilts which all the princely family
here wear to their swords. These we examined,
and found the work really good.

The most amusing incident of the evening,
however, and one which we were not at all prepared
for, was the sudden production by the Emir of one
of those toys called telephones, which were the
fashion last year in Europe. This the Emir caused
two of his slaves to perform with, one going into
the courtyard outside, and the other listening.
The message was successfully delivered, the slave
outside, to make things doubly sure, shouting at
the top of his voice, "Ya Abdallah weyn ente?
yeridak el Emir." "O Abdallah, where are you?
the Emir wants you," and other such phrases. We

expressed great surprise, as in duty bound; indeed, it was the first time we had actually seen the toy, and it is singular to find so very modern an invention already at Haïl.

At about ten o'clock, the Emir began to yawn, and we all got up and wished him good-night. He very kindly sent for, and gave me, a number of trengs and oranges, which he gave orders should be conveyed to our house, together with a new-laid ostrich's egg, the "first of the season," which had just been brought to him from the Nefûd.

EVENING WITH THE EMIR.

CHAPTER XI.

"I shall do well :
The people love me, and the Desert's mine ;
My power's a crescent, and my auguring hope
Says it will come to the full."

SHAKESPEARE.

Political and historical—Shepherd rule in Arabia—An hereditary
policy—The army—The law—Taxation—The finances of Jebel
Shammar—Ibn Rashid's ambition.

THE following is the result of our inquiries made
while at Haïl into the political condition and resources of the country. It has no pretension to
rigid accuracy, especially in the figures given, but it
will serve to convey an idea of the kind of government found in Arabia, and of the capacity for self-
rule of the Arab race.

The political constitution of Jebel Shammar is
exceedingly curious ; not only is it unlike anything
we are accustomed to in Europe, but it is probably
unique, even in Asia. It would seem, in fact, to
represent some ancient form of government indigenous to the country, and to have sprung
naturally from the physical necessities of the land,
and the character of its inhabitants. I look upon
Ibn Rashid's government as in all likelihood
identical with that of the Kings of Arabia, who
came to visit Solomon, and of the Shepherd Kings

who, at a still earlier date, held Egypt and
Babylonia ; and I have little doubt that it owes its
success to the fact of its being thus in harmony
with Arab ideas and Arab tradition. To understand ti rightly, one ought to consider what Arabia
is, and what the Arab character and mode of life.
The whole of the peninsula, with the exception,
perhaps, of Yemen, and certain districts of Hadra-
mant within the influence of the monsoon winds, is
a rainless, waterless region, in every sense of the
word a desert. The soil is a poor one, mainly of
gravel or of sand, and except in a few favoured
spots, unsuited for cultivation ; indeed, no cultivation is possible at all in Nejd, except with the help
of irrigation, and, as there is no water above ground,
of irrigation from wells. Even wells are rare.
The general character of the central plateaux, and of
the peninsula, is that of vast uplands of gravel, as
nearly destitute of vegetation as any in the world,
and incapable of retaining water, even at a great
depth. It is only in certain depressions of the
plain, several hundred feet lower than the general
level, that wells as a rule are found, and wherever
these occur with a sufficient supply of water, towns
and villages with gardens round them, have sprung
up. These, however, are often widely apart, showing
as mere spots on the map of Arabia, and uncon-
nected with each other by any intervening district
of agricultural land. Indeed, it is not too much to
say, that Nejd contains no agricultural region, as

we understand agriculture, and that all its production is garden produce. From this state of things, it happens that there is also no rural class, and that each town is isolated from its neighbours to a degree impossible with us. The desert surrounds them like a sea, and they have no point of contact one with the other in the shape of intervening fields or villages, or even intervening pastures. They are isolated in the most literal sense, and from this fact has sprung the political individuality it has always been their care to maintain. Each city is an independent state.

Meanwhile the desert outside, though untenanted by any settled population, is roamed over by the Bedouin tribes, who form the bulk of the Arab race. These occupy for the most part the Nefûds, where alone pasture in any abundance is found ; but they frequent also every part of the upland districts, and being both more warlike and more numerous than the townsmen, hold every road leading from town to town, so that it depends upon their good will and pleasure, to cut off communication for the citizens entirely from the world.

The towns, as I have said, are for the most part self-supporting ; but their production is limited to garden produce, and the date. They grow no wheat and rear no stock, so that for bread and meat they are dependent on without. They require also a market for their industries, the weaving of cloth, the manufacture of arms and utensils, and it is necessary, at least in Jebel Shammar, to send yearly caravans to the Euphrates for corn. Thus security of travelling outside their walls is essential to the life of every town in Arabia, and on this necessity the whole political structure of their government is built. The towns put themselves each under the protection of the principal Bedouin Sheykh of its district, who, on the consideration of a yearly tribute, guarantees the citizens' safety outside the city walls, enabling them to travel unmolested as far as his jurisdiction extends, and this, in the case of a powerful tribe, may be many hundred miles, and embrace many cities. The towns are then said to "belong" to such and such a tribe, and the Bedouin Sheykh becomes their suzerain, or Lord Protector, until, from their common vassalage, and the freedom of intercourse it secures them with each other, the germs of federation spring up, and develop sometimes into nationality.

This has, I believe, been always the condition of Arabia.

A farther development then ensues. The Bedouin Sheykh, grown rich with the tribute of a score of towns, builds himself a castle close to one of them, and lives there during the summer months. Then with the prestige of his rank (for Bedouin blood is still accounted the purest), and backed by his power in the desert, he speedily becomes the practical ruler of the town, and from protector of the citizens becomes their sovereign. He is now dignified by them with the title of Emir or prince, and though still their Sheykh to the Bedouins, becomes king of all the towns which pay him tribute.

This form of government, resting as it does on a natural basis, has always been reverted to in Arabia, whenever the country has, after an interval of foreign or domestic tyranny, succeeded in emancipating itself. Of very early Arabia little is known; neither the Persian nor the Macedonian nor the Roman Empires embraced it, and it is probable that Nejd at least existed till the time of Mahomet exclusively under the system of government I have described. Then for a short time it became part of the Mussulman Empire, and shared in the centralised or semi-centralised administration of the Caliphs, which substituted a theocratic rule for the simpler forms preceding it. But though the birthplace of Islam, no part of the Arabian Empire was sooner in revolt than Arabia itself. In the second century of the Mahometan era, nearly all the peninsula had reverted to its ancient independence, nor, except temporarily, has Nejd itself ever been since included in the imperial system of a foreign king or potentate. In the middle of last century, however, just as Mahomet had asserted his spiritual authority over the peninsula, the Wahhabi Emir of Aared once more established a centralized and theocratic government in Arabia. The Bedouin Princes were one after another dispossessed, and

a new Arabian Empire was established. This
included not only the whole of Nejd, but at one
time Yemen, Hejaz, and Hasa, with the northern
desert as far north as the latitude of Damascus.
For nearly sixty years the independence of the
towns and tribes of the interior was crushed, and a
system of imperial rule substituted for that of old
Arabia. The Ibn Saouds, "Imâms of Nejd,"
governed neither more nor less than had the first
Caliphs, and with the same divine pretensions.
But their rule came to an end in 1818, when Nejd
was conquered by the Turks, and the reigning Ibn
Saoud made prisoner and beheaded at Constantinople. Then, on the retirement of the Turks, (for
they were unable long to retain their conquest,)
shepherd government again asserted itself, and
the principality of Jebel Shammar was founded.

The Shammar tribe is the most powerful of
Northern Nejd, and the towns of Haïl, Kefar,
Bekaa, and the rest, put themselves under the
protection of Abdallah ibn Rashid, who had succeeded in gaining the Shammar Sheykhat for
himself. He seems to have been a man of great
ability, and to him is due the policy of rule which
his descendants have ever since pursued. He took
up his residence in Haïl, and built the castle there,
and caused himself to be recognized as Emir, first
in vassalage to the Ibn Saouds, who had reappeared
in Aared, but later on his own account. His policy
seems to have been first to conciliate or subdue the

other Bedouin tribes of Nejd, forcing them to become tributary to his own tribe, the Shammar, and secondly to establish his protectorate over all the northern towns. This was a simple plan enough, and one which any Bedouin Sheykh might have devised; but Abdallah's merit consists in the method of its application. He saw that in order to gain his object, he must appeal to national ideas and national prejudices. The tribute which he extracted from the towns, he spent liberally in the desert, exercising boundless hospitality to every sheykh who might chance to visit him. To all he gave presents, and dazzled them with his magnificence, sending them back to the tribes impressed with his wealth and power. Thus he made numerous friends, with whose aid he was able to coerce the rest, his enemies or rivals. In treating with these he seems always to have tried conciliation first, and, if forced to arms, to have been satisfied with a single victory, making friends at once with the vanquished, and even restoring to them their property, an act of generosity which met full appreciation in the desert. By this means his power and reputation increased rapidly, as did that of his brother and right-hand man Obeyd, who is now a legendary hero in Nejd.

Another matter to which the founder of the Ibn Rashid dynasty paid much attention was finance. Though spending large sums yearly on presents and entertainments, he took care that these should not exceed his revenue, and at his death he left, according to common report, a house full of silver pieces to his son. Nor have any of his successors been otherwise than thrifty. It is impossible of course to guess the precise amount of treasure thus saved, but that it represents a fabulous fortune in Arabia is certain; the possession of this, with the prestige which in a poor country wealth gives, is an immense source of power.

Lastly Abdallah, and all the Ibn Rashid family, have been endowed with a large share of caution. No important enterprise has been embarked on in a hurry; and certainly at the present day affairs of state are discussed in family council, before any action is taken. It seems to have been always a rule with the Ibn Rashids to think twice, thrice, or a dozen times before acting, for even Mohammed's violent deeds towards his nephews were premeditated, and thought over for many months beforehand. In their conduct with the Ibn Saouds and the Turkish Sultans, they have always waited their opportunity, and avoided an open rupture. It is very remarkable that so many members of this family should be superior men, for it is difficult to say who has been the ablest man of them, Abdallah, Obeyd, Tellál, Mohammed, or his cousin Hamúd. Nor is the rising generation less promising.

Having united into a sort of confederation all the Bedouin tribes of Northern Nejd, Abdallah became naturally supreme over the towns; but he was not satisfied merely with power, he aimed at making his rule popular. It is much to his credit, and to that of his successors, that none of them seem to have abused their position. Liberality and conciliation, combined with an occasional display of power, have been no less their policy with the townsmen than with the Bedouins, and they have thus placed their rule on its only secure basis, popularity. In early days the Ibn Rashids had to fight for their position at Haïl, and later in Jôf and at Meskakeh. But their rule is now acknowledged freely everywhere, enthusiastically in Jebel Shammar. It strikes a traveller fresh from Turkey as surpassingly strange to hear the comments passed by the townspeople of Haïl on their government, for it is impossible to converse ten minutes with any one of them without being assured that the government of the Emir is the best government in the world. "El hamdu lillah, ours is a fortunate country. It is not with us as with the Turks and Persians, whose government is no government. Here we are happy and prosperous. El hamdu lillah." I have often been amused at this chauvinism.

In the town of Haïl the Emir lives in state, having a body-guard of 800 or 1000 men dressed in a kind of uniform, that is to say, in brown cloaks and red or blue kefiyehs, and armed with silver-hilted swords. These are recruited from among the young men of the towns and villages by voluntary enlistment, those who wish to serve inscribing their names at the castle, and being called out as occasion requires. Their duties are light, and they live most of them with their families, receiving neither pay nor rations, except when employed away from home on garrison duty in outlying forts and at Jôf. · Their expense, therefore, to the Emir is little more than that of their clothes and arms. To them is entrusted any police work that may be necessary in the towns, but it is very seldom that the authority of the Emir requires other support than that of public opinion. The Arabs of Nejd are a singularly temperate race, and hardly ever indulge in brawling or breaches of the peace. If disputes arise between citizens they are almost always settled on the spot by the interference of neighbours; and the rowdyism and violence of European towns are unknown at Haïl. Where, however, quarrels are not to be settled by the intervention of friends, the disputants bring their cases to the Emir, who settles them in open court, the *mejlis,* and whose word is final. The law of the Koran, though often referred to, is not, I fancy, the main rule of the Emir's decision, but rather Arabian custom, an authority far older than the Mussulman code. I doubt if it is often necessary for the soldiers to support such decisions by force. Thieving, I have been repeatedly assured, is almost unknown at Haïl; but robbers or thieves taken redhanded, lose for the first offence a hand, for the second their head.

In the desert, and everywhere outside the precincts

of the town, order is kept by the Bedouins, with whom the Emir lives a portion of each year. He is then neither more nor less himself than a Bedouin, throws off his shoes and town finery, arms himself with a lance, and leads a wandering life in the Nefûd. He commonly does this at the commencement of spring, and spring is the season of his wars. Then with the extreme heat of summer he returns to Haïl. The tribute paid by each town and village to the Emir is assessed according to its wealth in date palms, and the sheep kept by its citizens with the Bedouins. Four khrush for each tree is, I believe, the amount, trees under seven years old being exempt. At Haïl this is levied by the Emir's officers, but elsewhere by the local sheykhs, who are responsible for its due collection. At Jôf and Meskakeh, which are still in the position of territory newly annexed, Ibn Rashid is represented by a vakil, or lieutenant, who levies the tax in coin, Turkish money being the recognised medium of exchange everywhere. Without pretending to anything at all like accuracy we made a calculation that the Emir's revenue from all sources of tribute and tax may amount to £60,000 yearly, and that the annual passage of the pilgrimage through his dominions may bring £20,000 to £30,000 more to his exchequer.

With regard to his expenditure, it is perhaps easier to calculate. He pays a small sum yearly in tribute to the Sherif of Medina, partly as a religious offering, partly to insure immunity for his outlying possessions, Kheybar, Kâf and the rest, from Turkish aggression. I should guess this tribute to be £3,000 to £5,000, but could not ascertain the amount. The Emir's expenditure on his army can hardly be more, and with his civil list and every expense of Government, should be included within £10,000. On his household he may spend £5,000, and on his stable £1,000. By far the largest item in his budget must be described as entertainment. Mohammed ibn Rashid, in imitation of his predecessors, feeds daily two to three hundred guests at the palace; the poor are there clothed, and presents of camels and clothes made to richer strangers from a distance. The meal consists of rice and camel meat, sometimes mutton, and there is besides a constant "coulage" in dates and coffee, which I cannot estimate at less than £50 a day, say £20,000 yearly, or with presents, £25,000. Thus we have our budget made up to about £45,000 expenditure, as against £80,000 to £90,000 revenue—which leaves a handsome margin for wars and other accidents, and for that amassing of treasure which is traditional with the Ibn Rashids. I must say, however, once more, that I am merely guessing my figures, and nobody, perhaps, in Jebel Shammar, except the Emir himself and Hamúd, could do more.

It will be seen from all this that Jebel Shammar is, financially, in a very flourishing state. The curse of money-lending has not yet invaded it, and neither

prince nor people are able to spend sixpence more
than they have got. No public works, requiring
public expenditure and public loans, have yet been
undertaken, and it is difficult to imagine in what
they would consist. The digging of new wells is
indeed the only duty a "company" could find to
execute, for roads are unnecessary in a country all
like a macadamised highway; there are no rivers to
make canals with, or suburban populations to
supply with tramways. One might predict with
confidence, that the secret of steam locomotion will
have been forgotten before ever a railway reaches
Jebel Shammar.

With regard to the form of government, it is
good mainly because it is effective. It is no doubt
discordant to European ideas of political propriety,
that the supreme power in a country should be
vested in Bedouin hands. But in Arabia they are
the only hands that can wield it. The town cannot
coerce the desert ; therefore, if they are to live at
peace, the desert must coerce the town. The Turks,
with all their machinery of administration, and
their power of wealth and military force, have
never been able to secure life and property to
travellers in the desert, and in Arabia have been
powerless to hold more than the towns. Even the
pilgrim road from Damascus, though nominally in
their keeping, can only be traversed by them with
an army, and at considerable risk. Ibn Rashid, on
the other hand, by the mere effect of his will, keeps

all the desert in an absolute peace. In the whole district of Jebel Shammar, embracing, as it does, some of the wildest deserts, inhabited by some of the wildest people in the world, a traveller may go unarmed and unescorted, without more let or hindrance than if he were following a highway in England. On every road of Jebel Shammar, townsmen may be found jogging on donkey-back, alone, or on foot, carrying neither gun nor lance, and with all their wealth about them. If you ask about the dangers of the road, they will return the question, "Are we not here in Ibn Rashid's country?" No system, however perfect, of patrols and forts and escorts, could produce a result like this.

In the town, on the other hand, the Bedouin prince, despotic though he may be, is still under close restraint from public opinion. The citizens of Jebel Shammar have not what we should call constitutional rights; there is no machinery among them for the assertion of their power; but there is probably no community in the old world, where popular feeling exercises a more powerful influence on government than it does at Haïl. The Emir, irresponsible as he is in individual acts, knows well that he cannot transgress the traditional unwritten law of Arabia with impunity. An unpopular sheykh would cease, *ipso facto,* to be sheykh, for, though dethroned by no public ceremony, and subjected to no personal ill-treatment, he would find himself abandoned in favour of a more acceptable member of his family.

The citizen soldiers would not support a recognised tyrant in the town, nor would the Bedouins outside. Princes in Arabia have, therefore, to consider public opinion before all else.

The flaw in the system, for in every system there will be found one, lies in the uncertainty of succession to the Sheykhat or Bedouin throne. On the death of an Emir, if he have no son of full age and acknowledged capacity to take up the reins of government, rival claimants, brothers, uncles, or cousins of the dead man, dispute his succession in arms, and many and bitter have been the wars in consequence. Such, quite lately, was the quarrel which convulsed Aared on the death of Feysul ibn Saoud, and led to the disintegration of the Wahhabi monarchy, and such, one cannot help fearing, may be the fate of Jebel Shammar, on Mohammed's. He has no children, and the sons of Tellál, the next heirs to the throne, have a formidable rival in Hamúd. The Emir, however, is a young man, forty-five, and may live long ; and if he should do so, seems to have the succession of the Wahhabi monarchy in his hands. He has effected, he and his predecessors, the union of all the Bedouin sheykhs, from Meshhed Ali to Medina, under his leadership, and is in close connection with those of Kasim and Aared. His authority is established as far north as Kâf, and he has his eye already on the towns still further north, if ever they should shake off the Turkish bondage. I look forward to the day when the Roala too,

and the Welled Ali, shall have entered into his
alliance, possibly even the Sebaa and Ibn Haddal ;
and though it is neither likely nor desirable that
the old Wahhabi Empire should be re-established
on its centralised basis, a confederation of the tribes
of the north may continue its best traditions. Hauran
and the Leja, and the Euphrates towns, were once
tributary to the Ibn Saouds, and may be again one
day to the Ibn Rashids. This is looking far afield,
but not farther than Mohammed himself looks.

NOTE.—That Mohammed ibn Rashid does not limit his ambition
to Nejd has been very recently proved. In the month of April
last, 1880, he marched with an army of 5000 men from Haïl, passed
up the Wady Sirhán, surprised Mohammed Dukhi ibn Smeyr in the
Harra and sacked his camp, and then went on to the Hauran. The
citizens of Damascus were not a little startled at learning one
morning that the Emir was at Bozra not 60 miles from the capital
of Syria, and there was much speculation as to his object in
coming so far northwards, no army from Nejd having been seen in
the Pashalik since the days of the Wahhabi Empire. Then it was
whispered that he had made friends with Ibn Smeyr, that the
quarrel between them had been a mistake, and that a Sherari
guide, held responsible for the blunder, had been beheaded ; lastly,
that an enormous feast of reconciliation had been given by Ibn
Rashid to the Northern tribes, at which 75 camels and 600 sheep
had been slaughtered, and that after a stay of some weeks at
Melakh the Emir had returned to Nejd.

Without pretending to know precisely what was in Mohammed's
mind in making this ghazú, or all that really happened, it seems
to me not difficult to guess its main object. Ibn Smeyr's success
over Ibn Shaalan, already alluded to, had placed him in a leading
position with the tribes of the North ; and his raid against the
Druses of the Hauran, a district once tributary to the Emirs of
Nejd, pointed him out for Mohammed's resentment. It is part of
the Ibn Rashid policy to strike a blow and then make peace ; and
by thus humbling their most successful chief, and becoming afterwards his host, Mohammed achieved exactly that sort of reputation

he most valued with the Northern tribes.   He has asserted himself
as supreme, where he chooses to be so, in the desert, and has moreover reminded the frontier population in Syria of the old Wahhabi
pretensions to Eastern Syria.   It is conceivable that having coerced
or persuaded the Anazeh to join his league, he may, in the coming
break-up of the Ottoman Empire, succeed to that part of its inheritance, and be recognised as sovereign in all the lands beyond
Jordan.

OUR HOUSE AT HÁYL.

IBN RASHID'S MARES.

CHAPTER XII.

"Je ne trouvai point en eux ces formes que je m'attendais à retrouver dans la patrie de Zeid el Kheil."—GUARMANI.

Nejd horses—Their rarity—Ibn Saoud's stud—The stables at Haïl
Some notes of individual mares—-The points of a Nejd head—
The tribes in the Nefûds and their horses—Meaning of the
term "Nejdi"—Recipe for training.

A CHAPTER on the horses we saw at Haïl has
been promised, and may as well be given here.

Ibn Rashid's stud is now the most celebrated in
Arabia, and has taken the place in public estimation
of that stud of Feysul ibn Saoud's which Mr. Palgrave saw sixteen years ago at Riad, and which he
described in the picturesque paragraphs which have
since been constantly quoted. The cause of this
transference of supremacy from Aared to Jebel
Shammar, lies in the political changes which have
occurred since 1865, and which have taken the
leadership of Central Arabia out of the hands of the
Ibn Saouds and put it into those of the Emirs of
Haïl.

Mohammed ibn Rashid is now not only the most powerful of Bedouin sheykhs, but the richest prince in Arabia; and as such has better means than any other of acquiring the best horses of Nejd, nor have these been neglected by him.

The possession of thoroughbred mares is always among the Arabs a symbol of power; and with the loss of their supreme position in Nejd, the Ibn Saouds have lost their command of the market, and their stud has been allowed to dwindle. The quarrels of the two brothers, Abdallah and Saoud, sons of Feysul, on their father's death, their alternate victories and flights from the capital, and the ruin wrought on them both by the Turks, broke up an establishment which depended on wealth and security for its maintenance; and at the present moment, if common report speaks true, hardly a twentieth part of the old stud remains at Riad. The rest have passed into other hands.

That Feysul's stud in its day was the best in Arabia is probable, and it may be that no collection now to be found there has an equal merit; but there seems little reason for supposing that it differed in anything but degree from what we ourselves saw, or that the animals composing it were distinct from those still owned by the various Bedouin tribes of Nejd. All our inquiries, on the contrary (and we spared no occasion of asking questions), tend to show that it is a mistake to suppose that the horses kept by the Emirs of Riad were a special breed, preserved in the towns of Aared from time immemorial, or that they differed in any way from those bred elsewhere in Central Arabia. They were, we were repeatedly assured, a collection recruited from the various tribes of the Nefûds,—a very fine collection, no doubt, but still a collection. Every Bedouin we have asked has laughed at the idea of there being a special *Nejd breed*, only found in Aared. In answer to our questions we were informed that in Feysul's time emissaries from Riad were constantly on the look-out for mares wherever they could find them ; and that the Emir had often made ghazús against this and that tribe, with no other object than the possession of a particular animal, of a particular breed. The tribe from which he got the best blood, the Hamdani Simri and the Kehilan el-Krush, was the Muteyr (sometimes called the Dushan), while the Beni Khaled, Dafir, Shammar, and even the Ánazeh, supplied him with occasional specimens. Abdallah ibn Saoud, his successor, still retains a few of them, but the bulk of the collection was dispersed, many of the best passing into the hands of Metaab and Bender, Mohammed ibn Rashid's predecessors. Mohammed himself follows precisely the same system, except that he does not take by force, but on payment. He makes purchases from all the tribes around, and though he breeds in the town, his collection is constantly recruited from without. Were this not the case, no doubt, it would soon degenerate, as town-

bred horses in Arabia, being stall-fed and getting
no sort of exercise, are seldom fit for much. There
is a false notion that the oases, such as those of
Jebel Shammar and Aared, are spots especially
adapted for the rearing of horses, and that the
sandy wastes outside contain no pasture. But
the very reverse of this is the case. The oases in
which the towns stand, produce nothing but date
palms and garden produce, nor is there a blade
of grass, or even a tuft of camel pasture in their
neighbourhood. The townspeople keep no animals
except a few camels used for working the wells, and
now and then a donkey. Even these must be fed
either on corn or dates, which none but the rich can
afford. Horses are a luxury reserved only for princes,
and even the richest citizens do their travelling from
village to village on foot. Longer journeys are
performed on dromedaries brought in from the
desert for the purpose, which are either the property
of Bedouins or held with them by the citizens on
shares.

The Nefûds, on the other hand, contain pasture
in abundance, not only for camels, but for sheep and
horses, and it is in the Nefûds that all these are
bred. Ibn Rashid goes every spring with the bulk
of his live stock to the desert, and leaves them
during part of the summer with the tribes, only a
few animals being reserved for use in the town.
It cannot be too strongly insisted upon, that the
upper plateaux of Nejd, where the towns and villages

are found, are a stony wilderness almost entirely
devoid of vegetation, while the Nefûds afford
an inexhaustible supply of pasture. The want
of water alone limits the pastoral value of these,
for the inhabited area is necessarily confined
to a radius of twenty or thirty miles round each
well,—and wells are rare. These facts have not,
I think, been hitherto sufficiently known to be
appreciated.

With regard to Ibn Rashid's collection at Haïl
we looked it over three or four times in the stables,
and saw it out once on a gala day, when each
animal was made to look its best. The stables
consist of four open yards communicating with each
other, in which the animals stand tethered each to a
square manger of sun-dried brick. They are not
sheltered in any way, but wear long heavy rugs
fastened across the chest. They are chained by one
or more feet to the ground, and wear no headstalls.
It being winter time and they ungroomed, they were
all in the roughest possible condition, and, as has
been mentioned, our first impression was one of disappointment. When at Haïl they are given no
regular exercise, remaining it would seem for weeks
together tied up thus, except for a few minutes in
the evening, when they are led to drink. They
are fed almost entirely on dry barley. In the
spring only, for a few weeks, they eat green
corn grown on purpose, and then are taken
to the Nefûd or on ghazús. It is surprising that

they should be able to do their work under such
conditions.

The first yard one enters in going through the
stables, contained, when we saw them, from twenty-
five to thirty mares. In the second were twenty
more, kept in a certain kind of condition for service
in case of necessity; but even these get very little
exercise. As they stand there in the yard, slovenly
and unkempt, they have very little of that air of
high breeding one would expect; and it requires
considerable imagination to look upon them as indeed
the *ne plus ultra* of breeding in Arabia. We made
the mistake, too common, of judging horses by condition, for, mounted and in motion, these at once
became transfigured.

Here may follow some descriptions of particular
animals, written after one of our visits to the stud;
these will give a better idea of them than any
general remarks. In our notes I find :—

" 1. A chestnut Kehîlet el-Krush with three white
feet (mutlak el-yemîn), 14 hands, or 14·1, but very
powerful. Her head is plainer than most here—it
would be thought a good head in England—lean
and rather narrow. She has too heavy a neck,
but a very fine shoulder, a high wither, legs like
steel, hind quarter decidedly coarse, much hair
at the heels. More bone than breeding, one is
inclined to say, seeing her at her manger, though
moving, and with the Emir on her back, one must

be very captious not to admire. She is Mohammed's favourite charger, and of the best blood in Nejd. Ibn Rashid got this strain from Ibn Saoud's stables at Riad, but it came originally from the Muteyr."

"2. A bay Hamdanieh Simri, also from Ibn Saoud's collection, a pretty head, but no other distinction. N.B. This mare is of the same strain as our own mare Sherifa, but inferior to her."

"3. A grey Seglawieh Sheyfi, extremely plain at first sight, with very drooping quarters, and a head in no way remarkable, but with a fine shoulder. This Seglawieh Sheyfi has a great reputation here, and is of special interest as being the last of her race, the only descendant of the famous mare bought by Abbas Pasha, who sent a bullock cart from Egypt all the way to Nejd to fetch her, for she was old, and unable to travel on foot. The story is well known here, and was told to us exactly as we heard it in the north, with the addition that this mare of Ibn Rashid's is the only representative of the strain left in Arabia." *

"4. A dark bay Kehîlet Ajuz, quite 14·2, one white foot, really splendid in every point, shoulder quarter and all; the handsomest head and largest eye of any here. She has ideal action, head and

---

* Abbas Pasha's Seglawieh is reported to have had two foals while in Egypt; one of them died, and the other was given to the late King of Italy, and left descendants, now in the possession of the present king.

tail carried to perfection, and recalls Beteyen ibn Mershid's mare, but her head is finer. She belongs to Hamúd, who is very proud of her, and tells us she came from the Jerba Shammar. It surprises us to find here a mare from Mesopotamia; but we are told that interchange of horses between the southern and northern Shammar is by no means rare."

"5. A dark brown Kehîlet Ajuz, no white except an inch in breadth just above one hoof, lovely head and thoroughbred appearance, and for style of galloping perhaps the best here, although less powerful than the Emir's chestnut and Hamúd's bay. It is hard to choose among the three."

"Of the eight horses, the best is a Shueyman Sbah of great power, head large and very fine. He reminds us of Faris Jerba's mare of the same strain of blood; they are probably related closely, for he has much the same points, forequarter perfect, hindquarter strong but less distinguished. He was bred, however, in Nejd."

"A grey Seglawi Jedran, from Ibn Nedéri of the Gomussa Ánazeh, is a poor specimen of that great strain of blood; but the Bedouin respect for it prevails here though they have now no pure Seglawi Jedrans in Nejd. It is interesting to find this horse valued here, as the fact proves that the Ánazeh horses are thought much of in Nejd. The more one sees of the Nejd horses here, the more is one convinced of the superiority of those of the Ánazeh in the points of speed, and, proud as every one here is of the ' kheyl Nejdi,' it seems to be acknowledged that in these points they are surpassed by the Ánazeh horses."

"Our own Ánazeh mares are looked upon as prodigies of speed.

"In comparing what we see here, with what we saw last year in the north, the first thing that strikes us is that these are ponies, the others horses. It is not so much the actual difference in height, though there must be quite three inches on an average, as the shape, which produces this impression. The Nejd horses have as a rule shorter necks and shorter bodies, and stand over far less ground than the Ánazehs. Then, although their shoulders are undoubtedly good and their withers higher than one generally sees further north, the hind-quarter is short, and if it were not for the peculiarly handsome carriage of the tail would certainly want distinction. Their legs all seem to be extremely good ; but we have not seen in one of them that splendid line of the hind leg to the hock which is so striking in the Ánazeh thoroughbreds. Of their feet it is difficult to judge, for from long standing without exercise, all the Emir's mares have their hoofs overgrown. Their manes and tails are thicker than one would expect.

"In their heads, however, there is certainly a general superiority to the Ánazeh mares, at least in all the points the Arabs most admire, and we were

both struck, directly we saw them, with the difference."

As I may fairly assume that few persons out of
Arabia have an idea what are there considered the
proper points of a horse's head, I will give here a
description of them :

First of all, the head should be large, not small.
A little head the Arabs particularly dislike, but the
size should be all in the upper regions of the skull.
There should be a great distance from the ears to
the eyes, and a great distance from one eye to the
other, though not from ear to ear. The forehead,
moreover, and the whole region between and just
below the eyes, should be convex, the eyes themselves standing rather " *à fleur de tête.*" But there
should be nothing fleshy about their prominence,
and each bone should be sharply edged ; a flat forehead is disliked. The space round the eyes should
be free of all hair, so as to show the black skin
underneath, and this just round the eyes should be
especially black and lustrous. The cheek-bone should
be deep and lean, and the jaw-bone clearly marked.
Then the face should narrow suddenly and run down
almost to a point, not however to such a point as
one sees in the English racehorse, whose profile
seems to terminate with the nostril, but to the tip of
the lip. The nostril when in repose should lie flat
with the face, appearing in it little more than a
slit, and pinched and puckered up, as also should the

mouth, which should have the under-lip longer than
the upper, "like the camel's," the Bedouins say.
The ears, especially in the mare, should be long,
but fine and delicately cut, like the ears of a
gazelle."

It must be remarked that the head and the tail
are the two points especially regarded by Arabs in
judging of a horse, as in them they think they can
discover the surest signs of his breeding. The tails
of the Nejd horses are as peculiar as their heads,
and are as essential to their beauty. However
other points might differ, every horse at Haïl had
its tail set on in the same fashion, in repose
something like the tail of a rocking horse, and
not as has been described, "thrown out in a
perfect arch." In motion the tail was held high
in the air, and looked as if it could not under any
circumstances be carried low. Mohammed ibn
Aruk declared roundly that the phenomenon was an
effect, partly at least, of art. He assured us that
before a foal is an hour old, its tail is bent back
over a stick and the twist produces a permanent
result. But this sounds unlikely, and in any case
it could hardly affect the carriage of the tail in
galloping.

With regard to colour, of the hundred animals in
the Haïl stables, there were about forty greys or
rather whites, thirty bays, twenty chestnuts, and
the rest brown. We did not see a real black, and
of course there are no roans, or piebalds, or duns,

for these are not Arab colours. The Emir one day asked us what colours we preferred in England, and when we told him bay or chestnut he quite agreed with us. Nearly all Arabs prefer bay with black points, though pure white with a very black skin and hoofs is also liked. In a bay or chestnut, three white feet, the off fore-foot being dark, are not objected to. But, as a rule, colour is not much regarded at Haïl, for there as elsewhere in Arabia a fashionable strain is all in all.

"Besides the full grown animals, Ibn Rashid's yards contain thirty or forty foals and yearlings, beautiful little creatures but terribly starved and miserable. Foals bred in the desert are poor enough, but these in town have a positively sickly appearance. Tied all day long by the foot they seem to have quite lost heart, and show none of the playfulness of their age. Their tameness, like that of the "fowl and the brute," is shocking to see. The Emir tells us that every spring he sends a hundred yearlings down to Queyt on the Persian Gulf under charge of one of his slaves, who sells them at Bombay for £100 apiece. They are of course now at their worst age, but they have the prospect of a few months' grazing in the Nefûd before appearing in the market."

"On the whole, both of us are rather disappointed with what we see here. Of all the mares in the prince's stables I do not think more than three or four could show with advantage among the Go-

mussa, and, in fact, we are somewhat alarmed lest
the Emir should propose an exchange with us for
our chestnut Ras el-Fedawi which is greatly admired by every one. If he did, we could not
well refuse."

With regard to Nejd horses in general, the
following remarks are based on what we saw and
heard at Haïl, and elsewhere in Arabia.

First, whatever may have been the case formerly,
horses of any kind are now exceedingly rare in Nejd.
One may travel vast distances in the Peninsula
without meeting a single horse or even crossing a
horse track. Both in the Nefûd and on our return
journey to the Euphrates, we carefully examined
every track of man and beast we met; but from the
time of our leaving the Roala till close to Meshhed
Ali, not twenty of these proved to be tracks of
horses. The wind no doubt obliterates footsteps
quickly, but it could not wholly do so, if there were
a great number of the animals near. The Ketherin,
a true Nejd tribe and a branch of the Beni Khaled,
told us with some pride that they could mount a
hundred horsemen, and even the Muteyr, reputed to
be the greatest breeders of thoroughbred stock in
Nejd, are said to possess only 400 mares. The horse
is a luxury with the Bedouins of the Peninsula, and
not, as it is with those of the North, a necessity of
their daily life. Their journeys and raids and
wars are all made on camel, not on horse-back;
and at most the Sheykh mounts his mare at the

moment of battle. The want of water in Nejd is a sufficient reason for this. Horses there are kept for show rather than actual use, and are looked upon as far too precious to run unnecessary risks.

Secondly, what horses there are in Nejd, are bred in the Nefûds. The stony plateaux of the interior contain no suitable pasture except in a very few places, while the Nefûds afford grass, green or dry, the whole year round. The Muteyr, the Beni Khaled, the Dafir, and the Shammar, are now the principal breeders of horses in Nejd, but the Ánazeh are regarded as possessing the best strains, and the Ánazeh have disappeared from Nejd. They began to migrate northwards about two hundred years ago, and have ever since continued moving by successive migrations till all have abandoned their original homes. It may be that the great name which Nejd horses undoubtedly have in the East, was due mainly to these very Ánazeh, with whose horses they are now contrasted. The Bisshr Ánazeh were settled in the neighbourhood of Kheybar, on the western edge of the Nefûd, the Roala south of Jôf, and the Amarrat in the extreme east. These probably among them supplied Nejd horses in former times to Syria, Bagdad, and Persia, and some sections of the tribe may even have found their way further south ; for the Ibn Saouds themselves are an Ánazeh family. So that then, probably, as now, the best strains of blood were in their hands. To the present day in the north the Ánazeh distinguish the descendants of the mares brought with them from Nejd as "Nejdi," while they call the descendants of the mares captured from the tribes of the North, "Shimali" or Northerners.

The management and education of horses seems to differ little in Nejd from what it is elsewhere among the Arabs. But we were surprised to find that, in place of the Bedouin halter, the bit is used at Haïl. At first we fancied that this was in imitation of Turkish manners ; but it is more likely to be an old custom with town Arabs. Indeed the Bedouins of the Sahara, no less than the Turks, use the ring bit, which may after all have been an invention of Arabia. Bad as it is for the mouth, it is certainly of use in the fancy riding indulged in at Haïl, the jerid play and sham fighting. Among the Bedouins of Nejd the halter alone is used.

Of anything like racing we could learn nothing. Trials of speed are no longer in fashion, as they must have been once, and skill in turning and doubling is alone of any value. That some tradition, however, of training still exists among the Arabs, the following recipe for rearing a colt seems to prove. It was given us in answer to our description of English racing and racehorses, and probably represents a traditional practice of Arabia as old as the days of Mahomet.

ARAB RECIPE FOR REARING A COLT.

" If," said our informant, " you would make a colt run faster than his fellows, remember the following rules :—

" ' During the first month of his life let him be content with his mother's milk, it will be sufficient for him. Then during five months add to this natural supply goat's milk, as much as he will drink. For six months more give him the milk of camels, and besides a measure of wheat steeped in water for a quarter of an hour, and served in a nose-bag.

" ' At a year old the colt will have done with milk ; he must be fed on wheat and grass, the wheat dry from a nose-bag, the grass green if there is any.

" ' At two years old he must work, or he will be worthless. Feed him now, like a full-grown horse, on barley ; but in summer let him also have gruel daily at midday. Make the gruel thus :—Take a double-handful of flour, and mix it in water well with your hands till the water seems like milk ; then strain it, leaving the dregs of the flour, and give what is liquid to the colt to drink.

" ' Be careful from the hour he is born to let him stand in the sun ; shade hurts horses, but let him have water in plenty when the day is hot.

" ' The colt must now be mounted, and taken by his owner everywhere with him, so that he shall see everything, and learn courage. He must be kept constantly in exercise, and never remain long at his manger. He should be taken on a journey, for work will fortify his limbs.

"'At three years old he should be trained to gallop. Then, if he be of true blood, he will not be left behind. Yalla!'"

HAMÚD IBN RASHID.

CHAPTER XIII.

" Babel was Nimrod's hunting box, and then
  A town of gardens, walls, and wealth amazing,
Where Nabuchodonosor, king of men,
  Reigned till one summer's day he took to grazing."
                                            BYRON.

"   .   .   .   .   Oh how wretched
Is that poor man that lives on princes' favours."
                                            SHAKESPEARE.

Mohammed loses his head—A ride with the Emir—The mountain
fortress of Agde—Farewell to Haïl—We join the Persian Haj—
Ways and manners of the pilgrims—A clergyman of Medina.

I HAVE hinted at a mystification in which we
found ourselves involved a few days after our
arrival at Haïl, and which at the time caused us no
little anxiety. It had its origin in a piece of child-
ishness on Mohammed's part, whose head was
completely turned by the handsome reception given
him as an Ibn Arûk by the Emir, and a little
too, I fear, by our own spoiling. To the present
day I am not quite sure that we heard all that
happened, and so forbear entering upon the matter
in detail; but as far as we could learn, Mohammed's vanity seems to have led him to aggran-
dise his own position in the eyes of Ibn Rashid's
court, by representing us as persons whom he
had taken under his protection, and who were in

some way dependent on him; boasting that the camels, horses, and other property were his own, and our servants his people. This under ordinary circumstances might have been a matter of small consequence, and we should not have grudged him a little self-glorification at our expense, conscious as we were of having owed the success of our journey hitherto, mainly to his fidelity. But unfortunately the secondary *rôle* which he would thus have assigned to us, made our relations with the Emir not only embarrassing, but positively dangerous. Our reception at first had been cordial to a degree that made it all the more annoying to find, that when we had been four days at Haïl, we no longer received the attentions which had hitherto been paid us. The presents of game ceased, and the lamb, with which we had hitherto been regaled at dinner, was replaced by camel meat. Instead of two soldiers being sent to escort us to the palace, a slave boy came with a message. On the fifth day we were not invited to the evening party, and on the sixth Wilfrid, calling at the palace, was told curtly that the Emir was not at home. We could not imagine the cause of this change, and Mohammed, usually so cheerful and so open-hearted, had become moody and embarrassed, keeping almost entirely with the servants in the outer house. Hanna, the faithful Hanna, began to hint darkly that things were not well, and Abdallah and the rest of the Mussulman servants seemed unwilling to do their duty. We remembered

that we were among Wahhabi fanatics, and we
began to be very much alarmed. Still we were far
from guessing the real reason, and it was not till we
had been a week at Haïl that Wilfrid, happening
to meet the Emir's chief slave Mubarek, learned
from him how matters stood. It was no use being
angry; indeed Mohammed's conduct was rather
childish than disloyal, and the *dénouement* would
have not been worth mentioning except as an
illustration of Arab manners and ways of thought,
and also as explaining why our stay at Haïl was cut
shorter than we had originally intended it to be ;
and why, instead of going on to Kasim, we joined
the Persian pilgrimage on their homeward road to
Meshhed Ali.

Matters of course could not rest there, and on
returning home from his interview with Mubarek,
Wilfrid upbraided Mohammed with his folly, and
then sent to the palace for Mufurraj, the master of
ceremonies, and the same dignified old gentleman
who had received us on our arrival, and having explained the circumstances bade him in his turn explain
them to the Emir. The old man promised to do this,
and I have no doubt kept his word, for that very evening we were sent for once more to the palace, and received with the old cordiality. It is, too, I think
very creditable to the arrangements of the Haïl court,
that no explanations of any sort were entered into.
Mohammed, though put in his proper place, was
still politely received ; and only an increase of

amiable attentions made us remember that we had
ever had cause to complain. As to Mohammed, I
am bound to say, that once the fumes of his vanity
evaporated, he bore no kind of malice for what we
had been obliged to do, and became once more the
amiable, attentive and serviceable friend he had
hitherto been. Ill-temper is not an Arab failing.
Still the incident was a lesson and a warning, a
lesson that we were Europeans still among Asiatics,
a warning that Haïl was a lion's den, though fortunately we were friends with the lion. We began
to make our plans for moving on.

I have said little as yet about the Persian pilgrimage which, encamped just outside the walls of Haïl,
had all along been a main feature in the goings on
of the place. On a certain Tuesday, however, the
Emir sent us a message that he expected us to come
out riding with him, and that he would meet us at
that gate of the town where the pilgrims were. It
was a fortunate day for us, not indeed because we
saw the pilgrims, but because we saw what we would
have come the whole journey to see, and had almost
despaired of seeing,—all the best of the Emir's
horses out and galloping about. We were delighted
at the opportunity, and made haste to get ready. In
half an hour we were on our mares, and in the
street. There was a great concourse of people all
moving towards the camp, and just outside the town
we found the Emir's cavalcade. This for the moment
absorbed all my thoughts, for I had not yet seen

any of the Haïl horses mounted. The Emir, splendidly dressed but barefooted, was riding a pretty little white mare, while the chestnut Krushieh followed him mounted by a slave.

All our friends were there, Hamúd, Majid and the two boys his brothers, with a still smaller boy, whom they introduced to us as a son of Metaab, the late Emir, all in high spirits and anxious to show off their horses and their horsemanship ; while next the Emir and under his special protection rode the youth with the tragical history, Naïf, the sole remaining son of Tellál, whose brothers Moham-med had killed, and who, it is whispered, will some day be called on to revenge their deaths. Mubarek too, the white· slave, was there, a slave in name only, for he is strikingly like the princely family in feature and is one of the richest and most important personages in Haïl. The rest of the party consisted of friends and servants, with a fair sprink-ling of black faces among them, dressed in their best clothes and mounted on the Emir's mares. Con-spicuous on his beautiful bay was Hamúd, who, as usual, did us the honours, and pointed out and ex-plained the various persons and things we saw. It was one of those mornings one only finds in Nejd. The air brilliant and sparkling to a degree one cannot imagine in Europe, and filling one with a sense of life such as one remembers to have had in childhood, and which gives one a wish to shout. The sky of an intense blue, and the hills in front of us carved out of sapphire, and the plain, crisp and even as a billiard table, sloping gently upwards towards them.   On one side the battlemented walls and towers of Haïl, with the palace rising out of a dark mass of palms almost black in the sunlight; on the other the pilgrim camp, a parti-coloured mass of tents, blue, green, red, white, with the pilgrims themselves in a dark crowd, watching with curious half-frightened eyes the barbaric display of which we formed a part.

Presently the Emir gave a signal to auvance, and turning towards the south-west, our whole party moved on in the direction of a clump of palm-trees we could see about two miles off.   Hamûd then suddenly put his mare into a gallop, and one after another the rest of the party joined him in a sham fight, galloping, doubling, and returning to the Emir, who remained alone with us, and shouting as though they would bring the sky about their ears.   At last the Emir could resist it no longer, and seizing a jerid or palm stick from one of the slaves, went off himself among the others.   In a moment his dignity and his town manners were forgotten, and he became the Bedouin again which he and all his family really are.   His silk kefiyehs were thrown back, and bare-headed with his long Bedouin plaits streaming in the wind and bare-legged and bare-armed, he galloped hither and thither; charging into the throng, and pursuing and being pursued, and shouting as if he had never felt a care, and never committed a crime in his life.

We found ourselves alone with a strange little personage whom we had already noticed riding beside the Emir, and who seemed even more out of place in this fantastic entertainment than ourselves. I hope at least that we looked less ridiculous than he did. Mounted on a sorry little kadish, and dressed in the fashion of European children fifty years ago, with a high waisted coat, well pleated at the skirt, trousers up to his knees, and feet shod with slippers, a little brown skull cap on his head, and a round shaven face, sat what seemed an overgrown boy, but what in reality was a chief person from among the Persian pilgrims. It was Ali Koli Khan, son of the great Khan of the Bactiari, who for his father's sake was being treated by the Emir with all possible honour. He, with the rest of the Haj, was now on his way back from Mecca, and it was partly to impress him with the Emir's magnificence that the present party had been arranged.

We did not long stay alone, for in a few minutes the galloping ceased, and we then went on sedately as before, and in due time arrived at the palm trees, which, it turned out, were the Emir's property, and contained in a garden surrounded by a high wall. Here we were invited to dismount, and a carpet having been spread under the trees, we all sat down. Slaves were soon busy serving a luncheon of sweetmeats,—boys were made to climb the lemon trees, and shake down the fruit, and coffee was handed round. Then all the party said their prayers except ourselves and the Persian, who, as a Shiah, could not join in their devotions, and we mounted again and rode home. This time we too joined in the galloping, which speedily recommenced, our mares fully enjoying the fun, and in this way we scampered back to Haïl.

On the following day Wilfrid called on Ali Koli Khan in his tent, going there with Mohammed, now once more a reasonable companion and follower. Indeed in the Persian camp assumptions of nobility on Mohammed's part would have been quite thrown away, for the Persians care nothing for Arabian nobility, and treat all alike as Bedouins and barbarians. Ali Koli, though only a younger son, was travelling in state, having his mother with him, and a multitude of servants, male and female, besides his *hemeldaria* or contractor, and the Arabs managing his beasts. His major-domo and interpreter was a magnificent personage, and his followers, dressed in felt tunics and skull caps, gave him the appearance of being an important chief. His tent was of the Turkish pattern, well lined and comfortable, with fine Persian carpets on the floor, and a divan. There Wilfrid found him sitting with a friend, Abd er-Rahim, the son of a merchant of Kermanshah, who is also British consular agent there. The young Persians were very amiable; but the contrast of their manners with those of the ceremonious Arabs struck Wilfrid at once. There were none of those elaborate compliments and polite inquiries one gets used to at Haïl, but rather a European *sans gêne* in the form of reception. They made Wilfrid comfortable on the divan, called for tea, which was served in a *samovar*, and at once poured out a long history of their sufferings on the pilgrimage. This they did in very broken Arabic, and with an accent irresistibly absurd, for the Persians speak with a drawl in their intonation, wholly foreign to that of the Arabs. Ali's natural language, he says, is Kurdish, but being an educated person, and an officer in the Shah's army, he talks Persian equally well. In Persia, Arabic plays much the part in education which Latin did in Europe before it was quite a dead language. Both he and Abd er-Rahim were loud in complaints of everything Arabian, and in spite of Mohammed's presence, abused roundly the whole Arab race, the poverty of the towns, the ignorance of the citizens, and the robberies of the Bedouins, also the extortionate charges of the Arab hemeldarias, contractors for camels, and the miseries of desert travelling. " Was ever anything seen so miserable as the bazaar at Haïl ; not a bag of sweetmeats to be had for love or money, the Arabs were mere barbarians, drinkers of coffee instead of tea." Every now and then, too, they would break out into conversation in their own language. Wilfrid, however, liked Ali Koli, and they parted very good friends, with an invitation from both the young

Persians to travel on with them to Meshhed on the Euphrates, where the Persians always end their pilgrimage by a visit to the shrines of Ali and Huseyn.   This seemed an excellent opportunity, and having consulted the Emir, who highly approved of the plan, we accordingly decided to travel with the Haj as soon as it should start.

Our last days at Haïl were by no means the least pleasant.   As a final proof of his goodwill and confidence, the Emir announced that we might pay a visit to Agde, a fortress in the mountains some miles from Haïl, and which he had never before shown to any stranger.   I do not feel at liberty to say exactly where this is, for we were sent to see it rather on parole, and though I hope Ibn Rashid runs no danger of foreign invasion, I would not give a clue to possible enemies.   Suffice it to say that it lies in the mountains, in a position of great natural strength, made stronger by some rude attempts at fortification, and that it is really one of the most curious places in the world.

One approaches it from the plain by a narrow winding valley, reminding one not a little of the wadys of Mount Sinai, where the granite rocks rise abruptly on either hand out of a pure bed of sand. On one of these is engraved an inscription in Arabic which we copied and which though not very legible may be read thus :—

"Hadihi kharâbat Senhârîb."
"This (is) the ruin of Senacherib ('s building)."

369

Such at least is its meaning in the opinion of Mr. Sabunji, a competent Arabic scholar, though I will not venture to explain on what occasion Senacherib made his way to Nejd, nor why he wrote in Arabic instead of his own cuneiform.

Inside the defences, the valley broadens out into an amphitheatre formed by the junction of three or four wadys in which there is a village and a palm garden. Besides which, the wadys are filled with wild palms watered, the Arabs say, "min Allah," by Providence, at least by no human hand. They are very beautiful, forming a brilliant contrast of green fertility with the naked granite crags which overhang them on all sides. These are perhaps a thousand feet in height, and run down sheer into the sandy floor of the wadys, so that one is reminded in looking at them of that valley of diamonds where the serpents lived, and down which the merchants threw their pieces of meat for the rocs to gather, in the tale of Sinbad the Sailor. No serpents however live in Agde, but a population of very honest Shammar, who entertained us with a prodigality of dates and coffee, difficult to do justice to. We had been sent in the company of two horsemen of the Emir's, Shammar, who did the honours, as Agde and all in it are really Ibn Rashid's private property. These and the villagers gave us a deal of information about the hills we were in, and showed us where a great battle had been fought by Mohammed's father and his uncle Obeyd against

the Ibn Ali, formerly Emirs of the Jebel. It would
seem that Agde was the oldest possession of the Ibn
Rashids, and that on their taking Haïl the Ibn Alis
marched against them, when they retreated to their
fortress, and there gave battle and such a defeat to
the people of Kefar that it secured to the Ibn
Rashids supreme power ever after. They also
showed us with great pride a wall built by Obeyd
to block the narrow valley, and made us look at
everything, wells, gardens, and houses, so that we
spent nearly all the day there. They told us too of
a mysterious beast that comes from the hills by
night and climbs the palm trees for sake of the
dates. "As large as a hare, with a long tail, and
very good to eat." They describe it as sitting on
its hind-legs, and whistling, so that Wilfrid thinks
it must be a marmot. Only, do marmots climb?
They call it the Webber.

We had a delightful gallop home with the two
Bedouins, (Mohammed was not with us,) of whom
we learned one of the Shammar war songs, which
runs thus :—

> " Ma arîd ana erkobu delul,
> Lau zeynuli shedadeha,
> Arîdu ana hamra shenuf,
> Hamra seryeh aruddeha."

thus literally translated :—

> " I would not ride a mere delul,
> Though lovely to me her shedad (camel-saddle);
> Let me be mounted on a mare,
> A bay mare, swift and quick to turn."

They were mounted on very pretty ponies, but could not keep up with us galloping. If we had been in Turkey, or indeed anywhere else but in Arabia, we should have had to give a handsome tip after an expedition of this kind; but at Haïl nothing of the sort was expected. Both these Shammar were exceedingly intelligent well mannered men, with souls above money. They were doing their duty to the prince as Sheykh, and to us as strangers, and they did it enthusiastically.

The level of Agde is 3,780 feet above the sea, that of Haïl 3,500.

This was, perhaps, the pleasantest day of all those we spent at Haïl, and will live long with us as a delightful remembrance. On the following day we were to depart. Mohammed, while we were away, had been making preparations. Two new camels had been bought, and a month's provision of dates and rice purchased, in addition to a gift of excellent Yemen coffee sent us by the Emir. Our last interview with Ibn Rashid was characteristic. He was not at the kasr, but in a house he has close to the Mecca gate, where from a little window he can watch unperceived the goings on of the Haj encamped below him. We found him all alone, for he has lost all fear of our being assassins now, at his window like a bird of prey, calculating no doubt how many more silver pieces he should be able to make out of the Persians before they were well out of his clutches. Every now and then he

would lean out of the window, which was partly
covered by a shutter, and shout to one of his
men who were standing below some message with
regard to the pilgrims.   He seemed to be enjoying the pleasure of his power over them, and it is
absolute.

To us he was very amiable, renewing all his
protestations of friendship and regard, and offering
to give us anything we might choose to ask for,
dromedaries for the journey, or one of his mares.
This, although we should have liked to accept the
last offer, we of course declined, Wilfrid making a
short speech in the Arab manner, saying that the only
thing we asked was the Emir's regard, and wishing
him length of days.   He begged Mohammed ibn
Rashid to consider him as his vakil in Europe
in case he required assistance of any kind, and
thanked him for all the kindness we had
received at his hands.   The Emir then proposed
that we should put off our departure, and go with
him instead on a ghazú or warlike expedition he
was starting on in a few days, a very attractive
offer which might have been difficult to refuse had
it been made earlier, but which we now declined.
Our heads, in fact, had been in the jaws of the
lion long enough, and now our only object was to
get quietly and decorously out of the den.   We
therefore pleaded want of time, and added that our
camels were already on the road; we then said
good-bye and took our leave.

There was, however, one more visit to be paid, this
time of friendly regard more than of ceremony. As we
rode through the town we stopped at Hamúd's house
and found him and all his family at home. To
them our farewells were really expressions of regret
at parting, and Hamúd gave us some very sound
advice about going on with the Haj to Meshhed
Ali, instead of trying to get across to Bussora.
There had been rain, he said, on the pilgrim road,
and all the reservoirs (those marked on the map as
the tanks of Zobeydeh) were full, so that our
journey that way would be exceptionally easy,
whereas between this and Bussorah, we should have
to pass over an almost waterless region, without
anything interesting to compensate for the difficulty.
But this we should see as we went on —the first
thing, as I have said, was to get clear away, and it
would be time enough later to settle details about
our course.

Majid was there, and received from Wilfrid as a
remembrance a silver-handled Spanish knife, whereupon he sent for a black cloth cloak with a little
gold embroidery on the collar and presented it to
me. It was a suitable gift, for I had nothing of the
sort, indeed no respectable abba at all, and this one
was both dignified and quiet in appearance. Majid
at least, I am sure, regrets us, and if circumstances
ever take us again to Haïl, it would be the best
fortune for us to find him or his father on the
throne. They are regarded as the natural heirs to

the Sheykhat, and Ibn Rashid's does not look like a
long life.

After this we mounted, and in another five
minutes were clear of the town. Then looking
back, we each drew a long breath, for Haïl with all
the charm of its strangeness, and its interesting
inhabitants, had come to be like a prison to us, and
at one time when we had had that quarrel with
Mohammed, had seemed very like a tomb.

We left Haïl by the same gate at which we had
entered it, what seemed like years before, but instead
of turning towards the mountains, we skirted the
wall of the town and further on the palm gardens,
which are its continuation, for about three miles
down a ravine-like wady. Then we came out on the
plain again, and at the last isolated group of ithel
trees, halted for the last time to enjoy the shade,
for the sun was almost hot, before joining the
pilgrim caravan, which we could see like a long line
of ants traversing the plain between us and the
main range of Jebel Shammar.

It was, without exception, the most beautiful
view I ever saw in my life, and I will try to
describe it. To begin with, it must be understood
that the air, always clear in Jebel Shammar, was
this day of a transparent clearness, which probably
surpasses anything seen in ordinary deserts, or in
the high regions of the Alps, or at the North
Pole, or anywhere except perhaps in the moon.
For this is the very centre of the desert, four

hundred miles from the sea, and nearly four
thousand feet above the sea level. Before us
lay a foreground of coarse reddish sand, the
washing down of the granite rocks of Jebel Aja,
with here and there magnificent clumps of ithel,
great pollards whose trunks measure twenty and
thirty feet* in circumference, growing on little
mounds showing where houses once stood—just as
in Sussex the yew trees do—for the town seems to
have shifted from this end of the oasis to where it
now is. Across this sand lay a long green belt of
barley, perhaps a couple of acres in extent, the
blades of corn brilliantly green, and just having
shot up high enough to hide the irrigation furrows.
Beyond this, for a mile or more, the level desert
fading from red to orange, till it was again cut by
what appeared to be a shining sheet of water
reflecting the deep blue of the sky—a mirage of
course, but the most perfect illusion that can be
imagined. Crossing this, and apparently wading in
the water, was the long line of the pilgrim camels,
each reflected exactly in the mirage below him with
the dots of blue, red, green, or pink, representing
the litter or tent he carried. The line of the
procession might be five miles or more in length;
we could not see the end of it. Beyond again rose
the confused fantastic mass of the sapphire coloured
crags of Jebel Aja, the most strange and beautiful

* We measured one, a pollard, thirty-six feet round the trunk
at five feet from the ground.

mountain range that can be imagined — a lovely vision.

When we had sufficiently admired all this, and I had made my sketch of it, for there was no hurry, we got on our mares again and rejoicing with them in our freedom, galloped on singing the Shammar song, " Ma arid ana erkobu delúl lau zeynoli shedadeha, biddi ana hamra shenûf, hamra seriyeh arruddeha," a proceeding which inspired them more than any whip or spur could have done, and which as we converged towards the Haj caravan, made the camels caper, and startled the pilgrims into the idea that the Harb Bedouins were once more upon them. So we went along with Mohammed following us, till we reached the vanguard of the Haj, and the green and red banner which goes in front of it. Close to this we found our own camels, and soon after camped with them, not ten miles from Haïl in a bit of a wady where the standard was planted.

Our tents are a couple of hundred yards away from the Haj camp, which is crowded together for fear of the dangers of the desert. The pilgrim mueddins have just chanted the evening call to prayers, and the people are at their devotions. Our mares are munching their barley, and our hawk (a trained bird we bought yesterday for six mejidies of a Bedouin at Haïl), is sitting looking very wise on his perch in front of us. It is a cold evening, but oh how clean and comfortable in the tent !

February 2.—It appears after all that only about
half the Haj left Haïl yesterday. There has been a
difficulty about camels some say, others that Ibn
Rashid will not let the people go, an affair of money
probably in either case. So we had hardly gone
more than two miles before a halt was ordered by
the emir el-haj, one Ambar, a black slave of Ibn
Rashid's, and the camels and their riders remained
massed together on a piece of rising ground for the
purpose we think of being counted. The dervishes,
however, and other pilgrims on foot went on as
they liked, and so did we, for we do not consider
ourselves bound by any of the rules of the Haj
procession, and Abdallah has orders to march our
camels well outside the main body. There was no
road or track at all to-day, and we went forward on
the look-out for water which we heard was somewhere on ahead, crossing some very rough ground
and wadys which were almost ravines. We have
become so used to the desert now, that from a long
distance we made out the water, guessing its
position from the white colour of the ground near
it. The whiteness is caused by a stonelike deposit
the water makes when it stands long anywhere;
and in this instance it lay in a sort of natural
reservoir or series of reservoirs in the bed of a
shallow wady. These must have been filled some
time during the winter by rain, and we hurried on
to fill our goat skins at them while they were still
clean, for the pilgrims would soon drink up and

pollute them. They are but small pools. We found
Awwad already there, he having been sent on in
front with a delúl to make sure of our supply, and
the process of filling the skins was hardly over
before the dervishes who always march ahead of the
Haj began to arrive. They have an unpleasant
habit of washing in the water first, and drinking it
afterwards, which we are told is part of their
religious ritual.

The wind has been very violent all day with a
good deal of sand in it, but it has now gone down.
Our course since leaving Haïl has been east by
north, and is directed towards a tall hill, Jebel
Jildiyeh, which is a very conspicuous landmark.
Our camp to-night is a pleasanter one than yesterday's, being further from the pilgrims, and we have
a little wady all to ourselves, with plenty of good
firewood, and food for the camels.

February 3.—Though fires were lit this morning
at four o'clock as if in preparation of an early start,
no move has been made to-day. Half the pilgrimage they tell us is still at Haïl, and must be waited
for. Wilfrid went to-day into the camp to find our
friend Ali Koli Khan, but neither he nor Abd er-Rahim, nor anyone else he knew had arrived.

The Persian pilgrims, though not very agreeable
in person or in habits (for they are without the sense
of propriety which is so characteristic of the Arabs),
are friendly enough, and if we could talk to them,
would, I dare say, be interesting, but on a superficial

comparison with the Arabs they seem coarse and
boorish.　They are most of them fair complexioned,
and many have fair hair and blue eyes; but their
features are heavy, and there is much the same
difference between them and the Shammar who
are escorting them, as there is between a Dutch
cart-horse and one of Ibn Rashid's mares.　In spite
of their washings, which are performed in season and
out of season all day long, they look unutterably
dirty in their greasy felt dresses, as no unwashed
Arab ever did.　Awwad and the rest of our people
now and then get into disputes with them when
they come too near our tents in search of firewood,
and it is evident that there is no love lost between
Persian and Arab.

My day has been spent profitably at home re-
stuffing my saddle, which was sadly in want of it.
Mohammed has become quite himself again, no airs
or graces of any kind, and, as he says, the air of
Haïl did not agree with him.　He seems anxious
now to efface all recollection of the past, and has
made himself very agreeable, telling us histories connected with the Sebaa and their horses, all of them
instructive, some amusing.

February 4.—Another day's waiting, the pilgrims
as well as we ourselves impatient, but impatience is
no good.　Wilfrid, by way of occupying the time,
went off on a surveying expedition by himself, with
his mare and the greyhounds.　He went in a straight
line northwards, towards a line of low hills which

are visible here from the high ground. They are
about twelve miles off. He met nobody except a
couple of Bedouins on delûls, going to Atwa, where
they told him there is a well. They looked on him
and his gun with suspicion, and did not much like
being cross-questioned. After that he found the
desert absolutely empty of life, a succession of level
sandy plains, and rough ridges of sandstone. The
hills themselves, which he reached before turning
back, were also of yellow sandstone, weathered
black in patches, and from the top of the ridge he
could make out the Nefûd, like a red sea. He
galloped to the ridge and back in three hours.
The ride was useful, as it enabled him to get the
position of several of the principal hills, Yatubb,
Jildiyeh, and others, and to mark them on his chart.
He did not say where he intended to go, but as it
happened, he returned before there was time for me
to become anxious.

In the meanwhile, Awwad and Abdallah had been
giving the falcon a lesson with a lure they have
made out of one of the nosebags. The bird seems
very tame, and comes to Awwad when he calls it,
shouting "Ash'o, ash'o," which he explains is the
short for its name, Rasham, a corruption of the word
rashmon, which means shining like lightning. We
may hope now with Rasham's assistance to keep
ourselves supplied with meat, for hares are in plenty.

In the afternoon visitors came, some Shammar
Bedouins of the Ibn Duala family, who have

preferred to camp beside us, as more congenial
neighbours to them than the Persians.   They are on
their way from Haïl to their tents in the Nefûd with
a message from the Emir that more camels are
wanted ; and they are going on afterwards with the
Haj as far as Meshhed Ali, or perhaps to Samawa
on the Euphrates, to buy rice (tummin), and wheat.
It is only twice a year that the tribes of Jebel
Shammar can communicate with the outside world ;
on the occasion of the two Haj journeys, coming and
going.   It is then that they lay in their provision
for the year.   The eldest of these Ibn Duala, a man
of sixty, is very well-mannered and amiable.   He
dined with Mohammed and the servants in their
tent, and came to sit with us afterwards in ours.
We are in half a mind to leave this dawdling Haj,
and go on with him to-morrow.   But his tents lie
some way to the left out of our road.

Besides the Ibn Dualas, there are some poor
Bedouins with their camels crouched down in our
wady to be out of sight.   They are afraid of being
impressed for the Haj, and at first it was difficult to
understand why, if so, they should have come so
close to it.   But they explained that they hoped to
get lost in the crowd, and hoped to have the advantage of its company, without having their camels
loaded.   They, like everybody else, are on their way
to Meshhed to buy corn.

There is a report that the Emir is coming from
Haïl to-morrow, and will travel three days with the

pilgrimage, going on afterwards, nobody knows where, on a ghazú. This would be tiresome, as now we have wished him good-bye we only want to get away.

February 5.—We have moved at last, but only another ten miles, to a larger wady, which seems to drain the whole country, and which they call Wady Hanasser (the valley of the little fingers), why so called I cannot say. Here there are numerous wells, and a large tract of camel pasture, of the sort called *rimh.* There are a good number of hares in this cover, and we have had some coursing with our greyhounds, aided by a sort of lurcher who has attached himself to us. The servants call him " Merzug," which may be translated a " windfall " literally a gift from God, an unattractive animal, but possessed of a nòse.

Two hours after starting we came to a curious tell standing quite alone in the plain. It is, like all the rest of the country now, of sandstone, and we were delighted to find it covered with inscriptions,*

* Mr. Rassam, who has been digging at Babylon, informs me that these inscriptions are in the ancient Phœnician character. It would seem that the Phœnicians, who were a nation of shopkeepers, were in the habit of sending out commercial travellers with samples of goods all over Asia; and wherever they stopped on the road, if there was a convenient bit of soft rock, they scratched their names on it, and drew pictures of animals. The explanation may be the true one, but how does it come that these tradesmen should choose purely desert subjects for their artistic efforts—camels, ostriches, ibexes, and horsemen with lances. I should have fancied rather that these were the work of Arabs, or of whoever

and pictures of birds and beasts of the sort we had already seen, but much better executed, and on a larger scale. The character, whatever its name, is a very handsome one, as distinct and symmetrical as the Greek or Latin capitals, and some of the drawings have a rude, but real artistic merit. They cannot be the work of mere barbarians, any more than the alphabet. It is remarkable that all the animals represented are essentially Arabian, the gazelle, the camel, the ibex, the ostrich. I noticed also a palm tree conventionally treated, but nothing like a house, or even a tent. The principal subject is a composition of two camels with necks crossed, of no small merit. It is combined with an inscription very regularly cut. That these things are very ancient is proved by the colour of the indentations. The rock is a reddish sandstone weathered black, and it is evident that when fresh, the letters and drawings stood out red against a dark back-ground, but now many of these have been completely weathered over again, a process it must have taken centuries in this dry climate to effect.

We were in front of the Haj when we came to this tell (Tell es Sayliyeh), and we waited on the top of it while the whole procession passed us, an hour or more. It was a curious spectacle. From the height where we were, we could see for thirty or forty miles back over the plain, as far as Jebel Aja,

represented the Arabs, in days gone by, anyhow of people living in the country. But I am no archæologist.

at the foot of which Haïl lies. The procession, three miles long, was composed of some four thousand camels (nor was this the whole Haj), with a great number of men on foot besides. In front were the dervishes, walking very fast, almost running; wild dirty people, but amiable, and quite ready to converse if they know Arabic; then, a group of respectably dressed people walking out of piety, a man with an immense blue turban, we believe to be an Afghan; a slim, very neat-looking youth, who might be a clerk or a shopkeeper's assistant, reading as he walks a scroll, and others carrying leather bottles in their hands containing water for their ablutions, which they stop every now and then to perform. Sometimes they chant or recite prayers. All these devotees are very rude to us, answering nothing when we salute them, and being thrown into consternation if the greyhounds come near them lest they should be touched by them and defiled. One of them, the youth with the scroll, stopped this morning at our fire to warm his hands as he went by, and we offered him a cup of coffee, but he said he had breakfasted, and turned to talk to the servants, his fellow Mussulmans, but the servants told him to move on. Among Arabs, to refuse a cup of coffee is the grossest offence, and is almost tantamount to a declaration of war. The Arabs do not understand the religious prejudices of the Shiyite Persians.

Some way behind these forerunners comes the *berak,*

or banner, carried in the centre of a group of mounted dromedaries magnificently caparisoned and moving on at a fast walk. These most beautiful creatures have coats like satin, eyes like those of the gazelle, and a certain graceful action which baffles description. Not even the Arabian horse has such a look of breeding as these thorough-bred camels. They are called *naamiyeh,* because one may go to sleep while riding them without being disturbed by the least jolting.

The berak, Ibn Rashid's standard, is a square of purple silk with a device and motto in white in the centre, and a green border. It is carried by a servant on a tall dromedary, and is usually partly furled on the march. Ambar, the negro emir el-Haj, generally accompanies this group. He has a little white mare led by a slave which follows him, and which we have not yet seen him ride.

After the berak comes the mass of pilgrims, mounted sometimes two on one camel, sometimes with a couple of boxes on each side, the household furniture. The camels are the property of Bedouins, mostly Shammar, but many of them Dafir, Sherârat, or Howeysin. They follow their animals on foot, and are at perpetual wrangle with the pilgrims, although, if they come to blows, Ibn Rashid's police mounted on dromedaries interfere, deciding the quarrel in a summary manner.

A Persian riding on a camel is the most ridiculous sight in the world. He insists on sitting astride, and seems absolutely unable to learn the ways and habits of the creature he rides; and he talks to it with his falsetto voice in a language no Arabian camel could possibly understand. The jokes cut on the Persians by the Arabs never cease from morning till night. The better class of pilgrims, and of course all the women except the very poor, travel in *mahmals* or litters—panniers, of which a camel carries two—covered over like a tradesman's van with blue or red canvas. One or two persons possess *tahteravans*, a more expensive kind of conveyance, which requires two mules or two camels, one before and one behind, to carry it. In either of these litters the traveller can squat or even lie down and sleep. The camels chosen for the mahmals are strong and even-paced; and some of these double panniers are fitted up with a certain care and elegance, and the luxuries of Persian rugs and hangings. A confidential driver leads the camel, and servants sometimes walk beside it. One of the pilgrims keeps a man to march in front with his narghileh, which he smokes through a very long tube sitting in the pannier above. There are a few horses, perhaps about half a dozen. One, a white Kehîlan Harkan, was bought the other day by a rich pilgrim from a Shammar Bedouin of the escort. This horse seems to be thoroughbred as far as can be judged from his head, tail, and pasterns; the rest of him is hidden by a huge *pallan*, or pack-saddle, with trappings, in which his new owner rides him. I have seen no others worth mentioning.

The whole of this procession defiled before us as we sat perched on the Tell es Sayliyeh just above their heads.

THE MECCAN PILGRIMAGE LEAVING HAÏL.

8
Charles Huber, 1883-4

Charles Huber of Alsace has been described by
Victor Winstone (in *Captain Shakespear*) as "the
greatest explorer of them all", but his writings
have never been translated from French before the
present volume appeared, and neither he nor Julius
Euting finds a mention in the index of Jacqueline
Pirenne's *À la découverte de l'Arabie* (Paris, 1958).

Huber, who had become accustomed to Arab society
and manners in Syria, was commissioned by the
French Ministry of Education to explore Najd as
thoroughly as possible. A naturalist by vocation,
he became an archaeologist by force of circumstance
and growing enthusiams. He arrived in al-Jawf from
Damascus late in May 1878, and on 1 June set out
across the Nafud to Ha'il. He reached Jubbah from
the Shakik wells in seventy-six hours, eleven fewer
than Wallin's record. Guarmani said he had taken
no more than fifty hours, whereas Palgrave admitted
to eighty-five.

Muhammad ibn Rashid, encamped at Umm al-Dulbhan
on the desert edge, received Huber's transparent
repetition of the Muslim profession of faith, and
supported the French Alsatian to the end.

Huber's first travels are described in contributions entitled 'Voyage dans l'Arabie Centrale:
Hamad, Šammar, Qacim, Hedjaz' in the *Bulletin de la
Société de Géographie* (Paris), vol.5, 1884, pp.
468-530 and vol.6, 1885, pp. 92-148; and 'Inscriptions recueillies dans l'Arabie Centrale, 1878-1882'
ibid., vol.5, 1884, pp. 289-363. These touch only

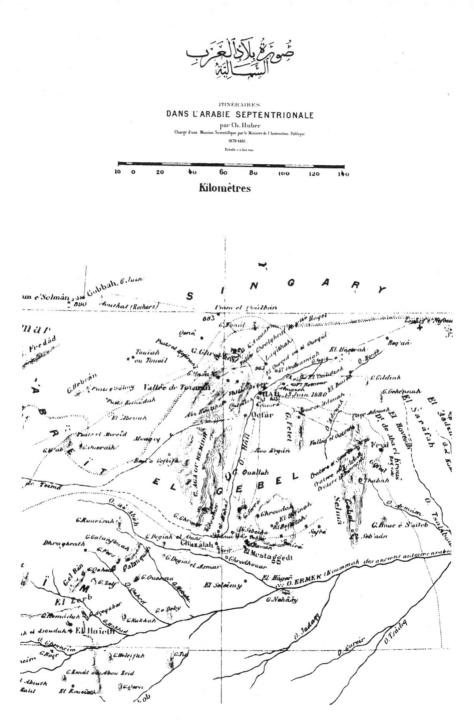

صورة بلاد العرب
السمالية

ITINÉRAIRES
DANS L'ARABIE SEPTENTRIONALE
par Ch. Huber
Chargé d'une Mission Scientifique par le Ministre de l'Instruction Publique
1879-1881.

Echelle 1:2.500.000

10 0 20 40 60 80 100 120 140

Kilomètres

in passing on Ha'il and the Jabal Shammar. But
when Huber returned to Najd the following year with
Julius Euting, they stayed at Ha'il for some time.
I have thought it opportune to abridge Huber at
points, for many of his comments are outdated,
trivial or repetitious: Euting is by far the more
vivid narrator.

On Sunday 21 October 1883, Huber records departing from his overnight camp at 5 a.m. in a S.S.E.
direction, arriving at 7.30 a.m. to a reception by
the Amir Hamud al-ᶜUbaid, Majid, and everyone else
of consequence: 'nothing could have been better'.
It had rained for the first time that season during
the night and, as it coincided with the party's
arrival, they were credited with having brought the
rain with them. Huber notes: 'The Amir kept me at
his palace until about noon, and then had me taken
to the house I was to occupy, which Mahmud had already arranged. It is one of the finest houses in
the Mashhadis' quarter'.

Between 22-25 October Huber made and received
courtesy calls. On the morning of the latter, the
Amir visited Huber from 9 to 10, saying that he was
about to leave on a *ghazu*, or raid, and asking
whether Huber would like to take part. Storm-clouds
appeared in the area at 5 p.m. and it rained. At
10.30 p.m. the storm broke over Ha'il. The following
is a selective translation of Huber's diary from 26
October 1883 to 23 January 1884, when Huber left
Ha'il, based on pages 61-209 of the *Journal d'un
Voyage en Arabie* published in a limited edition at
the Imprimerie Nationale (Paris, 1891). It may
strike the reader as strange that his companion
Euting is never mentioned.

26 Oct. Mid-day altitude of the Sun: $99°39'10"$.
Temperature: $+30°$; barometer: 675 mills. Truffles.
They are generically called *qima'* in the mountains.
The little red truffles are called *jiba'*, the white
truffles are known as *zubaidi* or *baluh*, and the

smallest, often found in clusters of three or four,
are called *hubar*. The first truffles appear about
a month after the October or November rains, and
the period during which they grow, lasting about
fifty days, is known as *al-wasm*. Truffles in the
Ha'il region are found on the plain between the
mountains of Futaiqa and Salma', in the Jabal Sarra,
between the Jabal Tuwal and the Jabal Aja' (before
the Nafud), but the largest and most numerous are
in the region of Hijr (near the wells of al-Jil and
Shubrun) and in Adhafir and Salman. The truffles
found in the Nafud are red and have a slight smell.
Truffles as large as a camel's head are said to be
found in the region of Abu Khuwaimah, between Salman
and Samawa. Hamud explained that Abu Khuwaimah is
a rocky area which receives and retains a good quantity of rainwater: not a *sha'ib*, nor a *ghadir*, but a
thaghab. When truffles are plentiful they are sold
in Ha'il for 1 piastre the *sa^c*, and when the harvest
is meagre they can fetch up to 4 or 5 piastres the
sa^c.

In Ha'il the truffles are peeled, washed, boiled
in water, and eaten with bread or rice. In the
desert, if the nomads have no cooking-pan, they
throw the truffles into the hot ashes, and eat them
with bread. In Ha'il, those not eaten at once are
cut into slices for drying and keeping, but then
lose some of their quality.

Today my camels have been taken away for several
days: their herd will be ^{c}Ayyad at-Tumi. 27 Oct.
Mid-day altitude of the Sun: 99°0'0". Temperature:
+34°; barometer: 676 mills. Knowing that the Amir
is preoccupied with his *ghazu*, I had avoided a meeting for two days but, realising that he was soon to
depart, I requested at noon an audience for this
same evening. At 4 p.m. Hamud called to say that I
had been invited to dine.

At dinner the Amir is charming. He tells me
that he will be away no more than ten days, and in

my presence instructs Sulaiman (brother of his
mother), Salih ar-Rakhis, Sulami and ^cAnaibar to
cater to my every need during his absence. He adds
that he will leave at dawn tomorrow.

28 Oct. Mid-day altitude of the Sun: 98°29'30".
Temperature: +32°; barometer: 676 mills. Very clear.
29 Oct. At Ha'il, the north-east wind is called an-
Nisri (from the star an-Nisr, reddish in colour),
the south-east wind Janub [*lit.* 'south', Ed.], the
south-west al-Mansha', and the northwest ash-Shami
['the Syrian', Ed.]

31 Oct. Excursion to Jabal ^cAqda. Depart at 9.35
a.m.; arrive 10.45 at the entrance of ^cAqda. 11.10.
Stop at the spring called ^cAin al-^cUwaimar. 11.25
on the move again, N. 84° W., then at 11.31 S.W.,
and 11.41 N. 85° W. through the pass sixty feet long,
built by ^cUbaid. 11.50 at the Amir's castle, the
keys to which he had given me. A tree common in the
^cAqda zone is the *qarriah*. Its wood is white both
inside and out, and it looks rather like a fig tree.
Its fruit, the *qurri*, is red and it too resembles
a fig.

November 1883

1 Nov. Climbing Jabal Far^ca. At 9.45 I left the
Amir's castle of ^cAqda and by 10.25 entered the
ravine which carries the Far^ca waters towards ^cAqda.
At 10.40 I rested by four palm-trees collectively
known as al-Khashaibah. The bed of the mountain
stream is covered with huge blocks of granite which
make progress difficult. Under one such block the
stream has hollowed out a beautiful pond, survivor
of the last rains: the water is cool and very welcome. 10.50 continued, arriving at 11.30 at a
passage obstructed by daunting boulders behind a
small plateau fifty metres long and 5-6 metres wide,
the whole called al-Jaziyah. Through al-Jaziyah at
11.35, then a descent of 40 metres into a small

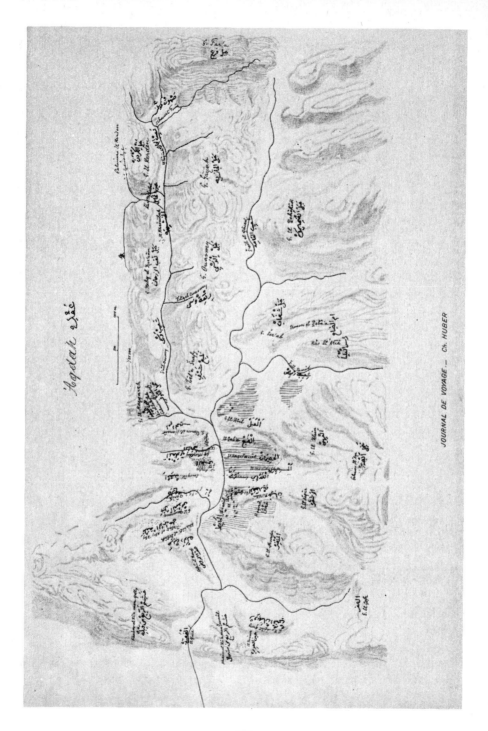

valley called Sahwat Fawwaz. Rest at 11.45, then
climbing again, arriving at the summit of Jabal
Far^{c}a at 12.50. After taking numerous compass
bearings we descended at 2.30. At 3.25 ^{c}Ain al-
Muhabil on our right, below Jabal al-Kardan. About
100 metres below the crest of the Far^{c}a we find
three hollows full of rainwater. I'm very relieved,
because I've lost my voice. Rest from 3.30 to 3.38.
At 4.30 we are back at al-Khashaibah, and at 5.14
at the Amir's castle of ^{c}Aqda. 2 Nov. On the subject of the ravine leading to Jabal Far^{c}a, one of
guides, ^{c}Abdullah, tells me that the rock walls
were originally straight, and the path of the mountain stream clear and direct; but, during the Flood,
Noah's Ark sailed above the Jabal Aja' and knocked
off the highest peaks into the ravine below, de-
forming it and filling it with blocks.

While one is still on the plains of Ha'il, and
before entering the Aja' massif, one sees about 1
km. to the right, a hill near the Aja' with a sharp
peak and gentle slopes, its brown face contrasting
with the black background of the massif. This is
Samra Dhaqaqa. Left of it, between the hill and the
massif, there is a tiny stream with a small natural
rainwater basin where rich Ha'ilis occasionally come
to picnic and take coffee before sunrise in the
Spring. After lunch I climbed Jabal al-Mandar, starting out from the Amir's castle at 1.30 and reaching
the summit at 1.41. I was back at the castle at
3.46. The population of ^{c}Aqda is about fifty, only
three of whom are at all wealthy, each with a fortune
of about 200 riyals. They have no camels to draw
water, and are consequently forced to hire camels
from the bedouin, who take their tribute in dates.
The marriage dowry for either a girl or a woman is
generally 2 riyals, but occasionally, 4, 6 or 8
riyals is paid, 10 being the maximum. Husbands do
not seek beauty or moral qualities in women but physical strength, for it is they who have to climb the
rocks for vegetation to be used as animal fodder, or
wood for fires. They carry their wares to Ha'il,

where they sell a load for 3 or 4 piastres, with which they buy the day's bread. Of all Arabia, it is my belief that it is at ʿAqda that the condition of women is at its lowest.

3 Nov. At 10.50 I left the castle to return to Ha'il, reaching the access to ʿAqda at 11.33, and the outskirts of Ha'il at 12.51. Last year, the Amir of Ha'il received as his 5% tax from ʿAqda a total of 70 camel-loads of dates: this year he has only *one* camel-load from them. The rocks near the entrance to Ha'il called Umm al-Masajid are the scene every year of the first morning prayer of the Great 'Id.

4 Nov. Cold and occasionally misty day. Fully occupied in house repairs. After the departure of the Amir and retainers on the *ghazu* the town appears quite lifeless.

5 Nov. Brought my journal up to date and cleaned my theodolite. Spent the night in astronomical observation. Shammaris returning from Mecca this morning say that there has been a great deal of rain over the desert north of Medina.

6 Nov. Another night spent in astronomical observation.

7 Nov. Mid-day altitude of the Sun: $92°0'40''$. Temperature: $+30°$; barometer: 678 mills. I receive a visit from Shaikh Muhammad ibn ʿAtiyah, chief of the Mu'izz, who has been here three days awaiting the Amir's return in order to persuade him to make a raid on the Huwaitat who have been persecuting his people for several years. I invite him to dinner tomorrow evening.

8 Nov. The sky is clearer than usual, but I missed making my noon observations because of the visit of Sulaiman. I prepare for an excursion to Jabal Jildiyah and think about setting out tomorrow. In the afternoon a visit from Mufarriq, whom I had asked to call so that I could let him know that Shaikh Muhammad would be my guest this evening. He shows

me his various wounds: a bullet in the right thigh,
spear-cuts in the right arm and the left shoulder,
and a smart sword-wound on the forehead above his
left eye. He adds philosophically: 'There is not a
single man serving the Amir who is still in one
piece'. *As-samaq*, at the end of Spring and beginning of Summer, is the recognised season for blood-
letting.

[On 9 November, Huber left Ha'il for Jabal Jildiyah,
spending several days on topographic surveying and
the copying of inscriptions reproduced in his
Journal. He returned to Ha'il at 5 p.m. on 16
November.]

17 Nov. The messenger sent by the Amir arrived at
Ha'il last night. The substance of his news seems
to be that the *ghazu* has failed. It appears that,
two or three days' ride south of the wadi, the
Shammar *ghazu* came on ten Mutair riders who were
probably part of a larger *ghazu*. Seven of the Mutair was captured and shot after they had killed
three Shammari horses; the other three Mutair were
able to warn just those tribes against whom ibn
Rashid had planned the raid - tribes were at that
time gathered in strength on a flat plain. They
saw the raiding Shammar from afar and had time to
get away with all their camels and some of their
flocks of sheep.

18 Nov. I receive a letter from Na'if ibn ^cAtiq,
Shaikh of Jubbah, replying to my request of twelve
days earlier asking him to obtain for me two *baqar
al-wahash*.

A visit in the afternoon from Muhammad ibn Bisis,
Shaikh of the Munt, owing allegiance to ibn Rashid.
His territories lie between Wadi Shara and near to
Sadus. He doubts whether a Christian could arrive
at Dorama without being killed. A little later, a
visit from Yusuf al-^cAtiq, brother of Nasr, the
Amir's secretary, who returned yesterday from al-
^cUla, where he had been to collect taxes. He saw

evidence of rainfall the whole way, proving that rain
has been widespread throughout Najd this year. The
sky is overcast all day, and the barometer has been
sinking since morning. At 5 p.m. the storm breaks
from the north and at 8 p.m. crashes with all its
force above Ha'il. Our main courtyard is suddenly
transformed into a lake.

19 Nov. It rained all night, causing two cracks in
the terrace wall. The water which fell in the plain
between Jabal Aja' and Ha'il forms a river that
floods through the town, transforming the Suq Mashhadi into a floodstream 70 cm. high. As always,
many terraces and walls have crumbled. Everyone is
jubilant, crying a perpetual *al-hamdu lillah!* The
second messenger, called an-Nattaf (literally, one
who warns the women to remove the veils they have
worn since their husbands left home, because they
are nearly home), arrived yesterday and announced
the Amir's arrival this morning. The *ghazu* party
had spent the night by the massif of Arkan, beyond
Qafar. At 9 a.m., the Amir and a few others, had
arrived on horseback at the Mashab, where a crowd
had collected to greet him. One after another they
approach, take his hand, offer *as-salamu ᶜalaikum,*
and then step back or sit on one of the stone wall-
benches. I arrive several minutes after the Amir,
who smiles when he sees me, and then I go to embrace
Hamud al-ᶜUbaid, Salih ar-Rakhis, and Sulaiman seated a little way off, near the castle gate.

At 9.30 the *bairaq* arrives with its escort and
roughly 200 riders on *daluls* (racing camels), who
have only to cross the square to reach home. The
Amir remains seated until 10 a.m., then enters the
palace. A fine rain falls the whole time.

20 Nov. The fine rain again falls from 8 to 10 a.m.,
but the sky is overcast all day. Here is the raid
narrative from the lips of Hamud al-Ibrahim:

Day 1 (28 Oct.) Departure from Ha'il before dawn.
        Night camp beyond Qafar.

Day 2 (29 Oct.) From Qafar, a short day's march to camp halfway between Jabal Sarra and Mustajiddah, on the territory called Qaᶜa-Harad.

Day 3 (30 Oct.) Near Mustajiddah.

Day 4 (31 Oct.) Near as-Sulaimi.

Day 5 (1 Nov.) Camped just this side of at-Tarfawi, a *sha'ib* on the way from al-ᶜAlim. The encampment took place 3 hours beyond al-ᶜAjajah.

Day 6 (2 Nov.) Camped 3-4 hours before an-Nuqrah.

Day 7 (3 Nov.) Camped near Jabal Khashm ar-Rik.

Day 8 (4 Nov.) Camped in the *sha'ib* Abu Mughair, where there are currently wells with good water. Left before sunset and marched throughout the night.

Day 9 (5 Nov.) Continued the march up to mid-day, when the *ghazu* encountered, near Jabal Qarnain, the Mutair, Hutaim, and the tribe of Bani ᶜAmr of ibn Hamud. Meal near Qarnain, then departure with the raid's booty to N.N.E., camping halfway between Karb and Qarnain at 4 p.m.

Day 10 (6 Nov.) Breakfast, then departure at sunrise. Night camp at 3 p.m. at al-Wabra, where the *ghazu* surprises another party of ad-Dawaiba, enemies belonging to the Bani ᶜAmr. Al-Wabra is one day's ride east of Karb, and possesses a well with good water. Departure an hour before sunset arriving after a forced march at al-Khadra a little after sunrise. One well, with very bitter water.

Day 11 (7 Nov.) On leaving al-Khadra, the Amir sends scouts to all points of the compass to reconnoitre for possible enemy camps. The Amir, and those without horses, stay within reach of al-Khadra. Eventual camp at Masrah al-Bal, 10 km. S.E. of al-Khadra.

Day 12 (8 Nov.) Departure after sunrise to camp just north of al-Khadra.

Day 13 (9 Nov.) Departure at sunrise to the south, arriving towards mid-day at a well called al-Kharb (a *sha'ib* between al-Khadra and Ruwailia). March from here over the Harrah (basaltic plateau) by way of two wells called as-Sasa, where the *ghazu* met and surprised another party of enemies: al-Khalawi, Mutair, and ʿUtaiba, all known generically as al-Khalaita. Passed the night near as-Sasa.

Day 14 (10 Nov.) Departure after first prayer to the N.W., arriving at mid-day at the only well of Ruwailia. Water very bitter. Half-hour's stay, then continued march till the ʿasr prayer, camping in the *sha'ib* roughly half-way between Ruwailia and al-Khadra.

Day 15 (11 Nov.) Departure after first prayer, stopping a little later in the small *sha'ib*, near the 15-20 wells of al-Kharb, where the noon meal was taken. After 1½ hours, en route northward arriving at 4.30 p.m. among the friendly ad-Duwaibi.

Day 16 (12 Nov.) Departure at sunrise. Camped at mid-day just before Karb. The first rain of the expedition fell at ʿasr.

Day 17 (13 Nov.) Departure at sunrise. Camped between Karb and Balagha 2 hours later. After a short stop there, another stop at 3 p.m. for prayer at Balagha. At sunset, camping for the night in a small *sha'ib*, where very heavy rains fell all night.

Day 18 (14 Nov.) Departure before sunrise immediately after the first prayer and no stop until 4 p.m., when the *ghazu* camped for the night halfway between the wadi and Balagha.

Day 19 (15 Nov.) Departure before sunrise, marching all day and camping for the night at Umm ar-Ruqaibah, just before the wadi.

Day 20 (16 Nov.) Departure after the first prayer. Two hours later a stop for lunch in the wadi. En route again 9-10 a.m., camping just before the *sha'ib* called al-Gharbia.

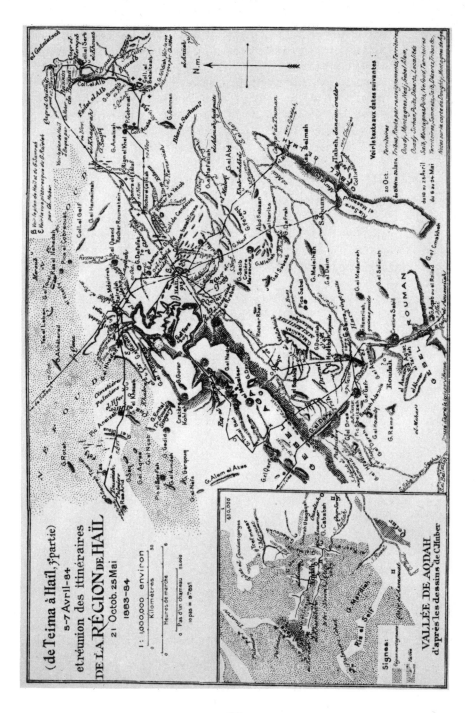

(de Teima à Haïl, 3ᵉ partie)
5-7 Avril-84
et réunion des itinéraires
DE LA RÉGION DE HAÏL
21 Octob. 25 Mai
1883-84

1 : 1,000,000 environ

Voir le texte aux dates suivantes :

VALLÉE DE AODAH
d'après les dessins de C.Huber

401

Day 21 (17 Nov.) Departure after the first prayer.
    March until mid-day, stopping for prayer on
    the territory known as Hamar, near Mustajid-
    dah, that is to say halfway between the Jabal
    Hamar and the Jabal Faghana. Then march from
    noon until ^{c}*asr* near ar-Rawda.
Day 22 (18 Nov.) Departure after sunrise. Camping
    at ^{c}*asr* near the massif of Arkan.
Day 23 (19 Nov.) Departure at sunrise and arrival
    at Ha'il at about 9 a.m.

The Shammar themselves contributed only 100 riders to the *ghazu*; the majority consisted of 1,000
allied riders, that is in addition to the *rajajil*,
or infantry. The victims had had time to save most
of their camels, losing only about a hundred, but
they had lost 5,000 to 6,000 sheep. In the evening
Shaikh Muhammad ibn ^{c}Atiyah comes to say goodbye;
he is returning to Tabuk with ^{c}Anaibar, who is collecting the *zakat* (religious tithe).

The plain between Jabal Tuwaiq and the Nafud is
called Hammada Tuwaiq. The eponymous mountain is
oriented N.E.E. to S.W.W. The petrified shells
brought today come from Jabal al-^{c}Abb, a hill between the Nafud and Jabal Tuwaiq.

I pass the evening in conversation with the Amir,
who describes the *ghazu* day by day, while I relate
my expeditions to ^{c}Aqda and Jabal Jildiyah. He enquires whether I have found any new springs. Talking of mountains, he mentions one whose peak is
higher than that of Jabal Far^{c}a, and quite inaccessible. This is a peak rising sheer from the plain
in the territory of al-Hamaliyah: its name is Jabal
Tummiyah.

21 Nov. The sky is still overcast, and the weather
cold and wet. In the evening, the Amir speaks at
length of a place called as-Salailiyah, between Faid
and Kahafah, to the west, with numerous inscriptions.

22 Nov. Mid-day altitude of the Sun: $84^{\circ}12'10''$.
Temperature: $+26^{\circ}$; barometer: 678 mills. Light mist.

23 Nov. Mid-day altitude of the Sun: 83°47'20".
Temperature: +26°; barometer: 674 mills. Very light
mist. In view of the heavy rains in the ᶜAqda district, the Amir has today given permission for the
inhabitants to sow corn, forbidden for the last six
years lest waters used for irrigation of the cornfields reduce the level of the wells in Ha'il.

Here are the names of the seasons and their duration in the Jabal Shammar:

al-Wasm	50 days
al-Murabbaᶜniyah	40 days
ash-Shubt	50 days
Bard al-ᶜUjuz	30 days
as-Saif	50 days
al-Qaid	50 days
Suhail	50 days

Then al-Wasm returns - the season now in progress.

24 Nov. Rain again last night. A storm raged over
the east, where a great deal of rain fell. Spent
the night in the Amir's winter *diwan (rawshan)*,
speaking of Sudair and Sadus; of the difficulty of
reaching them, and of the intolerance of the Wahhabis, condemned by the Amir.

26 Nov. I am caring for Ahmad ibn Juhaim, a rich
inhabitant of ᶜUnaizah, who is suffering from a
dangerous fever. Several days later I am laid low
by the fever, and can hardly write.

27 Nov. Still suffering, with severe headaches and
worse pain in my arms and legs. Two emissaries of
the Hajj arrive.

28 Nov. Still ill. The last two nights there has
been plentiful rain on Qafar. Today, storm and rain
at 3 p.m.

29 Nov. Still ill. The Hajj arrives. A violent
storm over Ha'il at 7, another at 9.30, and finally
a hailstorm at 10.30 p.m. Just after sunset, my
fever heightens, with delirium.

30 Nov. Still ill.

December 1883

1 Dec. Still feverish. No sun: it is cold and wet.
But I must nevertheless write several letters to
Europe. The hail of 29 November destroyed the
^cashab (grass) everywhere it struck.

3 Dec. My fever had almost subsided, and in the
afternoon I visited the Hajj market. No sooner was
I back home when the Amir had me summoned to discuss the political news from Europe brought by the
pilgrims, and also the rebellion which has cut communications between Mecca and Jiddah. Then about
the French (?) steamer reported to have touched
recently at Yanbu^c and al-Wajh. He also gives me a
stone found in the stomach of a *wabr*. Then he suggests a stroll around the stables, to examine some
of the horses. The Amir reiterates that I must ask
him for anything at all that I might need, and then
I leave by the Hamud Gate.

Hardly have I opened my front door when a gift
arrives from the Amir: an ivory-handled dagger for
which I had bargained with a pilgrim. The Amir had
ordered it to be purchased and given to me.

4 Dec. Sulaiman Mirza, son of Hassan Mirza, has
arrived with the Hajj from Medina, where he has
lived for a dozen years. He visits me this morning,
an extraordinary honour in the view of the Mashhadis
who are his fellow Shi^ca Muslims. Hassan Mirza is
still alive and residing at Mashhad: his fortune is
said to be 80,000 pounds. I feel a little better
today: the sun does me good.

8 Dec. Mid-day altitude of the Sun: $79°2'30''$. Temperature: $+21°$; barometer: 679 mm. Overcast sky.

9 Dec. Too misty to make astronomical calculations.
Fever recurs at noon, and lasts until 5 p.m.

10 Dec. No fever today. Evening as a guest of the

Amir. I request horses and men to visit Jabal Sarra
and around Jabal Aja' three or four days from now:
he promises to do everything in time. Then acrobatics and mime by some negroes, interrupted by the
arrival of the Shaikh ^cAbdullah the Khatib.

11 Dec. In al-Qasim, the corner of a courtyard, or
the whole of a small courtyard is used for ashes,
kitchen refuse and all other domestic trash. After
a certain time the whole is taken away, usually for
use as manure at seed-time. Here in Ha'il, by
contrast, the usual practice is to open a ditch in
the ground for garbage, then it is closed when full
and another is dug in another part of the courtyard.
It is only seldom when someone buys the refuse, for
there are few cornfields or barleyfields (the only
cultivation in Jabal Shammar), and that even those
are not sown when winters are dry.

12 Dec. Mid-day altitude of the Sun: $78^{\circ}17'50''$.
Temperature: $+19^{\circ}$; barometer: 678 m. Overcast sky.
Evening at the Amir's Palace. Hamud inveighs against paintings and drawings that Christians produce, and claims that they are strongly forbidden.
The Amir again speaks to me about his eyes and
liver. He urges me to delay my departure until
after the arrival of Amir Hassan Muhanna, due in
two or three days from Buraidah. I should do
better, instead of leaving for Qafar and Qasr, to
go with him northward, and staying with him five
or six days. I should give him pleasure, he says,
and I too should probably find it relaxing.

13 Dec. After the ^casr prayer and the *majlis*
gathering, I visit the Amir. He complains bitterly
about trying to govern the beduin who are all, he
declares, both adults and children, devoid of intelligence and only come to the Amir when they are in
difficulty. He then tells me to accompany him to
visit ^cUmran ibn Said Musa, who arrived a few days
ago from Mecca, with about forty different kinds of
European goods: white cotton, cotton cambric, drugs,

405

candles, paraffin lamps, pottery, porcelain, glass, perfumes, and so on. We stay with ᶜUmran about half-an-hour, then, as sunset approaches, the Amir returns to the palace. Throughout the recent Ramadhan, the Amir was on a campaign in the south against the Al Saᶜud, so he was unable to fast: he thus began his delayed fast some days ago. In the morning a Sharari, sent by Juhar, announces the presence in the north-east of an ᶜAnaizah raiding party. In the evening, the Amir dispatches ᶜAid, head camel-keeper, with his men to east and north east, to warn all the tribes in the area and to cut off the *ghazu's* progress if possible.

14 Dec. Yesterday and today the weather has become milder. At 3 o'clock the sky darkens and at 5 some rain falls. After dusk, lightning strikes north of Ha'il. In the afternoon, the Amir rode out into the plain, where a *fantasia* was held, during which Majid fell from his horse. I note that when someone falls because his horse falls one says of the rider not 'waqaᶜa min ᶜala 'l-faras' but 'taqantara min ᶜala 'l-faras'. When a horse slips on wet ground, one says 'al-faras zalqat' and if it slips on a rocky surface one says 'al-faras saffahat'.

15 Dec. I still feel very ill, with some fever. Today the air is heavy, and the wind strong. The peaks of Jabal Aja' are covered with mist the whole day.

Spending the evening with the Amir, I heard that visitors have arrived in Ha'il from many directions: two Aslam Arabs have come with news of the ᶜAnaizah *ghazu*, and some Ruwala and Sinjara from the north, Majmaᶜa Arabs from the east, some Harb from the south, and a Ha'il Shammari arriving from Riyadh. The last had been kept prisoner by ibn Al Saᶜud for more than a year so that he could not warn Rashid of his raiding plans. Rain has not fallen in abundance anywhere but in the Shammar and the allied lands for the last six to seven days southward, and

for the last seven to eight days northward. The
Muntafiq lands have received the most rain, especially in the district around Jabal Suman.

16 Dec. Another bout of fever today. The sky remains leaden day and night, and Jabal Aja' still
covered in mist. Hamud tells me that when clouds
are found only on the very summit of the Aja', near
Qafar, at the point called Khashm ad-Dibl, rain will
certainly come to Ha'il city; but if the clouds are
somewhat left or right of this point, they will
drift east or north of Ha'il, and there will be no
rainfall in the city boundaries.

17 Dec. The weather is overcast again, and I remain feverish. A storm passes over the Jabal from
south to north between 6 and 8 o'clock. I spend the
evening with the Amir. The news there is of the
ᶜAwaji and the Hutaimi. Some time ago the ᶜAwaji,
also called the Muqataᶜa, of the Awlad Sulaiman, had
raided the Hutaim of ibn Sumairah, carrying off
hundreds of sheep and camels. Ibn Sumairah immediately took the road to Ha'il, to lay the charge
before the Amir. Two days later Mashal al-ᶜAwaji
arrived in Ha'il. Since the sheep had obviously
been eaten, the Amir reconciled them as best he
could. Returning home, ibn Sumairah learned that
twenty-odd camels from the ᶜAwaji were on their way
to the Red Sea port of al-Wajh to bring back corn
and rice. Ibn Sumairah intercepted the caravan on
its way back, and massacred the leaders. It is
usually the Sulaimat of Shaikh ᶜAsi ibn Shitaiwi
who carry out the caravan trade between the Awlad
Sulaiman and the Red Sea. During my first journey,
I passed a night with Mashal (and his two sons
ᶜAskar and Takhimr) at Taima. It is Takhimr who
suffers from elephantiasis.

18 Dec. The weather is threatening all day, and
all are hoping that *in sha' Allah* it will rain.
The Amir himself asked me last night if there was
going to be a great deal of rain. Storms broke
in many places in the vicinity of Ha'il, and in the

oasis city itself there were sudden showers. The
rains we have had so far, which have enabled grass
to emerge everywhere, are considered enough for an
ordinary year, but to make the year a good one we
should need two or three more storms as heavy as
those we have enjoyed already. The present rains
will provide enough forage for the Spring, but then
nothing. The best fodder, ^{c}ashab, will only grow
with more rain. It will grow in two months and will
last all Summer, reaching a height of 50-60 cms.,
when the weaker grass succumbs to the Summer heat.
The fodder-grass will be found, unless more rains
come, in the sandy earth or the sand itself, but
not in the granitic or basaltic rocks of the Jabal.

19 Dec. I leave Ha'il at 9.45 a.m. for a modest
excursion into Jabal Aja', accompanied by ^{c}Abdullah
al-Muslimani. We make for al-Maslukh, a barren out-
crop at the extreme edge of the massif. So far
proceeding N.N.W., we turn abruptly west, and then
see the ravine al-Maghawat, some 200 metres deep
and 30-40 metres wide. The first sign of life is
a group of forty-odd palms planted twenty years ago,
but seeming to be only ten years old, so feeble are
they. The ravine rises rapidly, but is blocked by
huge granite boulders from 15 to 20 cubic metres
each: no passage is possible by this route. Under
one of the nearest and largest of these boulders the
mountain cascade has hollowed out a *ghadir*, or pool,
which is always full after winter rains, and may
remain so for several months. I can hear the tric-
kle of a rivulet which ends in the *ghadir*, though
the latter does not overflow.
It is here that Amir Talal used to come on fine
Spring days for holidays of up to 10 or 20 days at
a time, bringing with him the whole court. Some
Ha'ilis still come here to picnic in Spring, even
though they have to bring their own firewood from
the city, or go to the trouble of picking it from
the upper rocks, since none can be found nearby.
We had brought charcoal with us to make coffee and
enjoy the hubble-bubble.

After coffee, we resumed our exploration of the valley westward. It took us just one hour from 12.45 to the upper part of the valley, called al-Maghawat al-Fuqah. Never more than 100 metres wide, the valley occasionally narrows to 20 metres. Not only is there no path, but the ascent is actually dangerous, and I cannot imagine how the landowners gather their dates and take them home. In certain places the fall of rocks is indescribable.

Wherever the rockfall has spared a few square metres one or more palm-trees has been planted. In three places, where there are open spaces of 100 to 150 square metres, enchanting palm groves have been laid out. The grass is relatively thick, and the palms are grouped charmingly, often in a ring. At al-Maghawat al-Fuqah the valley broadens on both sides to form a triangle, and it is there that the greatest number of palm-trees are found.

There are no inscriptions whatsoever in this area, if one discounts a camel-rider brandishing a lance. The descent takes 42 minutes.

The palms, called Sharatin after their owners, total about 350, of which roughly two thirds are in the upper valley. The Abu ash-Shartan (literally 'those who make palm-fibre rope') live in the village of al-Wasitah, with ten houses and fifteen families.

At 4.35 we start back for Ha'il, arriving at 5.50.

20 Dec. After the asr prayer I visit the Amir. Three Arabs of the Majma'a bring news of the situation in their area, south-east of Ha'il. 'Abdullah ibn Al Sa'ud is ill, and has received nobody for several days. The rain has been very infrequent near them. Then a messenger arrives from Hassan Muhanna of Buraidah, announcing that the Amir is due in Ha'il tomorrow. Muhammad ibn Rashid tells me of news from the Sinjari (currently in the north) about the $ghazu$ made by the 'Anaizah against the Tuman and

Sinjari, near Jumaimah. Ten men of the Shammar have
been killed (among them four *shuyukh*), and three
horses lost. The ^{c}Anaizah are said to have lost
eight men and fourteen horses out of the 160 on the
raid.

21 Dec. At 8.30 a.m. Amir Hassan of Buraidah makes
his official entry, preceded by the Ha'il Amir's
secretary, Nasr al-^{c}Atiq, and Fahd, both on horseback. Amir Hassan rides a racing-camel, as do his
eight retainers. He brings an Omani racing-camel
and two horses as gifts.

Four of the chief Sharari *shuyukh* have also arrived this morning, bringing a dozen riders with
the Amir's *zakat*, or taxes.

A banquet in the evening at Salim al-^{c}Ubaid's,
for he is marrying today for the first time. Hamud,
Majid and Salim are charming. After the banquet
there is a reception at the Amir's, where Hassan
Muhanna is also found. There is a good deal of
discussion about Sadus and its famous column, and
then the conversation passes to the history of the
Shammar region, and the Amir reminisces about the
occupation of Ha'il by Khurshid Pasha. Storms over
the entire Jabal at 10 p.m.

22 Dec. Here is the genealogy of the Rashid family.
^{c}Ali ar-Rashid, of the tribe of Khalil, of the
^{c}Abdah, had two sons, ^{c}Abdullah and ^{c}Ubaid. ^{c}Abdul-
lah married the daughter of Muhammad al-^{c}Ali, his
relative, and governor of Jabal Shammar under the
authority of ibn Al Sa^{c}ud. He had three sons:
Talal, Mit^{c}ab and Muhammad.

Talal died in Safar 1283 after Hijra (16 May
1866-5 May 1867) and left these sons: Bandar (killed by Muhammad in 1289=1872/3); Badr (killed by
Muhammad in 1289); Sultan (killed by Muhammad in
1289); Maslat (killed by Muhammad in 1289);
^{c}Abdullah and Nahar (both killed by Muhammad in
1293=1876/7); and Na'if, who was killed by accident
in a fantasia in 1298 (=1880-1), and left a son.

Mitʿab was assassinated at the age of 35 by Bandar on 20 Ramadan 1285 (=1868/9) and left a son, ʿAbdulʿaziz.

Muhammad is the present Amir, born in 1289 (= 1872/3); he is childless. Zaid, son of Talal, died of an illness in 1288 (1871/2) at the age of 21, one year before Bandar and Badr.

ʿUbaid died in 1286 (=1869/70), a year after Mitʿab, aged about 80. His sons were: Sulaiman, who died aged 22; Hamud; ʿAli, who died aged 30; Fahd, born in 1845 who is insane; Faid, born in 1855; another Sulaiman, who died aged 20 in 1882; and ʿAbdullah, born in 1862. The eldest surviving son of ʿUbaid, Hamud, has the following sons: Majid, Salim, Sultan, ʿUbaid, Saʿud and Muhanna.

ʿAli, the father of ʿAbdullah and ʿUbaid, used to occupy a large estate at al-Wasitah.

ʿAbdullah had taken to wife the daughter of Muhammad al-ʿAli, governor of the Jabal; nevertheless relations between the two families became very strained, and ʿAli's two sons considered it politic to leave their home and take refuge in the Jabal Aja'. They used to come down at night to visit one of their female relatives at Ha'il for a meal. This course of action continued for some time, but as Muhammad ʿAli caused his son-in-law and ʿUbaid to be watched, the device was discovered and men were placed at night to trap them as they entered the city. One night, after the last prayer, ʿAbdullah was seized as he entered Ha'il by a negro called Khairallah, one of Muhammad ʿAli's close confidants. Khairallah had gripped ʿAbdullah by the neck, and was dragging him to the Amir, when ʿAbdullah drew out his dagger in the darkness and buried it in the negro's belly, then escaped.

Following these events, Muhammad ʿAli invited his relative ʿAli to leave the environs of Jabal Shammar, and the whole family went into the desert, finally seeking refuge at Hillah, in Iraq, where they passed two years. He was a man of energy and intelligence, who quickly gained the confidence of the Pasha, had soon been entrusted with lucrative positions and had amassed large funds. According to others, he had left Hillah in haste, taking with him the funds with which he had been entrusted. In short, from Hillah he made his way to Riyadh, then ruled by Saʿud Abu Faisal, who made ʿAli as welcome as befitted one of the most influential families of Jabal Shammar. Some time afterwards, Saʿud sent his son Faisal on a raid in al-Hasa, and with him ʿAbdullah, whose military and political qualities were recognised.

The *ghazu* were resting roughly halfway to al-Hasa, when one evening a rider arrived with a letter for ʿAbdullah. Written by one of his confidants who had remained behind at Riyadh, the letter announced that Abu Thunayyan, a cousin of the Amir, had assassinated the Amir and usurped his throne. ʿAbdullah immediately disclosed the contents of the letter to Faisal. They agreed to keep the new secret, announcing instead that the Amir had written to them to stop the *ghazu* and return immediately to Riyadh. This precaution was necessary, because if they had made known the contents of the letter, at least half of the raiding party would have dispersed to their respective tribes.

Returning to Riyadh, they naturally found the gates closed. For several days they exchanged desultory gunfire, but as the beduin with them were beginning to desert Faisal and ʿAbdullah, ʿAbdullah resolved to carry out a bold plan. One night he approached the castle where the usurper lived and threw some pebbles through a window which he knew separated him from one of his friends, Suwaid. ʿAbdullah made himself known to Suwaid and asked, "Are we still friends? May I count on you?"

"As on yourself," replied Suwaid. "Come back tomorrow night at the same hour, and I shall let you in."

^{C}Abdullah exultantly told Faisal of his success, and since Faisal trusted Suwaid no less than did ^{C}Abdullah, they picked out twenty faithful friends and agreed to meet them the following evening. They scaled the wall with rope and ladders and, with the first six friends, climbed on to one of the castle terraces. A few slaves were alerted by the noise, but in the darkness it was difficult to tell friends from enemies, and the usurper's retainers fell, some killing each other. At a certain moment ^{C}Abdullah was unable to draw his sword, and seized an enemy from behind. This was Abu Thunayyan's favourite slave, a huge man of great strength who withstood the attack from behind and tried to hack at ^{C}Abdullah's dagger with his sword. ^{C}Abdullah shouted to Faisal to come towards him in the dark and kill the man he was holding. Faisal leapt towards him and, grasping flesh without being able to see it, asked: "Is this your stomach that I'm holding?" "No," answered ^{C}Abdullah, and Faisal ripped the bodyguard's belly from side to side. This was Abu Thunayyan's last surviving trusty, and when the lights were lit, Abu Thunayyan himself was found hiding under a staircase. His throat was cut immediately, and Faisal restored to the throne of his forefathers.

It can be understood that Faisal was anxious to reward ^{C}Abdullah's loyalty with the governorship of Jabal Shammar, but asked him to wait until the incumbent should come to Riyadh (which he did once every two years) and, in the meantime, ^{C}Abdullah should attend to his wounds.

A year later Salih ibn Muhammad al-^{C}Ali, governor of the Jabal, came to Riyadh, duly bringing Faisal ibn Sa^{C}ud tribute and presents. Faisal did not wish to antagonise Salih, so allowed him to retain his powers, while giving equal powers to ^{C}Abdullah, in the dilemma of having to keep his word.

The two governors travelled together, and

arrived together in Ha'il, but ʿAbdullah was not a man to relish sharing authority, and amid rising discord, Salih finally decided to retire with his family to Buraidah. ʿAbdullah's arrival in Ha'il took place in 1246 [=1830-1. But E.C. Ross and others date the event to 1250 = 1834-5. Ed.] and it is therefore from that year that the ibn Rashid dynasty of Jabal Shammar is said to date. But he was not long to enjoy the fruits of his power struggle. Khalid, cousin of Faisal and son of Saʿud ibn Al Saʿud and a negress, obtained authority to invade Najd with troops. He was given a further 200 cavalry in Medina, and set out for the Jabal. Hearing of his approach, ʿAbdullah was caught with his men out in the desert and fled from Ha'il with ʿUbaid, seeking refuge at Jubbah with the father of Salih ar-Rakhis. So Khalid took Ha'il without bloodshed. Learning of ʿAbdullah's stratagem, Khalid sent three different assaults on Jubbah to surprise and seize the sons of ʿAli, but the attempts all failed because they were found out in advance.

After staying in Ha'il for three months, Khalid nominated ʿIsa ʿUbaidallah as Governor of Jabal Shammar, he being allied to the Rashid family. ʿUbaid had married ʿIsa's daughter, and it was she who gave birth to Faid who is still living [in 1883. Ed.]. After Khalid's departure, ʿAbdullah and ʿUbaid left Jubbah for Qafar; they had friends in the quarter of Suq Dabat al-ʿAyyadah there, but enemies in the Suq Dabat al-Khashmat. The friendly quarter joined forces with them and soon a war began between them and Ha'il, the other Qafari *aswaq* remaining neutral. This situation lasted two months.

One day a Ha'ili returned from Medina with the news that a fresh contingent of about 150 soldiers was about to leave Medina to reinforce Khalid's troops, and that there were only four or five days to spare.

^{c}Abdullah, who enjoyed considerable support in Ha'il, learnt the news the same day and that night left Qafar to visit the Ha'ili who had brought the intelligence. The latter said: 'If you want to know the truth, it is you and not Khalid whom the Turks want here; if you are wise, go straight to them, win them over, and you'll take possession of the Jabal once again.'

At once ^{c}Abdullah returned to Qafar and, after conferring with ^{c}Ubaid, left with two devoted men at sunrise to meet the Turkish soldiers. Next day he came across them near Mustajiddah. The Ha'ili had been right, and ^{c}Abdullah quickly sided with the Turks, sending one of his men back to tell ^{c}Ubaid about the happy outcome. ^{c}Ubaid did not wait until ^{c}Abdullah's return but made straight away for Ha'il with his followers, establishing them in the Lubdah quarter, which was on his side. Without delay they attacked the Amghidah quarter, which supported ^{c}Isa ^{c}Ubaidallah. ^{c}Ubaid's chief ally in Suq Lubdah was Muhammad al-^{c}Ali, Shaikh of Lubdah, who was allied with the powerful tribe of al-Quraish as well as with the Zamil and Salamah. Many shots were fired (a few falling within the castle precincts), and a few men fell on both sides, while a few houses were looted, but eventually the day was won by ^{c}Ubaid, who now planned to attack the castle. But a voice was heard high on a terrace saying that they could enter the castle without opposition: all the inhabitants, including the Governor, had abandoned the castle at 9 p.m.

When ^{c}Abdullah arrived with his soldiers later that day he found the mission accomplished, and took possession of Ha'il for the second time. In escaping by night from Ha'il, ^{c}Isa ^{c}Ubaidallah had managed to get as far away as al-Qasim, where he found Khalid ibn Al Sa^{c}ud and not only described what had happened during the last few days, but also reported the news that a second force of infantry was due from Medina to reinforce his troops. Khalid decided to intercept these reinforcements en

route in order to divert their strength to himself,
so they set out immediately with a few loyal retainers. Once ʿAbdullah and ʿUbaid learnt of this fact,
they resolved to kidnap them, and ʿUbaid left for
the south with a small detachment. Near Jabal Salma
they were told that Khalid ibn Al Saʿud and ʿIsa
ʿUbaidallah had agreed to pass the night at as-Sulaimi. ʿUbaid's men descended on al-Sulaimi during
the middle of the night, killing all the enemy except for ʿIsa ʿUbaidallah, who was spared at the
intercession of his friend ʿAbdurrahman al-Jabr, who
was of ʿUbaid's party.

With the reinforcements from Medina, ʿAbdullah
made five or six raids on the Harb and the Hutaim
so profitable that he was able to keep all his promises to the soldiers who, barely four months after
their arrival, returned to Medina enriched with
money, horses and camels.

Hitherto, ʿAbdullah had lived in the former
palace belonging to Muhammad al-ʿAli in the Amghidah quarter. After the soldiers had finally left
for Medina, however, he bought the then palace of
Muhammad al-ʿAli, with the ground in front and the
gardens at the back, for a thousand riyals from the
women of the family of Muhammad, all the men having
been killed or pursued into exile. The palace as
we know it today did not yet exist, for it was begun by the soldiers who killed Muhammad al-ʿAli,
and taken up only three metres. Later on, Salih
ibn Muhammad al-ʿAli raised the palace to a height
of 8-10 metres and built rooms on the ground floor.
ʿAbdullah continued the additions, then Talal completed the palace as we see it now.

When ʿAbdullah had built this second palace, he
demolished the first in Amghidah, and planted a
palm-garden in its place, now called al-Jumishah.

ʿUbaid, ʿAbdullah's brother, who had done so
much towards the foundation of the dynasty, survived him, dying at about 80 or 82 in the year 1286

(=1869/70) still in full possession of his facult-
ies. Six months before his death he made a *ghazu*
on the Suqur, some ninety of whom had penetrated
as far as Yatib. The Suqur were surrounded, and
all but five were killed, the survivors managing to
escape.

During the fifth or sixth year of Talal's rule,
Medina made another attempt to seize the Jabal. A
hundred to a hundred and fifty soldiers arrived
without warning at Mustajiddah. Talal was for
leaving straight away to fight; but ᶜUbaid, anxious
to avoid confrontation with the Turks, persuaded
Talal to negotiate and he left for Medina with
Zamil, their bags full of riyals. They were totally successful in their shrewd negotiations, because
Medina summarily recalled their troops.

23 Dec. The sky is a little brighter today, and
I took the mid-day altitude of the Sun: 77° 36'10".
Temperature: +20°; barometer: 676 mills. Dinner
with the Amir.

24 Dec. Left Ha'il at 11 a.m. to return to al-
Maghawat. Salih ar-Rakhis assures me that the inscriptions sought during my last expedition should
be near a small hill, somewhat farther off than al-
Maghawat, called Turaif Mashar. Further left and
at the side there are four characters, but they are
illegible. The hill is of yellowish basalt exposed
on the east, and darker with beautiful striations
of violet on the west. Here is my route: 11.05.
At N. 60° W. reached the basalt hills which run in
a straight line from the Jabal Samra' to the Jabal
Aja'. Now a change of direction to N. 40° W. At
11.20 reach the cultivated area of at-Turaifi, formerly known as al-Huqs, which has been sown with
corn for about twenty years whenever the winters
have been wet. There is a score of palms. The
water is near enough to the surface, but there is
not much of it.

At 11.26 reached the second row of basalt hills,

parallel to the first, and struck out from there at
N.50° W. At 11.31 passed the hills and turned towards the summit of Jabal al-Maslukh at N. 30° W.
At 11.55 reached al-Maslukh and turned N. 60° W. to
the yellowish-tinted hill Turaif Mashar. At 12.22
reached the summit of Turaif Mashar, stopped to
copy the inscription and to search for more. Two
hundred metres before arriving, one passes a *talh*
tree about thirty years old, east of which is a
ditch measuring about 1 m. 50 by 0 m. 80, and between 0.30 and 0.40 metres deep. A story is told
at Ha'il about this ditch.

Five years ago, an inhabitant of Qana happened
to pass this way on his way to Ha'il just after the
time of the evening prayer (^{c}asr). At the foot of
the tree near the ditch he found two men who were
slaughtering a black goat. They called out rudely
to the man of Qana, asking him roughly what he
wanted. He answered that, in the manner of all
Arabs, he simply wanted to greet them with 'as-
salamu ^{c}alaikum'. He judged by their speech that
they were foreigners, and by their baggage that
they were wealthy. They gave him a morsel of the
meat and told him to continue on his way. The next
day, passing the same spot on the way home, the man
of Qana saw the ditch that I had observed, but deeper. He then realised that the two travellers he had
seen the day before had been Moroccans, well known
over the whole world as sorcerers and especially
skilled in the art of discovering hidden treasure.
Passing near the hill of Turaif Mashar, they had
read the inscription which had enabled them to find
and carry off the buried treasure from that spot.
Moroccans are attributed with the skill of being
able to decipher all inscriptions.

At 12.36 left Turaif Mashar S. 80° W. towards
the ravine of Tala^{c}at as-Sawiyan. At 12.52 camped
at the foot of the gorge. While ^{c}Abdullah was
lighting a fire to make coffee and heat the hubble-
bubble, I climb up the rocks hollowed out by a

waterfall, and discover some pools with water, near
which inscriptions were said to have been carved;
but I found nothing and I am sure there is nothing
there. After an hour and a half, we packed up to
return, arriving in Ha'il at 3.58. The Amir had
left Ha'il a little earlier than we, riding eastward with Amir Hassan and Hamud.

25 Dec. Christmas today, alas! The weather is
melancholy, dark and cold: the festival is far away
from here. My digestion has been very poor for
several days, and I eat almost nothing. If Amir
Hassan stays here much longer I shall die of starv-
ation. This morning witnessed the arrival of Rakan
ibn Hathlain, the great Shaikh of the ^{c}Ajman. After
^{c}asr, I go back to the Amir, who invites me to dine
and keeps me with him until 8 p.m. At 4 p.m. he
summoned the Sharari *shuyukh,* asking them if they
had reached a decision as to whether they preferred
to pay the *zakat* tax at Taima or at al-Jauf. Four
of the six preferred Taima, while the other two op-
ted for al-Jauf. The Amir listened to each one in
silence, then ruled in a few words that he was obliged to call them all to al-Jauf, where they would
be taxed together. Those choosing Taima protested
that the proximity of the Ruwala would cause them
problems, but the Amir relieved their anxiety, asserting that the Ruwala were under his control. He
summoned the Sharari to appear again before him the
following morning, when they would receive their
last instructions, provisions for the journey, and
a letter for Juhar, his governor in al-Jauf. I
noted that one of the Sharari *shuyukh* had addressed
him *'Ya, akhur Nura'* (brother of Nura, the name of
his sister married to Abdullah ibn Al Sa^{c}ud). This
was the first time I had heard an Arab called by the
name of his sister.

26 Dec. The day is cold and dark, with not a
ray of sunshine. After lunch I visit the Amir until
^{c}asr. ^{c}Aid, the Amir's chief camelherd, had returned after a few days' tour of inspection, and reported with great satisfaction that fodder is plentiful

and the camels are healthy. This year will be better than average in Jabal Shammar. Without rain
this Winter, the Amir would have been incapable of
making a single raid during the coming year.

After sunset, Barghash ibn Atwal, Shaikh of the
Aslam, arrived to report to the Amir that nine days
earlier he and the Aslam had been surprised by a
ghazu led by ^cAbdullah ibn Al Sa^cud. The latter,
however, had been pushed back with the loss of 25
men and 10 racing camels. The Aslam had lost only
two men and three camels.

27 Dec. The Amir summons me before sunrise through one of his retainers called Yaqut. I find him
alone in the *rawshan* with ^cAid, Subhan, and Nasr al-
^cAtiq. On my arrival he sends these three away and
starts speaking to me of a certain camel of mine
which is infected with satyriasis, and cannot recover enough to be used for at least three or four
months. Then he says that the excursion we had
planned together in Jabal Aja' cannot now take
place, because he is going on a raid from the 6th
or 7th of the coming month, and I can leave immediately after that. He asks me what my plans are,
and I describe them in detail. He opposes my project for Tabuk, which he says is too far away, and
also my other project, to reach Jiddah via Mada'in
Salih and Khaibar. I snould do better, he says, to
aim for Jiddah direct. At last he agrees to everything, but I find him less well disposed to me than
usual. Amir Hassan soon arrives with Hamud, Salih
ar-Rakhis, and Sulaiman, and the Amir keeps me to
lunch, and I then stay until the general *majlis*.
After the *majlis*, Hamud al-^cUbaid details a man to
follow me home and dictate to me the Arab tribal
names of the south. This man is Khalid abu Thalathin, of the al-Azm tribe of the Qahtan, who has been
in Ha'il for five years, serving the Amir solely to
transmit messages to the *shuyukh* of the south and to
Riyadh. Khalid is a robust man aged between 55 and
60, with that rarity in these parts - a fine white

beard. His name was given him because of his strong
constitution and a reputation for sexual prowess:
('thalathin' means thirty, and the reference is to
a twenty-four hour period). Despite this reputation
and this name, he seems ultra-Wahhabi, his mouth always full of pious utterances. In the evening I was
invited by Amir Hassan, through his chief retainer
and favourite negro, to spend the evening with him.
Amir Hassan is exceedingly polite, excusing himself
for not having done me enough honour on my visit to
Buraidah two years ago, and promising a more generous reception on my next visit. He tells me that
when the town of Buraidah was founded, roughly a
century ago, water lay only 4 or 5 b^cas deep; later
on it was necessary to dig down 6, 8 and 10 b^cas;
and now it is found fully 12 b^cas below ground level.

28 Dec. I visit the Amir at dawn. He says he
is taking on his *ghazu* not only his European tents
but also his large beduin tents. After the *ghazu*
he will stay in the desert, returning to Ha'il
after two or three months.

29 Dec. All strangers arriving at Ha'il are
guests of the Amir unless they already have a
friend there who can accommodate them. But it is
customary, whenever any great person comes, *shaikh*
or not, for the leading lights of the city to invite him to take coffee during the day or after
the evening meal.

At such an occasion one serves fruit in season
before the coffee. When, as now, one has fresh
milk and butter, these are served with dates, followed by coffee and perfumes. Even the wealthiest
provide no more.

I had instructed my steward Mahmud to do everything properly, and since he had wanted nothing so
much as to display his talents to the full, he
excelled himself. I had invited the Amir of al-
Qasim and Shaikh Rakan ibn Hathlain, the great

chief of the ^cAjman, to dine with us after the final prayer. Thanks to Mahmud's ingenuity I was able
to offer my guests and their escorts first tea,
then lemonade, then pastries with sugar and almonds,
or with dates, called *sambusak*, then pastries in a
sweet juice called ^cAwamah, then lemon slices dipped in sugar, and finally coffee. I added *zabad*
and rose essence by way of perfumes. My hosts finally left, enchanted, at 10.30.

30 Dec. The weather is unchanged: without a
single ray of sunshine. After ^casr, I spend an
hour with the Amir, then to Hamud's, where I stay
to dine with Majid. I have already mentioned that
one of my camels is affected with satyriasis; today
I learn that my favourite camel, which I ride myself, is so far pregnant that she too cannot be
ridden for some considerable time. The Amir again
complains of his liver. I prepare some doses of
calomel.

31 Dec. As I had surprised Majid yesterday by
arriving at a meal unannounced, he promises to
treat me better today, and invites me to dine with
him formally this evening. I had mentioned to the
Amir, before dawn this morning, my desire to start
my own journey before his departure to the desert.
It will be difficult he says, but he will do what
he can. As regards my animals, I should patiently
await their return from pasture, then we'll see.
The real difficulty, he says, is to find someone
intelligent to go with me. At 6 p.m. there is a
light shower. Before sunset I visit Hamud al-^cUbaid,
where Majid is still eating. Hamud is there, and we
chat until the *muaddin* summons the faithful to evening prayer. Then Hamud performs his ablutions and
goes to the mosque, whence he will make his way to
the Amir's for dinner. After he had taken his
leave, the Amir's almoner Khairallah takes the prayer in the *diwan* and all present pray with him except for myself and young ^cUbaid, Hamud's son. Then
Majid calls for the plate of rice with a quartered

sheep on it, its tail turned towards Majid and me. The rice is overcooked, and I prefer to eat at home. At 6.30 p.m. I return home and work on a map of the Jabal Jildiah up to 10 p.m., when I retire and the year glides into oblivion.

January 1884

1 Jan. I have no New Year visits to make, for it is not the Islamic New Year, but I nevertheless make one - before dawn - to Hamud al-ᶜUbaid's, where I soak up tea and coffee and drown in perfumes. At noon there is a ray of sunshine, and I take advantage of it by leaving town for an hour, as far as the rock called al-Buwaidah, whence one has a fine view of Jabal Aja' in the west, and over Ha'il and Jabal Samra' in the east. From Buwaidah to the city limit, the little alley at the back of Suq al-ᶜAbid, I have counted 925 steps, each of 0.65 metres, so the distance is 601.25 m. About 4 p.m. the sky again darkens and rain sets in, becoming heavier about 9 p.m.

2 Jan. The rain persists all morning and is particularly heavy at 11 a.m. The rains are considered heavy: so far the depth is 0.025 m. At 10 a.m., the Shaikh of the Aslam dictates his tribal structure to me, and says that he was the victor in a *ghazu* made against him some days ago by ibn Al Saᶜud. Husain, the Damascene camel-merchant, who came here with me from Damascus, has completed his purchases, and is going back home tomorrow. I gave him four letters, for MM. Suquet, Ch. Metzger, Maunoir, and Hasenkener, enclosed in a letter addressed to M. Gilbert.

3 Jan. The weather is cold and wet. Yesterday and today the wells cannot be used because the rain has so saturated and weakened the well-walls that the usual pulley-structure would make them collapse if the attempt were made. Half the town is there-

fore without fresh water. After ^{c}asr I go back to
the Amir and again stress how anxious these delays
are making me, but he only counselled the customary
patience.

4 Jan. The weather is still cold, wet, and
rainy. After the evening *majlis* the Amir summons
all before him into the main courtyard in front of
the kitchens, and announces the *ghazu*. Today is
Friday: the provisions will be distributed on Saturday and Sunday. The date of departure is not
yet fixed. After the recent rainstorms all the
town and house walls are weakened, and two houses
crumbled today, one burying a man whose only injuries were broken ribs.

5 Jan. The weather is unchanged: rain from yesterday evening till this morning. In the evening,
after ^{c}asr, I discussed my itinerary in the Hijaz
with the Amir, who described it as impracticable.
It is easy enough to reach Taima and al-^{c}Ula, he
says, but it would be impossible to go to Tabuk and
then via Khaibar and Medina to Jiddah. I am determined to go to Tabuk, but as regards the route to
Medina, in which I have no especial interest, I
suggest that on quitting al-^{c}Ula I should make instead for al-Hayit and the lands of the Harbi on
the way to Jiddah. We end by agreeing on this itinerary. To dissuade me from attempting to reach
Tabuk, the Amir recounts how ^{c}Anaibar, who left here
for Tabuk some time back with three Shammaris and
Muhammad ibn ^{c}Atiyah, was surprised several hours
before arriving at Tabuk by a *ghazu* of the Bani
Sakhr comprising 35 horsemen and 50 camel-riders
led by ^{c}Aitan, Shaikh of the ^{c}Isa; the victims
were stripped of all they had. When the Amir had
finished this cautionary tale, I expressed the
pious hope that 'in sha' Allah' I should not suffer
a like encounter and, on turning to his cousin
Hamid, he burst out laughing and added 'Allah - he
fears nothing!!

6 and 7 Jan. The thunder began to roar at 9 p.m.
on Sunday 6 January and continued throughout the
night and all through Monday. I visit the Amir before *^casr*, and he invites me to dine. Everybody is
emotionally affected by the great rains, which
threaten virtually every building in Ha'il. The
Amir is moreover indisposed with a slight fever.
Nobody living recalls such abundant rains. The last
remotely comparable Winter was that of 1260 (1844-5),
known as the Lucky Year because of the prosperity
assured by the harvests of the following Summer.
After 1260, 1280 (1863-4) was the wettest in recent
years, and was known as the Year of the Market Flood
because of the flash floods which crashed through
the Mashhadi Suq, demolishing all the shops and a
great number of private houses. In my own dwelling,
no damage has been caused except to two staircases,
open to the sky, which lead to terraces, but throughout the night streams of rain have run along the
terraces and poured into my three main rooms: the
qahawah, diwan, and store-room, especially into the
last. There is a laconic rhyme bringing together
the three chief irritations of a restless night:
drops of water, the cry of a baby, and the bite of
a bedbug. On leaving the Amir, I am reminded that
I shall have to delay my departure for several more
days, like the Amir's own departure on the raid,
because of the heavy rains.

8 Jan. The rain has fallen without a break
throughout the night, but stops this morning at dawn,
though the strong wind from the north persists.
Many houses have crumbled during the night. The
sky is still overcast, the sun appearing through the
mist only twice. The only other good year recalled
in Jabal Shammar is that of 55 years ago [i.e. 1849.
Ed.], after a period of three years without a drop
of rain. Only a light rain fell at last, but it
was enough to turn the desert green and ensure prosperity for the coming season. That year was called that of 'Camel-dung Spring', for it was noticed

425

that the rain sufficed only to dampen the top of
camel-dung, but left it dry underneath.

After the last prayer, I spend the evening with
the Amir, whom I know to be alone at that moment,
and we chat until 10 p.m. He was -just bidding adieu
to Sanad ibn ^cAbhil, Shaikh of the Tuman, those
Shammaris who possess the greatest number of horses.
The Amir describes the origin and course of his sickness at length, and then changes the subject to that
of the aerolite which fell on Ha'il at the hour of
^casr in the Suq al-^cAbid. He asked me as many as
three times whether it is possible that stones can
fall from the sky, and was amazed when I answered
in the affirmative, and still more amazed when I
explained that they were tiny fragments of stars.
"Are the stars then black?" asked the Amir. I had
to avoid further explanations, since they would
have contradicted that in the Qur'an. Then the Amir
reverts to my itinerary, which he would again like
to modify. He grants me Tabuk, but asks me to
return from al-Hijr to Ha'il in order that I should
make my way to Jiddah via al-Qasim. But I stick
out for my plan to travel via al-Hayit. At last
we agree that I should await further instructions
at al-Hayit, so that if the desert situation is too
dangerous I can return to Ha'il, where I should be
given an ample escort as far as al-Qasim. At al-
Qasim I should be given an escort by Zamil as far
as Jiddah.

9 Jan. The sky is cloudless for once, but the
Sun gleams through a light haze, allowing me to take
the following midday altitude of the Sun: 80° 8'20".
Temperature: $+13^{\circ}$.

The Dafir have always been the most faithful
and constant allies of the Shammar; several times
each has come to the rescue of the other. Their
lands lie between those of the ^cAnaizah and the
Shammar, and thus they can always avert the threat
of a surprise attack by the ^cAnaizah on their Sham-

mari allies. Hence the Dafir have frequently been attacked by the ^cAnaizah, with loss of life.

One of the most remarkable plots was that of eight years ago (1876). There had been drought throughout Central Arabia for two long years, and even the best camels were enfeebled. The ^cAnaizah chose that moment, in Spring 1876, and the Fida^can and the Suba^cah, together with the Suqur, confronted the Dafir who, forewarned, had sent their families southward and awaited the enemy alone. They had also sent a messenger to inform ibn Rashid, and to secure his aid. This courier rode two days and two nights without rest, and Muhammad left Ha'il with only two other riders that same day. Meanwhile the Dafir and the ^cAnaizah faced each other, with their mounts behind them, which gave the *ghazu* its name: Manakh an-Nuqairah.

Amir Muhammad arrived from Ha'il in fifty hours, and all the Shammar had joined him four days later. Now the Amir resolved to attack: the allies fell upon the ^cAnaizah and Suqur, who fought only an hour before fleeing for their lives, abandoning fifty or so dead and a great booty. Next Spring the ^cAnaizah were back to pursue their feud with the Dafir, whose Shaikh wrote an urgent letter to ibn Rashid with the message 'hadha waqtuk' (this is your hour). Again the Amir did not hesitate and the *ghazu* left Ha'il in five days. This time the ^cAnaizah were not only beaten but pursued for two days. From that time on they have not emerged *en masse* as an attacking force.

10 Jan. The temperature dropped in the night below zero, and there was ice in the plain. I recorded +2° in my courtyard, but the Sun heated the atmosphere quickly.

At 8 a.m. my male camel is brought before me, having just arrived from the desert. He has been in rut for a month, and has lost some of his fat, but could still manage to reach Jiddah. But since a camel is often bad-tempered in rut, I reject it

for the time being, and ask for it to be returned
to pasture. At ^{c}asr I spend an hour with the Amir,
who tells me that one of his retainers, sent away
to bring milk, died of cold during the night north
of Laqitah.

11 Jan. At noon, despite a sky still slightly
misty, I take the altitude of the Sun: 80° 40'20".
Temperature +17°. Barometer: 682½ mills. Lunch
with the Amir, who again invites me to dine with
him in the evening. I had myself invited Khalid
al-Qahtani and Sa^{c}adun of the Sinjari, who had to
dine alone.

12 Jan. The Shaikh of the Tuman comes to visit
me this morning.

13 Jan. The temperature turns milder this morning. Noon altitude of the Sun: 81° 22'50". Temperature: +20°. Barometer: 681 mills. Good observation conditions.

14 Jan. During the night there were five star
occultations observable at Ha'il. I had established my theodolite on my southern terrace yesterday,
hoping for good astronomical observations, but at
9 p.m. a wind suddenly blew up and the sky was dark
until midnight, so I had seen nothing.

In Ha'il, the suq passing in front of the house
Khairallah al-Humaid, the butcher's, and the Bab
Saffaqat, the gate of Salamah, and along the gardens of the castle, is known as Suq al-Jarad, and
divides the town into two equal halves. The southern sector, with Suq Lubdah, is inhabited by the
Qawm al-Quwa^{c}a, and the northern sector, with the
Barsan quarter, by the Qawm ar-Rishan. These two
sectors have always been in conflict, and nowadays
this fire is covered with ashes. During his raids,
the Amir sedulously keeps men of the two sectors
apart from each other. Each qawm has its own shaikh, that of the Quwa^{c}a being Fahd ibn Muhammad al-
^{c}Ali, and that of the Rishan being Mubarak al-
^{c}Ubaid. Whenever the Amir plans a ghazu, he calls

428

both of these *shuyukh* together, checking whether each adult male can go on the raid, or whether for instance he is sick, or needed to cultivate fields or to go a commercial or other mission. Some, like ͨAbdullah al-Muslimani, are always excused from service on the *ghazu* because of their lack of skill with arms or camels, but they must in compensation pay a certain sum of money or pay in kind, and this compensation is settled in advance for each man and each *ghazu* in turn. Thus, ͨAbdullah must offer the loan of a gun and pay between 2 and 3 riyals. In 1882, before the raid on the Majmaͨa, ͨAbdullah had to supply three guns, all of them returned to him after the raid was over.

The different areas of the Jabal are called upon to supply a certain number of armed riders and provisions for a given number of days. Ten years ago Qafar was expected to provide 30 to 40 armed horsemen towards each *ghazu*, but nowadays, since Qafar is much reduced in circumstances, the village is expected to offer only ten men. Rawdah, to the south, was last year expected to offer twelve armed men, with provisions.

15 Jan. My new watch bought specially for this journey suddenly stopped this morning, twenty minutes after I had wound it up. I now have only one gold watch, bought for Muhammad Ibrahim at Najaf, which I am obliged to use at once. I am ill all day with the dysentery which began last night.

In addition to the pure Arab or beduin population devoid of any alliance with commoners, and the black slaves, there are the following classes in Ha'il, listed in descending order of caste: al-ͨAmamah, al-Jabara, al-Jazay, al-Khazam, al-Juray, and al-ͨAbid. 'Juray' is the name of a kind of puppy. Long ago, at Ha'il, runs the legend, a woman died in childbirth, having been delivered of a son. The baby's father, not knowing how to save the baby's life, thought of putting him to suck with a bitch which was then suckling her puppies.

429

The puppy's name 'Juray' stayed with the boy, who
became founder of the most impure race of whites
in Ha'il. The 'ᶜAbid', which are not as elsewhere
the negro slaves, are in Ha'il a population whose
negro ancestors became successively more pale-
skinned by intermarriage. The ᶜAmamah are the
noblest of these commoners, such that all the inferior castes try to pass for them. But since all
are artisans of one kind or another, even the most
ragged of the beduin treat them with contempt, as
if they were no better than Juray.

The ᶜAmamah say they come from the north. The
Jaᵤara and Khazam claim to be indigenous to the
Jabal Shammar. The Jazay derive from a dervish
of that name who came from outside but married a
low-caste Ha'ili woman. About a third of the population of Ha'il is Arab or *rafiᶜa*, the rest being
artisans or slaves. The population of Mustajiddah
is of Hamran origin, like that of Samirah, though
the latter has an admixture of Qasimis.

16 Jan. After *ᶜasr* yesterday, one of the Amir's
men arrived back from Satam ibn Shaᶜlan, who is
camping at present with ibn Sumair in the wadis.
He brings news of a great raid on them by the
Fidaᶜan; apparently the Fidaᶜan were so successfully pursued that all the booty was recaptured.

I learnt today the names of three of the Amir's
four wives: Lu'lu'a, the sister of Amir Hassan;
ᶜAmushah, the daughter of ᶜUbaid; and Dushah,
daughter of ibn Jabrin, Shaikh of the Sunaidah.
Hamud al-ᶜUbaid has only three wives at the moment:
Binayah, daughter of Mitᶜab; Munirah, daughter of
the Amir Hassan; and Latifah, daughter of Talal.
The predecessor of the present religious leader,
Muhammad al-Ghunaimi, was a certain ibn Khazam, who
had been sent by ibn Al Saᶜud; but, since he was
considered too strict by Talal, he was sent back
to Najd. Whenever this pious man saw a *kafiyah*
being worn in the street, he assumed that there was
a strand of silk in it, snatched it from the offen-

der's head in full view of the populace, and confiscated it. Muhammad al-Ghunaimi, who has now been
here fifteen years, has a reputation for greater
tolerance. He comes from Naʿam in Najd. Though
his grandfather was a negro, he himself is almost
white in complexion but retains the physiognomy of
his ancestor. He is called 'the Shaikh' in Ha'il.
His annual income, derived from the Amir, is 500
*sa*ʿ of dates (five camel-loads), 200 *sa*ʿ of rice,
150 *sa*ʿ of wheat; 150 *sa*ʿ of barley, 12 *sa*ʿ of
coffee, and 30 riyals before the onset of Winter
to buy firewood. He also receives on occasion
gifts of clothes, money, and several sheep after
each raid. His duties are to conduct the ʿasr
prayer every day in the Friday Mosque, (except on
Fridays, when he conducts the noon prayer; and on
festival days, when he conducts the morning prayer).
As regards teaching, every morning but Friday he
receives ʿAwad, ʿAbdullah and Yaqub to read a passage from the Qur'an and then to comment on it. In
addition he is responsible for passing judgements
at the morning and ʿasr Majlis on cases referred
to him by the Amir because they are dealt with in
the *Shari*ʿa or Holy Law, as for example matters
affecting the law of succession.

The three other ʿalim - those learned in the
law - of Ha'il are ʿAwad, son of a soldier called
Masri [but this could simply refer to his nationality: *Masri*= Egyptian. Ed.] who remained in Najd
after the campaign of Ibrahim Pasha; ʿAbdullah,
son of a Damascene who came to Ha'il half a century
past; Yaqub, son of Shammar parents. The first
two, the most intelligent, make the pilgrimage to
Mecca with the Persian caravan every year, and
carry out the Hajj duties for one of the relatives
of the ancestors of the Rashid family. Each receives 30 *majidi*s for this service. Yaqub, the
most fanatical, runs a school. All three, together
with their families, are given their food by the
palace and very little else. ʿAwad and ʿAbdullah

carry the title of Shaikh. All these men, and all
the *khatibs* wear their *kafiyah* without an *aqal*; it
is only al-Ghunaimi who, on Fridays alone, wears an
aqal with a little white cotton. All wear an ^{c}*aba*
made of white wool on Fridays.

Every Friday al-Ghunaimi comes to Hamud's morning reception, which takes place before sunrise.
Half-an-hour after sunrise he accompanies Hamud to
the Amir, who entertains him to lunch and keeps him
for the following *majlis*. These are the only direct contacts between the Amir and the local religious leader who, incidentally, is no favourite. I
should add that the opinions of these holy men in
my regard seem wholly favourable. They speak of me
as intelligent, serious, experienced and self-
controlled. There is no doubt that the Amir's
kindly attitude towards me has influenced these opinions. It is only Yaqub who fails to respond to
my 'as-salamu ^{c}alaikum'.

Commodity Prices Now and in Recent Years

	Dates	Wheat (Ha'il)	Iraqi Wheat	Barley	
Jan. 1884	10	6	8	12	*sa*^{c} for 1 riyal
1879-80	5	3	4	4-5	
1878-9	25-30	8-9	10	20	
1870	3-5	3	4	5	

It should be noted that the years 1870 and 1879
were the most expensive of the last fifteen years.
In 1870 (under Bandar's amirate) butter cost 4
majidis the *sa*^{c}, after which the price varied between 2 and 2½ *majidis* until a fortnight ago, when
it tumbled from 2 to 1¾ and then to 1½. It is predicted that it will fall again in Spring to only
1 *majidi* the *sa*^{c}. Two days ago three inhabitants

of Medina arrived to purchase butter and sheep, two
commodities continually in short supply down there.
Last night I invited the Shaikh of the Tuman with
his two companions to dine with us, and all of
them were impressed by Mahmud's excellent pastries.

17 Jan. This morning, before daybreak, I visit
the Amir on his own. Before I say a word, he remarks that, *in sha' Allah*, he will start his *ghazu*
on Monday (today being Thursday), and that probably
I too can leave Ha'il that day, even if ^cAnaibar
has not by then arrived. I stay for lunch with him.

With the Ruwala *shuyukh* who came yesterday there
was a Sulubi called Dirbish, of the Bannaq tribe,
who gives me information on the composition of the
tribes in his area: at-Tarfah, al-Musamah, al-Bann-
aq, al-Majid, and al-Qabwan. These tribes live in
the territory of al-Hijra, between the valleys of
al-Hayaniah, Hazal, Turbah, Linah, al-Jill, ash-
Shubrum, al-La^cla^ch, ash-Shabka, Sharaf, al-Makman,
al-Barit, an-Nukhaib and Luqah. The Tarfah prefer
to stay north of Sakakah, with their northern
limits near Hazal and Luqah. The Musamah keep to
the Widian, and in preference near ad-Dhubaib. The
Bannaq stay near Jabal Shammar, between the Nafud
and the Darb al-Hajj. The Majid keep close to the
Dafir eastward, to the other side of the Wadi. The
Qabwan wander northward as far as the Sha'ib abu
Khamsat.

The Sulaib prefer to keep close to Jabal Shammar
if there has been enough rain to foster the growth
of vegetation. Dirbish assures me that there are
at least a thousand tents in the vicinity of al-
Hijra, but I have good reason to suspect that there
cannot be more than half that number. Each family
in that area has three or four camels and several
sheep; they also raise fine donkeys which are sold
on average at 50 *majidi*s each. For the last two
years Amir ibn Rashid has permitted them to raise
camels and thus these particular Sulaib are much
better off than their fellows in the north. Their

manners are gentle and pacific, while their women
are reputed the prettiest in the whole desert, but
they have generally speaking few children. All are
childlike, with weak voices. The Sulaib hunt gazelle and ostrich so skilfully and patiently that
ten to fifteen gazelle may be caught and killed in
a single day.

Their costume, which distinguishes them from all
other beduin, is a single cloak of gazelle-skins,
the hair on the outside, with narrow sleeves covering the hands as far as the palms. Rich Sulaib
often wear a cotton shirt below their robe. The
robe itself lasts up to ten years and is currently
worth about 3-4 *majidi*s.

The Sulaib never raid other Arabs, and raids are
never made against them. If, as sometimes happens,
some of their animals are carried off during a
raid, they have only to seek their restitution from
the victors and reclaim what was theirs, a wish
immediately granted. The other Arabs regard them
as an inferior race, and only a few ^cAjman and
Qahtan Arabs kill them as infidels. There is no
intermarriage between them and the other Arab
tribes. They have no religion, and their language
lacks the range of holy formulas which Arabic uses
so profusely. But since they are fearful and timid,
whenever they happen to be resident in Ha'il, they
visit the mosque at the hours of prayer to mimic
the ritual.

They suffer from the detestable reputation of
eating the blood of animals with the dead flesh,
and of eating dogs. I have often been told the following story: if two Sulaib find in the desert an
animal that has been dead for two or three days, one
of them seizes the beast and imitates its cry, while
his companion, facing Mecca, slits its throat. Then
they eat it. This is all denied by the Sulaib themselves, and is hardly to be given credence.

The generic name of the Sulaib of al-Hijra is

Bani Ghanaimi, while that of the Sulaib found in
Harbi lands is al-'Amira.

Tribute for war is given to the Amir of the Jabal
Shammar as follows: 30 to 40 men by Ha'il, 4 or 5 by
Rawdah, 4 each by Muwaqqaq, Qafar and Qasr, 3 each
by Mustajiddah and Saba'an, and 2 or 3 by Ghazalah.
None of the other villages of the Jabal give money
or men. War tribute is neither constant nor identical; for instance, last Spring, in the campaign
against Ibn Sa'ud, the Amir requisitioned neither
men nor money, but employed only his own forces and
the Bedu who responded to his call.

18 Jan. There is no rejoicing or feasting over
the birth of a child, girl or boy, in Ha'il. A boy
is usually circumcised between the ages of 2 and 4
or 5. The locksmith Hassan and one of my friends
from Muwaqqaq are the men who normally perform this
operation. The latter also vaccinates, bleeds and
applies leeches. The poor give him half a *majidi*
or a quarter when he circumcises, and invite him to
the lunch given for relatives and friends. The
rich kill between one and six (and even up to eight)
sheep for the occasion, and serve the meat with rice.
Whatever is left is given to the poor.

The boy has no subsequent feast-day until he
goes to school, and until he completes learning of
the Qur'an and all the prayers by heart, normally
between the ages of 12 and 14. Then more sheep are
slaughtered in celebration, and eaten after sunset.
From that moment the youth has the privilege of
taking his place at coffee-drinking in the presence
of the host.

Whenever a man is so sick that everyone realises
he is about to die, each visitor declares on entering "Tayyib in sha' Allah, khair in sha' Allah"
("Well, if God wishes; better, if God wishes").
All, including the sick man, repeat the same sentence. When the death agony begins, his mat or
mattress is aligned east to west, and his face set

435

to the south. When he is dead, he is washed and placed inside cotton cambric a little longer than his body, its two ends knotted above his head and below his feet. Two or three extra bands of the material are wound round the body in the form of a shroud.

If the corpse is poor, and without relatives or friends, Salamah gives the necessary cloth from the Amir's treasury, and sends one of the Amir's servants to wash the body. Many of the poor beg the necessary material for a shroud from a rich citizen or from a cloth merchant. The Amir is also responsible for sending a servant to dig the hole for burial, if the poor man has no kindred. Otherwise, the relatives do it themselves, or pay someone else a quarter of a *majidi* to dig the grave. When washed and shrouded, the corpse is carried to the local mosque where friends and relatives are gathered. The Katib then conducts the prayers for the dead, repeated by the congregation. There is no kneeling or prostration in the funeral rites.

The corpse is borne to the cemetery by four men on a bier without legs called a *na'ash*. The bearers are friends who take the weight in turns according to oriental custom. The corpse is washed on a bier with four legs called a *murshal*. Every mosque in Ha'il possesses both a *murshal* and a *na'ash*. If the corpse has no kindred, he is carried to the cemetery by servants of the Amir.

19 Jan. The Sulaibi Darbish comes back this morning to give me further details of the wadi-system between here and Iraq. The tributaries east of the wadis are the *sha'ib* Abalqur and 'Ar'ar, and those west are the Tabal, al-Abaid, al-Hamar, al-Mara and al-Hauran. The desert around the head of the wadis is called al-'Ait, north east of the Jabal Misma. The Sulaib hunt in the borderlands between Ha'il and Iraq the baqar wahash, gazelle, and the ostrich. The everyday diet of the Sulaib comprises rice, bread, milk and gazelle-meat. They only kill

a sheep when a guest arrives. Daughters are married
as soon as they reach the age of puberty, that is
between 13 and 14 years of age. The dowry for a
girl is 10 *majidis*, and for a woman 6. If a girl
is divorced within a few days of marriage, she returns only half of her dowry, keeping the rest for
the loss of her virginity. A woman returns all six
majidis.

If a stranger to the Ghanaimi, whether Sulaibi
or not, desires one of their daughters, he must pay
a dowry of forty, fifty, or even a hundred *majidis*.
Grazing lands in the Sulaib territory bear the following plants: hamd ruth, ramat, damran, shih,
'arfaj, bakhtary, rablah, sam'a, khazam, nafl,
rughal, khasab, and ja'da. Nafl is one of the best
desert grasses, fattening rapidly, with a firm fat,
but it is scarce, and is found abundantly in northern Arabia only in the Jaulan.

For the first six months after a baby is born it
is given each evening a little butter with sugar.
During the next six months it is given each evening
a little bread or ground rice. After one year, a
child receives with its mother's milk some solid
nourishment. It is weaned at the age of two.

20 Jan. Before sunrise, we spoke at the Amir's
about 'Anaibar.

The Amir attributes his long absence to some misfortune, but in any case the *ghazu* is fixed for
tomorrow, and I depart with it: that is the main
thing.

21 Jan. Before removing my theodolite from the
terrace, I read off: at 274°27, Ras Samra, the nearest hill to Ha'il. From 268° to 259°1'40", the
Emir's fortress. Mid-day altitude of the Sun by
the sextant, 84°32'30". Temperature +23 ; barometer:
673^{1}/3 mills.

22 Jan. Still busy with my preparations for
departure.

I say goodbye to the Amir, who is himself leaving at noon on his *ghazu*. I shall leave tomorrow, in sha' Allah.

23 Jan. At nine a.m. I leave home, and make my route via Samah, Qafar and as-Silf.

The unfortunate Huber, who suffered from fever in Ha'il, was killed on 29 July 1884 by his own guides at Rabigh, on the way to Jiddah.

9
Julius Euting, 1883-4

Julius Euting accompanied Charles Huber on the latter's second journey to Ha'il. Euting was born in Stuttgart in 1839, and died in Strasbourg in 1913. He took courses in Theology and Oriental Studies at Tübingen in 1857-61, followed by postgraduate Oriental Studies in Paris, London and Oxford in 1863-4.

Euting's gift for sketching and inclination to drawing led him to study inscriptions, palaeography and epigraphy, fields which were amplified by an abiding interest in ancient history and archaeology. The work of Gesenius (1786-1842) on Semitic epigraphy formed the basis for Euting's chief contributions throughout the rest of his life, and he spent long hours in difficult conditions copying and sketching some thousand pre-Islamic inscriptions. He left 23 diaries and 9 sketch-books of his journeys and accounts of Oriental Congresses (1869-1905) to the library of Tübingen. In 1869 he travelled by way of Sicily to Tunis and Carthage, and in 1870 to Athens, Smyrna, Constantinople.

But his most ambitious journey was that undertaken to Central Arabia from May 1883 to August 1884, sponsored by the Governor of Alsace-Lorraine, Count Manteuffel, and by King Karl of Württemberg. Euting's way took him through central Syria (for three months, including important studies at Palmyra), from Damascus to the south-west Hauran, the Wadi Sirhan, al-Kaf, al-Jauf, and to Ha'il, where he stayed for three months as the rather fretfully impatient guest of the Ruler of Jabal Shammar, Muhammad ibn Rashid.

After leaving Ha'il, Euting passed through al-^cUla
(for Mada'in Salih), the Red Sea and Qusayr in Upper
Egypt. The scientific results of Euting's travels
comprised 900 Aramaic, Nabataean, Sabaean and Lihyanite
inscriptions. The Lihyanite script (dating to more
than 1,000 years before the Prophet Muhammad, s.a.w.),
a link between Old Phoenician and Sabaean, was hitherto
quite unknown. Euting published *Nabatäische Inscriften
aus Arabien* (Berlin, 1885), with contributions from
Nöldeke and A. von Gutschmid, and *Epigraphische Miszel-
len* (Berlin, 1885-7). The Nabataean inscriptions
afforded a new insight into the vanished culture of
that Arabian kingdom, into its tribal relationships and
migrations, and show the close connection between the
late Nabataean cursive and the earliest Arabic script.

Sinaitische Inscriften (Berlin, 1891) was the principal product of a journey to Upper Egypt and Sinai in
February-May 1889, but his epigraphic plates grace a
large number of publications, including the *Corpus
Inscriptionum Semiticarum,* Zimmern's *Vergleichender
Grammatik der Semitischen Sprachen,* Chwolson's *Corpus
Inscriptionum Hebraicarum* and many more. His scholarly work on inscriptions gives little or hint of the
man's waggish sense of humour, flashing but kindly
eyes, his passion for coffee and tobacco and abhorrence
of alcohol. The marble tablet designed for his grave
in the Black Forest, but currently in Stuttgart's
Linden Museum, reads "He is the Living One, the Eternal! When my bed has turned to dust and I dwell beside
the All-Merciful God, congratulate me, my friends, and
say: Good news, for you have gone home to a kindly
one". He funded not only a scholarship for calligraphy
in his own Grammar School in Stuttgart, but also the
gift of a cup of real Mocha Coffee for all who came as
a pilgrim to his grave.

The chronological catalogue of Euting's works runs
to 202 items, of which the most popular has always been
the amusing, anecdotal *Tagbuch einer Reise in Inner-
Arabien,* with numerous sketches by the author. The
first volume was published in 1896 but the second, left

ready for the press, was edited by Enno Littmann and
published the year after Euting's death. Of the first
volume, pages 173-240 are concerned with Ha'il, and are
here translated for the first time in their entirety.
Of the second volume, pages 1-106 are devoted to Ha'il,
and are likewise rendered here in full. Together they
constitute the fullest account of Ha'il yet penned by
any writer in any language.

Ha'il
21 October 1883 - 23 January 1884

We were of course full of excitement at the thought
of coming face to face with the ruler of northern Arabia
who had just been described to us, and in whose hands
rested our fortunes for the next few months. While our
luggage was being carried into the house allotted us,
we ourselves were conducted into the castle through a
court-yard past an old cannon into the reception-hall
(*madif*) where we were entertained with qahwah helu (p.
128) and coffee. The large crowd of people going out
and coming in to greet and gape at us was kept under
control by a reverend old man with a long snow-white
beard. He was the old Mufarriq, the Master of Ceremonies and Inductor into the Palace. We might have been
sitting on show in the hall for about half-an-hour -
during which the Amir had been receiving a preliminary
report from our travel-manager Hamud al-Mijrad - when
Mufarriq appeared with the announcement that the Amir
wished to receive us. He led us through a long dark
passage, past the guard-room, across a half-open vestibule, where there stood on the right-hand side a pair
of ludicrously European armchairs (thrones?), some gilt
garden-furniture, and other useless junk from the west,
into the qahawah, i.e. the reception-room of the
Prince. After leaving our shoes and sandals at the
entrance, we stepped forward towards the Amir in the

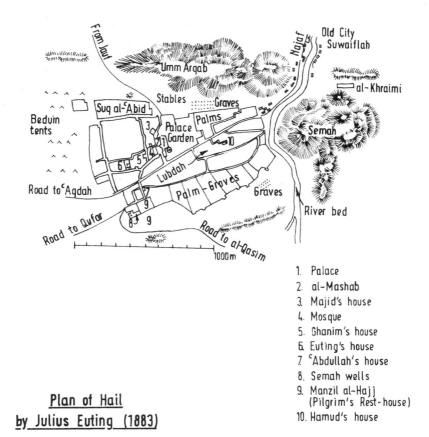

**Plan of Hail
by Julius Euting (1883)**

1. Palace
2. al-Mashab
3. Majid's house
4. Mosque
5. Ghanim's house
6. Euting's house
7. ʿAbdullah's house
8. Semah wells
9. Manzil al-Hajj
   (Pilgrim's Rest-house)
10. Hamud's house

left-hand corner without bowing or any other ceremony
beyond a simple *'Salam* ᶜalaikum'. As soon as he saw us,
he stood up to return the greeting, 'w' ᶜalaikum as-
salam', came forward to meet us, stretched out his hand
and while we kissed him on each cheek, he exclaimed
several times 'Kaif ent, Kaif ent?'. So too did the
Prince's cousin Hamud al-ᶜUbaid. 'Tafaddalu' ("Be so
good") was the signal to sit down. Greetings all round
with "Good morning!" Huber and I took our places on
the Prince's left, followed by Salih ibn Rakhis, the
warrior, and the young Princes; on the right sat Hamud

442

al-^cUbaid and some older relatives; against the wall
opposite (just to the left of the entrance) were what
we should call the Ministers and Palace officials, and
soldiers with drawn sabres. As Huber, being an old
acquaintance and former guest, had to do most of the
replying, I was able to look around at my leisure. The
reception-room consists of a white-washed rectangular
chamber 16 m. long, 10 m. wide, and about 4 m. high.
The ceiling is formed by palm-trunks supported by four
mud pillars, and with four paraffin-lamps hanging from
it,[1] the floor is carpeted with mats of palm-leaves,
and all round the walls are Persian carpets with
piled-up cushions as arm-rests. In front of the
Prince's seat, in a cavity 2 m. long, a fire is kept
blazing the whole time. On a small, low table in front
of this there stand 3 paraffin lamps and 2 candles in
globes. A further lamp hangs in the dark corner on
the right, where the coffee is prepared. In the day-
time there is little light in the whole room, for outside the door there are only a couple of narrow slits
in the wall opposite.

The Amir Muhammad ibn 'Abdullah ar-Rashid is a man
of about 48, of fairly light complexion like all the
princes of his family, with a black (or at any rate
faultlessly black-dyed) beard, energetic expression,
and lively eyes constantly in motion.[2] Almost completely without external adornment, he usually wears
over his white woollen shirt only the black woollen
^caba (cloak) embroidered at the neck, on his head a
red woollen kafiyah with ^cakal (head-band) worked in
gold; beneath this there are to be seen two, or sometimes four, black plaits. He walks without stockings
in ordinary leather sandals. His only articles of
luxury are fine weapons: the sabre, leaning against
the wall beside him, might contain 2000-3000 marks'
worth of gold on the studs of its sheath and on the
threaded work of the hilt. Intellectually he stands
head and shoulders not only above his subjects, but
also above his relatives. Though a believer in the
Qur'an, he is quite unprejudiced towards the unorthodox,

whom he often has the opportunity of seeing and observing in Baghdad. He speaks with equal fluency Arabic,
Persian, and Turkish; he knows the old Arabian poets to
a large extent by heart, and similarly all the satirical poems and gutter-songs, both old and new, of the
Beduin. He kept us there amused for a good half-hour,
during which coffee and various qahwah helu were handed
to us. From there we were conducted by Mufarriq into
another part of the Palace for a reception by ᶜAbd al-
aziz ibn Mitᶜab. He is a young, somewhat girlish
prince, 16 years old at most, with his own household
and special administration. Here there was - again! -
qahwah helu and coffee. I must confess that I now
really had enough of the pappy stuff inside me, and
was longing for some more solid support for my stomach;
whereupon I could not help thinking of "Mayer in
Constantinople", whose visit to the Sultan was so well
described to me by a friend of mine.[3] At last we were
saved by the appearance of Mufarriq with the announcement that dinner was ready. On the other side of the
courtyard, where ordinary Beduin were fed, we climbed
the stairs to a gallery reserved for guests of distinction. All those who had travelled with us from al-Jauf
hither were counted worthy of the honour of being
entertained like us on the gallery. As soon as we had

taken our places on the narrow passage-way, the food
was brought in: 4 tin copper plates more than one metre
in diameter, and piled high with rice and camel-meat,
were carried in by 4 slaves each. The plates themselves rested on a round mat of plaited straw with four
handles for carrying. We were just going to reach out
to our plate, when we had to make room again for the
other plates to be carried past us, for the room was so
narrow that the slaves grazed our mountain of rice with
the hem of their long robes and the ends of their
sleeves! I had, to be sure, a good appetite myself, but
what our Beduin companions, the Shararat, polished off
from the plate next to ours, beggars description. With
the painful thought that it would probably be some time
before they were treated to a similar meal, they did
their utmost and the ten of them emptied a plate intended to satisfy the hunger of 15 famished men. Before
and after the meal water was offered the guests to wash
their hands with, and, as a luxury, towels for drying
them. The latter were so dirty that Huber could not
refrain from asking our chief guide whether they had
recently been unable to procure any clean towels in
the qasr. That worked: fresh ones were immediately
brought. After dinner we had to admire in the court below 6 cannons, old iron barrels with the European dates
1793, 1794, which had once been left behind by Ibrahim
Pasha in al-Qasim. The gun-carriages were in such a
defective condition that no shot could be fired from

them without danger to the crews. Moreover, it was extremely unlikely that any ammunition for these guns could be found anywhere in Central Arabia.

Now at last we could seek out the house which the Prince had put at our disposition. Hamud al-Mijrad had revealed to us as early as our first meeting in Ithrah that the Amir left the choice to us, whether to stay in the qasr or in our own house; we had of course chosen the latter, because we thought life would be more informal there. This house, situated in the Persian quarter, was the property of a Mashhadi who had returned to his native town: his Wakil (attorney), for lack of anything better, had let it provisionally to the Prince for the sum of 6 majidi (20 marks) a year, and hopes that he will purchase it. In order to give an idea of the structural layout of an Arab house, I want at this point to present a plan and cross-section and try to give a view of the inner court.

Along a curved corridor in the right-hand corner one comes first to the front or outer court, in the middle of which on the right the entrance-door leads to the qahawah, the reception-room at once our sitting-room and our bedroom. Walls and floor consist of pressed clay. The servant Mahmud had given a good shake-out to the straw mattresses received from the qasr, and also arranged the carpets and the camel-saddles; all our luggage had been put in the adjoining Makhzan al-Qahawah, which could be locked, so as to keep it from the curious and covetous eyes of visitors. Besides the usual qahawah, a special Winter-qahawah had been carpeted, which had once been allotted to Mahmud as a bedroom. Separated from the first court by a protruding transverse wall there lay the inner, larger court, surrounded by various rooms devoted to cooking. It was here that the slaves assigned to us by the Amir had their quarters, namely the 15-year-old Matar and his sister Frayhah, and later another female slave. These were expected to help Mahmud in the kitchen, to fetch water from the Samah well, and to bring over from the castle wood, rice, meat, and whatever else we needed. They did not live in our house, but every evening after

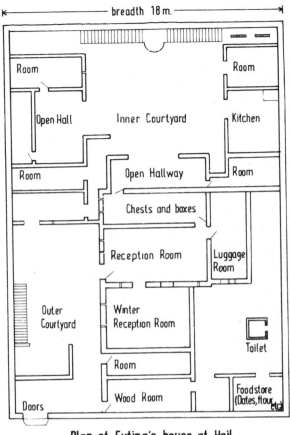

breadth 18 m.

Room

Room

Open Hall

Inner Courtyard

Kitchen

Room

Open Hallway

Room

Chests and boxes

Reception Room

Luggage Room

Outer Courtyard

Winter Reception Room

Toilet

Room

Doors

Wood Room

Foodstore (Dates, flour etc.)

<u>Plan of Euting's house at Hail</u>

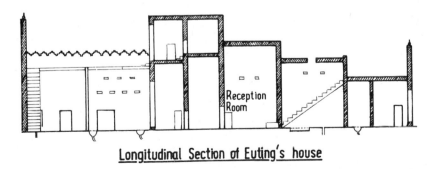

Reception Room

<u>Longitudinal Section of Euting's house</u>

supper returned to their parents, who lived in Suq al-
^cAbid (Slaves' Quarter).

Of course we should have liked most to settle in
comfortably in our lodging and to unpack the first
necessities for our own needs; but that was not possible. Today and on following days it was a continuous
coming and going of visitors of greater or lesser importance. The real purpose of these visitors, or rather
beggars, was to make the most of our presence and to
relieve us of our absurdly ample luggage in a peaceful
manner. It must have been a disappointment for them to
realize that they had come much too soon, and in any
case were in each other's way. There were presents for
none, either openly or slipped into the hand. So they

were all certainly bitterly disappointed, and while
each one secretly cursed the other and waited in vain
for his withdrawal, they remained seated with unshake-
able resolution and drank coffee with fond thoughts of
what they were going to receive. It was essentially
always the same competitors, except that, in order to
get the better of the others in the race, they strove
to come earlier every morning, that is, one hour before sunrise! - which moreover in this country is a
perfectly respectable and normal visiting time. For
this day we got rid of the hordes of beggars quite comfortably because the Amir invited us to the Castle for
supper at sundown.

The Prince received us very kindly in his closest
family-circle, eight persons in all. Hands washed, he
invited us with a sammu[4] to sit down on the floor and
begin the meal. I was astonished to see that the
Sovereign and the young princes hardly differed from
their subjects as regards the simplicity of the food:
a single large plate of rice soaked in butter and
covered with mutton and cakes of bread was laid on the
ground. Anyone thirsty could ask for water,[5] which
would then be offered him in a brass bowl by a slave.
The Amir urged us several times to help ourselves without ceremony, we must be hungry, etc., meanwhile laying before each of us round the table with his own
hand the fattest pieces of meat. At the conclusion of
the meal a copper basin was brought in, as is the custom in the civilized East, for hands to be rinsed: the
water was poured over the hands out of a slim-necked
copper jug, but the basin had a double bottom, the
upper one of which had holes in it and was detachable
so as to allow the dirty water to drain off into the
belly of the basin. Soap and this time clean towels
were not lacking. The meal might have lasted a quarter-
of-an-hour, and as it is not the custom to linger after
a meal unless there is some particular reason, we returned at dusk to our house. We were just thinking of
going to bed and were discussing what present to give
the Sovereign on the next day, when Hamud al-Mijrad
knocked violently on the front-door to summon us once

more to the qasr. Of the 24 flint-locks[6] of which
H.M. King Charles of Württemberg had made me a present,
12 were taken along with us, together with a Mauser
revolver and a sabre blade from Solingen. Mahmud and
the slave Matah bore them behind us. In the Amir's
qahawah there was a party going on and the house was
festively illuminated. While we took our places the
Sovereign had the guns laid before him, and with visible pleasure picked one up to test its fire-lock. As
he was doing this, his eye fell on Mahmud, who was
going to withdraw: "Stop! Ah! By God, I know you
from al-Jauf. Hum? Is it not so?" Mahmud paled; he
knew only too well that he had indeed at that time been
serving as interpreter in the unlucky expedition of
the Turks against al-Jauf; there was therefore no possibility of denial, so he stammered a few words. The
Amir gloated over his fear for a moment, and then called
out to him: "Eh, you don't need to be afraid!" and nodded to one of his entourage, whereupon the terrified man
was dismissed with the quiet delight of 15 majidi (52
marks). He examined the Mauser revolver with pleasure
and was delighted with the weapon's simplicity and
safety. The Solingen blade he handed over to the has-
tily-summoned armourer Ghanam, with orders to prepare
it immediately. While the remaining guests were allowed to look at and touch the weapons in turn, the Prince
turned to the two of us and asked: "What is your opinion? A Persian doctor visited me recently and prescribed a course of treatment for me. Is it good for me,
I wonder?" He bared both forearms as he spoke, and
showed that they were tightly bound by narrow silver
clasps. Two servants came up and unfastened the simple
lock; beneath the band there protruded some green plant-
leaves, which covered some issue-peas. Huber pointed
out to him that the treatment was not harmful, to be
sure, but a useless discomfort; he might just as well
drop the whole thing. However, the Amir wanted to give
the treatment another try, and had fresh peas put into
the artificial wounds, these covered with fresh leaves,
and the silver bands relocked. At ten o'clock in the
night we were finally able to get to bed.

Monday, 22 Oct. 83. After a long and restorative

night's sleep there appeared Hamud al-Mijrad, previously our chief guide and now our permanent adjutant during our stay in this place. Having grown up with the
Prince as his devoted follower, he has had the right
of entry into the qasr from his youth up; and though he
is invested with no official duties, his natural intelligence and a good nose for the truth win him employment on many an extraordinary service. At the same
time he still cannot avoid falling from time to time
into disfavour, in which case he is of course no longer greeted by any slave. He always surfaces again
however, and at this particular moment, when he has
been assigned to us as adjutant, he is enjoying the
greatest respect. Our servant Mahmud of course, being
his sworn foe, asserted that that respect does not go
very far; that he is reckoned a regular sponger
(mahrum), who out of miserliness hardly ever eats at
home and tries to feed in other people's houses. We
ought to be on our guard, he said; his friendliness
was just pretence, he was trying in the most shameless
way to exploit us for his own gain and that of the
qasr (the ruling family in the castle). Certainly he
was not slow to exploit his position with us now. As
soon as he came in, he complained querulously that he
had to feel ashamed when people asked him about the
presents he had received; for he had always to say that
up to now he had received no recognition in the form of
a present. Surely it could not be a matter of indifference to us, what people thought of us! Accordingly,
we promised him that he might keep as his own property
the flint-lock which he had been carrying on the journey as a loan. However, as he had already laid up
this equipment in his house, he obviously did not regard it as a new present, and although he had to give
up his complaint for the moment, he did not seem particularly cheered. Covetousness is a conspicuous
feature of even the best Beduin, and no attempt is
made by them to conceal it. If one *can* have something, why not take it? One man does it with violence,
another with cunning, and a third with begging. It is
quite typical of a Beduin that when Hamud al-Mijrad in

the course of the day received a Mauser revolver as a token of our satisfaction, he immediately asked whether we had not also another double-barrelled gun for him.

Today was to be the day for making the necessary visits. First of all Muhammad carried us off to the Prince; the reason for this, as it seemed to me, importunate visit, was soon to become clear to me. On our way there Hamud informed me that the Prince had made urgent inquiries of him concerning our repeaters; there would be nothing for it but to present them to him. And when we were received by the Prince, he disclosed to us that he was very curious to see our rifles, for he had heard wonders about them. A slave was forthwith despatched to bring back one of the rifles exactly as it was. On the removal of the leather case I had to explain the mechanism; I showed the weapon first as a single-loader, then as a repeater, or as "Father of nine", as the Amir put it; his eyes lit up with admiration at the way the nine cartridges were finally ejected one after the other with a jerk. I had to go through the whole procedure once more, and then at the end I laid the gun down in front of my place. Such an academic ending the matter was not to have, however. Hamud al-Mijrad, who was sitting next to me, whispered: "You must present it to him". Seething with rage, but controlling myself, I retorted: "Is your Amir a beggar then? Did I not give him last night twelve guns? Will be expect another one or more from his guests every morning?" With a significant gesture, putting his finger against his forehead, he uttered the ambiguous words: "ᶜAndak ᶜakl?" ("You have intelligence?") "Yes, I have enough intelligence to know that I need my guns myself!" "Good! But you have other guns, and you do not need more. Look! I was born in the same night as he, I have known his facial expression from my youth up; did you not see his eye when he was examining the gun? I tell you, he must have the gun!" I was silent. Hamud perhaps felt that the ground was a little loosened, and after a short pause he began again: "ᶜAndak ᶜakl? What do you want in our country? What can you do without the

452

consent of the Shuyukh?" "You know, I want to see the ruins of Taima, al-Hijr, al-^{C}Ula; I desire nothing else!" "Fine! Do you believe then that you will get to see those places, if you do not satisfy his desire? You will be received with hospitality as long as you like, but the real purpose of your journey you will never achieve. So give it to him!" I had a hard struggle in my mind: the incidents for which I had to be prepared were such that it was certainly not a matter of indifference what sort of weapon I possessed; my life was at risk with or without a repeater; the only question was: should I make the fulfilment of my journey's task easier, more difficult, or quite impossible? Hamud, you are right! I took the gun - it absolutely broke my heart - and laid it at the feet of the Amir with the customary "Khud" ("Take it"). He seized the weapon and leant it against the wall without betraying his feelings and without a word of thanks. The cartridges, 300 per gun, he was to receive in the course of the day. His cousin Hamud al-^{C}Ubaid then asked whether the second gun was of exactly the same kind as this one. Huber and I exchanged a glance of intelligence, and ten minutes later the second, our last, repeater stood beside the first. Hamud al-Mijrad had worked well for his master.

After giving away the most effective protector of my life, I could now be confident that apart from my scientific equipment I possessed nothing more in all my coffers, the loss of which I would in some way have found painful. How right I had been to leave some objects at home, the loss of which I would have felt deeply! I had, for example, originally intended to take with me the oriental ceremonial sabre given to me by H.M. King Charles of Württemberg for my journey as a token of his gracious homage. Fearing to lose this wonderful piece (erstwhile gift of Viceroy Muhammad ^{C}Ali to King William[7] of Württemberg) in one way or another during the journey, I had left it at home. Yes, if the Amir had seen this sabre, it would have gone the way of the two guns: he would have wanted and had to have it. He would have presented me with another fine sabre, plus 30 or, if I wanted them, more camels - and what was I supposed to do with those in Strassburg or Stuttgart? Either I should have per- force agreed to the bargain, and then should have lost the sabre; or I should have been foolish enough politely to refuse his request,[8] and then I should probably have completely frustrated the whole aim of my journey, as explained above, and if not the Amir himself - for I should like to acquit him entirely of the suspicion - at least his cousin Hamud al-^{c}Ubaid, to be described later, goaded by impatience in nights rendered sleepless by greed, would have found a means of ensuring that in the course of my journey an acci- dent would befall me, as a result of which I should have lost my head and thereby the sabre too. So I could well be glad to ensure that that sabre was safe in Strassburg.

After the Prince in high good humour had dismissed us, we were carried off to his cousin Hamud al-^{c}Ubaid in another part of the palace. He is the son of the al-^{c}Ubaid nicknamed "the Wolf", and has inherited from him many qualities, though he is perhaps a little less martially cruel by nature than his father. A strong Wahhabi, he likes to make a show of his piety, and so has the habit of murmuring pious formulas[9] at every pause in the conversation: for example, he will easily say 50 times in a row under his breath Subhana'llah, subhana'llah etc. ("God forbid!") or Istaghfir Allah, istaghfir Allah etc. ("I ask God for forgiveness.") A good dose of hypocrisy lies behind the mere habit, of course, and this is a worthy counterpart to his cunning. He is praised by the poor because of his generosity, and Doughty could see in him a benevolent protector. He is the Prince's right hand and constant- ly close to him; as the second man in the Kingdom no- one dare contradict him or refuse him anything. His greed is boundless, downright childish: for example, he is supposed to have more than 200 watches in his house, nearly all of which he has broken by eternally messing about with them. To give the Amir his due, once he had received the repeaters, he never asked

for the least thing again, whereas his cousin Mr.
Insatiable was not ashamed to play the beggar with us
every day, either personally or through an intermediary. The Amir is not fond of European manufactured
goods apart from weapons; for him they are baubles of
no interest: his cousin, on the other hand, when he
has acquired all attainable European articles, thinks
up the existence of uninvented ones, and begs for them
at least on the off-chance. I often had the greatest
difficulty in concealing my abomination of this man,
who did not make his repulsive qualities any more
tolerable by a mawkish grin. In addition it was I who
more often than not had the pleasure and honour of
sitting right next to him. Unlike the Prince, he was
richly blessed with sons, the eldest of whom, Majid,
has been selected as successor to the throne. As the
Amir would presumably bequeath one Mauser repeater to
his cousin, the latter had to be content on the present
visit with a Mauser revolver, a Solingen blade and a
bottle of snuff[10] from the Royal Tobacco-factory at
Strassburg.

From here we were commandeered by Prince Abdulaziz
ibn Mit^cab, for whom however we had no presents with
us. His reception-room was bright and comfortable; a
well-maintained rococo pendulum-clock and a bronze
samovar testified to a certain culture. He had us
served qahwah helu and tea.

I felt quite at ease only when I had the gate of
the qasr behind me and could order my coming and going
as I liked. I was inquisitive to look up the armourer
Ghanam ibn Bani, a man whose name is, for the Beduin
throughout Najd and beyond, a synonym for artistic
skill.   I found him together with his 20-year old son
Muhammad at work in his workshop; there he sat, with
two magnifying lenses on his nose, and working with piti-
able tools at the engraving of the silver plates of a
sabre-sheath. Naturally, he wanted to get up and conduct me into the reception-room and could hardly get
over it that I preferred to watch him at work. It
was really unwise of me to show so much interest and
admiration for him, and still more rash, to reveal to

Ghanam ibn Bani

him that I had with me tools of all sorts that were ten
times better and more perfect and would gladly give
him one or another of them. From then on the fellow
stuck to me like a leech, despite receiving repeated
gifts, until I made it clear to him in no uncertain
terms that henceforth I could do without his visits
and had no more gifts for him. His son Muhammad had
inherited his skill, but was his inferior in begging;
he had a long way to go to catch up there. As it happened, it was this young man who came with me to our
house to fetch the 300 cartridges for each of the two
repeaters, as instructed by the Amir. He declared
himself able to refill the metal cases of the cartridges each time and to equip them with new percussion-
caps, so that each case could be used at least ten
times. He was remarkably quick in understanding the
mechanism of the guns, certainly quicker than I had
been; after a brief introduction he could take the
lock to pieces, clean it, tighten it, and replace it.
At the same time I handed him various tools that belonged to the gun; only the cleaning-brush he stubborn-
ly refused with the instinctive revulsion felt by all

Muslims for any brush (on account of the hog's brist-
les) and promised to keep the gun clean and free of
dust(?) even without a brush. He could be got to
accept the good pig's lard for the greasing only by
the assurance that this was valuable deer-grease. A
few days later he cast in bronze a smart bullet-mould
for the bore of the guns and carried out the work with
astonishing neatness.

As visitors and sick persons of all kinds pushed
their way in after us, whenever we entered the house,
I used to flee on to the roof as soon as we had got
rid of Muhammad ibn Ghanam, in order to set down
there undisturbed the bare minimum of notes on the
events of yesterday and today. In the two days I had
seen and experienced so much that was new that I could
not but fear I would lose the correct sequence of
events or completely forget some details. It was mid-
day before the house was free of visitors, and we
seized the moment to look up a friend of Huber's from
earlier times, ᶜAbdullah al-Muslimani. Originally a
Jew, he had moved to Ha'il from Baghdad as Elia ben

457

Rahamin 15 years before, and had there been converted
to Islam. An unrivalled merchant and experienced in
business matters, he was greatly honoured by al-^{c}Ubaid
the warrior-father of Hamud: he administered his estate
and successfully increased it, held all the keys of
his house, desired nothing for himself, and enjoyed the
unlimited confidence of the "Wolf". When al- ^{c}Ubaid
rode to Qafar, ^{c}Abdullah was his escort mounted on a
richly caparisoned horse with embroidered saddle-cover.
It was no wonder that many envied him. With al- ^{c}Uba-
id's death, however, this magnificent state also came
to an end: in the same minute that the mighty one closed
his eyes, the son Hamud took the keys from ^{c}Abdullah and
drove him from the palace. He was no longer greeted by
the high and low of the country, hardly even recognized;
he had become a simple shop-keeper again. Yet in
those 13 years he has been quietly working for himself; by the diligent conduct of his business, by his
dealings in loans and the profits which he affords the
resident Beduin, he has augmented his estate to such an
extent that he can gradually call his own large gardens
and houses in Qafar and ^{c}Aqda. Unfortunately, he can
enjoy his possessions only to a limited extent. He
will of course take care not to show his wealth; he
cannot sell the property, or if he could convert it
into money, what good would it do him in Ha'il? Neither the Amir, nor and even less his cousin Hamud,
would ever allow him to spend the country's currency
abroad; the money is to stay in the country. In any
case, only with the abandonment and sacrifice of his
real estate could he hope to be allowed to withdraw
from the territory of Shammar. He is extremely fond of
women, as emerged from his own accounts of his adventures, and he is one of the few in Ha'il who allow
themselves the luxury of two wives. His philosophy of
life is of course much broader than that of the Beduin,
his manners more polished and less restricted and what
is most attractive about him is that he does not beg;
having grown up in a large town where not only Arabs,
but Turks, Persians, Indians, even Europeans come and
go, he has seen and heard much that he is fond of recalling in memory and conversation. Huber had there-

fore been on friendly terms with him at his very first stay and had him to thank for many small services and favours discreetly shown. This was not to go unrewarded this time: by Huber's request I had brought with me a silver watch for him, and had it on my person for today's greeting. After a long interval this man finds favour and honour again thanks to us; all the distinguished people, with Hamud al-ᶜUbaid at their head, who play the beggar round us and achieve nothing, seek to have better luck through ᶜAbdullah, they invite him to their houses and give him presents in the expectation of seeing their stock rise in our books and of making progress. The information which he gives us is more reliable and less biased than we could obtain from any other source.

His house, not far from ours, differs externally in no way from the usual houses of the town; inside however I was astonished at the unusual expenditure on decoration in the reception-room. The brown foundation of the only clay walls was overlaid with a good finger-thick layer of lime, and out of this the decorations had subsequently been carved. These consisted of proverbs, mathematical figures, lamps, birds, quadrupeds, human beings. The necks of all the larger animals had been cut through, in order to eliminate the idea of a living object, which would make the representation sinful. The master of the house was very pleased at our visit and with the watch that I had brought him. We did not stay long, drank a coffee, and smoked a hookah.

459

House Interior at Hail

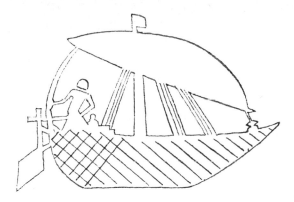

At sunset we had to take up our invitation to supper
in the house of Hamud al-Mijrad, where were assembled
besides ourselves all the travellers who had made the
journey from al-Jauf here with us. I presented our
host with a bullet-mould; instead of thanking me, he
asked whether he could not have the relevant rifle; I
pointed out to him that he already had it, for the
bullets to be cast by him would fit the barrel of the
flintlock he had already received.

My hope of being able to spend the evening quietly
at home was in vain: hardly had we returned when we
were fetched by Hamud al-Mijrad to go to the qasr.
The Amir inquired whether we had no wishes and needs;
I asked for one of the fly-brushes which were hanging
on the wall in the hall; together with that he presented to us also other things that happened to be
ready to hand; for example, eight camel-sticks of
tamarisk wood, two wooden inlaid rosaries, three exqui-
sitely beautiful amber chains, as well as a brass bowl.
He was within an ace of adding two sabres with silver-
gilt plating, but he considered them somewhat beneath
us, and promised us more beautiful ones later, which
were forgotten. To his request to see some pictures
I replied by showing a number of woodcuts, which I had
brought with me on my journey as samples. The drawings
were however too small for the long-sighted eye and a
little too complicated for what he was used to. Hamud
al-ᶜUbaid had so little *savoir-faire* that, having not
the slightest idea of what was represented, he held
most of the pages upside down in his hand and admired
them.

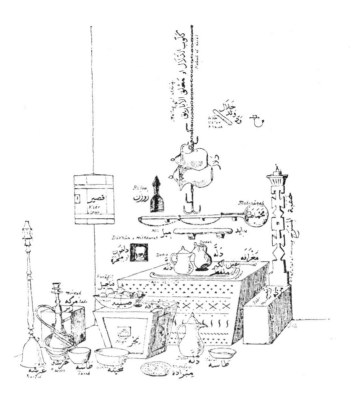

It was past nine o'clock at the earliest when we
left the qasr. A striking patch of red, which I at
first took to be a sort of Northern Light, appeared
in the night-sky, and (though I could not determine
this till daytime) in a westerly direction. For the
next 14 days this inexplicable phenomenon was regularly visible, first very bright, then gradually decreas-
ing in brightness. At that time I could not have been
aware of the explosion of the volcano Krakatau in the
Sunda Strait (27 August 1883) and the phenomena that
followed it in the twilit-sky.

Just as we were turning into our street, Ghanam was
already lying in wait at the corner, in order to pay us
another visit. He had vainly hoped that I would have
found time meanwhile to open the chest with the tools
intended for him. He stayed there till 11 o'clock.

Tuesday 23 Oct. 1883. An hour before sunrise:
visit to Hamud al'^{C}Ubaid the Prince's cousin. On returning home we found the princes Majid and ^{C}Abdulaziz.
As soon as these had gone off, we sought out ^{C}Abdullah
al-Muslimani, who regaled us with a delicate bread
baked in the Baghdad manner. Hardly back home, we were
to accept an invitation from the armourer Ghanam ibn
Bani. I begged to be excused on account of my injured
foot, which I was just then treating with carbolic
water, but was honoured by having the meal sent over to
me. In the course of the day there was an unbroken
stream of visitors, time-wasters of all sorts, and sick
people who wanted medicine from Huber. I fled as yesterday to the roof, to have a few undisturbed minutes
for the writing up of my notes. We sent a request to
Hamud al-^{C}Ubaid for bedding, such as quilted blankets
and cushions. As I intended to paint the walls of our
reception-room (qahawah) with proverbs and pictures, I
had the brown clay walls first overlaid with white lime
two metres high.

Towards evening the Amir sent for us, in order to
show us his Castle and to parade his horses. I do not
know much about horses and therefore will not tell
stories about the famous Arab horses, about which so
much has been written by experts and laymen. I would
however like to correct various widespread errors.
Above all, believe me: the number of horses in Central
Arabia is surprisingly small. At the very most they
would total 500 in Najd, and these, with the exception
of 30 or 40, are to be found exclusively in the possession of the Amir and his family. It may well be that
40 years ago there were 100 more in Najd; ^{C}Abbas Pasha
of Egypt, a great fancier of thoroughbreds, then however bought up through his agent sent to the spot
whatever good animals he could lay hands on at incredibly high prices. Unfortunately, the 80 or so animals
taken to Egypt have completely degenerated under the
changed living conditions, and as a result of the abundant green fodder in the Nile Delta have acquired thick
necks and finally lost nearly all of their lauded
virtues. There is no question of any real horse-

breeding in Najd; everything there is left to Nature,
so long as the race, i.e. the stock, is pure. In the
last analysis it is the poets who have seen to the
fame of Arab horses and who must answer for it; the
rare, precious, and outstanding horses are the proper
subjects for song. It must also be remembered that
the merits of the Arab horse are in the first place
relative, compared with the camels, which are to be
counted in thousands. In war, for the attack and the
pursuit, or as saviours in flight, the horse is far
superior to the finest dalul, not in stamina, but in
the immediate show of strength, speed, and handling;
the poetic imagination therefore gladly seizes on
its performance, but mostly exaggerates it. The
Prince's few hundred horses spend the whole year in the
best and best-watered grazing grounds 5 to 10 days'
journey north (and N.E.) of the Ha'il region, and there
have to make do with the usual fodder of the desert,
as camels and sheep also do. As soon however as there
is the suspicion or the report of a raid on even the
most remote frontier of the kingdom, the precious animals are immediately withdrawn a few days' journey
nearer to the oasis-city. Should the Amir himself be
planning a *ghazu*, the horses are fed with a couple of
handfuls of barley every day for weeks before; and if
the raid moves off with 3000-4000 participants on
camels, the horses, loose beside the camels, which have
to carry water and barley for them, are led along for
the 8 to 10 days it lasts, at the rate of 20 to 22
hours' march a day, and are mounted only at the moment
of the attack and for the pursuit. The situation is
of course quite different as regards the horses of the
Beduins outside Najd, as for example the ^cAnaiza',Ruwala,
Wuld ^cAli, who live in the Syrian desert near the
Euphrates, and therefore have better conditions in respect of water and fodder; it might be possible to speak
of a certain wealth of horses in their case, but all
the less for that very reason of purity of race. On
this latter point however it is not for me to judge.

And now for the Prince's horses. In the huge building attached to the Castle and forming a complete

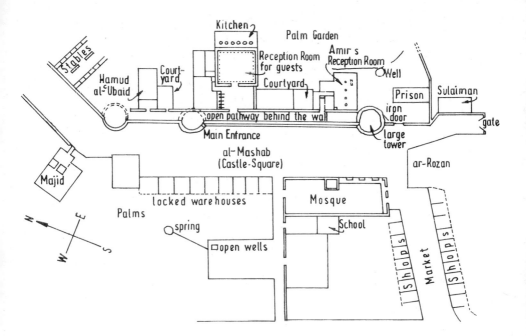

Labels in image:
Kitchen · Palm Garden · Reception Room for guests · Amir's Reception Room · Well · Stables · Hamud al-Ubaid · Court-yard · Courtyard · Prison · Sulaiman · open pathway behind the wall · iron door · gate · Main Entrance · large tower · Majid · al-Mashab (Castle-Square) · ar-Rozan · locked warehouses · Mosque · Palms · spring · School · open wells · Shops · Market · Shops · N E S W

Plan of the Amir's Palace
at Hail and surroundings

quarter of the town surrounded by continuous walls
there are on the north side a number of courts with
stables. Thither we betook ourselves, led by the Amir
and with a large escort of princes. The horses were
standing there in the open, separated according to age
and sex, hobbled and covered with heavy rugs. At a nod
from the Amir the rugs were removed and we were now to
give judgement. The first impression was anything but
favourable: the animals were pitiably thin, mean-looking,
and not well groomed. Somewhat impatient at our reserve
the Amir pressed us for an expression of opinion.

Acting as spokesman, I declared to him that I was no
connoisseur, but the animals seemed to be to be
absolute thoroughbreds. Confirming this, he explained to me some of the characteristics of the Najdi
breed. Challenged to compare them with European

horses, I took the liberty of observing that the
horses in Christian countries were in any case superior in size. "Yes, that is quite possible, and
in compensation they want to eat more and cannot
endure thirst; soft horses however are no use to us
in our country." He is not so wide of the mark in
that; in toughness and stamina the horses in Najd,
like their Beduin masters, can surely not be excelled.
In another court a huge black stallion, richly saddled and harnessed, was led forward, and I did not
conceal my admiration. It may well be however a
Saqlawi from Mesopotamia. In a separate area, there
were a dozen foals in a large room. In accordance
with local custom their tails had been cut completely
off, as those of all horses under 3 years always are,
leaving only the bald stump. What the purpose of that
is, I do not know; in any case the sight to the uninitiated is downright ludicrous. Finally we were shown
in a small courtyard the Amir's favourite camel, a mare
of the Nu^{c}maniya breed. The animal, wearing for the
first time today a new ornament, namely a magnificent
turquoise set in silver and screwed into its right
nostril, might gradually have convinced itself that
that was very beautiful, but was not quite reconciled
to the novelty, and therefore twisted its head to one
side every now and then, in order the better to be able
to squint at the turquoise.

From the horses we proceeded to the neglected
Castle-garden; among palm-trees there were growing, for
purely ornamental purposes, dispersed here and there
some others, fig-, lemon-, orange-, pomegranate-, and
peach-trees. For irrigation the necessary water was
raised by three camels out of a well 17·fathoms[11] deep.
At other times the Amir used to keep in a hedged-in
part of the garden a few animals such as gazelles,
ibexes, or even baqar al-wahsh (big white beasts like
antelopes), but had them removed, partly on account of
their vicious temper.

We were then shown, not without pride, the Castle-
kitchen, containing 7 copper cauldrons, each big enough
to boil the meat of a whole camel. The usual daily

average fed in the qasr on mutton and Iraqi rice[12] is 150 to 200 persons. There are however times - for example, shortly before setting out on a raid or when the Persian pilgrim-caravan passes through - when the number being fed on several consecutive days is 800 to 1000. Passing by the prison, an ordinary clay-brick building, in which behind the open door there was nothing to be seen beyond a pair of notched beams (for fastening criminals in the stocks), we left the Castle through a gate in the S.W. corner. Throughout the whole walk to see the horses and now finally up to the Amir's qahawah the young Prince ᶜAbdulaziz had held me by the hand. He seemed to have taken a great liking to me and urged me to visit him soon. For the evening we were left, oddly enough, untroubled by visitors.

Wed. 24 Oct. 83. In the morning we were taken by Hamud al-Mijrad to see the Mashab, i.e. to the large open space in front of the Castle. There was being held there the ceremonial Majlis or General Assembly in the presence of the Amir. On the raised clay benches along the Castle-walls sat the Amir and his household. We took our places farther on. A little farther out in the open space, squatting on the ground in a semicircle, were the spectators each with a sabre or at least a camel-stick in front of him. The Majlis is regularly attended without invitation by all those in the town who count, so far as we can judge, as high society, or by any who have some particular reason for showing themselves, such as one who wishes to make a personal request. The Prince surveys the crowd, accepts messages, opens letters, and reads out as much of them as he thinks fit, he listens to begging requests and accepts presents, settles disputes, administers justice, mark well, without any paperwork, since an individual's criminal record, if any, is well known to all his fellow-countrymen. The most frequent crime is theft. Someone steps forward and announces that a couple of sheep or camels have been stolen from him by such and such a person. The Amir promises him that he will see to it that they are given back or replaced, and has the shaikh of the tribe to which the thief be-

longs informed of this with the observation that he
must clear the matter up. This simple announcement
implies the tacit threat that in case of delay the
shaikh in question, together with his tribe may, at
the next year's distribution of grazing-grounds, be
allotted a region inferior to their previous one.

At today's assembly there stepped forward a man who
the previous evening had been struck by another with a
stick over the left eye and been injured, in proof of
which he showed his blood-stained shirt. The Amir
merely remarked that he knew about it already; next
please! Then some fellows were brought in who were
deserters from the Turkish garrison in San^{c}a' in the
Yemen; they wore only shirts, torn to shreds, and some
wretched head-cloths; in exchange for these they received new clothes and also a present of money and a
promise that they were to be fed here for a few days.

After half-an-hour the Majlis was over. The Amir
stood up and invited us to follow him. Adjoining the
Castle is the dwelling of the Finance Minister Sabhan.
We went up to the upper storey and into a large room
(rawshan) which had only narrow slits at floor-level in
the wall on the side of the street. Whenever the Amir
heard anything particular down below, he would turn suddenly round and shout something through the slit into
the street. In a short time the fellow who had struck
his companion and injured him the previous evening was
dragged through the Suq (market) into the street; the
Amir ordered him through the embrasure to be flogged.
That was immediately seen to. From my seat I could not
see this order carried out, but I did hear the swish of
the cane and a great shouting; but after a few strokes
the miscreant succeeded in running off. Then the Amir
took up the subject of my inscriptions and with his own
hand wrote in my note-book the names of a few localities
where inscriptions were supposed to be on the cliffs;
he would have me conducted thither.

After insistent entreaty we moved from there to the
house of Hamud al-^CUbaid, where we found boring company. This hypocrite once again let the beads of his
rosary slip through his fingers and churned out his
pious mutterings. He annoyed me so much today by doubting our veracity that I resolved it should be a long
time before I accepted another invitation to his house;
he asked not only us, but for safety's sake also our
servant Mahmud who happened to come in, whether there
were really no more cartridges for the two Mausers than
those we had handed over. I exchanged glances with
Huber, we took an abrupt leave, and betook ourselves
home. Arrived there I complained to Hamud al-Mijrad,
our adjutant, about this kind of questioning, as though
we were liars; whether out of greed or for pleasure we
wanted to take with us on the rest of our journey the
bare lead? With tears in his eyes he explained to us
the difficulty of his position; he was the object of re-
proaches from both sides, he said; in the Castle he
considered it his duty as our travelling companion to
defend us at all times, but in doing that he had to lis-

ten to ^CUbaid's complaint that he was not squeezing
enough out of us for the Castle (i.e. for him), and now
here was I belabouring him with such complaints. With
this conflict of duties he reminded me of Count Rüdiger
von Pechlarn in the *Nibelungenlied*. An end was put to
this unpleasant discussion by a succession of visitors;
first came the Finance-Minister Sabhan with his son
Nasir, then the inquisitive Prince Majid with his suite.
I had not time to put aside my mazwadah (camel's travel-
bag) and so he shook out the whole of its contents on to
the carpet, rummaging through the trinkets in the expectation that I would present him with them. I remained
as rigid as a goat. Towards midday it was peace at last.

In the afternoon I painted on the wall of the qahawah
(the reception-room) on a specially prepared white
ground, in red foot-high Arabic letters, the following
maxim from the Qur'an (Sura 2, verse 59):

> "See those who are believers (Muslims) and those
> who are adherents of the Jewish religion, and
> the Christians, and the Sabaeans: he who believes
> in God and in the Last Judgement, and does good
> works shall have his reward with the Lord; they
> have nothing to fear and shall not be afflicted."

Towards evening I betook myself alone to a place outside the town in order to sketch the town of Ha'il.

On the way I met some of Hamud al-^CUbaid's sons with
two hunting falcons, both chained and with the leather
hood (burqa') on their heads. The view of the mountain-
chain, on which a storm was just gathering, was beautiful.

After supper the inevitable Ghanam, who was gradually
becoming a thorough nuisance, returned, followed immediately by the smith Husain. I teased them with the
"Oriental Puzzle", two crossed and interlaced half-open
brass rings. They wished naturally to separate them by
force - which is impossible - and could be restrained
from trying to do so only by the threat of taking the
trick from them without explanation. Finally there
appeared our travel-escort through the Nafud, the black

Euting's drawing of Ha'il from the south

Ibrahim. He had gone on ahead towards the end of the journey and ceased to look after the camels and the luggage properly. Before his departure for Damascus with Hamud al-Mijrad he had driven out his wife, and the Amir had promised to give him another on his return. The wedding was to take place this evening, and he came now to fetch his promised wedding-present.

Thurs. 25 Oct. 83. Even before sunrise visitors were knocking indefatigably at our front door; with equal persistence on our side the house remained locked. Towards 9 o'clock the Amir appeared, without warning, in order to pay us a visit. He noticed the quotations from the Qur'an painted on the walls, nodded approvingly and recited them out loud. I presented him with a traveller's grip, and he asked also for a little box with Japanese cups. Huber asked me to give the Amir my copy of the Qur'an bound in red morocco with gilt edges. The Amir then wanted to see what kind of books we had brought with us. That we received this visit from the Amir today was to be appreciated all the more because he was otherwise quite absorbed in preparations for the raid due to take place on the following day. Its destination is still a secret, probably into the territory of Ibn Al Sa^{c}ud towards Riyadh. An unexpected invitation to take part in this threw me into a state of no small excitement. For all the discomforts and privations involved, what new and interesting experiences such a Beduin campaign would have given us: something in which no European had ever taken part before! I hesitated for a long time, but finally, thinking of my injured foot,

had to declare that I could not accept, but Huber reserved the right to take part. During this conversation
tea was served in two cups with handles and two small
Japanese cups. In the afternoon Prince Majid came to
ask for the two Japanese cups for his father. He also
wanted to have my little revolver. These friendly robbers! Heavens! it was not long before there came,
after supper, the cleverest beggar of them all, Hamud
al-Mijrad, to inquire (allegedly in the Amir's name)
whether it was not our intention to present the Amir
with the six-volume geographical work of Yakut and the
two volumes of al-Bakri. When I assured him that it
was not so, that that was a mistake, he said that I
could at least give one of the volumes as a gift. On
hearing my definite declaration that I needed these two
Arabian geographers as much as I needed my daily bread,
it occurred to him that he had seen yet other books in
our house. Yes, one is the *Thousand and One Nights,*
the Amir has that himself, and the other is Qastalani's
Life of Muhammad. Well then, give the *Life of Muhammad*
and lend us the other volumes to read one after another.
In the evening we had some peace at first. Soon Hamud
al-Mijrad was back, but this time he was given a well-
rehearsed sermon on the greed of the Shammar, so that
for today we were spared further demands. Time and
again I think how glad I am that I did not bring the
sabre which I had been given by H.M. King Charles; I
do not think it would have been possible to save it from
these claws. At a later hour the sandals ordered from
a shoemaker were delivered. They had turned out well
and cost 3/4 majidi the pair. In mine I had had a piece
of gold trimming, which I had brought along, sewn into
the heel, so that when I visited the Castle or somewhere, where according to circumstances there might be
40-50 identical sandals laid out in the vestibule, I
might on leaving be able at once to find the ones I was
looking for. Several brief rain-storms having occurred
during the day, the night was marked by brilliant flash-
es of lightning, accompanied by violent thunder-claps,
later by pouring rain.

Fri. 26 Oct. 83. Everyone in the town is completely

taken up with preparations for the *ghazu*, so that today we have a fairly undisturbed house. I seize the opportunity of painting one wall of our reception-room with a landscape in colours of clay: in the foreground a lofty grove of date-palms, around the springs gushing out among them some Beduin wearing richly ornamented weapons, while in the background camels were grazing in luxuriant pasture.

At 4 o'clock in the afternoon we took ourselves to the Mashab. Despite the light rain the square was unusually animated because of the imminent departure on the *ghazu*. We chased two Beduin away from a nice dry seat and took their place, in order to be able to watch all the activity in comfort. Sacks were being dragged along, provisions being piled up, weapons prepared, saddles and clothes patched, cords borrowed, animals fed and watered. Though stuffed full with camels, the Mashab was nevertheless very clean, because little girls vied with one another in immediately gathering into baskets the freshly deposited camel-dung, in order to lose none of the precious fuel. You should know that the area round Ha'il for a radius of several hours' travel has long since been stripped of every out-door plant, so that the poorer inhabitants have difficulty in procuring even the most essential fuel. To be sure, camel-loads of firewood are brought to market from the desert now and then, but each load costs from one half to one whole riyal (1 mark 60 to 3 marks 20). In Ha'il however few families can afford to spend so much. Accordingly, at every opportunity children are taught the value of the hunt for camel-dung. At one of the Castle gates money was being distributed to the needy among the participants in the *ghazu* (1-20 riyal), partly to procure the equipment still lacking, partly to support the families left behind. Not far from us there squatted alone a foreign bedu, conspicuous by his swarthy skin. Hamud al-Mijrad, who was busily giving orders to the throng of people, was beckoned over and informed us that the man was a Qahtani named Salim ibn Fatnan, from al-Qasim, the most southerly part of Najd, who had been deliberately kept in the town, because subjects of a

foreign tribe, even if it were friendly, are not allowed
to return to their homeland until a few days after the
start of a *ghazu*. Huber wanted information from him on
the tribes and organization of the Qahtani. The man
showed no inclination to give it, naturally; indeed
at first he gave no answer and then only an evasive
one, until Hamud conveyed to him the fact that we were
the special guests of the Shuyukh and he could confidently give us whatever information we asked for. In
order not to be disturbed and to loosen his tongue, we
invited him to a meal and regaled him generously. He
made his grateful satisfaction known through the usual
belches, and prepared to undertake the complete washing
of his body in the qahawah. Saying that it would be for
his greater comfort, we suggested he undertook this re-
freshing operation outside in the yard. He returned
after a considerable time, strengthened and cleaned,
and allowed himself quite willingly to be questioned
on all details of his tribe. Our literate servant
Mahmud recorded as usual the Qahtani's statements in
Huber's diary. The business, as a matter of fact, did
not proceed entirely smoothly, for the Qahtani had
hardly mentioned a few names when he stopped and complained of the water that he had in his head; we should
give him some medicine for it. The natives' idea of
sicknesses and their cures is as simple as it is naive:
every sickness has its seat in a specific part of the
body, and for every part there is a special medicine,
which the doctor only needs to take out of his medicine-
chest and administer. A particular description of the
illness or personal presentation of the sick person is
not considered necessary. Consequently we said we
would talk about the water in his head later; in the
meantime he should continue with his account of the
leading men in the tribe and its families. It may well
have been an hour before the information, constantly
interrupted by laments over the water in his head, was
concluded. Then we gave him on leaving a portion of
senna-leaves. After him came the camel-dealer Husain
who offered to forward letters for us via Medina and,
through the Hajj, to Damascus. He wanted to pick them
up one of these days.

Sat. 27 Oct. 83. Very early in the morning ᶜAbdullah
al-Muslimani came to report a large pool of blood in
front of our house-door. The camel-dealer who came in
just after him confirmed this, adding that there was
the same beastly mess on the threshold of the house
where he had put up, and the door itself had blood smeared all over it. The general opinion in the town was, he
said, that the Mashhadi (Persian merchants who had immi-
grated from Mashhad, in whose quarter our house was
situated), had committed this outrage against us doubtless out of resentment at being left to knock more than
once in vain at our house-door. Muhammad, the son of
the armourer Ghanam, was of the same opinion. Hardly
had this young man withdrawn with a present of 4 metal
capsules of the best gunpowder, when his father Ghanam
appeared, to beg for some powder for himself too. The
observation that we had just given his son 4 boxes full,
he rejected with indignation: what we gave his son was
no concern of his! A few other small presents were made
to the camel-dealer Husain in exchange for taking charge
of and delivering the letters home. For the morning
meal ᶜAbdullah sent us some choice Baghdad bread baked
by his wife, together with some pistachio-nuts and some
sweets.

The house-servant we had had hitherto, Matar, had
gossiped so much that we replaced him by another named
Khairullah. The lad however is so stupid as to be absolutely no use: he understands neither Huber and me nor
our servant Mahmud, he knows no words and understands
only when he is asked for fire or water; his greatest
skill consists in filling the holes in the floor with
clay and sand and then in patting it down with his ape-
like hands. The two female slaves who help in the
kitchen are much more intelligent.

Towards evening Hamud al-Mijrad announced that the
Amir was expecting us to supper at sunset. While Hamud
was begging, there arrived the Wakil, the plenipotentiary
of our landlord, to apologize for the insult paid to our
house; he was a Mashhadi himself, but could not find out
by whom and for what reason the deed had been perpetrat-

475

ed. Hamud interrupted his begging for several minutes
in order to discuss the incident; only after the departure of the Wakil did he carry on with his begging. A
few moments later a fine living gazelle was delivered to
us, a present from the Wakil.

On our way to the Amir all was quiet in the streets:
the main body of men, with flags (bairaq) flying at their
head, had left for the raid before midday. We found the
Amir in the Castle in high good humour; he enjoined the
four worthies who were being left behind to see to our
every need. Letters and newspapers that had arrived from
Medina were read out, others were given to us to read.
The meal provided a pleasant variety of dishes: besides
rice and meat, of which the Amir broke off some pieces
with his fingers and himself laid them before us, there
was some excellent unleavened bread and a kind of ris-
sole in broth. On account of my lack of dexterity in
the use of my fingers I was handed a spoon. The food
had not been prepared in the court-kitchen, but came
from the Harem. With our best wishes for the success
of the *ghazu* we left the Castle even before the last
prayer. Hamud al-Mijrad accompanied us to our house.
Recalling the fact that I had requested him to draw my
attention to everything that I should do or not do, he
asked me on leaving to take more account of local manners: owing to the influence of Wahhabi priests it was
not the done thing in his country to express one's joy
out loud, even to the extent of singing. In his presence I could do as I liked, but in the presence of
others (except perhaps that of ᶜAbdullah al-Muslimani)
I must not sing again.

Lastly came Muhammad ibn Ghanam to explain and
apologize for the pool of blood in front of our house.
He had himself been the obviously unwitting doer of the
deed: he must have trodden on a piece of broken glass
or something similar in the darkness on the previous
evening, without noticing it. Standing in front of our
house he had knocked several times in vain; he did as a
matter of fact have the impression that he was standing
in a puddle, and had then wiped dry on our door the wet
(blood-stained) hand with which he had rubbed his foot;

then, assuming from the lack of response to his repeated knocking that we were spending the evening with the
camel-dealer Husain, he had betaken himself to the latter's door, where, still standing in the wet, he had
cleaned foot and hand on the threshold and the door, so
as not to risk entering the house with wet feet. Having vainly knocked here too for a long time, he had gone
home to bed. Only the next morning had he noticed that
he had a wound in his heel. So saying, he showed us the
sole of his foot. There in the hard part of the sole
there was a gaping cut 3 cm. long and nearly 1 cm. deep.
One must have a healthy hide to notice such a thing only
the next day!

Sun. 28 Oct. 83. Since we have been here in Ha'il,
the weather has taken on a wintry look: the sky is more
or less cloudy, the nearby mountains are mantled in mist,
the smooth dripping walls of granite, when a ray of the
sun strikes them, glisten with a pale silver colour
through the light drizzle.

So, early this morning the Amir has set out on the
ghazu with his leading men, and will meet the rest of
the horde at Jabal Sarra this evening. After breakfast
we decided to pay a visit to the Amir's uncle on his
mother's side, Sulaiman al-Khuraishi. When the front
door was opened we found ourselves confronted with some
unprepared women, who fled screaming. We were received
in the upper storey of the house (*rawshan*), and regaled
with dates of wonderful sweetness. The light-coloured
wooden doors were attractively studded with iron and all
of them painted with decorations in red and black.

In the evening ^CAbdullah al-Muslimani prepared a
fine meal for us, enhancing the solemnity of the occasion by hanging up the silver clock that I had given
him. He dared not show it out of doors, nor indeed at
all before the departure of the raiders, otherwise its
existence would have been reported to al-^CUbaid in the
first quarter-of-an-hour, and he would have incorporated
it in his collection of clocks by expressing a quite
unmistakeable admiration: Huber produced as his contribution to the feast a bottle of champagne, which was to

be emptied to the health of its giver, i.e. Dr. Schröder, the Imperial Consul-General in Beirut. Our broad-minded host watched the uncorking expectantly, and drank one glass after another without any pricks of conscience. In vain I hoped he would get a little drunk; in spite of his being unused to it for so long, a good schooling in Baghdad obviously stood him in good stead. Only by repeated belching did he give his sense of well-being its natural expression.

For the next day we planned the ascent of Jabal Samra', situated just outside the town, and for that purpose ordered two donkeys for 8 o'clock in the morning from the Finance Minister, Salamah.

Mon. 29 Oct. 83. Of course the donkeys did not come. Twice we sent a message to Salamah in vain. At noon we abandoned the plan for today. At 3 o'clock our servant Mahmud had to write a letter to Salamah: it was regrettable, that since the departure of the Amir, from whose lips he had himself heard the command, our needs were neglected. Since the donkeys were not to be had, would he at least be so good as to send for our camels, who were on the pasture (a day's journey from here), in order that we might have at our disposal our own transport. After despatching the letter, we walked N.W. from the town up the Umm al-Masajid hill; from there I sketched part of Jabal Aja'.

On our return we found ͨAbdullah al-Muslimani in our house; he told us that in our absence Salamah had called twice and with tears in his eyes had lamented that he was very sorry that he had not been able to send the donkeys; two slaves had taken them without permission, one to Laqita and the other to ͨAqda. (Those chaps will get a good thrashing for that!) By tomorrow early the donkeys will certainly be available, he said.

In the evening after supper the smith Husain came. My large metal box, which served to keep the copies of inscriptions in, had in the course of the journey suffered various nasty dents and had been hammered by him back into shape. To reward him, I presented him with various tools and some emery-paper. Asked about his iron, he informed us that it all came from India by sea via Kuwait on the Persian Gulf; similarly cotton and coffee, called therefore *bahri*. The finer coffee from South Arabia (Yemen) was brought from Mecca and Medina over the Hajj, never however transported by land from Yemen itself, but shipped to Jiddah or Yanbu^c. When, after a good long drink of water, I lay down on the carpet to rest, he leapt up, pulling me up anxiously and begged me not to sleep, lest the water flow into my head!! Later on the venerable Master of Ceremonies Mufarriq paid us a visit. At midnight there was the sound of clattering: the gazelle had penetrated into the qahawah and was walking around among the cups and the crockery. Only after putting up considerable re-sistance and practising every sort of prank could she be chased out.

Tues. 30 Oct. 83. At 8 o'clock in the morning a Hutaima called ^cAid ad-Dursi appeared with the two donkeys. We rode out from the southern end of the town, and after half-an-hour reached the foot of Mount Samra' to the east of the town. Leaving the donkeys to bro-wse below, we climbed to the summit, which rose to 400-500 feet above the plain. It was a good spot for orientating oneself; in the west Jabal Aja', in the east Jabal Salma. I sketched a panorama of each while Huber measured a few angles. Our local escort was well informed as to the names of individual peaks. Some remarkable granite ridges, extending parallel from west to east, rose to quite a low height above the plain.

After spending four hours on the summit, we climbed down to the animals and rode to one of the Amir's walled gardens, called Huraimiyah, then back to the town by the N.W. through the quarter called ^cAinat, now ruined and uninhabited.

At supper-time the Qahtani presented himself in order to bid us farewell, because he would be allowed to de-part the next day. Till then all foreign Beduin were detained in the town, so that no news could leak out about the forthcoming *ghazu*. His laments about his catarrh were ridiculous; at least five times every quarter of an hour he would say: "Look! There is water in my head and it is always flowing down through my nose; if I shake my head, I can hear the water splashing about, and others hear it too." Huber assured him that he could hear nothing, and that he need not worry, no water had flowed into his brain while he slept; moreover, he wanted to follow up this advice with a medicine (it was nothing special). We were delivered by the appearance of the chief Overseer of all servants, the sinecurist ᶜAli. I questioned him about the number of servants in the town, all of which without exception belong to the Amir and live in a special quarter (Suq al-ᶜAbid) in the N.W. of the town. As to the number of adult men servants he estimated 160, and in addition 30 eunuchs, a total of 1000 head of servants.

Excursion to ᶜAqda

Wed. 31 Oct. 83. The house was locked up and the gazelle left alone in the yards with barley, dates, and water. Bedding and cooking utensils, laden on two donkeys, together with a wether to be slaughtered, were sent on ahead under the escort of three drivers. At about half-past nine ᶜAbdullah, Huber, and I, and then the servant Mahmud, rode behind them on donkeys. On the way ᶜAbdullah gave me a piece of a stick of palm which had been hardened in the fire, in order to keep the donkey up to the mark by a jab in the withers. The route lay westwards over the plain, and brought us after 1½ hours to the foot of the completely denuded Mount Aja'. There began the valley-floor of ᶜAqda about 100 m. wide, excavated horizontally by the coarse granite sand. A group of cliffs, al-Qaᶜayid, rose up from the centre, and seemed to block the entrance.

Behind on the right we turned off to one side towards the spring ᶜUwaimir, and camped for some time under the shady palms. A handsome bird, black with a

The Valley of ʿAqda

white head (*Abu mughairah*) was gaily and confidently
going about its business round the water. The spring,
once copious, is supposed to have dried up significantly
in the last three years. At 12 o'clock we struck camp;
while the cliffs drew ever nearer together, we soon came
up against a wall 50 m. long which straddled the narrow-
est point.

A door on the left was opened; behind it lay the
houses of the oasis ʿAqda, hidden in a grove of palm-
trees and enclosed by a circle of bare cliffs. We
dismounted at the qasr which had been built by the
shuyukh and was completely unfurnished. The luggage
had already been off-loaded; while the carpets with the
seats were being arranged and the wether slaughtered,
we called on two houses and drank several coffees. In
one garden a whole palm trunk lay with one end in the
fire; it burned slowly away and was pushed forward into
the fireplace according to need. Towards evening an
ibex appeared on one of the cliff-tops nearby; it was
clearly intending to climb down to some water-hole. A
huntsman immediately set off with a gun, glimpsed him
several times, but returned home after a considerable

time empty-handed. My physical condition left much to
be desired today; I had a bad headache and dizziness,
my upper lip and nose were much swollen, and what's more
the wounds in my foot hurt even more.

Thurs. 1 Nov. 83. In the morning I found great relief through bleeding of the nose. For today's proposed
excursion to Jabal Far^c, the highest peak of Jabal Aja',
I made several unsuccessful attempts to shape my sandals so that they would press less on the wounds in my
feet. The simplest method was the last to be tried: to
leave the sandals off altogether. We had taken along
with us two guides and experts in names, Muhammad al-
^cAid and Mufaddi. These sat on a single donkey, ^cAbdul-
lah stayed behind in the qasr, and Huber and I mounted
the two donkeys of the *shuyukh*. So at about half-past
ten we rode out of ^cAqda. The way led south-westward
through the sandy hollow of the valley; to right and
left were a few free-standing date-palms. Soon the
cliffs closed in; after an hour's ride we dismounted
and sent the donkeys on by a more comfortable roundabout
way. We ourselves turned to go straight up between the
granite blocks and in the hollow of an overhanging rock
we came upon a basin of clear water, enlivened by half
a dozen small black frogs. The water was balm to us.
From here down we had to slither at times under great
rounded cliffs, until we reached a basin-shaped grazing-
ground (al-Jaziyah), which had been selected as the place
where our animals could be left. The donkeys soon
arrived and set about the rush-like tufts (musi^c) with
delight. The animals could be left here unsupervised
without fear, since no-one would steal the property of
the Amir. The route climbed up the narrow ravine ever
more steeply; in the cliff-wall on the left the guide
pointed out a hole, which he called a spring, accessible
only with difficulty. I scrambled up to it: the hollow
was about 30 cm. in diameter and 15 cm. deep and filled
with water, and to my astonishment there was moss on
its walls, the only moss I had seen on the whole of my
journey. After a further half-hour we climbed over a
cliff-bar and over there on the right, separated from
us by a fold in the mountain, we saw the steep stone
boulder-strewn wall of the Far^c.

On a sloping surface a white mark was noticeable,
laid bare by some freshly crumbled stone. Our people
related how years ago a star (meteor) had fallen here
and had thrown down the fragments, while the other
pieces of cliff lying around in boulders had been there
from olden times – thrown down by Noah's ark as it
grazed the mountain-tops. Through the fissure in the
cliff that led upwards just before us, a camel that had
escaped from ^CAqda had a few years ago found a way over
the mountain; the path climbed so steeply that I would
have thought it impossible. As the ascent to the peak
threatened to become ever more difficult, we took off
all superfluous clothes and contented ourselves with a
shirt and a head-piece of white cotton-weool (*takiyah*).
Having climbed by the sweat of our brows the last slanting wall of smooth sheets of cliff, we stood on the
peak at 12.50 and enjoyed an extensive view of the
absolutely bare narrow-ribbed masses of granite. The
houses of Ha'il could be easily recognized out there in
the ocean-like plain; the light-blue line of Jabal Salma
bordered the horizon. However, I was in no condition to
enjoy this wonderful prospect in all its details: tor-
menting thirst forced me soon to climb down again to a
stone cavity forming a small water-hole, which I had
noticed lying far below us on the way up. While Huber
undertook angle-measurements on the peak and ascertained

483

the names of individual mountains, I did my sketching
below in the Shauwat Fawwaz. I felt ecstatic, wandering utterly alone in this magnificent mountain-landscape:
no baggage, hardly a garment on the body, a sketch-book
and a switch in the hand, no possibility of losing one's
way, no danger from any source, no being plagued, the
only clock the stomach. Having reached the donkeys in
the al-Jaziyah basin, I just had time to sketch the ravine leading down to ^cAqda. Thick banks of cloud were
threatening and thunder, beginning to roll in the ravines, warned that the time had come to depart. Huber had
hurriedly descended from the peak with the two escorts.
The animals, which had now fed for five hours, willingly
let themselves be mounted. The sky became ever darker,
and night was closing in when we reached the qasr in
^cAqda.

After supper people continued to come from the village, played the *rababah* and sang excruciating songs to
its accompaniment. The crackling of thunder and the
flashing of lightning lasted all night, but little rain
fell, the centre of the storm discharging itself on
Gha'ila in the north of the mountain chain. An unusual
guest that visited us in the darkness, a frog, was
assigned a more suitable abode outside the house.

Fri. 2 Nov. 83. After yesterday's march my foot hurt
so much that I had to stay indoors; I used the time to
do some painting. The sky was cloudy the whole day, but
only a little rain fell in spite of violent thunder.
During the night the same cold frog who turned up yesterday came to me in my bed, but suffered the same treatment
as the first time.

Sat. 3 Nov. 83. In the morning our belongings were
packed and the qasr thereby completely emptied. At
10.50 we rode off, and in barely two hours had reached
the town of Ha'il. While Huber dawdled on the way, I
had ridden ahead with the servant Mahmud and the servant
Khairullah.

The house had just been opened up and the baggage un-
loaded, when a number of people started pushing their

way into the courtyard again. Just as I was busy with
the unpacking of a travelling bag and had leant my sabre
up against the wall, and had ordered the servant to see
to it that unwanted people left the house, a man suddenly strode in, richly attired with a ceremonial sabre in
his hand, and accompanied by five retainers; he looked
round the court with an expression of dissatisfaction
and went straight into the reception-room. Without
preliminary greeting he uttered the question: Where is
Huber? Annoyed by his conduct, I answered without
turning round: "Huber is not here; kindly take yourself
off." A burst of anger greeted this and a flood of
extraordinary abuse, of which I understood only: "Ya
Nasrani, Ya Kafir, Ya Kalb!" ("You Christian, you
Unbeliever, you dog!") I cut in with the shout: "If I
were you, I should be ashamed to set foot in the house
of a Christian, or a dog; get out or ride off into your
paradise!" Then he called the servant Mahmud names,
among them a disguised dog of a Christian, whose head
should be cut off. As I turned round, my anything but
pleasant expression provoked him; with the artery in his
forehead swollen with rage he roared: "Here you slaves,
cut his head off![13] Have I not already told you once?"
At the same moment he snatched his sabre from its scabbard, and I with equal speed leapt to take up mine and
would have attacked him. While the spectators of this
scene, frightened and shouting, seized us in their arms
and kept us apart, one of the madman's escorts made me
a sign behind his back indicating that he was not quite
right in his head. Only with difficulty did they succeed in getting the furious man out of the court and in
calming me down. Seething with rage, I shouted after
him that I would inform the Amir of his fine performance
and tell him how his guests here were annoyed in their
own house. Then I had the front-door locked. Shortly
afterwards ʿAbdullah returned with Huber and informed
me that it had been the mentally sick Prince Fahd, the
son of the High ʿUbaid, and so a brother of Hamud al-
ʿUbaid. As long as the Amir was resident in the town,
this man had a house and garden allotted him as a
dwelling; only when the Prince and Hamud were out of
town could be emerge with the sabre. He would often

485

fall into a frenzy and would then have to be restrained with chains. As all these circumstances were unknown to me before, I had also failed to understand why the man asked after Huber. The unhappy man wanted to find and consult him as a *hakim* (doctor). I asked Huber to have a look at him tomorrow.

Sun. 4 Nov. 83. When Huber sought out Fahd this morning, he denied having said or even done anything. The wounds in my foot were becoming noticeably more painful and gradually a real source of anxiety.

Mon. 5 Nov. 83. Temperature only 14°C. The servant Mahmud had his hair cut this morning. I was surprised to hear the two talking to each other in Turkish, and learnt that the man was a Kurd by birth, from Siwas, a Turkish deserter from the garrison in San^ca', who had been resident here for the last two years. I thought I would do him a great favour and handed him an excellent European razor; but with that he was incapable of practising his craft, and preferred to wield his wretched scraper, which was simply a blade bound to a piece of wood. We spent the evening in ^cAbdullah's house, on the roof of which Huber set up his theodolite to make some astronomical observations.[14] It was 10 o'clock when we returned home; the gate to our quarter was already closed; the watchman, who had been fast asleep, spoke of the strictest rules and the sheer impossibility of opening, but after much arguing back and forth he nevertheless performed the miracle, opened the gate, and let us through.

Tues. 6 Nov. 83. Gloomier, mistier morning with 15°C, not a ray of sunshine the whole day. I adorned the walls of our reception-room with more paintings and made a sketch of the female slave Frayhah.[15]

The wounds in my foot continue to deteriorate, and in addition a nasty boil is forming on the left calf, of which people say 'that is a good thing' (as though a person by that very fact - or as a result of the local diet? - must have been stuffed full of uncleanness, for the discharge of which one should thank God!). However I have cut a great hole in the upper leather of my

right shoe above the little toe; now the wound can no longer be pressed on by the leather.

On the way to ^cAbdullah I saw in the distance the lunatic Prince Fahd. We had to pass one another at close quarters at the street-corner. He lived up to his name ("Panther"); with his sabre in his hand he looked at me as if he wanted to devour me; I had no weapon with me, but passed him proudly by, and looked him straight in the face. Each measured the other, thinking: If you want peace, that's all right with me; but if you start anything, I'm quite ready too.

Wed. 7 Nov. 83. The senior shaikh of the Bani ^cAtiyah or the tribe of the Ma^cazah, named Muhammad ibn ^cAtiyah, from the district of Tabuk, paid us a visit with an escort of four; he had come here to try to persuade the Prince to undertake a raid against his northern neighbours, the Huwaitat, who were becoming an increasing embarrassment. The servant Mahmud knew him of old, from the time when he had still been the scribe in the Pilgrim-caravan, and had to distribute the presents to the Beduin. As the shaikh may be, in certain circumstances, very useful to us on the occasion of a later journey to the west, we wish to show him every mark of respect, and begin by inviting him to a festive meal tomorrow.

Thurs. 7 Nov. 83. The walls of our reception-room are still too bare for me: they need some more painted adornment on them. Meanwhile, on the front side of a pillar in the courtyard passage I painted on to a green medallion the words Ya ^{c}Ali ("O Ali") in beautifully intertwined letters of yellow gold. That serves at the same time as a courteous gesture towards the landlord, who is a Shiite, and who will be very pleased when he next catches sight of the pious exclamation.

When old Mufarriq called on us today, I asked him to sit for me. He was quite prepared to do so. The old man is an outstanding phenomenon; he is one of the few persons here who disdain to dye their hair red;[16] at the same time his beard is unusually thick and long for

a Beduin, and it must certainly cost him a good deal of
time every day to keep his magnificent moustache extended so beautifully horizontal. In earlier years he took
part in all raids and carried off several mementoes of
flintlocks, sabres, and lances. On the left half of his
forehead he bears the deep scar of a sabre-blow (*falqah*).

After the Prince and his cousin Hamud he is the
best-known personality among all the Shammar. Wherever
I met with Beduin in the course of my later wanderings,
I was always required to show the picture of Mufarriq
in my book. Everyone recognized him immediately and
would shout out: Yes, that's he! Look at his moustache
and the *falqah* on his forehead; and his stick![17]

The invitation which he had conveyed to Muhammad ibn
ᶜAtiyah for this evening caused us some embarrassment,
as we had omitted to make sure in good time that we had
something decent to set before our guests. In the course of the afternoon it was impossible to rustle up an
edible animal either in the Castle or anywhere else in
the town. Meat at all costs had to be found; the nearest sheep were however pasturing 4 hours' ride away.
There was no alternative; our gazelle would have to be
slaughtered. I was sorry for the animal; in the last
few days it had become trustful and this morning it had
been frisking about so amusingly and with such joie de
vivre. Towards evening Muhammad ibn ᶜAtiyah arrived
for supper with his escort of four. We discussed our
travel-plans and with that in mind concluded a solemn
pact of brotherhood. This was sealed by a particular
pressure of hand and thumb common to the Beduin, i.e.
the hands were not merely lightly touched in the usual
way or the palms drawn over each other, but the hands
were grasped in their entirety and then the thumbs were
entwined. Conversation turned chiefly on the likely outcome of the *ghazu*; in two days' time at the latest a
bashir (messenger) from the Amir would certainly arrive.
We parted in the hope of meeting again in good health
after three months in the Hijaz, in the territory of
Tabuk.

Late in the evening the smith Husain came and re-

quested a medicine for some malady or other. Closely
questioned, he admitted that it was not really for him,
but for a very pious Khatib, who was uneasy at the
thought of directly applying to us (Christians!). That
is very kind of these Wahhabi priests, and reminds me
of similar timid conduct, as practised at the beginning
of the 'Seventies in respect of the Royal University and
Regional Library at Strassburg.

Excursion to Jabal Jildiyah and to Biq^{c}a' (9-16 November)

Fri. 9 Nov. 83. The camels ordered for early today
had naturally not been delivered, but had to be sought
out in their pasture by a special messenger. Surrounded
by travelling bags, bedding, cooking utensils, and victuals, we sat for a couple of hours in expectant boredom, so that even the visit of the otherwise annoying
Ghanam was not at all unwelcome. Around midday the three
camels from ^{c}Ar^{c}ar arrived, poor specimens of their
kind: limping, worn out, and under-nourished. It would
have been quite impossible to obtain better ones, for
all the animals anything like capable of work, including
our own splendid dalul previously bought in ^{c}Urman, had
been taken on the Amir's raid. On the other hand, all
the equipment was brand-new, except that the saddle did
not suit my beast and after the first quarter-of-an-hour
had to be adjusted afresh. At one o'clock we rode slowly out of the town. Besides the servant Mahmud we had
with us as our real guide a Beduin called Shawardi. As
always in the vicinity of permanent human settlements,
all fodder had long since been exterminated in the whole
area; only colocynths[18] were growing luxuriantly undisturbed all around. At about 5 o'clock there appeared
near the sandstone hills Sanduq and Hasaniyah a spot
where some scanty fodder and a little fire-wood were to
be found, and which was therefore chosen as our place
of encampment. Ominous clouds were hanging in the sky,
but it was only later, when we were asleep, that heavy

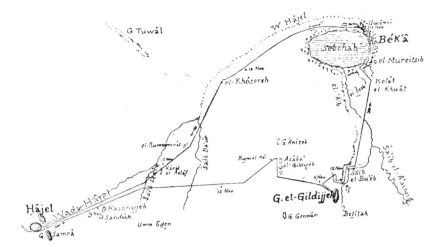

drops fell from them onto our faces. Supper consisted
of rice, some gazelle-meat (left over from yesterday),
dates, and bread baked in the embers.

Sat. 10 Nov. 83. In the grey light of morning we
drank coffee. The saddle was such a bad fit on my camel
and had been placed on it so badly that on mounting the
beast I was within a hair's-breadth of being hurled into
the still glowing fire, saddle and baggage and all. At
half-past seven we rode off. Mahmud put it to Shawardi
with a serious expression that it would indeed be a pity
if he allowed the rice in the leather pouch left over
from the previous evening (estimated at 5 helpings) to
go to waste, and he persuaded him (what he himself had
thought impossible before), to stuff himself with the
remains at intervals of a quarter-of-an-hour. Towards
10 o'clock we turned off into the Sha^{c}ib Shaqiq, a tributary of the Wadi Ha'il which flows westward and emp-
ties into the saltpan of Biq^{c}a'. In the sheets of
sandstone of the flat valley-channel there were some
holes here and there filled with fresh rain-water. This
circumstance moved us to prepare the meal here. A miserable Sharari, who was driving a flock of goats about
nearby, seized the opportunity to make himself useful
by fetching fire-wood, in the justified hope of being
invited to the imminent meal. The poor devil was

obviously famished, for he licked out of the spoon every last grain of corn. Having climbed up out of the Sha^c ib again, we followed the route over a monotonous sandstone plain strewn with small multicoloured, glass-like pebbles.

Asâbâ el-Gildijjeh   el-Gildijjeh

At 4 o'clock we camped. As some rain-drops fell more than once during the night, I spread my raincoat over my bed, but could not hold out long under it due to the dampness.

Sun. 11 Nov. 83. Turning north-east from our easterly direction, we made for a number of peculiarly-shaped pointed sandstone cliffs, which are situated in front of Jabal Jildiya to the north and bear the name Asaba^c al-Jildiyah. On these cliffs Huber had seen during his first journey some inscriptions and figures of animals chiselled in the stone. After quite a long search we succeeded in finding them again. Between the inscriptions there were crude carvings of innumerable camels, gazelles, baqar al-wahsh, ostrich-hunts, and similar things; only in the representation of a horse could a slight smattering of artistry be detected. I show here a sample of these oft-repeated designs.

Thanks to the thoughtlessness of our servant, who had believed the chatter of the Beduin[19] about the abundant water in the region, we found ourselves in the course of the day suffering acutely from lack of water. Had we not quite by accident discovered in the far distance and called over a lonely traveller, we might have been looking for water for a long time. Thus he seemed to us a real saviour, and in exchange for a present of tobacco he agreed to turn off his way and show our

Beduin escort where the water was - quite near, so he
said. It was two hours, however, before Shawardi returned from Qalat on his camel with the filled water-
skins. Our camp-site was splendid, on a gently sloping
plain on the fine sand of the Nafud, with the mighty

anden A sâba' el G.&   im W Bu'éb

massif of Jabal Jildiyah gleaming golden-yellow in the
evening-light in front of us.

There was firewood in abundance, so that we rather
over-confidently maintained three huge fires. In this
country the wind mostly drops at sunset, but today it
grew to a sandstorm such as I had not experienced since
the days of the simoom in Palmyra (July - August 1883).
The sand was driven rattling onto our camp. To protect
myself, I crawled completely under the carpet and muffled my head in it; nevertheless the sand penetrated
everywhere and filled my mouth, nose, eyes, and ears.
At 3 a.m. the storm abated; it had overwhelmed our camp
with a layer of sand two fingers thick.

Mon. 12 Nov. Today Jabal Jildiyah was to be climbed.

When I came to the foot of the mountain and dismounted
from the camel, I realized that it was impossible for
me to climb with my wounded foot; so I decided to stay
down below and search the cliffs for inscriptions. But
even that was too painful; I soon desisted, and slowly
made my way back to the camp, which was not so easy to
find in the low but thick scrub. At 11 o'clock Huber
came down from the mountain; he had had to abandon the
ascent to the peak on account of the steepness.

In the afternoon we moved off again, filled our water-
skins on the way, and reached the Sha^{c}ib Bu'aib as the
sun went down.

A shepherd called ^{c}Anaizan ibn Zaid was grazing a
few camels there. He had lived for a long time under
the Ruwalah, which naturally awoke the suspicion that
he had some motive for seeking the open spaces on account of some dirty work or other; his present occupation
too, the tending of a few inferior camels for strangers,
is, in the eyes of the Beduin, no particular recommendation, indeed rather suspicious. Not without a selfish
purpose, i.e. in the expectation of being allowed to
share our meal, he advised us to dismount in this area
so well provided with fodder, and to spend the night
there. He could offer us nothing himself except some
fresh camel-milk; could he bring some? He was told:
yes, he could bring some.[20] After a short time he
appeared with a square wooden container filled with
milk, and he offered it first to me. Although I was by
this time fairly used to camels and the milk looked.
quite clean, I could still not suppress a vague shudder,
something like that before a menagerie-drink. Huber
advised me just to try it; I must after all, he said,
make its acquaintance, and sooner or later will be quite
glad of it. I still had misgivings, but I put the bowl
to my lips and glanced at the same time over to Huber.
When he did not move a muscle, I swallowed some, and
really the luke-warm milk tasted quite good, indeed I
must confess that I noticed really no difference from
any other. Very pleased with my heroic deed, I took on
in two or three draughts quite a respectable quantity.
Likewise Huber. But we were unable to enjoy with any

peace of mind the meal brought half-an-hour later by our
servant Mahmud; rather I thought my last hour had come
and that I should suffer the sad end of the arch-heretic
Arius.[21] I lay down to sleep under the mild light of the
moon feeling as if I were nothing but mere spirit and
enfeebled soul.

Tues. 13 Nov. 83. In early morning the temperature
was only 14° C. At sunrise we rode down north-north-
west into the valley. Where the Sha^{c}ib ^{c}Aiwij discharges
itself on the right, there lies a ruined tower, the remains of an abandoned settlement. Here we camped till
11 o'clock. The ground was saliferous and covered with
large crystals of gypsum, among them a large amount of
granular iron ore (*rashrash*).[22] Here and there the
ground was as level as a dance-floor, quite cleanly
flattened, elsewhere the stone-flags were smaller in
shape, and partly worn by the weather as thin as paper,
or piled up in great heaps of half rolled up sheets 1 to
5 millimetres thick, so that one could think one was
riding through the cleanest dump of waste-paper in the
world. If the wind down in the valley freshened, it
inevitably involved gusts of rain and sand on the plateau; to the south dark clouds with slanting strips were
hanging over the Jildiyah. Having arrived at the top,
we were surprised to see in front of us lying in a hollow a great white lake surrounded by dark palm-trees
with *durah*-fields among them and half-ruined wells,
scattered groups of houses, and the watch-tower Muraiqib
on the top of a cliff. That was the important locality
Biq^{c}a' with its salt lake.

For an hour and a half we rode round the upper rim of
the hollow, and then gradually descended to the salt
lake. At that time of year it was rather a salt marsh,
where the salt blazed snow-white. Uncertain paths,
some for animals, some only for pedestrians, crossed
the flat surface like light-grey lines, with slippery
subsoil to left and right of them. The desire to cut
the last corner at the northern end nearly cost us dear.
Huber's camel, startled by a sudden blow with the
stick, swerved to the right, slipped, and hurtled into
the grey viscous bog. The only thing that gladdened me

was the fact that the lazy and gluttonous Shawardi, who
for three quarters of every day would ride behind Huber,
was a little roused by the sharp fall and found himself
gradually obliged to take a few steps on foot again.
The road went on and on, and the longed-for house of
Shaikh ^cUbaid still refused to come into sight. In
addition, as the air grew darker, the storm increased in
strength and clouds of sand were driving along like a
northern blizzard. Finally, just as the rain came down
in torrents and Huber's camel stumbled for the second
time, we reached the house. Another rider dismounted
at the same time.²³ It was a merchant from Baghdad
or Semawa, who had to bring to Ha'il 200 camel-loads
of rice for the Amir and 100 loads for others. The
Shaikh led us into the house of the Khatib, so that
we might settle in there. Of course, the space allotted to us was narrow and low (about 6 m. long and 2¼ m.
wide), but we were at least protected against the storm
and the rain. We betook ourselves over to the common
guest-room only for coffee while, opposite, the servant
Mahmud prepared supper. Having got used to life out of
doors after several days there, we found it a hardship
to sleep in an enclosed space, and a low-roofed one at
that.

Wed. 14 Nov. 83. As it was still raining, we decided to wait till after breakfast for departure. Under a
dark, watery sky we rode off at 11 o'clock. When we had
climbed the slopes which surround the hollow of Biq^ca'
on the north-west side, a fantastically illuminated
scene presented itself to us: in front of us the Nafud,
plunged in a dazzling sulphur yellow, over our heads
indigo-coloured clouds, boding no good and bordered with
trails of rain red with anger. In the motley change of
colours, enhanced by chasing shadows, the otherwise monotonous landscape seemed to be richly varied, extending
into the infinite. Violent gusts of the north wind soon
tore the glorious tapestry to shreds and misted the bare,
insignificant zone in characterless grey. Suddenly behind us there appeared six Rajajil ash-Shuyukh; as the
escort assigned to the rice-caravan, they were now unnecessary in this secure country, and were hurrying on

to the capital. As they rode past, they greeted us and shouted out various questions, especially whether we had any news of the *ghazu*. The raging wind, however, cut off all communication. On their nimble camels they passed out of sight with enviable speed, whereas we on our half-lame animals had to stick it out under the storm that was now breaking. The showers of rain whistled over horizontally, and the water penetrated under the inflated rubber cloak. It dripped down from the tasselled camel-bags like the taut chords of a harp. At the sight of so much wetness Shawardi could not refrain from saying optimistically, It will certainly be a blessed, well-foddered spring-time; to which I could only reply: in sha' Allah. At 4 o'clock it was all over; half-an-hour later we turned off from the way leftwards, in order to camp. The sand was still damp, but the sky was clear. Gratefully we stood round a rapidly kindled fire and warmed our frozen limbs. Our possessions too could do with drying. But now, where could we sit down, where lie down to sleep later? A scratching of the ground revealed the surprising fact that at this spot the rain had penetrated into the sand no more than 10 to 12 cm. That could be dealt with. With the long-handled wrought-iron shovel (*mahmasah*), each of us dug out his own resting-place; each sought to excel his predecessor through the artistry with which he executed his Trappist work.

Thurs. 15 Nov. 83. The night was cold (10° C), added to which everything was damp and covered with thick dew, which dripped onto the carpet in big drops during the morning. In the light morning-mist we surprised a line of partridges; Shawardi threw his stick at them but missed; by the time I was ready to fire, they had flown to safety. Such a bird would have once more done us good after so long a period of privation. Far more painful for me, however, was the discovery that I had nothing left to smoke: the two pieces of plaster which, being no good at patching, I had carefully stuck over a big hole in my tobacco-pouch, both outside and inside, had not been proof against yesterday's rain. The contents, saved up and anxiously protected for so long, had unnoticed all been ruined. As a slave to the vice of smoking I declined into melancholy and sullenness as a result of this bitter deprivation. A weak gleam of hope quivered in me, when a detachment of the disbanded rice-caravan approached from behind us. I, who had so often spoken ill of the Beduin for their shameless begging for tobacco, had no scruples about confidently trying my hand at this hitherto unpractised art. And in fact, I succeeded; one of them gave me forthwith a handful of golden yellow Persian *shawari*, which he had brought from Hillah. In the joy of my heart I gave him a pocket-knife, and then had my whole tobacco-pouch filled, after having fastened the torn place with a thread like the tip of a sausage. We had passed the skeletons of camels on our journey yesterday; today these markers of well-trodden ways increased in number. Two animal corpses from the last Persian Hajj were still lying there; the flesh had been devoured by beasts of prey, the skin over the bones was almost untouched. Is there then no use that one can make of such a big hide? I have up to now never seen or heard of camels' hides being treated in the East or in our country in leather-factories. Or am I mistaken?

Passing the spring Khasarah, we came to the double cliff Rumaiminat. While I was copying the inscriptions here, isolated units of the rice-caravan hastened with song through the plain. Towards evening we came again to a *ghadir* which, having been fed by yesterday's rain, formed a considerable stream. Mahmud and Shawardi had dismounted in order to find the best place for crossing it. I was just conversing with Huber who was riding on my right, and had my left leg hanging down sideways. It did not take much persuading to get our two camels over the stream. The third animal, on the contrary, which was supposed to follow without a rider, could only be brought to cross the water by blows with the stick, and then of course' with such impetuosity that it overtook us in a couple of leaps. In dashing past it crushed my wounded foot between two pieces of baggage, so that I screamed out with the pain. The skin of the

498

little toe was hanging in strips, and the flesh was torn
down to the bone. It was as good as a surgical intervention, and had, it turned out a few days later, the
most favourable influence on the recovery of my ability
to walk. We camped in Qarat al-Islaf in the vicinity
of Sha͞ʿib Shaqiq.

Fri. 16 Nov. 83. The cold and dampness of the night
caused us to strike camp before sunrise. A few inscriptions on the rock-face Sa͞ʿlika were soon copied; then we
marched fairly quickly the whole day, finally going faster and faster till we reached Ha'il with exhausted animals
shortly after sundown. ʿAbdullah, informed of our arrival, appeared at once, and gave us not only a meal, but
also the most diverse and mutually contradictory pieces
of information about the course of the *ghazu*. Such was
my hunger and the long privation that even the goat's
meat tasted good, but the real cordial was the Baghdad
bread and the good dates. Having submitted our bodies
to a thorough and highly necessary cleaning-process,
we settled down late to a well-deserved night's rest.

1) *American paraffin was imported from Basra or Baghdad.*
   The empty tins and the wooden crates of the packing
   are used for various purposes afterwards, and con-
   stitute therefore a much sought-after ware. The
   empty crate is still worth one majidi (3½ marks).

2) *Is it habit or suspicion, that at the slightest move-*
   ment or change of position on the part of anyone
   present he at once turns his head and freezes the
   man to the spot?

3) K.A. Woll, _Pfälzische Gedichte_ 3, A. Heidelberg.
   K. Gros 1881, p. 69 ff.

4) That is: "pronounce the name of God", i.e. say
   Bismillah "In the name of God", the formula with
   which every new action is introduced.

5) One simply calls out, without addressing oneself to
   any particular person, "hat ma'" ("bring water!").
   The servant, as a sign that he has heard the request,
   answers sam ' ("obeying") "At your service", and
   brings it. The drinker will hand back the basin not
   forgetting an al-hamdu lillah ("God be praised!"),
   whereupon all those present will look at him and wish
   him in turn haniyyan "Health", to which the first
   replies separately with hannak "May He (God) make
   you healthy".

6) Provenance: the Stuttgart Town Hall, whence H.M.
   had them bought for me.

7) King William carries this sabre in the picture well-
   known in Württemberg, where he is portrayed standing
   in the long Russian coat, with his orderlies in the
   background - and again on the bronze equestrian
   statue in Stuttgart Castle.

8) That cost the traveller in Africa, Eduard Vogel, his
   life at Wara in Wadai, when he refused to give his
   dun stallion to the local ruler.

9) An even more annoying mutterer of this species I met
   later in the Castle at al-Hijr.

10) He had asked Huber for this on his first visit to
    Ha'il in case of his return.

11) Ba^c, pronounced Bu^{c}a.

12) Demen; only Indian rice is called ruzz.

13) <u>Ta^{c}al, ya ^{c}abid, ukta^{c}u ra'suh</u>.

14) Absente Hubero Abdullah prolis ab uxore sua (quinta!)
    obtinendae cupidissimus medicamentum aphrodisiacum
    a me petiit. "Abusu vires consumuntur, continentia
    crescunt. Uxor autem rarius compressa filium, Deo
    juvante, tibi gignet." (In Huber's absence Abdul-
    lah, being very desirous of having children by his
    (fifth!) wife, asked me for an aphrodisiac. "Streng-
    th is used up by excess, increased by continence.
    A little less intercourse, and your wife will, God
    willing, bear you a son."

15) The dark-blue chemise is called <u>thawb</u>, the head-
    gear, likewise blue and pulled down over the face at
    the approach of a strange man: <u>bushiyah</u>.

16) It had struck me the very first day what a youthful
    generation was living in Ha'il. Old people are
    hardly to be seen. In view of the numerous raids in
    which a man takes part in his lifetime, he is lucky
    if he survives 20 or 30 of them. Grey beards are

usually dyed red with henna; hence an 'older generation' seems not to exist.

17) With which he signalled to the foreign Beduin encamped on the Mashab that the lucky ones had been
invited by the shuyukh to a meal in the Castle
court.

18) Hanzal, a kind of small light green gourd, bitter
and inedible.

19) If one asks a Bedu whether there is water on this
or that route, one usually receives the answer:
wajid! wajid! (there is! there is!), but may as a
result experience some painful disappointments.

20) One must know - though at the time I did not - that
the milk of these animals is for the Beduin not
only the most important source of nourishment, but
also at the same time the most natural remedy for
the most common illnesses. Besides ailments of the
eye (deriving from sand and heat) and indigestion
(from being hungry for a long time and then suddenly stuffing oneself), the most widespread are
dysentery and constipation. And now Nature provides
in camel's milk the best remedy. One must, as in
the case of the Carlsbad waters (but vice versa),
understand how to judge the temperature of the drink
in correct relation to one's own need. Drunk at
camel's heat, the sweet milk (halib) is more certain
than rhubarb and castor-oil; cold sweet milk arrests
diarrhoea immediately. For normal conditions and
the average man the most beneficial nourishment is
the sour milk from which the butter has been removed

(*laban*). If a female camel is to be weaned from milk, it is taken from her only every two or three days; such fresh milk is called muhaiyanah; it works more thoroughly than the warmest Hunyadi Janos. What the shepherd brought was in fact muhaiyanah.

21) *Ille cum sederet, gravissimo repente dolore cruciatus, omnia sua viscera, et ipsum cor, quod erat thesaurus impietatis, effudit in stercora, atque ita, mirabile dictu, internis omnibus evacuatis, attenuatus est, ut per angustias foraminis et sedilis totus ipse laberetur.* (When he was on the seat, he was suddenly stricken with excruciating pain, and discharged with his excrement all his intestines and his very heart, the treasure-house of his impiety, and having evacuated all his innards, he was so shrunken that, wonderful to relate, he slid completely through the narrow passage of the hole and the seat.)

22) The Beduin collect the lumps of granulated ore, and sort out the regularly-formed ones according to size, then swap these among themselves according to the calibre of their guns, thereby saving the cost of expensive lead.

23) In such an enclosed community as that of the Beduin, not only dress, but facial lineaments and gestures have a uniform and single stamp, so that when a foreign type suddenly appears among them, he stands out conspicuously. This observation impressed itself upon me even more strongly later when the Persian Pilgrim-caravan passed through Ha'il.

Preface to the Second Part

When the First Part of Euting's *Diary of a Journey
to Central Arabia* appeared in 1896, during my student
days, I had no idea that I should one day have the
task of editing the Second Part of the Diary. But
when, in 1913, I was given the opportunity to undertake the work, I readily and happily accepted.

Euting's friends, who not only respected the epi-
grapher and palaeographer in him but above all else
the unflagging traveller and the splendid human being,
long awaited the completion of his diary. During the
years when I was with him in beautiful Strasbourg, I
often saw him as he worked on it, and sometimes he
read aloud to me isolated chapters and descriptions
from the carefully-written manuscript. We discussed
many of his experiences, mostly in his workroom in
Castle Rohan, where many orientalists have gained
their knowledge. Thus in some respects part of the
contents of the diary was entrusted to me. At the
same time, through my own travels in Palestine, Syria,
the Syrian-Arabian desert, Egypt and Abyssinia, I
have had personal contact with the Orient and could
even imagine myself in Euting's description of his
experiences.

The man's amiable character is revealed in his
descriptions of his experiences, impressions, and
observations, which were always unpretentious, truth-
ful and natural. How he enthused over every one of
nature's small flowers! He was interested in all the

insignificant happenings of daily life which surrounded him. As an artist he had learnt to be observant,
and with delicate humour he knew which things to omit
and which to include. The real value of this diary
lies in the brilliant evocation of life in Central
Arabia, as well as in the pictures and sketches from
so distant a country.

For Central Arabia is still to a certain extent a
little-known country. But in our time the terrible
Europeanisation of the Orient is just beginning.
Syria and Palestine will soon be covered with a network of railways, which began with the first two
short lines in 1900. Even Damascus and Medina will
soon be connected by rail. This will naturally have
the effect that many old customs and life-long habits
will be discarded, and that the country and its
people will alter in many ways. Accounts such as
Euting's will always be of value - even if made public
30 years after the manuscript was written. Therefore the editing of his work is not only a labour of
love for my friend: it is also a duty to everyone
keen to enhance their knowledge of Arabia and the
Arabs.

As regards my editorial function, I have taken
Chapters IX-XIII direct from Euting's original,
while Chapters XIV and XV have been reconstructed
on the basis of Euting's travel diary.

In Chapters IX to XIII I have carried out only
minimal work on the punctuation and the orthography.
Those who read through Part I carefully will soon
notice that Euting's choice of orthography is arbitrary. For this reason therefore I prepared an index
of the various writings, to keep as faithfully as
possible to Euting's original. I found that the
German spelling of a country has limitless possibilities. And Euting had made abundant use of these
possibilities: some words are written at times with
s, at times with ss, at times with sz, other times
with tz, with z, again another time with ck, there

with k and so on. In order to introduce a certain
amount of consistency I have used as a reference the
old German Orthography from 1860 to 1880 and have
sought to use throughout one of the number of different possibilities proffered in the First Part.
But I have not succeeded in everything; I have, for
instance, allowed the word "Nichts" to be written
sometimes with a small letter. The name of the
finance minister in Ha'il, which Euting wrote as
Nasr Sabhan, is actually Nasr as-Sabhan according
to Hess, and I have chosen the latter.

For all the rest, I have added Euting's words,
in Chapters IX-XIII, in closed square brackets thus
- [ ]. I am indebted to Prof. J. J. Hess for the
majority of the notes. The latter worked together
with a Central Arabian by the name of Muhidh ibn
^cAjjaj, and he had the kindness to answer my many
questions either directly from his notes or by con-
sulting Muhidh. Everything which has come from him
is distinguished by an H-.

In Chapters XIV and XV I have used my discretion
more. Naturally I had to ensure that the diary
appears word for word in the manuscript; but then
these chapters would have remained disjointed.
Euting wrote some sentences in telegraphic style.
In order not to leave such a big gap between IX-XIII
and XIV-XV, I have tried to follow on in the same
style as Euting had written his own manuscript. The
reader can judge whether I have been successful.
Verification of this is possible, as Euting's travel
diaries, together with his sketches in the Orient,
are preserved in the library of the University of
Tübingen.[1] But everything which I have added in the
last two chapters is also enclosed here in square
brackets [ ].

The illustrations have been almost entirely reproduced from Euting's own drawings by D. Krencker,
who has, himself, spent a long time in the Orient.
I have drawn the inscriptions myself. In Chapters
IX-XIII the sketches have been exactly copied; in

XIV-XV most of the diary drawings have been reproduced. On the other hand the "Atlas", which has been used more times in Part One and has also been referred to in the manuscript of Chapters IX-XIII, has, with justification, been omitted.

The Jud Süss mentioned on page 171 is the financier, Joseph Süss Oppenheimer, who played an important part in the Duke Karl Alexander of Württemberg's government (1733-1737) as secret financial advisor. His memory still lives in Württemberg today.

A number of South German expressions which give Euting's style of writing a special charm and character of its own, but which might be unintelligible for North Germans and foreigners are:

Als weiter! = still further;
Als zu! = always shut;
gäh = steep
Kaib = carcass(invective)
Muhr = moor
mulzig = spongy, like melting snow;
Runse = cess pit;
Sack (in a suit) = pocket;
Springerle = small pastry;
Stundenhalter = Pietist, who conducts prayers;
ungrattig = awkward, uncomfortable.

It would also be helpful to include an index, for Part II, explaining Arab words which have not been encountered in Part I page VII. Darb al-Hajj, - pilgrim's route; majidi - Turkish Taler (coin); diwan - reception room; majlis, council assembly; Hajj - pilgrimage to Mecca, pilgrim; rababah, bedu khanjar, (thus with kh) - wood dagger; rajajil - soldiers; makhzan - warehouse, storeroom; riyal - Taler (coin); sha'ib - dried riverbed; suq - bazaar.

The title Shuyukh (pluralis majestatis of Shaikh) has also been used here several times for the Prince of Ha'il. It was quite logical, in German as well as Arabic, to put the verb in the plural, but my own feelings are that this contradicts good German diction.

I have corrected the transliteration of the Arabic words in accordance with the table in Part I, pages VII and VIII and I have taken the trouble to be consistent. But several times I have used, as Euting, s and sch, t̲ and th next to one another for the same speech, most from the Manuscript in question. Also, ghazu and beli should have been written; both words, from the beginning, mistakenly given accents. The city called ᶜAnezeh on page 226 should have been written as ᶜUnaizah on page 14. The name of the city al-ᶜUla I wrote without an accent, copying Euting, but there should have been an accent on the final vowel. The slave Mubarak mentioned on page 262 is really the same as Mabruk.

To begin with I have chosen to base the index on the same format as Part I; I have compiled it, however, in some detail and have listed in it the proper names together. In the Arabic index I believe I have satisfied the orientalist with my arrangement of word stems and explanations. The places visited by Euting have been in part visited and explored since the building of the railway, by Frs. Jaussen and Savignac. They had more spare time and more favourable working conditions in al-Hijr and al-ᶜUla than Euting enjoyed. Their work, *Mission en Arabie* is indispensable to those who wish to study in detail the ruins and inscriptions. It should be noted here that the Arabic inscriptions at the forts of al-Akhdar, al-Mu'azzam and Tabuk, which they have published, have confirmed Euting's data.

My thanks go to President A. Euting, the brother of the author, to J. J. Hess, D. Krencker and the firm of E. J. Brill, Leiden.

It is hoped that this book will serve as a remembrance of Euting and his travels to his friends and it may gain him new friends, even after his death.

Göttingen, April 1914 E. Littmann

LIST

of the diaries, etc. of Julius Euting, preserved in the library of the University of Tübingen, compiled by A. Euting:

1. Journey to Tunis, 2 Sept. - 24 Oct. 1869: 1 Diary, 1 Sketch Book.

2. Turkish Journey 10 Nov. - 31 Dec. 1870: 1 Diary, 1 Sketch Book.

3. Orientalists' Congresses in London 1874, Berlin 1881, Vienna 1886, Stockholm 1889: 1 Diary.

4. Journey to Central Arabia, May 1883 - August 1884: Diary I-VI, VIII; 1 book of inscriptions, 1-65 and 1-95; Arabic notes No. II; Sketch Book I-V; 1 landscape book; 4 water-colours, 1 Panorama from the summit of the Samra, 1 General map.

5. Journey to Egypt-Sinai 15 Feb. - end of May 1889; Diary I-III.

6. Journey to North Syria (Sendschirli-Urfah-Aleppo-Sendschirli) 27 Dec. 1889 - 27 May 1890, Diary I-IV; 1 Sketch book.

7. Journey to Port-Said-Jaffa-Jerusalem-Petra-Udruh (Brünnow Expedition) 23 Jan. - 22 April 1898: Diary I-II.

8. Journey to Jaffa-Jerusalem-Mashatta-Jerusalem-Cairo 16 Sept. - 23 Nov. 1903: Diary I-II.

9. Orientalists' Congress in Algiers 9 April - 15 May 1905: Diary I-II.

17 November 1883 - 22 January 1884

Saturday 17 Nov. Our first thoughts on waking
were: "How has the *ghazu* gone?" We must clarify
the nature of a *ghazu*.[1] It is a bedu campaign of
plundering or warfare. A *ghazu* can be undertaken
by any isolated beduin who band together, owing
allegiance to no-one, to try their luck at robbing
and stealing goods and chattels belonging to other
tribes. Such freebooters avoid bloodshed whenever
possible, for simple robbery is very honourable in
Central Arabia, and some of the poor tribesmen have
no other way to provide themselves with the few
necessities of life, such as a new shirt, coat,
weapon or something to ride. But if only a few
drops of human blood are spilt during the campaign,
there is an everlasting vendetta of family and tribal feuding. It is an established custom for a
ghazu to be enacted between all the tribes. The
power and the wealth of a tribe is directly related
to the frequency and success of their plundering
campaigns; the power and authority of a great Shaikh
was achieved by this means, and he thus increases
the wealth of the members of his tribe and the numbers of the cattle through lucky raids. A *ghazu* can
of course only be undertaken against those belonging
to a foreign or enemy tribe, or in any case against
those with whom they have so far contracted no alliance or to whom they do not pay any tribute. Nowadays, as Central Arabia is governed by the strong
horde of Muhammad Ibn Rashid, the *ghazu* is a rare
event. What used to be a small annoying enclave on
the borders of the Shammar state, has long since
been removed or amended, and now makes regular pay-
ments of tribute, or *zakat*.[2] It applies only to the
most powerful tribes, such as the ʿAnaiza in the
north, in particular the Ruwala, in the West the
'Al-Aidah, Bili, Juhaina; in the south the Mutair,
Harb, and Qahtan; and in the south-east, Rashid's

old rival Ibn Sa'ud of Riyadh in the Wahhabis' homeland. All of these are at least 500 km from the capital city of Ha'il, and extend spreading themselves just as far over their changing grazing lands, and must have been searching for the ideal moment. Accordingly, it is not possible to contemplate a return home in under three or four weeks. No-one is exempt from military service except in certain extenuating circumstances, and in any case he must then pay a war levy, which can consist of money, the loan of weapons, animals or other equipment. The people must be equipped with food (dates) for one month, and should have with them only those animals that have grown accustomed to the unusual hardships encountered. As soon as a *ghazu* has been planned, any outward indication of it is strongly avoided and the identity of the time and victim is known only to the prince and his council of war. At the appointed place and time 4000-5000 camel riders are assembled, and as soon as the prince himself arrives there, the campaign is set under way. For 21 to 22 hours a day the caravan of men and animals makes its way through the desert, two hours having to be sufficient for sleep, and at the same time the camels must be fed with pressed dates or a few handfuls of meal, and the horses strengthened with barley and watered from the supplies brought along. Following the assumption of a successful example, by the evening of the tenth day, the two scouts appointed as vanguard to the *ghazu* who would have hurried on ahead, will have reported the enemy tribe's encampment at a place two to three hours away, spread out in three or four large groups. But it is feared that early tomorrow morning they will break camp, because all the pastures in the region have been exhausted. Now everything is prepared to surprise the enemy before daybreak. The exhausted animals are used in the final decisive effort: they will be caught in a wide pincer movement. Like a whirlwind the camel-riders break into the camp. Within a few minutes there is a wild confusion of people and animals, the war-cries of the men, and the wailing of the women and children mingling with the snorting of the animals, tents are overturned, the fattened sheep and goats stampede through the dying embers of the camp fire; and those defending themselves are either stabbed or cut down. The victims disperse in all directions, taking with them everything they can get hold of. But escape is made uncomfortable for them. The best marksmen of the attackers have mounted their horses which were brought along with them, and hunt them down. What they believed to be saved, is finally lost. Possibly a few individuals escape, with the aid of a racing camel or *dalul* under the cover of darkness; hundreds of sheep and camels break free. This is insignificant compared to the mass of people and animals hemmed in together.

Before anything else the conquered are dispossessed of their weapons, while the slaves, women and children who are still of any use, are separated. The men, half naked, are driven with insults into exile and deprived of their goods and belongings. Nothing is left to these unfortunate ones; even a louse-ridden coat, a leaky pot, an ordinary tent peg, a piece of wood about a foot long, will be carried away as booty. Then the booty is shared out according to rank and merit. For some time there is only eating and drinking, followed by sleep. Next the great Shaikh gives the order to cut the throats of a thousand sheep or goats - as one can reckon on one such animal for five beduin stomachs.[3] Almost instantly the fire is rekindled and the meat gulped down half cooked, then the last gulp from the water bottle before sleep and more sleep! Only the sentries, posted to keep watch, rekindle the fire to keep their weary eyes open, until their uncertain relief arrives. The camels, tired and full, have thrown themselves on to the sand, eyes closed, and necks stretched out horizontally among the warriors, who still cradle their weapons in their arms while snoring. The raiders are kept awake neither by the bleating of the hungry sheep nor the complaining of the camels. There is nothing wrong in an artillery regiment having a good sleep; the youngest lawyer blowing his own trumpet would be hardly noticed here: they are all dozing, sleeping, dead to the world.

As for the vanquished, the plundered unfortunates! Their goods and belongings, wives and children are gone; exposed to terrible hunger, spurred on by thirst for revenge and despondency, having only one thought: how to get even; where are the nearest strong allies to be found? Still a few good runners have escaped. They might have worked together to make a go of it. Ma ikhalif? (What is the use?) There is not enough time, then one finally makes out quite clearly in the east, on the blue mountain slopes, the dark line of friendly tents. Where have they moved to? Who will be the first to find out? Twenty-four hours are subsequently lost by the youngsters looking for signs. They have travelled 200 kilometers. As they come within sight of the tents at daybreak they will be taken for the advance party of a *ghazu*, then recognised, their arrival awaited with anxious excitement. At the Shaikh's tent the animals collapse. Surrounded by armed men, the youngsters excitedly relate what has happened, and ask their friends for help. It is not the exiles' moving account of what had happened which impresses them, but the glittering prospect of booty. It does not require a long meeting of the tribe's elders to make the decision to embark on the dangerous adventure. Within half an hour all the preparations are made, then something to eat, and away! On the second day they come across a courier from a friendly tribe, grazing four days away to the west, and having learnt that the robbers with their booty have moved to the north, they issue the order to try at all costs to encircle the mountains from the east and block the exit of the narrow pass from the north, whilst their friends from the west would pursue them from the south. On the afternoon of the fifteenth day the northern pass is sealed. They have taken positions in the rocks, and the marksmen have excellent cover. It is high time. Out of the barely passable ravine in the distance comes the heavily-

laden camel train. The crackle of gunfire forces the
enemy back. The trapped mass of people are caught
in crossfire. Attempts at heroism are useless in
this desperate situation. Enough of the victims have
fallen to make further resistance quite hopeless. A
declaration of unconditional surrender by the robber
is demanded. Before the sun goes down the tide has
turned. The proud robbers have become naked beggars.
They move off into the night, taking the wounded with
them, and the scornful songs of the happy victors
ringing in their ears. One utters curses, the other
murmurs: There is no power but the power of Allah.
They are aware of the buried dead behind them, as
they are covered by a heap of stones. The victors
must decide how the retrieved property, as well as
the booty, is to be shared out. A Deborah stands up
amongst the women and *ad lib* sings of the latest valorous deeds of her tribe. This goes on through the
night until the fire burns out and the singing dies
down.

Now how has the latest *ghazu* of the Shammar fared?
In spite of the prince's Bashir, or victory messenger, who had arrived the previous night, taking the
trouble to give an exaggerated account, the *ghazu* had
met with only meagre success. The raid had been aimed at the Mutair in al-Qasim, south of Wadi ar-
- Rummah.[4] On the seventh or eighth day, in the early
morning darkness, the prince's people came across a
small company of Mutair riders, who were themselves
just going out on a raid. A few lives were lost in
the ensuing exchange of shots, whilst a few others
managed to escape. The main body of the Mutair was
camped on a distant plain with their herds; the distance from the oncoming Shammar gave them a two-hour
start. Quickly the alarm rang through the camp: "Dis-
mantle and pack up the tents, gather the herds together!" A round-up of this hastily dispersing mass
of people is unthinkable. What fell into the hands
of the Shammar may have been a few hundred camels and
perhaps 3,000 sheep. Not more than eight days supply
of meat. The rest of the proceeds, in tents, supplies,

weapons and clothes seems also to have been hardly
worth a mention. In short the *ghazu* has failed. The
prince's messenger also brought along for us a letter
from Hamud al-Mijrad, in which had been recorded all
the interesting places, mountains, valleys and especially the camp-sites along the way. Although riddled
with spelling mistakes, it was still a mine of information.

I have been drawing and painting the whole day.
Towards evening a man arrived on crutches. He had
received five bullet wounds in the body six months
ago; four of the wounds had already healed, but the
fifth which had shattered the top of his upper thigh
bone was still in his body, and out of this wound,
near the groin, a great deal of pus and bone splinter
had been discharged. A superficial examination with
a probe failed to reveal any trace of the bullet.
With the exception of a terrible leanness he had
recovered well from the wounds, and was quite contented, but found it difficult to accept that even with
the best will in the world his wound could not possibly heal. He had not long been lame before Ghanam
was in the position of a beggar and repeatedly asked
for a revolver. What could I say? Nothing. I was
pleased when Mufarriq appeared and put a stop to
the continual begging. He said that the 200-strong
camel train which arrived yesterday with rice, was
sufficient for 20-25 days. A load (himl) contains
90-100 sa'.[5] At times, when the pilgrimage is well-
supported, they need up to 800 sa' in the castle for
the entertainment of pilgrims and bedu, that means
about eight camel-loads of rice. Mufarriq wanted to
see his portrait and was very satisfied with it;
Ghanam and his son Muhammad, who meanwhile had just
arrived, demanded the pictures of Gyohar and
'Abdullah al-Muslimani. When Ghanam saw the picture
of 'Abdullah, he made a rude, disapproving remark
(quwad, ibn Qahba) which neither I nor Huber had
understood. Unfortunately 'Abdullah had been standing, unseen, for a long time, at the threshold of
the open door and had heard it all. Suddenly he

entered in a great rage and swore profusely at both of them: they cursed each others' parents and children, and Ghanam called 'Abdullah a Jew (*"Ya, yahudi li'an Allah wa aladaik anna na'ik ummuk wa ukhtuk"*); to this replied: "You are correct, my father and my brother are Jewish; I have little belief in religion, but who are you? You are a Ibn Sharari, you do not even know your father." For us this was all extremely embarrassing and even more so for the old man Mufarriq, who tried to use the influence of his age to end the quarrel between them, and had trouble restraining 'Abdullah from attacking Ghanam. Finally Ghanam left the house with his son, and Mufarriq did the same shortly afterwards; only 'Abdullah remained a few moments to compose himself. As he wanted only an apology, the Amir was to be told, on his return, about Ghanam's insulting behaviour.

Finally the blacksmith Husain came. When he saw me occupied with my foot wound he showed me, on his left thigh, the beginnings of a boil which was similar to mine; he thought it was because of the water, and he has had it now for forty days. He told me about a Christian who had his throat cut in Mecca and another Christian who not only managed to stay in Mecca by bribing the Sharif but has even bought a house there. Under pressure from the inhabitants the Sharif ordered him to pack up and move to Jidda. On the way he had been butchered by the beduin. Because of this a fight broke out between the beduin and Turkish soldiers, as a result of which up to 50 men from each side had fallen, after which the beduin contined to Jidda unmolested. This had happened a few months ago and was no more savoury a piece of news in Damascus than the storming of Jidda by the beduin had been.

Sunday 18 November. Who would have thought we should have had a strike on our hands? Our servant, Mahmud, had informed us yesterday that he must have an increase in pay. Huber had not told him in Damascus that he would have to serve two masters; he would be quite content with the previously agreed

price of 300 piastres per month (equal to about 3
Napoleons) for one but not for two. He named his
price for this: 500 piastres (4½ Napoleons). He
deceived himself about our dependence on him and
might soon be forced to come back, cap in hand. After
he had proudly strutted around the city for a couple
of hours, he came home at 3 o'clock in the afternoon
as quiet as a mouse, handed over, with downcast eyes,
his rifle, revolver and house keys and left the house
with his few personal belongings. 'Abdullah provided
him with a home out of kindness and will bring him to
his senses. Meanwhile we were at the same time both
masters and servants. Shaikh Naif ibn 'Atiq from
Jubba advises us by letter that he is unable, for
the time being, to meet our request for one or two
baqar al-wahash[7] also called *wudahi*, because at the
present time they do not have any, but he will try to
capture some for us as soon as possible. The letter
had been brought by Hamid Ghanam, whom we had met
when he was one of Shuyukh's soldiers in Jauf. After
him came his brother Muhammad ibn Ghanam, who apologised on behalf of his father as best he could for
the scene with 'Abdullah in our home last night.

Afterwards it rained the whole night and between
8 and 9 o'clock there was a remarkable cloudburst.
The whole courtyard lay 6 inches under water, so that
we could not even venture across the threshold. For
once Huber was not looking out from his usual night
quarters in the attic, but had to stay downstairs.
During the night I was woken up by the noise of rain
pouring in through the ceiling of the next room onto
our baggage.

The second of the Amir's messengers, called Nattaf
(an - nattaf = *depilator*) early in the morning announced the arrival of the Shuyukh, proclaiming to all
womenfolk that now was the time to beautify themselves for the imminent return of their husbands
(*Pubem depilandem jubens*).

Monday 19 November 1883. The damage caused by
overnight rain in the courtyard and to the roof of

the house was soon repaired by the slaves. 'Abdullah reported that everything was ruined at his house and a deep stream was running through the main street of the *suq*. At 9 o'clock the prince made his entrance on horseback, with his retinue, into the Mashab (Castle Square), and half an hour later the standard entered. As it was still drizzling with rain I excused myself from making an appearance at the welcome reception. Since I attribute my foot pains to the excessive use of cold water, I have acquired the traditional Arab wariness of washing and bathing. When the rain stopped I made a visit to Nasr Sabhan but did not find him at home,[8] so instead went to see Yusuf al-^{c}Atiq and his brother Nasr al-^{c}Atiq, to whom I had given presents of a sabre sword and a Spanish parasol.

On going through the suq I came across a Persian merchant, in formal attire, crouching on the floor, making a water pipe. It was none other than our former servant, now his own master, Mahmud! Solemnly he got up and greeted me respectfully; to which I responded courteously. The stupidity of his insubordination must have become apparent to him, after only a short period of greatness. What kind of life would he lead, with his few Napoleons in his pocket, amongst the beduin? The Prince had packed him off to Ma'an, as he was Turkish, to his family! Doubtless even 'Abdullah had in the meantime thoroughly washed his hands of him. It happened as was expected: in the afternoon he returned to us and after a short question and answer session about the earlier conditions of service, was reinstated in his employment. O quae mutatio rerum!

Hamud al-Mijrad supplemented the earlier news of the *ghazu* with the following colourful account: the campaign had been directed at the Mutair. At midday they came across ten members of this tribe, who fired at them and killed three horses from under the Shuyukh. By giving immediate pursuit, seven of them were caught and without further ado, decapitated.

But the other three were closely pursued until nightfall, throughout the following day, and until the
second night fell without being caught. It was quite
inconceivable that they would not be able to warn
their fellow tribesmen of the raid. On the morning
of the third day they came across an open plain, without a single secret approach, upon which the Mutair
were camped far away. The Mutair had time to escape
into the mountains leaving behind only their goats
and sheep. Hamud maintained that the Shammar had
slaughtered 10,000 (a round figure for an Arab) of
them in a night. Later on they came upon a number
of enemy Harb, of whom they shot 20 with Martini
rifles. Hamud had lost his way in the pursuit; on
orders from the Prince, arrangements were made to
look for him. Hamud's horse collapsed as a result
of exhaustion, but he hopes to obtain another from
those owned by the prince.

In the evening we discussed with Hamud our travel
itinerary for the future in detail. He thought that
if we wished to go to Sadus and Shaqra' a single
letter of introduction to the Shuyukh would be of
more value than all the gifts which could be taken
with us. "For", he said, "you should know the Arab
by now: when you give him a needle, they want a
knife; you give him the knife, they want a pistol;
they have the pistol and still need a flint; they
have the flint, they crave a cannon. You see what I
mean: you gave me a revolver, but I should have preferred a double flintlock".

Tuesday 20 November 1883. Ghanam delivered a silver case, which Huber ordered for his chronometer,
and received 10 majidi for it. From two Persian merchants (Mashahidi) I received a valuable pipe bowl.
At midday we had to endure a long visit from Prince
Majid, who had inherited or had learnt the art of
begging from his father Hamud al-^{c}Ubaid. First of
all he wanted my air pillow. Then, even though he
has received from me a present of a Mauser revolver,
he wanted my small revolver as well. I refused him
both. The old man has also again got hold of a really

nice little piece of workmanship. In the evening
'Abdullah related how he had earlier received a messenger ·from Hamud al-'Ubaid, with word that it has
come to his ears that he had been given a watch by
us for a present. He would like to see the watch
now, that is if we had no objection. Certainly
'Abdullah had every reason to fear 'Ubaid's displeasure. We advised him he should say that he has
not been given the watch, but only lent it temporarily for state occasions. Finally, Hamud al-Mijrad
offered painful advice that the most prudent course
would be to present the watch to 'Ubaid as soon,
and in as friendly a way, as possible.

The Shaikh Muhammad ibn 'Atiyyah took his leave of
us; he will be leaving for home accompanied by
'Anaibar, who is to collect tax due from the western
tribes.

Wednesday 21 November 1883. Under cover of the
morning darkness, the deed is done. 'Ubaid visited
'Abdullah, and simply took the watch from him. He
pressed into his hand, in exchange for it, a sacri-
legious American watch which, because of its unsavoury origins, he was not unhappy to have given away.
There was an enamelled picture of President Lincoln
on the watch face; and it had the wicked habit of
losing ten minutes every day. I could not, with my
weak practical knowledge, carry out repairs; also it
has to be thoroughly lubricated, in the absence of
any fine grease, with oil.

Hamud al-Mijrad very naively thought that luckily
for him the *ghazu* lies behind him, so there could be
really no harm if he resumed the internal general
cleansing of his body. He was not intimidated by
the strength of the treatment and, remarkably, added
that it would be best if he finished the course of
treatment in our house. Over a period of ten hours
we gave him three drops of croton oil on sugar.[9]

In the afternoon the Amir sent for my sketch-book
to inspect the pictures of Mufarriq, Ghanam, and
'Abdullah. In the evening we were sent for by the

Amir himself, who however appeared tired and aged.
Various kinds of minerals were on show which he had
collected for us on the *ghazu*: granite, glasslike
stone, a small fossilised shellfish, also a glittering shard which gave rise to the faint hope that
it could contain gold. My intolerable friend Hamud
al-'Ubaid, whom I had the honour to sit beside,
enquired whether we had come across any coal on our
trip to Jildiyya; then he wanted to have information
about modern explosives (Nitroglycerine) and how to
use them, about bomb outrages and so on. Then he
asked for an explanation of the construction and
operation of the air gun, a present which had been
lying around the castle for some years without anyone's having understood its secret. On our departure
the Amir honoured us with 50 sweet lemons and a bag
of stoned dates, prepared exclusively for him in the
city of 'Anaiza. On being asked if there were anything else we required, we begged for a larger
lantern.

Thursday 22 November 1883. Prince Majid, who is
not one to miss the opportunity of a further begging
visit, we have not allowed to enter. It is truly a
most dreadful experience to have to hid quietly behind a door, allowing someone outside to knock unin-
terruptedly for five minutes, as well as to call out.
On the other hand it is quite amusing to watch him
doing this unobserved. Thus I amused myself and
climbed up on to the roof of the house, lay down on
my stomach, lit up a pipe and watched the soulful
expressions and utterances of the discontented
Prince: "Nonsense! They must be at home! The neighbours were positive they had been seen shortly
before; the servant Mahmud, had just gone into the
house. He is at home in any case, probably at the
back in the courtyard, where he cannot hear. For
that reason, more loud knocking! Everything quiet.
Still louder knocking! Now. they *must* have heard
that! It is probable that Mahmud has left the house
again!" At last Majid ran out of patience, and went
off with his slaves. As soon as the coast was clear,

and I could be sure that I would not bump into him, I slipped over to the armourer, Ghanam, to see the sabre which I had ordered from him for myself. From there I went out alone to the cemetery, to the north, outside the city, where amongst others the members of the present ruling family are buried. Unpretentious square stones record the names of the buried. For example:

عبد الله ابن رشيـد رحـمـه اللـه	توفـي طلال ابـن رشيد قـدس الله روحه سـنـة ١٢٨٤ ١٧ ذ ا -+-	فيصل ابن رشيد رحـمـه الله سنـة ١٢٧٨
توفـي زيـد ابـن طلال قـدس الله روحه سنـة ١٢٨٨ ٢٥ ص	هيا بنة عبد الله ابن رشيد	-+- مـنـيـرة الـبـدر

Not far from there a grave, in which, as I was subsequently told, are buried two of the inhabitants of the city slaughtered by the present lord during his accession to the throne. I could not find the gravestones of Bandar and Mit'ab. There were many stones to be found without any inscription, or at the most showing which family they belonged to.

In the evening we were summoned to the Amir and handed over to him a supply of powder and shot. To be courteous he called me by my western name: "Kaif khatrak [how are you], Julius Euting?" When I told him that I had been to the cemetery and had written down the inscriptions on the gravestones, Hamud al-'Ubaid enquired about our burial and embalming practices. As a result of an argument about a saying in the Qur'an, the Khatib (house priest) was called, and had to recite the correct version of a long passage out of the holy book. The Amir ordered a delicate tea to be brought from the harem; in addition sweet lemons were handed around for dipping in it. At the end we all took part in a great communal prayer.

Hamud al-Mijrad, on being asked about the geographical extent of the Najd, gave the information: the following localities can be reckoned to be in the Najd:

1. Gebel en-Nîr جبل النير
2. Er-Rass [H.: ér-Rass] البرس
3. Ed-Dawâdimî الدوادمى
   [H.: ed-Dwâdmî]
4. Es-Sîr [H.: és-Sirr] السير
5. Eš-Ša'rà الشعرا
6. 'Arwà [H.: 'Ärwä] عروا
7. 'Argà [H.: 'Ärgà] عرجا
8. Wâsiṭ واسط
9. Ḥalabân [H.: Ḥĕlebân] حلبان
10. Šêtsîr (?) شيقير(?)
    [H.: Ušêdzir, أَشَيْقِر]
11. Šâḳrà شقرا

12. El-Khanûḳah الخنوقه
    [H.: el-Ḥanûge]
13. Ṛaul [H.: Ġoul oder Ġâl] غول
14. Šbêrmeh [H.: Šbârme] شبيرمه
15. Kebšân كبشان
16. Ḍerijjeh ضيريه
    [H.: Ḍerije, ضريه]
17. Mis-tse مسكه
18. El-Ḥaid الحيد
19. Nifî [H.: Néfî.] نفى
20. Uḍâḥ [H.: Uḍâḥ, أُوضَاح] وضاح
21. El-Iṭleh [H.: el-Eṭle] الاثله
22. Er-Rebkijjeh الربقيه
    [H.: er-Ribdzije]

23. Dikhneh	دخنه	26. Wâdî Sbê‘	وادى سبيع
[H.: Ḥesjân Dyḫne]		[H.: Widjân Sbâ‘] ¹)	
24. Eš-Šebaikijjeh	الشبيكيه	27. Wâdî ed-Dawâsir	وادى الدواسر
[H.: eš-Šbētsîje]		28. Abû Gelâl	ابو جلال
25. Ed-Dâṭ	الداٌت	[H.: Obū Gelâl]	

It was established by a consensus of opinion that
the last four places are not universally considered
as belonging to Najd.

In the afternoon Majid called for me and dragged
to his home. In the evening, on my return from
'Abdullah's house, I discovered once again an amazing colony of lice in my shirt. The item of clothing
was out on the roof in the wind. This could not have
attracted them.

Saturday 24 November 1883. I have presented
'Abdullah with a Chinese cup today. The Persian
merchants (Mashahidi), like Shi'a everywhere, are
ill-disposed towards Christians, but appear to have
received a nod from the Amir to be very obliging towards us. When I walked out of the house, 'Abid our
neighbour on the left side, humbly invited me to come
in. I refused at first because I wanted to visit
'Abdulaziz. But as there was no-one at home I called
in on 'Abid on my return journey. The furnishings
of the reception-room were as simple as possible. On
the floor, straw mats and a single narrow carpet along
half the left wall, framed by two earthen armchairs;
next to them an oven, with a few pieces of crockery.
I am convinced that the Mashhadi has reserved this
room with its meagre furnishings especially for receiving non-Shi'a guests and that for example a
Persian had never, before or since, drunk out of the
cup which I had contaminated by touching it and drinking coffee. It might also be that the meagre appearance of the reception rooms gives the impression, to
the uninitiated, of a shopkeeper's collection of

items which will be sorted out in due course.

From there Huber and I called upon Hamud al-'Ubaid. I wished to see his swords, two of which are famous, as well as his father's. He took them out of the cloth wrapping in which they were given to him, and described them. He claimed that with one of them he had cut off a head and arm at a single stroke. Also various kinds of wide daggers were laid out on display - beautiful pieces from Bahrain and Oman; but I was unfortunately unable to examine them carefully because of the gloom which prevailed in his Kahawah. He continually asked what he could present to us; we refused everything politely. Hardly had we arrived back at the house when he sent us, through our friend 'Abdullah, of whom he tended to make use as an influential go-between, an *abba* (coat) and an India *qumboz* or *zabun*, worth altogether at least 50 *majidis* (175 marks). The old biblical-type clothes given to me are all much too long and would have to be sewn up or shortened. After an hour 'Abdullah came again as ambassador of Hamud and the Amir: a Japanese cup had been broken, as Hamud wanted to clean it with his own hands on the Diwan of the Shuyukh. I sent them as a consolation a Limoges cup and a Chinese cup. They believe that if poisoned tea or coffee is proffered in real Chinese cups, they break in pieces, and this is why they are so highly treasured.

After the evening meal, Muhammad ibn Ghanam came along and brought some work from his workshop. I have always found that the drawing of water from a suspended animal skin bottle, through a wooden peg (jaza), held in place by the tightened neck around it, an exacting and laborious operation. I had therefore given him a brass tap which had been brought with us, which he could, on his return home, connect to a piece of pipe with a soldered connection, so that one could easily insert it into the neck of the bottle and secure it. His handiwork had turned out quite well and also produced at the same time an amazing example of his ability. Moreover he had just finished a pair of silver safety pins, as well as a

large rubber ring, in pieces, fitted with silver
clasps, which I had not long ago thrown away. He
had brought with him his daughter's son, the little
'Abdullah, a nice little five-year-old boy, whom I
delighted with my many animal drawings and a few
peppermint dainties.

Then there was an unexpected thunderstorm which
hardly touched the city. At a quarter to ten Hamud
al-Mijrad came, but he was in a foul mood because of
the fast and my negative answer to his arbitrary request for the highly-regarded field glasses for the
Shuyukh. He received a fitting reply from me: one
should not visit people when in such a temper.

Sunday 25 November 1883. Early every morning
ᶜAbdullah always comes with the offer that Hamud al-
ᶜUbaid would make some clothes for us. I was quite
busy, drawing from memory, a large map of Europe,
North Africa and the Near East, when the paymaster and
finance minister Nasr as-Sabhan arrived and was very
interested to see how the project was coming along.
When he took it upon himself to correct and become
insolent, I asked him if he would be able to show the
provinces in the southern Najd in their respective
sizes and positions to one another. Without a moment's
thought he replied "Of course!" I handed him paper
and pencil and, after a little hesitation, he produced
a few lines, and the place-names Sudair, al-Mahmal,
Tuwaiq, Nafud, and al-Washm.

Then the real reason for his visit emerged: he wanted scissors from us; he thought we must have at least
twenty pairs of them in our trunks, and we should not
miss a few. This however was not true, I had only one
pair and Huber had begged for one for himself from
Hamud. When he had gone I caught a louse: a fine
example! If I had glued it to a piece of paper I could
certainly have gained everybody's respect as a collect-
or and specialist!

At three o'clock I went for a walk to the Samah

wells. Just then, as a storm began to brew to the
south and south-east, I climbed up a nearby rocky hill
to enjoy a better view. Soon the Amir came along
with Hamud and a certain 'Aid ^{c}Ali[17] on horseback, and
behind them many followers on foot. Hardly had he
caught sight of me when he shouted "Ya Julius! kaif
khatrak, kaif halak?" (Oh! Julius, how are you? how
is it going?), upon which I hurried down from the hill
to greet him. He was riding a beautiful black horse
and wore a marvellous wide dagger with a gold sheath
and handle. I had only just climbed back to my position up in the rocks, when Hamud al-Mijrad emerged from
the city. He soon discovered me, clambered up, and
was amazed to see me all alone: it would be preferable
if I always took someone with me. I replied that he
should not be concerned on my account; but for once I
was pleased with his company, and asked if he would be
kind enough to show me Samah.

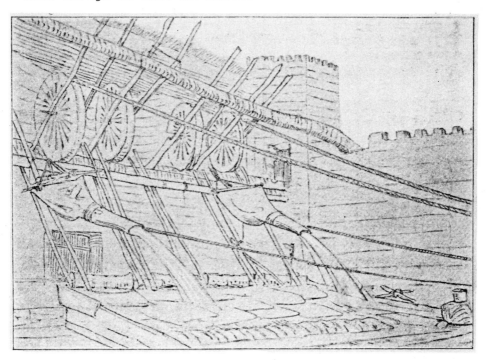

Situated on the south side of the city, the Samah well

527

is quite a compact system. It consists of 1) the actual well, with a shaft 25 m deep and 4 m in diameter in the granite rock, up which the water is drawn in leather buckets; 2) a 35-metre long walled walkway, along which two camels pass backwards and forwards pulling up and letting down the leather buckets over the wooden pulleys; 3) a long narrow building, with a room on the first floor, from which one can look over the well, the adjoining garden, and the square beyond the wall. At one end, stairs lead up to a slender tower. All these three sections are secured by doors. Originally intended only for watering the garden, the well is so productive that the Amir, who meets its running expenses for the whole year, allows the city's inhabitants free use of the excess supply. For this reason there is 4) a courtyard, approximately 40 square metres in area constructed next to the well room, on whose walls the well-water runs through channels, and before it flows off into the channels serving the garden, it can be tapped off into hoses. For the major part of the day the well courtyard is thronged with women fetching water, at their leisure and with a great deal of gossip: there is no reason to hurry, and it is preferable if the water is allowed to stand or hang for one or two hours, otherwise, so the people say, the warm floor (28°-29°C) causes 'drinking fever'. I went home with Hamud through the garden which, although it does not receive any special attention, is filled with vines, pomegranates, oranges, lemons, peaches, and other fruit trees.

We had to go to the castle after the evening meal. I presented the Amir with the field glasses and the map of Europe which was duly displayed upon the wall of the anteroom. The Amir gave us a manuscript of old Arab praise-poems, the so-called Mu'allaqat, with a commentary, and he also showed us a beautiful manuscript, with an interpretation, of the poems of Mutanabbi. He read aloud long passages from both of these. A toad which had wandered into the room was gripped with coal tongs by a slave and thrown into the air.

Monday 26 November 1883. Miserable day. Hamud
al-Mijrad brought along his twelve-year-old son Fahd,
and his eight-year-old nephew Musa ibn ᶜAli; I fetched each of them a little note book and a majidi.

I wanted to finish some sketches of the reception
room in ᶜAbdullah's house. The occupant had to go off
to his shop and left me alone. As I completed my drawing in peace, I was sure his wife was watching me,
inquisitively, through the doorway. I pretended not
to have noticed.

The Persian Hajj (pilgrim caravan from Mecca) is
supposed to be arriving here in two days.

In the evening lightning. Towards the morning
rain.

Tuesday 27 November 1883. When I walked into
the inner courtyard to visit Prince ᶜAbd al- Aziz,
I thought I noticed the man I was looking for had
disappeared to the sovereign's corner. Therefore
I asked the slave at the prince's door "Is 'Abd
al-Aziz at home or is he with the sovereign?" and
received the reply "No, he is at home" and then
with raised eyebrows, slightly lifted head and
barely perceivable clicking of the tongue added
"Ash-Shuyukh iqay". That is to say, the Amir has
taken an emetic and one cannot visit him. This is
made known then, to the whole city, by word of mouth.

ᶜAbd al-Aziz was delighted with my visit and
sought all the possible ways to honour and entertain me. I stayed a couple of hours with him; we
rummaged around in the various courtyards of the
castle, in the kitchen, in the prison, in the garden
and finally we examined the horses.

In the afternoon I completed the sketch which I
had begun yesterday at the Samah well.

In the evening we were invited to dinner by
Prince Majid. We were of course received in his
home, but - as if he could not trust the skill of his
kitchen or as if he planned to quarrel with his wife -

we had to eat over the road, in the gloomy hole of his avaricious father, in the castle. Four slaves carried in the huge plate with the meal. Out of respect to myself, Swabian soup amongst other meat soups had been prepared, and the servant Mahmud had to bring over from my house my own tablespoons.[18]

After the meal Majid wanted to show us a few examples of his artistry, which in no way rises above the level of that practised by the beduin for centuries.

As I could hardly proffer the expected recognition for his work, but on the contrary I was certain that one would give a European schoolboy a cuff on the head for such terrible work, he admitted that this was not the best he had done. This excuse only made me the more determined to force him into a corner until he was compelled to show me a second picture with which I declared some satisfaction.

A drawing by Prince Majid

I think he was quite glad when he heard the general call to prayer. After the prayer we went over to the sovereign, and so we returned home late. I found sleeping difficult, not only because I had drunk so many coffees, but more especially because ᶜAbd al- Aziz had perfumed my beard that morning so heavily I was terribly irritated by the nauseous smell. Finally I

530

made an end to it: I got up again (I might have done it
long before), washed my whole head with soap, rinsed it
thoroughly, blew my nose ten times, and put on a clean
cloth over my bald head, which had been shaved yesterday. Then all went well.

Wednesday 28 November 1883. Nasr as-Sabhan came in
the morning. There was probably too much lemon in the
tea he was offered. Suddenly he became afraid; wondering if there might have been wine or arak in it. Assurances to the contrary did not help. Our uproarious
laughter pricked his conscience and he was soon obliged
to leave.

I completed a few drawings at the home of ᶜAbd al-
Aziz ibn Mit'ab, among them a sketch of the prince himself.[19] They had taken from the Harem in the meantime
a two-year-old boy named Talal ibn Naif. His father
Naif (a son of the former ruler Talal who died in 1868)
had an older son who died before he was eighteen; he had
stood in the way of Prince Majid as the next in line to
the throne and because of this was shot accidentally,
while indulging in horseplay with someone, with a
flintlock supposedly loaded with blanks. I should gladly have painted the nice young lad; but they protected
their charge, in case any harm befell him, and before
he did anything they had to ask the Amir's permission.
For this reason I did not pursue my scheme.

Today the roof of the house was repaired; then as
luck would have it, after dark a storm blew up again.

Late in the evening, Ghanam, Hamud al-Mijrad and
the smith Husain paid a visit. Husain brought a pair
of coal tongs and a poker for the fire; he received
for them a ball extractor and a large saw blade which
my friend Ferdinand Schmidt, a distinguished financier
from Neuenburg (Württemberg), had had made for me from
the best Sensen steel.

Thursday 29 November 1883. The Persian Hajj has
arrived on its return journey from Mecca and has
pitched camp on the walled-in piece of ground, to the

north, adjoining the Samah garden. I hurried there,
but must admit I was very disappointed. I had not
thought it would be so pitiful. The Shi'a Persians
are missing again this year, otherwise they form the
main contingent of the pilgrims travelling overland
in Central Arabia. Throughout the year the Persians
bring 8-10,000 corpses in shrouds to Karbala and
Mashhad on the Euphrates, to bury them in consecrated
ground next to the mosque, with its golden domes,
where the martyrs Hasan and Husain, sons of the Caliph
'Ali, lie buried. Many of those accompanying this
funeral caravan have the wish to visit the Shi'a holy
of holies as well as to complete the pilgrimage to
Mecca and Medina. The next part of the journey - about
60 days ride - cuts diagonally across the Arabian desert, most of it in the Amir of Ha'il's territory. The
Amir sends his people, at the right time, to Najaf on
the Euphrates, to meet the Persian pilgrims and escort
them safely to the equally sacred Mecca and Medina.
The pilgrims have to pay, for the supply of camels, the
water and the escort, 30 majidis on the outward journey,
and, should they choose to return the same way, half
as much again, that is 45 majidi for the whole trip of
about 150-160 miles. The greatest proportion of this
money goes to the sovereign's coffers, which could mean,
with the usualy 800-1000 participants, and after the
deduction of living expenses for themselves, a quite
respectable sum of money. Now in previous years the
leader of that escort had taken it upon himself, two or
three days before the pilgrims' return to Najaf, to indulge in the pleasure of extorting from the odious Shi'a
a totally unreasonably high bribe or bakshish. The
majority of the Shi'a who, through their visit to the
cities of Mecca and Medina - where one appreciates the
useful purpose of the florin - soon realised that they

were being overcharged, explained that they were unable
to pay any more. The obvious proof, of empty pockets
and purses, was demonstrated with derisive laughter:
"Right! You dogs, God curse your fathers, you will die
here in the sand or sweat out the money; it is all the
same whether you die of hunger or thirst. If you will
not or cannot, then we keep our camels and water bottles
to ourselves and leave you to rot here; then you will
see!" This dishonourable bargain, even by beduin standards, forced the few Persians who still had money to
pay for themselves, as well as for the others, whatever
sum of money was demanded. On returning to their homeland the pilgrims made their complaints to the government. The caravan leader, for his part, handed over
the extortion money to Ha'il, but instead of the hoped
for praise and reward for his financial skill, was
sharply rebuked by the sovereign for his shameful and
at the same time impolitic behaviour, and summarily
imprisoned. The sovereign sent by special messenger
a letter to the Persian Wakil (consul) in Najaf for
delivery to Teheran, in which he apologised, stating
that the robbery had happened without his knowledge
or approval, the culprit had been punished, and the
money is herewith returned to the victims giving
the assurance that the Persian subjects would in future be accompanied through the bedu region as safely
and honourably as in the past. A similar letter was
sent to the Sharif in Mecca and to the Persian Wakil
of that city. However, before the letter arrived
in Teheran, the Shah of Persia had already made the
Wakil in Mecca, to whom the Amir of Ha'il had written,
aware that in view of the shameful treatment of his
subjects, they were forbidden until further notice
to take the route through the Shammar district. And
thus things stood, as was evident with the arrival
of the so-called Persian Hajj this year.

About 30 tents were pitched at the afore-mentioned
place, some round, some long and rooflike, as well as
simpler forms of shelter which were tents in name
only. I even detected a portable lavatory (*mikhr*)
with folding walls. Washing and clothes soaked in

the heavy storm had been hung out to dry on the tent
ropes; all kinds of sacks and tied-up bundles lay
around between the docile camels and donkeys; the odd
reed baskets with wooden legs, and high arched lids
covered with kerchiefs, were new to me. The furled
banner leant in a corner to the right of the gate.
Further away a small market had opened up for the day.
There could only have been at the most 150 pilgrims,
among them 4 or 5 women including one negress. The
people appeared to be of extremely civilised stock,
their facial features noticeably different from those
of the bedu. Such careful dress and neatly trimmed
beards I had not seen since leaving Damascus, such
half-military demeanour, in surplus Turkish army
trousers, fez, laced boots, Persian shoes and stockings. With the exception of 4 Persians, evidently
merchants from Mashhad, who joined on the way, I
could not discover any wearing Persian felt or sheep-
skin caps at all. Most of the people had been busy
drying out and repairing their belongings, others went
on a shopping expedition to the city; everybody
appeared to be at ease, for once enjoying a few days'
rest after the exertions of the journey.

At 7 o'clock in the evening there was a first storm,
so violent that the rain poured through the roof in
really unusual places, even for example making our
books wet; after 9 o'clock came the second storm, and
at half-past ten the third and heaviest of all. I had
stayed in the room below the door. The incessant
streaks of lightning and cracks of thunder were frightening, water streaming off the roofs and steps down
into the courtyard. For a time hailstones rattled down,
forcing me to stay behind the bolted door. But I heard
them quivering with excitement as they crashed down in
torrents, some finding their way through the narrow
slit in the wall (*fadwah*) into the *qahawah* (coffee-
house). I had an almost childish fantasy that this
arid land would in the end be completely flooded, but
there was not enough rain for that. As soon as the hail
shower subsided, I opened the door again, and saw that
water was still streaming down. The lamp, with which

Mahmud wanted to illuminate the lake in the courtyard, was extinguished by the draught, however there was just enough light to be aware of the danger: the mass of water with a layer of ice as thick as a man's hand was rising ever higher, and threatened to flow over the threshold into the house at any moment. The carpets and what lay on the floor were quickly gathered together and piled up on the hearth or on the stone armchair. As luck would have it the rain stopped. One moment - what is that? A chilly atmosphere: the lull before the storm? Then Mahmud shouted in horror: The *sail* is coming, the *sail* (flash flood). I did not want to believe it at first, but soon found that he was right. The water cascaded down from the mountains an hour and a half away, first as streams, then as a torrential river, and finally as a rising wall of water hurtling towards the city. Next morning, we found that it had even demolished the beduin tents outside the walls. Meanwhile during the night we noted with relief that the main stream had passed by to the east of the city.

Huber, already ill for several days, had a serious attack of fever today, and complained especially about the pain at the back of his head. When he became delirious I gave him three doses of quinine but I had to try the medicine myself to be sure it was the correct one.

Friday 30 November 1883. Hamud al-Mijrad rushed in early: the Sha'ib (normally a dry riverbed to the east of the city) is full to the brim, an event not seen for the past two decades at least. The Shuyukh and many others had just ridden out there to see the strange spectacle. I made it clear I would be ready to go with Hamud as soon as possible; but he did not want to wait for me, I was too slow for him. (He has not seen me walking about on account of my sore feet, now healed). You wait, I thought, I shall soon catch you up, and give you a run for your money! I went past him like the wind, through the front door, and realised that he was panting behind me. I let him shout a few

535

times: *shuwayya, usbur!* (slow down, patience!), then I
glanced over my shoulder and jeered at him, "I cannot
wait for you, you are too slow for me!" I had circled
the south side of the town in ten minutes. Indeed a
reddish-yellow torrent flowed down the narrow ravine
between the Umm Arqab and Samra mountains (which were
enveloped in mist) probably 60 m. wide and at least
2 m. deep. The people, who stood around at the edge,
were sure that it had already subsided by 1 ell.

High tide in the desert

I was impressed by the sight of this moving wave of
water, something I had not seen for a long time. Most
of the population were standing there; on the bank,
wives filled their water bottles with the precious
drinking water, whilst the children clung timidly to
their mothers' clothes.

During the afternoon I finished my letter to Europe
which the Persian caravan will take to Baghdad, and
Majid came to get hold of some gunpowder and the sketch-
map of Europe which I had drawn for the Amir. His

father ^{C}Ubaid took advantage of the favour shown to
^{C}Abdullah by sending messages to our home and scroung-
ing from us; thus today he was told to say that we had
honoured and given presents to everyone here, with the
exception of his much-loved second son Salim. For
that reason the third last revolver (ostensibly the
last) would be appreciated by him. As a reply he sent
a ram to the house late in the evening, which will have
to be slaughtered tomorrow.

As so much rain had fallen and it was also possible
to gather water from a thousand puddles, the operation
of the well at Samah was discontinued, as a consequence
of which there was a drought at home for the whole day.
I do not know where the concoction we received to drink
came from.

At 10 o'clock at night Hamud al-Mijrad came, in a
foul mood. I did not show much concern for him: when
he left the thermometer was still registering only 8°C.

Saturday 1 December 1883. Hamud al-^{C}Ubaid's sadness
that we still have not divested ourselves of all our
European lordliness began to be quite amusing. Huber
still has a beautiful mirror which he refuses to give
away and they know that I still have a small Mauser
revolver (7mm). ^{C}Abdullah brought us the bad news from
^{C}Ubaid, with trepidation, and full of apologies, as he
feared we should consider it harsh. We consoled him,
for we knew that if he had not delivered the message a
dozen others would soon be found, who would gladly play
the part of a little 'Red Riding Hood'. He was
relieved by this and appeared to be back to normal.
Aha, now what is wrong? He brought out from under his
coat, what appeared to be a parcel wrapped in a cloth:
^{C}Ubaid wants to offer me, instead of my own little
revolver, another one as a replacement. I was dumb-
founded. "My revolver is just right for me. I do not
need a replacement, and I have no desire for such
dubious rubbish." Obviously expecting this answer he
had a new question ready; whether I should take money
or something else for it. If there were nothing I
required, with which he could supply me, he would

537

immediately send something else to the house. For
fear of becoming saddled with an expensive piece of
rubbish, which annoyed me, apart from the obtrusive
way of seeking our thanks, as well as his daily presence, I allowed myself to be betrayed by a thoughtless
expression. My only *zebun* (long coat), which I had
brought with me from Damascus, had gradually become
quite worn, it would surely not be presumptuous if I
wore a new one; preferably I would like a white one
decorated in gold, like the ones which are imported
for the princes of this country, for example, similar
to the one his son Majid owns. Luckily ^cAbdullah,
realising what I wanted, wrapped up his parcel again
and hurried away. After half an hour he returned -
with two new shirts over his arm as the intended
acceptable present. ^cUbaid was extremely apologetic,
they had run out of gold ornamented white *zebun* in
the castle, and a search among the Persian merchants
had proved fruitless, so he is already taking the
coat of his son Majid, and having it adjusted to fit
me. Otherwise they had a large number of Syrian and
Indian *zebun* in the castle, amongst them a red silk one
which is perhaps nicer than the white one, in any case
a little daintier; did I want it? I replied that I
could not say until I had the opportunity to look at
it; there was no urgency. One thing was certain, that
I could not save the revolver from his clutches for
long, and so I was determined to torment the man for
as long as possible in anticipation, but I was only
sorry that I was unable to see the face of the old "so
and so" and his protracted agony.

In the evening, Hamud al-Mijrad presented himself,
and stayed for almost three hours. I read once again,
until 2 o'clock at night, the first part of Goethe's
Faust at one sitting. This was a pleasant relief
for me, for I was able to transfer myself into a wholly
different world.

Sunday 2 December 1883. Before dawn ^cAbdullah came.
Is it possible? Without a message? Without a political revolution? Yes, it is possible - Huber is com-

plaining again of fever and looks bad. I went outside
to the pilgrim encampment for amusement and looked at
the market, where I made a few sketches. At midday I
wanted to visit Prince Majid with ^cAbdullah, but it
transpired that he was with his wives in the castle, so
we turned back to ^cAbdullah's house to sit up on the
roof in the sun. Before we went up the stairs,
^cAbdullah called his youngest wife, who was from
Baghdad, "Ya, Jawa!" She hurried out of a nearby room
with innocent obedience, wearing only a blue shirt and
ran straight into me. With a cry of surprise, she
rushed out again, hiding her face, while her husband
called after her with a command. As far as I could see,
she had big, beautiful brown eyes, and what is very
strange here, red cheeks and lips; certainly her hair
was in need of some more attention. It was really painful for me, that he had so severely embarrassed the
creature, and I refrained from making a remark although
he appeared to be waiting for it. Thus we went up the
stairs quietly. When we were upstairs he put to me the
frivolous and confidential question: "Have you seen
her?" Without moving a muscle I simply said, "Yes,
with one eye". We had just made ourselves comfortable
on the roof, and were sharing the comfort of the sunshine with the flies when there was a knock on the door,
and a message from Majid that we should go to him. I
had to tell him the length of a cannon, and draw a few
animals. Four young brothers of Majid listened and
watched attentively, with the appropriate modesty of
their youth.

The bubble pipe, which has been brought, at
^cAbdullah's around midday, he smoked in the evening;
Hamud al-Mijrad also came with Huber.

Monday 3 December 1883. The Mashahidi brought one
of their countrymen, Sliman Mirza, who had arrived
from Medina with the caravan, for a visit. He and even
more his father, who was living in Mashhad, had got to
know Huber during his earlier travels, and are highly
respected people because of their wealth.

On the way to the pilgrim encampment a stranger

stopped me on the street and held up to my face three
fingers of his right hand with the words "Smell that!"
On my nodding approvingly he suddenly stroked my beard
with his finger and while I stood there amazed he continued "Is not that beautiful rose oil and *zabad*?"[21]

I brought ᶜAbd al- Aziz his portrait, which had been
done in watercolours, in my drawing book. He did not
seem at all satisfied - who is satisfied when one is
given a picture of himself? - but put it on display for
his inquisitive wives, in the peace and tranquility of
the harem.

He did not personally suffer from the same fear as
his relative, ᶜUbaid, who immediately sensed evil from
the useless and sinful pictures and was evidently worried by the thought that this noble cousin and uncle,
could use it to influence the Amir against him. It
would surely be easier for him, if I took the page out
of the sketch book, in front of him, and promised that
I would not talk to anybody about it or allow anybody
in this country to see it.

Prince ᶜAbdulaziz

^cAbd al- Aziz made his way to the garden; there we amu-
sed ourselves in various ways, throwing lances and
stones. The beduin had no experience of this, as they
use lances only for stabbing at short range. I had a
beautiful direct hit in the middle of the trunk of a
palm tree. As the bamboo shaft quivered along its
length for a few seconds in the air, everybody gasped
in amazement. We ran to the tree to see the hit. The
point had penetrated so far into the trunk that the
slave Fendi had difficulty pulling it out again, and
as a consequence the iron was bent. To show his accom-
plishment in the art, the Prince suggested a running
race. I advised him against it, as the way things
were, I should have soon left him behind; but he wanted
to go ahead, for he is 'as quick as a gazelle'. Good,
then I shall be as fleet as a panther. With the exception of our shirts and felt caps (taqiya) all our
clothes were put on one side. Ten paces advantage;
one, two, three, go! Jumping barefoot over the bushes
and leaving the accompanying slave far behind, I caught
him by his pigtail after about eighty strides. We were
both quite breathless and had a lot of mutual respect
for each other; but the race had played havoc with my
feet; I was bleeding in several places, and pulled a
splinter out of the sole of my foot. After the physical exercise, and while we were still feeling its
effects, someone from the important ^cAbdeh tribe came
into the Diwan with us. Straight away he began to boast
about the incomparable superiority of the beduin over
the Christian soldiers, although he had never seen any
of the latter. Whereas we have all the weapons possible, so the Arabs are in a position to fill their deci-
mated ranks with masses of people. I painfully
restrained myself from correcting his arrogant and
stupid ideas, but I declared that I must abandon it,
as it is pointless to argue with a bigot. I maintained an obstinate silence in the face of his various
tirades and outpourings, but on the contrary actually
enjoyed aggravating him with staring. No one, except
those in a lunatic asylum, can stand this for long,
and so he excused himself, after 5 minutes, and left

us. For the master of the house, who had evidently
feared that we might have come to blows, this was in
any case the most agreeable solution.

At 4 o'clock the Amir sent for us. He sat before a
bright blazing fire in a gold embroidered, fur-lined
coat, with Hamud al-ᶜUbaid next to him, dressed as
usual in a tasteless new robe. Under the sovereign's
fur coat a silk shirt was visible. I expressed my
astonishment: "Is that silk?" The sovereign nodded.
That is surely a sin? What does the house priest say
about it? I should not like to advise him to say anything at all. The sovereign wanted to know whether I
had been painting again today and had my sketch-books
brought to him. He did not appreciate the countryside;
he wanted the slaves to see whose portrait I had
painted. I was relieved that ᶜAbd al-ᶜAziz's picture
had been torn out, for it was highly probable that he
had heard about it. They brought along a special
stomach stone from a *wabr* (rock badger)[22] which had been
shot the previous year. Then the sovereign began to
talk about the news which had been brought to him from
Mecca by the caravan pressing us for our opinion of the
significance attached to the European battleship which
was causing alarm in the region of the Red Sea between
Yanbu' and al-Wajh. We could only say that it was the
first we had heard of it: perhaps it is trying to locate
a port for bunkering. He then added that the Pasha in
Mecca had spoken to the leader of the caravan, a certain
'Abdurrahman, and was told to enquire of him (the Amir)
how the two Christians he is entertaining as guests in
Ha'il are getting on. Even here the Turks were doubtless afraid of political intrigue. From there we went
over to the horses. I had expressed to the sovereign
my wish to draw his black stallion but I noticed at
once that this was not agreeable to him (from fear
based on superstition) and so I did not mention it
again.[23] As compensation I drew, in his presence, his
favourite *dalul*, a thin creature of the Nu'manya camel
breed. At the same time he wanted to see the colours
with which I paint; I showed him the small tin box with
the damp watercolours. Huber had seen a beautiful
khanjar (dagger) on one of the pilgrims, and had given

the order to Nasr as-Sabhan to buy it for him. As soon
as the Amir heard about it, he ordered it to be bought
from his purse. On our departure he offered us still
more, constantly asking if there was something else we
wanted.

Tuesday 4 December 1883. A number of wood carvings
of horses were presented to the Prince Majid. On the
way home I paid a visit to Hamud al-ᶜUbaid, who presented me with the red and gold decorated *zebun*. So
one more step forward: timeo Danaos! In the afternoon
I visited a few Persian merchants.

Wednesday 5 December 1883. In the morning I was
invited in by a Mashhadi, but was soon called away,
because Majid wished to visit us with two of his brothers. In the afternoon to Ghanam; later made a walk
to the rocky hill to the south-east of Samah, from
where one could see the activity in the pilgrim encampment. At 'Abdullah's for the evening meal, a little
light relief from the disconsolate boredom of living
in this country.

Thursday 6 December 1883. The Amir sent for us
because of the letter destined for Europe. Out of
special courtesy he did not want it delivered by the
returning caravan but by express messenger. We had
already sewn the letter up in linen, with a special
accompanying letter to the Inspector of Quarantine in
Mashhad Ali (Najaf) on the Euphrates, a certain Dr.
Lubitsch; as well as a roll of tin which had a few of
my completed casts (from Murduk, ᶜUrman and Jubba)
soldered to it. The three items were sewn up together
in another linen bag in front of our eyes, addressed
by the sovereign's secretary and handed to an express
messenger who will deliver it to Najaf within 10-12
days. The post will possibly be delivered to Europe
from there via Bombay. I wore around my neck a red
silk tie from which hung a fountain pen in an ivory
case. Hamud al-ᶜUbaid came up to me and asked, catch-
ing hold of the pen, with a meaningful glance, whether
I had another one. What did I see in these people?
Go to the devil! I thought. Evidently I could not

control my facial expression. The Amir angrily waved him away with the words "Ah! hadha haqquh" ("that belongs to him" = he needs it himself).

A large Majlis was held in front of the castle. After the meal I went to see ᶜAbd al-Aziz, Ghanam and ᶜAbdullah. I heard there that the Shaikh of the ᶜAtaiba[24] had arrived here yesterday to negotiate an alliance or some form of treaty. The raids are becoming too violent and too frequent for them. Husain, the camel-driver, came in the evening, and at my request dictated information about the camels, their names, sicknesses, way of moving and so on. The smith Husain and the servant Mahmud were interested in his detailed account. Also from today on the Amir began to fast, that is forsaking food and drink as long as the sun was in the sky. The previous *ghazu* had taken place during the actual fasting month of Ramadan (at this time July to August). The Muslim is excused fasting during sickness, journeys, or in time of war, but he has to carry it out at a convenient time later on, the so-called after-fast. For this reason the majority of the warriors are fasting nowadays. Hamud al-Mijrad fasts today for the fourteenth day; he carries with him, for want of a calendar, a scrap of paper on which he makes a mark every evening after sundown for record purposes. The person fasting, if coming into contact with a smoker, must avoid getting the tobacco smoke up his nose;[25] hence I have seen today two, who, because of this, pulled their Kafiyas right over their faces. They even refuse to use incense, with the words "I am fasting".

Friday 7 December 1883. I am seldom able to observe either the armourer Ghanam or his son Muhammad practising their art. There is a constant stream of visitors to his house and because of this the man is called away from his work and compelled to receive the idle in his *Kahawah*. It is a wonder that he is still able to complete such beautiful things. As I saw that he swept out the chippings and shavings on to the clay floor from time to time, I asked him what he did with the remains

of the precious metal as he carried out engraving and
other work. What could he do with it? It is all swept
into the waterhole (bi-'la'a) in the courtyard and into
the jackdaw's nest. I tried in vain to make him explain the reason for this inexcusable waste and folly.
Among our goldsmiths and workshops the precious residue
is painstakingly collected because, when melted down,
it represents quite a considerable value. Cleaning
clothes and tools, tables and floors, and extracting
precious metal from dirty water, is even a business in
its own right. Although it might seem to be only
paltry, there is sufficient metal obtained to ensure
the workshop cleaners require no remuneration, in fact
they even pay for their privilege of cleaning. Father
and son laughed disbelievingly about such a trivial
matter: in their own work such filings and shavings are
not even considered. Ah, well!

In the afternoon I made a farewell visit to Sliman
Mirza, who supposedly wishes to return to Iraq in a
year; but it seems to me that he has a comfortable life
among the beduin and does not wish to know any other.
In the afternoon I went out to look for the smith
Husain, but as he was not at home I glanced around his
workshop.

Majid, who was in pain because of a cavity in his
tooth, sent a slave around for some medicine. Huber
sent him over carbolic acid with the instructions
that he was to put a drop on a piece of dry cotton
wool, form it into a small ball, and press it into the
cavity of the tooth, being careful not to touch the
gum or the tongue as it burns. He was hardly in possession of the remedy, however, before he became inquisitive and made a slave stick out his tongue to try
out the effects of the carbolic acid.

His father Hamud al-^cUbaid has two upper front teeth
missing. He has heard that there is a dentist in
Damascus and would like to obtain two false teeth from
him. I am really surprised that he has not hit upon
the idea long ago to experiment with a number of slave's

teeth in order to see whether any of them would fit. It was extremely difficult to make him understand that the art consists of exactly matching the tooth with the jaw bone, so that he had to send a wax mould of his upper jaw bone to the Damascan. Of course it would be much more sensible if he went to Damascus himself, but nothing in the world would make him do that. On the other hand, the thought occurred to him that perhaps the man would visit Ha'il if he sent him a racing camel for the journey and the princely present of 200 majidi (750 marks). He was quite angry when I expressed any doubt as to whether the dentist would be satisfied with that. "What do you say? Heavens above. That is enough for two teeth!" - "Really, consider it for a moment: if the man rode like a maniac without stopping for breath, he would need 20 days to get from Damascus to Ha'il. In point of fact he would need at least 30. Then, arriving here exhausted, he would need time to recover. Then another ten days until your teeth are completed and fitted. He needs 30 days again for the return journey, making a total of 70 days in all. During that time he would have been earning at least 4 majidi per day, that is 280 majidi for the whole period, (980 marks) without taking into account the hardship and exertions of his ride." He could not fault this businesslike calculation, but I am convinced that he has dismissed my whole argument, for what it was worth, as just theory: Fool! Laughable!

Saturday 8 December 1883. Husain the smith, whom I missed yesterday, came in the morning; he accompanied me to the three old tamarisk trees near his house. After I had painted them in watercolours, he took me to his workshop, where I drew his nephew, Hamud ibn Khalaf. On the way home I came across a palm tree in the Sarha quarter which had up to half of its trunk surrounded by boards and stakes securely bound together by rope. Husain told me the name of the disease it is suffering from and gave a long explanation, of which I understood very little. He accompanied me as far as ᶜAbdullah's house. At 3 o'clock in the afternoon the Amir suddenly paid us a visit. He appeared with Hamud

al-ᶜUbaid, ᶜAbd al- Aziz and a few bodyguards. As he
was fasting we could not offer him anything. After a
quarter of an hour he made the suggestion of a stroll
in the direction of the Samah well. The Amir went
ahead with Hamud, half a step behind Huber and me, with
ᶜAbd al' Aziz in attendance, followed by a mass of
swordsmen and slaves in wide rows. We knocked at the
Samah well, surprising five women who were lying on the
floor sunning themselves. They were given quite a
start by our entrance, covered themselves and were very
roughly ejected by the slaves. The Amir spoke about
the well and the garden, and then we all crouched on
the bare earth by the inner wall; some-one took off
his coat and spread it on the ground for the Amir. At
his request I drew, very reluctantly, a one-eyed servant and a slave. From there we made our way on to
the plain towards ᶜAqda. On the way an old beggar
called out to the Amir, who stopped and exchanged a few
words with him. A couple of hundred paces further on
we came to a low stone wall with a Qibla, the niche
indicating the direction of Mecca. Here they formed
into two rows for common prayer; the Katib raised himself up on a couple of stones and led the prayers,
during which Huber and I, sitting farther away at the
back, amused ourselves. Likewise the Amir, at the end
of the prayers, sat down on the floor together with his
followers. He asked how is it that people maintain the
sun remains stationary, while the earth moves around it?
He listened to the explanation of the world-shattering
theory with interest but appeared not to be able to
follow it, to the point of becoming upset, for with a
sigh of relief he mentioned that nothing is said about
it in the Qur'an and in any case it is better if one
leaves it to the old people. Afterwards he gave the
order for a pair of donkeys to be brought from the
city to ride home on. Meanwhile the Khatib from the
village of ᶜAqda came along and they had to crouch
in a semi-circle and render something learnt by heart
from the Qur'an. As this was going on a young man
approached and put forward a complaint; the Amir promised to look into it himself, then the man was push-

ed aside. When the donkeys arrived we excused ourselves and walked back home with Hamud al-Mijrad. In
front of the house we met Prince Majid who stayed
with us a whole hour, until dinner time.

In the evening ꞌAbdullah told us that Hamud al-
ꞌUbaid had told him that I had a watch. ꞌAbdullah
replied that he has not seen me with one. I let him
say quite openly that I have one, but even though it
is made of cheap copper, I am not giving it away.
Can't the maniac for watches get enough? He is con-
tinuously whining in the ear of our courier Hamud
al-Mijrad: why don't you bring us more from Huber and
ꞌAbdulwahhab? A few days previously I presented the
five-year-old grandson of Ghanam, ꞌAbdullah ibn Hamd
az-Zuhavi (the child of the sovereign's bodyguard),
with a small pen in the shape of a musket, with a
mother-of-pearl handle, which was also fitted with a
knife blade. (Mrs Alfred Jobst from Stuttgart had
given it to me, together with some other things, as
a farewell gift for the journey.) Today I hear that
ꞌUbaid, having got to know about this gem, has run
over to Ghanam and, asserting that he has enough
children to whom I could and should have given preference, has taken the thing away from the little boy.
God - these people!

Sunday 9 December 1883. Prince Majid, really not
a gifted artist, is unusually perceptive. When I
was drawing in his reception-room this morning he
asked me why, in a row of posts, the end ones always
become smaller and yet they are all the same size. I
made him close one of his eyes and demonstrated the
relationship of receding size with distance and soon
he grasped the notion of lines above and below the
horizon meeting at a point, so that within ten minutes
he had learnt about perspective. Just as he was about
to demonstrate, by drawing a picture, that he could
correctly represent lines and angles on paper, he was
summoned to the Amir, who wished to go out riding.
The door of the house was opened, the horses brought
out one after the other from the stables opposite,
the princes buckled on their *khanjars* (daggers), and

went out to the street dressed informally, while I
and others who happened to be present, watched them.

I really wanted to hear from Ghanam how ^cUbaid
had managed to get hold of the "musket-pen". I
probably had such an angry expression on my face when
I entered his house that Ghanam was quite taken aback
and maintained that the Amir and not ^cUbaid had taken
the present away from his grandchild. What would the
Amir want with such a toy! Cursing I left the house.
I calmed myself down on the stony hill, Buwaida, to
the south-east of the city.

Monday 10 December 1883. Before breakfast I drew
from behind Samah a great panoramic view of Ha'il.
In the afternoon looked for the wolf's son in his
gloomy lair. He had the effrontery to dangle the
"musket-pen", which he had taken out of his pocket,
before my nose as soon as I came in. "Look I have got
it now! Why did not you give it to me in the beginning?" It took a great deal of effort to control
myself: "I had no idea that you hankered after such
little toys and even so I wanted to give it to this
young boy because I like him." "Ah! What is there to
like about a young boy who is just a silly lad!" Good
Heavens! One could quickly go mad here! I believe
it is quite impossible to give anybody a personal
present in Ha'il. Within three days the present has
found its way into the castle; the safe harbour into
which everything is tempted or compelled to flow. The
crafty hoarder was still not satisfied with all that;
he even began to scold Hamud al-Mijrad, that trustworthy champion of the castle's interest, who has
thoroughly plundered us, and who has had taken away
from himself, all the presents we have given to him.
Evidently he had blackened the man's character in the
eyes of the Amir and wanted to do the same to me, in
vain however, as I allowed nothing to happen to our
old *rafiq* (travel companion), and defended him ever
more strongly.

In the evening we were invited to the castle by the
Amir. After prayers more slaves had to come in and

perform for us. One of them imitated all kinds of
animal noises, then a Shi'a prayer which he delivered
in a ponderous way (Crepitum imitans). Another one
laid the palm of his hand in his armpit and by pressing on it with his arm produced the familiar rude
noise which everybody knows from childhood. A third
knew how to impersonate the mannerisms and speech of
various well-known personalities; he also did a fine
imitation of the wailing noise of the *rababah* and
finally followed this with a folk dance from his homeland. After all of this the whole audience laughed
in accordance with their importance, finally the
sovereign, heartily. At the end another slave, whose
name was Khumayis, gave a display of considerable

Arab acrobats

physical strength. He had to dance on one foot while
at the same time holding the big toe of the other
foot in his teeth; then to jump backwards and forwards·
over a horizontal stick, which he held himself, using
a footstool to balance himself, bending his head down
at the same time and picking up an object from the
floor with his teeth. The Amir assured us that this
slave's best turn could only be performed in the Nafud
(drifting sand desert): this is to dive head first
into the sand from the hump of a camel, with his legs
sticking straight up into the air until he falls over.
The person sitting next to me, the sovereign's cousin,
Hamud al-^{c}Ubaid, evidently through just watching this
show of strength experienced a feeling of superiority
due to his nationality and religion, that he wanted

to wring from me the concession that there is no one
so strong and so skilful in all Christendom. To that,
I looked at him quietly for a moment and said "Send
one of your best slaves over to me to see whether he
can bend my knee." Straight away two slaves were signalled to come over. Very proudly I half-turned upon
my left side, stuck out my naked right leg from under
my robe, and offered it to them. Well, one of them
placed his foot behind my knee and grasped my foot and
shin-bone in order to bend my knee. I made fun of
their desperate efforts: "You can have two to help you
and if this does not do the trick, then a third." At
once two others jumped up. "Come on, then!" But all
the pushing, pulling and straining were to no avail,

Gymnastic trick

and one in rage hit upon the totally inadmissible
solution of suddenly paralyzing one of my thigh
muscles with an angry blow of the fist so that the
knee jerked and all three toppled forwards. Highly
amusing. Hamud was still not satisfied with that and
wondered if I could perform one of the tricks just
performed by his negroes or something similar. "Certainly!" I asked for one or two branches such as are
used in roofing if possible and straight and yet not
too thick. Hastily a few ran off, and brought back
half a dozen samples from which I selected one as a
horizontal bar. As the bark was not very suitable for
my purpose I scraped it to obtain a smooth surface.
Two pairs of slaves had to hold the stake on their
shoulders; I thoroughly tested the pole. Afterwards

I laid aside my coat and scarf, wrapped the shirt
around me like a belt, and ordered them "Hold it
steady!" Then I swung myself up within a hair's-
breadth of the slaves on the floor: for safety's sake
four more slaves were standing by. I was now in the
position, before a breathless audience, for acrobatics
which I had not practised for more than 20 years, and
I must confess not without painful damage to the un-
protected skin behind my knee joints.

In the middle of performing a few further astounding
tricks the visit of a very pious man, the Khatib
ᶜAbdullah, was announced. The Amir hastily called out
to me: "Ilbis!" ("Dress yourself!"); I had just enough
time to slip on my coat and return panting to my
seat when the Khatib entered. Strangely, without
asking for any explanation, he took the seat which was
offered to him. There was an embarrassing silence in
the room, and everyone having cursed the good man under
their breath rather than greet him, as the evening had
been annoyingly interrupted. I had time to reflect
upon the brevity of my artistic career: Qualis artifex
pereo! Whether he noticed the performance, or whether
it had become apparent to him by the silence, I do not
know; in either case the Khatib wished to be kind to
me, and told me that he had copied at Mount Sara' (a
good day's journey to the south from here) an inscription in unknown lettering on the rock face, and will
show me his copy when convenient.

Wednesday 11 December 1883. I was quite surprised
to receive early in the morning a slip of paper, by
messenger from the sovereign, with the writing of the
Khatib ᶜAbdullah on it: "I found an inscription upon
the rock face of Mount Sara', near the water in the
countryside of Taj. It is certainly seldom that a
bedu puts pen to paper, but what is even more unheard
of is that he willingly draws out the letters. How
accurately and correctly he had done it, I was able to
verify by a visual inspection on 27 January 1884, when
I myself stood before the rock face at Sara'.

The steady decline in the temperature is becoming
noticeable (7°C); today I put on woollen underwear and
even socks. At 9 o'clock I told Majid, we should like
to go to ^cAbdullah's, upon which we set out together.
From there Majid dragged me to his garden, enquiring
on the way what I had hidden in the breastpocket of my
shirt. The mysterious answer "a rubber drinking cup"
stirred up his inquisitiveness and avarice to such a
degree that he could no longer control himself, and
actually snatched the wonderful thing with a lucky
grab. My protests that it was not for him and he would
break it in a minute, was to no avail. The beaker
had to be pulled and stretched until it was ruined;
I could not watch this childish vandalism and turned
my head away. As a replacement, he promised to send
me from the castle, a brass drinking beaker or bowl,
although I strenuously denied that I wanted any luggage which could only be a further burden. In one of
the courtyards adjoining Majid's house I caught sight
of hunting falcons. There were six of them, sitting
chained to a raised wooden platform. I had to paint
them as well as the slave named Fanaisan who looks
after them. In addition I clearly wanted[27] to have
explained to me how they are trained, but had to admit
that as it was a strange business, I have hardly under-

553

stood a word of it. The people use their own hunting
language for which there is as yet no dictionary
available.

In the afternoon I visited Hamud al-^{C}Ubaid, who
could not pass up the opportunity to beg for something
else, this time a silver safety pin which, by mistake,
I had left stuck in my coat; he promised to get Ghanam
to make me another one. On returning to the house I
came across one of Majid's slaves, who had brought over
for me a crude, sickly green coloured, drinking glass.
To the question, "Are you all still pulling the rubber
beaker about?" he answered: "Ah, no, it is broken; as
soon as you had left Majid wrenched at it with all his
might and tore it apart. Every one of us has received
a piece. Look!" That's how the rascals are.[28]

Hamud al-Mijrad and ^{C}Abdullah arrived for a meal.
The latter explained that Hamud al-^{C}Ubaid had told him:
"I will be in the way, tell Huber - it appears he
feels much more awkward in front of me - that he should
give you a nice watch, or a revolver, or a flintlock
for me." - Ah I have had enough of these people! - Huber
went later to the castle, in order to take the promised
medicine. Hamud al-Mijrad, when I asked him why he did
not go with Huber, said he thought that at present he
was not welcome in the castle.

Wednesday 12 December 1883. I did not stay up long
because of the fearful cold (7°C). I paid a return
visit to a Mashhadi, Ahmad Rashid, and also met the
brother of Mirza, our neighbour who has gone to Mashhad.
Ahmad let us smell a few of the sweetmeats, which origi-
nated from his homeland, for example, white cakes
(*sinubar*)[29], red pasties (*kanati*), very sweet pistachio-
nuts (*fustuq*), bonbons (*mlabbas*), roasted almonds and
other nuts.

I wanted to visit ^{C}Abd al- Aziz but could not get
in; the house-key had snapped off or the bolt mechanism had seized up. The prince appeared in person behind
his front door to apologise. But a conversation bet-

ween two people who cannot see each other soon becomes
tiresome, and the dialogue was soon abandoned.

The Amir summoned us to the castle at half-past
seven. Hamud al-ᶜUbaid, for whom I have little affection, and he no more for me, again remarked, when the
Amir asked me to fetch my sketch-book, that it is a sin
for people to draw. When I replied that it was not
sinful to us, he continued: "You are not in your own
country." However I hardly believe that his remarks
are likely to stir up the priests. The Amir called out
to me, after Hamud had gone off to prayers: "La takhaf!"
(Don't be afraid) and explained that I had been summoned to draw the slave Fanaisan with his falcons. It
was the ideal opportunity to have brought Majid and his
brother along, as they wanted to see how one handles
paint. But he quietly told Huber that it would be
better if I did not draw anybody else here; Huber who
advised me that I should get my diary and sketch-book
safely to Damascus or Baghdad at the first opportunity.
The stupidity which arises out of religious superstition is truly the worst kind of evil.

On the way home the sky again glowed wonderfully red
as it had yesterday and on previous days.

Thursday 13 December 1883. The Katib Salih, Hamud
al-Mijrad, Nasr as-Sabhan, and the Persian Ahmad Rashid
Mirza paid us a visit in the morning. The Katib, being
a cleric, had the place of honour on my carpet; and as
the Shi'a entered, I thoughtlessly offered him my place
(next to a Wahhabi priest). Huber tacitly corrected my
clumsy error and led the heretic by the hand over to
his carpet. After a short stay the Katib left with
Hamud.

Huber went alone to the sovereign's cousin, ᶜUbaid.
He greeted Huber with a reference to the difference of
opinion we had yesterday, with the question: "Qum?"
(are you hostile?),[30] but was pacified by Huber:
"Istaghfir Allah" (God! What could you be thinking
of!)

Today a Sharari, Mubarak by name, sent from Jauhar

in al-Jauf, arrived in Ha'il, having ridden day and
night to warn the Amir that the ^cAnaiza are embarking
on a *ghazu* against the Shammar to the north and north-
east of here. Immediately a number of *rajajil* had to
mount and ride out as far as possible to warn all the
Shammar encamped in the path of the *ghazu*. Then 'Aid
as-Sitr the commander of the flocks was summoned and
given the command to make certain that the sovereign's
horses and camels were safe, and to bring them closer
to the city.

The Chief Shepherd ^cAid as-Sitr

Hamud al-Mijrad must have been alone with the sovereign and ^cUbaid at least a whole hour during the
course of the day. We had the evening meal at
^cAbdullah's house for a change.

Friday 14 December 1883. Hamud al -Mijrad was very
perverse, even rude to me. He brought the Sharari,
Mubarak, to the house. Huber got him to name the tributaries of the Wadi Sirhan; our servant Mahmud who had
written down the Arabic names afterwards maintained
that half of the information was falsified at the instigation of Mijrad. I also had the impression that the
man had been lying out of habit, fear and mistrust.

^cAbdullah told us about the various beheadings which
he had witnessed. One of those executed had fallen
over at the first strike on the neck and since he was
still alive, the executioner had to cut his throat.
As the blood was gushing out he had left him for dead.
After a short while the victim recovered and the Amir
was asked what should be done with him. The Amir de-
creed that he should be allowed to live but should go
into exile. They treated his wounds, and he disappeared into al-Qasim. The beheadings, often five, six and

seven at once, actually ceased altogether at one time, but then increased from the accession of Muhammad ibn Rashid. But if ᶜUbaid were on the throne today there would probably have been an excessive number of beheadings, and a Christian might find it hard if he put in an appearance in Najd.

ᶜUbaid's brother, Fuhaid, had bought from a Persian pilgrim a silver watch for 13 majidis (45 marks), but unfortunately it bore a portrait of the Tsar and Tsarina on the dial. When he took it with him into the mosque, and unwittingly took out the watch in front of the Katib he was told it was a sin to enter with such a watch on his person, to pray. Now he wants to try to encumber our friend ᶜAbdullah with the watch; it remains to be seen how he can sell it.

The Mashhadi, ᶜUmran, to whom I lent 1800 francs a short while ago, paid a visit to the Amir and displayed before him goods which had recently been brought in by the caravan from Mecca. He selected - naturally free of charge (*bi la shay'*) - a few lamps. This is a convenient method for the sovereign to collect tax from the Persian merchants, who are becoming rich here.

Saturday 15 December 1883. I lunched with ᶜAbd al- Aziz, and dined with the Amir. When we entered, the Katib and religious tutor Jairullah was solemnly reading an enthralling extract out of *The Life of Muhammad* by Kastallani, which I had bought for him, as a present, in Cairo. I found even stranger the sing-song chanting style, with which Jairullah delivered sections from the *Mu'allaqat* (the best pre-Islamic poetry). I was happy, as the incantation came to an end, that I was in no way responsible for its hasty conclusion. As a contrast there followed modern battle songs and taunts.[31] Our friend ᶜAbdullah had himself announced to the Amir. Some time after he had taken his seat, he approached the Amir and crouched down before him. He explained that he had lent someone 35 riyals years ago and now the man is dead and his son will not repay it but is adopting a 'Jewish' attitude to it all.[32]

He therefore requests a letter from him (demand for payment). The secretary then wrote a letter, and rubbed some ink into the left hand of the Amir who dipped his ring in it, and made his mark on the letter, upon which ^cAbdullah immediately withdrew. He is then going to the defaulter with the letter; should the borrower's son still not pay up, ^cAbdullah will bring him before the Amir who will then send them both to the Qadi (judge).

Sunday 16 December 1883. I went to Majid, who was not at home, and then to Ghanam. I asked him to dictate to my servant Mahmud all the Arabic names of the weapons and their parts. During the evening, while ^cAbdullah was naming all the kinds of clothing to Huber, and Mahmud was writing them down, Hamud al-Mijrad came in. It annoyed him to see something going on without him. With every item which was mentioned he said very angrily: "*biss*!" (that's enough) in order to expedite the work and bring his boredom to an end. He would rather indulge in idle chatter.

Monday 17 December 1883. Nasr as-Sabhan and Majid came in the morning with their followers. They later sent for my use, a large Arabic dictionary, the *Qamus* of Firuzabadi, a vocalised edition printed in Lucknow (India) in 1298 A.H. = 1881 A.D. in 4 volumes folio, and was bought in Mecca for 6 *majidi* (21-22 marks). One of our Persian neighbours, Mahmud N.N., invited me home and, wonder of wonders, let me smoke his own pipe. Towards evening Hamud brought a Singari, who had to describe his tribal divisions. This was a great headache, causing so many moans and some anxiety that it was both laughable and pitiful; he had not displayed such fear when confronted with the most gruesome of operations with bone saw, chisel and drill! One had to come to the conclusion that there was little to be got out of him.

In the evening he was summoned to the Amir. Roars of laughter were audible in the distance, for they were already practising the game with bottles and lighting a candle at the same time, which I had shown

Majid and Nasr this morning. Beside the object of
mirth sat   the negro mimic attentively watching
every unsuccessful attempt of the clumsy ones to
light the candle.

I brought this stupid business to an end by promising to show them something more remarkable. I

Party trick in Ha'il

borrowed a bottle cork, pressing a sewing needle, by
the eye, into it, and stuck two knives, directly
underneath and opposite to one another, in the cork.
Then I made a slave come forward, who had to hold a
drawn sabre perpendicular. With bated breath and
growing amazement the whole company watched, as I
placed the needle with its attachments on to the
point of the sabre, and then set the whole contrap-
tion into a wobbly rotating motion, with my finger.
Why doesn't it fall off?! "Ma sha'llah! La quwwata
illa billah!"

The Amir asked me whether it is true that we have
paper money in Christendom, and how we actually
manage with it, whether such a quantity of paper can
be so expensive, for otherwise the paper would have
no value, and whether the people do not object to
accepting it instead of coins. I could only answer
the questions by resorting to elementary examples:
"If for example you write on a piece of paper: I
order Nasr as-Sabhan (the finance minister), to pay
to the bearer a sum of 100 riyals and make your seal

underneath it, Nasr as-Sabhan will not give it a
moment's thought but hand the man the 100 riyals in
silver. Hence you can say that that piece of paper
is worth 100 riyals, or is as good as silver money.
Now our Kaiser has a lot to do, and delegates much
of the work to his grand Wazirs. Thus for example,
the Wazir in charge of finance - who, you must
understand, is far more important than your Nasr
as-Sabhan - must put his name and seal on the paper
money. Naturally he has to be sure in his own mind
that everything is in order. Hence everybody, as
long as he has such a piece of paper, can go to the
treasury and demand to be given gold or silver for
it. The merchants are not happy to carry around
heavy metal, but prefer to exchange paper from hand
to hand." "Yes, yes, quite right; I would now like
to see an actual piece of paper money." With the
words "You can see one right now," I got up, went
into the house and fetched out a hundred-mark note.
The Amir felt the paper and examined it thoroughly.
It did not seem heavy enough to be worth 100 marks
and to be worthy of the signatures of the various
officials of the great Wazirs such as high stewards,
chief treasurers and accountants. When he asked
the identity of the boy with the wings or the little
angel holding the wreath, I saved myself with the
bold assertion that they are just Jinns (genies).
"What!! Is that what a Jinn looks like? Everybody
come here; now you can see for once a Jinn!" With
shouts of: "ma sha'llah", and "subhana 'llah", or
"ya sattar" (Good heavens, whatever next!) they
allowed their inquisitiveness and secret fear a
free rein. Of course every single person had to
have the paper in his hand until he had had a good
look at it. Then, as if I possessed the latest and
most reliable news about Jinn, I gave out all the
information required with an air of indifference.
"Actually the Jinns are of course much bigger, and
many times more frightening, but because of the
restricted space on the paper only the smallest
have been used, moreover they have been chosen from

the harmless, even benevolent, order". I got back
my hundred mark note after about 3 or 4 days, as
Hamud al-^CUbaid passed it through his harem, and
from there it made the rounds of Majid, ^CAbd al-
^CAziz and so on; they evidently all wanted to see
their wives' horror at being shown real Jinn.

Tuesday 18 December 1883. Today I wrote down
various word groupings for conversational exercise
which produced clumsy mistakes when hastily repeated, similar to the standard catch phrases in German.

Wednesday 19 December 1883. I was very surprised when two donkeys appeared in front of the
house: they were apparently to be used by Huber and
^CAbdullah for their excursion to the east today.
At 9 o'clock I visited Majid, and later Ghanam.
At midday I was invited over by Hamud al-^CUbaid,
whose words were ingratiating indeed. He was eager
to aquaint himself with Germany, Württemberg and
the Alsace Region. As an explanation I embarked
on the following: Germany consists of four kingdoms: Prussia, Bavaria, Saxony and Württemberg;
each is self-governing and has its very own king,
but the King of Prussia is the greatest of the four,
and in the event of war has all of them in his
pocket, that is why he is called the Kaiser. I
let slip something earlier about Alsace which he
brought up again. Then, as I had every reason to
mistrust my knowledge of the constitution of
Germany, I avoided any further discussion by ig-
noring the period after the King of Prussia's
Alsatian war. He wanted to know everything possible about Kaiser Wilhelm I, such as whether he has
many sons, how beautiful his horses are and how
old the Kaiserin is. It seemed incomprehensible
to Hamud that the Kaiser has not taken a new wife,
as a 50-year-old woman could not produce any more
children.

Thursday 20 December 1883. In the morning
Jairallah al-Humaid put in an appearance; he spoke
about the Hajj, in which he had taken part, and

said that the people in Mecca think the Pasha ('Aun Pasha, Wali of Hijaz) is in reality a God. He confirmed what had already been reported on many occasions, that a great explosion had been heard in the air, throughout the whole of Arabia, on one of the days in the month of Sha'ban the previous year 1300 (6 June - 4 July 1883). Everywhere they maintain it was not far away and was probably gun-fire in the next town. It was only at Khaibar that they were positive it crackled in the air directly overhead. Obviously it was caused by a meteor falling to earth unobserved.

In the afternoon I again climbed a hill outside the city to enjoy the quietness there, for in the city it is seldom possible to be alone. As soon as one takes a step outside the home, without a ser-vant in attendance, it is considered shocking. Everyone has his eye on you and feels compelled to ask "What are you doing? Where have you come from? Where are you going?" It is even considered im-polite not to have a companion in attendance. The easiest way I have found to get rid of the people is when I said "I have to go outside the city, to check on air and rain conditions." They think that their presence might have an undesirable effect upon this mysterious business.

On my return, through the *suq*, Majid called out to me as he sat among his slaves in the well-stocked shop of a Mashhadi. He told me the Amir has expres-sed astonishment to Hamud al-ᶜUbaid, that ᶜAbdullah and not I had ridden out with Huber to the moun-tains yesterday. He had made the donkeys available for Huber and myself but not for ᶜAbdullah. I believe it. The casualties which the ᶜAnaizah had inflicted on the Shammar in their raid comprise 10 people and 3 horses.

Friday 21 December 1883. At 9 o'clock in the morning Hasan Muhanna, the Ruler of Buraida, made his entry into Ha'il, the visit having been

expected for weeks. A crowd of people came by
foot to see this spectacle. In front came two
riders on horseback, whom the sovereign had sent
out to greet his guest, the secretary Nasr al
-ᶜAtiq and Fahd; then up high on a *dalul* came
Hasan Muhanna himself, in front of eight companions, on reluctantly ambling camels. There were
some really choice animals, beautifully decked
out and harnessed. A great mass of people were
moving amid it all, and bringing up the rear were
a lot of children. On the same morning Nasr as-
Sabhan called; he wanted to know whether I had
already drawn Hasan Muhanna. I dearly wanted
to do so but, telling him a fib, I said "No, I am
not drawing anything any more; that's all finished. You are too peculiar in that you consider
drawing a sin." He replied "Ah no, that it is a
sin only in the eyes of Hamud; the Amir is much
more tolerant." ᶜAbd al-Aziz had expressed a
similar opinion in his time. In view of the
cool temperature we decided to transfer our
living quarters to the so-called Qahwa ash-Shita'

Hamud al-ᶜUbaid describes the swords

(winter rooms). The room is warmer as it is not directly facing the exit to the courtyard. Two storms broke during the night.

Hamud al-^cUbaid's second son Salim took a wife for the first time today. Because of this event a special holiday had been declared, and he had also, as a sign that he was now conducting his own domestic affairs, invited all the guests to the meal. We had to wait a long time in his father's chambers until the meal was ready.

His father, Hamud al-^cUbaid, passed the time with us, by displaying various swords and describing them. The recollections of ancient heroic deeds appeared to have got the better of him, and to the astonishment of his last but one offspring, the 14-month-old Sa^cud, he paced the room, slashing the air and brandishing the supple blade. O Atta Troll! At last we were summoned to the meal. The food - which was served by the young domestics - was almost cold and partly burnt. There were five plates of rice and goats' meat brought in. Slaves lit the lamps, while others held the water bowls in readiness for the thirsty.

The food is served

From there we were taken to the Amir. In
front of the door we met Hasan Muhanna from
Buraida. He appeared to be blind in one eye.
I went to sit between him and the old man
Sulaiman. The latter, my neighbour on the right
hand side, told how on more than one raid, to
the east of Jabal Tuwaiq, he had seen outside
the city of Sadus, 20 days to the south-east
from here, a column covered with strange inscriptions. The following day I especially sought out
Sulaiman, to be quite certain, in the hope perhaps
that I could get more details from him; however
he was not able to be of any further assistance;
he only said that everybody in the length and
breadth of the region knew of the column, and promised me, that at least on the next *ghazu*, part of
the writings would be copied for me. From which
race of people did that column originate? Was it
the Phoenicians, who on their way from Gerrha on
the Persian Gulf to Petra, could have erected the
monument? Neither the Nabataeans nor the Sabaeans
nor Himyarites could be considered. I should

Dinner party at Salim's

sooner believe it is a victory monument set up by
Assyrian conquerors passing through. In any case
this column may become very important for ancient
Arab history. But how long will it be before a
brave traveller manages to penetrate that dangerous region? Palgrave has been there, but did not
notice it.

Saturday 22 December 1883. For quite a while
our friend ^cAbdullah has been complaining about
his worsening rheumatism. I wrapped him up in a
wet shirt and covered him with five coats. But
the last one was so stiff and inflexible that the
'sweat cure' did not work properly, so the result
was a failure. I had a fancy to make some fireworks, an art which I had not practised for a long
time. Accordingly I prepared a flour paste, which
I made myself, by covering with writing paper, a
pen smeared with soap, a supply of squib and
cracker casings. At Ghanam's I obtained some fine
iron filings and made him grind some porcelain
fragments into a powder for me. I twisted together
the narrow neck of the squib and tied it up and
made the whole thing solid, then stuck in a fuse.
It was a nice piece of work; also the crackers
could stand testing. Since the contents were still
damp, the fireworks had to be dried for several
days near the fireside.

Sunday 23 December 1883. I climbed up the mountain Umm Arqab, opposite Samra' alone and enjoyed
the view of the mountain peaks of Jildiyya and
at-Tuwal to the east and north-east. On the way
down I met Prince ^cAbd al- Aziz with his falcons.

I had made for myself special mountain sandals,
as Hamud al-Mijrad's brother, the ibex-hunter ^cAli,
is going to take me with him in the morning on a
hunting trip. At the same time I ordered myself a
pair of beduin boots. In the evening we were
visited first by the man who looks after the camels,
a native of Damascus, and later on by a Mashhadi.

Monday 24 December 1883. It was still not 4
o'clock, when the huntsman ^cAli ibn Ibrahim ibn
Musa al-Mijrad was ready at my door. He had with
him his eight-year-old son Musa and his nephew
^cAbdullah, son of ^cAbd al- Aziz al-Mijrad, who had
been shot in the thigh by the 'Ataiba eight years
ago when travelling with the Hajj, and who now was
laid up in Mecca with his wounds. Three donkeys
stood tied together at the front door. Besides the
rifles and cartridges, our supplies consisted of
ground coffee, a jug, a cup, some rice, a tin of
sardines, three pieces of bread and a few dates, as
well as a few pieces of clothing. Without any delay
we mounted the donkeys. We rode through the howl-
ing wind and darkness of the night, out of the city
towards the south-west. Wearing only a shirt, coat,
head-scarf and sandals, I was freezing to death;
after a short while my legs were so numb with the
cold that in the absence of stirrups I could no
longer tell if my sandals were still on my feet or
had already fallen off with the jolting of the donkeys. To bring this uncertainty to an end once and
for all, I took them off and stuck them in my saddle-
bag. We rode for two hours across the plain and up
the mountain. Before the entrance to a ravine we
dismounted from the animals. Standing on the rough
granite sand with my feet numb and frozen I gazed
on the glorious dawn over the rocks. No matter
whether they were rose-red or gilded! What was
supremely important at that moment was a warm drink.
We ate bread and dates with the coffee. Almost
with melancholy I opened the tin of sardines, which
had accompanied me as a true mascot in my knapsack
through six long years of my wanderings through the
Black Forest and Vosges Mountains. My companions
had never seen fish before in their lives, and probably thought them worms, but they eat worms as a
delicacy, so the young boy longed to have the last
oil remains out of the tin. All that was left to
do now was to change into hunting clothes: ^cAli put
on a yellowy brown shirt and head scarf, which by
their natural colour and dirt did not stand out in

contrast with the colouring of the rocks; I wore a
grey woollen hunting shirt and identical pants,
with a head scarf; we both left our coats behind.
Cartridge belts were buckled on, and I hung my sandals on a piece of cord over my shoulder. ^CAli
with his rifle led the way, while I followed with
my Lefaucheux. Now we could start: only the ibex
were missing! In a rocky fissure there was a sudden

On the ibex hunt

ascent. ^CAli obviously had thought of running me
into the ground – to no avail. It amused me that he
had from time to time to get his breath back just
like myself. After half-an-hour we approached the
highest ridge of the mountain; and carefully crept
up to the edge. We peered all around in vain, at the
same time looking over the bare empty precipices
towards ^CAqda. There was not a single ibex to be
seen anywhere. The most recent spoor were two, or
possibly even three days old. We came across many
recent panther tracks. We made our way along innumerable winding paths up and over the mountain ridges,
northwards towards Mount Mardiyya, and there lay down
behind a Menteris a hunter's hide of rough stone,
with concealed apertures to shoot through. On the
opposite rock face was the burrow of a *wabr* (badger)

but he did not show himself. I pulled a beautiful
rock crystal out of a crevice and put it in my pocket. There was growing here the *Hauaban* plant which
is the favourite food of the ibex. There was another plant there: *jalwa.* ^CAli broke the silence,
showing me the yellow wood with the red interior;
he praised its virtues as eye medicine, but it burns
when put into the eye with a little stick (*mil*) and
makes the eyes water. There was not much doing here,
so we gave the whole thing up as a waste of time.
^CAli wanted to have one last try and turned towards
the south, climbing over the steep Kishriyya ravine.
I climbed down through a treacherously difficult
ravine, too quickly, down into the valley. I knew

Kishriyya mountain

I was near the point of departure by the song of the boy who in any case had seen me up high above as he was preparing the coffee when I arrived. How comforting was the black drink! As it would be at least an hour before ᶜAli could return, to pass the time I went down on to the plain to draw the entrance to the ravine: in the background the Mardiyya and the pointed summit of Kishriyya. ᶜAli returned from the mountains without having seen a single ibex. Somewhat ill-tempered, he only wanted a cup of coffee. Then we remounted the donkeys. The ride home was cold and windy, and yet the journey back seemed shorter than the journey out in the morning. ᶜAbdullah was waiting for me at the house and took me out for the evening meal. It tasted wonderful. Later the Amir sent the head of a powerful ibex, whose antlers had a span of 4½ metres.

Tuesday 25 December 1883. I wanted to celebrate Christmas with a solitary walk which was of course not possible for me without going some distance outside the city. For first of all Majid caught me on the way to Ghanam the armourer; then a slave ran up and gave me an invitation to take coffee with the standard-bearer Mubarak al-Furaikh. From there I managed to creep away to the freedom of Mount Umm Arqab where I indulged myself in dreams of home, the decorated Christmas tree, the delight of the children, on the thick snow. Without hesitation I should have given all the palms below for a single white fir tree. I climbed over the ridge, towards the south-east, down into the valley and returned to the city through the Lubda quarter, where I met my hunting companion from yesterday, ᶜAli al-Mijrad, and made him dictate to me the song he had sung yesterday, the ibex-hunter Jasir's song. From there I took myself to the Amir to thank him for the antlers he had presented me with yesterday. He politely enquired about yesterday's events, and whether I had been satisfied with ᶜAli. When I told him about the huntsman Jasir's song he demanded to see what I had written down, took it out of my hand and began to read it aloud. "Wait a minute. There is a mistake, there should be two more verses." He dictated the whole thing again to me with four further verses, which ᶜAli had not known or had forgotten.

Wednesday 26 December 1883. Visited Prince ᶜAbd al-ᶜAziz. The room was full of beduin guests, the most important being Rakan ibn Hathlain from the ᶜAjman tribe which lives to the east of Ha'il, towards Hasa. As I left I again ran into my hunting companion ᶜAli al-Mijrad, and another cup of coffee! When I left him I wandered off to the Samra mountain, or more accurately to its spur. From the summit I gazed down over the desolation which had been caused by the previous four weeks' rain along the valley. Down there lay the Khuraimi, one of the sovereign's youngest palm gardens, sadly neglected. ·I clambered down to inspect the damage close up, entering through a wide breach in the clay wall. The fallen trees protruded from the débris, in the midst of which were the ruins of the caretaker's house, with gaping cracks. From there I descended farther, to the now dry water-course of the Ha'il stream. The ruins of the former suburb of the city, ᶜAinat, stretched out in a long narrow line, interspersed with neglected tamarisks and dilapidated wells. I came home thirsty and limping, for a stone, fragment of glass or something or other had cut my ankle.

Thursday 27 December 1883. Huber went to the Amir before sunrise. There appears to be some kind of plot afoot to prevent me from both travelling alone to acquaint myself with the country and from visiting al-Hijr and al-'Ula. Who and what was behind it? The noble cousin of the sovereign, Hamud al-ᶜUbaid, is the person who first springs to mind. Is he so upset about my alleged witchcraft and sinful drawing?

After breakfast I looked for Majid, but instead was caught by Hamud al-ᶜUbaid. I had intended to visit him in any case, to thank him for the little

571

silver box with *zabad* (civet) in it. He was over-
courteous and begged me to visit him daily (Oh no!
not that!). On my return home I met a Qahtani,
named Khalid, with the surname Abu Thalathin, who
had followed in his father's footsteps. He is a
sturdy man with a snow-white beard, and comes from
the south, but has lived in Ha'il for 5 years and
is used by the sovereign, whenever necessary, to
convey messages to Ibn Sa'ud in Riyadh. He dictated to Huber (that is to the servant Mahmud) the
names and regions of the southern tribes in central
Arabia.

Amir Hasan Muhanna

    In the evening, after the last prayers, we were
invited to visit Amir Hasan Muhanna of Buraida.
The sovereign had made available to him a house,
next to that of the armourer Ghanam. I was quite
surprised when a camel kneeling on the floor bel-
lowed at me as I walked through the dimly-lit
hallway. It was Muhanna's pet and, unusually in
Central Arabia, was kept and fed in the house. As
well as ourselves a number of other people were

invited, and even our servant Mahmud came smartly
dressed with a lit lantern. Soon the reception-room
was full of people and it was becoming so hot that
the Amir Muhanna threw back his kafiya half across
his head.

The conversation naturally centred upon the rain
and the lush grazing, then to the markings, value
and pedigree of our horses; someone wanted to know
how we obtained in our country such animals as
gazelle, ostriches and ibex. Also Hasan Muhanna
knew all about the column at Sadus; he promised to
have the markings on the stone copied for me by an
expert. After a short while we took ourselves to
the house of Ghanam's son-in-law, Hamd Zuhairi, the
sovereign's valet. Coffee was prepared there as
well and even served with some kind of lemon or
melon with sugar.

Friday 28 December 1883. The strong wind discouraged us from going outside, so the usually
troublesome visits of the Persian merchants were
therefore not quite so inconvenient.

Saturday 29 December 1883. I spent the morning
without talking to anybody, going out alone on an
ibex hunt with only a flintlock and a knapsack. My
destination was the peak Munif in the Jabal Aja'.
At first I travelled for one and a half hours
across the barren plain, crossing a small water-
course near the mountains which flowed down to the
north east between low rocks sticking out of the
sand. Soon there opened up before me a ravine,
called al-Jibbah, where I came across a small house
which I learnt later was designated for housing
people with smallpox or leprosy, as well as a con-
valescent home. To the right was a small cave full
of recently carved names. The ravine narrowed
until it finally ended in an impassable gully in
the form of a deep rock basin. I therefore chose
another route, which took me towards the south west,
preferable because the strong south wind made it
pointless to approach wild animals from another

direction. I struggled on for quite a time trying to get up higher. I had chosen a route which
turned out to be blocked with great boulders after
a short climb. Ever upwards! Then I came across
a second cave, this one with moss on it! The delicate plants were as if fossilised by the granite
sand around them. Resting at the entrance, I found
at first no possibility of pressing on further.
Above me stretched an inaccessible stone wall in a
wide semi-circle, part of it with a dangerous overhang. Never mind. Fortes fortuna juvat! Back into
my knapsack went my sandals and then I started to
climb up the sheer rock. Carefully, with outspread
arms, I set out on the slope of about 40 degrees.
It was manageable in bare feet but under my feet the
granite crumbled and peeled away in thin strips. It
must have been quite a long time since either people
or animals had passed that way. Gradually I disturbed more substantial débris, which tumbled down

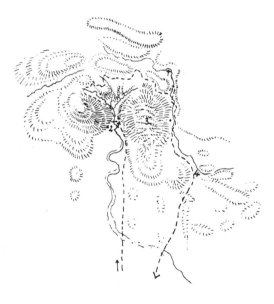

Map of the mountain peaks
1. al-Jibbah   2. smallpox house
3. mountain peaks   4. al-Maghawwat

574

into the depths. But then my adventure changed
into a nightmare as the whole rockface broke away
in one mass, and began to crash down. As I was only
a hair's breadth away from death I threw myself
shocked to the ground on the slope. However the
rumbling rocks crashed past me left and right down
into the abyss. I was relieved to emerge with only
a few scratches on my arms and hands. Twice more I
threw myself down on to the ground when in similar
danger, then I finally encountered solid rock again,
and breathed again as my mild flirtation with eter-
nity had run its course. But now to reach my goal;
through a gap I climbed up to a rocky ridge, but was
a little disappointed to say the least to see Mount
Munif, which I had assumed to be quite near, as a
high jagged wall, rising out of a deep ravine, far
away. So much was clear to me: if it were at all
possible - which was highly doubtful - to climb up
the Munif along its front face, then it would
require more hours than I had available. I also
did not wish to return by the route along which I
had come, so I had to wind my way around towards
the north and north-east behind the Needles of
Mushamrakha and from there look for a good descent.

I moved slowly and with great difficulty, pushing my
way for about 20 metres down a steep watercourse, and
was uncertain whether I should follow this doubtful
route or climb upwards. I bent down and, pushing myself forwards an inch at a time and looking for a way
out, suddenly saw on the left 60 metres in front of me
two beautiful ibex which, having caught sight of me at
the same time, quickly trotted with clattering steps
along the rocky slope. My heart beat audibly in my
breast. I was not in any position to take the flintlock from my back, and in fact dared not move a muscle.
I had to watch, impatient and infuriated, as the creatures were in no hurry, having understood my predicament. Only once, before they disappeared around a
corner, did they turn their heads: did one of the so-
and-so's stick out his tongue and laugh? Ha! the
wretch!

It was useless to get angry at their mockery and
the thoughts of revenge, for I had more important
things to do. The first was to rescue myself from my
difficult situation. Any sideways movement was out
of the question: there could only be a straight descent. My goal must be down in the depths of the
ravine with the boulders, even though I could perceive
no space between them. I had reached quite a distance
downwards when a dark abyss gaped open in front of me:
a wedge-shaped piece of rock was jammed in front of
the gully, and its edge extended ominously downwards.
Carefully I laid down flintlock, knapsack, and coat
to make a careful investigation. I convinced myself
that there was no alternative but to creep through
behind the stone blockage and try a vertical leap
downwards, of about 2½ metres, on to a stone boulder.
Thus I climbed back up again in order to pick up my
equipment, which had been left behind. The flintlock
was tied to a rope and gently let down, followed by
the coat and knapsack. The stone boulder stared up
at me, frighteningly round. Julius, your legs must

stand the leap! I limbered up for a moment or two
and then - bismillah! - down!

Thank God, my plan had succeeded but it occurred
to me to write it down as a warning. What is meant
by a warning? Hardly had I saved myself when my
thoughts again lingered on the ibex. However I had to
admit that I ought to refrain from all further hunting
today because the day was drawing to a close, but
curiosity spurred me at least to explore the floor
of the valley a little further, to the left. Before
anything else I had to complete the rest of the
descent, now safe, then I turned to the left and climbed wearily between man-high boulders. After about
twenty minutes I could move no further forwards, for
the whole ravine was solid with boulders. I could
only see, peering between the boulders, that a group
of wild palm trees were standing in a crater filled
with sand, in front of a sheer rock wall with no sign
of any ibex. I had to put up with my melancholy
thoughts on my return journey. The descent of al-
Maghawwat, because of its difficulty, went slowly.
At last the sandy basin appeared, then past the small
cave, over hillocks, I hastened back home across the
plain.

By now I had certainly, in all honesty, deserved a
drink, something to eat, a smoke and a rest, but
found only water, dates and tobacco. The whole household was concerned with one thing and one thing only:
the visit of Amir Hasan Muhanna, who wanted to put
in an appearance at our house after the last prayers.
Crockery, cups, and samovar had all been borrowed
from ᶜAbdullah; lamps, copper plates and stearine
candles from our Persian neighbour ᶜAmran. Our servant, Mahmud, had made it clear that he would produce
his finest cuisine, but declined to give any further
information; in short it would turn out to be a magnificent feast. After the meagre evening meal I could
hardly keep awake, all the company could go to hell.
The last prayer was long over and the Amir with his
followers were still keeping us waiting. The hasty

preparations for his reception had been completed in
an air of calm; all it required now was his appearance.
Three oil lamps burned on the walls, three further oil
lamps on a shaky table, while at the back of the
courtyard ᶜAbdullah and Hamud al-Mijrad stood expectantly and two freshly-cleaned lanterns were illuminated by stearine candles. Could any other house here
by so brightly lit? I had a sudden inspiration to
carry out a piece of theatricals. Almost my whole
supply of home-made squibs, probably four dozen of
them, must be sacrificed for it. Hurriedly I planted
them in suitable positions on the wall and stairs; a
slave was detailed as the fireworks operator and
waited impatiently to discharge his duty. Finally at
half-past nine the guests, ten in all, approached.
Frankincense and myrrh wafted from the coal bucket
at the entrance. Squibs crackled from the right and
left, from above and below. Universal astonishment
and amazement. The Amir of Buraida, striding through
the smoke, took his place on Huber's carpet, next to
him Shaikh Rakan of ᶜAjman; I led two of the latter's
people to my carpet. During the conversation with
one of the people next to me, I noticed, when he
turned his head, that he had hanging down in front,
next to his cheeks two pairs of pigtails. [44]
When I asked him how many pigtails he had got, he
proudly threw his head scarf in the air, without
uttering a word, and showed me his neck: I counted
ten of them. First we served lemon tea, which had
become bitter, through standing for a long time,
and was barely pourable through the large amount
of sugar in it, yet it was fully in keeping with
Arab tastes. I was really surprised when the Shaikh
Rakan spoke a few words of Turkish with Mahmud, and
learnt afterwards that he had spent seven years as
a prisoner in the Nish fortress (in Serbia, Turkish
until 1878). About twenty years ago he was enticed
into Hasa (on the east coast of Arabia) as mediator
under a guarantee of safe conduct by Midhat Pasha
but as soon as he arrived there he was imprisoned
and hauled off to Europe. It is on account of just
such treachery and breaking of their word that the

Turks have brought upon themselves the everlasting
hatred of the beduin which is understandable. Lemonade followed the tea, then came a great platter,
piled up with Mahmud's culinary achievement; lemon
slices with sugar, carnival cakes, glacé dates and a
kind of barn cake (*Pfizauf* in Swabian dialect) together with four bowls of thick sugar water. At the
beginning six of us sat up to the plate or platter,
then, after everybody had had his fill, came the
next ones in the queue. Then the bowls of sugar
water were set down in front of them, and impatiently drunk; in the same way the greasy pastries were
gobbled up. Such a delicacy does not come their
way every day. Now came the coffee, then the smoking,
finally zabad. This time Mahmud did not hand round
the little silver box with his usual frugality, but
allowed it to be passed around to each individual,
to stretch out their finger, and each dabbed on the
amount they thought they should have. After hand-
washing, a towel was needlessly offered to everybody; this seemed to wind up the proceedings. Highly satisfied, the guests got up to depart; they
found their sandals easily in the brightly-lit
courtyard. A pair of remaining squibs which had
been forgotten crackled a farewell salute and raised
a forlorn hope of a repeat performance, then everything subsided into silence. There was still a lot
of activity: the cleaning and putting away of the
crockery took a great deal of time. I gave one last
thought to the ibex that got away, then fell into a
deep sleep.

Sunday 30 December 1883. If the sun does not
shine, one cannot have bright ideas. It is so
sad that we cannot achieve our goal of getting to
the ancient ruins and burial grounds in the west.
We are enjoying ourselves very much here but we
find ourselves being kept in honourable imprisonment for the entertainment of the "castle". In
a despondent and lazy mood I lay down on a hill
outside the city.

Monday 31 December 1883. Prince Majid had
sent a slave over to announce that he will be
calling on us soon, but after half an hour when
he had still not come, I went out and Huber locked the front door. I came across Majid in the
street and explained that it was now too late for
us, left him standing there and carried on walking. In his place there appeared Hamud al-Mijrad
on my heels, forcefully begging me to come to his
house. After having dark coffee and smoked a
pipe, I took his eight-year-old nephew, Musa ibn
ᶜAli, for a walk around the city walls. In the
evening we were again invited by Majid to the
castle, that is to his father's apartments. Meanwhile the latter had taken himself off to the
mosque, where all the guests assembled for prayer
in rows; Khairullah placed himself at the head to
lead the prayer, while Huber and I, and a very
young son of Hamud al-ᶜUbaid, remained sitting by
the walls.

During the solemn proceedings there was the
unbelievable sound of a belch - no-one paid any
attention to it.

Tuesday 1 January 1884. How happy I am that
it is not New Year here, no visiting cards, no
list of new year resolutions, no torture by the
bell ringers, hangover-faces, no hypocritical
visits by employers (and if necessary by their
wives). In spite of the feeling of relief, the
longing for civilisation came over me, and I had
the desire to be transported over to the good
city of Strasbourg for just a quarter of an hour.

At the turn of the year I must not dispel
serious thoughts of what I have witnessed and
done so far on this journey. It is merely a preamble, an overture in to the real work. Shall I
ever see the mysterious ruins of al-Hijr and al-
ᶜUla? Shall I find what I am looking for? Can
I do what everyone expects of me?

At 9 o'clock to Majid's. I was not long there before the Amir was announced, with Hamud al-ᶜUbaid, with Hasan Muhanna from Buraida, and many of his followers. The whole coffee-lounge was full up with people. In the afternoon I drew a map for Huber's diary. It rained heavily in the night.

Wednesday 2 January 1884. In the morning the rain was coming down in a deluge from the grey sky. The whole day was just as miserable as a winter day at home. Rain was running down the streets in such broad streams that one could not step over them without getting one's feet wet. I crouched in a small cave, on a small stone hill, called Qubbat ᶜAli, to the east of the city, and the roar of the water crashing between the rocks, over at Munif, 6 kilometers from here. Naturally I could not remain unnoticed; a number of young lads joined me and sang songs which I could not understand. At the house I met Barghash ibn Tuwaila, Shaikh of the Aslam from Majma'a; he explained the structure of his tribe, which was written down by Mahmud. In the night more rain fell. My tobacco was thoroughly saturated.

Thursday 3 January 1884. Those who have not collected rainwater are without a drink in the house today, for the well-walls are so fragile from the continuous rain that the machinery cannot be used without danger of collapse. I have been suffering for eight days with a mild but quite painful rash, which comes from the blood, that is from the predominance of dates in my food. Unavoidable scratching with my fingernails is in no way advisable; I use a brush for the more inaccessible parts of my back.

The Qahtani Khalid with the surname Abu Thalathin was to have described for us the structure of his tribe but instead he tried desper-

ately to convert us to Islam.[45] We are now
powerful and distinguished, in the position of
an Amir, such as the Amir of Buraida, or still
higher. If we became fully-fledged Muslims,
and did not go astray, we could have women from
the noblest of the tribes, sit the whole day in
a garden, eat as much sheep's meat as we wanted;
if it did not suit us we should not need to
undergo the rigours of a *ghazu*, could stay
quietly at home and yet take our share of the
booty from it. "I should be ashamed of myself!"
And then once in paradise, we should wear silk
clothes and be given all manner of wonderful
things which we might desire. We convinced him
that we attached even more value to his account
of the Qahtan tribe and its structure. He gave
the names, unhappily, with gaps, in snatches,
perhaps even intentionally incorrect, which were
written down by the servant Mahmud; during this
he digressed into further exaltations of paradise and constantly had to be reminded of the
task in hand. To these people, Huber and I are
in all probability the cream and model of
Christianity, yet we are hardly Christian at
all and really we are very close to Islam, and
in any event high above the Shi'a (who are here
represented by the temporarily resident Persian
merchants from Mashhad); it is incomprehensible
to our Muslim friends that we do not become full
converts and take the advantages available here
on earth and up in heaven. In the same way the
eight-year-old Musa expressed to me his admiration: we are Christians, having a book and a
religion but the Mashhadi (the Persian merchants)
are "Idolaters - God curse their fathers". He
knows from his father that we are almost Muslim
and must not be allowed to stray into hell fire.

Today the Amir of Buraida began his journey
home, and tomorrow Husain the camel-handler will
depart; he has promised to take a letter with
him and believes he will arrive in Damascus in

two months. We paid a visit to our Persian neighbour ^cAmran.

Friday 4 January 1884. Uninterrupted drizzle since yesterday evening, no sunshine since 24 December. One of the walls in Majid's house collapsed because of all the rain, with such a crash that it was heard in the castle. In the Lubda quarter a man was buried up to his neck but luckily they managed to drag him out alive.

The details of the next *ghazu* have been settled and riders were sent out to the great Shaikhs.

Out of boredom I made some squibs and crackers today, but they were rather disappointing because of the dampness in the air. I shall wait until morning, or throw them into the fire out of sheer annoyance. 'Abd al'^cAziz sent a packet of fine granulated kohl (mascara). I paid a visit to the Persian merchant ^cAli, brother-in-law of ^cAmran. In the evening ^cAmran came and returned the borrowed gold in the form of silver, that is he paid me $427\frac{1}{4}$ majidis instead of 90 Napoleons. Hamud al-Mijrad, our adjutant, seeing this money suddenly required 6 majidi to buy a carpet. As I could not truly maintain I had no money, I wrote off the 6 majidis.

Saturday 5 January 1884. As 'Abdullah had a fight some time ago with his second wife, the beautiful Jawah from Baghdad, without making it up again with the present of a new dress or something similar, for 10 days we have had to do without the good Baghdad bread; but even without this strike we have no bread of any kind for 4 days, because 'Abdullah's oven, which stands out in the courtyard, has been ruined by the rain. There were also light rain-clouds (*dim*) in the sky; once, towards midday, the sun came out. In the afternoon we took coffee at

^{C}Amran's house, and in the evening received a visit from the Mashhadi Mahdi.

Sunday 6 January 1884. This morning I once again found traces of lice. The hunt was very fruitful: at least 30 of them were burnt to death, a huge nest of them in the folds of my shirt was destroyed; the shirt was taken outside and spread on the roof in the wind, and they are leaving of their own accord. I paid Majid a short visit. He had more than once expressed a desire to look at a pair of gloves, but I could not satisfy his curiosity.

If only we could at last get away from here! It will soon be three months that we have been sitting around in Ha'il. These people have no conception of time, no idea of what torment they are causing us. What do we get from it, except dates, and as much sheep's meat and rice as we can eat? That we can sleep without any worries for as long as we like, as well as a few gifts and honours! We went to the sovereign to make him understand that we should like to leave for Taima, al-Hijr and Tabuk and that he ought to let us go! There is no problem with the first two, thought the sovereign, but it is dangerous to go to Tabuk. The sovereign laughed at Huber's remark that it will not be too bad: So? He has just received the news that Muhammad ibn ^{C}Atiyya and ^{C}Anaibar[46] together with the *rajajil* of the Shuyukh have been overpowered and robbed, whilst tax-collecting not far from Tabuk, by the more powerful Bani ^{C}Isa (a part of the Bani Sakhr). Hm?? The zakat tax, to a total of 7000 majidis, is gone! Still more sorry is our servant Mahmud, who had entrusted Muhammad ibn ^{C}Atiyya with the delivery of 10 Napoleons to his family living in Ma'an.

This evening we are summoned (for the first time since 21 December) by the Amir after the evening meal. He was exceedingly courteous;

his cousin Hamud al-ᶜUbaid, to whom we went
afterwards, made us uneasy with his friendliness.
There was a lot of smoke around in his coffee
lounge which stung our eyes. Arriving home I
tried out the squibs I made yesterday, which
were by now dry. Yes! they went off excellently, powerful and lasted a long time. I must
practise some more of this skill.

Monday 7 January 1884. In normal years the
bedu is never satisfied with the rain; if it
were up to him he would beg ten times the average rainfall. But now the people are getting
gradually fed up with it. In many well-built
houses, as for example the home of Prince ᶜAbd
al-ᶜAziz, there is hardly a dry place to sleep.
All the buildings are weakened to such an
extent, that no muezzin (the official who summons the faithful to prayer) trusts a wall, let
alone a minaret. At our house the rain penetrates most undesirable places. Our chests and
cases have had to be moved to a place of safety.
A large amount has come down the steps which lead
up on to the roof. In the winter room, which has
a hole in the ceiling for the smoke to get out
(*suwamah*; [Hess has *samawe*]), there is a large
puddle on the clay floor which was adorned with
splendid lumps of ice from this morning's hail.
Anybody who wants to go outside has to leave his
donkey behind and wade through the deep *sail*
(winter stream) by himself. I have not looked
outside the house all day, and had nothing better
to do than put fireworks together.

Tuesday 8 January 1884. It rained heavily the
whole night. The water came down through two
floors into our store-room where the cases are
standing. The floor is awash. Both of my new
zebun (coats), which were hanging on the walls,
were thoroughly soaked and soiled by the dampness coming through the clay walls. In the
afternoon I went out to the Sha'ib, where the
waters are 2 metres high. The people said that

20 houses have been totally demolished in the suburb of Lubda; I saw one of them which had been swept into a 17-fathom well. A marvellous rescue bid had succeeded. Most of the walls in the palm garden have been severely damaged, everywhere turrets and towers have crashed down, and heaps of broken clay bricks are blocking the way. Through the many gaps in the garden wall, climbing over the slippery heaps of clay and wading through the puddles, I came across a deserted building and wondered why these once splendid premises have been allowed to deteriorate. Hardly had I passed by when there was a tremendous crash and as I turned around, I saw water and mud spray up into the air between the walls which were still standing. I did not dare to approach it as the ground was slushy underfoot. In front of the city, to the west, as well as in the palm garden, crowds of people are forced in tents as their houses are threatening to collapse or have become unfit to live in. Even the Amir is not entirely safe in his solid fortress, for the rain is coming in everywhere and for safety's sake he has had a mighty tent erected outside the city, to enable him to escape there if necessary. Visitors, when they come to us, note that our house has suffered comparatively little damage. But the stairs which were interrupted by three storeys are no longer there, the clay steps having crumbled under palm tree trunks diagonally across them, and the wall against which they are leaning is no longer to be trusted. One is given to understand that the *ghazu* has been postponed or abandoned altogether. The sovereign showed us a black stone which, according to the people in the slave-quarter, fell from the sky yesterday afternoon. He anxiously enquired whether it could be true. I reminded him of the 'Elephant' chapter in the Qur'an, in which a flock of birds threw glowing stones down on to the army and destroyed it.[47]

Wednesday 9 January 1884. The lovely sunshine
lured me into the open air. I slung my gun over
my shoulder and made off towards the mountains
in the keen north wind (4½°C). I went again behind the Mushamrakhah mountain in the direction
of Munif, upwards along the route familiar to
me, but did not catch a glimpse of any game at
all.

On the Craggy Mountain

I climbed up the rocks more easily this time,
and even pushed on to the hollow above it, where
palm-trees were growing. After I had partly
circumvented and partly waded through more water
holes I found myself directly under the summit
of Munif, which towered about 80 metres above
me, an impenetrable wall. As I squeezed my way
back between the boulders on the descent, I was
surprised to bump into a negro, similarly armed
with a flintlock, who was hunting; later I met
a second negro; they too had seen no ibex.
Arriving below on the Maghawwat plain, I sheltered behind a slab of stone and smoked one of the

cigars I had saved up. Then I looked, not very successfully, for a route back different from my way out and reached home after ^{c}asr (about 4 o'clock). Tormented by hunger, I had no desire to wait two hours for dinner time, and called the servant Mahmud to bring me something to eat. As he had the audacity to refuse, reprimanding me severely to the effect that I could wait until the meal was ready like everyone else, I was provoked into cursing. On this, Mahmud's face went purple with rage, he waved his arms about in the air, and uttered a stream of hardly-intelligible rubbish: I have grossly insulted him, cursed his religion ("What?") yes, really, he knows this from Damascus; it is an evil thing, anyway he has finished with us. After he had calmed down somewhat, I explained to him, that things will not carry on like this for much longer as we must look for another servant. I sent him out of the room and got myself a handful of dates from the stores. Soon after that he came in again, apologised, and served me coffee. We were summoned in the evening, once more, by the Amir.

Thursday 10 January 1884. We had had a cold night: it was 2°C in the courtyard, but there was a frost everywhere outside the city. One of the Amir's slaves had been found frozen to death in

Plan of the Craggy Mountain
(the previous illustration was drawn from here)

the Laqita region. I was not very well today;
it appears that I have caught a cold in the wind
by going on yesterday's mountain trip with only
a shirt and coat; this made itself felt through
a headache. Now they had to hang up my only
woollen shirt on the inaccessible roof! A visit
from Majid was not welcome at all.

We were invited to a meal in the evening by
'Abdullah; in the meantime there had been a
reconciliation with his Baghdad wife. The host
brought the conversation round to Jinns (evil
spirits) and told me quite seriously - it still
frightened him - how late one evening, in the
bazaar in Baghdad where he owned a shop, he was
boxed on the ears for a whole hour by a Jinn,
and although familiar with the place was forced
in the confusion, by the head, into the corner.
No a^{c}udu billah! ("I appeal to God"), no subhan
Allah! ("God help me!")[48] had any effect. He eventually found his way home, struggling pitifully
through the deserted streets with bumps on his
head and blue bruises over his body. It was difficult not to laugh. As I had heard by his own
admission that he was susceptible to spirits,
his assertion that the foregoing had a ghostly
explanation had become immediately questionable.
But I did not want this possibility to be overlooked and asked, whether in fact he had done a
little too much on the night in question. He
fervently maintained however that he had been
sober throughout, and there can be only punishment for thinking otherwise, as he had earlier
expressed blasphemous doubts about the existence of Jinns. I agreed that this form of
punishment had been certainly very painful and
deplorable, but what had he been doing, in any
case, at that late time of night in the deserted
bazaar? Well, he had been late in cleaning up
his shop, and as he was closing it he noticed
that it had become pitch-black and the whole ba-

zaar was deserted and closed. The night-watchman, frightened by the strange banging noises and frantic screams, had further delayed in unbolting the door.

Friday 11 January 1884. To overcome my boredom by a cheerful change, I decided to alter my appearance to the outside world. For this reason, before daybreak, I spruced myself up as well as possible: red silk shirt with tassels, silk head-scarf, silk handkerchief, the new Indian coat I had received from Majid, finely-woven stockings (the first time I had worn stockings for more than four months), red bedu boots with blue tassels and iron buckles, inlaid with gold, eyes nicely tinted black with mascara, beard lightly trimmed. And so I went out into the street, after breakfast, with my sword at my side, and greeted the astonished inhabitants politely and with some pomp. What happened next was inevitable: the Amir was notified within 5 minutes that I had put on clothes of state which had never been seen before, so that there must be a special reason. Of course he immediately sent me a message, I should come to the castle. The whole court were already waiting there for me impatiently. I was examined, mauled about, and had to give all possible details. I told them it was my sister's birthday today and this was the usual way of celebrating it. They wanted to know then whether I went around all day in such a costume at home. It was not really possible to correct this false picture in so many words, so I made them give me some paper and made a few sketches. The wide-brimmed hat brought astonishment and bewilderment (was it made of iron?), the top hat and dress coat caused hilarity, while the hiking clothes, knapsack and such climbing gear as crampons and snow-shoes did not receive any approval but remained incomprehensible. How could I explain ice skates? Without knowing words for them in Arabic, I ran the

risk of being taken for a charlatan and therefore with regret stopped my explanations. The
Amir changed the topic of conversation to music,
asking whether we too have songs. I caused
consternation by saying that various nationalities, professions, ages, generations, had a
preference for different songs according to how
they felt, so that we had for instance Tyrolese
songs, and songs for soldiers, hunters, sailors,
girls in love, or children. I could not refuse
to give them examples from the Tyrol and elsewhere, such as 'Wohlauf, Kameraden aufs Pferd,
aufs Pferd'; 'Ich hatt' einen Kameraden'; 'Im
Wald und auf der Haide'; 'Auf dem Meer bin ich
geboren'; 'Gaudeamus igitur'; and so on. Although the German words were not understood, and
not very easy to render in Arabic, the melodies
themselves did not make any special impression
on them either. But as I sang Leonora from
Verdi's *Il Trovatore*, translating the verse into
Arabic with poetic licence (the easiest thing
to do),[49] everybody was delighted and called for
an encore. Prince Majid begged me to teach him
the song in his home. This matinée was brought
to an ignominious end by a performance from a
barrel organ, produced from the castle's
treasury. On the way back home I dissociated
myself from this masquerade.

The Amir invited us to an evening meal; there
was rice, meat soup, ibex meat (not very good in
the rutting season), a sort of sausage meat
wrapped in leaves. Everybody had next to them a
bowl filled with bitter lemonade, in which a
scoop was floating. The sovereign presented me
with ibex antlers over 4 m. in span.

Saturday 12 January 1884. Beautiful sunshine
again. Early in the morning Majid sent over a
slave to say that he would like a few squibs and
a pencil. I told him "All right, all right, he
will get them during the course of the day." Of

course it did not please me: he can buy a pencil in the *suq* and make the fireworks himself. The message was only a pretext, I discovered next day: he really wanted a visit to trap me into giving him a singing lesson.

Sunday 13 January 1884. Majid had meanwhile tried to reproduced the Leonora aria within his four walls. It was astounding how this gifted person (whom I also considered capable of all evil)[50] - apart from one mistake at the end, which I had repeatedly to practise for him - had correctly remembered the tune in its entirety. In the finale he could not reach the deep notes, and every time I patted him on the knee, and shouted: *^camiq!* *^camiq!* (deep! deep!). I could hardly believe that this Arabic word would be so necessary to the art of musical expression. Majid's younger brother imitated me, and just as we were coming to the finale, he would shout annoyingly at Majid, with his index finger jabbing downwards, *^camiq!* *^camiq!* Then soon the abused Leonora aria rang out from every corner of the house. I made myself scarce, and sent Majid, as recognition of his musical performance, a few fireworks.

Monday 14 January 1884. Early in the morning we had a visit from Majid with his brothers Salim and Sultan. Afterwards I roamed about the north-eastern quarter of the city. The Persian merchant ^cAli saw my rubber head-bands and asked me fearfully if they were made out of pigskin!

Tuesday 15 January 1884. I tried to find the armourer Ghanam, whom I had avoided a few times on account of his importuning and begging. When I asked about his five-year-old nephew 'Abdullah he replied: "The young boy has so many lice: he is with the wives who are finding them all for him." In the evening we had invited the Shaikh

of the at-Tuman, Sanad ibn Rub'a with two companions to a delicious meal. As Mahmud brought
in carnival pastries and syrup after the coffee
and rice with lamb, admiration was equal to appetite. After a drink of water one of our guests
let out a burp which he accompanied with a
faithful "Al-hamdu lillah!" (Thanks be to God).
The Shaikh, who has his grazing grounds all
below the Shatt (south of Basra), definitely settled a controversial issue, stating that the
Wadi ar-Rummah flows out towards Zubair, that is
much further east than is indicated on the map.

After the guests had taken their leave, I
took down the two volumes by Ritter about Arabia
and read again, the campaign against the Wahhabis, and then for the umpteenth time all the
information about the Nabataeans and the evidence from oriental geographers and pilgrims
about ruins at Mada'in Salih or al-Hijr. Oriental patience and an oriental frame of mind are
needed to come to terms with descriptions given
by orientals. Nothing is solid, accurately
measured or clearly described. There is no
sense of substance, time or direction, all is
idle chatter, with repetitious religious sayings:
it is enough to drive one to despair. It never
ceased to amaze me how Ritter found his way in
this daunting desert and how he made the conditions work for him. If only I could make some
sense out of it: how the Thamudaeans relate to
the Nabataeans; how does it all fit together?[51]
Are the inscriptions in al-Hijr Nabataean? It
was hard to tear myself away from this labyrinth.
Three quarters of the night had disappeared
before I reluctantly put out the light.

Wednesday 16 January 1884. I rose to my shame
at 11 o'clock. I visited a cemetery on a way
out to the east, amongst the outermost palm
plantations. The plain gravestones displayed
partial names (for example Salih ibn Ibrahim ibn

Mijrad 1296), but most of them just a Wasm, i.e.
tribal or family insignia.[52]

[The following inscriptions are given here
from the diary: 1), 2), 3), 4) that is 1)
Shaqra God rest your soul! 2) Hindi ibn Nasir;
3) Sulaiman ibn Muhammad (whose tribal insignia
is $\bar{\bar{\chi}}$), 4) ᶜAisah (whose tribal insignia is $\underset{\sqcap}{\perp}$).]

Ten strange dalul lay on the Mashab (the open
space in front of the castle); I did not recognise the tribal insignia. Some one told me a
number of beduin have arrived from the north,
Ruwala, Shuqur and elsewhere. Those from the
friendly tribes are bringing information about
the enemies' positions and anything else which
they have found out; who from the enemies, as
for example even from the Ruwala and Shuqur, is
bringing presents of horses or other things, and
in any case put in an appearance because their
tribe is grazing on the borders of the Shammar,
in the wudian. For as long as their ambassador
is staying with the Shammar, they can graze
there unmolested; a surprise attack at this time
would be considered dishonourable. They will
use this opportunity to use their eyes and ears as
much as possible. In the evening we met all of
them at the sovereign's as guests. One of them
had the impudence to smoke the water-pipe which
he had brought with him. No-one made a remark
about this preposterous act, but it was recognised as an offence against etiquette. The punishment followed shortly afterwards. Around the

deserted castle the night was pitch-black as we departed. The bedu with his water-pipe had forgotten the steps leading to the outer door. Hardly had the door been closed behind him, when he fell through the crowd of us, with his sinful equipment. He tried, with our help, to gather it up in all the parts, but it was too dark, so we knocked loudly and long on the castle door, in order to obtain a lantern. It was a long time before the guard appeared, shouting that someone would be coming soon. While the Shaikh was still moaning about the still missing pipe-bowl and lid, the Wahhabi priest Salih just passed by and asked the reason for all the commotion. It was explained to him that Shaikh N.N. had fallen down the steps with his water-pipe and he had lost parts of it but he will - *in sha 'Allah* - find it again. Full of vindictiveness against the delinquent who smoked, and pleased about the misfortune, Salih retorted: "And I say to you: he will not find it again *in sha 'Allah*; that serves him right."

Thursday 17 January 1884. Huber thought it appropriate, with the *ghazu* imminent, to present my last 11 flintlocks to the sovereign. It would not only lighten the load on our journey west, but it would also impress on him the urgency for us to be gone with a minimum of fuss. So Huber went off before sunrise (I had no inclination), accompanied by two slaves loaded up with the flintlocks, to the sovereign and laid the weapons at his feet as our contribution towards the *ghazu*. After two hours he returned home with the joyful message that we could set out next day, on our long-awaited journey, and would be equipped with animals, provisions and guide.

Hamud al-Mijrad brought a Sulubi (plural: Sulaib or Sulubah) by the name of Dirbish ibn Bannaq from the al-Hijr region (half-way between here and Iraq). The Sulaib live peacefully amon-

gst the beduin but are not to be trusted. They
are miserable wretches, shy, keep only sheep and
donkeys, and devote themselves to the hunting of
ostrich and gazelle. Dirbish gave an account of
the classification of his tribe and the localities in the Syrian-Arab region of the desert,
which our servant Mahmud wrote down for Huber.
I had amused myself in the meantime by observing
and drawing the Sulubi. He wore the usual Sulaib
coat of 15 or 20 gazelle skins sewn together, the
sleeves fitting closely around the wrist, then
extending as far as the fingers; in contrast to
the beduin ^{c}Aba, the Sulaib coat is not completely
open at the front but has just a narrow slit at
the chest and neck for putting it on. It is a
sign of luxury to wear a shirt under the coat.

The Sulubi Dirbish

In the afternoon I paid a visit to the smith
Ghanam and also met there Prince ^{c}Abd al-^{c}Aziz,
whom I had missed at his house. I gave Ghanam's
son-in-law, Hamd ibn Fadil az-Zuhairi, a box of
vaseline for my Mauser-repeater-carbine which
had I presented to the Amir, and with it an old
tooth-brush. In the evening a Harb came, by the
name of Faris; but there was no getting out of
him the details of his tribe or the name of his
Shaikh.

Friday 18 January 1884. I rose very early, for the prospect of what is about to happen is giving me energy, and prepared everything for departure. I drank coffee in the afternoon at 'Abdullah's house. It rained in the evening from a heavily overcast sky.

Saturday 19 January 1884. In the morning to Majid and his father Hamud al-ᶜUbaid,[53] who had complained at us yesterday through the mediation of 'Abdullah: we had now given more flintlocks to the Amir, so had not we something else for him to use in the raid, perhaps a revolver. (O te monstrum insatiabile!) I had to express my regret, that we had no further weapons left to give away.

As well as the Sulubi Dirbish, another Sulubi, a certain Fahad ibn Ghazi of the Durairat tribe, from the region south of Mustajidda visited us.

Sunday 20 January 1884. Yusuf al-ᶜAtiq brought one of the Hutaimi (pl. Hitman), who was able to dictate the constitution of his tribe and the number of its tents.

In the course of the conversation Yusuf displayed very marked scorn for the Hutaimi. These people usually liked to be boastful towards us foreigners, and for this reason generally cite only exaggerated round numbers, to which Yusuf always made a downward adjustment. Finally Yusuf lost his patience, and contemptuously said to him: "And if you see 100 of your tents before you, you will not have the audacity to maintain that they are beduin tents[54] but you can only say that they are *Hitman*." The Hitman are considered less than equal by the Arabs (Urban) and they are even detested by some who hold it against them, that they - at least those living on the coast - eat fish. They are thought of as even lower in the scale than the Sharari. Besides this Hutaimi, a widely-travelled Shammar turned up, by the name of Dughaim, who promised to give us the route, in advance, to the Wadi Najran, over the Wadi Dawasir as far as al-Aflaj. At last our companion on the journey, Hailan, introduced himself to us. He is the guide provided by the ruler for our journey to the west. He is a man over 60 years old, still very fit and active, who has taken part in all the raids up to now, and is honoured and valued as a scout by the sovereign. He is familiar with all the local routes, distances, mountains and wells and is able to list their names with certainty.

All of our acquaintances are flocking to us: having been given flintlocks and pistols they want powder and bullets as well! The preparations for a *ghazu* is the best opportunity for receiving and giving presents. Thus the Amir has to order the distribution, during these days, of many thousands of majidi to the *ghazu* participants for the upkeep of their families. We are able to buy ourselves out cheaply; a few tins of powder and some shot is enough. Other people, such as 'Abdullah, are lending a few flintlocks.

Monday 21 January 1884. Now everything is prepared! But three camels are led before the house, when we had asked for four and actually required four: two for Huber and me, one for the servant Mahmud and one for the guide Hailan. Although we are not carrying any tents or luxuries each of the animals has quite enough to carry, that is to say, besides the actual rider, all the bits of equipment such as carpet, cloth, clothes, weapons, food (1 sack of dates, 1 barrel of butter, rice, coffee, tea, sugar, salt, a bag of meal, a tin of cocoa powder, 2 tins of lentils, 1 pouch of tobacco, water pipe), cooking utensils, water-bottles, rope, tools, theodolites, sextants, medicine, books, 8 metre collapsible ladder, and naturally a number of bits and pieces. The animals were left, for the moment,

in the courtyard of the empty house. By the
evening their food had already been stolen from
them, probably by our Persian neighbour. There
was not only our own stallion, dangerous and un-
manageable because it was in the rutting season,
bought in ͨOrman, but the three mares borrowed
from the sovereign's stalls as well.

In the evening the sovereign sent a slave to
fetch me alone, expressly saying that no-one
else should accompany me. In the reception-room
he was alone with Hamud al-ͨUbaid, Sliman and
Salih ar-Rakhis. After the coffee was placed
on the floor and the servant was sent away, the
sovereign shocked me by stating that Huber had
tried to get to al-Hijr and al-ͨUla without me,
and I ought to be on my guard. I suddenly recalled that I had been asked a few weeks ago first
by the smith Ghanam, and later by Majid, whether
I had given up the visit of those ruined cities,
a question which I had dismissed as nonsense).

In a state of excitement I replied to the sovereign that I did not understand what he wanted.
Thinking that I had not correctly understood the
Arabic words, Hamud repeated or wrote down the
sovereign's words again. I retorted "I fully
understood your words, but I cannot believe it!
How could Huber entertain such an idea? Haven't
I undertaken the journey with him for a common
end, to search for those places; isn't he my
travelling companion, and even my guest from the
beginning? He will also be my guest until the
end!" The sovereign shrugged his shoulders;
I left the castle depressed.[55]

When I returned home, Huber asked me what it
was the sovereign wanted. I did not hide from
him what had been discussed, but explained to him
that those in the castle would not succeed in
sowing the seeds of mistrust and discord between
us.

Tuesday 22 January 1884. Huber went early in the morning to the sovereign, picked up from him the letters of introduction (including one to the Sharif of Mecca) and also received the requested fourth camel as promised. It came out that my silent opponent Hamud would clearly like me to get back to Damascus or Baghdad as soon as possible. Towards midday the Amir went off on the *ghazu*, ostensibly to the north. In the evening we finished packing for the difficult journey ahead. What will it bring?

1) *The Arab name has changed to Razzia, also in Western languages. It is typical of the Amalekite Razu as described in the first book of Samuel Chapter 30. [Both words "razu and raziya" are derived from the same root in Arabic and have the same meaning. The latter word has been transferred to European languages, in which the r was already pronounced as a "rolling" r; evidently it came to France from Algeria. However as in "Gazelle", the r ('ghain') has become a g.]*

2) *Hess writes <u>zikah</u> = tribute, here, and cites the tribal names thus: ^cAnize, Ruwala, el-Eida, Bili, Gehene, Metar, Harb, Gehatan (or Ghatan).*

3) *Even the Abyssinians reckon on one goat for five men, see Littmann, 'Publications of the Princeton Expedition to Abyssinia', Volume IV, p. 606.*

4) Hess's note: The Mutair were originally from al-Qasim, but moved to the east, so I have been informed.

5) H: Himl had been suggested to me as being 150-200 wizna, that is 219-292 kilogrammes, as also according to Burckhardt (p. 359), who says that a camel carries over short distances, 3-4, or even 4-5 hundred kilogrammes. My estimate is from Hadar (Arabs living there); Muhidh thought it was too much. In Leonard's The Camel (London, 1894, p. 187), I see that the Kebabis in the Sudan load their camels on average with 300 sa'. A sa' in al-Qasim = 3 midd, that is 3 x 1.33 litres = 4.00 litres.

6) Objiciens, eum non e patre legitimo stirpis shammaricae, sed a vagante quodam Scherario quocum mater lignans in deserto convenisset, genitum fuisse, ya walad az-zina'.

7) Oryx beatrix J.E. Gray.

8) H: Nasr as-Sabhan - according to Hess, Beduinennamen auz Zentralarabien, p. 28.

9) Sursum ac deorsum efficacissimum.

10) 'Abdullah ibn Rashid, died on a Friday in 1843.

11) Talal ibn Rashid, died 17. Du'l - kadeh 1284 = 11 March 1868. The name accompanied by the words - "The power of God and the Holy Spirit" is only required when mentioning mystics and holy men of the highest order but here it is

also used for people who in a fit of depression or madness have taken their own life, whereby it is rightly presumed that God has taken
their ghosts beforehand.

12) Faisal ibn Rashid died 1278 = 1861/62.

13) Zaid ibn Tabal died 25 Safar 1288 = 16 May
1871.

14) Hajja, daughter of 'Abdullah ibn Rashid.

15) Munirah [daughter of] Bedr [ibn Talal].
[The 1 + over the names is the family sign
of Ibn Rashid - Hess notes "The signs do not
stand next to one another when branded on a
camel". The cross (al-Urga') is put upon the
calf of the right hind-leg, the dash (al-mutraq)
on the right fore-leg. On these family signs
see Littmann, Zur Entzifferung der thamudenischen Inschriften, Supplement.]

16) Also called Mit'yb, see Hess Beduinennamen,
p. 13.

17) Hess: One says ^CAjid, Najif, but the j is virtually elided.

18) This made me think of the town beggars in
Tübingen during my student years when they
turned up on Sundays and Thursday at the refec-
tory for their free meals, and brought with
them their own knife, fork and spoon in a case.
I can still see them, as they carefully cleaned
the implements after using them and then replaced
them in the case. Here my tablespoon would be
cleaned by one of the slaves on the cuff of his
shirt.

19) On my asking if he had done his plaits himself,
he replied, no, his mother and sometimes his
wife. How often? Perhaps every three weeks -
whenever it is necessary.

20) One does not get to know the wives here at all:
their manner of dress and the customs make it
hardly possible. If our women were forced to
wear a long heavy cloth over their head the
whole day and pull it quickly over their face
on the approach of a strange man, they too
would seem mischievous and enchanting.

21) Musk oil. [In fact zabad (or as Hess writes it,
zibad) is civet, which is the secretion of the
civet-cat and a very popular perfume throughout
the Orient].

22) Hess, waber, rock badger-dog Hyrax Syriacus
Schreber.

23) Huber explained afterwards that the Arabs here
are not really quite so openly distrustful if
one looks at a horse correctly; I shall never
mention drawing again.

24) According to Hess, who lived a long time with
this tribe, they called themselves ᶜOtäbe.

25) This makes sense, that one says in Arabic for
smoking "Smoke drinking". Drinking is forbidden [In Turkish too one says "Smoke
drinking" for smoking and the same expression
was used in olden times in Europe].

26) Fifteen years ago, when various theories using
meteorological instruments were expounded from
the platform of Strasbourg Meteorological
Society, the 83-year-old tower caretaker,
Bernard, assured me that all these modern
interpretations were worthless and stupid nonsense but the saddest thing is, every lunatic
is adopting it as their hobby. Not long ago
he was approached by a stranger wishing to

convert him to the idea that the earth revolves
around a stationary sun. What do you say to
that?

For more than 40 years I have clearly seen,
day after day, the sun rising up in the morning
behind the Black Forest, and then there comes
along this impertinent greenhorn who thinks he
can make a fool out of an old man. "So you see,
Herr Euting, there must be such cattle." The
stranger was corrected. [From Egypt I have
heard the following story: "A policeman came
across a drunk standing in the street. He said
to him: "Why are you loitering here, lad?" The
answer came back "I have heard that someone said
the earth revolves, however I did not believe a
word of it. But now I see that the world turns
around; and common sense told me: "Instead of
tiring your feet going home, rather stay where
you are; then, when you see your house going by,
grab hold of one of the windows and climb inside! Cheerio!" From <u>Kitab mi'at hikaya wa-
hikaya</u>, by Muhammad Effendi ^cAbid al-Fattah,
Alexandria, n.d., page 13].

27) Saqar - falcon; burqa' - leather hood; mitkakah
- leather strap; mirkabah - seat (plate); sikh
- seat's handle; diss- glove, made from the hide
of the grey fox called <u>husni</u>; murbat as-silsilah
- leather strap with chain.

The names given to the falcons are: ^cArjan,
Hazza^c (marauder), Ghanam (distributor of
booty), ^cAzzam, Suwaid, and Jirdan.
[Hess also knows the falcon names Khattaf
("thoroughbred"), Saffaq ('he who strikes with
the wings".) On the other hand he thinks that
Jirdan is a name given only to a working camel.

28) Names used for hunting dogs (<u>saluqi</u>, plural
<u>sulqan</u>) are cited as follows: Turfah, Sathah,
Shallah, Shalhah, Ruddah. The master of the
dogs is called Arbitah.

29) *Sinubar* are pine-kernels which are eaten on *hilw*, that is together on little cakes.

30) Hess notes that *qum* means a troop of soldiers, or enemy.

31) For example the Amir rendered a verse which made reference to the kinds of truffles which grow in this country: al-ghalasi li-rasi - the *ghalasi* are for me; al-jibad li-umm al-banat - the *jibad* for the girls' mother; az-zubaidi li-^{c}ubaidi - the *zubaidi* for my little slave; al-bulukh, li-ash-shuyukh - the *bulukh* for the Shaikhs.

The individual kinds of truffle, according to Hess, are as follows: *ghalasi*, the red truffle, just beneath the ground; *jiba* or *jibad*, reddish outside, white inside, deep below the ground; *zubaidi*, white truffle; *bulukh*, red (?) truffle, but Huber says white.

32) How one can settle this is hard to see.

33) tahin hantah tahi dukhn [that is, Cornmeal and millet].

34) ^{c}Ammi Taraman dabah kabshuh tabakh ^{c}ala kirsh kabshuh kishk; [that is, My uncle Taraman killed his duck, he cooked milk dumplings with the duck's stomach].

35) brrr ya matyab kirsh kabsh ^{c}ammi Taraman litabakh ^{c}alaihi 'l-kishk; [But how nice is my uncle Taraman's duck's stomach when he cooks milk dumplings with it].

36) qadib al-qaidalandab wa^{c}asaiyat al-^{c}asalansab watairun taqafqaf waqaf ^{c}ala qafa qafas min al-qasab al asfar; [The branch of qaidalandab and the trunk of ^{c}asalansab, and a bird quivered and sat in the back of the golden bird-cage. Hess has maintained from the beginning that these particular words have no meaning; someone told him they were made up

for conversational exercise only and do not make any sense.]

37) Sab^c khashabat buqs bisaqf bab habs Homs; [seven beech trees at the high threshold of the prison door at Homs.]

38) You need the following verse for the characteristics of the various nationalities:

The Arab is a spray from the sea,
The Turk a hole in the stone,
The Frenchman a ball of fire,
The Persian a bunch of flowers,
The Kurd a ball of shit.

39) Asl lafz ^carabas, turki honaras, farsi shakaras, ^cajami duraras.

Neither ^cAbdullah nor anybody else was able to give an explanation of the last verse. It is a ditty. [The verse in reality is Persian, and it is remarkable that none of the Arabs in Ha'il could understand a word of Persian, yet Persians were living amongst them. On the other hand it is possible that one did not wish to translate the verse out of politeness, that it expressed the arrogance of the Muslim over the non-Muslim. With the minimum of alteration I have had the previous verse translated thus:

The oldest language is Arabic
The Turkish is excellent;
The Persian is (sweet as) sugar;
The foreigners'[1] is like the twittering of
$$\text{birds.[2]}$$

---

1) *The foreign language referred to here is that of all non-Muslim as opposed to the three Muslim languages, according to Dr R. Tschudi.*

2) *Assuming the reading is correct one could infer that taghr denotes a bird.*

This saying appears to be quite widespread throughout the Orient. My friend G. Jacob heard it in Constantinople. At my request, my former pupil H. Ritter, now in Hamburg, had the kindness to make inquiries about it with a Persian living there, Dr Nisan. This person knew of it in the following form:

> Asl lafad lafad ^carab ast,
> turki hunar ast,
> farsi shukr ast,
> kurdi gawi khar ast.

This is firstly an improvement on Euting's text; secondly, the word <u>lafad</u> appears twice in the first line. The last line means "The Kurdish is donkey shit." Whether <u>kurdi</u> or ^c<u>ajami</u> is the original, I don't know. But instead of dughri, gawi khar is to be read.

40) _Nimr_ Felis pardus. According to Hess this beast of prey still inhabits Arabia.

41) Hess metres, plural: metaris known to the ^{c}Anaiza as mitras, is a mound or a heap of stones, which the hunter uses as protection or a hiding place.

42) Hess: This name is really incorrect. I know of a huwwa and even huwwa ad-dib = Picridium t^ingitanum L; huwwa al-ghazal = Zollicoferia glomerata Cass.; huwwa al-^{c}arab Zollicoferia nudicaulis L. - Perhaps hauabau was a mistake for "huwwa buh": "there is a huwwa".

43) Hess notes: "Unknown to me, perhaps _jala'_ Collyrium, Antimony.

44) It is usual for a bedu to have four pigtails: two in front and two hanging down at the back over the shoulder.

45) Mahmud servus noster, lingua gallica utens, suasit: Parate jam novaculam ad amputandum tarbusch.

46) The insolent slave, who had behaved himself so badly during his time with Doughty. I can telegraph Doughty this satisfying piece of news.

47) This alludes to the Ethiopian vassal, the Christian king or viceroy of Yemen, Abraha by name, who (according to legend) under- took a fateful campaign against Mecca with a huge army including 15 elephants, in the year of the Prophet Muhammad's birth.

48) Actually "God be praised".

49) *"Get up my love, up from your sleep, get up from your sleep, Oh my gazelle, oh gazelle".*

50) *He is reputed to have poisoned his uncle, Amir Muhammad ibn Rashid, at the end of 1897.*

51) *The Nabataeans and Thamudaeans were two different Arab tribes, the first belonging more to the west and the latter more to the east of Arabia. The Nabataeans became a greater power and founded a state in north-west Arabia, South Palestine and eastern Jordan, which appeared to threaten Rome itself. The greatest period of the state was approximately between 50 BC to 50 AD. The chief cities of the state were Hijr (al-Hijr) and Petra. In 106 AD the state was destroyed by the Romans under Cornelius Palma, and the greater part of it made into the Provincia Arabia. The Nabataeans had adopted the writing, and for official use also the language of the Aramaeans and managed to keep their autonomy to some degree. The Arabic script we know today evolved from the Nabataean variant of the Aramaean alphabet. The Thamudaeans by contrast always remained within their original borders, taking little or no interest in the culture of the ancient world. Their writing and language were pure Arabic; but their inscriptions are for the most part scratchings containing for the most part mere proper names. In al-Hijr Thamudaeans and Nabataeans came into contact with each other, and indeed many Thamudaeans might have belonged to the Nabataean state at the height of its power.*

52) With reference to the names and explanation
    of the tribal insignia see Littmann, "Iden-
    tification of the Thamudic Inscriptions",
    Berlin 1904 page 78 et al.

53) De puero quodam Aethiope, novem vel decem
    annos nato, coffeae pocilla ministrante se
    excusarunt; quia omnes servi adolescentes
    abessent e palatio expeditionis impedimenta
    curantes, illium puerulum, revera eunuchum,
    e gynaeceo arcessitum esse. Quum rogassem,
    numne liceret, eum visere, Magid accitum
    illum tunica sublata oculis meis praebuit.
    Ferro testes caudulamque innocentem adeo
    radicitus misero demessuerant, ut tantum-
    modo orificum urethrae aegre conspicuum
    ac cicatrix laevis a cutis colore vix
    discrepans sedem pristinae majestatis
    indicarent.

54) He only grudgingly allowed him to use the
    word tent.

55) Huber had in fact cheated on his fellow-
    traveller, at whose expense the greater part
    of his travels had been achieved. This
    brought Euting much grief, having been veri-
    fied by Euting's own publisher as well as
    by Professor Nöldeke. It even appears from
    Nolde's Reise nach Innerarabien, Kurdistan
    und Armenien (Brunswick), that Huber had
    described Euting as his servant. See the
    diary entries under 16 and 25 March.

10
Eduard Nolde, 1893

A book appeared at Brunswick in 1895 with the intriguing title *Reise nach Innerarabien, Kurdistan und Armenien 1892.*

Its author was one Eduard Nolde, and his journey from Damascus led him to Ha'il before turning north to Kurdistan, and ending in Armenia. The German Baron, about whom very little is known beyond what we read in his only book, committed suicide in England not long after making the journey.

The translation below is of pages 29-103 of Nolde's *Reise*, including his journey from Hayaniah to Ha'il (Chapter II of the original), considerations on the political situation in Central Arabia (Chapter III), an absorbing account of life in the camp of Muhammad ibn Rashid (Chapter IV), and finally Nolde's departure from Ha'il towards Meshed ᶜAli at the beginning of Chapter V. As far as can be traced, this is the first translation of any part of Nolde's narrative into any language, so readers are asked to forgive the presence of any material which may be repeated elsewhere, since it is intended to let Eduard Nolde speak in his own words, and voice his own opinions. They derive from a cultivated European who, suffering the usual inability to appreciate the vastly different value-system of desert Arabs, nevertheless displays more than a rudimentary knowledge of their history and political circumstances.

Nolde's Journey to Ha'il

From Hayaniah to Ha'il

*Unpleasant News - Absence of the Amir - Ha'il in
view - Message to the Regent Hamud - Refusal of the
same to let in a stranger - Resolution of the
difficulties by the Dragoman Nasrullah - Entry into
Ha'il - Smoking forbidden in Central Arabia - First
reception - The people of Ha'il praise Manek's
beauty - Home in Ibn Rashid's old private castle -
Alternative use of the same as a state prison -
Importance of Ha'il - Government palace - Splendid
kitchen arrangements - Ibn Rashid's wealth - The
wells and their importance for cultivation of the
fields - Schools in Ha'il - A mild form of
slavery - Humorous slave story - Strange
incidents - Information about the murder of the
Alsatian Huber - Ibn Rashid's clear conception of
European ideas - Mistrust of the Arabs - Sudden
change of public opinion in favour of the
travellers - Rain - The Amir's effective weapons -
Visit to the mosques - Excursion to Aidah - The
mountains of Ha'il - Ibn Rashid's invitation to the
rendezvous in the desert - Departure from Ha'il -
Affectionate farewell from Hamud.*

Some really unpleasant news came to my ears in
Hayaniah. The Amir, as he is called, is absent from
Ha'il on a campaign somewhere far into the south,
almost halfway to Aden; in Ha'il a regency has been
installed under Ibn Rashid's cousin Hamud. All of
this could very well lead me into a really
embarrassing situation. The regency in Ha'il might
perhaps not wish, or even feel themselves strong
enough, to receive a foreigner. In any event there
was no alternative but to continue my journey.

On 9 February I was within sight of Ha'il and its
picturesque background formed by the mountains of
Jabal Shammar.

Nasrullah, who had been sent on in advance, had a very stormy discussion with the Regent Hamud, who refused to allow me to move freely in Ha'il.

All the difficulties and wars that Ibn Rashid has experienced with the recently-conquered Wahhabis, and with the other inhabitants of Najd, have arisen solely as a consequence of their dissatisfaction at the Amir's maintaining friendly contacts with the Turks, unbelievers of all kinds, other Arabs and allegedly favouring the interests of distant foreigners. The great majority of those of Ibn Rashid's age, indeed most residents of Ha'il, are Wahhabis, so the government of Ha'il several years ago decided irrevocably not even to allow foreigners to enter Najd. If he, Hamud, had known in time, he would certainly have issued orders for me to be held up in Jawf.

Although quite shocked, luckily Nasrullah did not lose his head, but answered firmly and resolutely that I had come to Najd with a letter of introduction from the Sultans and Caliphs and it would after all be unworthy and not in keeping with genuine Arab hospitality if I were to be driven back into the desert after such a long march; the Amir, if he had been at hand, would certainly not have contemplated such a thing; and more protests of a similar nature. Finally Hamud tried to make some changes with regard to the manner of my first arrival and of my European appearance which could well have provided the reason for disturbances and even insurrection by the inhabitants. Such a thing was all the more frightening since Hamud maintained that he had very few soldiers at his disposal. Besides, the few foreigners who had ever been to Ha'il (Palgrave, the Blunts, Doughty and Huber) not only had not demanded a public and official reception but out of regard to public feeling had worn exclusively Arab dress. Thus Hamud proposed that I should consider wearing a white leather helmet as well as a sword with a golden handle otherwise it could not be foreseen how things might develop, even with the best will of the Regent himself. Nasrullah, recovering from his first shock, did not give in but thought it might not be too disagreeable; besides, with the exception of a few white clothes, I did not have any Arab style garments and the Regent must have realised that I should not in any event have agreed to disguise myself in such a laughable and unworthy manner as an Arab, besides God knows how, and from whom, to borrow the clothes. At the worst I could pitch my camp outside the town, giving up Ha'il entirely, and next move further towards ^CUnaizah, as the first step towards a meeting with the Amir. Finally the Regency abandoned all their objections and hastily made ready the Amir's old palace. Soon afterwards I rode into Ha'il.

A large crowd, numbering at least several thousand, filled the streets and the square in front of the government building, before the gate of which Hamud, surrounded by his followers, very politely waited to invite me to the first state reception.

In Ha'il, as indeed throughout the whole of Central Arabia, smoking is strictly forbidden and in the Wahhabi region it is considered an evil equal to that of drinking wine. Selling tobacco and even the accidental possession of the "devil weed" incurs severe punishment and can lead to cutting off the ears in the case of persistent offenders. Under such circumstances it was an important question whether I should smoke in public and in the courtyards or not, or whether my being foreign would permit me to be an exception. To smoke under these conditions would be a provocation while on the other hand not to smoke would certainly be regarded as a sign of weakness. However it was well known, and I had even conferred with Nasrullah about this, that I both smoke and drink wine.

The first reception however was so polite and civil that I considered it ill-advised to rush things. Thus I decided at the first reception neither to smoke nor even to ask permission to do so. At the last minute,

as I put on my gloves in readiness for departure,
Hamud appeared to consider this question. He
apologised for having completely forgotten to ask if I
smoked, and perhaps on account of this had no wish to
smoke, whereupon I naturally replied 'of course' and
the next time I should avail myself of his kind
invitation.

   As I left the palace to go home, I noticed that the
crowd had greatly increased. At first I was allowed
to pass by in a foreboding silence, then came the
breakthrough with the Arab enthusiasm for horses.
Manek's beauty had so completely won all their hearts
that a murmur of appreciation ran through the crowd
which finally culminated in a loud shout of
"Mashallah, Mashallah! what a magnificent horse!"
What a relief! I was so touched by this, my very own
darling receiving such admiration, that I showed my
appreciation with a few waves of my hand whereupon the
praise increased. At least we had a common
enthusiasm and it was as if this incident had broken
the ice favourably for me in Najd, for Manek's beauty
had often enough served as an invaluable asset in
contact with horse-lovers. To a European reader this
may well appear to be absurd but in the Orient, and
wherever the Arabic language is spoken, it is a fact.
In view of this a first-class horse is nowhere in the
world as expensive as in Arabia, which explains the
answer I received to my question of how much this or
that horse might be worth: it is worth as much as whatever would be offered to buy it. In other words,
every Arab, whether rich or poor, would give up everything for a particular horse, whatever he possessed at
the time in money, other horses, tents, camels,
carpets and so on.

   The collection of dwellings which were made available for my stay constituted the private palace (Qasr)
of Ibn Rashid, naturally a palace only in an Arab
sense, in reality however an agglomeration of
numerous (from 200 to 300) frequently dark chambers,
closets, garrets, corridors and galleries; and, in

addition to many very large courtyards, a truly
beautiful and extensive garden. A wall with towers
surrounds the whole complex and even on the inside
there is an abundance of towers, defensive
balustrades, and suchlike. In a certain sense it is
Ha'il's 'Tower of London', insofar as twenty bloody
years of Arabian history have been enacted here.

Ibn Rashid stayed there until 1891, in which year
he built himself a small house connected by a gallery
to the government building, as he wished to be near
his treasury, his cannon, his armoury.

Most of Ibn Rashid's important state prisoners had
been locked away under his personal supervision, and
Hassan Ibn Muhanna, the Shaikh and Mayor of Buraidah,
had been transferred, on my account and on the day of
my arrival, to the government building.

The Amir's former reception-room was situated on
its own on one of the terraces, and it was this which
I chose as the best place for a combined bedroom and
main reception-room. It was a large room, with a
number of carpets spread out on the floor, decorated
with pillars and a few simple Persian frescoes. As I
learnt later and was even told by Hamud himself, it
was here, twenty years earlier, that Ibn Rashid had
ordered the murder of eight of his uncles and cousins
together with their servants.

Ha'il is not a large place and probably may not
number more than 10,000 to 12,000 inhabitants.
Ibn Rashid spends most of his time in the desert and
stays in Ha'il only during the two or three hottest
months of the year, when the desert is so parched that
not even a thistle can be found for the camels to eat.
Thus Ha'il certainly does not play the part of a
capital city in this Arabian state but much more that
of a storage place where wives, children, money and
provisions are kept. Everything that one sees in
Ha'il (buildings, walls, gardens and wells) are in
perfect condition and seem as clean and neat as if
everything was new and had only just been built or
completed. The whole city is completely surrounded by

a wall of thick clay which was not intended as a
serious defence, but more for law enforcement, to
enable the town to be made secure, and also if
required to provide its only protection against raids
by plundering horsemen or surprise attack at a time
when there were few or no soldiers in the city.

In conclusion, Ha'il is the only city in Arabia
which its rulers could think of as the Prussian kings
thought of Berlin, whose best defence lay in the
aggressive mastery of the surrounding countryside.
The government palace is a large fortified building
and, although gloomy, of a very distinguished
appearance. Like all Arab forts it has windowless
walls with only parapet openings. The walls are at
least 25 metres high as I recollect, with six towers.
The whole reminded me instinctively of the old French
and Spanish donjons whose architectural style might
well have had Arab origins.

The extraordinarily clean and purpose-equipped
kitchens of Ha'il Castle may justly be described as
magnificent. They have to be, since while Ibn Rashid
is in Ha'il he feeds not only his retinue but also
his personal guards who are normally always with him:
a total of more than 2,000 people. The daily cost of
running the kitchen comes to £100 sterling. In
addition to a well-stocked armoury of guns, swords
and ammunition I saw in the fort eight quite old-
fashioned cannon which could hardly be of any use
except for defending the fort with grapeshot, a ruse
which might be of decisive importance against a
determined hostile mob.

Ibn Rashid's treasure is kept in this castle and
consists mainly of Turkish and English gold pieces,
worth between 1½ - 2 million pounds sterling, a very
large sum, especially in cash, in Arabia. Of course I
am not certain if this is accurate, but it is quite
possible since Ibn Rashid is very rich and one can
estimate that after deduction of his outgoings there
is an annual surplus revenue of approximately 60,000
to 75,000 pounds sterling.

The upkeep of the existing wells in addition to the establishment of new ones takes up most of the time and expenditure of the administration. This is very important since in the absence of any water on tap, and until the arrival of the annual rains, well-water is not only the source of life for the people but has to be used for watering the gardens and the fields. The water is drawn out of the deepest wells, normally the most productive, by camel-powered wheels and then taken through small channels on to the land which is to be irrigated. It is a laborious process to water even the small number of fields surrounding Ha'il, but even so it appears to produce corn which yields an extraordinarily high price and therefore the area under cultivation would be increased if in Ha'il, as in all Arab oases, the suitable land were not restricted by the encroaching desert. The main crop is barley, which, in a good year, would fetch a firm price of 1 Majidiah for 4 Constantinople Okka.[1] In Central Arabia their own production is not nearly enough to cover their consumption and so everything else must be purchased, not only barley but also rice and other necessary foodstuffs from as far away as Baghdad and outside Iraq.

There are four schools in Ha'il which are described as very good in Arab terms and Ibn Rashid has indulged himself at great cost in this intellectual luxury. During the course of time he has brought several teachers from Syria and Egypt and is trying with their help to widen the scope of the education provided to his own people.

In addition to knowledge of the Qur'an and the Arabic language, which naturally form the main subjects of the syllabus, some geography and arithmetic are also taught. Two beduin boys were introduced to me as being especially well versed in the latter, understanding it with such ease that they were able to use decimals. One finds sometimes amongst the beduin a considerable awareness of the stars, and the Amir in particular really surprised me

with his extensive knowledge of this subject as he
knows hundreds of stars by name, described exactly how
each of them changed their position by the hour, and
how all this is taken into consideration with
reference to checking one's position and course. He
occupies himself with such matters even to the extent
of checking and comparing daily his various watches
and compasses. As to his barometer, he suggested
laughingly that such instruments were useless to the
Arabs, and its only interest to him was its
inaccuracy, with reference to the rain, which could
not really be shown, for when the barometer occasionally falls, it signifies the end of the wind and storm
of which one has had enough.

Slavery exists throughout Central Arabia; as a rule,
however, in such a mild form, that the slaves are
rather looked upon and treated as spoilt children,
although still slaves in the European sense of the
word. Once I had the opportunity to become actively
involved in quite an amusing slave story.

It happened about two days away from Kaf. I had
fallen some distance behind the caravan when I made
out in the distance some kind of chase in progress.
One man ran after another. A few soldiers in the
advance guard, thrilled by the excitement of the
chase, joined in and caught the fugitive, as they were
on horseback, so that when I rode up to them he was
already tied up. I was very angry as I felt that the
captive (a black Somali boy) was a slave, running away
from his master, who would have certainly escaped if
it had not been for the interference of my soldiers.

Now it came to a decision, as I had once before
experienced, although with a different outcome, in the
case of a runaway boy and his father. The slave was
freed from his bonds and both he and his master were
placed in the same positions as they had been prior to
the time of the intervention of the riders. Furthermore, the fugitive was given a small advantage to
compensate for his fatigue on being pursued by the
riders. It was not much, as he gave himself up almost

immediately, but I wished to do something for him. After quite a long deliberation this extra advantage was set at 125 m. The slave-owner argued forcefully against this as it could cost him his slave. He was so angry that he swore that if he only had his gun, which had been left behind in his house, he would rather, without any further argument, shoot the slave (worth about £50-£60) than lose him as a result of my interference. As it was, this man had only besides his sabre, a quite useless pistol, which did not appear to be of any danger to the boy. Still this possibility gave rise to a fresh discussion in which I made it clearly understood that the life of the slave was considered to be in his master's hands as soon as he succeeded in getting within five to six steps of him, in which case I should intervene and hand the slave, bound, back to his owner. The slave's owner considered his pistol good enough to only require someone to be within a minimum range of ten steps, so he was not a little startled when the slave thereupon declared, that he was ready to stand within such a shooting distance of his master on the condition that, if he were neither to be killed nor injured, I should take the slave with me.

Finally the race started; both proved themselves to be runners as good and tireless as one usually sees in Arabia. At the beginning the slave lost some ground but after a short time not only regained it but succeeded even in putting one kilometre between himself and his exhausted pursuer.

Now it was evident that the slave could not possibly be overtaken and I therefore continued my journey, I am sorry to say, without thinking what became of them. Normal people would soon collapse under such conditions in the desert, but this is not true of Arabs or negroes, for it is really incredible what such people can endure, particularly in the winter when they are capable of going without water for days.

In Hayaniah I once saw a recently recaptured slave.
He had stolen his master's camel and had used it to
make his escape. Five days and five nights he had
ridden without a break through the Nafud without food
or water, and would probably never have been caught if
the beduin robbers whom he encountered had not
dispossessed him of his camel as valuable booty. Full
of courage he continued his flight on foot but was
recaptured just in view of Hayaniah by his pursuing
master.

After this long digression it is high time that I
returned again to my stay in Ha'il.

Hamud made his return visit to me the morning after
my arrival but, during the first few days, I noticed
on more than one occasion, an almost sinister coldness
about him..

Amongst some other strange occurrences was the
following, which appeared to be very suspicious not
only to my Dragoman but also to Shaikh Muhammad.
Hamud sent, for interest sake, the photograph of the
Alsatian Huber who was murdered in 1885, between Ha'il
and Medina. This photograph, which is still in my
possession, had Huber's signature on it, and had
obviously been removed from his belongings after his
murder. Exactly how it arrived in Ha'il will never be
fully explained, for there appears to be a great deal
of interest in circulating different versions of the
whole story. Pressed for time on account of the
strong influence of the French Foreign Ministry on the
Porte government the latter, in order to gain time,
had entered into correspondence with Ibn Rashid on
this subject. However, he was not prepared to be
bothered with it and the blame lay, as he maintained,
much more on the dreadful insecurity and conditions of
life in all Turkish territory and especially around
Medina. In any case he considered that Huber had been
murdered in Turkish territory and it is hard enough to
maintain order there as well as being wearied with
such stories. Moreover he accepts very little of the
responsibility as he had accorded Huber the highest

regard and courtesy, and amongst other favours, as
everybody knew, had built with great difficulty and
expense large platforms in the mountains to enable the
Frenchman to obtain copies and impressions of the
ancient inscriptions which can be found on the rock
walls. Finally, all notions about this story were
completely confused when a Prussian, Huber's servant,
was brought into it. Huber had been twice to Ha'il
and had lost his life when he was on his way there for
the third time. It appears to be a dangerous undertaking to have on him such an unnecessarily large
amount of money for this journey, especially as he did
not travel with sufficiently strong protection. Later
Ibn Rashid told me himself that, after Huber's death,
his servant had appeared in Ha'il and asked for the
things which the deceased had earlier left behind.
The Amir agreed, after he satisfied himself after a
few inquiries that Huber really was dead. After this
was verified the things had been handed over, as he
naturally considered that he wished to avoid all
involvement with the matter, and also as the afore-
mentioned servant was the only European to have been
previously seen together with Huber. I discovered
however, after fruitless inquiries in Syria, Baghdad,
Basra and elsewhere, that such a servant with such
papers and belongings had never left Arabia and in all
probability had never existed.

One one occasion I asked the Amir, "How did you
know that Huber's servant was German or more to the
point, a Prussian?". That they both spoke German to
one another proves nothing at all since Huber himself
was from Alsace and his servant could well have been a
fellow-countryman. The Amir answered almost angrily,
"Well of course I know all about Alsace: why should I
not? It is that country which was taken away from the
French by the Germans 20 years ago as a result of
which the famous city of Paris had been shelled and
the French are now so angry with Germany that they
have allied themselves with the Moscow government and
this uncertainty forms the centre point of all
European politics, politics, upon which the fate of

the Daulah[2] depends, a fate which is of sufficient importance and interest to us here in Arabia so as to be to a certain extent a warning."

I had already found Ibn Rashid to be an astute and well informed bedu: his clear understanding of European affairs was really astonishing considering the frequent strange mixture in Arabs of political shrewdness and barbarism, of savagery with traditional civility and hospitality, of Semitic understanding and cleverness with ignorance and prejudice - a really very strange and surprising hotch-potch.

The fact that the portrait of Huber was sent to me did not seem to be so bad in itself, but its condition appeared somewhat strange and my people thought it highly suspicious that the throat of the unlucky man had been scratched out with a sharp instrument, evidently to show that his throat had been cut. There arose the question as to whether this mark was old or new and, if the latter, whether the memento had any significance for myself or perhaps even for us all. Therefore, as I did not wish unnecessarily to increase its seriousness I declared that it required a thorough examination through the magnifying glass to accurately determine its age and hence, for the moment, shrugged away its significance.

Sometimes one experiences a sense of foreboding when these and similar questions are considered late at night in gloomy surroundings. The vast area and strange gloom of the building complex in which I lived; my own great room, really a hall, almost eerily lit by a great blazing fire in the middle of it; the many bloody stories, as well as the probably exaggerated accounts of the many chained prisoners in the castle; added to these dreads were the dark night and, from outside, the muffled sound of marching feet belonging to the night patrol.

During the first day I left my room only to visit the castle; otherwise I stayed quietly at home awaiting further developments of the affair.

As with all mistrustful and initially reserved people, it is always advisable with Arabs to allow them time to get used to new people, new contacts and new ideas. Afterwards, they are not in the least obstinate and one can get along with them quite well.

Meanwhile all kinds of things began to happen which were to benefit me. Of all things, it began to rain soon after my arrival in Ha'il: a really heavy rainstorm flooded everything and lasted for 36 hours. This combination of wet and quite cold weather was uncomfortable for me personally, but for the Arab it was the rarest, greatest and most gratifying of all imaginable gifts from heaven.

Hamud had suffered for months with a cough which had kept him awake at night. Soon after my arrival, however, this cough had disappeared, probably as a result of the change in weather following the rain. Nevertheless this was a good omen. Likewise Manek's conquests followed their usual course. All kinds of distinguished people in Ha'il asked for, and naturally received, permission to visit the magnificent horse, even offering him dates and sugar. This forced them to visit me as well, even if only to thank me for allowing them to admire my horse. Gradually in this way half the town had visited me; it became popular and soon the coffee and tea parties at my place became endless.

At last came important news: the Amir had won a great battle against the combined tribes of the ᶜUtaibah and the Mutair and, as a result, he had captured a great booty of 6,000 camels, 300 horses, etc. When it was further established that Ibn Rashid's enemies had been put to flight, at three hours before sunset, on the very day and at the very hour of my arrival in Ha'il, then my people were so filled with pride and confidence that for example Nasrallah, Qidu and Shaikh Muhammad began really to relax and smoke in the courtyards. There now surfaced true oriental imagination and charlatanism as, apart from the people first in line to see the coming of him blessed by Allah, now every child knew me to be an auspicious person and to enjoy the same special favour as Allah's chosen people. The rain as well as Hamud's recovery - all this would be simply attributed to my store of good luck. In a few days I had suddenly become, to my own pleasant surprise, a very popular man in Ha'il.

I began to smoke in the street and it seems that this was accepted so smoothly that the people from the Bazaar, the shops and the houses brought me out a light whenever I needed one. Finally came the greatest of all my triumphs.

The town's imams and learned men asked Hamud to explain why I, who make as many visits as possible and am interested in all kinds of things, do not enquire about the mosques and schools? Was my attitude to be understood as lack of interest or instead as disrespect for such important institutions. "What?" I replied, appearing to be at least outwardly very angry, "in the whole of the Islamic world it would only be tolerated with reluctance if Christians and other non-believers entered Mosques; the European is allowed only into the common ones (not into the Friday Mosque) in Turkey and Persia, and only then when compelled to do so against the will of the Muslims. It was for this reason that I had decided to show special consideration and therefore I had not touched on the subject of a visit to a Mosque's being arranged for a non-believer purely out of scandalous curiosity. And now is it to be so twisted, that my consideration is taken for contempt? That is quite unbearable and unfair - quite uncalled for. If therefore my not visiting the Mosque is taken as an insult hence the converse of this must be taken for the truth." That very day my visit to the Friday Mosque, a new and really beautiful building, was arranged. Thus everything turned out for the best in Ha'il and I began to enjoy myself. Shortly before my departure we made an excursion with Hamud, who in the meantime had always been hospitable, to Aidah, a stone castle in the mountains about two hours from Ha'il. The mountains of Ha'il, the Jabal Shammar, lay close to the town, standing out as a solitary mountain chain or mass. I should estimate the length of this mountain range to be 30 to 40 kms. and its width about 10 kms. Ha'il lies about 1100 m. above sea level and the summit of the Jabal Shammar is probably 700 m. above that, at a height of about 1800 m.

In these latitudes there is of course no snow, which is unfortunate for the Ha'il oasis, as otherwise the people would have abundant supplies of water on tap. These mountains rise perpendicular out of the desert without a transitional slope. The whole thing, consisting of rock pyramids and needles piled up one upon the other, has a very majestic appearance, and even its colour, a dark lilac sprayed with pink at sunset, is extremely beautiful.

Soon after my arrival, both the Regent and I myself had written to Ibn Rashid. On February 16 his answer came. He suggested that I met him in the desert, about halfway between Shaqra' and Riyadh. From the place from which he had written he would go north-east to the agreed meeting-place.

Five horsemen from the Amir's retinue were sent to accompany me to the proposed place so that I should be in the hands of Ibn Rashid even during the journey.

Early the next day, that is February 17, I left early. Hamud accompanied me for about an hour and, as we drank our last farewell coffee, he suddenly became so emotional that I really believed he had grown quite fond of me as he cried and sobbed so much that it became a real farewell scene.

Against all Arabic tradition, that one must not turn back after a departure, Hamud did so, at the last moment coming up to me again, laying his hand on my shoulder, and saying: "Do not forget that I am and

always will remain a proven sincere friend to you in
this country. And I have written about this to my
eight sons, whom you will meet in the Amir's camp.
All of them, from my eldest Majid, are amongst the
most brave and feared people in all Arabia as you will
soon see for yourself. In any case you have my word
that my sons will be your sincere friends and in this
respect I have charged them to be at your service."
This sounded like a sincere promise, and was quite
considerable since not long ago this same bedu prince
had been a stranger to me. Furthermore it was so
unexpected that I really did not know how to take it.
Was it simply one of those peculiar characteristics
common in orientals and especially so amongst the
Arabs, or should it be taken as an assurance of
protection against some kind of danger, protection
even against Ibn Rashid himself, against that 'Desert
Lion' about whose outrageous actions and erratic
behaviour so many lurid stories circulate? This
seemed hardly credible to me, at least since Hamud and
Ibn Rashid are devoted kinsmen and long-standing
comrades-in-arms. I have never had a full explanation
of the meaning of Hamud's last assurance, probably
because I did not have any reason to call upon the
protection of his sons.

In any case they came up to me at the first
opportunity and with great politeness explained that
they had received special orders to be helpful and of
service to me in every respect.

The Political Situation In Central Arabia

The borders of that part of Arabia inhabited and
governed by the beduin - Listing of beduin tribes -
The warlike Harb - Their attacks on the Mecca
caravans - The Sultan's obligation to protect
them - Attempt by the Turks to make Ibn Rashid
responsible for the Harb's robberies - Ibn Rashid's
explanation that the Harbs are independent -
Possibility of a remedy for this inconvenience -
Ibn Rashid's defence treaty with the Harb -
Estimate of the population of Central Arabia -
Number of warriors - The Wahhabis and their
religious views - The growing power of the
Wahhabis - Their plundering of Karbala and Medina -
The Egyptian war against the Wahhabis - The latter
finally overthrown - Evacuation of Arabia by the
Egyptians in 1842 - The subsequent internal wars -
The beginning of Amir Muhammad's government in
Ha'il - His atrocities - Happenings in Riyadh -
Alliance of various tribes against him - Even
fighting strength of the opponents - Desertion of
Buraidah from Ibn Rashid - Ibn Rashid's vulnerable
position - Magnificent victory of Ibn Rashid over
his opponents - The punishment of Riyadh.

Before I continue with my travelogue, it might be
of assistance to the reader to have at least a superficial geographical and historical survey of the Arab
situation.

Arabia is taken to be the whole country inhabited
by beduin and governed by them, of which the northern
border runs in a semi-circle formed by a line drawn
through Damascus - Aleppo - Urfa - Mosul, and of
which the southern border would lie in the unimportant
Dahna desert. The eastern boundary would run from
Mosul to Baghdad on the Tigris, then to the Persian
border and finally to the Persian Gulf, including the
Qatar peninsula. To the West would be Palestine and
the undefined borders of the Turkish possessions of
Hejaz and Asir. Oman, as far as Hadramaut and the

south coast, is not taken into consideration, as this region, even if occupied by beduin, is separated from the focal point of the Arab state by the great uninhabited southern desert, and one can assume that they have little or no connection with each other. The Arabs who inhabit the aforementioned region are split up into a number of large or small tribes, partly independent of one another and partly connected by blood relationships or treaties.

Even a superficial description of these relationships would involve us in a confusing discussion of internal Arab politics; for that reason I shall mention here only the most politically important, and for the European reader sufficient mention of the influential main groupings and their relative significance. There are in Mesopotamia the Northern Shammar, ruling to the south-west and south of the Euphrates, the whole region between Syria and Baghdad, the great tribe of CUnaizah; in Iraq the Muntafiq; and finally in Najd the Southern Shammar, who are the original founding tribe of the Ha'il state, which however of late has annexed so many extraneous parts that they could hardly be given the name of the Shammar people. The remaining beduin of Central Arabia, the CUtaibah, Mutair and the rest, are named after their towns, thus for example the CUnaizah, the Harik or Hutah, and so on. Finally at this point one must take account of the still-feared Harb, who inhabit the region east of Mecca and Medina. The powerful, war-like and savage Harbs can put into the field between 15,000 and 18,000 warriors, mostly armed with flintlocks - people who are the main source of fear on the part of pilgrims to Mecca, as almost annually they fall upon the Mecca caravans, robbing them all, or some of them, or occasionally delaying them for weeks and months. The armed police force, numbering a thousand, which accompanies the pilgrims cannot always do much against the bold, incessant attacks of these beduin. In fact, because of the incredibly long drawn-out line of pilgrim caravans, it would be

difficult for even a much larger number of Turkish
soldiers to provide adequate cover. Thus during night
attacks it quite frequently happens that through the
ensuing panic and confusion, the different parts of
the caravan are separated from one another and robbed.
The only successful means of defence is to take
charge of the caravan and move it along in the midst
of the troops, which however is not always possible.
If, as happened three years ago, these caravans are
held up for approximately two full months until the
arrival of fresh troops, the caravan suffers the worst
kind of suffering through shortage of water and food,
and as a consequence the most horrible kinds of sickness.

Never, or only very rarely, do the Turks release
any news about these happenings, for fear of
embarrassment in Europe. Among the many titles of the
Sultan is that of protector and escort of the Mecca
pilgrims, a title alluding to his most important and
responsible obligation, and it is thus under his
banner and accompanied by his soldiers that many tens
of thousands make the pilgrimage of all pilgrimages.
If the caravan could not reach Mecca, or in doing so
many thousands perish, then naturally the blame for
this state of affairs lies, in the eyes of the
Islamic world, with the Turks, that is with the Sultan
himself.

Because of the relentless grip of the Harb on the
Mecca caravan, on more than one occasion the question
has been broached whether these beduin are in fact the
subjects of the Amir of Ha'il, or should be considered
as such and if one should therefore put pressure on
Ibn Rashid, perhaps very quickly, so that some
security could be obtained for the pilgrims. Ibn
Rashid's various opponents always return to the
following theme: the Amir maintains he is a true
friend of the Sultan, while the Harb are the greatest
annoyance to him. The Amir further maintains he has
no control over the Harb, which seems however very

strange, since everybody knows the relationship which exists between them. The Harb had always collaborated with the Ha'il state, not only from the beginning of the present Amir's administration but over the past twenty years or more, and they appeared year after year, on the battlefield under the command and banner of Ha'il. This is by no means all that is surprising, in this affair. The Persian pilgrim caravan arrives from Baghdad or Basra and then after a difficult head count in Ha'il, goes from there to Mecca or Medina through the territory of the Harb. It is these caravans, carrying Ibn Rashid's mail and accompanied at the most by a handful of his riders, which are the least attacked. Thus one might conclude that, even if the Harb are not direct subjects of Ibn Rashid, the Amir's wishes are their command and, if he really wishes, he could quite easily make an end to all these attacks on the holy caravans, which are causing such a great scandal throughout the Islamic world.

This all sounds quite convincing, until one hears Ibn Rashid's quite different explanation of these events. When I was with him in the camp he explained to me that he had no control over the Harb. They are an independent and warlike tribe, whose interests have of course coincided with his, as far as his campaigns were, and still are, concerned. They have always been good company when they took part in his campaigns and raids, for he had so far always been victorious on the field of battle and not mean in the sharing-out of the booty. As far as attacks on the pilgrim caravans are concerned - he continued - he certainly did not agree with the Harb in this matter and it is quite conceivable that these problems are of great annoyance to the Turks. However what can one do against it? The Harb maintain that it is their ancient bedu right of plunder (in fact their only means of existence) to ride out of their camp when there is the greatest likelihood of reward, in the same way as they rule the streets of Mecca.

In such circumstances there are only three
alternatives:

i. The Turks should provide an even larger number of
    troops as protection for the pilgrim caravan,
    which is impossible on account of the shortage of
    water and severe problems of supplies;

ii. The Turks should decisively destroy the power of
    the Harb in their hiding place - another apparent
    impossibility, against a people who have neither
    a town nor any definite area of settlement and in
    any case can withdraw, in the face of any strong
    expeditionary force, into the comforting desert
    with its huge expanse; finally,

iii. The Turks could sue for peace with the Harb.
    This of course is possible only with large pay-
    ments of money and therefore not compatible with
    the honour and dignity of a great military power.
    The Amir further told me, very forcefully, about
    his long-standing alliance with the Harb, which
    provided mutual aid in all circumstances, with
    the sole exception of a Turkish attack on the
    Harb due to the Mecca caravan incidents.

'I am', the Amir so often explained, 'a devoted
admirer and servant of the Sultan Hamid; however, it
would obviously be madness for me to use my strength
against my own, and to me very important, Arab allies.
In any case it would be quite useless, when it is
considered that even I cannot get close to the Harb,
against whom, in those terrible mountains, all my
riders and force of camels would prove powerless.'
'After all', he added, full of humour, 'you have
already become acquainted with some of the important
Harb Shaikhs present here in the camp. You can tell
them everything yourself personally, and you will
enjoy it as they are unbelievable devils, who are not
even afraid of me; they are subservient to me only
because of their certain promise of reward and
because here in the desert, anyway, I am master, even
over them.'

A population census is naturally something unknown in Arabia. Once the warriors and camels are counted, however, one can make quite a good estimate of the population of this country, or more precisely of this desert, by multiplying this number by 5, since the beduin form the majority of the population.

The total number of warriors, in that region which I consider to be beduin land, comes to approximately 120,000 which would certainly mean a total population of around 600,000.

Of course this figure is not very high for a country which has quite probably an area double that of Germany (540,000 square kilometres).

The bulk of the 120,000 warriors can be divided into tribes as follows: the Northern Shammar have about 15,000 warriors; the whole of the ^CUnaizah 30,000; Ibn Rashid with all the forces of the Najd (except the Harb, ^CUtaibah and Mutair) 30,000; the Harb 15,000 and the Muntafiq in Iraq - Arabia 10,000; and all the remaining tribes about 20,000 warriors.

Here is an outline of the recent history of Central Arabia. In the middle of the last century (about 1746) Abdulwahhab created the Wahhabi sect. They opposed and still oppose orthodox Islam roughly as Protestants and Puritans opposed the Roman Catholic Church.

The Wahhabis accept only the Qur'an and not only reject the Traditions (even the Sunnah) but detest them as being groundless and insolent arrogance, an enlargement of the revelations found in the Qur'an under the pretext of giving an explanation, and even 'improving' on the reports of the Prophet's words and deeds, and what is still worse, according to the Wahhabis, making changes to the extent of falsification. Again using the analogy of Protestantism and Catholicism, the latter were charged with enlargement and development of theological doctrine and creed, as distinct from the Protestant Gospels, to the detriment of the authority of the apostleship.

Orthodox Islam is however not in a position to claim that the protestations of the Wahhabis detract in any way from the dignity of the Qur'an, as they cannot prove that something not written in the Qur'an, as a sequel or innovation, must be accepted as ·fact. Hence the Wahhabis declare that everything not written in the Qur'an, but acknowledged by the Sunnis or even by the Shi'as as religious laws, is an outrageous abomination against the true religion and the originator of such abominations are shameless frauds and opponents of the only true religion, and are therefore to be regarded in the same way as the worst idolaters.

There are countless examples and proven charges, according to the Wahhabis, of how so-called orthodox Islam has falsified the pure religion or has set itself up in direct opposition to it.

The worship of saints, monasteries (*tekkes*) and similar things are expressly forbidden in the Qur'an, yet all are present in Ottoman orthodoxy. Circumcision, which also plays a significant in orthodox Islam, is hardly mentioned in the Qur'an; the importance of the Caliphate is less than claimed in the Qur'an, and so on.

These, and similar arguments in themselves totally logical, must quickly have found approval by the desert Arab, with his clearly defined thinking and thus it happened that the teachings of Muhammad Abdulwahhab spread quickly throughout Arabia.

The prince of Dira^{C}iyah, Muhammad Ibn Al Sa^{C}ud made himself, as the first Amir of the Wahhabis, political head of the new teachings. Supported and elevated by the popularity of the new doctrine, which at the same time revitalised his troops, he instilled in them a real fanaticism as well a matching death-defying bravery; Muhammad and his successors (^{C}Abdul ^{C}aziz and Sa^{C}ud) were able quite quickly to bring the whole of

the Arabian interior under the influence of Wahhabi
doctrine. Gradually the holy cities of Mecca and
Medina fell into their hands and the orthodox Muslim
pilgrims were forced into the position of being able
to visit these holy places only after all kinds of
humiliation and only by the grace and favour of the
Wahhabis.

In the course of about sixty years they built themselves a great Wahhabi empire comprising almost all of
Arabia, the Hauran and all the land to the west of
Jordan, as well as a substantial part of Syria.
Damascus was held to ransom, temporarily, for a great
deal of money, against the threat of plunder and
attack. Karbala in Iraq was stormed. It is, like
Mashad ^CAli (Najaf), one of the two most holy of
pilgrimage shrines for Persian as well as for all
Shi'a Muslims and hence there was great dismay when
the Wahhabis not only put the whole of the male
population to the sword but even, after robbing them
of all treasures, opened the grave of Husain and
scattered the remains of this revered martyr and holy
man to the four winds.

The Porte had taken much too long, through their
involvement in European politics, to carry out a major
campaign against the Wahhabis and were quite happy to
have at least held on to Baghdad. However the
Wahhabis had set their sights on this important city
as the next main target of their campaign and a great
army was already prepared for this purpose.

The Wahhabis had crossed the Euphrates many times,
laying waste to Iraq - Arabia and besieging Baghdad,
and moreover their success would have continued still
further in this region, had they not experienced their
first reverse. This was their vain siege of Mashad
^CAli. All their attacks, came to grief on the
impregnable walls of this city, and they were forced
to withdraw empty-handed. Finally the worst of all
happened. The third Amir of Najd, since 1801 the
ruling Sa^Cud of the Wahhabis, allowed the Prophet's
grave in Medina to be opened in 1810. The remains

were laid to rest again, and under the pretext of cleansing the treasure - defiled grave, the valuables which had been stored there for hundreds of years were removed. A cry of horror and anger went up throughout the whole of Islam and even though the power of the Wahhabis has not yet been destroyed, this event marked the end of all designs on the Caliphate by the Turkish Sultans.

The Turks were still very active in Europe, but Mehmet CAli, the energetic Viceroy of Egypt, received the order to overthrow the Wahhabis. Hence in 1811 the first division of Egyptian troops appeared in Arabia. At the beginning it consisted of about 10,000 men, mostly Albanian troops under the command of the Viceroy's eldest son Tusun Pasha. At about the same time the main strength of the Wahhabis lay in the north-east of their empire, where SaCud was preparing himself for the capture of Baghdad, which again had to be given up. It came to a long and bloody war. In spite of all the reinforcements brought in from Egypt Tusun could only just maintain a presence in Hejaz. Actually he captured Mecca for a short while, but suffered setbacks in other battles, so that Mehmet CAli had twice to enter Arabia himself in order to retrieve the situation with new troops, which he more or less succeeded in doing, occupying Medina in 1815.

Without going into too many incidents of this war, I shall mention only briefly that as there was no successful Egyptian breakthrough it seemed as if the Turks had fulfilled their original plans. These had been to retrieve the Holy Places through the power and determination of Mehmet CAli and to destroy the power of both the Wahhabis, and the Turks' increasingly powerful subject, the terrible Lord of Egypt. It was however not to be; for there appeared in 1816 a first-class field commander on the battle-front in Ibrahim Pasha, who had previously made his name in Greece, Syria and Asia Minor.

This determined man quickly made up his mind to attack the Wahhabis in their own desert. In the battle of Wyah he not only heavily defeated them but also ordered the slaughter of many thousands of those captured at the time. From there he moved on to the siege of Ras, where he was to make the first mistake of his military career. He began, with his French engineer, to surround what he thought to be an unimportant city, following all the rules of the art. However it was of no more use to him than were his bombardments and assaults. For four months he persevered, losing more than 3,000 men, some in great numbers as a consequence of the increasingly ferocious sorties of the Wahhabis from Ras as well as attacks by the army at his rear. While awaiting fresh reinforcements he had to enter into an armistice; soon however he renewed his operations.

Leaving Ras to one side for the time being he now went into the interior. After many days of bombardment ^CUnaizah surrendered to him and after many months of siege Buraidah and Shaqra', after which Ibrahim Pasha began the siege of Dira^Ciyah - the capital city of the Wahhabis.

After the death of Sa^Cud in 1816, his son ^CAbdullah acceded to the Wahhabi throne and the task of defending Dira^Ciyah against Ibrahim now fell to him. Dira^Ciyah held out for over six months and once Ibrahim was in the greatest danger, when almost a complete powder-store blew up, which as a result severely limited Ibrahim's defence of his own position. His personal bravery and determination triumphed in the end against all the difficulties. After the arrival of new reinforcements and stocks of powder, Dira^Ciyah finally had to surrender under harsh conditions. All the treasure robbed from the Prophet's grave had to be given up, Dira^Ciyah was to be razed to the ground, and the Amir of the Wahhabis had to go as a prisoner to Cairo and Constantinople where the Sultan would decide his fate. In spite of Mehmet ^CAli's interceding on his behalf, ^CAbdullah was executed in Constantinople in 1818.

From now on the whole of the Arabian interior as

far as the Gulf was controlled by the Egyptians. All the important towns were held by Egyptian garrisons, and Arab princes and leaders were dispossessed or installed as Egyptian vassals or governors, according to the circumstances. These few changes took place during the uprising and the various disturbances and lasted until 1842.

Egyptian attention and power had meanwhile been diverted towards a greater goal. Ibrahim had once beaten the Turks decisively in the Battle of Konya. Unopposed he ruled Syria and Palestine, from where he launched a second campaign against Constantinople, as a result of which the Turks could be protected only by the combined might of the great powers. The Egyptians had become weary of the distant campaigns, always supplying new soldiers for the unrewarding and thankless Najd, until it was gradually abandoned, the last of the Egyptian troops having left by 1842. This marked the beginning of a further period of war in Central Arabia which was to last for almost 50 years.

For a time it appeared as if the old Wahhabi government would rise from the ashes. Faisal, a son of the beheaded ^cAbdullah, came to Riyadh and was gradually acknowledged as Lord by almost the whole of Najd, although in many areas in name only. From 1842, the year of the withdrawal of the last Egyptian troops, until the years 1870-72, there were battles in Najd among the following powers: 1. the old house of the Wahhabis in Riyadh and al-Hasa under Ibn Al Sa^cud; 2. the increasingly strong Amirate of Ha'il; 3. the city of ^cUnaizah together with its tribe and dependents; 4. the city of Buraidah; 5. the virtually-demolished city of Shaqra'; 6. the southern state and city of Harik - Hutah; 7. the Harb; 8. the ^cUtaibah; and finally, 9. the Mutair.

After Ha'il, which belonged to Ibn Rashid, had grown in stature through the perseverance and statesmanship of the two regents Talal and Mat^cab (1843 to 1870), the present Amir Muhammad, fifth in his

dynasty, took over the government in 1872. He had
stabbed to death the Amir Bandar, his nephew, in a
quarrel and thereupon was ordered by his cousin
Hamud - ruler in Ha'il at the time of my visit -
straight to the castle and recognised as the new Amir
of Ha'il.

He very quickly strengthened his authority through
bloodshed and fear. On the very day of his enthrone-
ment he had six members of his family, who seemed to
him to be dangerous, executed in Ha'il castle, and a
few days after that, as previously mentioned, eight
more relations (uncles, cousins and nephews) were
murdered in Ibn Rashid's private house. However even
these victims were not the last to be sacrificed to
the strengthening of Ibn Rashid's power.

Having an already quite well-organised state as one
important asset, the new Amir quickly began to make
his presence felt in all internal Arabian affairs. For
twenty years he appeared year in year out on the field
of battle, besieging and blockading ^CUnaizah, then
seeking battle with the ^CUtaibah and the Mutair, and
then intervening in Riyadh again. Ibn Rashid's
beloved sister and boyhood playmate, Nura, whose
beauty had become famous throughout Arabia even during
all these events was married to ^CAbdullah, Amir of
Riyadh, who was dethroned for the first time in 1872
and imprisoned with his wife Nura in a tower by their
own son and would have died of hunger. However, Nura
managed to let her brother know of their terrible
predicament with the aid of a messenger on horseback.
At that time Ibn Rashid happened to be in the vicinity
of Shaqra' and as he was able to arrive so quickly and
unexpectedly in Riyadh, taking them by surprise, he
not only saved the life of his sister, but also
succeeded in reinstating the Amir from the position of
hostage in the power of his insubordinate son. However this did not last for long as he was again
deposed two years later and was fortunate this time
to escape to Ha'il, where he entered into an alliance
with the Turks. Midhat Pasha, the current Grand

Vizir, was at the time Governor-General of Baghdad; he made clear his government's intentions to march into Arabia, especially since he would now have the full co-operation of Ibn Rashid.

Thus, in spite of England's stated desire for peace in the Gulf, the Turkish campaign against al-Hasa went ahead in 1874 and 1875. The Turks wanted to march against Riyadh but at the last moment held back from marching through the 300 km. wide Hasa Nafud.

Ibn Rashid who, in this case, had the same aim as the Turks, namely to instal ^CAbdullah on the throne of Riyadh once more, now had to accomplish this alone. As luck would have it, the outcome of these events was to be regretted by the Arabs to this day, as there was an unacceptable Turkish rule over the whole of the Hasa coast and, from a Turkish point of view, a domination which had the purpose of isolating the interior of Arabia from the sea. So the wars, uprisings and interference have continued since time immemorial. The Turks themselves have found their occupation of Hasa a thorn in their side, as they suffered there a severe setback in the previous year (1893) which proved that they can neither rule this desert directly nor indirectly through a knowledge of the correct way to handle the Arabs.

Three times Ibn Rashid interfered in the affairs of Riyadh and innumerable were his campaigns against the other powers of the Najd, against whom he was always lucky, for the various sieges and blockadings of ^CUnaizah were the only misfortunes of all his operations.

Finally, in the spring of 1891, something happened which seemed as if it would determine the fate of Najd for a long time to come. A great alliance had been formed against the ever more powerful Amir of Ha'il. The prominent powers of this alliance were ^CUnaizah, under its old and warlike Shaikh Zamil; the whole house of Riyadh which had put aside all internal disagreements because of the need for vengeance; the cities of Buraidah, Ras and Shaqra'; and the combined tribes of the ᶜUtaibah and the Mutair.

Many old enemies and rivals had to sink their differences and about a hundred ancient families had to seal blood-bonds by embracing their opponents before this important alliance could be formalised. It was the common hatred for Ibn Rashid united them, but the driving force behind this whole conspiracy was the aforementioned Zamil, a giant of a man who, in spite of his 60 years of age, enjoyed the reputation of being a war hero, the strongest, the bravest man in Arabia. He was appointed supreme commander; there took place in his government fort the final council, after the alliance had sent its declaration of war to Ha'il.

The alliance had assembled a force of 30,000 men between ᶜUnaizah and Buraidah, and soon Ibn Rashid appeared before them. He had approximately the same strength as his opponents. Among his important allies were the Harb with over 10,000 men, and about 1,000 horsemen sent by the Mesopotamian Shammar, to their so-called cousin; the Amir of Ha'il, in all haste.

Thus on this occasion there must have been assembled 60,000 warriors - for Arabia a quite extraordinarily large number, which I doubted at first in view of the oriental imagination and propensity for exaggeration. But having corroborative evidence from different sources, I now believe it was quite possible that so many warriors really were ranged against one another, an unprecedented battle array in Arabia as far as anyone could remember, since the time when all able-bodied Arabs had joined together under the Wahhabi banner to defend their desert against Ibrahim.

On that day, however, a situation arose which Ibn Rashid had not foreseen and which was to be of the utmost importance to him. He had believed that the chief of Buraidah, Hassan Ibn Muhanna, had been won over to his side, through his diplomatic skill and by offering several gifts, including six hundred pounds sterling in cash, a large sum of money for an Arab chieftain in those days.

Instead of Buraidah and its Shaikh joining his alliance or at least remaining neutral as Ibn Rashid had expected, he saw himself betrayed at the last moment and Buraidah a member of the opposing alliance. This unexpected setback was not only very disturbing because of the imbalance of numbers that it brought about, but still more important was the defensive position of the towns favouring the alliance.

The Arab alliance of the opposing Amir stood in a line about 30 km. long, both its flanks supported by ᶜUnaizah and Buraidah and with a 12,000 strong company of infantry in the centre. Against such a force there was no alternative but to use expert horsemanship: to outflank the enemy, causing panic amongst them, when the opportunity arose.

Human life is precious in Arabia and its passing must follow a respected Arab tradition, for even a victor must be prepared to lose between 50 and 100 dead. In this instance Ibn Rashid realised that he had to attack the positions of the ᶜUnaizah infantry with his cavalry. These foot soldiers were, in the tradition of European infantry, quite poorly armed – with muzzle loaders and occasionally even only flintlock-muskets, which however proved sufficient against lancers. In addition, Zamil had brought up a great amount of brushwood and had dug small trenches in the sand to protect himself and at the same time to bear the brunt, to a certain extent, of the first impact of Ibn Rashid's horsemen. Victory went to the alliance.

The war, which had already lasted a month, was to drag on even longer. The beduin require very little in the way of food and supplies on their campaigns, however it is worth noting how they managed to get such a great mass of people to Buraidah. As far as the alliance was concerned this was simple to achieve,

since they were not on their own but had the support
of two of the most important towns, ^CUnaizah and
Buraidah, which had been prepared for such an
eventuality for a long time. For Ibn Rashid, however,
the situation was quite different as his troops in the
desert were 200 km. from the nearest point of supplies
and water. Many thousands of his camels were used day
and night to bring all supplies and finally even the
water into his camp.

This could not go on for long, especially since the
hot season was approaching. Another reason was that
Ibn Rashid had to be able to withdraw from this camp
if threatened with defeat. But this appeared to be
impossible. For the last twenty years he had always
been victorious in all his battles without exception,
a record dependent to a great extent upon his
appearance, fear of his good fortune, and his bloody
reputation. If he had retreated from the Buraidah
positions defeated, it would have been the beginning
of the end for him. His allies, the Harb, who had
hoped for great booty under his banner, had already
returned home. As a consequence of this, Ha'il was
now practically defenceless and the alliance would
certainly march on it.

Ibn Rashid was so well aware of this that he was
determined in no circumstance to survive a retreat and
for this reason he kept a revolver and poison under
his saddle and pillow, to end his life at a moment's
notice.

At the end of March 1891, the Amir tried in
desperation a few night attacks on the ^CUnaizah
positions but these yielded only a few casualties.
Everything now seemed completely hopeless, when a new
and final attempt was decided upon in the Ha'il camp
and carried out. Twenty thousand camels were moved in
one day from all sides, against the ^CUnaizah infantry.
Ibn Rashid's people rode deep in amongst and behind
this infantry, which then lost its head when it
realised what was happening and, without causing any
notable damage to its enemy, discharged a volley of

shots from flintlocks which were not easily reloaded. Thousands of camels died - and even now the desert is still strewn with their remains - but the objective was achieved.

A terrible panic broke out among the ^CUnaizah people, who threw away their muskets and even their lances. They fled unarmed across the open plain, before victorious and merciless horsemen, who butchered them in their thousands. Even the rest of the alliance did not fare much better. They had taken for granted the impregnability of their infantry centre and had been too long in arriving from the distant parts of the battlefield to be able to intervene decisively in the action. As it now appeared to be too late, first the cavalry from Riyadh then the ^CUtaibah and all the rest in turn, decided to return quickly to their tents and supplies, collect them together, and make a cautious retreat, each into his respective desert. Yet they did not succeed even in this, as in the meantime their tents had been removed.

Thus it happened that after a few hours nothing of the whole alliance remained. The defeated, in terrible fear and confusion, soon gave up any thoughts of fleeing and rested all their hopes of survival on begging for mercy when brought before the Amir. Shaikh Zamil, the supreme commander of the alliance, was killed with his eldest son, who had arrived from Basra on the first day of the disaster, after hearing the news of his father's battle with Ha'il near Buraidah. The princes of the house of Riyadh were also killed and the rest were captured by the Amir. On the same evening ^CUnaizah and Buraidah surrendered to Ibn Rashid and soon afterwards emissaries from Ras, Shaqra', and Riyadh met him to announce their surrender and asked him for his orders with respect to the 'wakils' or deputies.

Hassan, the Shaikh of Buraidah, who tried to escape into the desert, after many hours also fell into the hands of the Amir and was condemned to life imprisonment in Ha'il.

Apart from the allies' encampment with all its many thousands of horses and supplies, Ibn Rashid had the opportunity to seize as booty 12,000 flintlocks. However, since these were not as militarily valuable as rifles, they did not seem worth keeping and were therefore given, together with a lot of other booty, to his allies the Harb. This action later led to a new charge's being brought against him by the Turks, who maintained that he had armed the Harb with new weapons for their attacks on the pilgrim caravans.

As a result of Ibn Rashid's victory, the whole of Central Arabia lay at his feet. He chose Buraidah as his temporary court and from there reorganised everything to his liking. Meanwhile, CAbdurrahman, one of Ibn SaCud's prisoners, made a lucky escape from Ibn Rashid's camp to Riyadh, where he proclaimed himself prince and at the same time Ibn Rashid's deputies there were thrown into prison. But this episode ended as quickly and pitifully as it had started. After a short forced march from Buraidah, Ibn Rashid appeared again at the gates of the hapless Riyadh, which had to surrender for the fourth time to the mercy or displeasure of this enemy. CAbdurrahman escaped to the Turks at Hasa, but Riyadh had to pay dearly for its fickleness. The old fortified town of Riyadh was burnt to the ground and the citizens had to work hard to make ends meet. The worst of all was that Ibn Rashid cut down and set fire to half of all the date - and other plantations in and around Riyadh, a blow from which the unfortunate oasis will take a long time to recover.

After many months of direct rule, Ibn Rashid installed a member of the Ibn SaCud family, a certain Muhammad, as so-called Amir, but in reality since the battle of Buraidah a puppet of the effective lord of Najd. On asking him why he had done this, I was told by Ibn Rashid: 'You must understand that one has to do something which is politically right and yet accept-

able in the eyes of God; for almost one and a half
centuries the Ibn Sa^{c}ud have been sultans of Arabia,
even my own father was their vassal; therefore I did
not wish to make this family into fugitives and
homeless beggars. They have already had enough
misfortunes.'

In Ibn Rashid's Camp

*Excursion to ^CUnaizah - Greetings from Ibn Rashid -
Reason for the disparagement by the beduin of their
country - Meeting with 300 horsemen - Received by
Ibn Rashid - His opinion concerning the rebellion
in the Yemen - Inspection of the camp - The Amir's
bodyguard - His favourite colour - The standard
bearer - Conversations with Ibn Rashid - Camel
couriers - Supplying the camp with provisions -
Giving and receiving gifts - The Amir's last
advice - Departure in the company of the Amir -
Last farewell coffee - Ibn Rashid's assurance of
friendship.*

Four forced marches brought me to the outskirts of
^CUnaizah, the most populous city in Arabia, and in
spite of my exhaustion I wanted to visit it. From
Arab reckoning, al-Jawf, Sakakah, Ras, Ha'il, Riyadh,
Buraidah, Shaqra' and Hofuf (al-Hasa) have between
8,000 and 12,000 inhabitants. ^CUnaizah and Hutah on
the other hand must be three times as big and have
about 35,000 inhabitants.

^CUnaizah has two surrounding walls: an inner wall
surrounding the city itself, and an outer wall. Between them lies a belt of gardens and plantations two
to three km. wide. Both of the surrounding walls have
towers and the walls themselves are of a double mud-
wall construction. In fact, the 10-12 m. space
between these walls is filled with earth, effectively
making one wall 10-12 m. thick: quite a respectable
barrier against any artillery. After a tour of the
two main mosques, I attended the reception in the
government building. The Shaikh Faisal, of the Bassam
family, head of state and Ibn Rashid's representative,
presided over the proceedings and showed me a few of
the interesting parts of the city, including the well-
stocked bazaar.

After three further forced marches, in which I
passed Shaqra' on my left, I crossed the so-called

small Nafud of Buraidah and pitched my camp on 23 February about five hours from the agreed meeting-place with Ibn Rashid.

As I was lying in bed, the Amir's messenger entered with news that he had arrived at the agreed place yesterday and sends me five great Salams (greetings), with the hope that I should care to join him for breakfast on the following morning.

When I left in the morning to make the final ride into Ibn Rashid's camp, I became quite excited and curious at the thought of coming face to face at last with this strange man, a kind of Richard III - the 'Desert King' as he is known in Baghdad and Constantinople.

Of course, to comply with his command in this instance I had to leave my caravan behind and hurry on ahead. About an hour from the camp I came across a splendid company of horsemen, who had been sent by the Amir to meet me. There were 300 of them under the command of Ibn Rashid's successor and heir-apparent to the throne, his nephew, CAbdul Caziz Ibn MitCab. With him were all those of any importance who were present at that time in Ibn Rashid's camp: Majid, Hamud's eldest son, together with his seven brothers - two of Ibn SaCud's princes from Riyadh, whom Ibn Rashid has always with him as hostages; the Shaikh of Hutah; many Shaikhs from the Harb, as well as the Wahhabis from Shaqra' and Riyadh, Nasr (Ibn Rashid's private secretary) and Fahad (the chief treasurer).

In their unruly and as it were barbaric robberlike way of living the Arabs are as much afraid of an invasion as of a ghost. What happened in the Egyptian invasion, as well as in the subsequent Turkish attempts, was interference in their affairs and the gaining of an advantage from their traditional internal discord.

Such apprehension is given credence by the beduin, who see no point in allowing foreigners to tour their country and take every opportunity to portray their homeland, in every respect, as more poor and fearsome than it really is. Each and everything has to be criticised and treated, according to their way of thinking, in a contrary manner. An example of this in Ha'il was my amazement at the splendour of the kitchen arrangements as well as the great size and number of the pots and pans in the castle, leading me to calculate how many poor people has the Amir to feed in this terrible land. Even every good and productive well must have been dismantled.

As far as the ambassadorial cavalcade sent to meet me is concerned, oriental splendour and conceit had won the day, in contrast to what was said above. Their wealth and elegance was an indication of what Arabia is capable of putting on show, in the way of horses and saddlery, finely-dressed people and weapons. Apart from the horses, of which the best available in Najd were here assembled, the opportunity was taken to display the people and the saddlery in their gold brocade and embroidery, richly-coloured silks and velvets.

After having dismounted for a moment to make my first acquaintance with those who had come to meet me, I resumed my journey to the camp in their company, while the riders were displaying their abilities in a 'fantasia'.

This spectre was truly beautiful, especially against the backdrop of such magnificent scenery. The great desert, bounded in the far distance by a few picturesque mountain chains, the camp of the Amir before me, all illuminated by the clear sun of Arabia: this spectacle was more than ample reward for having come so far.

Having reached the camp, I was welcomed by Ibn Rashid in the following manner. A very beautiful Indian tent, three times the length of a normal tent, was pitched on a plateau in the sand. The front entrance was then thrown open, giving the impression of a verandah standing in a podium. This formed one side of a square of which the other three were framed by 2,000 soldiers, as the guard of honour. The whole picture, together with the general layout of the camp and the arrangement of the onlookers, displayed a considerable talent for theatrical effect.

I rode through this living square into an open space, accompanied by ^cAbdul ^caziz and Majid, the two premier princes of the Ha'il household. After I had dismounted and approached his tent, Ibn Rashid rose, came a few steps towards me and then invited me into his tent.

Ibn Rashid, now 53 years old, is hardly of medium height, being thickset and well-built. His facial features are delicate and refined; but his eyes are so keen and penetrating, that sometimes they have an almost tigerish look about them. The Amir's black beard, not too long, was trimmed to just below the cheeks and tapered to a point just below the chin, a style which would be known in Europe as the "Spanish". He told me later that his beard is already going quite grey, and only appears so black because it is tinted.

Our first conversation turned to the usual preamble of civilities about our health, the difficult ride and so on, yet the Amir could not avoid touching on a few sensitive areas.

He skilfully brought the discussion around to the rebellion in Yemen, asking whether I had yet seen in my journey any Turkish deserters fleeing from Yemen. It would not be acceptable to him if Najd should become known as an asylum for all the soldiers escaping from the Sultan, but at the same time he did not know what to do about it. For instance, could one refuse to offer help to some of these people, who arrived half dead after unspeakable hardships? 'I will send some of these people to you', he added. 'You will learn much from them. There are some amongst them who speak an unknown language[4] and are not even able to properly understand their Turkish companions. Perhaps my Nasrullah would be able to understand these people, since he knew so many languages, then at least I should be certain that they had not been ordered to tell me certain stories, for it would be something well worth doing, if somehow I could manage to get some of these strange people back to their homeland, on my further travels.

'Yemen', confessed the Amir, 'is really no concern of mine, but I cannot help feeling a sense of indignation at the outrages going on there.'

About sixty battalions of regular troops are said to have been engaged in that hellish land now for two years and still there is no end of this war in sight. Of course this is not so disagreeable for the Pashas, as the longer and more extensive are the expeditions and disorders, so the more will be stolen, to fall simply and solely into the hands of the Turkish government. The Sultan, being a knowledgeable and admirable monarch, can hardly be aware that all the Pashas without exception are evil men and are destroying everything in their path.

The Amir continued in this heated manner, showing the inner bitterness of all Arabs against everything Turkish, a rage which only requires the slightest provocation to make them violently angry. I was happy when the conversation came to a temporary halt and Ibn Rashid invited me to inspect his camp.

There were altogether about 10,000 men there, more than half of whom would be leaving the next day as they relied upon the available supply of rainwater in two natural pools.

As mentioned earlier, the Amir can deploy over 40,000 warriors. Since the battle of Buraidah, nothing of importance has happened in Central Arabia which would require the maintenance of anything approaching such a large force, and I even believe that, as things are at the present time, the force of 10,000 assembled here is superfluous, or at the most a calculated luxury for reasons of prestige.

The Amir is surrounded at all times by a bodyguard of 2,000 picked men consisting of well-armed camel riders with the best and fastest camels. With this exceptionally well-trained Praetorian Guard, which is ready to break camp at a moment's notice, it is possible for Ibn Rashid suddenly appear a hundred kilometres away, and frighten any beduin who rebel against him, or do not pay their taxes. The reward for service in the Amir's guard is a supply of victuals and clothing far in excess of what other beduin can only dream about. Each of them has his house and family in Ha'il and is treated generously with a share of the booty from the wars and plundering raids.

When one considers that behind this power there is some sort of state, with unheard-of treasure in Arab terms and with allies, one can understand how a bedu who rules everybody, even a European, like a strange desert king and statesman, must appear to the oriental as the personification of a magnificent, fortunate and therefore enviable robber-chief.

The Amir's favourite colour is a dark golden orange, and all those in his service and surrounding him wear long cloth robes of the same colour. Ibn Rashid must have grown accustomed, in earlier times, to luxurious clothing, but I have never seen him dressed in any other way than in the most unpretentious fashion and it is only when one makes a closer inspection that it becomes clear that his clothing material is mostly very expensive; a few of his coats, for instance, are made out of very expensive, although plain-looking, Kashmir shawls. Ibn Rashid's flag of state is blood red with the well-known saying embroidered on it: "There is only one true God and Muhammad is his Prophet".

The bearer of this standard is considered the most important person in Ibn Rashid's entourage and is paid and treated accordingly. He lives in a special tent erected close behind that of the sovereign and leads a very curious life guarding the banner. During my time

the holder of this office was quite young, probably
not more than 20 to 21 years of age, very well-groomed
and elegant looking. The Amir went out of his way to
introduce him to me, explaining that only in
exceptional circumstances is it possible for such a
young person to hold such an important position. His
father had been the standard-bearer at Buraidah, where
he had been killed in the battle. The standard was
almost lost, as a result, but the 17-18 year old son
of the old standard-bearer, the young man in question,
had rescued it and brought it to safety. For such a
service, and in memory of his fallen father, one
naturally had no choice but to award him the position.

I stayed ten days in all in Ibn Rashid's camp and
of course saw much of him during this time. Every
morning, before I had risen, he came to visit Manek,
to bring him sugar and dates. I became tormented by
the thought that his excessive admiration for my
horse meant that I should have to give away my
darling, in the form of a gift.

When I cautiously approached the Amir on this
subject I received the comforting as well as fitting
reply: he had already taken various gifts from me, and
when it came to horses it would not be appropriate if
he, the first lord of the world's premier horse
country, were to accept one from a foreigner. There
was no reply to that.

Every morning as soon as Ibn Rashid had heard that
I had risen, he regularly sent word over to me, asking
where and when we should meet, and whether I preferred
to come over to him for breakfast or to wait for him
to pay me a visit. Naturally I always hurried to
answer him, although he did not intend to put any
pressure on me, then I would dress and appear before
him. Many times he did not wait for me but came
across himself, and on two occasions even all alone,
that is without his ever-present companions, armed
with a few swords and hatchets. However this was not
a mistake on his part for, as he laughingly remarked,
neither myself nor my people would kill him or poison

his coffee and I should protect him just as well as his own people against the surprise attack of a madman. Such a remark required a few of my people to stand watch in front of the tent while he was present, which greatly pleased the Amir. The longest meetings, however, took place in the evenings, in which the tea and coffee sessions with Ibn Rashid, after the completion of prayers and the evening meal, dragged on long into the night and occasionally until the following morning.

The Amir is not only a very clever and unbiased man but also an outstanding storyteller and portrayer of people and events, so that I spent many hours listening to him in astonishment. With the exception of the Sultan, he was often relentless in his description and angry criticism of the laziness and stupidity of the Turkish administration and politicians. With great humour and caustic jokes, he ridiculed the orthodox Sunnis or Shi'a priesthood, and, as he put it, the worship of holy and absurd legends.

One of his chief hobby-horses is a fierce condemnation of the inhabitants of Mecca and Medina. He criticised them ruthlessly in detail, as in these two holy cities the true religion is systematically falsified and commercialised, resulting in all kinds of abominations: hypocrisy, depravity, poisoning, murder, and all kinds of violent death. These were exactly the same kinds of argument which one had earlier read and heard from Luther and all the other Puritans against Jerusalem and Rome, but it was quite fascinating to hear from the lips of a bedu such phrases concerning Islamic ideas and concepts.

The Amir subscribes to a number of Arabic and Turkish newspapers from Egypt, Syria and Constantinople and enters into extensive correspondence. During my stay at least one camel courier arrived daily in the camp, and occasionally even two or three from different regions.

In addition to my conversations a couple of hunting
and falconry trips were arranged as well as a few
evenings of sword and war-dancing, performed by more
than a thousand armed men. The desert was illuminated
in the background by a great fire, and the dull and
gloomy noises of the horn and drum music, dancing and
war chanting: everything was tremendously exhilarating,
wild and romantic.

On March 2 the Amir of Riyadh, Muhammad Ibn Sa^{c}ud,
came to the camp for a day. He is a man of about
forty years of age and has the reputation of being an
accomplished Arab intellectual, but politically a
puppet of Ibn Rashid. As far as I and my camp's food
requirements were concerned, these were admirably
taken care of by the Amir, who gave lavish assistance
to my cook Hajji Salah.

Shaqra' and Riyadh, which are approximately sixty
km. from the camp, had to provide fresh meat and
butter, but as soon as it began to get significantly
hotter during the day, these provisions were brought
in at night with the courier camels. He had learnt
from my people that I prefer milk and cream of the cow
to that from sheep and goats, and because of this a
cow was soon brought into the camp. The expert
hunters managed to procure wild game (antelope,
gazelle, hares and a few edible birds) with the help
of their marvellous hunting dogs and falcons. This
was all very hospitable and kind, in spite of which
however the time had arrived for my departure.

Naturally I had brought with me for Najd and
especially for Ibn Rashid himself a number of gifts:
an expensive sable coat covered with velvet and gold
embroidery, various scarce military pieces, a number
of revolvers and other weapons, field-glasses and a
number of other things of this kind, as well as a
hundred metres of scarce rope and cable, a valuable
item for the deep Arab wells, as the ordinary cable is
soon worn through by the camel's raising the water up
over the sharp stones. Moreover there a large
amount of money, which had to be divided out amongst

various of the Amir's people as 'bakshish', which began with his 'kafeji' (coffee-brewer) and his standard-bearer down the line to all the lesser personages.

However the Amir was also very generous. All of my people, without exception, were presented with clothes, gold pieces, and camels.

On the day before my departure I also received the Amir's own present to me: one stallion and three mares of pedigree blood, descended from Ibn Rashid's very own favourite horse, the mare Farha, which is officially premier horse of Arabia. As an Arab prince, this was the most valuable thing he could give me. Moreoever he sent me many other things such as camels, useful large water bottles, and adequate supplies for my journey: a mountain of rice, barley, dates and butter which were brought to me and into the camp. The boxes packed full of Marseilles sugar-loaf were so big that not even the strongest camel was able to carry two of them and the camels had to be loaded up again the next day. On my suggestion that the supplies were excessive, Ibn Rashid told my cook that if my camels could not haul supplies away then the necessary extra camels could be supplied.

On the evening of 4 March, when I had my last tea-drinking session with the Amir, he took the opportunity to offer me his final advice on the journey.

'Everything possible', he said 'has been done to make your journey to Baghdad safe and comfortable. All my subjects and Arab allies have been made aware of your route and have been ordered to be of assistance wherever possible. Hajji Hassan (Governor-General of Baghdad) has written to Ibn Haddal (a Shaikh of the CUnaizah Tribe) and hence everything is as it should be at that end. I am providing you with fifteen of my best people including CAbdurrahman,[5] one of my most trustworthy and experienced servants. It is highly improbable that anything could happen to you on your journey. A large bedu tribe will do nothing, either for fear of the Turks or even against me, and as far as the possibility of meeting a small robber band is concerned, with my people yours will be a much stronger force. The possibility of meeting such a danger could only arise during the last three marches before Mashhad ^CAli. Remain dressed during this period, even at night, and have your four best horses saddled all the time. Should the superior strength of the attacking band be evidently too great, then forbid your people to shoot, preventing any bloodshed as it would be totally unnecessary, since you have my assurance that any stolen luggage will be returned to you. However, it would be better if you were not caught yourself and so I advise you to escape from any fracas. I must leave the choice of your horse to you, whether it be my mares, Manek or Leila. Your choice, something which is of great importance to an Arab, perhaps should be on this occasion Manek, for as well as his strength, he had proved for many years, when he still belonged to Muhammad Pasha in Baghdad, to be the fastest horse in Iraq and Mesopotamia. At least ensure that my two mares and the other two horses do not fall into the hands of your pursuers. A gallop of between 10 to 12 hours would get you to Najaf; do not tire your horse completely as conditions are such that the last four to five hours before Mashhad ^CAli would be the most dangerous section. If it came to this, you would be all alone and have no other weapons, against a pair of opportune robbers, than your horse. By day you have your compass, by night you simply go by the North Star and then you will arrive without fail in sight of the golden cupola of Mashhad ^CAli.'

The Amir spoke to me in this fashion for a long time, covering all conceivable eventualities.

Ibn Rashid had gradually began to show some affection towards me, in spite of the fact that he is one of those people who is thought never to allow his true feelings to come to the surface. However I must repeat that he was always kind to me, right to the end, and the friendship between us lasted long after my departure.[6]

On 5 March I left Ibn Rashid's camp to set out upon my march which, after 19 days uninterrupted by a single day's rest, brought me to Mashhad ^{C}Ali, a distance of about 840 km.

The Amir accompanied me for about an hour, with his great retinue of followers, hunting dogs and falcons to the fore, a truly majestic sight.

When the carpet was laid out for the last farewell coffee, Ibn Rashid repeated with some emphasis all the assurances of friendship, which had been made earlier. If I still wanted horses, dogs, falcons or anything else, I was at liberty to choose them, from any of those present. Moreover if I wrote to him, I could count on any request which lay within his power in the whole of Arabia being granted. Also, if I needed horses in the future he would send some to me. He took a number of examples of my signature and personal seal and promised me that anyone who came to his country would be treated as an intimate friend - and should it be my cousin,[7] with whom I had done so much travelling in the past, he would be treated in exactly the same way as myself.

Finally it came to our last farewell embrace and it took place strictly in accordance with Arab etiquette - without looking back.

To Mashhad ^CAli

Horned viper as an omen of good luck - Abundance of
snakes in Mesopotamia and the Arabian interior -
Charm of the desert journey - Camp by the prickly
trees - The Darb Zubaidah - Lack of water -
Performance of a racing camel - Within sight of the
golden cupola of Mashhad ^CAli - A sand storm - Rest
in ^CAin Sa^Cid - Inhospitality of the inhabitants -
The sea of Najaf - The Hindiyah camel - At the
gates of Mashhad ^CAli - Persian colony - Prohibi-
tion of the movement of bodies - Body smuggling -
Saffron used as wrapping material for bodies -
Persian insolence - Conflict with the Turkish
authorities - The ^CAli mosques - The fanaticism of
the mob - Departure from Mashhad.

In the morning of the next day, one of the feared
horned species of viper was discovered on the carpet
of my tent, where it had probably spent a comfortable
night. All of my people were quite naturally
ecstatic over this good luck omen, which signifies in
Arabia that one has overcome and left behind all
danger. For this reason a snake discovered at the
beginning of a journey should not really be killed. In
spite of all the feelings to the contrary, I refused
to allow myself to be influenced by such superstitious
beliefs, and with the greatest of pleasure had the
snake killed and referred to the Qur'an, where it is
said that all those beliefs in magic, omens and suchlike are the worst kind of abomination and godless
lunacy.

In my opinion I had been in such danger from the
snake, which had been killed by someone in a few
minutes, that I hung my bed up every night about four
to five feet above the ground, and wound double around
its posts, a special spiked belt as a means of
preventing these reptiles from climbing up on to the
tent posts. Because of my great fear of snakes and my
aversion to them, I have not only taken extreme
measures against these horrible animals but every

killing or even a mere glimpse of them is meticulously recorded.

Accordingly, Mesopotamia is in my experience the worst of all countries, with its average of 45 snake observations per month. Central Arabia[8] came next with one snake per day and then, with a far smaller amount, the United States, Mexico and Kurdistan. By comparison in maligned India and Burma in the course of nine months, half of which were spent camping in the jungle, I saw no more than four cobras.

It was a long desert march to Mashhad [C]Ali, interrupted only by minor incidents, but it is improbable that anyone could find such a journey and way of life as agreeable, and appreciate it, as I did, being able to meander alone in such magnificent solitude, breathing uniquely pure air, and yet feeling totally surrounded by an impressive world of its own, in the midst of which one not only feels one is the master but really is so.

There are a few names on the map but there is not a single inhabited place, over a distance of 120 miles. Only once did I see a clump of eight large trees. I immediately put to the two with me what must have seemed to be an astounding question: how is it that these trees just suddenly appear and, what is more remarkable, how is it that they have not been used up long ago by beduin as firewood during the cold desert nights?

I quickly galloped up close to this strange apparition, whereupon its secret was quickly revealed to me. Each of these trees which, to judge from its circumference and height, must have been about a hundred years old, was like an ornate trellis-work fence of spikes. The trees had thin supple branches, thickly interwoven, which made it impossible for even a hand to penetrate, while the distance between the outermost part of the branches and the trunk was probably between 15 and 20 m. Thus it became clear why these trees had been left untouched for perhaps hundreds of years, since it would require great bravery and ingenuity to get near the trunk.

As we had divided the available water for the night among us, I shortened the march by an hour this time, merely to pitch the camp in the shade of these strange trees, which could be described as a wood. After seven marches from Ibn Rashid's camp I came to the so-called Darb Zubaidah. A thousand years ago, Zubaidah, the favourite wife of Harun ar-Rashid, had installed a large number of cisterns (*birkats*) in a line between Mecca and Baghdad. She, the mighty empress, had almost died of thirst along this road, and had consequently decided to spare all subsequent pilgrims the same hardship. One can still see that the cisterns and wells she built must have been magnificent, but unfortunately they have been systematically destroyed by the Wahhabis in the defence of their country and now most are only ruins.[9] On my journey I found water in only two of her cisterns, and elsewhere in only a couple of wells or water holes. In general we had water every three days on this stretch of the journey.

I had become gradually careless and lazy as to the exact state of our water supply, leaving it to the care of my people, who in turn were relying on ^cAbdurrahman. This almost precipitated a great calamity, which I think is worthy of mention at this point, as it provides the ideal opportunity to prove what a dalul (racing camel) is capable of doing.

One evening it was agreed that we should lack water for the next three marches, whereupon I ordered that enough water be taken for four nights. In the circumstances this appeared to be a great amount; most of the water bottles had dried out, were torn or in a state of disrepair so that the additional load of a few hundred buckets would not be very light. I did not give much thought to this, however, and became so annoyed by the objections of Shaikh Muhammad, Nasrallah and the others that I demanded that something must be done, if the bottles proved to be

useless, after all the stitching, patching up and
testing. This was very necessary as we should
certainly be without water during the·fourth march.
The gravity of the situation had now come to light for
the first time. ^CAbdurrahman, who was repeatedly
riding back and forth, appeared to be suddenly so
wretched and dispirited that I asked him what was the
matter. "Well", he confessed, "my head is full of
suspicious thoughts." "What kind of suspicious
thoughts?" I asked. "About the water, of course", was
the reply, "for who knows if we shall really find some
tomorrow night?"

Suddenly it dawned on me: "How can that be?" I
asked him. "You have asked for three nights' water
and I have supplied, as a contingency, four nights'
supply and now all of a sudden we do not know whether
we shall have water even after the fifth march. That
is really hard and if I understand you correctly, if
we find no water tomorrow night, we shall probably all
perish."

"No", ^CAbdurrahman retorted, "it is not that
desperate, if you listen carefully, I shall explain
our predicament. I had hoped to have come across some
familiar or helpful beduin and asked them for
information on the whereabouts of a supply of water.
This has not happened, as we have not met a single
living soul in this desert, with the exception of a
solitary horseman who is coming along with us for the
time being. He does not know and one could not rely
on his guess or even his story. I believe", he
continued, "that we must find some water 9½ hours from
where we are pitching our tents tonight, that is by
tomorrow night. Should that not happen, the situation
is still not hopeless. This evening, thank God, you
still have water. In one hard gallop of eight to ten
hours, your twelve horses can reach certain water the
evening after next. The camels of your caravan do not
need any water, and as far as the people who would be
left behind are concerned, they will have to endure,
in such circumstances, a certain twenty-four hours of

thirst. However something as difficult as that is not really necessary at all, as I have the following, far better, proposition for you. As already mentioned we have sufficient water for this evening's requirements. Now, if you gave up one of your courier daluls, which were a present from Ibn Rashid, Ghata (our first leader) could, overnight get to the place where I expect there will be some water for tomorrow night. Should there be sufficient for our needs, he will bring us back the news, whereupon, at our leisure, we can march there and have water tomorrow night. But if there should be insufficient for us there, then we will obtain it from somewhere else. There is a well to be found, some ten hours from our night quarters here, which has an excellent supply of water. Finding this well will involve us in a small diversion and, as each well is also unfortunately 270 m. deep, this means a further 24 hours of hard work to pull up the necessary quantity of water."10

ᶜAbdurrahman quite naturally put these proposals into effect and very early next morning, I was awoken with the news, that Ghata had returned with the glad tidings of a water supply at the place originally supposed. This camel, which had travelled 100 km overnight from 10 o'clock to 5 o'clock in the morning, had already come forty-five to fifty km. daily for many days and had been given water on only five or six or these days. On the day before its night trip of 100 km. in seven hours it had already travelled 45 km. and again a further 50 km. to return again with the caravan to the place which it had visited the previous night, a total of 195 to 200 km. in 32 hours. We moved out at 8 o'clock in the morning on the day when Ghata had finished his ride, and arrived at the water discovered by the leader, at 4 o'clock in the after-noon on the next day.

1) "1 Constantinople Okka = 3 1/3 pounds;
1 Majidiah = 3.60 marks; consequently for 4 Okka,
the day's ration for a horse (13 pounds),
3.60 marks!! that is 1 Centner at 100 pounds or
about 25 marks!!"

2) The 'Daulah' in the sense of the former Holy Roman
Empire, and in the other sense of the Turkish
state, which assumes a like position in the
Islamic world, when the Sultan also wishes to be
Caliph. The Persian and the Indian Shi'a, the
Wahhabis, and many others, although Muslims, are
political opponents of the Turks, and so do not
acknowledge this. Under normal circumstances, and
when one does not wish to be shown as being in
open opposition to Turkish politics, it always
remains as the Turkish Empire, the Caliphate, thus
the 'Empire'.

3) Ibn Rashid has no children, an affliction which is
God's punishment, so the Arabs whisper amongst
themselves, for all the blood split by the Amir.
In all the Orient, childlessness is known as
probably the worst of all evils (to a certain
extent even as a disgrace) which can be inflicted.

4) Apart from a few Kurds, actually two came from the
region beyond Ahmadiyah and spoke only Chaldaean.
I took them, together with a few others, with me
and luckily was later able to return them to their
mountain homes.

5) He usually leads the Persian pilgrim caravan from
Baghdad to Mecca as Amir of the Hajj.

6) Amongst others was the following instance: two
young sons of Zamil, the Shaikh of ᶜUnaizah who
was killed at Buraidah, lived as fugitives in
Kuwait on the Gulf. From there they came to
Baghdad to beg me to intercede with Ibn Rashid on
their behalf. This I did, by letter, whereupon
the Amir very quickly arranged for all their
wishes to be granted, as I received the news,
before I left Baghdad, that they had been given

back all the various houses and herds, which had been confiscated over two years ago and even their wish to set foot once again in ᶜUnaizah had been granted.

7) Count André Kreutz originally wanted to make this journey with me, but was prevented from doing so by paralysis of his right arm.

8) My last journey through this country to Ha'il was in any case during the cold weather and even on my return the hottest season of the year had not yet begun; it was in Ha'il that I first saw snakes but after having made enquiries I discovered that there must be many snakes in the desert in summer. During my stay in Ibn Rashid's camp there were a few snakes killed, which were shown to me, amongst them as many horned vipers as cobras.

9) There are only a few in number left, all in need of repair.

10) I have myself seen a well 200 m. deep and have carefully measured it.

11
Hajji Abdullah Williamson, 1895

In 1895, at the age of 23, the Muslim convert William Richard Williamson, who now called himself Hajji Abdallah, made his first pilgrimage to Mecca, via Ha'il. (His second pilgrimage of 1898 and his third, in 1936, did not pass through Ha'il.)

Williamson, whose marvellous stories are recounted in W.E. Stanton-Hope's *Arabian Adventurer* (Robert Hale, 1951), had run away to sea as a boy, and spent some time panning for gold in California, hunting whales in the Arctic Ocean. After more adventures in the Philippines, Williamson found a job in the British colonial police force in Aden. After conversion to Islam he left Aden for Iraq, and it was while living near Basra that he decided to make his first *Hajj*.

On reaching Ha'il, Williamson enjoyed that magnificent hospitality for which the Amir Muhammad ibn 'Abdullah Rashid was renowned. 'Hardly had the vast caravan encamped', writes Stanton-Hope, 'than the Amir invited the thousands of pilgrims to a feast of the prodigious kind that only an Eastern potentate would contemplate as a matter of course. The feast was spread in the square between the Ruler's palace and the bazaar. Many camels and sheep were killed. Huge stacks of rice and chapatties were prepared. The shopkeepers in the bazaar were given supplies of coffee, milk and sugar to make liquid refreshment for the guests'.

Williamson was allowed to accompany the Amir al-Hajj to view the cooking areas of the Ruler's palace.

The huge enclosure was like no ordinary kitchen, for it was an open space on which numerous fires were blazing. On each fire a pot was boiling, each with a whole camel carcase in water. The carcase was first covered with clarified butter, and then roasted for a short time. It was then lowered by a chain and pulley into a boiling pot, the same water being used again to boil rice. Sheep carcases, also covered in clarified butter, were roasted on spits. The ravenous pilgrims were encouraged to eat until fully satisfied.

The day after this feast, the pilgrim caravan from Baghdad arrived at Ha'il, joining the Zubair caravan to which Hajji Williamson belonged. He estimated that another four thousand meals were served that day. Williamson took advantage of the reception to beg clemency for a camel thief under sentence of execution, Muhammad Misfar, a shaikh of the Beni Harb. The people of Ha'il were disappointed of their promised entertainment when the Ruler graciously accorded Misfar his life.

We learn virtually nothing more of Ha'il from this extraordinary man, who was to work for the British Government after the conquest of Iraq, and end his working life as an interpreter for the company now known as British Petroleum. He visited Ha'il not for political motives, like Palgrave and Guarmani, nor for the pure love of learning, like Euting or Wallin, but for the fulfilment of the Muslim's sacred duty of pilgrimage to Mecca. Ha'il was merely a stepping-stone on Williamson's road to salvation.

12
Gertrude Bell, 1914

When the intrepid Englishwoman Gertrude Bell arrived
in sight of Ha'il, on 25 February 1914, no Christian
European had been seen in the area for more than
twenty years, and no Christian woman for more than
thirty. The tale of her journey to Ha'il was recorded in *The Geographical Journal* of July 1927 by David
George Hogarth, then President of the Royal
Geographical Society. The Society has kindly granted
permission for the whole of his lecture to be reproduced here, with all the plates, and the verbatim
discussion which followed delivery of the paper on
4 April 1927.

Before the paper the PRESIDENT said : I have no one to call upon to-night
but myself, and I shall spare you any effort at self-introduction. But may I
say a few words by way of introduction to my discourse ? You will understand,
without my impressing it upon you, from the circumstances of this paper, that
I am speaking of what I have not myself seen ; and that I am entirely dependent
for what I am to say to-night upon the notebooks and diaries of Miss Gertrude
Bell, written in the desert under every conceivable circumstance of difficulty
and in every sort of weather. They contain mere *memoria technica* which
her remarkable visual memory and mind richly stored with the experiences
of the desert and of the desert men would have been able to clothe with flesh.
I cannot clothe them with anything like the same flesh, and I hope you will
not expect much more than the bare bones of an itinerary.

GERTRUDE BELL'S JOURNEY TO HAYIL

Dr. D. G. Hogarth, C.M.G., President R.G.S.

Read at the Meeting of the Society, 4 April 1927.

THIS journey was carried out in the winter of 1913–14. When Miss Bell reached England again, less than three months before the outbreak of the Great War, she was physically worn out ; nor had she recovered completely when called to perform war service in Boulogne and London. She proceeded late in 1915 to Cairo and, early in 1916, to Basra ; and from this moment to the day of her death, in 1926, she was engaged in exacting political work, taking few and brief holidays. It is, therefore, not surprising that she published no narrative of her journey to Hayil. When urged to write it at Baghdad she pleaded lack of time, of books, and of other facilities ; but before her death, intending soon to return to England for good, she looked forward to realizing various literary projects, and among these, I have little doubt, was the composition of the desired narrative. In the meantime, she put the cartographic material which she had collected on that journey at the disposal of the War Office and the Royal Geographical Society, and her route was plotted throughout and incorporated in the " Million Map." Also during the War her social and political information was communicated to the Intelligence Services concerned with Arabia, 'Iraq, and Palestine. Taking these facts into consideration, together with the remarkable character of her single-handed achievement and its value for geographical and ethnographical science, I felt, after her death, little hesitation in asking her representatives to approve an attempt to put together, from diaries and letters and recollection of conversations, a narrative of her Arabian journey. For assurance of such approval I have to thank her father, Sir Hugh Bell, and for facilities to inspect and use documents in the possession of her family, I am beholden not only to him but also to Lady Bell and Lady Richmond.

Miss Bell arrived at Damascus on 25 November 1913, hoping to fulfil a long-cherished desire to penetrate Central Arabia and traverse Nejd to the borders of the great south desert. Since she had reason to know that such a project would not be approved either by the Ottoman authorities or by the chief representative of Great Britain in Turkey, she avoided officials so far as possible during her three weeks' stay in Damascus, and discussed her plan only with unofficial friends and such Arabs as she thought would be both useful and discreet. These included the local agent of Ibn Rashid of Hayil, through whom she arranged to draw money on arrival at that town, and others who, like Muhammad el Bassam, the son of Doughty's 'Aneiza friend, might be supposed well informed about Central Arabia and the way thither. On such matters, however, she obtained contradictory and often unsound information, although she heard much of good authority on Arab politics and especially the activities of the Arab Unionists and the Wahhabis, which was to be of great service after the entry of Turkey into the Great War. Among other things she learned that the Desert was united for the first time since the Prophet's day—a sanguine anticipation of what would come true for a brief space three years later.

Her original plan was to slip into the Hamad desert on the east of the Damascus oasis and swing due south by such tracks as Musil had followed in 1908 and Leachman in 1912. Thus she would avoid altogether the Hejaz Railway, with its inquisitive officials and police. An illness, however, which struck down Fattuh, her indispensable Armenian body-servant, after his arrival from Aleppo, led her so to modify this plan as to render his rejoining her possible by use of the railway; and her final route was laid out in such a curve round the east of Jebel ed Druz and its eastward lava tracts (*Harrat*), as, after two or three weeks of desert marching, would bring her into touch with the railway at Ziza. She purchased twenty camels, engaged three cameleers, and sent all eastward on December 15. Following herself next day with two personal servants, one of whom was the same Muhammad Merawi who had travelled with Carruthers in 1909, she camped at 'Adhra. This place, and its larger neighbour, Dumeir, lie on the north-eastern edge of the Oasis; accordingly the Ottoman authorities seem to have supposed that Miss Bell was bound for some point in the northern Hamad or Mesopotamia, and would go by the Qaryatein–Tadmor road. But when, after delay by rain all the 17th, she entered the desert, she headed at once south of east (forward bearing 102°) for Jebel Sais, intending, after examination of the extinct volcano and early ruins reported by Oppenheim to exist there, to turn due south. Her party had been increased by a fourth cameleer and an Arab of the Ghiyadh tribe of the Jebeliya group, who was to serve as *rafiq* (guarantor) till some tribesman of the more important Beni Hasan could be procured. She was well aware that a Druse, whose people were then at peace with all the tribes which range the Safa and the Hamad immediately to east of the Jebel, would have afforded better assurance; but none could be found at the moment. The largest local Bedouin tribe, the Walad 'Ali, was reported gone east, and not likely to be in her path.

Jebel Sais was reached at noon on the 20th, the way having lain through desolate but not untrodden desert of volcanic formation on which *fellah* Arabs of Dumeir raise sparse crops. One of these was seen to sow first and plough afterwards. This tract was rendered the

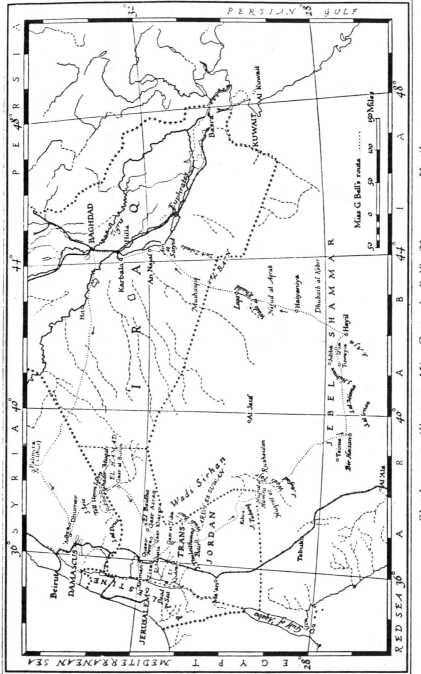

Sketch-map to illustrate Miss Gertrude Bell's Journey to Hayil

672

more inhospitable by very cold weather conditions, which coated all hilltops with snow, and at Jebel Sais itself brought down the night temperature below 20° Fahr., the tent canvas having to be thawed by fire in the morning before camp could be struck. Miss Bell found at Jebel Sais a very perfect crater and below it a two-towered fort, a mosque dating from the first century of the Hegira, a bath curiously constructed of mingled stone and brick (she wondered whence the latter could have come), and house-ruins of finely cut stone. Good well and pond water and sufficient grazing were at hand.

Next day (forward bearing about 136°) progress was resumed under the eastward face of the *harra* of Umm Idhn; and presently the party fell in with armed shepherds of the Masaid tribe, who, being at feud with the Ghiyadh, held up the party and began to plunder. In the nick of time, however, two of its members were recognized for friends; and sheikhs, coming up, called off the attack, restored the booty, and supplied a *rafiq*. Ahead lay a very repellent region. " The stony hills," wrote Miss Bell on the 22nd, " draw together in front like the gates of an abandoned Hades ! "; and to add to the dreariness heavy mist and cold rain came up next day, when the large wadis Muqati and Umqad, running west to the Ruhbe marsh, had to be crossed. But Burqu was duly reached on the 24th, and Miss Bell camped there over Christmas Day, taking several latitude observations (32° 37' 19" N.), and finding extensive ruins to study and measure and inscriptions, Greek, Safaitic, and Kufic (one being of the Umaiyad Caliph, Walid) to copy. The fort, she concluded, had indeed seen a Roman occupation, far though it lies beyond the eastern limit of Provincia Arabia.

On the 26th she breakfasted in a temperature of 25° Fahr., and then followed across a *harra* patch the trace of an ancient road (bearing about 230°) which led down the Wadi Resaya towards Qasr el Azraq. On the 28th she sighted the southern end of Jebel ed Druz and reached camping-grounds and dry wells of the Ruwalla 'Anaza, a great tribe of the Hamad, whose headquarters lie some three days to the east. They come thus far to westward only when at full strength. She actually encountered, however, not those tribesmen but their sworn foes, the Serdiya, a branch of the large Beni Sakhr group, and was hospitably entertained by their sheikh, Ghalib ibn Mit'ab, famous (or infamous) in the Arab world for having betrayed the paramount Ruwalla chief, Nuri Sha'lan, to the Turks. On the 30th, after hearing the women wail at the cenotaph of Mit'ab, she emerged at last from the volcanic country, crossed the main track between Jebel ed Druz and Wadi Sirhan, and reached the Roman fort and springs of Baida, from which place to Qasr el Azraq there remained but a short ride, on the last day of the year. We need not linger with her there (lat. 31° 49' 4" N.), for this large

The crater of Jabal Sais

The Hammam, Jabal Sais

Pinnacles of volcanic rock (Ḥarra)

castle, whose existing ruins, though they contain an inscription of Diocletian, are of the period of the Egyptian Mamluks, has been well described, together with its palm grove and reedy pools. The place became famous, in 1918, as the rendezvous or rallying-point of the Emir Feisal's force which afterwards took Damascus. Lawren·e spent many days of that winter and spring in its ruinous keep. Miss Bell found it, as usual, in the hands of outlaws, and experienced some difficulty. It has since harboured Druse refugees.

She was now on a doubtful frontier between the range of greater tribes. Certain graveyards of the Ruwalla, who had used fragments of Byzantine and Umaiyad architecture for headstones, and some horsekeepers of the Sherarat, who, as landless men without feuds, frequent frontiers, were met with on January 2 as she moved down towards the well-known ruins of Qasr el 'Amra, Kharana, and Meshetta—the last a " ghost," stripped of the lacework façade which adorns a room in the Kaiser Friedrich Museum at Berlin. There she was well within the range of the Beni Sakhr, the Ruwalla's chief foes. At Kharana, less well known than Meshetta, but dating in part from the first century A.H. full of Kufic texts and, as she wrote, " splendid surprises," she camped and worked for two whole days, postponing her appearance in the neighbourhood of the railway till January 7.

This first stage, completed in twenty-one days had, she confessed, tried both her body and her soul. Continuous cold and the absence of Fattuh, who knew her ways, made for acute discomfort ; and this had been aggravated by the uncertainties of passage through the ranges of small and lawless tribes. To make matters worse, it looked for some days as if that trial had been endured in vain ; for, though Fattuh duly joined her at Ziza, there followed on his heels a sergeant and posse of soldiers, sent to stop her further journeying in the desert and bring her to 'Amman. Ten weary days, therefore, had to be spent in interviewing officials (the *Kaimmakam* of Salt, fortunately for her, was a Christian), in telegraphing to Damascus, and in waiting—too familiar process !—for the Turkish official will to weaken. A powerful local Christian family, the Bsharras of Judeida, befriended her ; and returning to Ziza on the 14th, she was able to persuade the chief of police to accept a document absolving the Ottoman Government from further responsibility for her fate. That same day also she received a message from her friend, Sir Louis Mallet, H.M. Ambassador at Constantinople, warning her that the British Government would likewise disclaim responsibility if she persisted in the way to Nejd. The thought that she was about to re-enter the desert (it " always looks terrifying from without," she wrote) as an outlaw threw her for a few hours into deep despondency ; but reflection followed that, after all, in no case could either Government, Ottoman or

The keep of Burqu

The castle of Bayir

Qasr al-ᶜAmra

British, do anything to protect her in that desert ; nor could it, if she came to grief, take measures that would give the smallest satisfaction to any one. Eventually, though she failed to induce the police officer to return her document, and her three 'Aqail cameleers refused to continue, she slipped away on the 17th, in good spirits, with help and fresh men from the Bsharras, and rode south-east over recently tilled lands of the Beni Sakhr for Tuba, a small Umaiyad palace visited and planned by Musil. This place, which lies within the drainage basin of Wadi Sirhan, is known as the " gate of the 'Anaza," being on the line between the *dira's* of the Beni Sakhr and the Ruwalla. On the 19th the party descended the Wadi Mukhaiwir, and reached the black and dreary Ard es Suwan (Land of Flints). Here three pointed and white-capped hillocks, known as the Thuleithuwat, make a conspicuous landmark. She passed close to them but on the west, not the east side from which Carruthers, on his outward ride from Qatrani, had seen them in 1909. Crossing several tributaries of the Wadi Bayir, the party dropped, on the 21st, into the main valley which contains much tamarisk scrub, several wells, and the ruin which Carruthers saw on his return journey. He guessed it to have been a caravanserai on a Roman trade-route to the Persian Gulf, but Miss Bell thought it an early Islamic castle like Tuba, and the last that the desert-loving Caliphs of Damascus had pushed out into the Syrian waste. Lawrence, however, who visited it more than once in 1917, believes it to date back to the Ghassanids. As the first halting-place of importance on the path to Arabia, Miss Bell thought well to fix its latitude at 30° 40′ 43″ N.*

Thenceforward, until she entered the Nefud, three weeks later, Miss Bell, unlike her predecessors, Guarmani in 1864 and Carruthers in 1909 (their tracks ran respectively to east and to west of hers almost to Tor at Tubaiq, and both to westward of hers south of that point) was enabled, by the certainty of finding *khabra's* (ponds) after recent heavy rains, to avoid the dangerous proximity of wells, which too often are rendezvous of raiding parties. Bayir itself is such a rendezvous, but less in winter than in summer, when the Beni Sakhr frequent it. Though it is the resting-place of this tribe's *jidd* (tribal forefather), it lies near the limit of its southward and eastward range and is apt to be occupied from time to time by its enemies. At all seasons, indeed, the tract of desert north and south of Bayir is dangerous, and especially so when (as at the moment of Miss Bell's passage) it is *khala*, *i.e.* empty of shepherds.

* Miss Bell carried a 3-inch transit theodolite, in whose use she had been instructed at the R.G.S. Judged by a subsequent observation at Hayil, which, when computed, agreed within 42″ with another obtained by Charles Huber, her latitudes may be relied upon.

Moreover, it is of a melancholy monotony. No outstanding feature relieves a dreary succession of shallow sandy wadis, declining towards the Sirhan, and of dusty, flinty levels between them. Over this waste the party zigzagged from *khabra* to *khabra*, not keeping on one course, as travellers do between wells whose position is fixed and known, but seeking rain-waters which might have collected and remained unexhausted.

On the 25th came a change. The party was approaching the northern verge of Tor at Tubaiq, the Itbaik of Carruthers and Tobeyk of Doughty (who knew it by report alone)—a knot of hills to which Bedouins resort all the year round for pasturage. Here the sandstone has been protected from denudation by a lava-cap, now largely wasted and lying in the form of great boulders on the valley-floors. Smoke was seen, a portent of terror in so silent and vacant a land; but it heralded nothing worse than a camp of Howeitat shepherds, who reported that many of their great tribe, of both the Tayi and the Jazi sections, were pasturing in the hills ahead. Reassured, Miss Bell rode on over ground covered with green plants and starred with little flowers, white, purple, and yellow, and up between broken hills into the heart of the Tubaiq, which she describes as " rusty red hills with a dropping of coal-black stones down their steep sides " and with sands, at first red and then yellow, on their valley-floors. She found it a real hill region where dews, not met with since the Jordan valley, soaked her tent-flies, and frost sparkled at dawn. The most important chief, 'Auda abu Tayi, was away raiding the Shammar; but she was well received on the second day by another sheikh, Harb ad Darausha, at whose tent in the evening arrived 'Auda's cousin, Muhammad adh Dhailan, who was " sheikh ad Daula " *i.e.* agent for the collection of camel-tax for the Ottoman Government and responsible for the safety of a section of the distant Hejaz Railway.

Miss Bell was disturbed to find that even here she was not quite beyond reach of the Ottoman arm, and to hear her men questioned whether she was or was not travelling with the leave of the " Daula." But no harm followed, and in the end she spent no less than eight days in and about the Tubaiq, of which " very interesting region," as Carruthers called it, her diary gives the best account we have. The keen-eyed Howeitat— Doughty's " stout nomad nation " which he guessed to be of Nabathæan descent—seem to have pleased her. The time was passed partly in the hospitable tents of Harb and Muhammad, she being, as she said, " baptized of the desert " in the camel's milk of the Tayi; partly in taking, without let or hindrance, many photographs and a latitude observation (this worked out at 29° 52' 53" N.); partly in excursions to two neighbouring ruins; partly in climbing heights from which she could " look over fold on fold of golden red sand and smoke-grey ridge "; and always in making

The defile of Habrun

Sa^cud in Abu Tayi's tent

Auda abu Tayi's harim

and re-making plans for the journey ahead. After long debate between the Jauf and the Taima routes, she elected the first, being warned that the Bishr, Hutaim, Fejr, Wad Suleiman, and others ceaselessly raid the second ; and with Harb's brother, Awwad, as *rafiq*, she actually made a start ahead on January 28. But next day came news that the Wadi Sirhan, by which she must pass, was full of Ruwalla tents, among which Awwad might neither go safely nor frank his charge. So she turned back after calling on the *harim* of 'Auda, who told her of the "burden of woman" in nomad life ; and she abode other four days with Muhammad adh Dhailan, beguiling part of the time with an excursion to the walled pool of Kilwa, where are a small stone cistern of uncertain date and a sacred High Place. This ride took her beyond the Tubaiq which she saw, on the south, "break down abruptly in great riven crags" to a plain of red sand spotted with vegetation and diversified by rain-pools, left over from the downpouring of November. Meanwhile she had been advised so strongly to give Taima a wide berth (Carruthers had had to fly thence in 1909) that, when finally she started south on February 2, she intended to try to reach Hayil by the directest line that the Nefud desert would allow, *i.e.* by cutting across its south-western angle, where she heard of two wells—Haizan and Thoza—and of dunes less high and intervening horseshoe hollows less deep than they become farther east.

Besides a Howeiti *rafiq* her caravan now included two starveling families of Shammar folk with tents, children, and livestock. Though mendicant and graceless, they were welcome as unofficial *rafiqs* in the event of encounter with Shammar elements ahead. All went well for four marches slightly east of southward over steppes of sandstone and gravel cut by deep wadis falling east. "I read 'Richard Feverel,'" she noted on the first afternoon. The next day was beguiled by legends of the Tubaiq, and the next again by the red-gold sands and grey-green trees of the Nuqra depression. On the seventh day her march lay over a "regular garden" of flowers in the Aufad. But on the eighth came a check. After a party of Howeitat on the move had been passed, a camp of the Wad Suleiman (these nomads are Jeda'n of the 'Anaza group, and range to Tebuk and Taima) was seen ; and its sheikh, Saiya ibn Murted, barred passage unless Miss Bell would surrender a revolver and a Zeiss binocular to his greed. Even with these in his hands, he tried to induce her *rafiq*, by a promise of half the plunder, to abet a plot for leaving her to his mercy ; but, finding the Howeiti steadfast, he dared not provoke a great tribe, and in the end let the party go next day, with his own cousin and two men of the Fuqara—a tribe which befriended Doughty—for *rafiqs*.

On the third day—the eighth from Tubaiq—the first red dunes of the Nefud showed abreast ; and on the morrow, at a point only one long camel-march from Taima, the pebbly steppe was left for the sands. The pale yellow dunes, lying east and west with steep sides to north, were bare, but the lower sand was found well clothed with camel food. The change from the monotony of the steppe to a winding course, keeping a general direction south by east, round or through *qu'ara* (steep hollows between dunes), seemed pleasant enough. But in the absence of rain the going was heavy, and the weather continued cold. On February 13 the sands were white with frost. Many shepherds of the 'Awaji group were met, who had news that the Rashid Emir ex-

Drawing water at Haizan well

pected the *sitt* (lady), but was himself, at the moment, far from Hayil, raiding in the northern Nefud. On the 14th Miss Bell reached Haizan, where many of those shepherds were watering from a brackish well, evidently of great antiquity, to judge by its cemented upper part, and its depth (150 feet) into rock. A sweeter well near by, called Haiyar, had lately been blocked. Jebel 'Irnan in Nejd had been visible for two days past; and now from dune-crests some bearings on its northern butt, called Dhurru, were obtained to south-south-east, and others on Jebel Misma almost due east.

Jabal Aja'

Next day the other reported well, Thoza, was passed.   On the 17th, to the general delight, heavy rain fell, and hardened the sand for that day and the following.   Gravel was near at hand on the south, but fear of raiding Hutaim—reckoned, like the Sherarat, landless men of tainted blood—and consideration of pasture moved the guide to keep within the shelter of the Nefud.   The party wound among dunes and horseshoe hollows at a rate of not more than one crow-fly mile an hour, and Miss Bell began to grow as tired of the sands as she had been glad to get into them.   Though, as she writes, she " brought the world back into per- spective " by reading Hamlet in the rain, she decided, on the 19th, to bear right-handed to harder ground, and so she came to the southern- most dunes, and between the black rocks of Misma at last saw Nejd.

" It was a landscape terrifying in its desolation.   Misma drops in precipices of sandstone weathered to a rusty black, and at its feet are gathered endless companies of sandstone pinnacles, black too, shouldering one on the other.   They look like the skeleton of a vast city planted on a sandstone and sand-strewn floor.   And beyond and beyond more pallid lifeless plain and more great crags of sandstone mountains rising abruptly out of it.   Over it all a bitter wind whipped the cloud shadows. ' Subhan Allah ! ' (said one of her servants), ' we have come to Jehannum ! ' ' "

That plain, however, proved by no means infernal.   Pasture and waterpools lurked among its sand-pillars and tables ; and for that day and the next it provided fair going.   Then a southward tongue of the Nefud projected far across the path, and the party, now bearing almost due east, had to wind again among dunes.   The defile of Habrun was passed late on the 21st, the soil became granitic, the long ridge of Jebel Aja showed ahead, and a mud-built village, Tu- waiya, the first seen since Ziza, invited the party to stay after sending out five riflemen to investigate it.   The course henceforward lay but little to north of that followed by Doughty on his ride eastwards from Taima in 1877.   Presently for the third time intervened dunes, from which there was no escape till, on the 23rd, the deeply worn track from Jubba and Jauf was struck.   Following this past the village of Qana with its palm gardens and cornfields into a sandy pass walled with black pinnacles, Miss Bell came through Jebel Aja down to red plains which support villages, mud-walled and palm-girt ; and on the 25th, entering a basin larger than the rest, she saw Hayil.   Well knowing the unwisdom of taking such a place by surprise, she had sent two men ahead at dawn. No European, other than a Turkish officer, was known to have been seen in Hayil for over twenty years, and no European woman for more than thirty.   The all-powerful Emir, Muhammad ibn Rashid, who protected more than one Western visitor, had died half a generation ago ;

and since his death murder after murder had thinned the princely house. Its power had been waning for some time in comparison with that of the Emirate of Southern Nejd; and one result of the growing preponderance of the Ibn Sa'uds in Central Arabia was likely to be accentuation of Wahhabism heretofore lukewarm. Miss Bell might well be doubtful how she would be received.

All however seemed to promise fair. The envoys were met returning to say that the party was welcome, and Miss Bell was guided in a half-circuit round the town wall with its machicolated brick towers and admitted by the south, or Qasim, gate. But, to her disappointment, she was directed to quarters allotted to her immediately on the left, in what had been a subsidiary palace of the great Emir Muhammad, and since his day used as a guest-house. An inclined way, open on one side, led to a roof court and a lofty *roshan*, or reception-hall, whose floor was spread with carpets and its divan with cushions, below a red and blue frieze of pious texts. A ladder to the roof tempted her to view the town; but, beyond the knowledge that her house stood within a large fivefold enclosure, which once had bloomed with gardens and cornfields but was now uncultivated, and that other gardens and fields occupied a large part of the town area, she gained little before being called down to receive two women told off to attend her. Of these a lively Circassian, once sent by the Sultan 'Abdul Hamid for a concubine to Muhammad ibn Rashid and now married, took her fancy. This woman's mission no doubt included espionage; but her reports, in the end, did Miss Bell some service, and she seems to have reciprocated the latter's liking. The Emir, Sa'ud ibn Rashid, proved indeed to be absent, and the town was nominally in charge of his uncle, Ibrahim as Subhan, but really in that of Fatima, the Emir's grandmother, the real power behind the throne. Presently an odour of attar of roses heralded the entry of Ibrahim himself, and a polite conversation about former European visitors, especially the Blunts and Doughty (under his Arab name, Khalil), and about the stormy history and present state of the Rashids, left Miss Bell with no nearer prospect either of cashing the draft for £200 which she had brought from the Rashidian agent in Damascus, or of penetrating farther into the town. In fact, Ibrahim warned her that the *ulema* disliked her presence, and next day a message enjoined her not to leave the house without express invitation. On the 27th, however, she was bidden after nightfall by Ibrahim to the Qasr or palace, and conducted thither through clean silent streets, empty but for a woman or two creeping under the wall. The way lay through the market-place, which was entered by a wooden gate, and past the columned façade of the chief mosque to a second and then a third barred gate. These passed, she found herself in the Qasr and was led to the main reception hall,

Villages near Ha'il

Ha'il from the northwest

The Suq and Mosque of Ha'il photographed
by Gertrude Bell in 1914

white of walls and of floor, below a high roof propped by stone pillars. The usual courtesies were exchanged, and she handed over the presents which she had brought.

But on March 1, the fourth day of her stay, she had seriously to consider her position. She was told that neither would permission to depart be given nor would her draft be honoured till the Emir should return at some unknown date. She had sold six of her weaker camels, and with their price held just £40 in hand. A request for an audience of Fatima was not answered, and the presents left overnight at the Qasr were returned. She could only sit and wonder what the dark minds of the Rashids might be meditating, the Rashids, on their side, evidently being equally at a loss to tell what was in hers. In Hayil she knew murder to be "like the spilling of milk," and no prominent head to rest easy on its shoulders. "To the spiritual sense," she writes in her diary, "the place smells of blood." The political situation in Nejd, she had learned, was as unfavourable to her plan of going south as it well could be. Rashid power was everywhere on the wane. In the north Nuri Sha'lan held Jauf in secure defiance, and in the south Ibn Sa'ud was mobilizing for an anti-Rashid campaign destined to materialize toward the end of the year. Contrary to much that she had heard in Damascus, North Arabia was full of war and rumour of war.

Therefore she came, either now or earlier, to the conclusion that it was useless to attempt to reach Southern Nejd, and formed a new plan for direct return to Baghdad with eight camels, while the rest, with her spare men, should take the road for Medina and regain Damascus by the railway. Exactly when she began to doubt of her original plan is not clear, nor does the question matter, except in so far as it affects another which puzzled and worried herself—why she was not more frankly welcomed at Hayil. During her first two days, at any rate, she seems still to have cherished hope of reaching Ibn Sa'ud; and, if so, she probably gave some hint of it to Ibrahim, even if she did not directly ask for permission. At any rate, it may be inferred from Fatima's remark, "Is that all?" made a week later than this to the Circassian Turkiya, when the latter convinced her at last that it was for Baghdad, not Riyadh, that Miss Bell wanted a *rafiq* and money, and also from that old queen's action in forthwith cashing the draft, that previously the latter had seen reason to think that the Englishwoman intended to proceed in some less acceptable direction. At this juncture the Rashids, menaced by Ibn Sa'ud, and anxious, as always, to stand well with the Ottoman Government, whose forces their enemy had just expelled from Hasa, could hardly help an Englishwoman to take her money, her prestige, and her knowledge into the Southern Emirate; and seeing that they had received forenews of Miss Bell's coming, they probably knew also that she had come without Turkish sanction.

A significant passage in her diary for the 28th reflects disillusionment about the utility, if not the practicability, of travelling in independent Arabia *à la franca*, as she called it, *i.e.* as a European notable without assumption of Arab character, but with train of servants and private tent, equipped with travelling comforts of the West. Thus Shakespear had gone to South Nejd, as she knew, but not Palgrave, Doughty, or Leachman. She questioned if it were at all worth while to travel like the first named. Doughty, at the price, it is true, of pain and ignominy, had succeeded in seeing all Hayil and much of its intimate life. What could she add to his picture, penned, as she was, like a plague-stricken patient, within an implacable cordon? She seems keenly to have felt a sense of isolation even before she reached Hayil, and during all the time that she spent in the town, an unwelcome consciousness of being alien and incongruous. " I was the one blot," she wrote, after describing the company gathered about the Emir's mother, Mudi, when audience of the *harim* in the Qasr had at last been granted. On all her previous journeys in the Near East, and especially among the Bedouins of the desert, Miss Bell had never failed herself to control her actions and those of her men, to disarm suspicion and to establish reasonable relations with whoever was in authority. Now her failure in all these respects galled her not less than did the inactivity enforced, day after day, on her energetic body, and her disappointment at having come so far to see so little. She wrote bitterly now and later of her " imprisonment " in Hayil.

It should be said on the other side, however, that while she was treated there from first to last as a great lady, with formal and even distinguished courtesy, her arrival in a Wahhabi town placed its rulers in a difficult position. No one of its existing generation had seen a Christian woman of this station before. Why this one had come and whither she meant to go were questions that were bound to be canvassed suspiciously. The princely house, none too safe or sure of itself, evidently felt her a grave responsibility. Had Miss Bell's nerves been as well under control as in her younger days (she was now forty-four, and showed clearly in her diary that, from the start of this journey, she was neither physically nor morally as fit for the road as once she had been), she might have allowed more for peculiar circumstances of the moment, social and political, governing the action of the Rashids in Hayil.

That visit to the Emir's ladies on March 5 was almost the only occasion, before the sky cleared on March 7, which offered her any further opportunity of seeing the life of Hayil. Except for one angry conversation

The Rawshan in the guest-house at Ha'il, 1914

with Ibrahim in the Barzan, on the 2nd, and an excursion outside the walls to his garden, she had to keep for nearly a week after the 28th to her house or its precincts, protesting to all and sundry and waiting for the camels which she had called back from their distant grazing-ground on the Nefud. The audience with Mudi, still young and attractive, though three Emirs, one after another, reeking of the blood of her husband or her son, had forced her into their beds, stirred all Miss Bell's sense of the strangeness of the place with its silent moonlit streets and blood-stained society—" the unadulterated East in its habit as it has lived for centuries." She received a visit from two princely children, and returned it to find herself confronted in a garden by five small cousins, scented, solemn and silent in stiff gold-embroidered robes, who stared at her with painted eyes.

Whether these visits broke the ice, or the accomplished fact of the division of her caravan added conviction to Turkiya's pleading, certain it is that late next day Fatima did open the Treasury, and Miss Bell did find herself free to go. But, greatly daring, she refused after all to budge unless allowed a sight of town and Qasr by daylight—a sight which Mudi had told her she might on no pretext enjoy till the Emir's return. On the 7th, however, this facility was accorded. Crowds beset the path, but none molested her. The Hayil zealots, whether spontaneously or under compulsion, were all smiles and benevolence, vying with one another to supply subjects for the Englishwoman's camera ; and she was conducted all over the Qasr, even to the kitchen.

Relieved of her late anxieties and cheered by serene weather, Miss Bell ended with a more kindly feeling towards Hayil. " In spite of imprisonment," she wrote, " I carry away a deep impression of the beauty and charm of it all." The sunset glow on Qasr and town ; the art of the palace gate ; the noiselessness and, strange to say, dustlessness of the clean streets ; the green of cornfields " shining like jewels within the walls " ; the atmosphere of Harun ar Rashid's Arabia—all these things brought balm, and coloured the descriptions which she would give to her friends after her return to England.

If northwards she must go, she desired to follow the Persian Pilgrim track along which over a thousand years before Queen Zubaida ordered wells and tanks to be provided. Not that these attracted her, but she had heard of " written stones " near Dhubaib, some two marches from Hayil. On the 8th, however, she learned that, on the double pretext of the insecurity of the Darb Zubaida and of her obligation to meet the Emir, her guide had been ordered to lead by a more westerly track to the Haiyaniya well, and thence as straight as might be to Najaf. She could only bow. But in the end her disappointment about Dhubaib, was to prove short-lived; on the second day out, she heard enough of its stones to recognize natural freaks or fossiliferous blocks, rather than cuneiform *stelæ*. Two days she rode east of north over the plain to a low sandstone ridge which marks the limit of Jebel Shammar, and then once more into the Nefud by a deep-worn track between daisy-starred dunes smaller than those of the west. Everywhere were to be seen abundant pastures and Shammar shepherds' tents. Two days up to Haiyaniya—where water was drawn from 150 feet depth before a castle built by the Emir 'Abdullah ibn Rashid in the middle of the nineteenth century—and two days beyond it the land was still sandy, and known as Nefud el 'Aqrab; but it soon changed to a gravelly steppe—a type of desert usually called Dahna—and, after the bush-grown Wadi el Khadd had been passed, to flat and stony levels. "Oh, but it's a long and weary way!" sighed Miss Bell, as soon as the hills of Jebel Shammar dipped below the southern horizon; and her one solace was found in steadily mapping a track which, except at Haiyaniya, diverged from any followed by previous explorers. At Loqa, on the 15th, were found wells; but for the most part the camels drank from rain-pools. At Haiyaniya Miss Bell had been told that the Emir had passed eastwards. Now it leaked out that his raid on Jauf had failed. All idea, therefore, of meeting him was abandoned.

On the 17th, in a low sandy tract called here (as on the Kuwait road) Batn (Belly), the limit of the Shammar country was left behind, and with it the careless security of the past nine days. The track, bearing now slightly east of north and converging towards the Euphratean border-lands, brought the party within the extreme range of small semi-settled tribes—Arab but not Bedouin—which, in search of spring pasturage, resume nomadic habits. This year, owing to the favourable rains of the past winter, they were pushing farther afield than usual. The first two groups met with—one of Ri'u tents and one of the Beni Hasan—were ready to loot the caravan, and only refrained from fear of the Shammar. A third group belonged to another small and ignoble tribe, the Beni Salama. Much nervous energy and time were spent in persuading each of these groups to find *rafiqs*, whose guarantee would serve for a few hours only and be doubtfully valid with the next group that might be met; and great was Miss Bell's relief on the 19th, after the usual tentative approach to a fourth camp surrounded by great numbers of grazing donkeys, to find it occupied by Ghazalat, a tribe of such repute and strength that robbers (more and more likely to be met as Najaf drew nearer) would be slow to ignore its safe conduct. The worth of the Ghazali *rafiq*, Dawi, was to be proved next day and the day after, when, deaf to bribes, he stood by his charge and twice stopped attempts by Madan tribesmen to loot. The track had now fallen into the high-road, the Darb Zubaida, and what with camel-herdsmen, who shot by way of precaution, and Najaf merchants, who shot from nervousness, the rest of the way did not lack incident. As the margin of cultivation drew nearer, grassy *wadis* set with sparse trees were met with. Najaf could have been reached on the 22nd had not Miss Bell set her heart on holding on to and camping at a historic spot, 'Ain as Saiyid, which was once called Qarqisiya. Its castle however proving of recent date, and the place being without other interest than its associations, Miss Bell rode on to within sight of Najaf, camped near a village two hours away, and on the 23rd coaxed her camels across irrigation channels and rotten canal bridges into the town.

We need not follow her further travelling by carriage to Karbala and Baghdad over well-trodden ways; and I shall not attempt to relate her return across the Hamad to Damascus, after she had spent some three weeks in Baghdad. To another European woman, in the days before desert motor services had been thought of, such a journey would have seemed adventurous enough. But to Miss Bell, who had been into Nejd, a crossing of the Hamad, though it offered hardships and some danger, and the chance of visiting one of the greatest of Bedouin chiefs—Fahd ibn Hadhdhal—at his camp in the broad Ghara depression, and also of seeing and studying many unrecorded ruins of early Islamic and even pre-Islamic times, seemed something of an anti-climax.

She was now very tired and lacked her old zest for the novelties of exploration. A fit of depression at Baghdad issued in self-reproach for her failure to go beyond Hayil, or, as she thought, to render services to science commensurate with the labour and risks of her journey. She had learned, for one thing, that her pet study, archæology, would find little to feed upon in Central Arabia. But this mood did not prevent her from registering then and there a vow to ride direct to Ibn Sa'ud at some future date—a date which, in the event, the Great War was to postpone for ever.

Of her journey she felt in Baghdad indisposed to write; but she admitted that after a while she might feel differently. Such change of feeling did, indeed, come to pass. Had she, however, lived to write her own narrative, she would have claimed less for her achievement than here and now I propose to claim. To my thinking its interest and value lie by no means only or principally in its mere demonstration that a Christian English-woman could penetrate Nejd alone and return unscathed, but more in all sorts of gains that accrued to the geographical and archæological sciences, and to our social and political knowledge of the Arabs. Her journey in its first stage from the Oasis of Damascus round the back of the

Syrian *harra*, was a pioneer venture, which not only put on the map a line of wells, before unplaced or unknown, and enabled account to be taken during the War of the strength and local ranges of the Jebeliya tribes, heretofore names in the void, but also cast much new light on the history of the Syrian desert frontiers under Roman, Palmyrene, and Umaiyad domination. It is to be hoped that Miss Bell's detailed notes on the ruins marking these frontiers may be made available for students of history and architecture. On the second stage from Ziza to Hayil, archæology gained less (since nothing ancient of importance was met with after Bayir), but geography gained more. Miss Bell gives in her diary much the best account that we have to date both of the steppeland forming the western half of the Sirhan basin and also of the isolated hill group of Tor at Tubaiq. She was the first European to find a way across the south-western angle of the Nefud and to prove the existence of wells there; the first, too, to discover the character of the denuded sandstone region of north-western Jebel Shammar, which escaped Doughty. But perhaps the most valuable result of that stage consists in the mass of information that she accumulated about the tribal elements ranging between the Hejaz Railway on the one flank and the Sirhan and Nefud on the other, particularly about the Howeitat group, of which Lawrence, relying on her reports, made signal use in the Arab campaigns of 1917 and 1918. There is more to be learned of Bedouin life, thought, and custom from this part of Miss Bell's diary than in any book except Doughty's 'Arabia Deserta.' It is especially informing on the subject of the women, of whom her sex enabled her to see more than her predecessors.

Her stay in Hayil was fruitful, not of fresh topographical matter—for the place had been well described a generation before and had not materially changed—but of political information, especially concerning both the recent history and the actual state of the Rashid house, and also its present and probable relations with the rival power of the Ibn Sa'uds. Her information proved of great value during the War, when Hayil had ranged itself with the enemy and was menacing our Euphratean flank. Miss Bell became, from 1915 onwards, the interpreter of all reports received from Central Arabia.

The final stage of her journey—the ride from Hayil to Baghdad—had less important results. Though her route was new to geographical science, and therefore has been of much interest to cartographers, trying to plot the wadis running eastward towards the Shatt by their occurrence on different north–south tracks, it proved singularly poor in scenic and social features. Moreover travellers over other tracks lying not far from it on either hand had informed us already about the general character of this eastern end of the Nefud, and of the Dahna and the Shamiya steppes. Indeed, whether for topography or for social anthropology and ethnology or, needless to add, for archæology, the entries in Miss Bell's subsequent diary kept between Baghdad and Damascus are more valuable than those made between Hayil and Baghdad. But what she had learned about the Shi'a tribes of the Euphratean fringe was to prove of much service in the War and after.

It remains to be said that, in addition to half a dozen latitude observations, Miss Bell took her bearings and kept her marching times, also daily readings of barometer and thermometer, without a break from one end of this journey to the other. These bearings and readings she noted and recorded in such workmanlike fashion that little difficulty was found in plotting her continuous route from and back to Damascus—a total march of about 1500 miles.

The jaded traveller, writing her diary and letters at Baghdad in April 1914, had no suspicion that, in little more than half a year, the knowledge and experience acquired during the past four months, which seemed to her then so little important, would become of national value. Nor could she foresee that, even after the War, Northern Nejd would return to the obscurity from which she had rescued it. Up to this year of grace, 1927, her visit to Hayil, thirteen years ago, remains the last that has been put on scientific record by a European traveller.

a discussion followed

Sir PERCY COX : Dr. Hogarth, when he commenced the paper, told us how difficult he found it to do more than give us the dry bones of Miss Bell's narrative. We all know that with her great command of English and her powers of description what an absorbing narrative she would have given us ; but as Providence did not spare her to tell her own story I think we are greatly to be congratulated on the material having been given to the hands of Dr. Hogarth. Apart from the fact that he is President of our Society and our great authority on Arabia in general, he was a close friend of Miss Bell's, and always in touch and in sympathy with her work and her ideals. We can all admire the extraordinary pluck and tenacity with which she went through this lonesome journey. It is a very great pity that none of our Arabian travellers are in England now, or with us to-night, who could have entered into the details of her narrative and commented upon its great value in many respects. Arabian exploration, indeed, seems to have a rather fitful history. The end of the 'seventies and the beginning of the 'eighties was the period which saw the great expeditions of Doughty, the Blunts and Huber. After that there came a lull for a number of years, and it was not until the early years of this century that English interest seemed to have revived. I cannot help thinking that the revival was in a great measure due to the extraordinary amount of interest taken in that sphere and in the Persian Gulf by Lord Curzon during the seven years of his Viceroyalty in India. I cannot say whether Miss Bell first got her inspiration from that source, but, at any rate, I know that some of her contemporaries did—for instance, Captain Shakespear and Captain Leachman, who had both made fine expeditions into Central Arabia. Unfortunately, they were both killed in the war, or they would, I am sure, have gone back to the field of their early expeditions.

Miss Bell's journey, of which we have heard such a graphic story from Dr. Hogarth, was the beginning of my acquaintance with her, in this way.

In 1909 I was home for a few months' leave from the Persian Gulf Residency. Sir Richmond Ritchie, a mutual friend of ours, arranged a meeting between Miss Bell and myself that she might consult me as to the possibility of penetrating Central Arabia from the Persian Gulf side. At that time politics among the tribal chiefs between the east of the Persian Gulf coast and Hayil were extraordinarily disturbed, and I was obliged to persuade her to postpone her project for penetrating from that side to a later date. That was in the winter of 1909. She went almost immediately to Asia Minor, and it was then that, finding herself unable to get southward, she made the journey from Aleppo to Baghdad, returning through Northern Mesopotamia to Konia, of which she gave an account on her return in a very fine book of travel, 'Amurath to Amurath.' After that she was unable to find any opportunity to realize her ambition until just before the war, in 1913, when she found herself in Damascus in November, and managed to slip away in the manner that Dr. Hogarth has described to us to-night.

Then Dr. Hogarth told us how, after this journey, she came home tired out and had barely had time to recuperate when came the outbreak of the Great War, and from that moment she was continually employed on Government service. In 1915 she went to Cairo, where she became a member of the Intelligence Bureau for Arab Affairs, and where she was associated with Dr. Hogarth (then Commander Hogarth, R.N.V.R.), as well as with Sir Gilbert Clayton and T. E. Lawrence.

After three months there, working up Arab questions on the Hejaz side, she was deputed as Liaison Officer at G.H.Q. of the Force in Mesopotamia. She came over to Basra and at first she was attached to G.H.Q. Intelligence, but after a few weeks working up tribal questions from our side of the desert she was transferred to my department, and so began those ten years of most devoted service to myself and my successors which were only ended by her untimely death in 1926. The great experience she had of Arab traditions, and Bedouin customs, and the knowledge of individuals which she had gained in this and previous journeys was an enormous asset to us all. For me she became, when she joined me, what I called Oriental Secretary. A very necessary part of my work at that time was that of interviewing innumerable sheikhs and tribal leaders whom we came in touch with as the Force advanced : it was impossible that I could deal with every one, and Miss Bell used to act as filter, with all these sheikhs, and send them to me with a note as to where they came from and who they were. Her work was of the very greatest value to me.

The great Bedouin tribes migrate right across the desert from Syria to the 'Iraq border, and some of the great figures that we have seen crossing the stage in Syria we meet again in 'Iraq. Fahd ibn Hadhdhal, for instance, whose photograph we have seen on the screen, was an old friend of mine in 'Iraq ; and tribal questions as between Syria and 'Iraq are entirely dependent upon one another, so that the knowledge we gained as a result of Miss Bell's previous work and travels was exceedingly valuable. There are many personal aspects of her work which I should like to touch upon, but which it is impossible to go into now, because it would take too long ; but I should like to say what a great privilege I feel it to have been associated with her and to have worked with her all those years, and how glad I am to-night to have had the opportunity in this company of paying some tribute to the great lady whose loss we so greatly deplore.

Brig.-Gen. Sir GILBERT CLAYTON : Although Arabia has intruded itself upon nearly all the work, and indeed a good deal of the so-called play, which have fallen to my lot during the last ten or fifteen years, I do not pose as an Arabian expert, and indeed he would be a bold man who would attempt to traverse or criticize any of the statements made by so eminent an authority as our President, and based on the notes of so great an explorer and traveller as Miss Gertrude Bell. But I should like to take the opportunity of paying a humble tribute to the value of Miss Bell's services in one particular phase of her many activities during the war, which happened to be closely connected with work for which I was responsible, and which brought her into close personal contact with myself. When the war broke out that much-maligned but none the less necessary institution, the Intelligence Department, realized that the Arabs were going to have a considerable influence on the result, at any rate so far as the Eastern theatre was concerned, and we endeavoured to establish an organization by which information should be collected, to enable us to take advantage of such pro-ally sentiments as might be induced by various means, pecuniary and otherwise, in that part of the world ; and the result of our efforts was the establishment of an Arab Bureau, which I may say owed much of its impetus—indeed, almost all of its impetus—to our President, who has given us the lecture this evening.

You have all heard of Colonel Lawrence's wonderful exploits ; and indeed they were wonderful, and are wonderful. But it is not always realized what a large amount of preparation had to be made before those exploits became possible, difficult though they were in any case. That preparation entailed a lot of very hard, perhaps to some extent uninteresting work during the earlier days of the war, and the collection of a very large amount of information. The Arab Bureau was engaged in that work, and you can, I think, after what you have heard this evening, realize our delight at hearing that Miss Gertrude Bell had consented to come out and give us her assistance—and very valuable that assistance was. Indeed, I attribute much of the success of Colonel Lawrence's enterprises to information and study in which Miss Bell had a very large hand, and I think no one would be more ready to acknowledge that than Colonel Lawrence himself, were he here to-night.

I will not make any remarks on the general statements that the President has made, except to put one thought into your minds in connection with the value of exploratory work such as Miss Bell undertook. I will give you these simple facts. The President mentioned Ziza as the starting-point of Miss Bell's expedition. That was just before the outbreak of the war. Ziza is now the starting-point of the air route between Palestine and Mesopotamia. Miss Bell undertook a camel-ride back from Baghdad to Damascus. A very fine performance for any woman, indeed any man. That journey can now be done, only ten to thirteen years afterwards, by motor-car. I think if you just ponder a little on those two facts, you will have some idea of the value of expeditions such as Miss Bell undertook.

Just one word in conclusion. I have had the privilege, and have the privilege, of the acquaintance of most of the leading Arab rulers and many of the chiefs in Arabia. I have never met one who has not either known Miss Bell personally or by repute, and I have never met one by whom she is not held in affection, in honour, and in reverence.

Sir HUGH BELL : Some years ago I had the honour to receive at the hands of your Society the Founder's Medal on behalf of my daughter, and now I have once again to thank the Royal Geographical Society for the honour that they have done her and her memory by the most excellent lecture you have heard from your President. We were of course aware, to some extent at all events, of the dangers which our daughter ran when she left Damascus on that journey into Southern Arabia. I remember after she had been some weeks, months perhaps, on the way I began to consider what I should have to do in the event of things turning out as unfortunately as at one time seems to have been possible. I went to Lord Cromer and consulted with him as to what course I should take should cause arise, and we agreed as to what should be done ; but Lord Cromer added, " You need not be concerned. She will come through all right." And so she did.

I have here to ask you to accord to your President your thanks for the most excellent and interesting lecture which he has delivered. To us, her relatives, her loss is quite beyond words ; to me, her father, irreparable. I think there never were father and daughter who stood in such intimate relations as she and I did to one another. And so, Sir, it gives me the greatest pleasure to hear you accord to her all that honour which you have been good enough to do this evening, and it gives me greatest satisfaction, therefore, to be permitted to move that the best thanks of this meeting be given to you for your lecture.

Admiral Sir WILLIAM GOODENOUGH : I have been asked to second and to support Sir Hugh Bell in his vote of thanks to the President for his lecture. It is not my intention to speak to-night of the travels of Gertrude Bell except, if you will allow me, Sir, to thank you for the way in which you have treated both her notes and her memory ; but I would, for a moment, speak of her as a personality, for although many notices have appeared of her in the newspapers, and also in the *Geographical Journal*, so far as I know no public estimation of her has been made at one of our fortnightly meetings here. What was it that caused such universal admiration and affection for her ? Not only her powers, great as they were. She was one of the first women to get a first class at Oxford ; a really great traveller, and not only one who travelled widely but one who observed with great intelligence, assimilated with discretion, and described with great skill all that she had seen and heard ; one of our best known archæologists ; an administrator who at once obtained the confidence of all those with whom she dealt, European or native ; one of the boldest riders to hounds that you can think of ; imbued with a courage beyond that ordinarily given to man or woman, and the most fascinating companion. There was another quality in her which was most endearing—her sympathy with and affection for all children. I can remember a day, long before the war, when she and Valentine Chirol sat on a bench in a garden in Wales and told stories, some serious, some amusing, some almost frivolous, while a group of children sat spellbound listening to the strange but absolutely true things that they heard.

But that was the product. What was the root and stem from and by which it sprang ? It was her absolute sincerity. Politically—and I speak in the broadest sense of the word, not of those petty matters of Press and Party, of which she took no count—broadly she was a Constitutionalist. She believed in and stood on the foundations on which the growth of this country has been laid—honour, justice, truth, freedom. Those were the qualities which actuated her life and which she inspired in others. Her mind soared high. Like other great spirits, she was prepared to build new things on those firm foundations. An enthusiast yet not a fanatic, an idealist yet not a visionary, she was not content to sit on the dry stones of convention hugging a sluggish security. Her belief in the progress of the world was unconquerable. I remember her saying, " We must go on ; if we stand still we go back."

Whether at the last moment she was conscious that her spirit was passing from us we do not know, but if she was so conscious I believe that her thoughts and hopes could be described in those words written by Masefield :

" Oh, given spirit now taken,
Keep to this faith unshaken,
That the good thing well willed
Becomes fulfilled."

Her life was an inspiration, her death a grievous loss ; but if ever man or woman left this world victorious it was Gertrude Bell.

The PRESIDENT : I am more than obliged to Sir Hugh Bell for proposing, and to Sir William Goodenough for seconding, a vote of thanks ; but a vote of thanks was really the last thing that I deserve for attempting to pay a tribute to one whom I knew for nearly forty years and in whose company I have taken greater pleasure than in that of almost any one else that I have known in my life. I was glad to hear Sir Gilbert Clayton's assurance that Miss Bell is still so well known throughout the length and breadth of the Arab world. I can endorse that. I do not think that any European has enjoyed quite the same reputation. She had all the charm of a woman combined with very many of the qualities that we associate with men. She was known in the East for those manly qualities. Fattuh, her servant of whom I spoke, was also my servant for one journey. He had gone with Miss Bell five years before he went with me. I remember an awful week in the north of Syria when it rained day after day, and day after day I told him we could not start because the weather had not lifted. Once he did not ask, but merely said, " I suppose we don't start to-day ? " I said, " No." He said, " No, *we* shan't start, but the *sitt* " (*i.e.* Miss Gertrude Bell)—with an expressive gesture—" *she* went through water and mud to her waist." In those days Miss Bell could outtire any man and had the courage of any two men. I shall not serve any good purpose by trying to say how much I, and many others, have felt her loss. Hers was the brightest spirit that shone upon our labours in the East during the War.

13
Eldon Rutter, 1929

Eldon Rutter, the American author of *The Holy Cities of Arabia* (2 vols., New York, 1928), travelled to Ha'il from Damascus in late October 1929, returning to Amman at the end of the rainy season in early February 1930. His purpose was to seek permission from King ^cAbdulaziz ibn Al Sa^cud to travel in southern and central Saudi Arabia, and he understood that the King was then in the vicinity of Ha'il, undertaking a campaign against the rebellious faction led by Faisal ad-Dawish.

The security situation at the time was perilous, and Rutter must have felt in danger with only two camels and a bedu guide from the Ruwala called Sahan. They joined the Ruwala on the afternoon of the second day, at Ahdilla (see the accompanying map), and from then on Rutter's safety was ensured by the migrating tribe whose camel herd covered a front of twenty miles. On the seventh day after leaving Damascus the party arrived at ^cAnqa, and after another week they approached the end of the limestone steppe of al-Hamad, some two hundred miles wide, and roughly 3,000 feet above sea-level.

By the end of the following day the Ruwala and Rutter had encamped 400 feet lower down, at 2,600 feet, within view of al-Jauf, the fertile depression including Sakaka, Daumat al-Jandal, and al-Qara. Like Musil, but unlike all other previous travellers, Rutter reached the Juba depression and al-Jauf from the north, and not by the usual route of Wadi Sirhan. Leaving the Ruwala territory, Rutter engaged Gubayil, a bedu of the Shararat tribe to ensure safe passage

as far as Bir Hazil, two days on, where he was to
take on a Shammar guide. Bir Hazil consists of some
twenty water-holes, and had been seen by no Westerner
before except Leachman (1912). Despite the early
report, Rutter found no Shammar at Bir Hazil, but
came across an encampment at Rijm Hazza', where he
paid off Gubayil, and hired ibn Rimal to take him as
far as Ha'il.

Rutter and ibn Rimal now crossed the loose red sand
sea called the Nafud, encountering a number of
encampments of the Shammar, who were migrating towards Labba in the north of the Nafud. Some of the
long narrow depressions in the Nafud were virtually
cleared of sand by the high winds, exposing areas of
limestone floor, with occasional outcrops of basalt.
Rutter's passage across the Nafud, which took five
days, followed a route never before followed by a
Westerner and ended at Bir Taiyim, five ancient wells
on the southern fringe of the Nafud with a recently-
established settlement of Wahhabi Ikhwan.

They crossed the ridge of as-Sabrawat by moonlight,
with the ridge of al-Jilf to the south and the cone
of al-Jildiya to the south-east, and rested until dawn.
The travellers baked bread at sunrise, ate a hearty
breakfast with coffee, and then began to ride towards
Ha'il. "As they sun rose behind the horizon," wrote
Rutter, "a beautiful view opened around us. The peaks
of the distant mountains stood faintly revealed against the pale sky. They seemed to float in the air, for
their bases were hidden in a pink mist. They presently turned to translucent red, and as the sun rose
higher they slowly became blue, while the plain in
front of them turned yellow. The sand which lay
heaped against the southern slope of the ridge of
as-Sabrawat, behind us, shone like virgin gold under
the ruby crests. Something else was slowly emerging
from the mists far away to our right front. It was
a mountain of granite, which rose almost perpendicularly from the plain to a height of some 5000 feet.
The mass of pinnacles and crags was now an ethereal

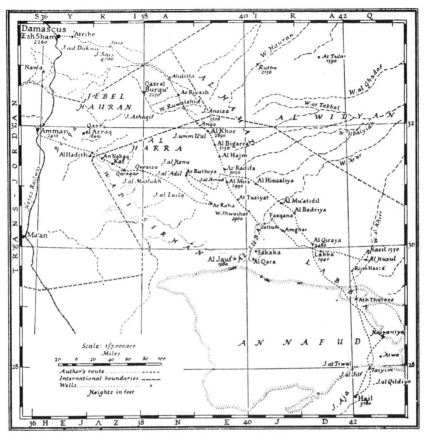

Mr. Rutter's route to Hail

assemblage of golden points and blue shadows, poised
in the sky. It was Jabal Aja'."

The keen impression of Jabal Aja', and even of the
lower double-crested hill of Samra, has made itself
felt on all visitors first seeing Ha'il from the
north. Rutter and ibn Rimal rode among the last red
sandstone hills, with thorny acacias struggling for
survival in the depressions nearby, and finally entered the settlement of Suwaiflah, with dates and tamarisk: the outskirts of Ha'il. It was the hour of
siesta, and they saw nothing whatsoever moving.

701

At the residence of the Amir, Rutter was invited to rest on a bench until the Amir was ready to receive him. Very quickly the Amir emerged, with a score of retainers, but after returning Rutter's greetings he passed on. Shortly afterwards Rutter was assigned lodgings.

Next morning he called on the Amir in his palace, and was told that King ^{C}Abdulaziz was pursuing ad-Dawish on the border with Kuwait. The Amir had no authority to allow Rutter to travel beyond Ha'il, but agreed to send a letter to the King, requesting such authority.

There now passed two weeks, which Rutter spent in exploring the oasis city and its environs, while sleeping in the house of one of the Amir's retainers.

"All the inhabitants wore the Badawin mantle and head-kerchief; the turban, tarbush, and other articles of clothing seen in the Arabian border countries were entirely absent. Even a Javanese barber, one of the two or three foreigners settled in the town, wore Arabian clothing." Rutter estimated the population of Ha'il at the end of 1929 to be about two thousand. This was much below earlier levels, since the rebellion by Faisal ad-Dawish had caused King ^{C}Abdulaziz to close the border with Iraq, thus curbing trade. Merchants had migrated to al-Qasim, to Medina, and even to Iraq, abandoning many houses, of which some of those in the northern district were already falling into ruin.

During the late 1920s all the officials in the local government were Wahhabis from Riyadh and al-Qasim, and Rutter observed that religious practice was rigorously enforced, following the example of King ^{C}Abdulaziz. Camel saddles of tamarisk wood were then made in Ha'il, using the timber found plentifully east of the town and in the surrounding oases.

At the end of Rutter's fortnight he was summoned to the Amir's presence and advised to leave Ha'il at once. He had not been able to send Rutter's letter of request to the King, saying that he did not know exactly where to send it, and gave the same reason for not permitting Rutter to proceed southward beyond Ha'il.

Two days were spent in fruitless argument, and then Rutter reconciled himself to the return journey, again crossing the Nafud, this time with two guides. Ten days later the party arrived at a Ruwala camp in the southern Hamad which was attacked by ʿAmara tribesmen on the same night. One Ruwaili man and four mares were killed, while the ʿAmara lost two men before being driven off. This 1929-30 winter was so cold that Rutter found his cloak covered with hoar-frost on rising at dawn, and the water in their goatskins was often frozen solid. On passing through Qurayyat al-Milh (The Salt Villages) in the Wadi Sirhan, Rutter noted huge expanses of white salt left by the evaporation of rainwater. The road to Jordan was now short, and Rutter entered Amman on 5 February 1930.

14
Bawden and Berman, 1944

Despite the advances in exploration after 1929 elsewhere in the Arabian Peninsula, Ha'il slips out of accounts by travellers until 1944, when curious circumstances involving World War II led Captain Edward Bawden (the celebrated English painter born in Essex in 1903) and Sergeant-Photographer Berman to record their visit to Ha'il in words and drawings, and in photographs respectively.

The occasion is most graphically described in a press release from the General Headquarters, Middle East Forces, dated 26 November 1943.

UNARMED TROOPS OPEN NEW FRONT

Britain is sending a force of unarmed troops to a neutral country to open up a new battle front with the agreement of the king of that country, Ibn Saud of Saudi Arabia. The war is against the locust plague, whic is likely to reach a peak this coming year. The Army is running the supply and transport services for the civilian experts of the Middle East Anti-Locust Unit.

Locust swarms vary greatly in size and extent each year, and it was predicted that 1944 would be a time of devastation in the Arab World. Since the food situation there and in Europe was becoming critical, it was decided that an especial effort should be made to exterminate the swarms of young 'hoppers' in the deserts during the early

spring, before they were ready to fly off in search
of food. While the Middle East Supply Centre was
co-ordinating the efforts of scientists from
several nations, including Britain, the U.S.A.,
the U.S.S.R. and India, the Ministry of Information arranged for a photographer and artist to
accompany the expedition. The only link with the
outside world was by radio, operated by a special
signal section with seven transmitting sets, to
keep posts in touch with each other, and with G.H.
Q., M.E.F., and G.H.Q., Paiforce. Supplies of
food, petrol and water were sent on monthly convoys
that also supplied Bahrain, Sharjah and Yanbu, with
their outposts.

Sa^{c}ad Muhammad al-^{c}Amiri, leader of the pilgrim
guides, Ha'il. Water-colour by Edward Bawden
(1944).

706

One convoy of 250 vehicles made its way from Egypt to the east coast of Arabia through Syria and Iraq. The other, of 100 vehicles, left Egypt for Aqaba and the west coast of Arabia. The thousand men were not to find the experience novel, for all officers and men had all at least two years' service in the Western Desert during World War II.

Distant view of the Amir's Palace, Ha'il, built after 1921 (Photo: Berman, 1944).

The methods of dealing with the locust swarms
were summarised in the press release as follows:
'The locusts seek a moist spot in which to lay
their eggs, and the young 'hoppers' hatch out in
from four to six weeks. For the next four to six
weeks they are unable to fly, but hop along in vast
swarms, often three or four miles wide, devastating
all the ground they pass over. It is during this
period that the poisoned bait, consisting of bran
with an arsenic compound, must be put down in their
path. The 'hoppers' eat it not because they like

The Castle of King [c]Abdulaziz, built shortly after
1921 (Photo: Berman, 1944).

bran, but because they want the water that the bait
is mixed with. Great care has to be used in laying
the bait line as the young locusts are sensitive to
disturbance and will deviate from their line of
march and by-pass the source of disturbance, thus
wasting many tons of previous bait.'

The series of photographs by Sergeant-Photographer Berman which follow first appeared in *The
Architectural Review* (1949) and are reprinted here
by kind permission. Of the drawings by Edward
Bawden, three are reproduced here by kind permission of the Imperial War Museum, which owns them:
Sa'd Muhammad al-'Amiri, leader of the pilgrim

guides at Ha'il; the Amir's Palace and Government
Buildings at Ha'il; and the Rest-house of the Anti-
Locust Mission at Ha'il with a Sudanese Locust
Officer (Mr.Shaddad), Salim the Arab guide to Ha'il
and the latter's son 'Abdullah. The Art Gallery and
Museum of Cheltenham possesses Bawden's drawings of
Ha'il Castle and The Amir's Palace, while the
Whitworth Art Gallery, University of Manchester,
possesses the drawing entitled *Ha'il: the Camel
Market and the Ruins of the Palace of Ibn Rashid*.

Edward Bawden wrote a letter to E.C. Gregory,
Secretary, War Artists' Advisory Committee, National
Gallery, London W.C.2 dated 18 July 1944, and the
first three pages of this beautifully-written letter
(the pages covering Ha'il) are reproduced here in
facsimile by kind permission of the artist.

Amir's Palace (Photo: Berman, 1944). The benches
around the walls have been described by Wallin and
Doughty, among others.

Embassy Public Relations,
Baghdad
5.5.44

Dear Mr Gregory, I received your letter of the 16th of February a week ago at Kut el Imara. In two days I shall have another set of photographs, & at the same time I will send the drawings; the two parcels will not arrive together in the same bag because the Publications Branch at Cairo, who incidentally made the trip arrangements for my trip to Saudi Arabia, have asked to see the work.

The first batch of drawings which I took to Cairo were given the security of a cupboard pending Col. Mason's decision on the question of an exhibition. I dont know what has happened. When I reached Baghdad I sent a letter by one of the officials of the Ministry who was returning to Mr Ryan's Office, but I have not yet received a reply. As I shall be seeing Col. Mason before the end of the week I will add a postscript. Anything put under lock & key may remain in custody for an indefinite sentence, despite instructions begging for a release: anyway I am sorry you have not received the work, unless it has arrived since the date on which you wrote.

The trip across Arabia from the Red Sea coast to the Persian Gulf took two months. On the map a few short straight lines might be drawn linking Jedda, Yenbo, Hail, Bureida, Rumaihiya & Dhahran, but on the face of the earth I found these journeys from place to place to be neither short nor straight. The general direction of the route was almost on a line with Riyadh. Like Mecca & Medina Riyadh the capital was strictly out-of-bounds, but it was possible to reach the town on an invitation of the King, & that, with luck was simple. If the King was hunting near the capital the guide allocated to the vehicle would ask to diverge temporarily from the main track to have the opportunity of paying his respects, the personnel on the truck would be put into the guest tent, fattened for a day or two on good food, given as a gift a complete change of Arab clothes, & then, on the appointed day properly attired, clean & rosy, ushered into the Royal Pavilion. In due course an invitation to stay at the Guest Palace at Riyadh for the duration of the King's pleasure might hopefully be anticipated. I was keen to work this racket, but Jordan, British Minister to Saudi Arabia worked another. It was a misfortune to be travelling with a journalist & a photographer, & at Jedda where we called at the Legation Mr Jordan gave my companions no encouragement; 'let no circumstances' said he 'must the King be interviewed or

711

Amir's Palace and government buildings.   Water-
colour by Edward Bawden (1944).

2

photographed," as an instance of what should not be allowed to happen he mentioned the article in "Life" written by, in his own words "two scurvy American journalists". (But not too scurvy: by observing the King's wishes the journalists behaved honourably but their scruples were not supported by the editorial staff.) The moral of that & another story (subsequently found to be false) was that journalists & reporters were untrustworthy. Towards me his attitude seemed to be a trifle more favourable as he admitted that a drawing of the King would have value, but he had suspicions, & these were confirmed when I appeared for dinner improperly clothed in my best lounge suit (war-time moths had removed the flys) & I failed to take a proper, only a polite interest in the recreations of the consulate class — fishing for barracuta in the Red Sea, pig-sticking in the wilder parts of Turkey, & losing money at cards. We wanted to hear of Arabia & of the people but the officials at Jedda who, no doubt recognised the existence of such things on paper, were unwilling, or they had had no experience of, or interest in these things, therefore no information to impart. We gave our countrymen a pain in the neck for four or five days, but the only practical result occured later when, after Mr Jordan's visit to Riyadh, a message was received from Ibn Saud expressing his regret that he would not be able to see the photographer.

Arabia has no rivers; or roads. To progress by any other means than on foot is by knocking around on a slow bone-shaking camel or donkey. The Anti-Locust Mission had cars & from Jedda to Yenbo, two hundred & thirty miles in a day on a track which was no more than the combined wheelmarks of other cars made me keen not to retrace any of my future journeys. On arriving by night at Yenbo I went to bed with malaria. Next morning Mohammed arrived from Cairo, luckily!— to hold the patient's pan. Five days on that sweltering saltmarsh & I was feebly strong enough to stroll by the shore for shells, but despite this interruption of good health I did not miss the first convoy leaving for Hail. It was a five days' ride. From sunrise to sundown it was a ceaseless tumble in the car, a respite for an hour at noon & another brief meal in the dark, then dossing down with a blanket on a piece of ground which, speaking for my own comfort, I cleared fastidiously of the larger stones. Going inland from the coast to Hail the track passes through Medina, & it was to avoid the city by twenty miles that a long detour had to be made through the tortuous valleys of the Hedjaz hills. The country was extremely wild & rocky;

Rest-house at Ha'il. Water-colour by Edward Bawden,
showing the Sudanese assistant locust officer, Mr
Shaddad, with the local guide Salim, and the latter's son ᶜAbdullah.

grim, desolate & forbidding as though a great fire had in a past age burnt up every sign of life, leaving the piled rocks blackened by smoke or scorched to redness, but with veins of more vivid colour where the heat remained. The toss & tumble of the largest rocks was often sensationally baroque, & by contrast, the volcanic reds & blacks austerely rich by juxtaposition had the dim fiery glow of a Russian ikon. From the car I watched the skyline which was always as unexpected in contour as the red line of a seismograph; the scenery though not of the first order of magnificence was exciting. The smaller pieces of rock everywhere thickly scattered upon the ground were not weathered, but retained an original sharpness of edge inimical to walking, or climbing in shoes soled with Egyptian leather.

At Hail we stayed longer than anywhere else, & most of my work was done there, either in or around the town, or at Jebel Selma, a range of rocky hills forty miles from Hail.

To live alone in an Arab house puts a strain upon the virtues of patience & forebearance. A day wasted in Arabia may be no more than an hour of laziness in London, the time passes slowly from the hour before dawn to the hour after sunset punctuated by the passing of the coffee cup & the hours for prayer: coffee & prayer are the diversions, for the rest, like Mr Eliot's Gumbie (at one just sits & sits & sits & sits until the European arse is sore. Sometimes, sitting uncomfortably cross-legged I saw in an inner mirage a Tottenham Court Rd armchair, at other times I wondered why the ingenious Arab had never invented a flytrap, or noticed the filth he lived with, or took such little trouble to be punctual, always this waiting for someone to come, waiting for something which has been arranged to take place, waiting — waiting which is so apt to make the temper testy, querulous or peppery. "What does it matter", says the Arab, & indeed, what does it matter! But though time passes slowly it does not limp as it does when regulated by Big Ben, & when my arse got tougher (I did not grow an enormous, irremovable corn) & I accepted the "never mind" attitude, placing upon the shoulders of Allah the shortcomings of men I found the life pleasant & sensible. The virtues of patience & forebearance can be stretched a little & controlled, but it is as wearing for the temper as a shortage of cigarettes; at first.

General Market, Ha'il (Photo: Berman, 1944).
    The 'rude' two-leaved gateway' seen by Doughty
in 1878 was still there in 1944.

Camel Market, Ha'il (Photo: Berman, 1944).

Camels were the ubiquitous companion of the
nomad until very recently, and the camel market at

Ha'il served a vast region centred on the Jabal
Shammar. The older Rashidi architecture is exempl-
fied by the tall round tower at the left of the
photograph, while the Saudi battlements on the
right date from after the conquest of the city by
King CAbdulaziz in 1921.

15
Ha'il Today

After the stories of Euting and Huber, Palgrave and
the Blunts, it is time to place a proper emphasis
on the ways in which Ha'il has adapted and is adapt-
ing to the needs of the present day.

The most obvious signs of change are in the face
of the city: its physical expansion, the tall new
buildings in traditional architectural styles which
blend so harmoniously with the environment, and the
elegant public gardens which emulate the green oases
of old with their green lawns and recently-planted
trees and flowerbeds.

The small local airport has been replaced with a
magnificent new terminal serving two runways 3,300
metres long, one 45 metres wide and the other 23
metres wide. Ha'il Airport sees on average sixty
SAUDIA planes and twenty private planes each week.

Four Boeing 747s and 3 Boeing 737s can be accom-
modated on the major apron, 225 metres x 75 metres,
while there is a small apron, 75 metres x 50 metres,
for helicopters. The aprons and runways are illuminated to IATA specifications, and as well as the
normal Fire Department equipment, there is an emer-
gency generator to provide 60 kw. of electricity
for the runways, and the air freight warehouse
covers 500 square metres. Passenger service, comfort
and security has always been of prime concern to
SAUDIA, and four air-conditioned halls offer such
facilities as restaurants and automatic baggage-
handling. The Passenger Hall covers 2,270 square
metres. The Arrivals Lounge is capable of proces-

sing 600 passengers an hour, and the Departures
Lounge some 240 passengers an hour. The V.I.P. hall
has a royal annexe.

Inside Ha'il Airport (1982)

This, then, is the view that most visitors to
Ha'il will first see. Their next view will probably
be one of wide avenues: dual carriageways illumin-

Car park, Ha'il Airport (1982)

ated at night and separated by trees and grass-
covered banks. Official figures for the 1981-2
financial year reveal that 240 million Saudi Riyals
(equivalent at the time to US$$_c$ 790 million were
allocated for the Ha'il - Biqa^c' road and the city
ring-road, while the road Ha'il - Jubba was under
tender to a value of about SR230 million. The first
part of the road Ha'il - 'Uqla as-Suqur is now ready,
passing through ash-Shinan, Abda, Fayd and Sab'an, and
the second phase is one of the three significant road
projects linking areas of Ha'il province to Medina

The Entrance to modern Ha'il (1982)

in the southwest and al-Qasim in the south-east.
The other two major projects are the second phase
of the Great Nafud Highway, linking Ha'il with al-
Jawf via Jubba, and the western link road to al-
'Ula. The agricultural roads within these projects
have a total length of 339 kms., including links
between the eastern and western agricultural zones,
and other minor connections to the Education Village,
Harir, Julfa, Hamima, al-Laqita, Naqbin, and Mashar.
The 105 km. Ha'il - al-Qasim road through Sha'lania,
Dawia and Khawir is already in use, as are the

The new dual carriageway entering Ha'il (1982)

connections off the Ha'il-Hanakiyah road to ar-Rawda, al-Mustajidda, as-Salimi, and al-Ha'it, to a length of 151 kms. Studies for further roads totalling 370 kms. are under way.

Sports Stadium, Ha'il

As regards details of the electricity projects, the most significant aspect is that four gas turbine units providing 40,000 kw. are already in place. The whole electric grid will be renewed, providing

Building the new Amir's Palace, Ha'il

sufficient power for the new industrial zone, and
the installation of a new city network connecting
all parts of the city and outlying suburbs. The
Project Research Centre of the Central Electricity
Project has decided to postpone construction of the
small diesel station originally planned and to abandon the 2 x 20 megawatt central generating station
in favour of a main 5 x 50 megawatt station.

Mountains near Ha'il

Agriculture has been the traditional cornerstone
of Ha'il society. Support to the farming economy has
strengthened the move from a structurally weak nomadic society to a strong urban economy. Interest-free
loans are available to encourage mechanisation and
long-term planning. Ha'il is now entirely self-
sufficient in agricultural produce and in fact is
even exporting to Kuwait. The Agricultural Bank

Tawarif - antiquities near Ha'il

offers farmers generous facilities, and the Ministry
of Agriculture and Water Resources has established
bureaux for technical assistance to farmers at al-
Biqa^C' and al-Khutta. A centre is in course of
construction as a Directorate of Veterinary Medicine
and Livestock, and other buildings are being prepared for storage and refrigeration. Two dams are

HRH Prince Fahd ibn Sa^{C}d ibn ^{C}Abdurrahman, Governor
of Ha'il from 1971 to 1972

being built on the flanks of Jabal Aja' to irrigate
fields near the city. Nurseries are being set up
in al-Qa'id to provide farmers with seeds and plants.
Exploratory wells are being dug west and south of
Ha'il, and a drinking-water project is under way in
six villages. A pasture-area is being planted near
Sabha' and al-Malikia.

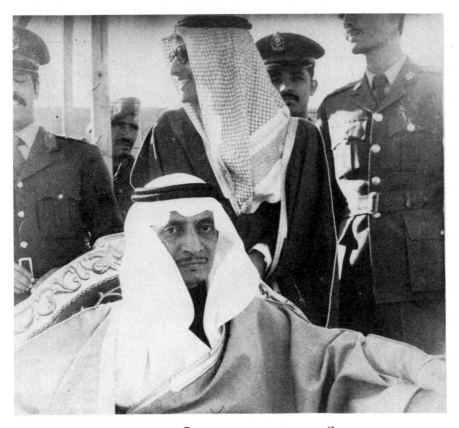

HRH Prince Sa^{c}d ibn Fahd ibn Sa^{c}d, Governor of
Ha'il from 1972 to 1974

One of the most exciting enterprises is the formation of an agricultural company as a collaboration between the Government and the ablest businessmen, with a capital recently increased from SR200 million to SR300 million. The purpose is to co-ordinate and strengthen farming in the Ha'il area by subsidies and interest-free loans to shareholders.

Social development goes hand-in-hand with economic and industrial progress in the Kingdom of Sa'udi Arabia. For instance, in the village of Quffar, some 12 kms. from Ha'il, a Social Development Centre has been set up to encourage communal action such as the improvement of housing standards, the organising of cultural competitions, health advice and campaigns (with instruction in first aid and the use of sprays against rodents and insects), agricultural co-operation (such as the distribution of fertilizer and field pesticides), and the provision of a library and wall newspapers. The Centre has a section for women, and supports study trips out of the district for school pupils.

Ha'il itself has a new Public Library building, a Vocational Training Centre established in 1395 (corresponding to 1975), and a Youth Welfare Centre. Sports and social activities are practised at eight clubs: al-Hablain, at-Tai, al-Liwa, al-Ghuta, al-Ha'it, al-Habba, Fayd, and Samra'.

The modern sports stadium can seat 25,000 spectators in covered stands. In addition to the soccer pitch surrounded by a running track, there are indoor facilities such as swimming pools for men and women, a lecture room and library: it claims to be the first purpose-built sports complex in the Kingdom.

As regards current health projects, the two most outstanding are the opening of 13 clinics in outlying villages, and the building of a model general hospital in Ha'il with two hundred beds and two hundred fully-furnished accommodation units for staff.

HRH Prince Muqrin ibn ᶜAbdulaziz, Governor of
Ha'il since 1980

Education has always been a great priority in the Kingdom, and Ha'il now has 201 primary schools for boys and 62 for girls (with 112 adult literacy programmes using the same facilities in the evenings), 37 intermediate schools for boys and 13 for girls; and 7 secondary schools for boys and 3 for girls. There is a Teacher-Training College for boys and another for girls. Stress has recently been laid on building more schools at all levels, and it is intended to open a tertiary-level college for men and some university departments in Ha'il.

Aspects of modernisation, Ha'il

The businessman visiting Ha'il has two excellent hotels at his disposal, as well as branches of the National Commercial Bank, the Real Estate Bank, the Agriculture Bank, the Rajhi Bank, and the Riyadh Bank.

Telephone communications are a vital sector in national development, and within the Ha'il district most of the targets have already been passed, including the addition of five hundred new telephone lines, four new public kiosks, and international

Roadside gardens in the heart of Ha'il

direct dialling. A new project to instal 600 more lines will ensure that all villages in the area can be reached by telephone. Postal services are also up to a high standard.

Provision of electric power for domestic and industrial use has been budgeted on a completely different scale during the Third Development Plan. In the last year of the Second Development Plan, to the year ending 30/6/1400 (corresponding to 1980), only SR2 million was allocated for the electricity sector. Including the cost of land, administration, consultants, equipment, materials and salaries, the budget for 1400-1 (1980-1) was SR547,025,000; for 1401-2 (1981-2) it was SR869,575,000; for 1402-3 (1982-3) it was SR782,815,000; for 1403-4 (1983-4) it was 408,685,000; and for 1404-5 (1984-5) it was 148,000,000, a total for the five-year period of SR2,756,100,000.

Altogether, the budget of the Ha'il *baladiah* (Mayor's Office) for 1401 A.H. (1981 A.D.) was SR317 million, spent on paving roads and pavements, electrification, car parks, garages, workshops and the building of the new Baladia, maintenance of the city walls and irrigation system and the reservoir, a food inspection laboratory, and the compulsory purchase of land, with a further SR180 million for improving and increasing the water supply.

Village centres have been built at Biqa^{c}' and ar-Rawda, and others are in progress as Muwaqqaq, al-Ha'it and as-Salimi. A factory to recycle city refuse as fuel and fertilizer will produce 150 tons of fertilizer each day.

All in all, the prosperous present and bright future of Ha'il, *in sha' Allah*, marks a sharp, poignant contrast with the city's turbulent past which has been chronicled in part throughout the foregoing pages. May Ha'il long enjoy peace and stability!

Appendix

Notes on the "Ibn Rasheed" family of Jebel Shammer,
and present position of Mohammed "ibn Rasheed"

The works of Mr. Palgrave and of Mr. and Lady
Anne Blunt have rendered the names of Jebel Shammer
and its capital, Háyil, familiar to many readers of
travel, and in the past year a more elaborate book
was published by Mr. C. Doughty, containing a very
full description of Central Arabia, and much valuable information. Indeed, Mr. Doughty's book must
take rank as the standard English work on Arabia
of modern times.

Mr. Palgrave visited Háyil about 15 years ago,
when Telál, eldest brother of the present Chief, was
Emir. Mr. Doughty travelled in Arabia from 1876 to
1878, and the Blunts in 1879. Since the latter date
the power of "Ibn Rasheed" has been extended, and is
now paramount in Nejd.

The word "Nejd", as is well known, means "high"
or "table-land", and according to Arabian geographers the region so named comprised all Central Arabia
from Hejáz to 'Irák. Whilst the power of the Wahhábi Emirs lasted, El-Hasa was, in a political
sense, a portion of Nejd, and now that a Turkish
Governor resides in El-Hasa that Turkish administration is called by the Turks the "Government of Nejd".
At one period, it may be, Nejd was held to mean the
provinces ruled by the Wahhábi; but, however that

may be, the names should now be regarded as a geographical expression, including in its scope Jebel
Shammer and all the provinces of Central Arabia
lying within the tracts of red-sand deserts [Dahná
or Nefood].

The Shammer tribe which is connected with the
Kahtán has risen to importance in Nejd within the
last half century. Some sixty years back the family
of the Shaikhs of the Shammer was divided into rival
branches, the Al-'Ali and the A'l-Rasheed. A contest for supremacy, as usual, occurred, which ended
in the extermination of 'Al-'Ali, and Abdallah-Ibn
'Ali-Ibn Rasheed became Shaikh of the Shammer, with
Háyil for his residence, *circa* 1835 A.D.

It is said that Abdallah succeeded through the
aid of the Wahhábi Emir, Feysal Ibn Toorkee. He
had also a staunch and able supporter in his brother 'Obeyd.

'Abdullah Ibn Rasheed, as he was commonly called,
a man of rare ability, inaugurated the policy which,
followed by his successors, has led to the establishment of the supremacy of the Shammer Chief over a
large portion of Central Arabia. By the Wahhábi
Emir, 'Abdallah was nominated "Muháfidh", or "Warden
of the Marches", and thus was in the position of a
Frontier Governor under the Wahhábi, Jebel Shammer
at that epoch being a province of the Wahhábi
Empire. Until his death 'Abdallah-Ibn Rasheed remained a vassal of the Wahhábi Emir.

In the year 1846 Abdallah Ibn Rasheed died, and
was succeeded by his eldest son Tilál, whose name
became so well-known through the eulogies of
Palgrave. Tilál became wholly independent of the
Wahhábi Chiefs of Riádh, and governed with consum-
mate skill and caution until A.D. 1867, when, tor-
tured by some internal malady, perhaps fearing loss
of reason, he committed suicide by shooting himself.

Tilál was succeeded by his brother Muta 'Ab-Ibn 'Abdallah, who lacked the prudence and skill of Tilál, and behaved harshly to his nephews, the sons of the latter. Two of these nephews, Bandar and Bedr, conspired against Muta' Ab and succeeded in putting him to death in the year 1868 A.D.

Bandar-Ibn-Tilál then assumed the reins of Government at Háyil.

At that time Mohammed Ibn Abdallah, younger brother of Tilál, and now Emir, was residing at Riádh as a fugitive, and was kindly treated by the Wahhábi Emir Abdallah-Ibn Feysal, who effected a sort of reconciliation between Mohammed and his nephew· Bandar.

Mohammed became the leader of pilgrims, and it was when entering Háyil in that capacity that he suddenly stabbed his nephew Bandar to death. This event, which occurred in 1868, was immediately followed up by the slaughter of all the remaining children of Tilál, and Mohammed Ibn Abdallah, or, as he is now generally called, "Ibn Rasheed", became Emir and Muháfidh in Háyil. A full account of the circumstances attending the accession of the present Emir is given by Mr. Doughty in his work "Travels in Arabia Deserta".

The reigning "Ibn Rasheed" is said to be now about fifty years old and vigorous. He has the misfortune, for such it is accounted, to be childless, but he is on the best terms with his able cousin Hamood Ibn Obeyd and that branch of the family, and Hamood is at present the most likely successor.

The Government of Mohammed Ibn Rasheed is firm and popular; his subjects boast of it as the best in the world. He may be reproached by enemies as the slayer of his kin, but by the majority of the townspeople he is respected and feared, and the security and prosperity enjoyed under his rule is certainly appreciated.

As to foreign policy Mohammed Ibn Rasheed has hitherto shown the same prudence and circumspection as his predecessors. His neighbours are the Turks on one side, and the Ibn Su'ood princes on the other. After years of fit-ful warfare Ibn Rasheed has crushed his Wahhábi rivals and established his supremacy over El ꜤAred. The slaughter of the sons of Su'ood in Khorj last year is recounted in another place, and the partizans of the Al-SuꜤood appear to be utterly crushed.

Ibn Rasheed is fully aware how necessary it is to *"menager"* the Turkish Government, and some semblance of recognition of the suzerainty of that power is accorded, but the small tribute paid to the Shereef of Medina may be regarded as having more a religious than a political significance.

At the present time Ibn Rasheed wields paramount power from the confines of Syria to El-Hasa, which is the residence of a Turkish Governor. An Agent of his resides at Riádh, and is virtually the Governor, but, with the caution of his race, Ibn Rasheed has not wholly dismissed the Wahhábi family from the scene. Perhaps out of gratitude for former aid, perhaps from other motives, Abdallah-bin-Feysal is still honored by Ibn Rasheed with the title of Imám, that is to say, religious head of the Wahhábi sect of Mohammedans. It may be regarded as almost certain that Ibn Rasheed will not undertake any important enterprize without full deliberation or without making sure of the approval of the Sublime Porte.

From "Administration Report of the Persian Gulf Residency and Muscat Political Agency for 1888-89," pp. 15-16, by E.C. Ross, *Colonel, Political Resident, Persian Gulf*

 Chronology

Rulers of Ha'il up to 1921

Dates in Arabian history are notoriously approximate, and cannot be depended upon. Sources conflict with each other (for instance Ross with Huber, and Euting with Musil), but the following guideline may be used with as much confidence as any other.

A.D.	A.H.	
1834–47	1250–65	^CAbdullah ibn ^CAli ibn Rashid appointed Muhafidh (Governor) of the Northern Frontier by the Prince of Riyadh, Faisal ibn Turki. Died from natural causes.
1848–68	1265–84	Talal ibn ^CAbdullah. First independent Amir (Prince) of Ha'il. Committed suicide.
1868–9	1284–5	Mit^Cab ibn ^CAbdullah. Murdered by his nephews Badr and Bandar.
1869	1285–8	Bandar ibn Talal ibn ^CAbdullah. Murdered by his uncle Muhammad ibn ^CAbdullah.
1869–97	1289–1315	Muhammad ibn ^CAbdullah. Died, without a son, from natural causes.
1897–1906	1315–24	^CAbdulaziz ibn Mit^Cab ibn ^CAbdulaziz. Killed at the Battle of Rawdat Muhanna.
1906–7	1324	Mit^Cab ibn ^CAbdulaziz. Murdered.
1907–8	1324–5	Sultan ibn Hamud ibn ^CUbaid. Murdered by his brother Sa^Cud.

1908–10	1325–7	Sa^cud ibn Hamud ibn ^cUbaid. Murdered by Sa^cud ibn ^cAbdulaziz ibn Mit^cab.

1908–10 1325–7 Sa^cud ibn Hamud ibn ^cUbaid. Murdered by Sa^cud ibn ^cAbdulaziz ibn Mit^cab.

1910–20 1327–38 Sa^cud ibn ^cAbdulaziz ibn Mit^cab. Murdered by his cousin ^cAbdullah ibn Talal.

1920 1338 ^cAbdullah ibn Talal. Immediately murdered by the party of Sa^cud ibn ^cAbdulaziz ibn Mit^cab.

1920–1 1338–9 ^cAbdullah ibn Mit^cab ibn ^cAbdulaziz. Surrendered to ^cAbdulaziz ibn Al Sa^cud.

1921 1340 Muhammad ibn Talal ibn Na'if. Surrendered to ^cAbdulaziz ibn Al Sa^cud on the fall of Ha'il, December 1921.

Rulers of Ha'il since 1921

1921–3 1340–2 Ibrahim as-Subhan. Named Governor of Ha'il by the Al Sa^cud.

1923–71 1342–91 ^cAbdulaziz ibn Musa^cd ibn Jiluwi.

1971–2 1381–2 Fahd ibn Sa^cd ibn ^cAbdurrahman.

1972–4 1392–4 Sa^cd ibn Fahd ibn Sa^cd.

1980 to 2.5.1400 Muqrin ibn ^cAbdulaziz (b.1943), date to date son of the late King ^cAbdulaziz and brother of King Fahd

Bibliography

Allan, Mea. *Palgrave of Arabia: the life of William Gifford Palgrave, 1826-88*. London, Macmillan, 1972.

Alusi, Mahmud Shukri al-. *Ta'rikh Najd*. Ed. by Muhammad Bahjat al-Athiri. Cairo, 1343, A.H. [1925].

Bell, Gertrude. *Letters*. 2 vols. London, 1927. *Description of her journey to Ha'il in 1914, pp. 301-347.

Bishr, ^CUthman ibn ^CAbdullah. *^CUnwan al-majd fi ta'rikh Najd*. Mecca, 1349 A.H. [1930]. Supplement in the 1373 (Cairo) edition: Ibrahim ibn^CIsa, *Iqd ad-durar fi ma waqa'a fi Najd*, a MS. of 1947'.

Blunt, *Lady* Anne Isabelle. *A pilgrimage to Nejd*. 2 vols. London, 1881. *Reprinted in 1968.

Bray, N.N.E. *A paladin of Arabia: the biography of Brevet Lieut.-Colonel G.E. Leachman, C.I.E., D.S.O., of the Royal Sussex Regiment*. London, John Heritage, 1936.
*Though Leachman did not visit Ha'il, his primary objective, he met many of the Shammar tribesmen, and described the twelve-year-old Prince of Ha'il Sa^Cud ibn ^CAbdulaziz of the Rashid dynasty.

Carruthers, Douglas. 'Captain Shakespear's last journey'. *Geographical Journal*, vol. 59, 1922, pp. 322-334 and 401-18.

Carruthers, Douglas. 'A journey in North Western Arabia'. *Geographical Journal*, vol. 35, 1910, pp. 225-248.

Doughty, Charles Montagu. *Travels in Arabia Deserta*. 2 vols. Cambridge, 1888. [Reprinted

1964].
* A new one-volume ed. was published by Cape in
1926, and has been reprinted several times.
Elmgren, S.G. *Georg August Wallins reseantecknin-
gar från orienten, åren 1843-1849*. Helsinki,
1865.
* In Swedish.
Encyclopedia of Islam, v. ḤĀYIL or ḤĀ'IL.
Euting, Julius. *Tagbuch einer Reise in Inner-
Arabien*. 2 vols. Leiden, Brill, 1896-1914. (Vol.
2 ed. by Enno Littmann).
* Ha'il is fully described in vol. 1, chap. 8
(pp. 173-240) and in vol. 2, chap. 9 (pp. 1-106).
Grimme, Hubert. 'Religiöses aus thamudischen
Inschriften'. *Le Monde Oriental,* vol. 28, 1934,
pp. 72-98. (To be used with caution)
Guarmani, Carlo Claudio. *Il Neged settentrionale:
itinerario da Gerusalemme a Aneizeh nel Cassim*.
Jerusalem, 1866.
*Before book publication, this work appeared in a
virtually complete French translation in the
Bulletin de la Société de Géographie (5th ser.,
Vol. IX, 1865) and in a German précis by H.G.
Rosen (with a map by H. Kiepert) in the
Zeitschrift für Allgemeine Erdkunde (New ser.,
Vol. XVIII, 1865).
The English version by Lady Capel-Cure (Arab
Bureau of Cairo, 1917) was published with a fine
introduction by Douglas Carruthers in an edition
limited to 475 copies by The Argonaut Press
(London, 1938), the latter reprinted by N. Israel
of Amsterdam and Da Capo of New York (1971).
Hogarth, David George. 'Gertrude Bell's journey to
Hail'. *Geographical Journal,* vol. 70, 1927, pp.
1-21.
Hogarth, David George. *The life of Charles M.
Doughty*. Oxford, 1928.
Huber, Charles. *Journal d'un voyage en Arabie
(1883-84)*. Paris, 1891.
Huber, Charles. 'Voyage dans l'Arabie centrale:
Hamâd, Šammar, Qaçim, Hedjâz, 1878-1882'.

Bulletin de la Société de Géographie (Paris), vol.
5, 1884, pp. 289-363 and 468-530; and vol. 6, 1885,
pp. 92-148.
  *Huber did not visit Ha'il during this first
  journey.
Leachman, Gerard Evelyn. 'A journey in North-East-
ern Arabia'. *Geographical Journal,* vol. 37, 1911,
pp. 265-274.
Littmann, Enno. *Zur Entzifferung der thamudenischen
Inschriften.* MVAG, Berlin, 1905.
  *Published 225 of the 800 Thamudaean inscriptions
  collected by Huber and Euting.
Lorimer, J.G. *Gazetteer of the Persian Gulf, ^cOman,
and Central Arabia.* Calcutta, 1908-15.
  *New edition, Dublin, 1970, in 5 vols.
Mengin, Félix. *Histoire de l'Egypte sous le
Gouvernment de Mohamad Aly.* Paris, 1823.
  *Mengin's account of Najd was derived from Shaikh
  ^cAbdurrahman, grandson of Muhammad ibn
  ^cAbdulwahhab.
Musil, Alois. *Northern Negd.* New York, American
Geographical Society, 1928.
  *Especially valuable on the history of the ibn
  Sa^cud and the ibn Rashid families.
Necd kit'asi meselesi. Istanbul, 1334 A.H. (=1915
A.D.).
  *In Turkish.
Nolde, *Baron* Eduard. *Reise nach InnerArabien,
Kurdistan und Armenien 1892.* Brunswick, 1895.
Palgrave, William Gifford. *Personal narrative of
a year's journey through Central and Eastern
Arabia* (1862-63). 2 vols. London, Macmillan,
1865.
Philby, Harry St John Bridger. *The heart of Arabia.*
2 vols. London, 1922.
Rashid, Dari ibn. 'Nubdhah tarikhiyah ^can Najd',
as told to Wadi^c al-Bustani. MS. in possession
of R. Bayly Winder.
Richards, James Maude. 'Desert city: an account
of Hail in central Arabia'. *The Architectural
Review,* vol. 105, 1949, pp. 35-41.

Rihani, Amin ar-. *Tárikh Najd al-hadith wa mulhaqatihi*. Beirut, 1928.

Ross, E.C. 'Memoir on Nejd'. *In* Administration Report of the Persian Gulf Political Residency and Muskat Political Agency for 1879-80, pp. 36-61.

Ross, E.C. 'Notes on the "Ibn Rasheed" family of Jebel Shammar, and present position of Mohammed "ibn Rasheed".' *In* Administration Report of the Persian Gulf Political Residency and Muscat Political Agency for 1888-89, pp. 15-16.
*Reproduced in the present compendium as an appendix.

Rutter, Eldon. 'A journey to Hail'. *Geographical Journal,* vol. 80, 1932, pp.325-331.

Saldana, J.A. 'Precis of Nejd affairs, 1804-1904.' *In Persian Gulf Gazetteer* (Simla, 1904).

Salih, Mutlaq ibn. 'Shadha an-nadd fi ta'rikh Najd'. Arabic MS. dated 1361 in the Library of the Arabian American Oil Company, Dhahran.

Shuwi'r, Muhammad Sᵃd ash-. 'Ha'il: muftah al-sahra' al-ᶜarabiyah'. *Al-Faisal* (Riyadh), no. 25, June 1979, pp. 35-49.

Stanton-Hope, W.E. *Arabian adventurer*. London, Robert Hale, 1951.
*On the Muslim convert (Hajji Abdullah) William Richard Williamson (b. 1872), who visited Ha'il en route to Mecca.

Tallqvist, Knut. *Bref- och dagboksanteckningar af Georg August Wallin*. Helsinki, 1905.
*In Swedish.

Van den Branden, Albert. *Inscriptions thamoudéennes*. Louvain, 1950.

Van den Branden, Albert. 'Les textes thamoudéens de Huber et d'Euting'. *Le Muséon,* vol. 69, 1956, pp. 109-137.

Wallin, Georg August. *Travels in Arabia (1845 and 1848)*. With introductory material by W.R. Mead and M. Trautz. Cambridge, The Oleander Press, 1979.
*Reprints, with a comprehensive new bibliography

by Philip Ward, Wallin's epoch-making contributions to the *Journal of the Royal Geographical
Society* (vol. 20, 1850, pp. 293-344 and vol.
24, 1954, pp. 115-207).

Winder, R. Bayly. *Saudi Arabia in the Nineteenth
Century*. London, Macmillan, 1965.

Winnett, F.V. *and* Reed, W.L.   'An archaeological-
epigraphical survey of the Ha'il area of northern
Sa^{c}udi Arabia'. *Berytus,* vol. 22, 1973, pp. 52-
101.

Winstone, Harry Victor Frederick. *Captain
Shakespear: a portrait*. London, Cape, 1976.
 *A clear account of Shakespear's wanderings as
a British negotiator with ibn Sa^{c}ud. He was
killed in 1915 by Rashidi raiders on a Sa^{c}udi
encampment.

Winstone, Harry Victor Frederick. *Gertrude Bell*.
London, Cape, 1978.
 *The chapter 'Hail' is on pp. 126-142.

Genealogy

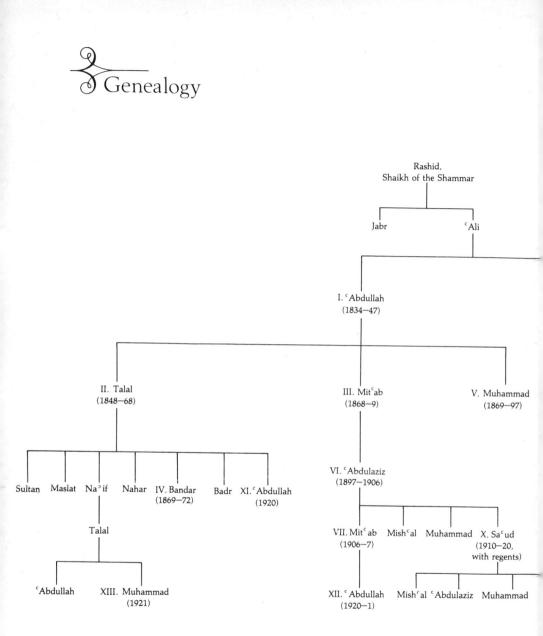

Rashid,
Shaikh of the Shammar

Jabr · ʿAli

I. ʿAbdullah
(1834—47)

II. Talal
(1848—68)

III. Mitʿab
(1868—9)

V. Muhammad
(1869—97)

Sultan · Maslat · Naʾif · Nahar · IV. Bandar
(1869—72) · Badr · XI. ʿAbdullah
(1920)

Talal

ʿAbdullah · XIII. Muhammad
(1921)

VI. ʿAbdulaziz
(1897—1906)

VII. Mitʿab · Mishʿal · Muhammad · X. Saʿud
(1906—7) (1910—20,
with regents)

XII. ʿAbdullah · Mishʿal · ʿAbdulaziz · Muhammad
(1920—1)

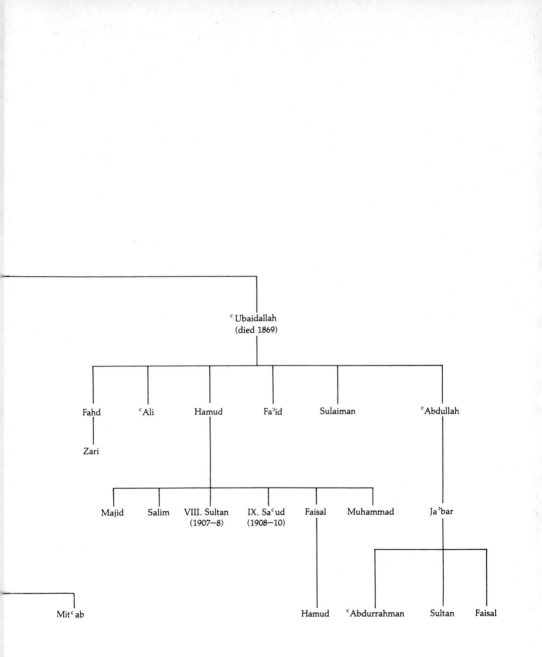

BOOKS FROM OLEANDER

MONUMENTS OF SOUTH ARABIA
D. Brian Doe
The definitive corpus of archaeological sites in
the two Yemens, Oman, and the southern district of
Saudi Arabia, with numerous maps, drawings and
photographs, bibliography and index, superseding
the author's *Southern Arabia*.

A LIFETIME'S READING
Philip Ward
According to *The Good Book Guide* (London), "a
supremely well informed, idiosyncratic reading pro-
gramme arranged year by year over 50 years, so that
by the time you finish you will not only have read
500 masterpieces of world literature, but travelled
in every continent and learned a few languages to
boot. An amusing read, a deadly serious undertaking, and a fascinating reference".

KING HUSAIN AND THE KINGDOM OF HEJAZ
Randall Baker
A history of the dynasty which rules the state now
forming western Saudi Arabia, and also ruled some
time in Iraq and Jordan, with a careful character
study of its longest-reigning monarch.

THE LIFE AND MURDER OF HENRY MORSHEAD
Ian Morshead
A solution is offered to the mystery of the murder
of Henry Morshead, the Everest climber and Survey
of India cartographer, with a complete biography
by one of his sons.

BOOKS FROM OLEANDER

THE GOLD-MINES OF MIDIAN
Sir Richard Burton
The original edition was marred by numerous misprints, and this new edition has been prepared from Burton's own annotated copy: an authentic Arabian travel classic.

THE AEOLIAN ISLANDS
Philip Ward
The Italian archipelago north of Sicily which includes Vulcano, Stromboli and Lipari is unspoilt, spectacular and hospitable, with easy connections from Messina or Naples: this is the only full travel guide to the Aeolians in English.

MARVELL'S ALLEGORICAL POETRY
Bruce King
New light is cast on the Nun Appleton period of Andrew Marvell by an allegorical interpretation of some of his most celebrated poetry.

BIOGRAPHICAL MEMOIRS OF EXTRAORDINARY PAINTERS (1780)
William Beckford
Beckford, called by Byron 'England's wealthiest son', is best known today for his oriental novel *Vathek* (1786), but he had already achieved fame at the age of 20 with the publication of the first edition of this parody. He satirises the popular art books of the day (and voluble if ignorant housekeepers!) in one of the most amusing contributions to art-historical parody.

BOOKS FROM OLEANDER

COME WITH ME TO IRELAND
Philip Ward
Between 'portraits of a city' devoted to *Tripoli*
and *Bangkok,* Philip Ward relaxed in the Republic
of Ireland and describes here what he did and saw.
Ireland of the Welcomes called it "A most desirable companion for an Irish journey, leading you
away from the highroads to the hidden treasures
off the beaten track". Uniform with the same
author's *Touring Cyprus.*

SABRATHA: A Guide for Visitors
Philip Ward
The only book in print in any language on the most
charming city of Roman Libya. "Orderly and
authoritative. No one will want to visit or study
this site without the help of this model guide" -
Archaeology. Superb photos by Hans Lafeber.

APULEIUS ON TRIAL AT SABRATHA
Philip Ward
The great Latin writer Apuleius, born about A.D.
125, who married a wealthy widow of Roman Tripoli,
was tried for sorcery in the law-court of Sabratha
in 157 at the height of his oratorical powers.

FRIULAN: LANGUAGE AND LITERATURE
D.B. Gregor
The first systematic grammar of this Italian regional language in English, with a representative
anthology of prose and poetry in Friulan, facing
translations by the author, and copious bio-bibliographical notes.

BOOKS FROM OLEANDER

ARABIA IN EARLY MAPS
G.R. Tibbetts
An authoritative bibliography of printed maps of
the Arabian Peninsula, beginning with the first
attempts, based on Ptolemy, and ending with the
modern cartographic methods of Bourguignon
d'Anville. With numerous plates.

TRIPOLI: PORTRAIT OF A CITY
Philip Ward
'The Arab World' wrote of Philip Ward's *Touring
Libya: the Western Provinces* (Faber and Faber:
now o.p.): "For anyone who has already booked a
trip to Libya or is contemplating one, I strongly
recommend they read Philip Ward's book and keep it
near at hand during their visit." This is a poet's
evocation of sights and sounds, pleasures and
surprises of the capital of Western Libya.

LIBYAN MAMMALS
Ernst Hufnagl
"This excellent field guide to the mammals of Libya
...[has]...a good key, many pen-and-ink sketches,
and notes on identification, habitat, behaviour,
food and distribution of the species" - *Times
Literary Supplement*.

MOTORING TO NALUT
Philip Ward, Angelo Pesce
"An excellent...motoring guide and pictorial atlas
of the Jabal Nafusa area and its contemporary inhabitants" - *Middle East Journal* (Washington).

BOOKS FROM OLEANDER

JIDDAH: PORTRAIT OF AN ARABIAN CITY
Angelo Pesce

The definitive scholarly work on the major Red
Sea port, and at the same time a spectacular
picture book, with a foreword by Freya Stark.
Forty-eight colour plates, numerous maps, 148
pages of text, 33 pages of appendices, and bibliography. 2nd ed.

BANGKOK: PORTRAIT OF A CITY
Philip Ward

A journey of fourteen chapters, stressing the
enchantment of the most exotic city of the Orient;
its temples and palaces, its river and canals, its
music, sport, art and drama. With excursions to
Ayudhya, U Thong, and the Bridge on the river Kwai.

HEJAZ BEFORE WORLD WAR I
D.G. Hogarth

A reprint of the enlarged Arab Bureau of Cairo
Handbook to Hejaz (1917), with a new introduction
by R.L. Bidwell. Even now the best route guide
to isolated oases.

TELEVISION PLAYS
Philip Ward

Hawklaw concerns the peculiar household of a famous
artist who has every reason to keep even his warmest admirers at a distance. Two brothers in *A
Fence Round the Property* are obsessed with the past
but differ (perhaps) on what to do about the future.
Words are used as benign bullets in a relentless
battle whose armistice cannot easily be predicted.

BOOKS FROM OLEANDER

TRAVELS IN ARABIA (1845 and 1848)
Georg August Wallin
The Fenno-Swede Wallin published the results of
his travels in Arabia in early volumes of the
Journal of the Royal Geographical Society, here
reprinted for the first time with introductions
by Professor W.R. Mead and M. Trautz.

COASTAL FEATURES OF ENGLAND AND WALES
J.A. Steers
Eight diverse new essays by the Professor
Emeritus of Geography and Emeritus Fellow of St
Catharine's College, Cambridge.

MEDICAL BOOK ILLUSTRATION: A SHORT HISTORY
John L. Thornton, Carole Reeves
A profusely-illustrated chronicle of the progress
of medical book art from ancient times to the
sophistication of the present day.

**JAN VAN RYMSDYK: Medical Artist of
the Eighteenth Century**
John L. Thornton
Jan Van Rymsdyk, a fiture so shadowy that even
now we cannot pinpoint his precise date or place
of birth, is the Dutch-born artist who was responsible for the magnificent plates in the
obstetrical atlases of William Hunter and
William Smellie.

ROMONTSCH: LANGUAGE AND LITERATURE
D.B. Gregor
Romontsch is - with German, French and Italian -
one of the four national languages of Switzerland.
Here is its grammar, with a generous anthology of
texts and translations.

BOOKS FROM OLEANDER

DIARY OF A JOURNEY ACROSS ARABIA (1819)
G.F. Sadleir
A major travel book by the first Westerner ever to cross the whole of the Arabian peninsula from east to west. Lost for 50 years, the book first appeared in a small edition at Byculla, near Bombay, in 1866. With a new introduction by F.M. Edwards. ISBN O 902675 59 1 Hardback.

A DICTIONARY OF COMMON FALLACIES
Philip Ward
Medical, mathematical, biological, astronomical and other fallacies drawn from all fields of human knowledge. "One of the most entertaining reference books ever written" (Daily Telegraph).

ROMAGNOL: LANGUAGE AND LITERATURE
D.B. Gregor
The first systematic grammar of the language of Romagna in English, with a representative anthology of prose and verse in the original Romagnol, facing translations by the author and copious bio-bibliographical notes.

CELTIC: A COMPARATIVE STUDY
D.B. Gregor
Celtic, a work of over 400 pages, is the first detailed comparison of Breton, Cornish, Irish, Manx, Scots Gaelic and Welsh.

THE ART & POETRY OF RAMUZ
David Bevan
The first major contribution to Ramuz studies in English, showing how the Swiss novelist integrates his message and style with admirable coherence.